Fundamentals of Financial Management

Fundamentals of Financial Management

RAMESH K. S. RAO
University of Texas, Austin

MACMILLAN PUBLISHING COMPANY
New York

COLLIER MACMILLAN PUBLISHERS
London

Copyright © 1989, Macmillan Publishing Company, a division of
Macmillan, Inc.

Printed in the United States of America

Macmillan Publishing Company
866 Third Avenue, New York, New York 10022

Collier Macmillan Canada, Inc.

Library of Congress Cataloging-in-Publication Data

Rao, Ramesh K. S.
    Fundamentals of financial management / Ramesh K. S. Rao.
      p.   cm.
    Includes index.
    ISBN 0-02-398151-2

    1. Corporations—Finance.   I. Title.
  HG4026.R364   1989
  658.1′5—dc19   88-30351
                                                              CIP

Printing: 1 2 3 4 5 6 7 8   Year: 9 0 1 2 3 4 5 6 7 8

To Anita, for her understanding, patience and support.

PREFACE

As the name implies, *Fundamentals of Financial Management* is an introductory treatment of managerial finance. To a great extent, this book is the direct result of my earlier book, *Financial Management: Concepts and Applications*. The enthusiastic response to that book was accompanied by several requests for a less quantitative and less detailed version aimed at a more general audience. Hence the *Fundamentals* book. Although the material itself has been changed, the pedagogical philosophy of the earlier book has been retained.

The audience for this book is the undergraduate business student who has not been exposed to issues of business finance. A special effort has been made to write the text in a manner that appeals to nonfinance majors and that, at the same time, motivates finance students to pursue a more detailed examination of the various topics. In many instances, nonfinance majors take a course in finance to fulfill their degree requirement; the burden is therefore placed on the instructor to motivate these students and impress upon them the relevance of finance.

In my experience, teaching finance to a more general audience requires a less technical and more intuitive approach to enable them to appreciate the interplay between their functional areas and the discipline of finance. The emphasis throughout this book is therefore on a general, intuitive examination of issues in financial management that relies on quantitative analysis only to the extent that it facilitates student understanding. A major pedagogical feature is the systematic, "stair-step" approach to introducing ideas with intuitive explanations and detailed examples. Great effort has been expended to explain why the issue under study is interesting and important, how it can be used, and how it ties in with other issues seen in other chapters. Over the years, I have made notes of recurring student questions and areas of confusion, and have explicitly addressed these issues in the book. For example, Chapter 2 addresses common student concerns about the usefulness of understanding time-value calculations when calculators are available, and Chapter 13 discusses the distinction between expected returns and required returns that so often confuses students.

The net impact of these efforts is a smooth, logical development that provides an integrated view of financial decision making and sensitizes the student to the potential for using this new knowledge in various areas of business management.

Structure and Pedagogy of the Book

The book is divided into eight parts. Each chapter starts with a brief introduction to the subject matter. The chapters are divided into several *sections*, each with a distinct objective. An *outline* of these sections, presented at the beginning of each chapter, is intended to serve as a "road map" for the student. The concepts in each section are explained, and their usefulness is demonstrated with a *minimum of mathematical detail*. Derivations of key formulas are relegated to the end of the book. *Key concepts* are highlighted, and *numerical examples* are provided wherever they serve to increase the students' understanding of the material. *Highlights* are provided either to reinforce a concept addressed in the text, to provide an interesting aside, or to clarify a potentially confusing concept. Each *section* ends with a *summary* of new terms introduced and some questions to test the reader's comprehension of the material. The *Summary* at the end of the *chapter* is a recapitulation of the broad themes addressed in the text. *End-of-chapter problems* are included to provide readers an opportunity to consolidate their understanding of the material. Many chapters contain *appendixes* that can be used to supplement the general discussion in the text with a more detailed examination of specific issues.

Supplementary Material

- *Instructor's Manual:* A detailed instructor's manual has been developed by Robert C. Duvic to accompany this book. It provides complete lesson plans for each chapter. It also includes a comprehensive collection of transparency masters than can be used as visual aids or as self-contained lecture notes. Additional features include teaching strategies, caveats for the teacher, section outlines, and so on.

- *Solutions Manual:* The end-of-chapter problems in the book are worked out in detail in a manual prepared by Kenneth W. Wiles. Special care has been taken to provide a detailed, step-by-step analysis of the problems. In addition, useful insights and comments concerning the problems are included.

- *Study Guide:* Professors John Jahera and Daniel Page of Auburn University have prepared a study guide to facilitate systematic assimilation of the text material. The guide includes a general discussion of the important ideas, numerical and verbal questions with answers, and outlines of each chapter.

- *Test Bank:* A detailed test bank with verbal and quantitative multiple-choice questions has been developed. This data base is also available on computer discs with a very flexible test-generation program.

- *Computer-Based Instruction:* A separate document with computer-oriented applications of the concepts and techniques developed in the book is also available to instructors who would like to explore this supplementary pedagogical method.

Acknowledgments

This book has benefited from the input of various individuals, and it may be impossible for me to thank all who have provided assistance in one form or another.

My deepest thanks go to Bob Duvic, who has contributed in many ways to the completion of the book. Not only has he taken a deep interest in the actual production, but he has been instrumental in my reworking of entire chapters to improve their pedagogical efficacy. His suggestions on earlier drafts were so insightful that I have incorporated several of his ideas into the text. His dedication to this project is also reflected in many of the supplementary teaching materials that accompany this book.

Special thanks are also due to Ken Wiles. Ken has provided useful feedback from class testing of the materials and has developed the comprehensive Solutions Manual.

I would also like to thank Ken Macleod, Bonnie Lieberman, and Bill Oldsey of Macmillan for their continued support of this book. Ed Neve's and Helen Greenberg's input and Jo Anne Ruhland's careful review has improved the final quality of the manuscript. Thanks are also due to Marilyn James and Nancy Rudisill of York Production Services for their help in the production stage. At the University of Texas, Michael Rebello, V. Venkat, Rachael Driskill, and Cathy Lucia provided assistance in various forms.

The manuscript has gained from the input of several reviewers to whom I owe thanks:

Haragopal Banerjee	Emporia State University, Kansas
James M. Block	Youngstown State University
John H. Crockett	George Mason University
George Gallinger	Arizona State University
Delvin D. Hawley	University of Mississippi
Glen V. Henderson	University of Cincinnati
Carol Keifer	Eastern Illinois University
Ginette M. McManus	Cleveland State University
John B. Mitchell	Central Michigan University
Thomas J. O'Brien	University of Connecticut
David J. Rystrom	Western Washington University
Paul J. Speaker	West Virginia University
John M. Wachowicz	University of Tennessee
Arthur G. Wentz	University of Akron
William L. Wilbur	Northern Illinois University
Douglas Wilson	University of Massachusetts
Joseph W. Wilson	California State University, Fresno

I welcome any and all suggestions and comments on this book.

Ramesh K. S. Rao
Austin, Texas

Contents

PART III

The Analysis of Financial Statements

PART VIII

Special Topics in Financial Management

PART I

A Valuation Framework for Financial Decisions

1

Society, Capitalism, and Financial Management

The discipline of finance has evolved significantly over the last three decades. Before the 1950s, finance was primarily descriptive, and financial management books relied heavily on institutional descriptions rather than on scientific observation and analysis. However, more recently, finance has evolved into a logically justifiable set of procedures to analyze several financial decisions. In our highly competitive business environment, good financial management becomes more important each day, since managers constantly have to make decisions in a rapidly changing environment. Although there is no substitute for business acumen, today's managers increasingly need a consistent framework for making decisions, especially because managers are being held more and more accountable for their actions, both by the owners of firms and by society as a whole.

Regardless of its nature—whether it be a service organization or a manufacturing plant, a massive corporation in Ohio or a roadside delicatessen in Alaska—every business makes financial decisions. Of course, the nature of the decisions that must be made will differ, but the guidelines and principles are basically the same. Financial managers have to adapt these basic guidelines and principles to the realities of the situation they confront.

This book is about financial decision making. It presents the conceptual as well as the practical aspects of financial management. Of course, no book can address every practical situation. However, with a solid foundation in the basic principles, financial managers should be able to develop a logical framework for solving the myriad problems they confront in day-to-day operations. In some instances the procedure for making decisions will be clear, and we identify certain techniques to help the manager make a decision. However, clear-cut, satisfying solutions may not always exist. In these cases, we distinguish these variables that are relevant for making a decision from those that are not. By identifying the variables that deserve close attention, managers become sensitized to considerations that can lead them to make an intelligent decision.

No decision-making framework can be developed in a vacuum. To understand finance, we must understand the environment in which financial decisions are made. In this chapter, we describe the major elements of this environment and show how they are closely interrelated. We first examine the general goals that society sets for itself. We then describe the economic organizations and relationships that exist to satisfy these goals and place the function of financial management in the context of the business firm. Our introduction to financial management concludes with a comparison of accounting profits and cash flows and the identification of stock price maximization as the goal of the financial manager.

This chapter is organized into six sections.

SECTION 1•1: *Societal Objectives and the Capitalist Philosophy.* This section discusses the goals and objectives of a free-enterprise society and explains how capitalism facilitates the achievement of these goals.

SECTION 1•2: *Forms of Business.* This section outlines the various organizational forms of business and identifies the advantages and disadvantages of each form.

SECTION 1•3: *Objectives of the Firm.* This section examines several possible objectives, or goals, of the firm and identifies the primary goal for businesses.

SECTION 1•4: *Financial Decision Making.* The role of finance in achieving business goals is the central theme of this section. Here we introduce the two basic decisions—what investments to make and how to pay for them—and identify the individuals within the firm who are responsible for making these decisions.

SECTION 1•5: *Types of Financial Securities.* Here we explain the importance of primary and secondary markets for financial securities, the important decisions central to financial management, the types of financial securities issued by corporations, and the risks and returns that these securities carry.

SECTION 1•6: *Maximizing Stockholder Welfare.* Here we demonstrate that stockholder welfare is maximized by focusing on stock prices rather than on profit maximization.

SECTION 1•1 *Societal Objectives and the Capitalist Philosophy*

The modern business firm exists within a complex social and economic environment. This environment exerts tremendous influence on the firm and determines the firm's organizational form, operating characteristics, and goals. Thus, to understand the firm, we must understand the society in which the firm exists. Because the United States is founded on the concept of individual liberty, we will take this free society as the environment within which the firm operates.

THE GOAL OF A FREE SOCIETY

The most important objective of an economy based on freedom of choice is to maximize consumer satisfaction. The United States is a free society; thus, to achieve its economic goals, businesses must produce the right quantity of the right goods and services at the right time. It is consumers who decide what "right" is. If consumers buy the goods and services produced, businesses have done the right thing; if, for some reason, consumers refuse to buy, then, by definition, businesses have made an incorrect decision. Consumers are thus the most important individuals for business, and businesses must constantly aim to please them. Consumers have the luxury of changing their values, preferences, attitudes, and habits at any time, and businesses must constantly attempt to guess consumers' changing preferences. If a business makes good predictions about consumer preferences, it is financially rewarded; if business predictions are consistently wrong, the economy will punish the firm.

WHAT IS A BUSINESS ORGANIZATION?

In a primitive economy, life is relatively simple and consumer needs are few. In such an environment, consumers' needs can be satisfied fairly easily by simple cooperative arrangements among individuals. However, in a dynamic, sophisticated economy, life is not that simple. Consumers' needs are virtually endless; they include an innumerable number of goods and services. Social and technological changes in society create new and ever-changing needs, and as a society becomes more and more affluent, it demands larger and larger quantities of most goods and services. Simple cooperative arrangements are not enough. Organizations that involve the collective efforts of many people and possess the ability to produce large quantities of goods and services become necessary. Society has reacted to this evolution of consumer needs by replacing informal cooperative arrangements between individuals with more complex formal contractual relationships that constitute a business.

KEY CONCEPT: A **business organization** is a collective endeavor consisting of contractual relationships among the various parties involved in some productive activity.

Businesses can be large or small. To produce a million light bulbs demanded by consumers, the economy could support 10,000 small businesses that each produce 100 light bulbs or 5 businesses that each produce 200,000 light bulbs. It does not matter whether these bulbs are made in small backyard operations by a family investing its life savings of $20,000 or in large industrial parks that cost $20 million to build. However, in a free-enterprise system, the light bulbs must be produced at the lowest cost. A fundamental concept called **economies of scale** suggests that large businesses may be able to produce goods at a lower average cost per unit than small businesses with smaller production levels. This naturally encourages large-scale production. But large-scale production requires more machinery, bigger plants, and more workers. These cannot be obtained without more and more money.

THE NEED FOR CAPITAL

Business organizations cannot produce goods and services without resources. These productive resources are called **capital.** Depending on the nature of the resource, it may be either **physical capital** or **human capital.** For large-scale production, businesses must have large amounts of both physical and human capital.

Physical capital includes **financial assets** (financial capital) and *real assets*, and these may be changed from one form into another. For example, cash, which is a financial asset, can be changed into plant and equipment, which are real assets, by using the cash to purchase the plant and equipment. Financial assets are required for businesses to purchase land, plant facilities, and equipment; to pay salaries; to buy raw materials; and so on. **Real assets** may be needed to produce the goods or services that the firm wants to sell. Human capital, unlike physical capital, is intangible. Human capital includes a company's productive human resources. For example, the intellectual and entrepreneurial skills of management, the enthusiasm of the employees, and so on, are human capital. Because it is intangible, the value of human capital is difficult to measure. In the remainder of this book, the term *capital* will refer only to financial capital. Depending on the amount of capital that a firm requires, different forms of business evolve. We will discuss these various business forms subsequently. However, regardless of the form of business involved, one thing remains the same—American businesses need capital and are constantly raising it from both individuals and other businesses. This reliance by business on private capital, or *productive wealth*, is the basis of the principle of capitalism.

WHAT IS CAPITALISM?

In the most simplistic terms, **capitalism** is an economic system based on capital that is the private property of someone else (the *capitalist*). Such a capitalist society (e.g., the United States) recognizes individual **property rights.** That is, individuals are allowed to own property in their own names and in almost any form. In a capitalist society, individuals and businesses are free to do as they please with their capital without fear of governmental intervention. Such an economy can also be called a **free-enterprise system.** The Soviet Union, on the other hand, is not a capitalist system because the state, that is, the government, sharply limits individuals' right to own property. Because most property belongs to the state, the Soviet economy does not meet our definition of capitalism.

THE DRIVING FORCE IN A CAPITALIST SOCIETY

How will individuals and businesses act in a capitalist society? What makes the economy tick? Is there one fundamental belief that suggests that a free-enterprise system will be the best possible economic arrangement?

Because they can own property and use their capital with few or no restrictions, all individuals will channel their capital to those activities that they expect will benefit them most. By investing their resources in what they view as the best alternative for them, all individuals help not only themselves but all of society. In fact, individual self-interest automatically helps improve social welfare. The reason for this is perhaps best stated in the words of the founder of modern capitalism:

Every individual endeavors to employ his capital so that its produce may be of greatest value. He generally neither intends to promote the public interest, nor knows how much he is promoting it. He intends only his own security, only his own gain. And he is in this led by an invisible hand to promote an end which was no part of his intention. By pursuing his own interest he frequently promotes that of society more effectively than when he really intends to promote it.

Adam Smith, *The Wealth of Nations*, 1776

KEY CONCEPT: Allowing individuals to pursue their own self-interest will improve the welfare of society as a whole.

These famous words clearly communicate the fundamental principle of the U.S. economy. As individuals work to improve their own welfare, they are, perhaps unconsciously, also improving the welfare of society as a whole. This *invisible hand* acts automatically and solves several basic economic problems simultaneously. Thus a capitalist economy is based on the principle that as long as the government does not interfere too much, the self-interest of individuals will benefit society as a whole. This powerful idea is not, however, new, as the highlight, "An Ancient View of the Invisible Hand," demonstrates.

■ *HIGHLIGHT*

ANCIENT VIEWS OF THE "INVISIBLE HAND"

The U.S. financial system is based on the philosophy of capitalism, the cornerstone of which is the private ownership of property and free enterprise without excessive governmental intervention. Although Adam Smith is generally considered to be the father of modern Capitalism, the elements of the Capitalist philosophy have existed for centuries.

Szuma Chien, a Chinese historian who lived in the 2nd Century B.C., justified free trade without governmental intervention:

> There must be farmers to produce food, men to extract the wealth of mountains and marshes, artisans to process these things and merchants to circulate them. There is no need to wait for government orders: each man will play his part, doing his best to get what he desires. So cheap goods will go where they fetch more, while expensive goods will make men search for cheap ones. When all work willingly at their trades, just as water flows ceaselessly downhill day and night, things will appear unsought and people will produce them without being asked. For clearly this accords with the Way and is keeping with nature.

The conclusion reached by this philosopher is the same as that reached by Adam Smith: without government intervention, individuals will pursue their own interests and thus unconsciously work to benefit society as a whole.*

*Records of the Historian, Written by Szuma Chien, translated by Yang Hsien-yi and Gladys Yang. The Commercial Press, Limited, Hong Kong, 1975. The author would like to thank Professor Leslie Young for bringing the work of Chien to his attention.

Financial management decisions in general, and the workings of financial markets in particular, are thus based on the self-serving behavior of individuals. Individual investors make decisions based on what is best for them. A major objective of this book is to show how investors determine what "best" is.

Learning Check for Section 1•1

Review Questions

1•1. What is the goal of a free society? Why is this goal appropriate?

1•2. What do individuals and business firms require from each other? What do they provide to each other?

1•3. How is the idea of efficiency related to Adam Smith's idea of the invisible hand?

1•4. Define capitalism, and explain why it encourages decision makers to act so as to increase societal welfare.

New Terms

Capital	Financial assets	Physical capital
Capitalism	Free-enterprise system	Property rights
Economies of scale	Human capital	Real assets

SECTION 1•2 *Forms of Business*

Although we have discussed the role of businesses in achieving societal goals, we have not yet discussed the various forms of business that exist. There are three legal forms of business in the United States: proprietorships, partnerships, and corporations. Each has advantages and disadvantages. As a firm grows, it may have to change its legal form. This may be necessary because the legal form of an organization affects the extent to which it controls its own operations, its ability to acquire funds, the risk its owners bear, and how it is taxed. Table 1•1 lists the size and receipts of the three forms of business organization in the United States.

PROPRIETORSHIP

The oldest, simplest, and most common legal form of business is the **proprietorship,** in which a single person has controlling interest. This person is re-

TABLE 1•1   The Mix of Business Organizations in the United States

Firms, by Gross Annual Receipts	Number of Firms (Thousands)		
	Proprietorship	Partnership	Corporation
Total	10,106	1,514	2,926
Less than $25,000	7,203	759	620
$25,000 to $50,000	1,117	178	218
$50,000 to $100,000	844	191	325
$100,000 to $500,000	838	293	1,021
$500,000 to $1,000,000	68	52	296
Over $1,000,000	36	42	446
	Receipts (Billions)		
Total	$433.7	$251.6	$6,157.0
Less than $25,000	45.0	1.7	2.9
$25,000 to $50,000	39.9	3.3	6.6
$50,000 to $100,000	59.2	7.8	21.5
$100,000 to $500,000	166.4	41.5	242.1
$500,000 to $1,000,000	47.0	23.6	203.3
Over $1,000,000	76.2	173.7	5,680.6

Source: *Statistical Abstracts of the United States,* 106th ed., U.S. Department of Commerce, Bureau of Census, 1986, Tables No. 875 and 876.

sponsible for the firm's policies, owns all its assets, and is personally liable for its debts. The success or failure of the firm lies entirely in the proprietor's hands. If the firm prospers, the owner receives all the benefits; if it fails, the owner suffers all the losses.

The advantages of a proprietorship pertain to its ease of formation, its control, and how it is taxed. Setting up a proprietorship involves no legal or organizational requirements. Therefore, organizational costs are virtually nil. One has only to "hang out a shingle" to start the business. Perhaps the most attractive feature of a proprietorship is that of being one's own boss, that is, having total control. Proprietors have complete authority unless they decide to delegate responsibilities to their employees. All earnings of a proprietorship are taxed at the owner's personal tax rate, which is often lower than the corporate income tax rate.

The disadvantages of a proprietorship are unlimited personal liability, limited access to funds, and a limited life. Because the firm's assets and liabilities belong to the owner, the owner and the owner's business are identical. In particular, if creditors' claims cannot be satisfied by the firm's assets, the owner's personal assets can be used to fulfill these obligations. Perhaps more important, the firm's growth is limited by the owner's personal wealth and access to short-term bank loans. Finally, the life of the business is limited to the life of the proprietor. Because of these factors, a proprietorship is usually a small firm and is found most often in retail, service, and construction areas. As proprietorships grow, their owners find a change to a partnership form of organization increasingly attractive.

PARTNERSHIP

A **partnership** is similar to a proprietorship except that is has several owners. Most partnerships are established by a written contract between the partners that is called the **articles of partnership.**[1] Although not formally required (an oral understanding can suffice), a written partnership agreement eliminates future problems with regard to salaries, contributions to capital, the distribution of profits and losses, and the dissolution of the partnership.

The advantages and disadvantages of a partnership are similar to those of a proprietorship. The major advantages are its low cost and its ease of formation. However, a partnership has the following additional advantages: More capital is available (because more than one person makes contributions) and creditworthiness is improved (because the personal assets of all partners stand behind the business).

A partnership's main disadvantages are its unlimited liability and limited life. If the business fails, all partners assume its liabilities, and their personal assets may be used to fulfill creditors' claims. Moreover, if one partner cannot

---

[1]Most states have adopted the **Uniform Partnership Act,** which lays out the legal rules pertaining to partnerships.

assume his or her proportionate share of the partnership's obligations, the remaining partners are obligated to meet them.[2] A partnership legally dissolves if one of the partners withdraws, goes bankrupt, or becomes mentally incompetent; a new partnership must then be drawn up if the business is to continue. The tax features of a partnership are, in many ways, similar to those of a proprietorship. Each partner must pay personal income taxes on his or her proportionate share of the partnership's earnings, even if he or she does not actually receive that share. Whether this is an advantage depends on the individual's tax bracket.

By and large, unlimited liability and the problem of maintaining continuity make it difficult for very large companies to operate as partnerships. Except for legal and accounting firms, very large partnerships are rare.

CORPORATION

In terms of size rather than numbers, the public **corporation** dominates the U.S. business scene, accounting for almost 90% of total sales. The sheer size of American corporations is overwhelming, and the influence of American corporations worldwide is impressive. To demonstrate the size of some major corporations, Table 1•2 lists the top 20 U.S. corporations in terms of sales and compares them to the gross national product (GNP) of several countries. As the table shows, only a few countries have GNPs that exceed the combined sales of the top 20 companies. The old saw "What's good for General Motors is good for America" is thus not entirely without merit. The immense size of corporations makes their influence on the economic well-being of the country more dramatic than that of proprietorships and partnerships.[3]

In contrast to other legal forms, a corporation is unique in that it is a legal entity created by state charter. A corporation is formed through **articles of incorporation,** which state its rights and limitations. It is an artificial being and a legal fiction in that it is separate from its owners. Much like an individual, a corporation can acquire property, issue securities, sue or be sued, and enter into contracts. Like individuals, it is guided by the invisible hand as it acts in its own best interest.

A corporation has three major advantages: **limited liability,** unlimited life, and easy **transferability of ownership.** An owner's liability is limited to his or

---

[2]The risks of unlimited liability can be reduced by forming a **limited partnership,** in which one or more partners' liability is limited to the amount of their contributions. However, at least one person must be a general (or regular) partner who has unlimited liability. The limited partners are essentially investors and are not involved in running the business. Moreover, the partnership does not dissolve if one of the limited partners dies, goes bankrupt, or becomes mentally incompetent. Although common in the oil and gas, leasing, and real estate industries, limited partnerships are not compatible with most other business activities.

[3]For an early account of how U.S. corporations influenced the culture, economy, and life-styles of Europe and the rest of the world, see J. J. Servan Schreiber, *The American Challenge* (New York: Atheneum Publishers, 1968).

TABLE 1·2 The Mighty U.S. Corporation

Country	Gross National Product (Billion dollars)	U.S. Corporation	Sales (Billion dollars)
United States	3855.00	**General Motors**	102.81
Japan	1200.00	**Exxon**	69.89
USSR	734.00	**Ford Motor**	62.72
West Germany	655.00	**IBM**	51.25
France	568.00	**Mobil**	44.87
United Kingdom	505.00	**General Electric**	35.21
Italy	350.00	**AT&T**	34.09
Canada	317.00	**Texaco**	31.61
China	313.00	**DuPont**	27.15
India	190.00	**Chevron**	24.35
Mexico	168.00	Chrysler	22.51
Switzerland	93.70	Shell Oil	16.83
East Germany	89.00	United Technologies	15.67
South Korea	78.90	Procter & Gamble	15.44
South Africa	76.80	Occidental Petroleum	15.34
Taiwan	56.60	Tenneco	14.59
Israel	23.00	Atlantic Richfield	14.59
North Korea	18.10	U.S. Steel	14.00
Ireland	16.50	Phillips Petroleum	9.79
Philippines	16.00	Sun Oil	9.38

Total sales of 10 top U.S. companies = $483.95 billion. Country names in boldface indicate
countries with gross product that exceeds the combined sales of the 10 top U.S. corporations.
Source: Corporate sales figures from *Fortune,* GNP numbers compiled from the *World
Almanac* and *Book of Facts,* published by the Newspaper Enterprise Association, Inc. (1987).

her investment. That is, the corporation can raise funds without exposing its
owners to the risk of having their personal assets confiscated. This feature encourages investors to provide funds to companies working on risky projects.
Since the ownership of a corporation is separate from its management, a corporation has virtually perpetual life. Finally, ownership is represented by shares of
stock, which permits the easy divisibility and transferability of owners' interests. In fact, a large corporation may have as many as 1 million owners, with
ownership changing almost daily.

Besides being more costly and difficult to organize, a corporation has a
potential disadvantage in how it is taxed. The primary drawback is the **double
taxation** of income. Because it is a separate entity, a corporation pays taxes on
its own income. If after-tax income is distributed to its stockholders as a cash
dividend, the stockholders must pay a second tax on this amount. An exception
to this is the S corporation, which is discussed in the highlight ''The Best of
Both Worlds.''

■ *HIGHLIGHT*

THE BEST OF BOTH WORLDS

Corporations have the advantage of limited liability, but the double taxation of income is a disadvantage. Proprietorships and partnerships avoid double taxation but have the undesirable feature of **unlimited liability.** Wouldn't it be nice for a firm to have the good features of corporations and proprietorships without having the bad features of either?

Indeed, one way to achieve this legally for stockholders in small businesses is to form an **S corporation** (known as Subchapter S corporations before 1982). An S corporation is taxed not at the corporate tax rate but at the shareholders' individual tax rate. The corporate profits (losses) are distributed on a pro rata basis to the owners, who then pay personal taxes on this amount. This organizational form has the advantage of limited liability.

So, why isn't every corporation an S corporation? Primarily because the Internal Revenue Code limits the number of stockholders to 35 or fewer. This largely restricts this form of legal organization to small businesses and startup companies.

In this text we will deal exclusively with the public, or profit-seeking, corporation. However, other organizations, which are also corporations, have different objectives. These nonpublic corporations are described in the highlight "The Many Faces of the Corporate Form."

■ *HIGHLIGHT*

THE MANY FACES OF THE CORPORATE FORM

Our primary interest in this text is the public corporation: the large legal organization that produces goods and services for profit and is owned by individuals who purchase its shares in a public market. However, other types of corporations that provide different benefits to society have different structures and ownership patterns.

• Nonprofit corporations: These institutions provide services but are not managed to make a profit. They enjoy limited liability but, having met certain requirements of the IRS, are not taxed.

• Professional corporations: Some high-income individuals, such as doctors and lawyers, may incorporate and be treated as corporations.

• Private corporations: These firms seek profits, but have few owners and their shares are not publicly traded.

• Quasi-public corporations: Some large endeavors are extremely important to society but are also extremely risky. To entice investors, the government takes a position in the firm either by investing in it or subsidizing it.

• Government-owned corporations: These corporations may be entirely owned by a governmental body and provide services, such as utilities, considered vital to society.

Learning Check for Section 1·2

Review Questions

1·5. What are the primary differences between the proprietorship and partnership forms of business organization?

1·6. What legal form of business organization most favors large-scale production techniques? Why?

1·7. Rank the forms of business organization in terms of their need for capital. How are the firm's need for capital and its ability to meet society's needs related?

1·8. How are taxes treated in the three forms of business organization? What are the advantages and disadvantages of these tax treatments?

1·9. You wish to invest in a business, but not to jeopardize your entire wealth. Which form of business would be to your best advantage? Why?

1·10. Summarize the advantages and disadvantages of the various organizational forms of business.

1·11. Table 1·1 suggests that corporations account for only about 20% of all U.S. businesses, yet the primary focus in this book is the corporation. Why do you think this is so?

New Terms

Articles of incorporation	Limited liability	S corporation
Articles of partnership	Limited partnership	Transferability of ownership
Corporation	Partnership	Uniform Partnership Act
Double taxation	Proprietorship	Unlimited liability

SECTION 1·3 *Objectives of the Firm*

Thus far, we have seen how society and the business organization are interrelated. We have also established that the goal of the capitalist society is to maximize consumer satisfaction. With society's goal in mind, we are now ready to establish the goal/objective of the business firm.

THE OBJECTIVE OF THE FIRM

The self-satisfying behavior of individuals in a free-enterprise system determines the objectives of the firm. We have already seen why businesses exist.

Businesses can often do what individuals cannot do on their own. For example, to get the benefits of mass production, large amounts of capital may be needed, which may be beyond the means of an individual. Yet the individual will still seek to get the benefits that the business can provide. How is this possible? By providing capital to the business in one form or another. That is, some people are willing to **finance** the operations of the firm.[4] In return for their capital, the company provides each such person with a document attesting to the transaction. These documents, called *financial securities*, will be examined in Section 1•5.

Note that the firm has now taken the place of the individual in Adam Smith's capitalist economy. Since the firm now acts on behalf of the individual, it, too, must operate in a self-satisfying manner. The firm must make the right decisions in almost every aspect of its daily operations to act in the best interests of its owners. To do this, the managers of the company need a systematic framework for making day-to-day decisions. The primary objective of this textbook is to provide the manager with a framework for analyzing financial decisions from the standpoint of maximizing the welfare of the owners of the firm: its shareholders.

KEY CONCEPT: The goal of the firm's management is to maximize the **welfare of the stockholders.**

PROBLEMS IN IMPLEMENTING STOCKHOLDER WELFARE MAXIMIZATION: THE THEORY OF AGENCY

Is the objective of **maximizing the welfare of the stockholders** of the firm always attainable? In large corporations the stockholders cannot make all the necessary decisions. Instead they hire managers, who act as the stockholders' **agents** to run the firm. Thus managers, not owners, are in day-to-day control of the firm, and may be interested in their own welfare, not just the welfare of the stockholders. In addition to the managers and stockholders, there are numerous other groups, or constituencies, with interests in the firm. Each group has resources, such as labor or capital, which the firm needs. Each group also has expectations of receiving assets or services from the firm.

The existence of these diverse groups may result in multiple financial goals, of which maximizing shareholder interest is only one (and not necessarily the dominant) part. Moreover, the financial interests of the various constituencies may conflict. **Agency theory** identifies these potential conflicts between participants in a business and examines how the undesirable consequences of these potential conflicts can be reduced. These conflicts cannot be ignored because

---

[4]When used as a verb, the term *finance* refers to the act of providing capital. This ability of the public to participate directly in the investment activities of large corporations by financing them has been dubbed *peoples' capitalism.*

they impose inefficiencies, called **agency costs,** on the firm. While we will not discuss agency theory in detail, we will give some examples of how conflicts between various groups with diverse interests may affect its goals.

KEY CONCEPT: **Agency problems** can arise when there is a separation of ownership and control of the firm.

Multiple Constituencies

As mentioned already, a firm is not only accountable to its stockholders, but in addition, it has a social responsibility towards its consumers, employees, the environment, and society in general. However, the criteria for social responsibility are ambiguous. Clearly, the firm has an obligation to protect the consumer and to pay fair wages. Yet social responsibility creates problems because it falls unequally on firms. If one mining company incurs significant costs in reducing pollution, whereas its competitors do not, its profitability will be compromised and its stockholders must bear the cost. They may respond by selling their shares in the corporation, causing the price of the stock to fall. To society, this situation may hamper an efficient allocation of resources and ultimately retard economic growth and increase unemployment.

How can this potential conflict of interests be resolved? Many feel that management should adopt policies that will maximize the firm's stock price, for only then can the firm attract capital, allocate it efficiently, provide employment, and create benefits that satisfy society's economic needs. After all, this is the basis of a free-enterprise system. Instead, society, through its governmental representatives, must make decisions on the relative trade-off between desirable social goals and the reduction in efficiency from reallocating the scarce resources necessary to realize these goals. Given these decisions, the firm should be left to maximize shareholder welfare subject to the mandatory constraints that society imposes on all firms. In this sense, the corporation may end up **satisficing** (i.e., meeting certain goals, such as achieving a certain level of sales) rather than truly optimizing.

Management Goals versus Stockholder Goals

In a provocative survey, Gordon Donaldson found that the primary concern of mature businesses is the creation and conservation of corporate wealth—not shareholder welfare—and that the two are not the same.[5] This means that the goals of management and shareholders may conflict.

A potential conflict occurs when other objectives supersede shareholder interests. Whether implicit or explicit, these objectives center on organizational and/or managerial survival. The managers of the company may be overly con-

[5]Gordon Donaldson, *Managing Corporate Wealth* (Cambridge, Mass.: Harvard University Press, 1984).

cerned, for example, with issues such as financial self-sufficiency (the firm may want to use only internally generated funds), independence for top management, job security, and personal success relative to competitors (a manager may strive to be the highest-paid employee in the industry). By expending resources to address these concerns, the officers of the company may not be attempting to maximize stock prices with every decision. Instead, they may be pursuing other goals.[6]

This situation can occur because ownership and control are often separated, since stock is widely distributed. Outside stockholders (other than management) can generally exert little direct influence on management decisions. Conflicts of interest can arise. For example, stockholders may prefer a higher cash dividend, but management may desire to preserve cash in order to enhance its ability to pursue other goals. Management normally has the upper hand in these situations.

Another area of potential conflict between stockholders and management involves corporate executive compensation. Most top corporate executives receive compensation other than salary. This usually takes the form of performance or incentive plans and options to buy company stock at below-market prices (see the highlight "Executive Compensation"). Do these staggering benefit packages work in the interests of management and against the interests of owners? Some critics would say "yes," but others argue that these benefits ultimately profit the corporate owners. If stockholders are not benefiting, they can always bring legal action against the firm. An outside firm may also attempt a takeover and oust management. Thus, in both the short term and the long term, management must act in the shareholders' best interests.

Exactly how does the firm go about maximizing shareholder welfare? An answer to this must await an examination of the financial decision-making process and the securities issued by the firm. This is because the firm's **financial securities** provide the link between managerial decisions and shareholder welfare. After examining these aspects in the next two sections we provide a more definitive answer to the above question.

■ *HIGHLIGHT*

EXECUTIVE COMPENSATION

Most major American corporations pay large salaries and provide money perquisites ("perks") to their executives. While some criticize such large compensation packages, others defend the need for them.

A 1984 *Forbes* magazine tally of 805 chief executives revealed that no fewer than 103 executives earned more than $1 million in 1983, with 27 earning more

---

[6]Besides survival or self-sufficiency, management may also be more concerned with maximizing sales or market share.

than $2 million. Phillip Caldwell, the chief executive officer of Ford Motor Company, was paid a total of $7.3 million. Warren Hirsch, president of Puritan Fashions, earned $1 million for eight weeks of work.

Peat, Marwick, Mitchell & Co. estimated that in 1980 the typical chief operating officer of a manufacturer with annual sales of $1.5 billion earned a base salary of $300,000, an annual bonus of $150,000 to $300,000 depending on the company's earnings, an assortment of stock options, a pension plan designed to provide 65% of the executive's salary and bonus during the last five years with the company, life insurance worth $900,000, a comprehensive health insurance plan, and a variety of other perks, including a car, memberships in a luncheon club and a country club, and access to professional help with taxes and financial planning.

Source: Adapted from Patricia O'Toole, *Corporate Messiah* [New York: New American Library (Signet), 1984.]

Learning Check for Section 1•3

Review Questions

1•12. What is the responsibility of the financial manager to the owners of a firm?

1•13. List four groups that have an interest in the firm, and identify the goals that each group would have the firm pursue.

1•14. Why would the interests of the corporation's managers differ from those of its owners? How would this conflict affect the decisions made by the manager?

1•15. How do societal goals influence the corporation's goal of maximizing shareholder welfare?

1•16. Why does management sometimes pursue goals other than maximizing shareholder welfare? Why may such conflicts arise?

New Terms

Agency costs	Finance	Stockholder welfare
Agency theory	Financial securities	maximization
Agents	Satisficing	

SECTION 1·4 *Financial Decision Making*

THE MAJOR DECISIONS

KEY CONCEPT: There are two major decisions that the financial manager must make—the **investment decision** and the **financing decision.**

Both of these decisions will now be discussed.

The Investment Decision

A firm needs to invest in real assets in order to produce goods or services. Therefore, decisions must be made on what assets to own—what mix of fixed assets (plant, equipment, and land) and what mix of current assets (cash, accounts receivables, and inventories) will best facilitate the firm's production of goods and services. In other words, how much should the firm invest, and in which specific assets should it invest? The answers to these questions involve the firm's **investment decision.**

The Financing Decision

The company needs to finance its assets by acquiring cash from the financial markets. Decisions must therefore be made about what securities to issue and what mix of short-term credit, long-term debt, and equity best facilitates the effort to meet the firm's objectives. These questions are answered by the firm's **financing decision.**

FINANCIAL MANAGEMENT

These two broad decisions—investment and financing—are the responsibility of the financial manager, and the art and science of making the right decisions for the firm are called **financial management.**

A successful manager must understand the function of finance. A firm's activities fall into three broad areas: production (operations), marketing, and finance. The finance function largely involves preparing cash budgets, monitoring performance, evaluating prospective investments, raising funds, and helping to establish marketing and pricing policies.

The Decision Makers

To perform these tasks, financial managers draw on the conceptual principles of economics and use information systems organized by accountants. The

financial manager attempts to obtain the best long-run benefits from the allocation of the firm's scarce resources. In this sense, financial decision making deals
largely with the future. Nevertheless, managers must also ensure that plans and
policies are followed and that the proper financial objectives are being pursued
at all times. Through these efforts, finance interacts with and helps to coordinate other functional areas. In other words, finance affects all areas of business.
This is why even nonfinance majors in business schools are required to take at
least one course in finance.

In smaller firms, the finance function may be performed by one person
(e.g., the owner-manager). Larger firms, however, tend to have individuals or
departments that specialize in different tasks. Figure 1•1 presents a simplified
organizational structure that illustrates the role of finance within a large corporation such as Exxon or IBM. The **chief financial officer** (CFO) is the vice-
president of finance and reports directly to the president. The CFO is usually a
member of the board of directors and is responsible for all financial operations.

Beneath the vice-president are the controller and treasurer. The **controller**
is concerned mainly with the firm's accounting activities. Accounting primarily
records past financial events and is not overly concerned with the future. The
controller's duties include providing information on the firm's financial position
and reporting on its progress to management and to outsiders such as creditors
and investors. In many ways, the controller's function involves maintaining an
internal information system that describes past and present developments
within the firm to facilitate an analysis of the firm's financial position.

In contrast, the *treasurer's* activities are primarily external to the firm—
developing and maintaining relationships with creditors, lenders, and stockholders, and monitoring financial markets. The **treasurer** is responsible for

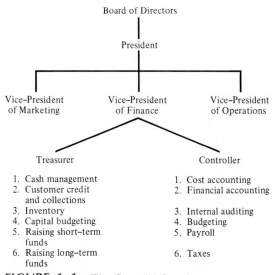

FIGURE 1•1   The financial function.

managing the firm's current assets, evaluating investment proposals, and negotiating with banks for short-term loans and with underwriters for long-term loans and stock issues.

In addition to these top-level managers, firms also have several middle-level managers who are responsible for certain specific tasks (e.g., internal auditor, credit manager).

Learning Check for Section 1•4

Review Questions

1•17. What two important decisions are the responsibility of the financial manager?

1•18. What are the specific elements of the firm's financial decision?

1•19. How is a typical corporation organized? What are the usual responsibilities of a corporate treasurer? Of a controller?

1•20. How does the financial manager's investment decision affect the firm's ability to produce goods and services?

1•21. Your duties in the firm include raising short-term funds and managing the firm's cash. What is your title?

New Terms

Chief financial officer	Financing decision	Investment decision
Controller	Financial management	Treasurer

SECTION 1•5 *Types of Financial Securities*

FINANCIAL SECURITIES

Different individuals in the economy have different needs for current and future consumption. Some will choose to consume more now and less later; in fact, they may need to consume more than their current wealth. These people will be borrowers. People with less need to consume now will provide capital by lending to the borrowers. Some will choose to invest in a business and share in the potential rewards or losses of the firm. Others may want to provide capital to a business but may not be willing to take on the risks of the firm. Thus, depending on their personal considerations, individuals provide capital to a business primarily in two distinct forms: as **equity** or as **debt.** Let us consider the specific case of a corporation. The two primary forms of corporate capital are equity capital and debt capital.

Equity Capital

When investors provide capital to a corporation in return for fractional ownership in it, the investor becomes an equity holder or common **stockholder.**[7] The company issues the investor a piece of paper that records this arrangement. This document is called a **common stock certificate** (or simply **stock**) or *share*, and the stockholder/shareholder is usually free to sell these certificates at any time through the financial market called the **stock market.** As part owners of the firm, stockholders have to share its losses and profits. However, all creditors must be paid off before they can claim any of the firm's earnings.

KEY CONCEPT: **Equity** is ownership; suppliers of **equity capital** (stockholders) are the owners of the firm.

Debt Capital

When investors lend capital to a company and the company agrees to repay the loan at a specified **interest rate,** the investor is a **creditor** of the corporation. The document that records the nature of the arrangement between the issuing company and the investor is called a **bond,** and **bondholders** can sell their securities at any time in the bond market. Bonds typically have a **face value** of $1,000 and a **maturity date** of several years. On the maturity date, the company agrees to pay back to the bondholders the face value of the bond. If for any reason the firm does not make its interest and principal payments on time, the firm is said to be in **default,** and the bondholders can sue the company to recover their money.

KEY CONCEPT: **Debt** is borrowing; suppliers of **debt capital** (bondholders) are creditors of the firm.

Other Forms of Capital

In addition to common stocks and bonds, companies issue other types of securities to investors. Some of the more popular securities are preferred stock, convertible securities, warrants, and rights. These securities are dealt with individually in later chapters.

---

[7]The term *common* in *common stock* is used to distinguish this financial security from another form of equity called *preferred stock*.

Collectively, the contributors of the different varieties of capital to the corporation are called *security holders*. In the remainder of this chapter, we restrict our use of this term to stockholders and bondholders and, unless otherwise specified, deal primarily with debt and equity financing (i.e., bonds and stocks).

PRIMARY AND SECONDARY MARKETS

When a firm issues new financial securities (i.e., raises new capital) directly to the public, the transaction is said to be a **primary market** transaction. In contrast, much of the activity that goes on daily in financial markets consists of **secondary market** transactions. Brokers and dealers buy and sell financial securities that were issued in the past for the clients. The existence of active secondary markets is extremely valuable. Individuals can get rid of their financial securities simply by selling them to someone else. Security holders do not have to wait for a company to pay them off. They can "cash in" and then turn around and invest in other securities instead of waiting for companies to issue new securities. Investors can thus make profits (or incur losses) in secondary-market trading. Companies also benefit from secondary markets: For example, a company with a surplus of funds may choose to avoid the interest payments on the outstanding debt. It can then "retire" the debt by buying back the bonds in the secondary market.[8]

THE REWARDS AND RISKS TO SECURITY HOLDERS[9]

Investors choose to become security holders for a very simple reason—they expect rewards for helping out the corporation. Yet these rewards are not guaranteed, and security holders take several risks.

The Rewards to Stockholders

Stockholders expect to get their rewards in one or both of two ways: via dividends and/or via capital gains.

Dividends Corporations may choose periodically to return a portion of their earnings to stockholders in the form of a cash distribution. This distribution is

---

[8]It is important to remember that companies are as interested in what happens to their securities in secondary markets as in primary markets. For one thing, the wealth of their stockholders is affected by the price of the stock in the secondary markets. The prices of the stocks and bonds in secondary markets also influence the firm's future cost of funds for future investment activity.

[9]The discussion of risks and returns here is confined to common stocks and bonds.

called a **cash dividend.** For example, if the Wellcor Corporation chooses to distribute 20% of its current earnings to stockholders, it declares a 20% cash dividend payout. However, instead of paying a cash reward to its shareholders, it may choose to issue a new share of stock for every five shares that a stockholder owns. This distribution is called a **stock dividend.** Unless explicitly stated otherwise, in this book the term *dividends* refers to cash dividends.

Capital Gains In addition to cash or stock dividends, stockholders may expect to sell their stock in the stock market for more than what they paid for it. For example, if you bought a share of Trombay stock for $55 on January 1 and sold it at a later date for $69, you would have a capital gain of $14.

The Rewards to Bondholders

Like stockholders, bondholders have two potential rewards: interest payments and **capital gains.**

Interest Payments Bondholders know exactly the amount of interest they can expect periodically for loaning capital to the company; this rate is stated on the bond. For example, if AT&T bonds pay an interest rate of 6% per year and you own a $1,000-face-value bond, you will get annual interest of $60, payable in semiannual payments of $30.

Capital Gains If you paid $1,000 for a bond issued by AT&T on February 6 and sold it for $1,100 2 years later, you would have a capital gain of $100. For both stockholders and bondholders, the expected capital gain may turn out to be a capital loss as the result of selling an asset for less than the original purchase price.

The Risks to Stockholders

Although stockholders can expect dividends, there is no assurance that a firm will in fact pay them. The contractual agreement between common stockholders (in contrast to preferred stockholders) does not specify that the firm will pay dividends. Thus stockholders may not be assured of this form of reward. There is also no assurance that the price of the stock will go up, resulting in capital gains when the stock is sold. Investors may be forced to accept a capital loss if they have to sell the stock at a given time. Common stockholders also face a risk when a company goes bankrupt. When a company files for **bankruptcy,** its assets are sold, and those with claims against those assets are paid off. Common stockholders are the residual owners and can expect repayment only if there is any "residue" left behind after the creditors have been paid. However, stockholders cannot lose more than their capital contributions even if the creditors cannot be paid in full by liquidating the firm's assets. That is, stockholders have the protection of **limited liability.**

The Risks to Bondholders

The interest payments and the repayment of principal to the bondholders are fairly certain. Uncertainty occurs only if the firm is in serious difficulty. If the interest and principal are delayed or not paid, the firm has defaulted on its terms, and its creditors may have to take the company to court. Thus bondholders take the **risk of default.** They also face one other risk if they attempt to sell their bonds in the bond markets. Depending on the level of interest rates in the economy at that time, bondholders must take a **price risk;** they may have to sell their bonds at a price either above or below their purchase price. Thus bondholders must recognize the possibility of a capital loss if they wish to sell their bonds before they mature.

Learning Check for Section 1•5

Review Questions

1•22. If you were to sell a share of stock, would you sell it in the primary or secondary market?

1•23. What role does the secondary market play in the economy?

1•24. Which type of security would you want to hold: debt or equity? Why? What trade-offs did you make in arriving at your decision?

1•25. What are the differences between the rewards to a stockholder and to a bondholder?

1•26. What are the differences between the risks borne by a stockholder and those borne by a bondholder?

1•27. What is a financial security? Distinguish between trading these securities in primary and secondary markets.

1•28. Summarize the ways in which corporations can raise capital. What are some of the features of debt and equity capital?

1•29. Why should a company be concerned with the price of its stock in the primary markets? In the secondary markets?

New Terms

Bankruptcy	Default	Price risk
Bond	Default risk	Primary market
Bondholder	Equity	Secondary market
Capital gains	Face value	Stock
Cash dividend	Interest rate	Stock dividend
Common stock certificate	Limited liability	Stockholder
Creditor	Maturity date	Stock market
Debt		

SECTION 1·6 *Maximizing Stockholder Welfare*

We have established that the firm's objective is to maximize shareholder welfare. This is achieved by making investment and financing decisions that maximize the price of the company's stock. After all, the common stock is the connection between the firm and the stockholders. Thus the only way that stockholder welfare can be affected by the firm is through the market price of the stock. Successful management decisions will cause stock prices to increase in the secondary markets and hence shareholder wealth increases.

KEY CONCEPT: Owners' welfare is maximized by maximizing the price of the firm's stock.

However, a major question still remains unanswered. In making these investment and financial decisions what should management be concerned with? That is, how do managerial decisions affect stock prices? Are stock prices maximized by increasing the firm's profits? Earnings? Dividends? As we will see next it is the firm's **cash flows** and not accounting profits that determine the market value of the firm's stock.

PROFIT MAXIMIZATION VERSUS WEALTH MAXIMIZATION

Profit maximization, or earnings maximization, is often offered as the appropriate objective of the firm. However, increasing profits will not always result in higher stock prices.

First, profits or earnings are accounting measures that may not reflect the economic realities of the firm. Because different accounting conventions, such as depreciation methods, permit flexibility in reporting firm activities, a different profit picture can emerge depending on which accounting method is adopted. A dramatic example of how a few accounting adjustments can change the profits picture of a company is provided by USX (formerly U.S. Steel) and its surprising turnaround.

In 1983, USX was the biggest money loser among the Fortune 500 companies, with a loss of $1.2 billion. Yet in 1984, the company showed $493 million in profits and was ranked number 37 in terms of profitability on the Fortune 500 list. However, this phenomenal performance was not the result of some miraculous recovery in the steel business. Nor were these profits the result of any changes in the oil industry, USX's biggest product line since it acquired Marathon Oil in 1982. Instead, these earnings were generated by some complicated accounting changes. According to an analyst's calculations, only $157 million in profits came from operations. The remaining earnings "can be attributed to a gallimaufry of nonoperating items, from asset sales to accounting adjustments."[10]

Putting it another way, finance managers should not use profits as a criterion for making decisions because they may not be serving the best interests of the owners. This is because profits are a *book* concept; they are sensitive to how the accounting books of the company are kept.

KEY CONCEPT: **Profit** is an accounting measure that may not reflect the firm's actual economic condition.

A simple example should convince you that decisions made using profit as a criterion may not be the best decisions. In fact, the owners may sometimes prefer losses to profits.

Example 1•1   Losses May Sometimes Be Preferred to Profits

Suppose that Graebert Company's financial manager is confronted with a choice between two decisions regarding its copper-rich land.

ALTERNATIVE A

Graebert Corporation sells the rights to copper mining on its land to Cupola, Inc., for $50 million in cash. However, the rights expire in 30 years, and Graebert must spend an estimated $51 million to eliminate the environmen-

---

[10]Robert E. Norton, *Fortune*, April 29, 1985. According to this author, U.S. Steel took in $265 million before taxes by selling off coal oil properties, two barge lines, and other assets. By trimming inventories and changing accounting methods, it generated more profits. In addition, by changing its actuarial assumptions and interest-rate forecasts, it was able to change the amount it put into its pension funds. Finally, it profited by repurchasing old debt at less than its book value.

tal damage caused by the strip-mining operation. Thus the profit on this alternative is $-1 million.

ALTERNATIVE B

Graebert can buy the strip-mining equipment for $75 million today, do its own mining, and end up with $76 million in 30 years after the cleanup costs have been paid. Since Graebert has no experience in strip mining, this alternative is very risky. The profit for this alternative is $1 million.

Which alternative is preferred? If the criterion for the decision is profits, alternative B is a clear winner. A profit of $1 million appears to be much better than a loss of $1 million. Yet this decision is incorrect. Alternative A benefits the company more. Graebert is better off with the alternative that results in losses.

Understanding why this conclusion is correct helps to identify the other weaknesses of profit-based decision making. By focusing on profits, the timing of the benefits to Graebert cannot be explicitly recognized. Suppose Graebert could earn 6% on its investments. Then the $50 million it would get under alternative A (even though it does not represent a profit) could be invested at that interest rate to amount to over $287 million in 30 years. Such an investment possibility might not exist with alternative B. Thus the cash flow generated under alternative A is of significant value—something totally disregarded by focusing on profits. Stockholders would be better off with alternative A because even though it has an accounting loss, the cash flow from this alternative increases the wealth of the stockholders. In addition, alternative B is risky, but there is no way to incorporate risk into the profit-based criterion. Thus profit-based decisions can work against the best interests of the firm's owners—the stockholders.

ARE PROFITS IRRELEVANT?

The preceding discussion should not be interpreted to mean that management should not seek profits. All firms are in business with the expectation of making a profit. However, what determines the market value of assets (in particular, the value of the company's stock, which determines the wealth of the firm's owners) is not profits per se, but cash flow. *Cash flow* calculations not only recognize profits but go a little further and measure the actual cash available for the firm. It is, after all, the available cash that determines the firm's future investments and growth. In fact, this is precisely the point illustrated in Example 1•1. The details concerning the estimation of cash flows are presented in Chapter 6.

KEY CONCEPT: Profits have no earning potential; cash flow does.

THE IMPORTANCE OF CASH FLOWS

The preceding discussion showed that wealth is determined by cash flows and not profits. Cash flows capture the economic impact of managerial decisions. Stockholders, in evaluating the firm, will therefore examine its potential cash flows in order to determine how much they are willing to pay for its stock. This fundamental relationship between cash flows and prices forms the basis for understanding how *any asset,* not just the firm's stock, is valued.

The precise connection between cash flows and prices is fairly complex. This relationship depends on not only the magnitude of the cash flows but also upon the times at which they occur and the degree of uncertainty (risk) associated with their receipt. These factors are examined in greater detail in the next two chapters.

Learning Check for Section 1·6

Review Questions

1·30. Is profit maximization consistent with maximizing the wealth of the stockholders? Why?

1·31. Distinguish between profits and cash flow. Explain why cash flow, in contrast to profits, has earnings potential.

1·32. What is the goal of financial management? Why?

New Terms

Cash flow   Profit   Profit maximization

SUMMARY

Societal Objectives and the Capitalist Philosophy

The primary objective of a free-enterprise society is to maximize consumer satisfaction. In a primitive economy, simple cooperative arrangements between individuals can satisfy their few needs. In more sophisticated economies, complex arrangements become necessary. A business is such an arrangement.

All businesses need capital, much of which is supplied by individuals and other businesses. This dependence on private capital makes the United States a capitalist society. In a capitalist society, all individuals and businesses are guided by an invisible hand to improve, simultaneously, their own and society's welfare. By allowing individuals to pursue their own self-interest, the economy solves several basic economic problems simultaneously.

Forms of Business

There are three legal forms of business: proprietorships, partnerships, and corporations. Each has its advantages and disadvantages. The corporate form is by far the most dominant arrangement in terms of size. Corporations issue financial securities to investors in return for capital, and investors expect the corporation to use this capital in the most productive manner.

Objectives of the Firm

A corporation is characterized by the separation of ownership and control and by the existence of several groups with potentially conflicting interests in the corporation. Corporate managers cannot afford to ignore a firm's social environment. Their activities must recognize the constraints imposed by society. There may also be conflicts between the interests of the managers and those of the stockholders. Agency theory studies these conflicts and their resolution. In resolving these and other potential conflicts, management must always act in the best interest of the shareholders.

Financial Decision Making

Financial managers must decide which assets to invest in and how to finance these investments. The art and science of financial management provides a framework for making financial decisions. The vice-president of finance, the controller, and the treasurer have the responsibility for financial decision making within the firm.

Types of Financial Securities

Investors provide capital to firms in the form of equity capital or debt capital and in return receive financial securities. Each type of financial security has risks and rewards. By buying equity securities, stockholders expect benefits from dividends and capital gains on their stock. By buying a company's bonds, bondholders expect interest payments and capital gains. Whereas bondholders expect a fixed-interest payment, stockholders cannot be assured of dividends. Primary and secondary markets are important for both individuals and firms.

Maximizing Stockholder Welfare

Managers who use profits as a basis for their decisions may not be acting in the best interest of the firm's owners. Since cash flow rather than profits has earnings potential, cash flow should be the basis for decisions. It is the magnitude of the cash flow and its associated risks that determine the market prices of stocks. Managers must focus on cash flow to pursue the goal of stock price maximization effectively because, by maximizing the firm's stock price, they are maximizing the welfare of the stockholders.

READINGS

BARNEA, AMIR, ROBERT A. HAUGEN, AND LEMMA W. SENBET, "Market Imperfections, Agency Problems and Capital Structure: A Review," *Financial Management*, Summer 1981, 7–22.

DEALESSI, LOUIS, "Private Property and Dispersion of Ownership in Large Corporations," *Journal of Finance*, September 1973, 839–851.

DONALDSON, GORDON, "Financial Goals: Management versus Stockholders," *Harvard Business Review*, May–June 1963, 116–129.

FRIEDMAN, MILTON, AND ROSE FRIEDMAN, *Free to Choose* (San Diego: Harcourt Brace Jovanovich, Inc., 1980).

HAND, JOHN H., WILLIAM P. LLOYD, AND ROBERT B. ROGOW, "Agency Relationships in the Close Corporation," *Financial Management*, Spring 1982, 25–30.

HILL, LAWRENCE W., "The Growth of the Corporate Finance Function," *Financial Executive*, July 1976, 38–43.

LEWELLEN, WILBUR G., "Management and Ownership in the Large Firm," *Journal of Finance*, May 1969, 299–322.

MANCUSO, JOSEPH R., *How to Start, Finance, and Manage Your Own Small Business* (Englewood Cliffs, N.J.: Prentice-Hall, Inc., 1978).

2

The Mechanics of Valuation

In Chapter 1 we established the importance of making financial decisions in terms of the firm's cash flows. In this chapter we provide the framework for *comparing* cash flows that differ in both magnitude and timing.

One of the most fundamental principles of financial decision making is the time value of money. In simple terms, this concept states that when faced with a choice between two identical cash flow amounts, an individual should prefer the cash flow that occurs earlier in time because the time value of money makes this alternative more valuable. For example, a dollar today is said to be worth more than a dollar tomorrow. This is because a dollar invested today will earn interest and be worth more than a dollar by the end of the year. Similarly, $5,000 to be received in two years is worth more than $5,000 to be received in three years. This is because, even though the magnitude of the cash flows is the same (both are $5,000), they occur at different points in time and the potential to earn interest on the earlier cash flow gives to time a value—commonly referred to as the *time value of money*. Thus it is because interest rates are positive that there is a time value to money.[1] (See the highlight "Why Is There an Interest Rate?")

The two preceding examples are fairly easy to understand because the magnitudes of the cash flows are the same. However, in practice, business managers

---

[1] Although this chapter is entitled "The Mechanics of Valuation," we do not discuss valuation until Section 3•2 because it is best understood after gaining familiarity with the time-value calculations discussed in the first part of the chapter.

have to make decisions about cash flows that differ both in timing and in magnitude. For example, one cannot readily compare $5,000 in two years with $5,500 in three years. Similarly, it is not easy to say whether a dollar today is worth more than $1.10 tomorrow. In general, comparing two cash flows that differ both in timing and in magnitude is like comparing apples and oranges; they are not simply and directly comparable.

KEY CONCEPT: To compare cash flows, we need information regarding both the magnitude and the timing of those cash flows.

HIGHLIGHT

WHY IS THERE AN INTEREST RATE?

We know that there is a time value to money because there is a positive interest rate in the economy. But why is there an interest rate? It is commonly said that the interest rate is the "price of money," but this explanation, although convenient, is not entirely correct.

The interest rate is the difference between the value of current and future goods, and this difference may be viewed as a premium for immediate as opposed to deferred consumption. The interest rate has nothing to do with money because it will exist even in a society without money. Thus as long as current goods are more valuable than future goods, interest rates will be positive.

But why are current goods considered more valuable than future goods? Several explanations and theories exist, but we discuss only two concepts that explain why.

Time Preference

Almost all individuals have a positive rate of **time preference.** This is a behavioral characteristic which states simply that for whatever reason, people prefer current consumption to future consumption. Some have argued that because of this, people are "irrational"; others have argued that this "bird-in-the-hand" attitude is a normal human condition. Whatever the intensity of the preference for "now" as opposed to "later" that different people may have, it is almost always positive, although it may vary from one person to another and from one society to another. This time preference alone suggests why positive interest rates will exist.

Productivity of Capital

This factor is technological rather than behavioral. Because capital has the potential for productivity, a positive interest rate will exist. Let us see why by considering Robinson Crusoe's life-style on his island. Crusoe barely survives by eating four clams per day—and he has to dig them out of the ground with his bare hands, an activity that consumes his energies the entire day, leaving him little time for TV. If he had a shovel, he could dig six clams per day and thus be better off. Yet to make a shovel will take five full days, and there is no way that he can do this without starving to death. It is clear, however, that Robinson will be willing to borrow 20 clams now and agree to repay more than 20 clams in the future. This is because Robinson will not go hungry with the borrowed clams and with the shovel he can dig more clams daily in the future. Robinson's shovel is *capital*, and because it has productive potential, he is willing to pay a premium (some extra clams) to acquire it. Thus a positive interest rate will exist.

Note that in our example no money was involved. All that was involved is capital and consumption.

It is extremely important to be able to compare cash flows that differ both in timing and in amount because virtually every financial decision involves a comparison of alternatives. One way to facilitate a comparison of cash flows is to find their values at the same point in time (be it today, next year, or two years from now) and then to compare their magnitudes. Because most individuals can relate to the present more easily than to any other point in time, cash flows are often adjusted to find their present value, and the magnitudes of their present values are then compared.

The remainder of this chapter is devoted to a more detailed look at the time value of money. This chapter sets the stage for the theory of value and forms the basis for other applications of financial decision making that we deal with in the remaining chapters. This chapter consists of three sections:

SECTION 2·1: *Finding Future and Present Values.* In this section, we describe the basic procedures for finding the future and present values of single cash flows and series of cash flows. Several examples reinforce the explanation.

SECTION 2·2: *Other Time-Value Considerations.* In this section, we explain the adjustments required for the case when interest is compounded more than once a year. Then we present the process of finding the present values of perpetuities. Finally, we briefly introduce the concepts of stock and flow variables because they motivate the process of valuation discussed in detail in Chapter 3.

SECTION 2·3: *Applications of the Time-Value Concept.* In this section, we introduce two important concepts: the net present value (NPV) and the internal rate of return (*IRR*)—methods used extensively in later chapters. We will explain the meaning and calculation of each method.

SECTION 2·1 *Finding Future and Present Values*

FUTURE VALUES AND THE COMPOUNDING PROCESS

Consider a person who deposits $100 today into a savings account that earns 12% annual interest. How much would his account be worth at the end of the first year; that is, what will be the future value of this lump sum?

$$FV_1 = \$100 + (\$100 \times 0.12)$$
$$= \$100 + \$12 = \$112$$

where FV_1 is the future value at the end of the first year. The future value is composed of the original principal amount, \$100, plus \$12 in simple interest. This result may also be obtained by multiplying the present value by $(1 + i)$.

$$FV_1 = PV + (PV \times i) = PV(1 + i) \tag{2-1}$$

Now, what will be the future value of the \$100 at the end of year 2?

$$FV_2 = FV_1 + (FV_1 \times i)$$
$$= \$112 + (\$112 \times 0.12) \tag{2-2}$$
$$= \$112 + \$13.44 = \$125.44$$

That is, his \$112 at the end of the first year will grow by 12% to \$125.44, and \$100 today is equivalent to \$125.44 in two years at an interest rate of 12%. However, from equation (2-1) we can write

$$FV_2 = PV(1 + i)(1 + i) = PV(1 + i)^2 \tag{2-3}$$

which will give us the same answer in one step rather than two (i.e., calculate FV_1 and then FV_2):

$$FV_2 = \$100(1.12)^2 = \$100(1.2544) = \$125.44$$

Moreover, equation (2-3) can be generalized to handle any number of years. Note that the important change from equation (2-1) to equation (2-3) was the exponent on the interest factor, $1 + i$, and this exponent always equals the number of periods that interest is compounded. So, for the general case shown in Table 2•1, the future value of a lump sum in n years is determined by

$$FV_n = PV(1 + i)^n$$

or

$$FV_n = PV(FVF_{i,n}) \tag{2-4}$$

where $FVF_{i,n} = (1 + i)^n$ is the future value interest factor for an interest rate i and n years. Equation (2-4) shows the preferred method for calculating a future value of a lump sum because we do not have to keep track of each future value, as the method shown in equation (2-2) requires. That is, if we wanted to calculate the future value of \$100 at the end of five years, we would have to calculate FV_1, FV_2, FV_3, and FV_4 separately. But with equation (2-4),

$$FV_5 = \$100(FVF_{.12,5}) = \$100(1.12)^5 = \$100(1.7623) = \$176.23$$

TABLE 2·1 Future Value Factor for a $1 Single Sum: $FVF_{i,n}$

Period	1%	2%	3%	4%	5%	6%	7%	8%	9%	10%	12%	14%	15%	16%	18%	20%	24%
1	1.0100	1.0200	1.0300	1.0400	1.0500	1.0600	1.0700	1.0800	1.0900	1.1000	1.1200	1.1400	1.1500	1.1600	1.1800	1.2000	1.2400
2	1.0201	1.0404	1.0609	1.0816	1.1025	1.1236	1.1449	1.1664	1.1881	1.2100	1.2544	1.2996	1.3225	1.3456	1.3924	1.4400	1.5376
3	1.0303	1.0612	1.0927	1.1249	1.1576	1.1910	1.2250	1.2597	1.2950	1.3310	1.4049	1.4815	1.5209	1.5609	1.6430	1.7280	1.9066
4	1.0406	1.0824	1.1255	1.1699	1.2155	1.2625	1.3108	1.3605	1.4116	1.4641	1.5735	1.6890	1.7490	1.8106	1.9388	2.0736	2.3642
5	1.0510	1.1041	1.1593	1.2167	1.2763	1.3382	1.4026	1.4693	1.5386	1.6105	1.7623	1.9254	2.0114	2.1003	2.2878	2.4883	2.9316
6	1.0615	1.1262	1.1941	1.2653	1.3401	1.4185	1.5007	1.5869	1.6771	1.7716	1.9738	2.1950	2.3131	2.4364	2.6996	2.9860	3.6352
7	1.0721	1.1487	1.2299	1.3159	1.4071	1.5036	1.6058	1.7138	1.8280	1.9487	2.2107	2.5023	2.6600	2.8262	3.1855	3.5832	4.5077
8	1.0829	1.1717	1.2668	1.3686	1.4775	1.5938	1.7182	1.8509	1.9926	2.1436	2.4760	2.8526	3.0590	3.2784	3.7389	4.2998	5.5895
9	1.0937	1.1951	1.3048	1.4233	1.5513	1.6895	1.8385	1.9990	2.1719	2.3579	2.7731	3.2519	3.5179	3.8030	4.4365	5.1698	6.9310
10	1.1046	1.2190	1.3439	1.4802	1.6289	1.7908	1.9672	2.1589	2.3674	2.5937	3.1058	3.7072	4.0456	4.4114	5.2338	6.1917	8.5944
11	1.1157	1.2434	1.3842	1.5395	1.7103	1.8983	2.1049	2.3316	2.5804	2.8531	3.4785	4.2262	4.6524	5.1173	6.1759	7.4301	10.657
12	1.1268	1.2682	1.4258	1.6010	1.7959	2.0122	2.2522	2.5182	2.8127	3.1384	3.8960	4.8179	5.3502	5.9360	7.2876	8.9161	13.214
13	1.1381	1.2936	1.4685	1.6651	1.8856	2.1329	2.4098	2.7196	3.0658	3.4523	4.3635	5.4924	6.1528	6.8858	8.5994	10.699	16.386
14	1.1495	1.3195	1.5126	1.7317	1.9799	2.2609	2.5785	2.9372	3.3417	3.7975	4.8871	6.2613	7.0757	7.9875	10.147	12.839	20.319
15	1.1610	1.3459	1.5580	1.8009	2.0789	2.3966	2.7590	3.1722	3.6425	4.1772	5.4736	7.1379	8.1371	9.2655	11.973	15.407	25.195
16	1.1726	1.3728	1.6047	1.8730	2.1829	2.5404	2.9522	3.4259	3.9703	4.5950	6.1304	8.1372	9.3576	10.748	14.129	18.488	31.242
17	1.1843	1.4002	1.6528	1.9479	2.2920	2.6928	3.1588	3.7000	4.3276	5.0545	6.8660	9.2765	10.761	12.467	16.072	22.186	38.740
18	1.1961	1.4282	1.7024	2.0258	2.4066	2.8543	3.3799	3.9960	4.7171	5.5599	7.6900	10.575	12.375	14.463	19.073	26.623	48.038
19	1.2081	1.4568	1.7535	2.1068	2.5270	3.0256	3.6165	4.3157	5.1417	6.1159	8.6128	12.055	14.232	16.776	23.214	31.948	59.568
20	1.2202	1.4859	1.8061	2.1911	2.6533	3.2071	3.8697	4.6610	5.6044	6.7275	9.6463	13.743	16.367	19.460	27.393	36.338	73.864
21	1.2324	1.5157	1.8603	2.2788	2.7860	3.3996	4.1406	5.0338	6.1088	7.4002	10.804	15.667	18.822	22.574	32.323	46.005	91.591
22	1.2447	1.5460	1.9161	2.3699	2.9253	3.6035	4.4304	5.4365	6.6586	8.1403	12.100	17.861	21.645	26.186	38.142	55.206	113.57
23	1.2572	1.5769	1.9736	2.4647	3.0715	3.8197	4.7405	5.8715	7.2579	8.9543	13.552	20.361	24.891	30.376	45.007	66.247	140.83
24	1.2697	1.6084	2.0328	2.5633	3.2251	4.0489	5.0724	6.3412	7.9111	9.8497	15.178	23.212	28.625	35.236	53.108	79.495	174.63
25	1.2824	1.6406	2.0938	2.6658	3.3864	4.2919	5.4274	6.8485	8.6231	10.834	17.000	26.461	32.918	40.874	62.668	95.396	216.54
26	1.2953	1.6734	2.1566	2.7725	3.5557	4.5494	5.8074	7.3964	9.3992	11.918	19.040	30.166	37.856	47.414	73.948	114.47	268.51
27	1.3082	1.7069	2.2213	2.8834	3.7335	4.8223	6.2139	7.9881	10.245	13.110	21.324	34.389	43.535	55.000	87.859	137.37	332.95
28	1.3213	1.7410	2.2879	2.9987	3.9201	5.1117	6.6488	8.6271	11.167	14.421	23.883	39.204	50.065	63.800	102.96	154.84	412.66
29	1.3345	1.7758	2.3566	3.1187	4.1161	5.4184	7.1143	9.3173	12.172	15.863	26.749	44.693	57.575	74.008	121.50	197.81	511.95
30	1.3478	1.8114	2.4273	3.2434	4.3219	5.7435	7.6123	10.062	13.267	17.449	29.959	50.950	66.211	85.849	143.37	237.37	634.81
40	1.4889	2.2080	3.2620	4.8010	7.0400	10.285	14.974	21.724	31.409	45.259	93.050	188.88	267.86	378.72	750.37	1459.3	5455.9
50	1.6446	2.6916	4.3839	7.1067	11.467	18.420	29.457	46.901	74.357	117.39	289.00	700.23	1083.6	1670.7	3927.3	9100.4	46890.
60	1.8167	3.2810	5.8916	10.519	18.679	32.987	57.946	101.25	176.03	304.48	897.59	2595.9	4383.9	7370.1	2055.5	56347	—

or just multiply the present value by the future value interest factor. $FVF_{i,n}$ can be determined in a number of ways. The term $(1.12)^5$ can be calculated on a calculator by multiplying 1.12 five times by itself (the fifth power) or using the exponential power key, y^x, where $y = 1.12$ and $x = 5$. Another way is to use a future value table such as that in Table 2·1 to read off $FVF_{i,n}$ directly.[2] Alternatively, the entire process could be done easily with a financial calculator.

In finding these future values, we use the **compounding** process. For a more detailed discussion of simple interest and how it differs from compound interest, see the highlight "Understanding the Compounding Process."

[2] A major disadvantage of using the present and future value tables in this book is that they are constructed for whole percentages (e.g., 10%, 12%). To find the interest factor for a percentage such as 12.5% requires the use of a financial calculator or the formulas contained in the mathematical appendix at the end of the book.

■ HIGHLIGHT

UNDERSTANDING THE COMPOUNDING PROCESS: SIMPLE VERSUS COMPOUND INTEREST

Look back at equation (2-3) for a moment. Notice that the future value at the end of two years is determined by adding the first year's interest to the principal, and this total amount in turn earns interest in the second year. This process illustrates the difference between simple and compound interest and the concept of "earning interest on interest."

Simple interest is the interest earned on the original principal. At the end of each period, interest is earned, but is not added to the principal.

Compound interest is the process of adding earned interest to the principal and basing the interest for the next period on this increased amount.

Compounding is a powerful means of increasing the effect of interest. Figure 1 depicts this process on $100 at 12% interest over five years. The medium-tone area represents the earning of simple interest and the dark area represents the earning of compounded interest, or "interest on interest."

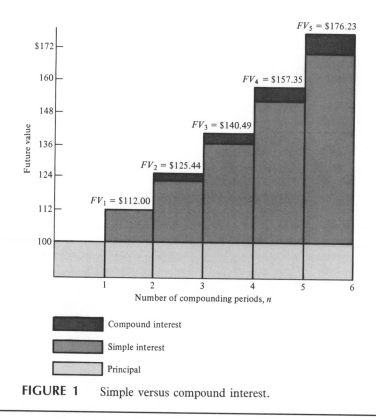

FIGURE 1   Simple versus compound interest.

SOME OBSERVATIONS ABOUT FUTURE VALUES

The curves in Figure 2•1 show how the future value interest factor increases as the number of compounding periods and the interest rate increase. From this graph the following observations can be made:

1. Since future values are greater than present values for positive interest rates, future value factors, $FVF_{i,n}$, are always greater than 1.

2. The larger the interest rate, i, the larger is $FVF_{i,n}$ for any given n, and consequently, the larger is the future value, FV_n.

3. The longer the investment (PV) is earning interest (i.e., the larger n is), the larger is $FVF_{i,n}$, and consequently, the larger is FV_n.

A common boast of someone attempting to sell you a risky investment is that it will "double your money" in a short period of time. A traditional means of determining just how much time this would take is covered in the highlight "The Rule of 72."

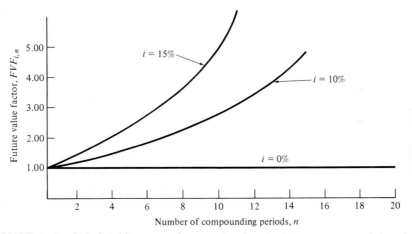

FIGURE 2•1 Relationship among future value factors, interest rates, and time for a $1 lump sum.

■ HIGHLIGHT

THE RULE OF 72

There is a very handy rule of thumb to determine how long it will take for a sum of money to develop. Called the "rule of 72," it states that the growth rate divided into 72 gives the time it takes for the quantity to grow by a factor of 2. For example, Hewlett Packard's average growth rate in dividends over the last 10 years was 10%. At this rate, it will take 72/10 or roughly seven years for its dividends to double.

Another potential use of the rule is to determine how long it will take for the dollar to lose half its purchasing power. In the late 1970s, inflation was around 9% per year. At this rate it would have taken 72/9 or eight years for the dollar to be worth 50 cents in terms of purchasing power. By the mid 1980s, inflation had decreased to about 5%. At this rate it would take about 14 years for the dollar's purchasing power to drop by 50%.

FUTURE VALUE OF AN ANNUITY

So far, we have only discussed how to determine the future value of a single cash flow (lump sum). Most financial decisions, however, involve the evaluation of a series of payments or receipts. When the cash flows are equal and the time between each cash flow is identical, we have the special case known as an **annuity.**

KEY CONCEPT: An **annuity** is a sequence of uninterrupted, equal cash flows.

A stream of payments that does not fit this description is called an uneven stream of cash flows and will be discussed shortly. First, we consider two different kinds of annuities.

Ordinary Annuity

KEY CONCEPT: An **ordinary annuity** is a sequence of uninterrupted, equal cash flows with payments (receipts) occurring at the *end* of each period.

To find the future value of an ordinary annuity, assume that $200 will be deposited at the end of each year for four years and will earn 10% interest. As the time line in Figure 2•2 indicates, valuing an ordinary annuity involves calculating the future value of a series of lump-sum payments, with the payments occurring at the end of each period. That is, we determine the future value of each $200 and then sum these individual values. Using Table 2•1, we obtain

$$
\begin{aligned}
FVA_4 &= \$200(FVF_{.10,3}) + \$200(FVF_{.10,2}) + \$200(FVF_{.10,1}) \\
&\quad + \$200(FVF_{.10,0}) \\
&= \$200(1.3310) + \$200(1.2100) + \$200(1.1000) + \$200(1.0000) \\
&= \$928.20
\end{aligned}
$$

However, since the $200 is a constant figure, we can factor it out:

$$FVA_4 = \$200(FVF_{.10,3} + FVF_{.10,2} + FVF_{.10,1} + FVF_{.10,0})$$
$$= \$200(1.3310 + 1.2100 + 1.1000 + 1.0000)$$
$$= \$200(4.6410)$$
$$= \$928.20$$

Because of this special property, we can create a new interest factor called the future value interest factor for an annuity, $FVFA_{i,n}$, which represents the sum of a series of future value lump-sum interest factors. Moreover, based on this insight, we can create a special table, such as Table 2•2, just for $FVFA_{i,n}$. Therefore, the general formula of the future value of an annuity becomes

$$FVA_n = A(FVFA_{i,n}) \tag{2-5}$$

where A is the constant cash flow or annuity amount.

TABLE 2•2 Future Value Factor for a \$1 Annuity: $FVFA_{i,n}$

Number of Periods	1%	2%	3%	4%	5%	6%	7%	8%	9%	10%	12%	14%	15%	16%	18%	20%	24%
1	1.0000	1.0000	1.0000	1.0000	1.0000	1.0000	1.0000	1.0000	1.0000	1.0000	1.0000	1.0000	1.0000	1.0000	1.0000	1.0000	1.0000
2	2.0100	2.0200	2.0300	2.0400	2.0500	2.0600	2.0700	2.0800	2.0900	2.1000	2.1200	2.1400	2.1500	2.1600	2.1800	2.2000	2.2400
3	3.0301	3.0604	3.0909	3.1216	3.1525	3.1836	3.2149	3.2464	3.2781	3.3100	3.3744	3.4396	3.4725	3.5056	3.5724	3.6400	3.7776
4	4.0604	4.1216	4.1836	4.2465	4.3101	4.3746	4.4399	4.5061	4.5731	4.6410	4.7793	4.9211	4.9934	5.0665	5.2154	5.3680	5.6842
5	5.1010	5.2040	5.3091	5.4163	5.5256	5.6371	5.7507	5.8666	5.9847	6.1051	6.3528	6.6101	6.7424	6.8771	7.1542	7.4416	8.0484
6	6.1520	6.3081	6.4684	6.6330	6.8019	6.9753	7.1533	7.3359	7.5233	7.7156	8.1152	8.5355	8.7537	8.9775	9.4420	9.9299	10.980
7	7.2135	7.4343	7.6625	7.8983	8.1420	8.3938	8.6540	8.9228	9.2004	9.4872	10.089	10.730	11.066	11.413	12.141	12.915	14.615
8	8.2857	8.5830	8.8923	9.2142	9.5491	9.8975	10.259	10.636	11.028	11.435	12.299	13.232	13.726	14.240	15.327	16.499	19.122
9	9.3685	9.7546	10.159	10.582	11.026	11.491	11.978	12.487	13.021	13.579	14.775	16.085	16.785	17.518	19.085	20.798	24.712
10	10.462	10.949	11.463	12.006	12.577	13.180	13.816	14.486	15.192	15.937	17.548	19.337	20.303	21.321	23.521	25.958	31.643
11	11.566	12.168	12.807	13.486	14.206	14.971	15.783	16.645	17.560	18.531	20.654	23.044	24.349	25.732	28.755	32.150	40.237
12	12.682	13.412	14.192	15.025	15.917	16.869	17.888	18.977	20.140	21.384	24.133	27.270	29.001	30.850	34.931	39.580	50.894
13	13.809	14.680	15.617	16.626	17.713	18.882	20.140	21.495	22.953	24.522	28.029	32.088	34.351	36.786	42.218	48.496	64.109
14	14.947	15.973	17.086	18.291	19.598	21.015	22.550	24.214	26.019	27.975	32.392	37.581	40.504	43.672	50.818	59.195	80.496
15	16.096	17.293	18.598	20.023	21.578	23.276	25.129	27.152	29.360	31.772	37.279	43.842	47.580	51.659	60.965	72.035	100.81
16	17.257	18.639	20.156	21.824	23.657	25.672	27.888	30.324	33.003	35.949	42.753	50.980	55.717	60.925	72.939	87.442	126.01
17	18.430	20.012	21.761	23.697	25.840	28.212	30.840	33.750	36.973	40.544	48.883	59.117	65.075	71.673	87.068	105.93	157.25
18	19.614	21.412	23.414	25.645	28.132	30.905	33.999	37.450	41.301	45.599	55.749	68.394	75.836	84.140	103.74	128.11	195.99
19	20.810	22.840	25.116	27.671	30.539	33.760	37.379	41.446	48.018	51.159	63.439	78.969	88.211	96.603	123.41	154.74	244.03
20	22.019	24.297	28.870	29.778	33.066	36.785	40.995	45.762	51.160	57.275	72.052	91.024	102.44	115.37	146.62	186.68	303.60
21	23.239	25.783	28.676	31.969	35.719	39.992	44.865	50.422	56.764	64.002	81.698	104.76	118.81	134.84	174.02	225.02	377.46
22	24.471	27.299	30.536	34.248	38.505	43.392	49.005	55.456	62.873	71.402	92.502	120.43	137.63	157.41	206.34	271.03	469.05
23	25.716	28.845	32.452	36.617	41.430	46.995	53.436	60.893	69.531	79.543	104.60	138.29	159.27	183.60	244.48	326.23	582.62
24	26.973	30.421	34.426	39.082	44.502	50.815	58.176	66.764	76.789	88.497	118.15	158.65	184.16	213.97	289.49	392.48	723.46
25	28.243	32.030	36.459	41.645	47.727	54.864	63.249	73.105	84.700	98.347	133.33	181.87	212.79	249.21	342.60	471.98	898.09
26	29.525	33.670	38.553	44.311	51.113	59.156	68.676	79.954	93.323	109.18	150.33	208.33	245.71	290.08	405.27	567.37	1114.6
27	30.820	35.344	40.709	47.084	54.669	63.705	74.483	87.350	102.72	121.09	169.37	238.49	283.56	337.50	479.22	681.85	1383.1
28	32.129	37.051	42.930	49.967	58.402	68.528	80.697	95.338	112.96	134.20	190.69	272.88	327.10	392.50	566.48	819.22	1716.0
29	33.450	38.792	45.218	52.966	62.322	73.639	87.346	103.96	124.13	148.63	214.58	312.09	377.16	456.30	669.44	984.06	2128.9
30	34.784	40.568	47.575	56.084	66.438	79.058	94.460	113.28	136.30	164.49	241.33	356.78	434.74	530.31	790.94	1181.8	2640.9
40	48.886	60.402	75.401	95.025	120.79	154.76	199.63	259.05	337.88	442.59	767.09	1342.0	1779.0	2360.7	4163.2	7343.8	22728.
50	64.463	84.579	112.79	152.66	209.34	290.33	406.52	573.76	815.08	1163.9	2400.0	4994.5	7217.7	10435.	21813.	45497.	—
60	81.669	114.05	163.05	237.99	353.58	533.12	813.52	1253.2	1944.7	3034.8	7471.6	18535.	29219.	46057.	—	—	—

Annuity Due

You may occasionally encounter another type of annuity, called an **annuity due.**

KEY CONCEPT: An **annuity due** is a sequence of uninterrupted, equal cash flows with the payments (receipts) occurring at the *beginning* of each period.

The only difference between an ordinary annuity and an annuity due, then, is in the timing of the cash flows. As the time line in Figure 2•2 shows, all cash flows are shifted one period closer to the current time. This means that each cash flow will receive one more period of compound interest. Therefore, the future value of an annuity due is found as

$$FV_n = A(FVFA_{i,n})(1 + i)$$

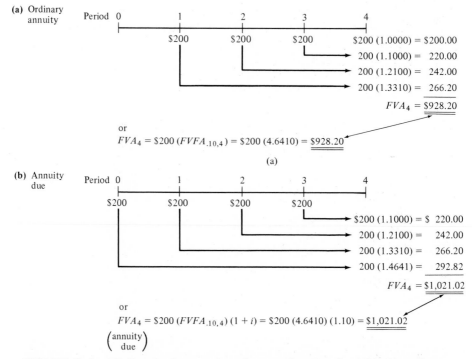

(a) Ordinary annuity

Period 0   1   2   3   4

$200 $200 $200

$200 (1.0000) = $200.00
200 (1.1000) = 220.00
200 (1.2100) = 242.00
200 (1.3310) = 266.20
FVA_4 = $928.20

or
$FVA_4 = \$200\,(FVFA_{.10,4}) = \$200\,(4.6410) = \$928.20$

(a)

(b) Annuity due

Period 0   1   2   3   4

$200 $200 $200 $200

$200 (1.1000) = $ 220.00
200 (1.2100) = 242.00
200 (1.3310) = 266.20
200 (1.4641) = 292.82
FVA_4 = $1,021.02

or
$FVA_4 = \$200\,(FVFA_{.10,4})\,(1 + i) = \$200\,(4.6410)\,(1.10) = \$1,021.02$
$\left(\begin{array}{c}\text{annuity}\\\text{due}\end{array}\right)$

FIGURE 2•2 Finding the future value of an annuity when $i = 10\%$: (a) ordinary annuity [note that since the last deposit is made at the end of four years, it does not earn any interest, that is, $FVF_{.10,0} = (1 + i)^0 = 1.000$]; (b) annuity due.

or, using our example,

$$FV_4 = \$200(4.6410)(1.1000)$$
$$= \$200(5.1051) = \$1,021.02$$

Note that in this case, the interest, 5.1051, is simply the sum of the lump-sum interest factors in Table 2•1. Since ordinary annuities are the most common in finance, we will use the word *annuity* to mean that the cash flows are received at the end of each period (unless otherwise indicated).

Example 2•1   Future Values

FINDING FUTURE VALUES

Lump-Sum Problem. If you invest $10,000 today at 8% and expect to use it 20 years from now for your child's education, how much will you have at that time?

In this example, we are asked to find the future value of $10,000 at the end of 20 years if the interest rate is 8%. From our formula, $FV_{20} = PV(FVF_{.08,20})$. Since $PV = \$10,000$ and $FVF_{.08,20} = 4.6610$ from Table 2•1, we have

$$FV_{20} = \$10,000(4.6610) = \$46,610$$

Annuity Problem. If Ima Cooper deposits $1,000 in her savings account at the end of each year for the next 12 years, how much will she have at the end of this period if the interest rate is 6%?

From our formula, $FV_{12} = A(FVFA_{.06,12})$. Since $A = \$1,000$ and $FVFA_{.06,12} = 16.869$ from Table 2•2,

$$FVA_{12} = \$1,000(16.869) = \$16,869$$

Notice that in this case $1,000 \times 12 = \$12,000$ represents her original deposits, while the difference ($4,869) is the interest earned.

On occasion, the future value will be known and you must solve for one of the other variables (i.e., PV, A, i, or n). The following examples demonstrate how this is done.

SOLVING FOR THE PRESENT VALUE LUMP SUM OR ANNUITY

Lump-Sum Problem. If the interest rate is 8%, what lump-sum amount would a person have to invest today if she wants to have $46,610 in 20 years?

$$FV_{20} = PV(FVF_{.08,20})$$
$$\$46,610 = PV(4.6610)$$

or

$$PV = \frac{\$46,610}{4.6610} = \$10,000$$

This is just a rewritten form of the first example. It helps you understand why \$1 today is worth more than \$1 received later. That is, \$10,000 today is preferred to \$10,000 received in 20 years because \$10,000 today could be invested to grow to \$46,610 versus the \$10,000 received in 20 years.

Annuity Problem. How much must Larry Crum deposit annually in his bank account, which pays 12% interest, if he wants to have \$2,858.76 at the end of five years?

$$FVA_5 = A(FVFA_{.12,5})$$
$$\$2,858.76 = A(6.3528)$$

or

$$A = \frac{\$2,858.76}{6.3528} = \$450 \text{ per year}$$

SOLVING FOR THE INTEREST RATE

Lump-Sum Problem. What interest rate must a \$5,000 investment earn to make it worth \$7,013 in five years?

The \$5,000 must equal \$7,013 after compounding interest for five years. So

$$FV_5 = PV(FVF_{?,5})$$
$$\$7,013 = \$5,000(FVF_{?,5})$$

or

$$FVF_{?,5} = \frac{\$7,013}{\$5,000} = 1.4026$$

From Table 2•1, the future value interest factor 1.4026 in the row for five years corresponds to an interest rate of 7%.

Annuity Problem. Assume that a retirement plan calls for \$3,500 to be deposited at the end of every year for the next 40 years. If this plan guarantees that you will have \$541,660 at the end of this time, what is the interest rate earned?

From this information,

$$FVA_{40} = A(FVFA_{?,40})$$
$$\$541,660 = \$3,500(FVFA_{?,40})$$

or

$$FVFA_{?,40} = \frac{\$541,660}{\$3,500} = 154.76$$

From Table 2•2, the future value interest factor 154.76 in the row for 40 years corresponds to an interest rate of 6%.

SOLVING FOR THE NUMBER OF ANNUAL COMPOUNDING PERIODS

Lump-Sum Problem. Jane Smart borrowed $7,200 a few years ago. If she owes $12,592.80 today, how long ago did Jane take out the loan if she has to pay 15% annual interest?

$$FV_n = PV(FVF_{.15,?})$$
$$\$12,592.80 = \$7,200(FVF_{.15,?})$$

or

$$FVF_{.15,?} = \frac{\$12,592.80}{\$7,200} = 1.7490$$

From Table 2•1, the future value interest factor 1.7490 for 15% corresponds to $n = 4$. Therefore, Jane borrowed the money four years ago.

Annuity Problem. An annuity contract requires that $1,000 be paid annually. If the interest rate is 14%, how long will it take before the total value of this contract reaches $8,535.50?

$$FVA_? = A(FVFA_{.14,?})$$
$$\$8,535.50 = \$1,000(FVFA_{.14,?})$$

or

$$FVFA_{.14,?} = \frac{\$8,535.50}{\$1,000} = 8.5355$$

From Table 2•2, a future value annuity interest factor of 8.5355 when $i = 14\%$ is found to correspond to $n = 6$ years.

By this point, some students may be questioning the necessity of these calculations. Can't a financial calculator do this "drudge" work? The highlight "Financial Calculators: A Means, Not an End," addresses this question.

■ *HIGHLIGHT*

FINANCIAL CALCULATORS: A MEANS, NOT AN END

Students often ask: With the easy availability of hand-held calculators, why is it necessary to study the mechanics of valuation in such detail? Moreover, why use present and future value tables when a calculator can provide the answers directly?

The answer to this question lies in an examination of how a time value problem is solved. There are two stages to this process. The first stage involves the *analysis* and *set-up* of the problem. This step requires an understanding of the principles of time value, of how these principles relate to the problem at hand, the ability to separate the problem into sequential steps and a knowledge of how each step is solved. Only when the first stage is completed can the second stage of the process, the *calculation*, be accomplished.

If finance was merely calculating numbers, taking a finance course and reading this text would be a waste! All you would have to do is purchase a good quality financial calculator, read its owner's manual, and start making financial decisions. As you progress through this text, you will see that the proper set up of the problem is the difficult part. Once this step is accomplished, the calculations are easily done. Thus, a student with a good facility with calculators but possessing only a superficial knowledge of the *process* of comparing cash flows may never get to the second stage if he cannot set up the problem correctly. Working out a few problems at the end of this chapter will convince the reader that this is true. Therefore, to be proficient in analyzing a time value problem a student must develop an understanding of the theory and interrelationships involved in the time value approach. Thus our emphasis on the mechanics of time value in Chapter 2.

Of course, once into the second stage, it makes no difference whether tables or calculators are used for computations. In this step a good calculator can be a great asset. However, given the wide choice of calculators currently available with different features, varying methods of data entry and different levels of programmable functions, we cannot examine methods specific to different makes of calculators. We therefore concentrate on the first stage, and provide the student with an understanding of the procedures required for solving simple and complex time value problems. The details of calculator usage may be obtained from the calculator's user manual.

Moral: Calculators can *compute*, they cannot *analyze* a problem.

PRESENT VALUE OF A LUMP SUM AND THE DISCOUNTING PROCESS

The process of finding present values (also known as **discounting**) is the reverse of what we have done so far. When we compute future values, we move forward through time; when we compute present values, we move backward. Until now, for instance, we wanted to know how much a single cash flow today would be worth after n years. Now, instead of starting with a current cash flow to find its future value, we will start with a future cash flow and find its value today. Figure 2•3 compares present and future values.

Look again at equation (2-4). If we want to find the present value of a cash flow occurring n years from now, all we need to do is solve for PV.

$$FV_n = PV(FVF_{i,n}) \qquad PV = \frac{FV_n}{FVF_{i,n}}$$

Note that this is exactly what we did earlier. Alternatively, since $FVF_{i,n} = (1 + i)^n$,

$$PV = \frac{FV_n \times 1}{(1 + i)^n}$$

or

$$PV = FV_n(PVF_{i,n}) \qquad (2\text{-}6)$$

where $PVF_{i,n} = 1/[(1 + i)^n]$ is the present value interest factor for a lump-sum cash flow received in n years with an interest rate of i. That is why $PVF_{i,n}$ values such as those in Table 2•3 are just the reciprocal of the $FVF_{i,n}$ values found in a future sum of a lump-sum interest factor table such as Table 2•1.

The concept of present value allows one to compare cash flows at different points in time by valuing them all at the present point in time. Recall the example from the beginning of the chapter: Which is preferred: $5,000 in two years or $5,500 in three years? Unless one knows the interest rate and then

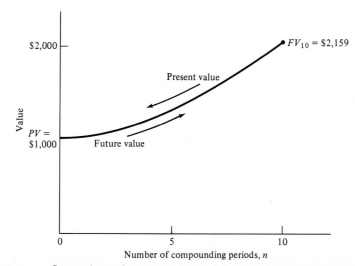

FIGURE 2•3 Comparison of present value and future value when $i = 8\%$.

45

TABLE 2·3 Present Value Factor for a $1 Single Sum: $PVF_{i,n}$

Number of Periods	1%	2%	3%	4%	5%	6%	7%	8%	9%	10%	12%	14%	15%	16%	18%	20%	24%
1	.9901	.9804	.9709	.9615	.9524	.9434	.9346	.9259	.9174	.9091	.8929	.8772	.8696	.8621	.8475	.8333	.8065
2	.9803	.9612	.9426	.9246	.9070	.8900	.8734	.8573	.8417	.8264	.7972	.7695	.7561	.7432	.7182	.6944	.6504
3	.9706	.9423	.9151	.8890	.8638	.8396	.8163	.7938	.7722	.7513	.7118	.6750	.6575	.6407	.6086	.5787	.5245
4	.9610	.9238	.8885	.8548	.8227	.7921	.7629	.7350	.7084	.6830	.6355	.5921	.5718	.5523	.5158	.4823	.4230
5	.9515	.9057	.8626	.8219	.7835	.7473	.7130	.6806	.6499	.6209	.5674	.5194	.4972	.4761	.4371	.4019	.3411
6	.9420	.8880	.8375	.7903	.7462	.7050	.6663	.6302	.5963	.5645	.5066	.4556	.4323	.4104	.3704	.3349	.2751
7	.9327	.8706	.8131	.7599	.7107	.6651	.6227	.5835	.5470	.5132	.4523	.3996	.3759	.3538	.3139	.2791	.2218
8	.9235	.8535	.7894	.7307	.6768	.6274	.5820	.5403	.5019	.4665	.4039	.3506	.3269	.3050	.2660	.2326	.1789
9	.9143	.8368	.7664	.7026	.6446	.5919	.5439	.5002	.4604	.4241	.3606	.3075	.2843	.2630	.2255	.1938	.1443
10	.9053	.8203	.7441	.6756	.6139	.5584	.5083	.4632	.4224	.3855	.3220	.2697	.2472	.2267	.1911	.1615	.1164
11	.8963	.8043	.7224	.6496	.5847	.5268	.4751	.4289	.3875	.3505	.2875	.2366	.2149	.1954	.1619	.1346	.0938
12	.8874	.7885	.7014	.6246	.5568	.4970	.4440	.3971	.3555	.3186	.2567	.2076	.1869	.1685	.1372	.1122	.0757
13	.8787	.7730	.6810	.6006	.5303	.4688	.4150	.3677	.3262	.2897	.2292	.1821	.1625	.1452	.1163	.0935	.0610
14	.8700	.7579	.6611	.5775	.5051	.4423	.3878	.3405	.2992	.2633	.2046	.1597	.1413	.1252	.0985	.0779	.0492
15	.8613	.7430	.6419	.5553	.4810	.4173	.3624	.3152	.2745	.2394	.1827	.1401	.1229	.1079	.0835	.0649	.0397
16	.8528	.7284	.6232	.5339	.4581	.3936	.3387	.2919	.2519	.2176	.1631	.1229	.1069	.0930	.0708	.0541	.0320
17	.8444	.7142	.6050	.5134	.4363	.3714	.3166	.2703	.2311	.1978	.1456	.1078	.0929	.0802	.0600	.0451	.0258
18	.8360	.7002	.5874	.4936	.4155	.3503	.2959	.2502	.2120	.1799	.1300	.0946	.0808	.0691	.0508	.0376	.0208
19	.8277	.6864	.5703	.4746	.3957	.3305	.2765	.2317	.1945	.1635	.1161	.0829	.0703	.0596	.0431	.0313	.0168
20	.8195	.6730	.5537	.4564	.3769	.3118	.2584	.2145	.1784	.1486	.1037	.0728	.0611	.0514	.0365	.0261	.0135
25	.7798	.6095	.4776	.3751	.2953	.2330	.1842	.1460	.1160	.0923	.0588	.0378	.0304	.0245	.0160	.0105	.0046
30	.7419	.5521	.4120	.3083	.2314	.1741	.1314	.0994	.0754	.0573	.0334	.0196	.0151	.0116	.0070	.0042	.0016
40	.6717	.4529	.3066	.2083	.1420	.0972	.0668	.0460	.0318	.0221	.0107	.0053	.0037	.0026	.0013	.0007	.0002
50	.6080	.3715	.2281	.1407	.0872	.0543	.0339	.0213	.0134	.0085	.0035	.0014	.0009	.0006	.0003	.0001	—
60	.5504	.3048	.1697	.0951	.0535	.0303	.0173	.0099	.0057	.0033	.0011	.0004	.0002	.0001	—	—	—

compares the two dollar amounts at the same point in time, the answer is not clear. If $i = 12\%$, the future value in year 3 of $5,000 that can be obtained two years hence is given as

$$FV_3 = \$5,000(FVF_{.12,1}) = \$5,000(1.12) = \$5,600$$

which is more than $5,500. Thus the $5,000 in two years would be preferred because it has a higher future value.

Alternatively, we could find the present value of both cash flows by *discounting* them at 12%. Referring to the second time line in Figure 2·4 and using Table 2·3 yields

$$PV = \$5,000(PVF_{.12,2}) = \$5,000(0.7972) = \$3,986.00$$

and

$$PV = \$5,500(PVF_{.12,3}) = \$5,500(0.7118) = \$3,914.90$$

Once again, the $5,000 in two years would be preferred over the other alternative because it has a higher present value. This is as it should be because the decision should not depend on the point in time at which the two cash flows

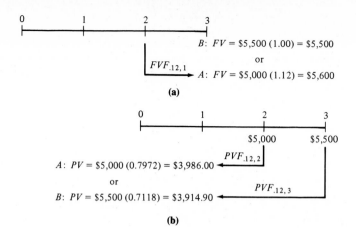

FIGURE 2·4 Comparison of two cash flows to be received at different future dates in terms of (a) future values and (b) present values. *A*, $5,000 in two years; *B*, $5,500 in three years.

are compared. What is important is that they be compared at the same point in time, whatever point is chosen for comparison (recall the apples–apples, oranges–oranges analogy).

Since we live in the present, which is when financial decisions are made, our discussion will rely primarily on present value comparisons.

SOME OBSERVATIONS ABOUT PRESENT VALUES

1. Since present values are smaller than future values for all positive interest rates, present value factors $PVF_{i,n}$ are less than 1.00.

2. The higher the interest rate, the smaller the present value factor, and consequently, the smaller the present value.

3. The further into the future the cash flow occurs (i.e., the larger the n), the smaller the present value factor, and consequently, the smaller the present value.

Use Table 2·3 and Figure 2·5 to confirm these observations.

A NOTE ON TERMINOLOGY

Finding the present value of a cash flow that will occur in the future requires a **discount rate.** At various times, the discount rate is also known by other names. These other names are used when time value techniques occur in a particular financial setting and a more specific meaning is needed.

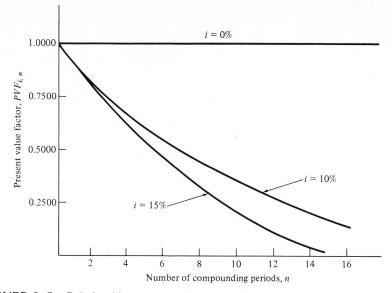

FIGURE 2•5 Relationship among present value interest factors, interest rates, and time.

PRESENT VALUE OF AN ANNUITY

To find the present value of an annuity, we need to reverse the process of finding the future value of an annuity. Conceptually, each cash flow is discounted back to the present, and then all cash flows are summed to get the present value. This means that the present value interest factor for an annuity, $PVFA_{i,n}$, is simply the sum of a series of present value interest factors for a lump sum. To see this, let us take the annuity problem described in Figure 2•2 and find its present value.

Referring to Figure 2•6, we see that

$$PV = \$200(PVF_{.10,1}) + \$200(PVF_{.10,2}) + \$200(PVF_{.10,3}) + \$200(PVF_{.10,4})$$
$$= \$200(0.9091 + 0.8264 + 0.7513 + 0.6830)$$
$$= \$200(3.1698) = \$633.96$$

Rather than sum the individual $PVF_{i,n}$ values every time, a special table for the present value interest factors for annuities, such as Table 2•4, can easily be constructed. The general formula then becomes

$$PVA = A(PVFA_{i,n}) \tag{2-7}$$

48

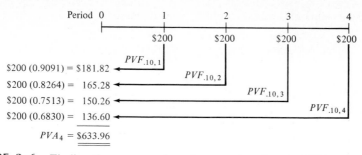

FIGURE 2·6 Finding the present value of an annuity when $i = 10\%$.

TABLE 2·4 Present Value Factor for a $1 Annuity, $PVFA_{i,n}$

Number of Periods	1%	2%	3%	4%	5%	6%	7%	8%	9%	10%	12%	14%	15%	16%	18%	20%	24%
1	0.9901	0.9804	0.9709	0.9615	0.9524	0.9434	0.9346	0.9259	0.9174	0.9091	0.8929	0.8772	0.8696	0.8621	0.8475	0.8333	0.8065
2	1.9704	1.9416	1.9135	1.8861	1.8594	1.8334	1.8080	1.7833	1.7591	1.7355	1.6901	1.6467	1.6257	1.6052	1.5656	1.5278	1.4568
3	2.9410	2.8839	2.8286	2.7751	2.7232	2.6730	2.6243	2.5771	2.5313	2.4869	2.4018	2.3216	2.2832	2.2459	2.1743	2.1065	1.9813
4	3.9020	3.8077	3.7171	3.6299	3.5460	3.4651	3.3872	3.3121	3.2397	3.1699	3.0373	2.9137	2.8550	2.7982	2.6901	2.5887	2.4043
5	4.8534	4.7135	4.5797	4.4518	4.3295	4.2124	4.1002	3.9927	3.8897	3.7908	3.6048	3.4331	3.3522	3.2743	3.1272	2.9906	2.7454
6	5.7955	5.6014	5.4172	5.2421	5.0757	4.9173	4.7665	4.6229	4.4859	4.3553	4.1114	3.8887	3.7845	3.6847	3.4976	3.3255	3.0205
7	6.7282	6.4720	6.2303	6.0021	5.7864	5.5824	5.3893	5.2064	5.0330	4.8684	4.5638	4.2883	4.1604	4.0386	3.8115	3.6046	3.2423
8	7.6517	7.3255	7.0197	6.7327	6.4632	6.2098	5.9713	5.7466	5.5348	5.3349	4.9676	4.6389	4.4873	4.3436	4.0776	3.8372	3.4212
9	8.5660	8.1622	7.7861	7.4353	7.1078	6.8017	6.5152	6.2469	5.9952	5.7590	5.3282	4.9464	4.7716	4.6065	4.3030	4.0310	3.5655
10	9.4713	8.9826	8.5302	8.1109	7.7217	7.3601	7.0236	6.7101	6.4177	6.1446	5.6502	5.2161	5.0188	4.8332	4.4941	4.1925	3.6819
11	10.3676	9.7868	9.2526	8.7605	8.3064	7.8869	7.4987	7.1390	6.8052	6.4951	5.9377	5.4527	5.2337	5.0286	4.6560	4.3271	3.7757
12	11.2551	10.5753	9.9540	9.3851	8.8633	8.3838	7.9427	7.5361	7.1607	6.8137	6.1944	5.6603	5.4206	5.1971	4.7932	4.4392	3.8514
13	12.1337	11.3484	10.6350	9.9856	9.3936	8.8527	8.3577	7.9038	7.4869	7.1034	6.4235	5.8424	5.5831	5.3423	4.9095	4.5327	3.9124
14	13.0037	12.1062	11.2961	10.5631	9.8986	9.2950	8.7455	8.2442	7.7862	7.3667	6.6282	6.0021	5.7245	5.4675	5.0081	4.6106	3.9616
15	13.8651	12.8493	11.9379	11.1184	10.3797	9.7122	9.1079	8.5595	8.0607	7.6061	6.8109	6.1422	5.8474	5.5755	5.0916	4.6755	4.0013
16	14.7179	13.5777	12.5611	11.6523	10.8378	10.1059	9.4466	8.8514	8.3126	7.8237	6.9740	6.2651	5.9542	5.6685	5.1624	4.7296	4.0333
17	15.5623	14.2919	13.1661	12.1657	11.2741	10.4773	9.7632	9.1216	8.5436	8.0216	7.1196	6.3729	6.0472	5.7487	5.2223	4.7746	4.0591
18	16.3983	14.9920	13.7535	12.6593	11.6896	10.8276	10.0591	9.3719	8.7556	8.2014	7.2497	6.4674	6.1280	5.8178	5.2732	4.8122	4.0799
19	17.2260	15.6785	14.3238	13.1339	12.0853	11.1581	10.3356	9.6036	8.9501	8.3649	7.3658	6.5504	6.1982	5.8775	5.3162	4.8435	4.0967
20	18.0456	16.3514	14.8775	13.5903	12.4622	11.4699	10.5940	9.8181	9.1285	8.5136	7.4694	6.6231	6.2593	5.9288	5.3527	4.8696	4.1103
25	22.0232	19.5235	17.4131	15.6221	14.0939	12.7834	11.6536	10.6748	9.8226	9.0770	7.8431	6.8729	6.4641	6.0971	5.4669	4.9476	4.1474
30	25.8077	22.3965	19.6004	17.2920	15.3725	13.7648	12.4090	11.2578	10.2737	9.4269	8.0552	7.0027	6.5660	6.1772	5.5168	4.9789	4.1601
40	32.8347	27.3555	23.1148	19.7928	17.1591	15.0463	13.3317	11.9246	10.7574	9.7791	8.2438	7.1050	6.6418	6.2335	5.5482	4.9966	4.1659
50	39.1961	31.4236	25.7298	21.4822	18.2559	15.7619	13.8007	12.2335	10.9617	9.9148	8.3045	7.1327	6.6605	6.2463	5.5541	4.9995	4.1666
60	44.9550	34.7609	27.6756	22.6235	18.9293	16.1614	14.0392	12.3766	11.0480	9.9672	8.3240	7.1401	6.6651	6.2492	5.5553	4.9999	4.1667

Example 2·2   Present Value of an Annuity

If you win a sweepstakes prize that offers you either (1) $50,000 today or (2) $7,000 per year for the next 12 years, which alternative would you prefer if your discount rate were 12%?

In this case, $50,000 is already a present value, so all we have to do is to find the present value of a $7,000 annuity for 12 years. From Table 2•4, we have

$$PVA = \$7,000(PVFA_{.12,12}) = \$7,000(6.1944) = \$43,360.80$$

Therefore, alternative (2) is worth less than alternative (1).

Learning Check for Section 2•1

Review Questions

2•1. Explain why compounding and discounting are essentially procedures for finding the value of cash flows at a later or earlier point in time.

2•2. What do higher interest rates indicate about people's preferences? What do they indicate about the productivity of capital?

2•3. What is the difference between simple interest and compound interest?

2•4. The interest rate on your investment has dropped from 12% to 8%. What will happen to the future value of your investment?

2•5. What is the difference between an ordinary annuity and an annuity due? Can you think of some examples? What is the significance of this difference for the computation of future values?

2•6. Your friend, who was supposed to pay back an interest-free loan in one month, has now informed you that she will pay it back in three months. What has happened to the present value of that loan to you? Why?

New Terms

Annuity	Discounting	Time preference
Annuity due	Discount rate	Time value of
Compounding	Ordinary annuity	money

SECTION 2·2 *Other Time-Value Considerations*

FREQUENCY OF COMPOUNDING PERIODS

So far, we have assumed that interest is compounded once a year, or annually. That is, at the end of the first year, the interest earned for that year is added to the principal and this larger amount earns interest for the second year. In contrast, savings institutions typically compound interest on their accounts quarterly or even daily. Bonds pay interest semiannually, and are therefore valued assuming semiannual compounding.

Suppose that a savings account earns interest quarterly. At the end of three months, interest is added back to the principal, and for the next three months, the larger amount earns interest. Thus quarterly compounding yields a larger sum at the end of the year than annual compounding. The reason, of course, is that the $FVF_{i,n}$ will be larger with quarterly compounding, which implies a higher **effective interest rate.** In this case the interest rate is divided by 4, but four times as many compounding periods are used because interest is earned four times a year.

To reflect the frequency of compounding periods, we must make two adjustments. First, the interest rate is converted to a per-period rate by dividing the annual rate by the number of compounding periods in a year, $1/m$. Second, the number of years is multiplied by the number of compounding periods occurring per year, mn. To illustrate, let us adjust $FVF_{i,n}$:

$$FVF_{i/m,mn} = \left(1 + \frac{i}{m}\right)^{mn} \tag{2-8}$$

Now assume that we deposit $100 in an 8% savings account that pays interest quarterly. How much would be in the account at the end of the year, and what is the effective annual interest rate?

$$FV_n = PV\left(1 + \frac{i}{m}\right)^{mn}$$

or

$$FV_1 = \$100\left(1 + \frac{0.08}{4}\right)^{4\times1}$$

$$= \$100(1.02)^4 = \$100(1.0824) = \$108.24$$

and the effective interest rate is 8.24%. Often the term **nominal** or **stated interest rate** refers to the annual rate, such as the 8% in our example, while the

annual percentage rate (*APR*) refers to the 8.24% figure. Finally, note that if the nominal interest rate had been 9%, the quarterly rate would have been 2.25%, which is a rate not contained in the interest factor tables. In such cases, the interest factor can be computed directly, using a financial calculator.

PRESENT VALUE OF A PERPETUITY

A perpetuity is a special type of ordinary annuity.

KEY CONCEPT: A **perpetuity** is a series of equal periodic payments that continues forever (to infinity).

One example of a perpetuity is the British consol. To finance its wars against Napoleon, the British government issued bonds, called *consols*, that paid the bondholders a stated amount in pounds sterling periodically as long as they (or their heirs) owned it. Sometimes preferred stock, an equity instrument that pays a fixed dividend and has no maturity, is also considered a perpetuity. The present value of a perpetuity can easily be found via a simple formula:

$$PV_{\text{perpetuity}} = \frac{\text{cash flow per period}}{\text{discount rate}} \qquad (2\text{-}9)$$

If the consol paid its holder £100 per year forever and if the discount rate is 10%, its value would be

$$PV_{\text{perpetuity}} = \frac{£100}{0.10} = £1{,}000$$

This is a surprisingly small value for an asset that will pay millions of pounds over time. The reason for such a small value is that the more distant cash flows do not have much present value, and therefore their contribution to the perpetuity's value is very small. For example, $1 to be received in 40 years is worth only about $0.02 at a 10% discount rate.

STOCK AND FLOW VARIABLES AND THE PROCESS OF CAPITALIZATION

At this point, we must take a small detour from the discussion of time-value calculations to understand the meanings of the words **capitalization** and **capitalize.** These concepts are vital to the development of subsequent chapters. To understand them, we must examine the concepts of **stock** and **flow variables.**

Consider the income stream that workers expect from their jobs. They typically get a monthly paycheck and then pay a monthly mortgage payment, credit card bills, and so on. These are examples of flow variables or cash flows per period. A stock variable, on the other hand, has no time dimension; it is simply a number at a particular point in time. For instance, stock variables include the wealth that an individual has today, the value of his or her house, and the current market value of Exxon's 10-year bonds.

In our discussion of time-value calculations, note that whenever the present or future values were computed, the answer was always a number. Thus finding the present value or future value of cash flows is nothing but the conversion of flow variables (cash flows) to a stock variable (a present or future value). The stock variable provides information that is equivalent to the information provided by the flow variable. This process is the basis of the concept of valuation.

The process of finding the value of a security or an asset that provides a cash flow stream (often referred to as an *income stream*) is simply the process of finding a stock variable that capitalizes this income stream (a flow variable). But as seen earlier, this can be done by finding the present value of the stream.

KEY CONCEPT: **Capitalizing** a cash flow stream is simply the process of finding the present value of the stream.

We discuss other aspects of the capitalization process in Chapter 3. For now, we just note that the process of finding the (present) value of an asset involves two steps:

1. Identifying the cash flows provided by the asset.

2. Capitalizing (discounting) these cash flows at the appropriate discount rate.

To put it another way:

KEY CONCEPT: **Valuing** an asset consists of transforming a flow variable (cash flows provided by the asset) to a stock variable (present value).

Learning Check for Section 2·2

Review Questions

2·7.   For a given interest rate on your savings, would a switch from quarterly to monthly compounding be to your advantage?

2·8.   What is the difference between a perpetuity and an annuity?

2·9.   Determine whether the following are stock variables or flow variables:
(a)   The amount of cash in your wallet
(b)   Monthly Social Security payments made to senior citizens
(c)   The value of your car

(d) The monthly payments on your car

(e) The gross national product of the United States

(f) Rent on an apartment

2•10. Explain how the effective interest rate is calculated with semiannual compounding.

2•11. "Valuation is the process of converting a flow variable to a stock variable." Explain.

New Terms

Annual percentage
   rate (APR)
Capitalization

Effective interest rate
Flow variable
Nominal interest
   rate

Perpetuity
Stock variable
Valuing an asset

SECTION 2•3 *Applications of the Time-Value Concept*

We are now ready to use time-value techniques in a more sophisticated manner. In this section, we examine two very important concepts that are useful in evaluating cash flows: **net present value** (**NPV**) and internal rate of return (IRR). However, before a detailed discussion of these concepts the reader may wish to examine a more lighthearted application of time value concepts in the highlight "Can Time Machines Exist?".

■■ *HIGHLIGHT*

CAN TIME MACHINES EXIST?

A science-fiction application of the time value of money.

Ever since H.G. Wells published *The Time Machine* in 1895, numerous authors and moviemakers have explored the potential consequences of time travel. Is time travel really possible? Might time machines have existed in the past? What about the future?

The answer is that as long as current economic conditions prevail, the effects of interest rates rule out the possibility of past, present, or future time machines. This implication of the time value of money is an amusing aside to the (perhaps less fascinating) discussion in the text.

One of the basic ideas underlying the theory of finance is that individuals prefer more wealth to less. Consider a "time traveler" who deposits $100 in a savings account in 1986 at an annual interest rate of 10%. In seven years, Equation 2-4 suggests that the value of his savings account will be $194.87. If time travel were possible, the investor could deposit the $100 in 1986, travel instantaneously to 1993, withdraw the $194.87, fly back to 1986, redeposit the $194.87 and repeat the process until he had infinite wealth. His time machine would really be a "money machine." In fact, if all citizens had access to time travel, the entire country would prosper—everyone would have infinite wealth! Negative interest rates are also inconsistent with finite wealth in a world of time travel because individuals could then travel backward through time to generate infinite wealth.

The only condition under which the time machine would not be a money machine is when the interest rate is zero. Only then can the economy support individuals who can travel forward or backward through time without generating wealth.

Since interest rates are (and have been) nonzero, this strongly suggests that time travel has never existed, and furthermore, will never.

Adapted from M.R. Reinganum, "Is time travel impossible? A financial Proof," *Journal of Portfolio Management*, Fall 1986.

NET PRESENT VALUE

The Definition of Net Present Value

The examples presented so far have not distinguished between cash inflows and cash outflows. In practice, cash flows are usually made up of both inflows and outflows. For example, a firm that buys a widget machine initially has to pay for it (a cash outflow). Once the widgets roll off the assembly line, they can be sold to generate revenues (cash inflows). When the machine cannot be used any more, the firm will sell it, perhaps for scrap value (a cash inflow).

If these cash flows all occur at the same time, we simply subtract the outflows from the inflows and see whether the result of the transaction is positive or negative. However, what if these cash flows occur at different points in time? In such situations, the firm is interested in finding the *net present value* (*NPV*) of these cash flows. We will discuss the economic meaning of net present value and its applications in greater detail later. At this point, we simply define it:

KEY CONCEPT: The **net present value** (*NPV*) of a stream of cash flows is the difference between the present value of the inflows and the present value of the outflows.

That is,

$$NPV = PV_{inflows} - PV_{outflows} \qquad (2\text{-}10)$$

55

Calculating Net Present Value

Because the use of this formula for calculating net present value is fairly straightforward and because we will see such calculations in greater detail later, we present only one numerical example here.

Example 2•3   Calculating the NPV of a Cash Flow Sequence

Suppose that an initial investment of $1,000 is expected to produce the future cash inflows shown in the following time line. What is the *NPV* of this investment if your discount rate is 10%?

0	1	2	3
−$1,000	$200	$450	$850

STEP 1

Calculate the present value of the outflows. The only outflow is the initial investment of $1,000. As it is already at time zero, no adjustments are required.

$$PV_{\text{outflows}} = -\$1,000$$

STEP 2

Calculate the present value of the inflows; that is, discount each cash flow amount back to time zero. Then sum these present values to get the present value of all the inflows.

$$
\begin{aligned}
PV_{\text{inflows}} &= \$200(PVF_{.10,1}) + \$450(PVF_{.10,2}) + \$850(PVF_{.10,3}) \\
&= \$200(0.9091) + \$450(0.8264) + \$850(0.7513) \\
&= \$181.82 + \$371.88 + \$638.61 \\
&= \$1,192.31
\end{aligned}
$$

STEP 3

Calculate the *NPV*.

$$
\begin{aligned}
NPV &= PV_{\text{inflows}} - PV_{\text{outflows}} \\
&= \$1,192.31 - \$1,000 \\
&= \$192.31
\end{aligned}
$$

Thus, the investment has a positive *NPV* of $192.31.

INTERNAL RATE OF RETURN (IRR)

What Does the *IRR* Mean?

The *IRR* is often misunderstood. What is it? What does it tell us? These questions can be best answered by comparing the rate of return computed using a naive approach with the *IRR*.

As a loan officer, you have agreed to loan $100 to the China Inn Restaurant. The loan will be repaid over the next three years, as shown in this time line.

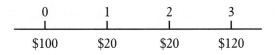

What rate of return are you earning on this loan?

A Naive Approach

A naive approach that is often used is to divide the inflows by the outflows. The general **rate of return** formula is

$$\text{Rate of return} = \frac{\text{net inflows}}{\text{outflows}} = \frac{\text{inflows} - \text{outflows}}{\text{outflows}}$$

Net inflows are used to give the dollar return we will receive above and beyond the original investment. Using this formula, the naive rate of return on the loan is

$$\text{Rate of return} = \frac{\$20 + \$20 + \$120 - \$100}{\$100} = 60\%$$

The bank appears to have earned 60% on the loan, a rate we would have obtained regardless of whether the largest cash flow of $120 occurred in year 3, in year 2, or in year 1. However, we would hardly be indifferent as to when this large cash flow is received. Therefore, the naive approach, because it does not properly take into account the timing of the cash flows, is not a correct measure of return.

The *IRR* Approach

The **IRR** approach differs from the naive approach in that it explicitly recognizes both the amount and timing of the inflows and outflows in determining the rate of return.

KEY CONCEPT: The *IRR* is the rate of return on an investment after adjusting for the timing of the inflows and outflows.

To calculate the NPV with equation (2-10), we have to know the discount rate to find present values. In certain situations, we are interested in finding the discount rate that makes the *NPV* equal to zero.

KEY CONCEPT: The **internal rate of return (IRR)** is the discount rate that makes *NPV* = 0. Alternatively stated, the *IRR* is the discount rate that makes the present value of inflows equal to the present value of outflows.

In words, the *IRR* is that discount rate that satisfies the following equation:

$$PV_{\text{inflows}} - PV_{\text{outflows}} = 0 \qquad (2\text{-}11)$$

Recall that our objective is to determine the rate of interest earned on the loan. Also recall from the discussion of "Present Value of a Lump Sum and the Discounting Process" that the discount rate relates present value and future value. Therefore the discount rate that makes the present value of the bank's cash inflows (from the loan repayment) equal to the amount it loans out (the $1,000 outflow) is the true rate of interest earned on the loan. Equating the present value of the outflows and inflows for our loan gives the following equation:

$$PV_{\text{inflows}} = PV_{\text{outflows}}$$

$$\$20(PVF_{IRR,1}) + \$20(PVF_{IRR,2}) + \$120(PVF_{IRR,3}) = \$100$$

or

$$\$20(PVF_{IRR,1}) + \$20(PVF_{IRR,2}) + \$120(PVF_{IRR,3}) - \$100 = 0$$

Solving this equation for the unknown *IRR* gives an *IRR* of 20%. (We will see shortly how the *IRR*s are calculated.) This is the rate of return that equates the present value of what the bank loans out with the present value of the payments it receives in return. This *IRR* is the correct rate of interest earned on the loan. It is called the *internal rate of return* because the only information needed to compute it is the magnitude and timing of the cash flows of the loan or asset. No other external information is required.

Calculating the *IRR*

Finding the *IRR* therefore involves solving equation (2-11) for the unknown discount rate. Depending on the cash flow pattern, the *IRR* can be found in a number of ways. Three such methods will now be discussed.

Method 1: Constant Annual Cash Inflows—An Annuity Problem If the only net cash outflow occurs immediately ($t = 0$) and the future cash inflows are constant, the *IRR* can easily be found to be the discount rate that satisfies equation (2-11). But in this special case, the present value of cash outflows is the cash flow that occurs at $t = 0$, represented as CF_0. Further, the cash flows in the future represent an annuity, so that in this case we can write equation (2-11) as

$$CF_t(PVFA_{IRR,n}) - CF_0 = 0 \qquad (2\text{-}12)$$

where $CF_t = A$ is the constant future cash inflow and CF_0 is the initial cash outflow (a present value).

Example 2•4   Calculating the IRR for an Annuity

Suppose that \$5,000 is invested today and will generate an annual cash inflow of \$1,319 for five years. Then, from equation (2-12),

$$\$1,319(PVFA_{IRR,5}) - \$5,000 = 0$$

or

$$PVFA_{IRR,5} = \frac{\$5,000}{\$1,319} = 3.7908$$

From the $PVFA_{i,n}$ table (Table 2•4), this present value interest factor for $n = 5$ indicates an implied interest rate (*IRR*) of 10%.

Method 2: Uneven Annual Cash Flows—A Trial-and-Error Procedure With the more common problem in which the cash flows are irregular, the *IRR* cannot be determined directly, as in method 1. Instead, we need a trial-and-error procedure. We begin with a best guess of a discount rate, and then if this "guesstimate" is not reasonable, we try new discount rates until equation (2-11) is approximately accurate.

Example 2•5   Finding IRRs by the Trial-and-Error Procedure

Suppose we are interested in calculating the *IRR* for the investment described in Example 2•3. The cash flows for this project are as follows:

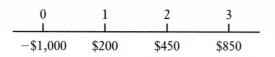

0	1	2	3
−$1,000	$200	$450	$850

Our first guess for an *IRR* is 24%.[3] This is, however, only a first approximation. The *NPV* of these cash flows at a 24% discount is −$100. Therefore, a 24% rate will be too high, and we must try a lower value for the *IRR*. If we try a discount rate of 20%, we find that *NPV* is less than zero ($−28.96). This suggests that the discount rate is close to 20% but slightly lower. So, if we try a discount rate of, say, 18%, we find that the *NPV* equals $+10. Because the *NPV* switched from negative to positive, it must be true that the *IRR* lies somewhere between 18 and 20%.

Method 3: Using a Financial Calculator or a Computer The *IRR* can be found most easily and precisely with the aid of a hand-held calculator because the procedures are preprogrammed and can thus be done more quickly and efficiently, especially for irregular cash flows, where method 1 does not work. In fact, this is the best way to gain precision in calculating the *IRR*. Readers with financial calculators should refer to their manuals for the calculation procedure.

Learning Check for Section 2•3

Review Questions

2•12. Define *NPV* and *IRR*.

2•13. "To find the *NPV* you need a discount rate, but not to find the *IRR*." True or false?

2•14. List the information needed to calculate the *NPV* of a series of cash flows.

2•15. Why is the *IRR* an "internal" rate of return?

New Terms

Internal rate of return (*IRR*)   Net present value (*NPV*)   Rate of return

---

[3] This guess is our best approximation of the *IRR*. It does not have to be accurate; it merely serves as the starting point for the trial-and-error method. Naturally, if, through experience or other approximation procedures, this estimate is close to the actual *IRR*, the procedure will be quicker.

SUMMARY

Finding Future and Present Values

Since interest rates in the economy are positive, there is a time value to money. Virtually all aspects of financial decision making call for a comparison of cash flows that differ in both timing and magnitude. Without a firm grasp of the time-value mechanics, these comparisons cannot be made in a meaningful way.

In this chapter we have focused on what is now commonly referred to as the *arithmetic of finance*—the calculation of present and future values. These calculations may be performed on individual lump sums or on a stream of irregular payments. They may also be performed on streams of cash flows, called *annuities*, which are regular in both amount and timing.

Other Time-Value Considerations

Although the factors provided in the present and future value tables assume that interest is paid once every period (year), the situation involving other (semiannual, monthly, etc.) compounding can be handled fairly easily by adjusting the interest rate and the compounding period appropriately. Perpetuities, which are streams of cash flows that continue indefinitely, can be valued easily by means of a simple formula. A stock variable is an amount at a given point in time. A flow variable, on the other hand, is the flow of cash over a period of time. Capitalization is the process of converting a flow variable into a stock variable.

Applications of the Time-Value Concept

In this chapter, we have also introduced certain concepts that are used extensively in later chapters: the net present value (*NPV*) and the internal rate of return (*IRR*). Net present value measures the difference between the present value of inflows and the present value of outflows of an investment. *IRR* is the rate of return on an investment after adjusting for the timing of the inflows and outflows.

PROBLEMS

2·1.   If you deposit $100 in the bank today and it earns interest at a rate of 8% compounded annually, how much will be in the account 50 years from today?

2•2.   Your uncle died recently and left you the money in his savings account. His only deposit was $100 made 50 years ago. The savings account paid 8% compounded annually. How much money is in the account today?

2•3.   A loaf of bread costs $0.79 today. If its price increases by 6% per year, how much will an equivalent loaf cost in 20 years?

2•4.   You ask a friend with some interest factor tables for $PVF_{.09,6}$. He tells you that the number on his table is 1.677, but the heading of the table is torn off, so he does not know if 1.677 is $PVF_{.09,6}$ or $FVF_{.09,6}$. Without looking at another table, can you tell which it is? Why? If it is $FVF_{.09,6}$, what is $PVF_{.09,6}$?

2•5.   How much money must you deposit in a savings account today to have $20,000 in 20 years if the interest rate is 8% compounded annually?

2•6.   A stock has paid dividends regularly for the last 20 years, starting with $0.75 in 1964 and rising to $4 in 1984. If these dividends have been growing at a constant rate, what has that rate been for the last 20 years?

2•7.   Your sister borrows $1,000 and promises to repay $2,000. If you want at least a 5% return on your loan, within how many years must she pay you back?

2•8.   Which would you prefer: $1,000 now, $2,000 in 5 years, or $3,000 in 10 years if your time value of money is 12%?

2•9.   Which would you prefer: $3,000 now, $2,000 that was placed in a savings account 5 years ago, or $1,000 that was placed in a savings account 10 years ago if
(a)   your time value of money is 12%.
(b)   your time value of money is 16%.
(c)   your time value of money is 8%.

2•10.   Using a discount rate of 12%, find the present value of $100 received at the end of each of the next four years
(a)   using only the *PVF* table.
(b)   using only the *PVFA* table.

2•11.   Using a discount rate of 12%, find the future value as of the end of year 4 of $100 received at the end of each of the next four years
(a)   using only the *FVF* table.
(b)   using only the *FVFA* table.
(c)   using only your answer to problem 2•10 and the fact that $FVF_{.12,4} = 1.5735$.

2•12.   You ask a friend with some interest factor tables for $PVFA_{.09,6}$ and she tells you that the number on her table is 7.5233, but the heading on the table is torn off, she does not know if 7.5233 is $PVFA_{.09,6}$ or $FVFA_{.09,6}$. Without looking at another table, can you tell which it is? Why?

2•13.   How much must you save at the end of each of the next 10 years to have $100,000 at the end of the 10th year if the interest rate is 10%?

2•14.   If the discount rate is 12%, what is the present value of $200 received at the end of each of the next 10 years except for the fourth year (i.e., you get payments at the end of years 1, 2, 3, 5, 6, 7, 8, 9, and 10)?

2•15.   If the discount rate is 14%, what is FV_{10} of $300 received at the end of each of the next 10 years except for the fourth year?

2•16.   What is the present value of a seven-year $1,000 annuity if the first $1,000 payment is made four years from today and the discount rate is 15%?

2•17.   What is FV_{12} of a 10-year $500 annuity for which the first $500 payment is made at the end of the 3rd year (and the 10th payment at the end of the 12th year) if the discount rate is 16%?

2•18.   What is the present value of a 20-year annuity due with $1,000 payments if the discount rate is 8%? [*Hint:* Assume that a payment made at the end of one year (as in an ordinary annuity) has the same present value as a payment made at the beginning of the next year (as in an annuity due).]

2•19.   What is FV_{10} of a 10-year annuity due with payments of $1,000 if the discount rate is 10%?

2•20.   How much must you deposit at the end of each year for 15 years to be able to withdraw $500 at the end of 10 years and $1,000 at the end of 15 years if your savings draw interest at an annual rate of 7%?

2•21.   You are buying a $100,000 home with a 30-year mortgage requiring payments to be made at the end of each year. The interest rate is 10% for the first 15 years of the mortgage but then increases to 15% for the last 15 years. How much will your annual payments be?

2•22.   If you deposit $100 in a savings account today, and keep it there for 50 years, how much would be in the account if the interest were 8% compounded semiannually? If it were 8% compounded quarterly? (*Note:* $FVF_{.04,100} = 50.505$ and $FVF_{.02,200} = 52.485$.)

2•23. A device is for sale that will save you 10% of your utility bill every year. Your time value of money is 12% and your utility bill is $500 per year. Assuming that your utility bill remains constant and that you (and your heirs) will be around to enjoy the benefits of the device forever, how much should you be willing to pay for it?

2•24. You plan to retire in 40 years, at which time you want enough in a savings account to allow you to withdraw $20,000 at the beginning of each of the subsequent 10 years (an insurance policy will support you if you live for more than 10 years after you retire).
   (a) If the savings account pays interest at an annual rate of 9%, how much must you have saved up by the end of the fortieth year?
   (b) If you deposit a fixed sum of money in the savings account at the end of each of the next 40 years to achieve the retirement goal of part (a), how much must you deposit each year?
   (c) Same as part (b), except that this time you only save for 20 years (at the end of each of years 21 through 40).

2•25. You are trying to decide whether to buy a $2,500 motorcycle on credit or to save money to buy it in 30 months. If you buy on credit, you will make 30 equal end-of-the-month payments at a finance charge of 2% per month. If you save money to buy it in 30 months, you will earn 1% per month on your savings. However, the semiannual inflation rate is 5%, so the motorcycle will cost more in 2.5 years. (Suppose that you don't care when you take possession of the motorcycle; that is, you will make your decision solely on the basis of which plan has lower monthly requirements.)
   (a) What will your monthly payments be if you buy on credit?
   (b) What must your monthly deposits be if you choose to save money and buy it in 30 months?
   (c) What should you do?

2•26. Your brother has just graduated from high school and is seeking your advice as to whether he should find a job immediately or go to college for four years and then find a job. He estimates that if he gets a job immediately, he will earn $15,000 per year for the next 40 years. If he goes to college first, he estimates that he can earn $30,000 for each of the 36 years after he gets out. (Whether he goes to college or not, he plans to retire 40 years from today.) He also estimates that the four years of college will cost him $8,000 each. Assume that his time value of money is 14% and that all cash flows are ordinary annuities. (If he goes to college first, he can borrow money at 14%, too.)
   (a) What will be the present value of his cash flows if he gets a job immediately?
   (b) What will be the present value of his cash flows if he goes to college first?
   (c) What should he do?

2•27. Consider an investment that pays $80 in interest every year plus $1,000 when it matures in 12 years. You can buy the investment today for $753. What is the *IRR* of this investment? (Use a financial calculator for this problem.)

2•28. An automobile costs $10,000 now, requires $1,000 annually to maintain, and has a salvage value of $2,000 at the end of eight years. Your time value of money is 9%. What is the *NPV* of these cash flows?

READINGS

FAMA, EUGENE F., AND M.H. MILLER, *The Theory of Finance* (New York: Holt, Rinehart and Winston, 1972).

FISHER, IRVING, *The Theory of Interest* (New York: Augustus M. Kelley, Publishers, 1965; reprinted from the 1930 edition).

HIRSCHLEIFER, J., "On the Theory of Optimal Investment Decision," *Journal of Political Economy*, August 1958, 329–352.

OSBORN, R., *The Mathematics of Investment* (New York: Harper & Row, Publishers, Inc., 1957).

3

The Concept of Value

Chapter 1 established the basic premise underlying this book: The goal of the finance manager must be to make the shareholders wealthier. That is, the objective of the manager should be the maximization of the value of the shareholders' stock. We also argued that this is achieved not by focusing on profits but by recognizing that values are determined by cash flows. In implementing this line of reasoning in day-to-day decision making, managers are constantly faced with the prospect of comparing cash flows that differ in both magnitude and timing. In Chapter 2 we suggested that the present value of these cash flows be compared after discounting them at an appropriate discount rate. Finally, we introduced the notion of net present value (*NPV*).

The previous chapters have not addressed several important issues. For one thing, while we said that cash flow rather than the book concept of profits determines values, our discussion was very brief. We need to discuss this and related ideas further. Second, we need to establish how one determines the discount rate used to find present values and which factors affect discount rates. The examples in Chapter 2 have already shown that discount rates are related to interest rates. However, this inference does not capture the entire picture; other factors are also involved. Finally, what is the special significance of *NPV?* While the method of calculating *NPV*s is straightforward, what is the economic meaning of this concept? Why and how can the financial manager use it?

This chapter answers these questions. To do that, however, we must introduce several new ideas. We begin this introduction with a preview of the chapter's contents.

SECTION 3•1: *What Is Value?* The primary objective of this section is to examine the concept of value and see why it depends on opportunity costs. After explaining these ideas in detail, we argue that the discount rates used in Chapter 2 are really opportunity costs. The concepts of economic profits and excess returns are introduced with the aid of a simple example. Finally, we explore the impact of risk on opportunity costs.

SECTION 3•2: *The Valuation Process.* In this section, we discuss the valuation process in general and the distinction between personal valuations and market valuations. Then we relate the net present value concept introduced in Chapter 2 to the excess returns concept developed in Section 3•1.

SECTION 3•3: *Market Values and Market Efficiency.* In this section, we discuss the meaning and implications of the efficient market hypothesis. It is important to recognize here that decisions based on market values are meaningful only if markets are efficient.

SECTION 3•4: *The Fundamental Valuation Model.* In this section, we present a fundamental valuation model. This model applies to the determination of any financial asset's value, irrespective of whether it is a stock, a bond, an oil and gas partnership, or real estate. All cases of valuation addressed in this book are specific cases of this formulation.

Although the discussion in this chapter may appear abstract at times, it is the basis of virtually every practical decision in finance. The concepts lend themselves to application not only in corporate finance and investments but also in everyday personal financial planning situations. We cannot overstate the importance of understanding the concepts presented in this chapter.

SECTION 3•1 *What Is Value?*

"What is value?" appears to be a very basic question, yet most people have trouble answering it. The early economics literature is replete with discussions on what this term means; even *Webster's New Collegiate Dictionary* gives eight different definitions of value, none of which is entirely satisfactory for financial decision making. In finance and economics, value is really **economic value.** Social, ethical, and moral values are not central in studying financial management. A definition of value that is useful for our purposes is the following:

KEY CONCEPT: The **value** of an asset is the maximum dollar price that one is willing to pay for it.

We will explore several aspects of this definition in greater detail.

THE DETERMINANTS OF VALUE

For an asset to have value, it must possess two characteristics: *benefits* and *costs*.

Benefits

A commodity or service has value only if it provides, or has the opportunity to provide, some benefits. For example, a piece of paper found on the sidewalk normally has no economic value. However, if this same piece of paper carried the signature of Abraham Lincoln, it has economic value because the owner can expect to sell the signature. Similarly, a piece of machinery has some economic value to a company because it can be used to produce goods that the firm can sell for cash. Even if the machine cannot be operated, it can still have some economic value because the company may get some benefits by selling it, perhaps to a scrap dealer. It does not matter how the benefits come. As long as one can derive some benefits from a commodity or service, it has economic value.

Consider some extreme examples. A glass of water can provide benefits, yet it is generally not regarded as being of value. Similarly, the air around us provides benefits, and yet it too is not regarded as having economic value. Obviously, something is missing from the discussion—something that will explain this apparent discrepancy.

Costs or Sacrifice

Value is associated with sacrifice. It is not enough for an asset to offer benefits in order to have economic value; obtaining these benefits in any other way must also involve some sacrifice. To get the benefits from owning Lincoln's signature (personal satisfaction and a certain amount of dollars) without having that piece of paper will involve time and effort (to get it from somewhere else) or money (if it can be purchased from a collector). Because the potential benefits are associated with some sacrifice, the piece of paper will have value. Air and small quantities of water can generally be obtained easily without involving any sacrifice (time or money) and hence have no economic value; they can be had free.

WHAT BENEFITS SHOULD BE CONSIDERED?

The benefits an asset provides can be either tangible or intangible. **Tangible benefits** are physical, easily quantifiable, and therefore relatively easy to deal with. For example, a metal worker at Bethlehem Steel draws a salary that is a tangible benefit. Working for the White House also provides a salary. In addition to this tangible benefit, however, the worker at the White House gets **intangible benefits** such as prestige and influence. Other examples of tangible benefits include the dividends and capital gains from owning stock and the services provided by a car in working condition. In finding the value of an asset in finance, we confine ourselves to measuring tangible benefits. The most common tangible benefit for our purposes is the cash flow stream (sequence) an asset provides.

WHAT COSTS SHOULD BE CONSIDERED?

The true cost of anything is the most valuable alternative given up or *sacrificed*. This cost is termed an **opportunity cost,** and this is the relevant cost for financial decision making. The trick to understanding the concept of opportunity costs is to recognize that every act of choice involves an act of sacrifice. Suppose that a manager has the choice of three different investment proposals: A, B, and C. If he chooses A, this choice is equivalent to a sacrifice of B and C. Suppose that of the two, B and C, B is the better alternative. Then, in choosing A, the manager has incurred a cost of the next best alternative, B.

The principle of opportunity cost becomes clearer if one considers another example. Do you prefer studying finance on Tuesday or on Saturday? The time involved in studying a chapter is the same on both days, but the cost of studying on Saturday is higher because the alternative use of your time is more valuable on Saturday; there are perhaps several other more beneficial activities open to you that day. (See the highlight "Benjamin Franklin on Opportunity Costs.")

◼ *HIGHLIGHT*

Benjamin Franklin on Opportunity Costs

Remember that Time is Money, He that can earn Ten Shillings a Day by his Labour, and goes abroad, or sits idle one half of that Day, tho' he spends but Sixpence during his Diversion or Idleness, ought not to reckon That the one Expence; he has really spent or rather thrown away Five Shillings besides.

Source: Benjamin Franklin's "Advice to a Young Tradesman," *Papers*, Vol. III, pp. 306–308: first printed on July 21, 1748. Reprinted in *The Political Thought of Benjamin Franklin*, R.L. Ketcham, ed. (Indianapolis, Ind.: The Bobbs-Merrill Company, Inc., 1965).

In contrast to the preceding examples, opportunity costs in finance are quantified and are usually measured as a percentage return. Suppose that a corporation has a $500,000 deposit in a bank earning 14% interest per year. All other uses of its money provide a lower return. But suppose the company is considering another use for the money—a project that will improve its computer facilities. The opportunity cost for this project (alternative) is 14% because, by taking the money out of the bank, the company has to forfeit a 14% rate of return. That is, the sacrifice involved, or the opportunity cost, is 14%. Therefore, to calculate a value for this project, the relevant cost is the opportunity cost of 14%. At first glance, this definition of cost appears nonintuitive and maybe even discomforting because people generally think that cost should be measured in dollars and cents rather than in percentages.

KEY CONCEPT: The relevant costs in finance are **opportunity costs**, and are calculated not by looking at historical costs and prices but by evaluating the available alternatives.

HOW VALUE DEPENDS ON OPPORTUNITY COSTS

Let us now use an example to see explicitly how asset values depend on opportunity costs. Consider the case of Mr. Trueval, who is contemplating the purchase of First Regional Bank's new certificate. If he buys the certificate today, he will receive $1,000 at the end of a year. No uncertainty is involved because the certificate is insured. The question is: What is the maximum amount that Mr. Trueval should pay for this certificate? He should pay, at most, the value of the certificate (whatever it is); if he pays more than the value, it is an unwise investment. Of course, he will want to pay less than the value, if he can.

To answer the question, therefore, one must calculate the value of the certificate. We know that value depends on the benefit of $1,000 at the end of the year and on the opportunity cost involved in making the investment. What is Mr. Trueval's opportunity cost?

Assume that Mr. Trueval has surveyed all the banks in his neighborhood and finds that the best interest rate he can get on a risk-free investment for one year is 10%. Then 10% is Mr. Trueval's opportunity cost for tying up capital in First Regional's certificate.

Since we do not know the value of the certificate, let us assume that it is X. If Mr. Trueval invested X at 10% for one year, he would end up with $X +$ $0.10X = $X(1.10)$. This is because of the interest earned for one year. Instead, if Mr. Trueval buys the certificate for X, he ends up with $1,000 at the end of the year. In order that Mr. Trueval not lose any money by buying the certificate, we must have

$$
\begin{array}{ccc}
\$X(1.10) & = & \$1,000 \\
\text{Proceeds (\$) from} & & \text{proceeds (\$) from} \\
\text{next best opportunity} & & \text{investment in the} \\
& & \text{certificate}
\end{array}
$$

or

$$
X = \frac{\$1,000}{1.10} = \$909.09
$$

Thus the value of the certificate is $909.09 for Mr. Trueval. If he pays more than $909.09 for it, he will lose money because he is paying more than the certificate is worth. If he pays more than $909.09 (say, $950) for the certificate, Mr. Trueval will end up with only $1,000. If instead he invests $950 in the bank at 10%, he will end up with $950(1 + 0.10) = $1,045$. Similarly, we can verify that any price below $909.09 for the certificate will be a bargain.

Note that if, instead of 10%, Mr. Trueval's opportunity cost is 12%, the value of the certificate will fall to $892.86 (1,000/1.12), whereas if his opportunity cost is 6%, the value of the asset will rise to $943.40 (1,000/1.06).

KEY CONCEPT: The value of an asset has an inverse relationship to its opportunity cost.

RELATIONSHIP TO DISCOUNT RATES

To extend the discussion to discount rates, assume that the First Regional Bank also has a three-year risk-free certificate that pays $1,000 at the end of the third year. How much will Mr. Trueval be prepared to pay for this certificate if his opportunity cost is 10%?

If Y is the value of this certificate, we know that Y must satisfy the equation

$$Y(1 + 0.10)(1 + 0.10)(1 + 0.10) = \$1,000$$

or

$$Y = \frac{\$1,000}{(1 + 0.10)(1 + 0.10)(1 + 0.10)} = \$751.32$$

Note that this relationship can be written as

$$Y = \$1,000/(1 + i)^3 \text{ where } i \text{ is the opportunity cost}$$
$$= \$1,000/(1 + 0.10)^3 = \$1,000[1/(1 + 0.10)^3]$$
$$= \$1,000(PVF_{.10,3}) = \$1,000(0.7513)$$
$$= \$751.32$$

Thus Y is obtained by multiplying the cash benefit of $1,000 by the present value interest factor for three years at a discount rate of 10%. Thus the opportunity cost of an investment is the discount rate to be applied to that investment. The value of the certificate, Y, is therefore only the present value of the benefits the certificate provides.

KEY CONCEPT: The discount rate for time-value calculations is the appropriate opportunity cost.

This conclusion should come as no surprise. In Chapter 2 we also explained the process of finding present values given a discount rate. However, we deliberately avoided discussing what this discount rate really is. Now we know that it is the opportunity cost of capital.[1]

The examples given so far are very simple cases—simple because only one cash benefit is involved. In addition, we have omitted risk considerations. In more realistic examples, benefits may occur over an extended period and in an uncertain way. For example, an investment in a machine may yield (uncertain) cash benefits annually for the next 10 years. When these cash benefits occur over several periods, they are often referred to as a *benefit stream, cash flow stream,* or *income stream.*

THE CONCEPTS OF ECONOMIC PROFIT AND EXCESS RETURNS

In the example of the $1,000 one-year First Regional Bank certificate, we calculated the value of the certificate to Mr. Trueval as $909.09. If he paid $909.09 for this certificate, he would be paying the right amount. If he paid more than $909.09, he would lose money; if he could buy the certificate for less than $909.09, he would make money.

Focus on the words *lose* and *make money,* and be sure that you understand these terms in the context in which they are used in finance. Table 3·1 shows three different prices that Mr. Trueval could have paid for the certificate. In all three cases, he gets back $1,000 at the end of the year. The third column shows the increase in wealth for Mr. Trueval by investing in the certificate for one year. In all three cases, his wealth has increased. This seems to imply that in all three cases he has made money. This conclusion is wrong.

It is true that Mr. Trueval's wealth increases in all three cases, but in only one case (when he pays $875) does he make money. At a price of $950 for the certificate he loses money, while at a price of $909.09 he neither makes nor loses

TABLE 3·1 Increase In Wealth for Mr. Trueval[a]

Price Paid for Certificate	Wealth at the End of the Year	Increase in Wealth
$875.00	$1,000	$125.00
909.09	1,000	90.91
950.00	1,000	50.00

[a]Opportunity cost = 10%.

[1] It is tempting to conclude that this result should have been apparent even in Chapter 2. However, this ignores a subtlety. In Chapter 2 the discount rate was not linked directly to the opportunity cost concept, as in this chapter. Chapter 2 linked the discount rate to the weak notion of an interest rate.

money. If this appears surprising, it is perhaps because you are not thinking of economic profit; perhaps your focus is really on accounting profit and loss.

KEY CONCEPT: **Economic profit** is the excess profit that is gained from an investment over and above the profit that could be obtained from the best alternative foregone.[2]

That is,

$$\text{Economic profit} = \frac{\text{wealth increase}}{\text{from an investment}} - \frac{\text{wealth increase}}{\text{from the best}}{\text{alternative forgone}} \qquad (3\text{-}1)$$

As we have just seen, the best foregone investment for Mr. Trueval yielded 10%. (That is why his opportunity cost is 10%.) If he had invested $X in this investment, he would have received $1.1X$, so we can now set up Table 3•2.

Instead of working with increases in wealth, one can work equivalently in terms of rates of return. In finance, rates of return are more widely used for analysis; Table 3•3 restates Table 3•2 in terms of rates of return.

Note from Tables 3•2 and 3•3 that positive economic profits exist only when there are **excess returns.** When an asset is purchased at its *fair value,* there is no economic profit or excess returns. This is an important observation. We will see later that the concept of market efficiency has something to do with this no-excess-return situation. For now, however, it is sufficient simply to state that when an asset is purchased at its fair value, there are no excess returns. Alternatively, when no excess returns are available in the marketplace, all assets are properly valued (i.e., *fairly priced*).

Summarizing the discussion so far, the term *making money* refers to the situation in which either economic profits or excess returns are generated. Thus, the age-old story of the old man who made money in the stock market without even knowing how to spell the word *stock* deserves closer scrutiny. Just because

TABLE 3•2   Economic Profits

Price Paid for the Certificate	Wealth at the End of the Year for Certificate	Wealth at the End of the Year If Invested at 10%[a]	Economic Profit
$875.00	$1,000	$ 962.50	$+37.50
909.09	1,000	1,000.00	0
950.00	1,000	1,045.00	−45.00

[a]That is, if the price paid for the certificate is invested at 10%.

[2]We will not pursue risk considerations at this point.

TABLE 3·3 Economic Profits in Terms of Excess Returns

Price Paid for Certificate	Rate of Return Provided by Certificate[a](%)	Rate of Return from Best Alternative Forgone(%)	Excess Returns (%)
$875.00	14.29	10	+4.29
909.09	10.00	10	0
950.00	5.26	10	−4.74

[a]Rates of return are calculated as ($1,000 − price)/price.

he bought stock at, say, $35 a share and sold it 18 years later for $145 does not necessarily mean that he made money even though there is no denying that he made $110 in accounting profits. Whether any economic profits were generated depends on his opportunity costs.

Risk and Opportunity Costs[3]

The discussion so far has not explicitly recognized risk. What if, instead of being a risk-free investment, the First Regional certificate were risky? In risky situations, the relevant opportunity cost of capital (i.e., the discount rate) will be higher than the return available on investments without risk. This is because most individuals are risk averse; they prefer a safer course of action to a riskier one if both alternatives have identical benefits. This does not imply that risk-averse individuals should not invest in risky investments. Risk, per se, is undesirable. If the expected returns are high enough, however, a certain level of risk may well be acceptable. However, risky alternatives should be evaluated at higher discount rates to calculate their values. Mr. Trueval will, in this case, evaluate any risky investment by assessing its risk and then adding a **risk premium** to the **risk-free discount rate.** Thus the *risky discount rate* will be higher.

KEY CONCEPT: The appropriate opportunity cost for a **risky investment** is the opportunity cost of capital for a riskless investment plus a premium for bearing risk that is proportional to the risk of the investment.[4] Or, in terms of discount rates,

$$\frac{\text{Risky}}{\text{discount rate}} = \frac{\text{risk-free}}{\text{discount rate}} + \text{risk premium} \qquad (3\text{-}2)$$

The higher the risk, the greater the discount rate, and therefore the smaller the value of an investment for a given stream of benefits. Consider an example:

[3]The question of how risk is defined and measured is not addressed until Chapter 12. The discussion in this chapter can, however, proceed without formalizing the notion of risk.

[4]See footnote 3.

If First Regional's certificate were risky and Mr. Trueval assessed a 5% risk premium for this investment, he should use a 15% discount rate. With a discount rate of 15%, the same certificate falls in value from $909.09 to $869.57[5] As long as Mr. Trueval can buy the certificate for $869.57 or less, the risk involved will be offset by the smaller price that the asset commands. Mr. Trueval can expect a 15% return instead of the 10% return earlier—a premium of 5% for bearing risk.

The example of First Regional Bank's risk-free certificate was used for purposes of illustration only. To calculate risky discount rates in practice, we must identify another risk-free asset whose rate of return can qualify for the risk-free discount rate status. In practice, the rate of return offered by short-term U.S. Treasury bills is taken to be the risk-free discount rate.[6]

All interest rates are not necessarily opportunity costs. The following example demonstrates the importance of using the correct interest rate as an opportunity cost in making a financial decision.

Example 3•1   Using Opportunity Costs in Day-to-Day Decision Making

Levitron, Inc., a maker of solar screens, has discovered that the insulation in its factory contains asbestos, a hazardous chemical. Regardless of the high cost of a complete strip-and-repair job, management has decided that it will have to be done. Two bids for the project are obtained. B&G Contractors will do the work for $240,000. With a $40,000 down payment, B&G will finance the balance over five years at 10%. Levitron will be required to make five annual payments. Harris and Company will do the job for $245,000 and will finance the entire amount over five years (annual payments) at 6%. If Levitron's best available use of money (i.e., its opportunity cost) is 8%, which contractor should it use?

One cannot conclude from the preceding information that B&G is cheaper than Harris by $5,000. Such a conclusion ignores opportunity cost considerations and the timing of the cash flows. The decision must be made in terms of *NPV*. Since these projects will involve no cash inflows, the *NPV*s will be negative. Levitron should accept the alternative that has the smaller negative *NPV*.

STEP 1: COMPUTE THE ANNUAL PAYMENTS

B&G: Amount financed = $240,000 − $40,000 = $200,000. Let the annual payment be X. It follows that $X(PVFA_{.10,5})$ = $200,000; $X(3.7908)$ = 200,000, or X = $52,759.31.

---

[5] The present value of $1,000 due in one year at a 15% discount rate is $869.57.

[6] U.S. Treasury bills are securities evidencing a U.S. government debt obligation. They are risk-free because the government cannot default.

Harris: Amount financed = \$245,000. Let the annual payment be Y. Then $Y(PVFA_{.06,5}) = \$245,000; Y(4.2124) = \$245,000$, or $Y = \$58,161.62$

STEP 2: COMPUTE THE *NPV*s

$$NPV(\text{B\&G}) = \$-40,000 - \$52,759.31(PVFA_{.08,5})$$
$$= \$-40,000 - \$52,759.31(3.9927)$$
$$= \$-250,652.10$$
$$NPV(\text{Harris}) = \$-58,161.62(PVFA_{.08,5}) = \$-58,161.62(3.9927)$$
$$= \$-232,221.90$$

Levitron should accept the bid from Harris because it is cheaper. In this case, we are not interested in making a profit, but rather in seeking the least expensive means of meeting our objective.

Example 3•1 shows the different ways to use interest rates. The rates at which Levitron could finance the repair job (10% for B&G or 6% for Harris) are used to determine the amounts Levitron will have to pay each year. However, these rates are not the opportunity costs for Levitron. Levitron's best available use of money is 8%; this is the interest rate that should be used to determine the present value of its payments.

Learning Check for Section 3•1

Review Questions

3•1. Why is the interest rate offered by U.S Treasury bills considered to be a riskless interest rate?

3•2. What does it mean to make money?

3•3. An investor bought a security for \$25 and sold it one year later for \$28. Did he make an economic profit?

3•4. Harriet Stone needs a loan and has been offered one by the Benefit Finance Company. Ms. Stone would like to evaluate this loan, using the concept of opportunity cost that she learned in her corporate finance class. She has a savings account at her credit union that pays 6%. The credit union is willing to lend her money at 8%. What is the relevant rate (6% or 8%) for evaluating the loan from Benefit Finance?

3•5. What is the relationship between risk and opportunity cost?

3·6.   Why does value have an inverse relationship to opportunity costs?

3·7.   "Discount rates for value calculations are opportunity costs." True or false? Why?

3·8.   What is the difference between accounting profit and economic profit?

New Terms

Economic profit	Intangible benefits	Risk premium
Economic value	Opportunity cost	Risky discount rate
Excess returns	Risk-free discount rate	Tangible benefits

SECTION 3·2   *The Valuation Process*

The process of finding the values of assets is called the *valuation process*. The valuation process is the same as the capitalization process, which was introduced in Chapter 2, and consists of two steps:

1.   Determining the benefits (cash flow stream) from the asset.

2.   Discounting this cash flow stream at the opportunity cost of capital. This opportunity cost is also known as the **required rate of return (RRR).**

Restating these steps more succinctly in the language of Chapter 2:

KEY CONCEPT: **Valuation** is the process of capitalizing a cash flow stream at the appropriate required rate of return (*RRR*).

The valuation process is an important tool for financial decision making. However, the inputs for the two steps of this process, especially the opportunity cost, must be selected with care. There are two ways this discount rate may be determined. We will examine each in turn, and see why only one of these is used for making corporate decisions.

THE PERSONAL VALUATION PROCESS

Personal valuation depends on the person making the decision and is based on the individual's estimate of the expected cash flows and his or her personal (subjective) discount rate. Hence these are personal inputs. The resulting valuation of an asset is a personal valuation, and the process is called the **personal valuation process.** Because of the personal nature of these two inputs, two individuals can arrive at two different personal values for the same asset; yet, both are correct. Value lies in the eyes of the beholder. Unfortunately, as personal valuations can differ among individuals, they are not very useful for corporate decision making. It is important to see why.

CORPORATE FINANCIAL MANAGEMENT AND ASSET VALUES

Consider the case of the financial manager of a corporation that is contemplating a new project—say, the opening of one more sales office. Since this project is an asset, the manager will want to know its value before deciding whether to invest in this project. This value assessment is necessary because the manager's objective is to maximize the value of the firm, and value-reducing projects are clearly to be avoided.

In calculating the value of this new project (asset), the manager will ask the marketing and accounting staffs for help in arriving at a forecast of the expected cash flows from it. This is the first step in calculating asset values. Let us assume, for this discussion, that all stockholders agree with the forecasts of the project's cash flow stream. The second step requires identifying a proper discount rate to capitalize this cash flow stream.

However, this step presents a serious problem. Whose discount rate should be used? The discount rate, as seen earlier, can vary from person to person. The owners of the company are the stockholders, and there may be thousands of them. Owners can calculate the value of this project by using their forecast of the cash flow stream and capitalizing this at their personal discount rates. Thus, if there are 10,000 stockholders, it is quite possible to have 10,000 different values for the project. Some will find the project attractive, whereas others will not. In other words, not all owners may support the decision of the financial manager.

Suppose that the corporation hires a pollster to poll the owners and find some type of "average" discount rate. Then the manager could use this discount rate and calculate the project's value. Of course, some owners will still be unhappy, but in any event, the manager's actions will reflect some consensus among the owners. However, for obvious reasons, actually polling all the owners is an impractical alternative. Financial economists solve this problem by developing a theory of asset valuation.

In Chapter 13 we explore the details of a theory, called the *Capital Asset Pricing Model,* for finding the average discount rate that will be used by investors.[7] This market valuation theory provides a market-determined discount rate that, in a sense, is like an average discount rate used by investors for a given risk. If this discount rate reflects the average opinion of all investors in the economy, we can assume that it also reflects the average opinion of the stockholders of a large, widely held company.

KEY CONCEPT: The financial manager should use **market discount rates** for financial decision making.

---

[7] The distinction between the average discount rate and the marginal discount rate is ignored in this discussion.

THE MARKET VALUATION PROCESS

Figure 3•1 depicts the **market valuation process.** The risk-free rate and the extimate of the project's risk are used as inputs for the **market valuation theory.** The theory provides a market-determined interest rate that can be used as a discount rate in the **valuation process.** The estimated cash flows provided by the asset are then discounted by this rate to determine the value of the asset. If the estimates of the cash flow stream provided by an asset are the same, personal value can differ from market value only because of differences in the discount rate.

The discount rates may be different for the two cases. In arriving at the personal discount rate, an investor has to estimate his or her personal risk premium. However, in the market valuation framework, all investors estimate the risk of the asset and the risk premium the same way. Then, given the asset's risk, the market valuation theory implies a risk premium that is an average for the market. In other words, given an estimate of the asset's risk, it is possible to go directly to the average discount rate that the market participants should use for the asset. Values computed in this manner are **market values**—the relevant values for decision making. They are market values because they are estimated using market valuation theory, which recognizes that market prices are determined by demand and supply considerations in the marketplace.

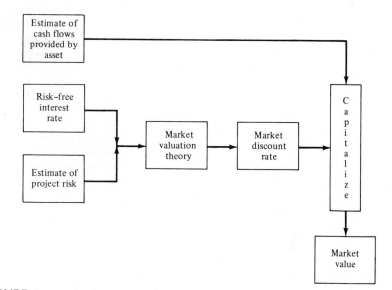

FIGURE 3•1   Market valuation.

EXCESS RETURNS AND NET PRESENT VALUES

The market valuation process just discussed describes the process of determining market values of assets. Let us recall the definition of net present value (*NPV*). It is the difference between the present value of cash inflows and the present value of the outflows. Because present values are involved, a discount rate is needed. If the *NPV* of an investment is determined by using a market discount rate, the resulting *NPV* is a measure of *excess market value*, or additional wealth created.

Recall that managers make money for their companies only when excess returns are generated. However, excess returns and economic profits are sensitive to the opportunity cost involved. For example, in Table 3•2, note that the third column uses the 10% opportunity cost to determine the economic profit in the fourth column. Consider the case of a company that is considering an investment in First Regional's one-year certificate that is currently selling in the market for $909.09. The management of the company has estimated that the market discount rate is 10%. What is the *NPV* of this investment?

$$
\begin{aligned}
NPV &= PV \text{ of inflows} - PV \text{ of outflows} \\
&= \$1{,}000(PVF_{.10,1}) - \$909.09 \\
&= \$1{,}000(0.909) - \$909.09 \\
&= \$0
\end{aligned}
$$

From Tables 3•2 and 3•3, we observe, from the numbers corresponding to this calculation of *NPV*, that when the *NPV* of an investment is zero, the economic profits from that investment are zero. Equivalently, the excess returns generated from that investment are zero. Financial managers who undertake a zero-*NPV* project are not making money for their companies; there is no net gain in market-value terms. This is not to imply that the acceptance of the project will hurt the company; a zero-*NPV* project simply recovers the firm's opportunity cost. It does not increase the value of the firm. To make money, managers should generate excess returns or economic profits. This can happen only when *NPV* is greater than zero. *NPV* therefore measures, in market-value terms, the economic profits, or increase in wealth, generated by the project. It represents the excess market value that the firm will have by taking on the investment. The link among market values, opportunity costs, economic profits, excess returns, and *NPV* is now complete. Figure 3•2 depicts the equivalence among these concepts. Since this figure is simply a pictorial summary of the discussion thus far, no further elaboration is necessary.

KEY CONCEPT: The **NPV** of an investment measures the potential increase in wealth from that investment.

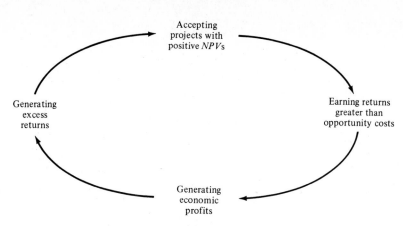

The easiest job I have ever tackled in this world is that of making money. It is, in fact, almost as easy as losing it. Almost, but not quite.

H. L. Mencken

"A Personal Note," Baltimore Evening Sun, *June 12, 1922*

FIGURE 3·2 Making money.

Learning Check for Section 3·2

Review Questions

3·9. What is (are) the essential difference(s) between the personal valuation process and the market valuation process?

3·10. $NPV = 0$ implies zero economic profit. Why? When will economic profit be greater than zero?

3·11. What are the differences between the personal valuation process and the market valuation process?

3·12. How should managers evaluate a project to ensure stockholders' support for their decision?

3·13. Under what conditions does NPV serve as a measure of economic profit?

New Terms

Market valuation process

Market valuation theory

Market value

Personal valuation process

Required rate of return (*RRR*)

Valuation process

SECTION 3•3 *Market Values and Market Efficiency*

A determination of market values requires estimates of the benefits and risks of assets. These estimates are based on expectations about the future characteristics of the asset (e.g., IBM stock). But how are these expectations formed? On the basis of available information. For example, if word got out that IBM was on the verge of a technical breakthrough, this might lead to expectations of higher future earnings. As a result, an investor's estimate of the future benefits from owning IBM stock could rise, and the market value of the stock could also rise to reflect this new information. Thus, a direct link between information and market values has been established.

The concept of an **efficient market** deals with the relationship between the market value of an asset and the information available about that asset. Traditionally, an efficient market is a capital market in which the market value of an asset reflects all available information about the asset. However, this statement has created an ongoing controversy, as some researchers have argued that prices may not fully reflect all available information. Rather than get into this controversy, we will work with a more widely accepted definition of an efficient market.

KEY CONCEPT: An **efficient** capital market is one in which it is not possible to generate excess returns *consistently.*

To be precise, this description is really an implication of efficient markets. However, it is sometimes useful to focus on this "definition" in order to get a better understanding of the market efficiency hypothesis. The hypothesis that U.S. capital markets are efficient is called the **efficient market hypothesis (EMH)**. We will now discuss the different degrees of market efficiency and the implications of the EMH.

FORMS OF MARKET EFFICIENCY

There are three forms of market efficiency, depending on how *information* is defined: weak, semistrong, and strong.

Weak Form Efficiency

The market is **weak form efficient** if the market value of an asset already reflects **historical** price and trading volume **information.** That is, in a weak form efficient market, there is nothing to be gained by looking back through time to study the previous price behavior of the asset. One cannot make money by studying the behavior of stock prices or trading volume over the preceding years. The current price of the asset (security) subsumes all history of prices. Thus **technical analysis,** the name given to the study of stock price forecasting by looking at historical patterns of stock price behavior, is a useless exercise. Most researchers now agree that the stock market is at least weak form efficient. The words *at least* are used advisedly. Being weak form efficient does not preclude U.S. markets from being either semistrong form efficient or strong form efficient.

Semistrong Form Efficiency

In a semistrong market, stock prices reflect all historical and publicly available information. Stock prices already incorporate any information (publicly held) that may be contained in balance sheets, income statements, earnings announcements, dividend declarations, and so on. Professional analysis of these *fundamentals* (i.e., **fundamental analysis**) of the firm is also useless. The general consensus today is that U.S. capital markets are **semistrong efficient.** In other words, it is not possible to generate consistent excess returns in U.S. financial markets today by using **publicly available information.**

Strong Form Efficiency

A capital market is **strong form** efficient if the stock price already reflects both publicly available and private information. U.S. capital markets are not strong efficient. In other words, it may be possible to generate excess returns consistently by using private information. **Private information** refers to specialized information. For example, an oil industry analyst may know better than other types of analysts how to evaluate the impact on oil prices of developments in the Middle East. Private information should not be confused with insider information, the use of which is illegal. *Insider information* refers to the information that corporate insiders (e.g., directors) may possess about their own company.

IMPLICATIONS OF EFFICIENT MARKETS

What are the consequences of an efficient market? In other words, what does the statement that markets are semistrong efficient imply? The EMH has important implications, which we now examine.

Stock Prices Cannot Be Predicted

For one thing, the EMH implies that stock prices cannot be accurately predicted.[8] Why? If current stock prices reflect all available information, these prices will change only to reflect future events that are not anticipated today. If future events cannot be anticipated, future stock prices also cannot be anticipated. If an event is anticipated, it becomes publicly available information and is immediately reflected in current stock prices. An immediate consequence of these observations is that in an efficient market no strategy will consistently yield excess returns. Recall that this was, in fact, stated as a definition of efficient markets.

This implication is often misunderstood. Efficient capital markets do not imply that it is impossible to make money (generate excess returns) in the market. If this were true, investors would soon disappear from stock markets. The key is in the use of the word *consistently;* in efficient markets, one cannot make money over an extended period of time and over several transactions. On any particular transaction, one is as likely to make money as to lose it. In the long run, the excess returns will dwindle to zero. This means that investors and mutual fund managers who have generated excess returns in the past were probably just lucky; there is no *guarantee* that they will continue to generate excess returns in the future. Their success in the past is not necessarily a result of their superior skills in using publicly available information.

All Investments Will in the Long Run Have a Zero *NPV*

If excess returns cannot be generated in the long run, our earlier discussion regarding the economic significance of *NPV* implies that in an efficient market all investments will in the long run have a zero *NPV*. This is particularly true of financial securities because of the efficiency of financial markets. The markets for real assets (e.g., machinery) are not as efficient as financial markets. This is particularly true of financial securities because of the efficiency of financial markets. The markets for real assets (e.g., machinery) are not as efficient as financial markets. The implication of this situation for the financial manager should be clear. Even if the company accepts an investment (say, software manufacturing for computer applications) because it has a positive *NPV*, in the long run this investment's attractiveness will decrease because of competition. As more and more companies find that software manufacturing offers positive *NPV*s, they enter the market, and the resulting competition forces down prices and cash flows to the companies. This lowers *NPV*s. Thus, managers must

---

[8] There is a general truth recognized by many Wall Street soothsayers: To predict the market correctly, you cannot go wrong if you do either of the following:
   1. If you want to predict the level of the market, don't give a specific time.
   2. If you want to discuss the market on any given day in the future, don't discuss the level for that day.

constantly evaluate new projects to identify new positive-*NPV* investments. A negative-*NPV* project today may turn out to be very attractive tomorrow as economic conditions change.

Market Values Reflect "True" Value

Another way to characterize an efficient market is to define it as one in which the market value of an asset reflects its *true* or **intrinsic value.** Financial decisions should be made in terms of market values precisely for this reason. Managers who announce a new investment plan for a company do so because they believe that this investment has an *NPV* of, say, $59,000. That is, the managers believe that the company, and consequently its stockholders, will be wealthier by $59,000 if the company takes on the project. However, stockholders are not better off by $59,000 unless the value of their stock goes up by $59,000. Only if stock prices reflect true values does this correspondence between *NPV* and the stock price make sense. Remember that investors do not get wealthier because the manager has estimated that the *NPV* of the investment is $59,000. Investors get wealthier only if this increase in *NPV* is translated into an increase in stock price. Financial managers do not have to worry about this in efficient markets; this translation from a firm's higher value to an increase in stock prices will indeed take place.

Corporate Decisions Can Be Evaluated Through Stock Prices

In efficient markets, corporate financial managers can evaluate the markets' assessment of their decisions by focusing on stock prices. If a corporate decision lowers stock prices, it is a bad decision because it also lowers the wealth of the stockholders. If a decision increases stock prices, it is a good decision. If the information regarding corporate decisions were not immediately reflected in stock prices (i.e., if markets were not efficient), decisions based on market values would be meaningless; the market value of the stock would not reflect the extent of approval or disapproval of the investors. In such cases, market values would not reflect true values. Luckily, as already noted, most evidence indicates that U.S. capital markets are semistrong form efficient.

Investment "Advice" Is Ineffective

The implication that stock prices cannot be predicted challenges the usefulness of the recommendations made by financial experts. When advisory agencies compile lists of "good buys" and "bad buys," what is the basis of these recommendations? People who believe in efficient markets often ask: If a stockbroker or an investment advisor knows how to make a killing in the market, does it make any sense for this person or company to sell this advice to someone else for just a few dollars? The EMH also suggests that you would be just as well off buying a random set of stocks and holding it for an extended period instead of letting an expert do this for you.

EMH ASSUMPTIONS

The EMH is naturally very controversial.[9] Although several arguments have been advanced to support it, the EMH rests on several assumptions that may not hold strictly in the financial markets. For example, the EMH requires that information dissemination be costless and instantaneous. While information is rapidly translated into price changes, some argue that certain parties still have enough time to act before prices react completely. Others point out that monopolistic elements in the markets may weaken the assumption of pure competition that underlies the EMH. Still others argue that prices may not reflect all available information regarding the asset.

TESTS OF THE EMH

The EMH has been tested extensively, and the results, in general, support it. There has been no strong evidence that over the long run any individual or institution has been able to generate excess returns consistently. There are certain exceptions, however.[10] These exceptions do not imply that the EMH is invalid. Although the EMH does not strictly hold for every situation at every point in time, current experience shows that, by and large, markets are efficient. Putting it another way, corporate financial managers who assume that markets are efficient are not making a totally unrealistic assumption. On the other hand, if they believe that markets are not efficient, they must have some very specific reasons (specialized knowledge) to justify their position. These considerations should be examined carefully before decisions are made that ignore the notion of financial markets' efficiency.

Learning Check for Section 3•3

Review Questions

3•14. Evaluate the statement "Corporate managers can look to stock prices for guidance in an efficient market."

---

[9] For an interesting perspective on the debate between the academic and practitioner viewpoints and related issues, see "Adam Smith," *The Money Game* (New York: Vintage Books, 1976).

[10] For example, the *weekend effect* suggests that if one bought stocks on Friday just before the stock market closed and sold on Monday just before the close, negative returns are generated. Other anomalies have been found in the context of closed-end funds and the performances of Value Line and Walter J. Schloss Associates. However, several of these anomalies are not as dramatic when transaction costs are recognized or if risk is defined differently.

3•15.   How do the weak and semistrong forms of the EMH differ?

3•16.   What does it mean to say that a market is efficient?

3•17.   List and explain two implications of the EMH.

New Terms

Efficient market	Intrinsic value	Semistrong form
Efficient market	Private information	efficiency
hypothesis (EMH)	Publicly available	Strong form efficiency
Fundamental analysis	information	Technical analysis
Historical information		Weak form efficiency

SECTION 3•4 *The Fundamental Valuation Model*

In this section we introduce the Fundamental Valuation Model. This model integrates the idea of cash flows (Chapter 1) with time value techniques (Chapter 2) and the opportunity cost concept of this chapter to yield a method for valuing assets. This model underlies our valuation of stocks and bonds in the next part of the book.

The present value of any asset, whether it is real or financial, is the discounted stream of future cash flows that it is expected to provide. To estimate an asset's value, then, the following information is needed:

1.   The magnitudes of the cash flow stream.

2.   The timing of the cash flow stream.

3.   The opportunity cost (or *RRR*) to apply to each periodic cash flow.

Once this information is available, the present value of the asset is determined by the following formula:

$$V_0 = CF_1(PVF_{k,1}) + CF_2(PVF_{k,2}) + \cdots + CF_n(PVF_{k,n}) \qquad (3\text{-}3)$$

where

V_0 = current ($t = 0$) or present value of the asset

CF_t = expected cash flow in period t

k = investor's opportunity cost (*RRR*)

n = number of periods over which the cash flow stream is expected (the number of periods could be the length of time an investor expects to hold the asset—the **expected holding period**—or the life of the asset).

If we assume that the *RRR* is known, we must then estimate only the magnitude and timing of the cash flows. This implies that we must know the life of the investment.

Example 3•2 Use of the Fundamental Valuation Model

Assume that the cash inflow from an asset will be a constant $500 per year for the next 10 years. If an investor requires a 12% rate of return, equation (3-3) suggests that the asset is worth

$$V_0 = \$500(PVFA_{.12,10}) = \$500(5.6502) = \$2,825.10$$

As you can see, the asset's value is simply the present value of an annuity. An investor should be willing to pay up to $2,825.10 for this asset. For example, if someone were willing to sell it for less, say $2,500, the asset would be undervalued to the investor and its purchase would yield a higher return than 12%. In the financial markets, the demand for and supply of securities by many potential buyers and sellers determine a market price that is, in effect, a consensus value of all investors in the economy.

Learning Check for Section 3•4

Review Questions

3•18. What information do you need to calculate the value of an asset?

3•19. "Equation (3-3) adds nothing new. It is essentially the same as the present value of a series of cash flows seen in Chapter 2." Do you agree?

New Term

Expected holding period

SUMMARY

What Is Value?

The value of an asset is the maximum price that one is willing to pay for it. The two fundamental determinants of value are potential benefits and opportunity costs. The opportunity cost is estimated by looking at the other alternatives available in the marketplace. Opportunity costs are the appropriate discount rates for time-value calculations.

The Valuation Process

The valuation process consists of determining the benefits (cash flow stream) from an asset and discounting these cash flows by the opportunity cost of capital. This opportunity cost is the sum of a risk-free interest rate and a risk premium. The valuation process may occur in a personal or a market setting. A financial manager should value assets via a market valuation process that uses a market-determined discount rate.

Market Values and Market Efficiency

The notion of *making money* has a very special interpretation in finance. One makes money only by generating economic profits. Earning an accounting profit may not amount to making money. To evaluate this further requires opportunity cost considerations. Economic profit (dollars) is often converted to a percentage in finance and is known as *excess returns*. When an investment provides excess returns, it is a positive-*NPV* project. This equivalence between excess returns and *NPV*s justifies the *NPV* rule: Accept projects with a positive *NPV* to increase shareholder wealth. A zero-*NPV* investment simply recovers the opportunity cost of taking on that investment; it does not increase the firm's value.

If financial markets are efficient, it is impossible to generate excess returns consistently. Since U.S. financial markets are efficient, positive *NPV*s will thus, in the long run, disappear. Managers must constantly reassess their analyses because an unattractive project today may become attractive tomorrow, and vice versa. Market efficiency also suggests that managers can look to stock prices to assess the extent of approval or disapproval of their decisions by the marketplace.

The Fundamental Valuation Model

In valuing an asset, estimates are required for both the expected cash flows and the appropriate *RRR*. In this chapter, we have considered the valuation of financial assets by assuming that the *RRR* is known. The fundamental valuation model requires that the cash flows from the asset be discounted at the *RRR* to find the asset's market value.

PROBLEMS

3•1.   A certificate of deposit (CD) offered by a new bank will pay $10,000 in three years. Your current bank offers a 9% rate on three-year CDs. What is the most you should be willing to pay for the new bank's CD?

3•2.   Now that you have graduated, your parents have offered to lend you the $12,000 you need to buy a new car. They will require you to pay them back $17,569 in four years. Your bank offers an 8% interest rate on four-year CDs and will make new car loans at a 12% interest rate. You have no other opportunities.
   (a)   What is the appropriate opportunity cost to use in making your decision?
   (b)   What should you do?

3•3.   After spending $300 on advertising, Van Harlow has found a buyer for his twin-engine plane. Van can sell the plane for $20,000, but he must then pay $500 to transport the plane to the buyer. Alternatively, he can keep the machine for use in a new project that came up after he placed the ads to sell. What is the appropriate cost (in dollars) of keeping the plane for the project?

3•4.   You have researched a new one-year project and determined that it has a $1,000 initial outlay and an *NPV* of $100 given a 12% opportunity cost of funds. A co-worker has argued that the $1,000 could more profitably be invested in a one-year CD yielding 11%. What is wrong with her argument? If $2,000 is available for new projects, should you adopt the project and buy the CD?

3•5.   Five years ago, you withdrew $2,000 from a money market fund paying 10% to place it in a mutual fund. Today your investment in the mutual fund is worth $3,000.
   (a)   What is your accounting profit from the investment in the mutual fund?
   (b)   What was the opportunity cost of your $2,000 investment? What was your economic profit from the mutual fund?

3•6.   You are trying to choose among three one-year notes of varying risks in which to invest your money. A has virtually no risk, and you have assigned a 0% risk premium to it. Note B has moderate risk, and you have assigned it a 5% risk premium. Note C has high risk, and you have assigned it a 10% risk premium. Note A sells for $9,300, note B for $8,850, and note C for $8,460 (each promises to pay $10,000 in one year). What should you do if the riskless rate is 5%?

3•7. You have done some research on a new project and found that it has a required initial outlay of $1,000 and an *NPV* of $10 given the opportunity cost of 10% for new projects. A co-worker argues that it is not worth going through the trouble of adopting the project for only $10. How do you respond?

3•8. Your firm is considering either of two tracts of land for a new warehouse. The decision about which one to buy will be based solely on cost. Hamman Realty will sell its tract for $200,000 cash, while the Wolff Investment Corporation will sell its tract for $190,000 subject to the condition that this amount be borrowed from Wolff and paid off as a five-year 14% loan with equal end-of-the-year payments. If the land is purchased from Wolff, the $200,000 that your firm has allocated for the land has no better alternative use than a 10% money market fund.
(a) What would be your annual payments to Wolff?
(b) What discount rate should you use to determine the present value of these cash flows, and what is their present value?
(c) What should you do? What would your decision be if Wolff offered the land for $185,000 under otherwise identical conditions? What price would Wolff have to quote on the land for you to be indifferent?

3•9. You have narrowed down your housing search to two apartments to lease for your last 12 months of school. The Cloisters will lease an apartment for $500 per month, with two months' rent required as a deposit. The Woodward Street Apartments will lease an apartment for $510 per month, with a one-month deposit. In either case, payments are made at the beginning of each month and the deposit is returned at the end of 12 months. The Cloisters will not give you any interest on your deposit; the Woodward Street Apartments will give you 1% interest per month. You have determined that your opportunity cost is 1% per month. What should you do?

3•10. You are trying to decide whether to purchase a tuxedo or simply to rent one as needed. For $1,000 you can purchase one that you estimate will last for 20 years. Alternatively, you can lease one for $60 each time you need one (you estimate that this will be twice a year). If your opportunity cost is 12%, what should you do? (For simplicity, assume that the rental expense is paid at the end of each year.)

3•11. Your brother has decided what model of car he wants to buy and is trying to choose between two dealers. Dempsey Motors will sell the car for $10,000 ($1,000 down, with the rest payable on a four-year note with a monthly interest rate of 1%). Tunney Motors will sell the car for $9,500 ($1,000 down, with the rest payable on a four-year note with a monthly interest rate of 1.2%). Your brother's opportunity cost is 1% per month. What should he do? (Note: You cannot use the tables for this problem. $PVFA_{.01,48} = 37.97$, $PVFA_{.012,48} = 36.33$.)

READINGS

FAMA, EUGENE F., "Efficient Capital Markets: A Review of Theory and Empirical Work," *Journal of Finance*, May 1970, 383–417.

HEYNE, PAUL *The Economic Way of Thinking* (Chicago: Science Research Associates, Inc., 1980).

MALKIEL, BURTON G., *A Random Walk Down Wall Street*, 4th ed. (New York: W.W. Norton & Co., 1985).

SMITH, ADAM, *The Money Game* (New York: Random House, Inc., 1976).

PART II

Raising Capital Through Equity and Debt

4

Equity Financing

Equity is simply ownership, and ownership is one of the cornerstones of the American economic system. It is the driving force behind the entrepreneurism that gave birth to this country's largest and most powerful corporations. With ownership comes the potential of unlimited return in exchange for the willingness to accept the risk of the investment.

The purpose of this chapter is to explain the different aspects of equity securities and the various sources of equity capital that are available. After introducing some new terms and concepts, we examine the ways in which firms raise new equity capital. Included in this discussion are private sources of capital and sources that are tapped when the firm *goes public* and sells securities that are traded in the market. We then use the procedures developed in Chapters 2 and 3 to determine a value for equity securities. Investment bankers have become a critical part of the process of raising capital, and their role in raising both equity and long-term debt is examined in Appendix 4A.

The chapter is divided into three sections:

SECTION 4•1: *Equity Ownership.* This section begins with an examination of the basics of stock ownership, some of which will be a review. We then introduce the accounting terminology associated with common stock before examining the rights and privileges that accrue to stockholders.

SECTION 4•2: *Sources of Equity Capital.* This section discusses various alternatives available to a company for raising new capital: seed capital, venture capital, and private and public placements of stock.

SECTION 4•3: *Common Stock Valuation.* This section demonstrates common stock valuation, using the fundamental valuation equation of Chapter 3. First, we present several cases of stock valuation under different assumptions regarding how long the stock is held (the holding period). Then we explain how different forms of stock valuation are made possible by different assumptions regarding the growth rate of dividends.

SECTION 4•1 *Equity Ownership*

Ownership carries with it rights and responsibilities that must be understood thoroughly by both managers and stockholders. In this section, we review the basic accounting concepts associated with stock ownership.

ACCOUNTING TERMS

This review covers the important terms found in the **stockholders' equity** portion of the corporate balance sheet. Table 4•1 gives the equity portion of Kimberly-Clark's balance sheet as of December 31, 1987. Under **"common stock,"** the balance sheet shows that the company is authorized by its stockholders to issue up to 300 million shares, which means that management must seek shareholder approval if it wants to issue more than 300 million shares.[1] As of the end of 1987, only 81 million of those shares were outstanding.

TABLE 4•1   Stockholders' Equity: Kimberly-Clark's 1987 Annual Report
Year ended December 31, 1987 (millions of dollars)

Common stock: $1.25 par value—authorized 300.0 million shares; issued 81.0 million shares on December 31, 1987 and 95.5 million shares on December 31, 1986	$ 101.2
Additional paid-in capital	144.5
Retained earnings	1451.4
Less: (1) Cost of common stock in treasury	(39.3)
(2) Unrealized currency translation adjustments	(85.9)
Total stockholder's equity	$1571.9

Source: *1987 Annual Report*, Kimberly-Clark Corporation.

[1]Companies rarely have trouble obtaining stockholder approval for increasing the number of authorized shares. Typically, when seeking approval, companies try to get a large number of shares authorized "for general corporate purposes" in order to avoid the time and expense involved in getting shareholder authorization when they do actually plan to issue the shares. The proposal for an increase in authorized shares usually shows up as an item to be decided at the annual meeting of stockholders, unless it is related to a merger, in which case special meetings are usually called.

The **par value** of the shares refers to a technical value placed on the shares to comply with state law and has little to do with the stock's market value. It is usually set very low because some states require that if a bankruptcy occurs, any shareholder who bought the stock for less than par value must contribute the difference between the price paid and the par value. That problem is easily avoided either by never selling the stock below par or by simply setting no par value, which is also permitted.

In the Kimberly-Clark example, the par value is set at $1.25 a share, so that for bookkeeping purposes only, the stock is valued at $101.2 million. The additional funds received beyond the $1.25 per share when those shares were issued is entered as the **additional paid-in capital,** which is $144.5 million.

The company's net income after payment of dividends was added to the *retained earnings account,* making it $1,451.4 million. This account includes all the net income since the corporation's inception that has been reinvested in the company rather than distributed to stockholders as dividends. **Treasury stock** consists of shares that were sold to investors but repurchased by the company and is recorded at cost. Treasury stock pays no dividends and has no voting rights. It may be retained in the account indefinitely, retired, or resold.

The *book value,* or accounting value, of a share of stock can be determined by dividing total common stockholders' equity by the shares outstanding. To illustrate the computation, the book value of Kimberly-Clark stock on December 31, 1987 was:

$$\text{Book value} = \text{stockholders' equity/shares outstanding} = \frac{\$1,571.9}{81}$$
$$= \$19.41 \text{ per share}$$

The actual market price of a stock at any time may easily be determined by examining a good newspaper. The highlight "Deciphering the Stock Pages" shows how to find the stock price and other useful information in the *Wall Street Journal.*

■ HIGHLIGHT

DECIPHERING THE STOCK PAGES

Suppose that a neophyte investor wants to follow the performance of certain stocks in the daily newspaper. The investor can look up major stocks in the business pages of his local daily newspaper. For more information and more obscure stocks, he would be more likely to find them in financial publications, such as the *Wall Street Journal* (see Figure 1).

First, to find the stock desired, one must first know where it is traded: New York Stock Exchange, American Stock Exchange, or in the NASDAQ Over-the-Counter Markets. The OTC stocks are further categorized by the amount of investor interest, with the most heavily traded listed in the National Market Issues followed by NASDAQ Bid and Asked Quotations and Additional OTC Quotes.

THE WALL STREET JOURNAL FRIDAY, MARCH 25, 1988

52-weeks				Yld	P-E	Sales				Net
High	Low	Stock	Div.	%	Ratio	100s	High	Low	Close	Chg.
56½	28	Tandy	.60	1.5	13	2827	41¼	40⅜	40½	−½
19	14⅛	Tndycft		...	19	50	17⅛	16⅞	17⅛	−⅛
18¾	9¼	TchSym		...	10	224	13⅜	12½	12½	−⅜
40¾	20½	Tektrnx	.60	2.1	41	548	29⅜	28½	28⅞	−⅞
3⅞	1⅝	Telcom		...	18	35	2	1¾	1¾	−¼
390	242	Teldyn	4.00	1.2	...	159	337¼	332¼	332¾	−4¾
29½	16	Telef n	1.09e	4.7	6	899	23½	23⅛	23⅛	−¼
26⅞	10	Telrte s	.32	1.6	25	2012	20½	18½	19¾	+⅝
93⅜	29½	Telex		...	10	27	50	50	50	...
68½	35	Templ s	.84	1.8	10	652	47⅜	45⅜	45⅞	−1½
10⅛	10	TmpGl n		...	...	4619	10⅛	10	10	...
62½	36⅛	Tennco	3.04	7.1	...	2304	43⅜	42½	42¾	−⅞
100	84¼	Tenc pr	7.40	7.9	...	2	93½	93½	93½	−⅛
36½	12	Terdyn		...	...	557	15½	15	15⅛	−⅜
16½	7¾	Tesoro		...	...	319	11⅜	11⅜	11½	−⅛
28¼	19	Tesor pf	2.16	10.0	...	3	21¾	21½	21½	−⅜
47½	26⅞	vlTexaco		...	...	17296	47¼	45½	46	−1¼
15¾	2⅞	TxABc		...	...	50	3⅜	3¼	3⅜	+⅛
41⅜	20⅓	TexEst	1.00	3.1	18	10585	32¾	31	32½	+⅜
36⅛	25⅜	TexInd	.80b	2.3	...	87	35¼	34½	34½	−¾
80¼	36¼	TxInst s	.72	1.5	17	4143	49⅜	48⅜	49⅛	−1¼
37¼	22⅞	TxPac	.40	1.4	39	129	28⅞	28¾	28¾	−⅛
34⅜	25½	TexUtil	2.88	11.0	6	8169	26½	25⅞	26⅛	−½
10⅜	4	Texfl s		...	12	297	6	5⅞	6	...
10¾	9⅜	Texfl pf		...	...	12	10¼	10¼	10¼	...
10½	9⅞	Texfl pfB		...	...	60	9⅞	9⅞	9⅞	...
39¾	17¼	Textrn s	1.00	3.7	8	10366	28⅜	26⅜	26⅞	−2⅜
79¾	41¼	Textr pf	2.08	3.6	...	1	58¼	58¼	58¼	−¾

NYSE HIGHS/LOWS

Thursday, March 24, 1988

NEW HIGHS – 14

Calmat s	HoughMlf	MooreMc	StevensJP
CarsPlr n	Intermed s	MooreMc pf	StrideRite s
Firestone	Koppers	SpclEco n	VanDam
Genmotr Hs	Larfarge		

NEW LOWS – 10

vlAlgin 11.25pf	DigitalEq	IrvingBk adj pf	Thortec
ChasMnh flt pf	FtFldBcp pfC	PutnamMIT n	Xerox 3.00pf
ChasMn fttF	GenData		

s–Split or stock dividend of 25 per cent or more in the past 52 weeks. High-low range is adjusted from old stock. n–New issue in past 52 weeks and does not cover the entire 52 week period.

EXPLANATORY NOTES

(For New York and American Exchange listed issues)

Sales figures are unofficial.

PE ratios are based on primary per share earnings as reported by the companies for the most recent four quarters. Extraordinary items generally are excluded.

The 52-Week High and Low columns show the highest and the lowest price of the stock in consolidated trading during the preceding 52 weeks plus the current week, but not the current trading day. The 52-week high and low columns are adjusted to reflect stock payouts of 10 percent or more.

u–Indicates a new 52-week high. d–Indicates a new 52-week low.

g–Dividend or earnings in Canadian money. Stock trades in U.S. dollars. No yield of PE shown unless stated in U.S. money. n–New issue in the past 52 weeks. The high-low range begins with the start of trading and does not cover the entire 52 week period. pp–Holder owes installment(s) of purchase price. s–Split or stock dividend of 25 per cent or more in the past 52 weeks. The high-low range is adjusted from the old stock. Dividend begins with the date of split or stock dividend. v–Trading halted on primary market.

Unless otherwise noted, rates of dividends in the foregoing table are annual disbursements based on the last quarterly or semi-annual declaration. Special or extra dividends or payments not designated as regular are identified in the following footnotes.

a–Also extra or extras. b–Annual rate plus stock dividend. c–Liquidating dividend. e–Declared or paid in preceding 12 months. i–Declared or paid after stock dividend or split up. j–Paid this year, dividend omitted, deferred or no action taken at last dividend meeting. k–Declared or paid this year, an accumulative issue with dividends in arrears. r–Declared or paid in preceding 12 months plus stock dividend. t–Paid in stock in preceding 12 months, estimated cash value on ex-dividend or ex-distribution date.

x–Ex-dividend or ex-rights. y–Ex-dividend and sales in full. z–Sales in full.

pf–Preferred. rt–Rights. un–Units. wd–When distributed. wi–When issued. wt–Warrants. ww–With warrants. xw–Without warrants.

vi–In bankruptcy or receivership or being reorganized under the Bankruptcy Act, or securities assumed by such companies.

FIGURE 1 Reprinted by permission of the *Wall Street Journal*, © Dow Jones Company, Inc. 1988, all rights reserved.

Suppose that the investor owns some shares in Texas Instruments. It is traded on the New York Stock Exchange, as are most major public companies. Looking it up in the pages of the *Wall Street Journal*, where stock quotations read from the back of the newspaper forward, he finds it listed as TexInst. Since it is easy to confuse the listing with TexInd and TexInt, which relate to Texas Industries and Texas International, respectively, he might consult a broker if he is unsure.

The newspaper gives 11 columns of information for each stock listed on the New York Stock Exchange. The first six columns give a bit of history and perspective on the stock: the last five columns give the results of the previous trading day's activities.

In the Friday, March 25, 1988, issue of the *Wall Street Journal*, the listings are for trading that occurred the day before, March 24. The first two columns give $80\frac{1}{4}$ and $36\frac{1}{4}$ as the highest and lowest levels, respectively, at which Texas Instruments stock was traded within approximately the last year.*

The next column simply lists the name of the stock. To distinguish trading of the common stock from the preferred stock in a company, the letters "pf" follow the stock name listing.† The fourth column gives the company's dividend payout at an annual rate, based on the company's last declared quarterly or semiannual dividend rate. A variety of footnotes, denoting stock splits, extra dividends, ex-rights, and others, may also appear here, with explanatory notes found at the end of the exchange tables. In Texas Instruments' case, its annual dividend payout rate is $0.72 and there are no footnotes.

The fifth column shows the dividend payout rate of $0.72 as a percentage of the company's current price, or 1.5% of the $48\frac{1}{8}$, where it closed, which will be explained shortly. The next column gives the company's price–earnings ratio (P/E) of 17, meaning that its selling price of $48\frac{1}{8}$ was about seven times its annual per-share earnings level.

The seventh column gives the trading volume, in hundreds of shares, that traded hands on Thursday, March 24. Thus the figure 4143 means that 414,300 shares of Texas Instruments traded that day.

The next three columns give the high, low, and closing prices for Thursday. These figures mean that Texas Instruments traded as high as $49\frac{3}{8}$, as low as $48\frac{3}{8}$, and closed at the end of the trading day at $49\frac{1}{8}$. If the low price is footnoted with a "d," it means that the prior day's closing price set a new 52-week low for the stock.

The final column shows the change in the stock's closing price from the day before. Texas Instruments dropped $1\frac{1}{4}$ points from the day before, meaning that the prior day's closing price was $47\frac{7}{8}$.

*Precisely, it means the prior 52 weeks plus the current week: that is, trading from March 23, 1987 through Wednesday, March 23, 1988, and excluding the latest trading day, Thursday, March 24.

†The abbreviation of the stock name is not the same as the stock's ticker symbol, which is used in executing trades and on instruments reporting the stock price changes.

RIGHTS AND PRIVILEGES

Stock ownership entitles its holders to certain rights and privileges. Table 4•2 gives a summary of the rights of stockholders, the most important of which are covered in detail in the following discussion.

Evidencing ownership is the *stock certificate*, as shown in Figure 4•1 for the Hickok Electrical Instrument Company. The information on the Hickok stock certificate includes the 35 common shares owned, the $1 par value, and the state in which the company is incorporated.

Control

First, the shareholders have the right to choose and replace management. The management is chosen by the board of directors of the firm, who in turn are elected by the stockholders. In small companies, the process is almost redundant, since the biggest shareholders are the directors and hold most of the top management positions. In large companies, however, the directors usually consist of a minority of internal management and a majority of outside owners. Often outside owners are managers of other companies, and some sit on several boards.

TABLE 4·2   Rights of Stockholders

Holders of common stock have certain fundamental rights or privileges that cannot be revoked. These rights may include:

1. *Limited liability.* Stockholders cannot lose more than they have invested.
2. *Proportionate ownership.* Stockholders have ownership in the company in the same proportion as their shares to the total of all shares outstanding.
3. *Transfer rights.* Stockholders may give away or sell shares to anyone they choose.
4. *Receiving dividends.* Stockholders share in the profits if dividends are declared. There is no guarantee, however.
5. *Inspecting corporate books.* Stockholders have the right to see annual reports. This does not include detailed books of accounts and minutes from internal meetings.
6. *Preemptive right.* Stockholders have the right to subscribe proportionately to any new issue of stock.
7. *Voting at shareholder meetings.*
8. *Residual claims to assets at dissolution.* If the corporation ceases to exist, stockholders have the right to corporate assets only after all debt claims and other security holders' claims are satisfied.

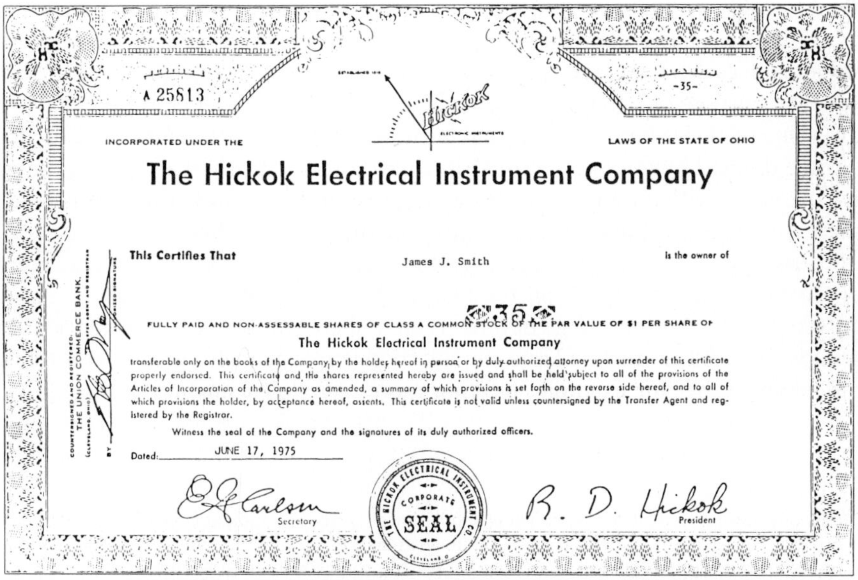

FIGURE 4·1   Stock certificate.

Corporations must hold annual meetings for their stockholders at which directors are elected, auditors are chosen, and other business is conducted. Management often gives a summary of the past year's performance and the outlook for the coming year. Usually these statements are found in the annual report, which the company must prepare for stockholders, or in the first-quarter statement. Stockholders may vote in person or by proxy. A *proxy* is a document that transfers the right to vote to another party, which under normal circumstances is current management. In large companies, very few stockholders actually attend the meeting; most vote by proxy.

Thus, when dissident shareholders wish to solicit the votes of other stockholders in their efforts to challenge management, they typically wage a proxy fight. These battles usually involve the dissidents' efforts to elect their own nominee(s) to the board of directors. Proxy fights typically take place by mail, telephone, and advertising in business periodicals. Thus they can be very expensive.[2]

Preemptive Rights

To protect current stockholders, corporations may, in their bylaws, give them **preemptive rights,** allowing them to buy any additional shares offered by the company. For example, if a firm has $50 million of equity outstanding and wishes to raise an additional $25 million in equity capital, it has to go through a **rights offering,** which is also called a **privileged subscription.** Each share is entitled to one right. The firm announces that shareholders as of a certain future date, usually within several weeks of the announcement, may purchase additional shares in the company for a certain number of rights plus a certain amount of cash. That cash price is set below the market price of the stock.

The purpose of preemptive rights is to protect stockholders from *dilution* of the value of their shares. Recall that earnings per share are determined by net income divided by the number of shares outstanding. If the shares outstanding are increased without a corresponding increase in net income, the earnings per share are reduced, thus causing dilution of the value of the shares.

Preemptive rights also protect stockholders from any attempt by managers or friendly third parties to control a larger percentage of the company's shares outstanding by issuing a large number of new shares to themselves or to friendly groups. This block may be large enough to give management greater control of the company by, for example, electing more of its own directors.

---

[2] The company has the advantage in such fights, since its defense campaign can be financed by corporate funds and it controls corporate information. For example, although dissidents are entitled to the corporation's stockholders' roster, companies have been known to delay producing it in an attempt to reduce the time available for dissidents to solicit proxies before the scheduled annual meeting.

Classes of Stock

On rare occasions, with shareholder approval, a company may wish to segregate stock, allowing a variance in the rights and privileges available to all stockholders. In these instances, companies may create new *classes* of stock to facilitate those needs, such as *class A common* or *class B common*. Such designations carry no standard meaning across companies. The highlight "Classes of Stock: All Are Not Created Equal" shows how firms may create separate classes of common stock for specific purposes.

■ *HIGHLIGHT*

CLASSES OF STOCK: ALL ARE NOT CREATED EQUAL

As discussed in the text, companies sometimes issue different classes of stock. The case of Waldbaum, Inc., a regional supermarket chain, is illustrative. The company's founders, owning 49% of the stock, wanted to keep control of the company even if some shares of the family block were sold. The Waldbaums devised a plan involving two classes of stock that would enable the family to retain control of the firm with as little as 10% of the outstanding stock.

Here is how it worked: Waldbaum shareholders were asked to approve two new classes of stock. They then were to choose the type of share they desired. Approval of the proposal was a foregone conclusion, since the Waldbaum family was to vote its 49% block in favor of its own proposal.

The two classes, approved in July 1985, were:

1. Class A shares, where holders would receive a 5-cent annual dividend and one vote per share.

2. Class B shares, where holders would receive no dividend but get 10 votes per share.

The essence of the two-class plan was that while most shareholders could be expected to choose the shares paying a 5-cent dividend, the Waldbaums said in proxy material accompanying the sale that they intended to convert at least 44% of their stock to the class B shares. By the family's calculations as expressed in the proxy material, less than a 10% ownership would still permit them to retain control of the company.

The separate classes may also be designated for other managerial purposes. For example, General Motors Corp. issued about 13.6 million shares of class E stock in October 1984 when it acquired Electronic Data Systems (EDS) in a transaction valued at $2.5 billion. The purpose was to give holders of this "GME stock," as it was called on Wall Street, a continuing stake in EDS's earnings by tying GME dividends to the income of EDS and its subsidiaries. Creation of the class E stock was also intended to help prevent key EDS personnel from leaving.

Sometimes classes of stock are established when the company's founding owners go public, permitting the founders to have, for example, the only voting power or twice as much voting power as new stockholders for a certain period. In exchange for the additional voting power, the founders may be prohibited from selling their stock for a certain number of years.

Return

As discussed in earlier chapters, common stockholders' right to income from the company is based on its performance. They receive a return on their capital only after creditors and preferred stockholders have been paid. Income may be received in cash dividends or stock dividends or from the sale of the equity owner's shares. The net return to stockholders will depend on the way the Internal Revenue Service taxes dividends and capital gains.

Learning Check for Section 4·1

Review Questions

4·1. What is the importance of par value to an investor?

4·2. How can the existing stockholders in a firm that is issuing new stock maintain control?

4·3. What is the significance of par value, paid-in capital, and retained earnings?

4·4. List the usual rights of common stockholders.

4·5. What are preemptive rights? Why are they issued? What is the dilution effect caused by these rights?

New Terms

Additional paid-in capital	Preemptive rights	Stockholders' equity
Common stock	Privileged subscription	Transfer rights
Limited liability	Rights offering	Treasury stock
Par value		

SECTION 4·2 *Sources of Equity Capital*

Most major corporations begin as startup organizations, turning to a widening variety of financing sources as they mature. In this section, we cover the genesis of new businesses and how they raise equity capital to finance their growth.

SEED CAPITAL

The startup funds for a new business are called **seed capital.** These funds may be obtained from such sources as an entrepreneur's savings, the sale of personal or business assets, or an inheritance. If the money is solely from the entrepreneur's family, the company probably began as a proprietorship or partnership.

Seed capital may also be raised from family members and friends who are willing to risk their capital in exchange for a "piece of the action." These sources often provide the easiest or only way to raise startup funds. When a startup company is established, the owners often incorporate the company. The process of incorporation costs about $200. These arrangements are still the most informal type of ownership agreement. But as long as a corporation is involved, these holders are entitled to the rights outlined previously.

VENTURE CAPITALISTS

Another means of raising capital for the entrepreneur or small businessperson is to approach **venture capitalists.** Venture-capital firms are owned by individuals or corporations that have raised funds to invest in portfolios of promising young companies. Some invest in startup operations, while others prefer one- to three-year-old businesses. Some even seek out ailing young businesses in order to turn them around. Venture-capital firms may also prefer certain industries or certain types of companies, as well as certain geographic locales. For example, U.S. Venture Partners of Menlo Park, California, prefers to invest in companies less than three years old in high technology or specialty retailing that are located in the northeastern or far western United States.

Venture-capital firms generally exchange their funds for substantial positions in the companies. If possible, they try to take a majority ownership position. The venture capitalists often anticipate that they will receive their return by taking the companies public some years later. This practice permits them to sell all or most of their ownership and receive capital gains on their shares.

One reason that new companies find venture capital firms attractive is that venture capitalists typically view their investment as long-term and are willing to wait several years before receiving their return. Another reason is that many venture capitalists provide connections, management, and marketing know-how that new companies often need very badly. On the other hand, since many new ventures must give up control to venture-capitalist firms, their management must sometimes accept big changes dictated by the venture-capital firm, including forced departures of some managers, eventually including the founders themselves.

Most venture-capital firms are not much older than the companies they finance. Although the origins of organized venture capital date back to the 1950s, most of today's firms were started in the early 1980s. In 1983, $4.5 billion in venture capital was raised, up from just $39 million in 1977.

Venture-capital firms raised $4.0 billion in 1984, reflecting the end of a boom period. By 1985, many of these firms had problem companies in their portfolios. Some venture-capital firms are subsidiaries of large manufacturing or banking companies. Others are privately managed firms that raise the money to invest in the new companies from pension funds, individuals, foreign investors, and corporations. Table 4•3 lists the venture-capital firms that made the largest investments in 1986.

Private Placements

As a firm becomes more established and builds a track record, it can remain private and still raise capital from new, more conservative sources. One means of reaching a limited number of investors is through **private placement,** in which the company finds a small group of large, usually institutional investors to provide the entire amount of new capital it seeks. The stock sold by the private company in return for the capital is called **letter stock** because the buyer must furnish the Securities and Exchange Commission (SEC), the securities regulatory agency, with a letter stating that it did not buy the stock for resale. The SEC requires the letter because it wants to ensure that the buyers are aware of the illiquidity of the investment.

TABLE 4•3 Ten Venture Capital Firms Making the Largest Investments in 1986 (Millions of Dollars)

Rank		Firm Name and Location	1986 Investment ($Millions)
1987	1986		
1	3	Citicorp Venture Capital, Ltd. (SBIC)/Citicorp Capital Investors, Ltd., New York	233.11
2	2	TA Associates, Boston	166.14
3	1	First Chicago Venture Capital/First Capital Corporation of Chicago (SBIC), Chicago	135.17
4	5	Warburg, Pincus Ventures Inc., New York	93.80
5	4	Hambrecht & Quist Venture Partners, San Francisco	93.40
6	8	Hillman Ventures, Inc., Pittsburgh	82.45
7	6	Security Pacific Capital Corporation/First SBIC of California, Costa Mesa, California	73.30
8	10	Aeneas Venture Corporation/Harvard Management Co., Inc., Boston	73.30
9	50	Manufacturers Hanover Venture Capital Corporation/ M.H. Capital Investors Inc. (SBIC), New York	60.83
10	15	Clinton Capital Corporation (SBIC)/Columbia Capital Corporation (MESBIC), New York	59.94

Source: Reprinted from the August, 1987 issue of VENTURE, For Entrepreneurial Business Owners & Investors, by special permission. © 1987 Venture Magazine, Inc., 521 Fifth Ave., New York, N.Y. 10175-0028.

Private placements have largely been the domain of small to medium-sized firms seeking equity capital of $500,000 to $5 million. However, in recent years, large, established public firms have used the private placement method to raise hundreds of millions of dollars.

The advantages and disadvantages of private placements of equity are similar to those of private placements of long-term debt, which we cover in Chapter 5. Typically, the private placement is faster and less costly than a public offering, since filings with the SEC, marketing, and other activities can be avoided. However, the fees levied in private placement reflect the risk assumed by the investors, including illiquidity and more intensive due diligence on the part of the investors.

PUBLIC OFFERINGS

As a company matures, it must eventually decide whether to become a public company. If it chooses to go public, the procedures and alternatives for raising equity funds differ significantly from those used by a privately held company or a closely held company, which is controlled by a small group. Most firms opt to go public, although there are many large private companies, such as the Bechtel Group, United Parcel Service, Hughes Aircraft, and Hallmark Cards.

Advantages of Going Public

Two major considerations underlie a company's decision to go public. First, the current owners often desire to take their capital investment out of the company and/or diversify their holdings into other companies. Sale of their stock is a means by which to obtain capital gains on the return they are receiving for their stock holdings.

Second, it is easier for the corporation to raise external funds. Investors find publicly held companies' stock more attractive than stock in private companies because it is liquid, so the investor may resell it at any time in the marketplace. In addition, the market value of publicly held stock is readily available, whereas valuation of privately held companies depends on independent appraisals or other subjective valuation methods.

Furthermore, a company that has been publicly traded is familiar to analysts and investors, and thus is more likely to attract their attention. Ultimately, the stock price is expected to rise because of the greater demand for it due to the higher interest in it. That attention level rises rapidly when the company chooses to raise its stature by trying to get its stock traded on one of the major stock exchanges. The process by which a firm obtains capital is described in the highlight "Financing Extremes." This highlight also demonstrates the risks assumed by those who take an equity position in a venture.

■ *HIGHLIGHT*

FINANCING EXTREMES: EXPLOSIVE GROWTH AND EXPLODING BUBBLES

Compaq: Financing Explosive Growth

Compaq Computer Corp. epitomizes the entrepreneur's dream. With sales of $111.2 million in its first year of marketing computers and $329 million in its second, Compaq established itself as the fastest-growing startup in American history. If the three founders of this company had sold their stock in 1985, they would have reaped roughly a 2,500% return.

The company's early rise to stardom could not have been achieved, however, without its frequent trips to the equity-capital markets. In fact, it might be argued that Compaq had two lines of business in 1983 and 1984: making computers and selling equity.

Compaq's growth had to be financed so quickly that the company did not experience the dilemma of most companies—choosing between obtaining fast funds and retaining control. Some companies finance their growth through internally generated funds, more commonly known as "bootstrapping," since the company is "pulling itself up by its own leather straps." The founders retain control, but the firm usually grows more slowly as a result. Other companies finance their business by selling equity ownership. This method, utilized aggressively by Compaq, usually entails sacrificing control to achieve faster growth.

Compaq, founded in Houston in 1982, has in its short lifetime tapped nearly all of the traditional equity capital-raising methods. In less than two years, the founders of this company raised $90 million in four rounds of financings. The company's first financing was for $1.5 million in March 1982, in which it gave up 55% equity ownership to Sevin Rosen, the venture-capital firm. Six months later, Compaq obtained $8.5 million from eight private investors. Six more months later, Compaq raised another $20 million, and finally, in December 1983, Compaq went public. Its initial public offering netted the company $60 million with an $11/share price on the over-the-counter market.

The South Sea Bubble: Most Spectacular Financial Crisis

The famous "bursting" of the South Sea Bubble is sobering fare for even the more fanatical of speculators. The scandal created by the South Sea Bubble was great enough to earn it a place in the *Guiness Book of the Business World* as the "Most Spectacular Financial Crisis." The South Sea Co. was formed in 1711 in Britain principally to trade with Central and South America. For some reason, speculation took off on a number of trading companies. Some of these new companies had bizarre objectives, such as "importing a large number of jackasses from Spain" and "fishing wrecks from the Irish coast." One company announced that it was being formed "for an undertaking which shall in due time be revealed." Speculation was rampant, and fortunes were made and lost.

The speculation peaked when South Sea Co. actually offered to take over the country's national debt and issued shares for this purpose. The entire country, including the king's Parliament, and many of London's well-to-do, got caught up in the excitement. Share prices were bid up to 10 times their nominal values.

Then suddenly in 1720, the bubble burst. South Sea Co. collapsed, leaving thousands of British subjects ruined and creating financial chaos across the nation. More than a century passed before Parliament allowed the formation of new companies again—and then only on very strict conditions.

Disadvantages of Going Public

The major disadvantages of going public are, first, the reduced flexibility management has in running the company, and second, the large increase in disclosure requirements and filings to the stockholders and the SEC.

Flexibility is reduced because management must exercise its fiduciary responsibility to shareholders to act in their best interests, not necessarily those of management. These responsibilities become particularly important when the company's performance is lagging, exposing management to criticism. Management must be able to justify to stockholders its salaries and benefits, as well as expenditures made on behalf of the company. In addition, the SEC prohibits management from engaging in any insider dealings. This includes trading the company's stock based on *inside information,* which is company information that has not yet been made public. In private companies, however, managers need only justify to their investor group or to themselves how they have spent corporate funds or arranged favorable deals for themselves with the company.[3]

The disclosure requirements of public companies can also be burdensome. Public companies are required by the SEC to make full disclosure of any material information relating to the company and to make sure that this information is fully disseminated. The intent of these requirements is to disallow any unfair information advantage to insiders over other people. The SEC also requires regular and timely filings of corporate activities with the agency.

Initial Public Offering

If the corporation decides to go public, its first offering is called, not surprisingly, an **initial public offering (*IPO*).** However, the firm will make a number of decisions long before going to market.

Decision to List on an Exchange

After a company has gone public, it is usually traded in the over-the-counter (OTC) market. The OTC market is not physically located in a specific place. Instead, trades are made by communications, usually by telephone, among bro-

---

[3] The Internal Revenue Service (IRS) does limit such dealings, but any penalization is associated with tax liability, not corporate bylaws. If the IRS views a salary as excessive, for example, it may treat the excess amount as a dividend, which, unlike a salary, is not deductible by the corporation.

kers across the country. Dealers act either as principals or as brokers for customers. The computerized system called the *National Association of Security Dealers Automated Quotations (NASDAQ)* displays many OTC stock bids and asked prices. Although most OTC companies are relatively young, OTCs also include such well-established companies as the Hoover Company.

Certain new issues that are purposely priced very low and are usually highly speculative are sometimes called **penny stocks.** According to the *PennyStock News,* a penny stock is any issue offered for less than $5 a share. Some stocks actually sell for a penny a share. These issues are considered highly speculative for two reasons. First, the companies are young, involving many startups. Second, the due diligence requirements of the underwriters involved are considered more lax than those for issues that are not marketed as penny stocks. As we explain in Chapter 5, **due diligence** refers to the verification that facts, projections, and other information regarding the company are not false or misleading. Denver, Colorado, is called the "Penny Stock Capital of the World" because many speculative issues, particularly mining issues, originate there.

At the opposite extreme from the penny stocks, the companies traded on the most prestigious exchange, the *New York Stock Exchange* (NYSE), or the "Big Board," command the most respect among investors. The NYSE possesses the most stringent requirements for listing of any of the exchanges, as illustrated in Table 4•4.

In addition to asset size, trading interest, and the other exchange requirements listed in Table 4•4, the NYSE requires some measures that are even more protective of shareholders than some corporate bylaws. If a firm fails to meet such requirements, it may be delisted by the exchange. For example, the NYSE began delisting proceedings against the Allis-Chalmers Corporation for converting $65 million in debt to equity without prior shareholder approval. Although the Big Board later finished a review of its own shareholder approval policies, its then-current policy required shareholder approval for increases in common shares outstanding of more than 18.5%. Allis-Chalmers' debt-equity conversion had the potential of increasing the outstanding common shares by 79%.

Traditionally, companies have tried to move up from listing on a regional exchange to the American Stock Exchange (AMEX), and then to the NYSE. In

TABLE 4•4   New York Stock Exchange Sample of Original Listing Requirements

- National interest in the company
- At least 1 million shares publicly held among at least 2,000 stockholders who own at least 100 shares each
- Had pretax earnings of at least $2.5 million in the preceding year and at least $2 million in the each of the preceding two years
- At least $16 million in net tangible assets
- The publicly held common shares have a market value of at least $16 million

Source: New York Stock Exchange.

recent years, however, many companies, such as Apple Computer and MCI Communications, have opted to remain with the NASDAQ rather than to step up to the AMEX and then the Big Board. Such developments have resulted in increasingly aggressive efforts by the exchanges and the NASDAQ to attract members.

Table 4•5 lists the various stock exchanges located in the United States and Canada. Note that the regional exchanges trade stocks listed on the NYSE and AMEX, as well as the stocks of local companies.

TABLE 4•5   Stock Exchanges

Exchange	Location
United States	
American Stock Exchange	New York
Boston Stock Exchange	Boston
Cincinnati Stock Exchange	Cincinnati
Intermountain Stock Exchange	Salt Lake City, Utah
Midwest Stock Exchange	Chicago
New York Stock Exchange	New York
Pacific Stock Exchange	San Francisco and Los Angeles
Philadelphia Stock Exchange	Philadelphia
Spokane Stock Exchange	Spokane, Washington
Canada	
Alberta Stock Exchange	Calgary, Alberta
Montreal Stock Exchange	Montreal, Quebec
Toronto Stock Exchange	Toronto, Ontario
Vancouver Stock Exchange	Vancouver, B.C.
Winnipeg Stock Exchange	Winnipeg, Manitoba

Learning Check for Section 4•2

Review Questions

4•6.   Why would a venture capitalist invest in a new firm?

4•7.   Why would a new firm welcome the participation of a venture capitalist?

4•8.   What are the main differences between a private placement and a public offering?

4•9.   Explain why going public can reduce the flexibility of management.

4•10.   Explain why raising additional equity capital can dilute the value of current stockholders' shares.

4·11. What are the advantages and disadvantages of a private placement of equity?

4·12. What are the advantages and disadvantages of going public?

4·13. What are some of the considerations in deciding to be listed on an exchange?

New Terms

Due diligence	Penny stock	Seed capital
Initial public offering	Private placement	Venture capitalist
Letter stock	Public offering	

SECTION 4·3 *Common Stock Valuation*

Thus far, we have examined the basic characteristics of common stock and have discussed the methods by which a firm may obtain equity capital. To complete our understanding of equity capital, we must understand how to use the fundamental valuation equation, introduced in Chapter 3, to value common stock.

The valuation of common stocks can pose two problems:

1. The future stream of cash flows is more uncertain than other financial assets, such as bonds.

2. These cash benefits to owners occur in perpetuity because the firm is viewed as an ongoing concern.

What cash flows are relevant to common stock investors? In Chapter 1 we identified the two cash flows: cash dividends and potential capital gains. It is the receipt of dividends and the price expected when the stock is sold at a future date that induce investors to buy stocks. To discount these cash flows, then, it is necessary both to make assumptions about when the stock will be sold and to forecast the future cash flows.

In the remainder of this section, we address two different situations. In the first segment, we discuss three cases under different assumptions about the holding period of the stock. In the second segment, we consider several cases under various assumptions regarding the growth of future dividends.

STOCK VALUATION UNDER DIFFERENT HOLDING-PERIOD ASSUMPTIONS

Case 1: Single-Period Valuation

Consider the simplest case of Bev Carlson, an investor who anticipates that she will hold Bering Company stock for one year before she sells it. Bering is expected to pay a dividend at the end of the year. Adapting equation (4-1) to this situation, the stock's current price, S_0, is given by

$$S_0 = \frac{(Div_1 + S_1)}{1 + k_s} \qquad (4\text{-}1)$$

$S_0 = \frac{(D \cdot v_1 + S_1)}{1 + KS}$

where Div_1 is the dividend expected in one year, S_1 is the expected stock price at the end of one year, and k_s is the RRR.[4] If Ms. Carlson expects a $1.20 dividend and an ending stock price of $38, and requires a 12% return, the stock's value is

$$S_0 = \frac{(\$1.20 + \$38)}{1.12} = \$35$$

It is instructive to view this situation from a different perspective and verify why a stock price of $35 leads to a 12% return. To see this, rewrite equation (4-1) in terms of the required rate of return as

$$k_s = \frac{Div_1 + S_1}{S_0} - 1$$

or

$$k_s = \frac{Div_1}{S_0} + \frac{S_1 - S_0}{S_0} \qquad (4\text{-}2)$$

Equation (4-2) demonstrates that Ms. Carlson's total percentage return is composed of two parts: an expected dividend yield, Div_1/S_0, and an expected capital gains yield, $(S_1 - S_0)/S_0$:

$$k_s = \frac{\$1.20}{\$35} + \frac{(\$38 - \$35)}{\$35}$$
$$= 0.034 + 0.086 = 12\%$$

[4] Note that $1/(1 + k_s)^n = PVF_{k_s,n}$. In this section, we are interested in examining the required rate of return, k_s, and will use the basic discounting formula rather than the PVF.

KEY CONCEPT: A stock's total return is composed of two elements: **dividend yield** and **capital-gains yield**.

Equation (4-2) can also be used to calculate the dollar return on the stock. Multiplying the initial stock price by the rate of return gives the dollar return. That is, from equation (4-2),

$$k_s S_0 = Div_1 + (S_1 - S_0)$$

and therefore, for preceding example,

$$k_s S_0 = \$1.20 + \$3 = \$4.20$$

Ms. Carlson therefore expects to receive her return in the form of a $1.20 dividend and $3 in stock appreciation. The financial manager of Bering thus affects Bev Carlson's returns through the dividend decision (how much of earnings to pay out) and the investment-financing decision (the change in stock price).

Case 2: Multiperiod Valuation

To extend the valuation model to more than one period, equation (4-1) can be applied, recognizing that dividends and the stock price (when sold) are the relevant cash flows:

$$S_0 = \frac{Div_1}{1 + k_s} + \frac{Div_2}{1 + k_s^2} + \cdots + \frac{Div_n + S_n}{(1 + k_s)^n} \qquad (4\text{-}3)$$

or

$$S_0 = \sum_{t=1}^{n} Div_t \, (PVFA_{k_s,t}) + S_n \, (PVF_{k_s,n}) \qquad (4\text{-}3)$$

In this case, the stock's current price is just the discounted value of a series of periodic dividend payments and the ending stock price.

Example 4•1 Multiperiod Stock Value

Michael Solt, another invester, expects a constant $5 annual dividend from SysTech Industries. He also expects to sell the stock for $55 after seven years and requires a 15% return. What is the maximum that he should pay for Sys-Tech stock?

The value of the stock, using equation (4-3), would be

$$S_0 = \$5(PVFA_{15,7}) + \$55(PVF_{.15,7})$$
$$= \$5(4.1604) + \$55(0.3759)$$
$$= \$20.80 + \$20.68 = \$41.48$$

The multiperiod valuation just described, although less restrictive than the one-period model, is still not entirely satisfactory. Since different investors retain a particular stock for different holding periods, all valuations that result must be personal valuations. A more general framework, which allows investors to have different holding periods and eventually leads to a market valuation of stocks, is warranted. The basis for such a market valuation model is now presented.

Case 3: Infinite-Period Valuation

The most general formula for common stock valuation treats the firm and its stock as if they will exist forever. In this case, the stock's value represents a stream of expected dividends in perpertuity. This means that equation (4-1) becomes

$$S_0 = \frac{Div_1}{1 + k_s} + \frac{Div_2}{(1 + k_s)^2} + \cdots + \frac{Div_\infty}{(1 + k_s)^\infty} \qquad (4\text{-}4)$$

or the sum of dividends from now to infinity. For obvious reasons, this formula is referred to as the *discounted dividend-valuation model*.

Note that the assumption of an infinite life has provided a valuation equation that does not require the estimation of a future stock price. Thus it can be used irrespective of the investor's holding period, be it one month or three years.

STOCK VALUATION UNDER DIFFERENT ASSUMPTIONS ABOUT THE GROWTH RATE

In addition to determining the time horizon used for valuing the stock, we must make an assumption concerning how the dividend payments of the stock will change over time. The **dividend growth rate** has a substantial effect on the value of the stock.

Case 1: Zero Dividend Growth

Often a firm is expected to pay a stable dividend, with little chance for growth in the foreseeable future. In this situation, a constant or zero growth dividend pattern is implied in which

$$Div_1 = Div_2 = \cdots = \overline{Div}$$

As we pointed out in Chapter 2, a constant cash flow to infinity can be valued as a perpetuity. Algebraically, this reduces the general stock valuation model in equation (4-4) to

$$S_0 = \overline{Div}(PVFA_{k_s,\infty})$$

or

$$S_0 = \frac{\overline{Div}}{k_s} \tag{4-5}$$

or, with zero growth, the value of a share of stock is equal to the value of a perpetual dividend dollar amount divided by the *RRR*. If all investors agree on *Div* and the required rate of return used is a market-determined *RRR*, the resulting stock valuation is a market valuation.

Example 4•2   Stock Value with a Zero Dividend Growth Rate

Suppose that the Senneco Corporation is expected to pay a constant $3 dividend indefinitely. If an investor requires a 15% return on its stock, the price per share of Senneco from equation (4-5) would be

$$S_0 = \frac{\$3}{0.15} = \$20$$

Even though few firms are expected to pay a constant dividend forever, this valuation model can be a useful approximation when the current level of dividends will continue indefinitely.

Case 2: Constant Dividend Growth

Perhaps a more realistic assumption for many firms is that dividends will increase steadily at a constant growth rate forever. Indeed, this is often the stated policy of management. From equation (4-4), the current stock price is found as

$$S_0 = \frac{Div_1}{1 + k_s} + \frac{Div_1(1 + g)}{(1 + k_s)^2} + \cdots + \frac{Div_1(1 + g)^\infty}{(1 + k_s)^\infty} \qquad (4\text{-}6)$$

where g is the constant rate of growth in dividends. Using the mathematical properties of the sum of an infinite series (the details of which are presented in the derivation appendix at the end of the text), Equation 4-6 may be simplified to obtain

$$S_0 = \frac{Div_0(1 + g)}{k_s - g} = \frac{Div_1}{k_s - g} \qquad (4\text{-}7)$$

Equation (4-7) is called the **Gordon valuation model** and is probably the most widely cited dividend valuation model, mainly because its application is so straightforward.

If all investors use the same estimate of future dividends and if the *RRR* used is the appropriate market-determined discount rate, the preceding valuation is a market valuation.

Example 4•3   Stock Value with a Constant Dividend Growth Rate

To illustrate, consider the no-growth example discussed earlier (Senneco Corporation), but now assume that future dividends will grow at a 5% rate. Since the current (constant) dividend is $3, the next dividend can be calculated as $Div_0(1 + g)$. Equation (4-7) therefore implies that Senneco's stock price should be

$$S_0 = \frac{\$3(1 + 0.05)}{(0.15 - 0.05)} = \frac{\$3.15}{0.10} = \$31.50$$

Small changes in dividend growth can have a dramatic impact on stock prices; in this example, the current stock price has increased from $20 to $31.50.

This valuation model can also be used to provide insights into the components of the investor's total return. That is, rewriting equation (4-7) in terms of the required rate of return, we obtain

$$k_s = \frac{Div_1}{S_0} + g \qquad (4\text{-}8)$$

This states that the total expected return is composed of an expected dividend yield and the future growth in dividends, which represents the expected capital gains yield. Therefore, for this example, the individual contribution to total return from these two components is

$$k_s = \frac{\$3.15}{\$31.50} + 0.05$$
$$= 0.10 + 0.05 = 0.15$$

A comparison of equation (4-8) and equation (4-2) shows that g is equal to $(S_1 - S_0)/S_0$.

ESTIMATION OF THE GROWTH RATE

To use the Gordon valuation formula, three inputs are necessary: the next period's expected dividend (Div_1); the *RRR* (k_s), which is assumed to be known (at least for this chapter); and the growth rate (g). How does one estimate g?

Consider the dividend payment process. Out of its earnings, a company decides to pay a certain proportion as dividends. This proportion (or ratio) of earnings paid out as dividends is called the **dividend payout ratio.** For example, if a company decides to distribute as dividends $0.20 on every dollar of earnings, the payout ratio is 20/100, or 20%. The **retention ratio** is given by (1 − payout ratio), which in this case is 80%.

What does the firm do with the dollars it retains within the business? Presumably, all of it is reinvested to earn more for the company next year. Since the retained earnings represent equity capital, and if we assume that the dividend payout ratio is fixed, the dividend growth rate can be readily calculated as

$$g = \text{retention ratio} \times ROE \qquad (4\text{-}9)$$

where *ROE* is the return on equity. *ROE* is calculated as

$$ROE = \frac{\text{net income}}{\text{equity}} \qquad (4\text{-}10)$$

Example 4•4 Determination of Dividend Growth Rate and Stock Price

Clarion Records has had a fixed dividend payout ratio of 25% for the last 15 years, and management sees no reason to change its policy. The book return on equity has been a stable 20%. If its last dividend was $2 per share and Laurence Booth requires a 20% rate of return, what is the maximum price that Mr. Booth would pay for Clarion Records stock?

STEP 1: Calculate g, the Growth in Dividends

$$g = \text{retention ratio} \times ROE$$
$$= (1 - \text{payout ratio}) \times ROE$$
$$= 75\% \times 20\% = 0.15 \text{ or } 15\%$$

STEP 2: Calculate Div_1

$$Div_1 = Div_0(1 + g) = \$2(1 + 0.15) = \$2.30$$

STEP 3: Use the Gordon Valuation Model to Find the Stock Price.

From equation (4-7),

$$S_0 = \frac{Div_1}{k_s - g} = \frac{\$2.30}{0.20 - 0.15} = \$46$$

Thus $46 is the maximum price that Mr. Booth should pay for Clarion stock.

WEAKNESSES OF THE CONSTANT GROWTH MODELS

A few aspects of equation (4-7) require special consideration. First, for the stock to have a meaningful price using equation (4-7), the *RRR* (k_s) must be greater than the growth rate (g). If k_s equals g, the stock price is indefinite, and if k_s is less than g, the stock has a negative price. A negative price implies that you will pay someone to take it. This situation should therefore be ruled out. Second, it is important to restate the critical assumptions underlying equation (4-7). These were that the growth rate in dividends is not only constant but also that the dividend continues to grow at this rate forever.

This is clearly unrealistic. The first difficulty is in determining the future growth rate. This itself is not an easy task. Then it must be assumed that this rate will be sustained forever. No company maintains a constant growth rate forever, especially if its current growth rate is high. For example, consider Pyrotech, Inc., a new company with a current dividend of $1 and a growth rate of 20%. Even if one believes that this growth will continue somewhat longer, it cannot last forever. After three years (say) the growth rate may come down to a stable 5% per year. How would we value this company's stock? The use of the Gordon valuation model is clearly ruled out because the growth rate changes after three years.

Case 3: Variable Dividend Growth

The two common stock valuation models just described are simple to use, but they do not allow for changes in expected growth rates. To find the current stock price when dividend growth rates are variable is a complex situation. Nevertheless, the process of valuation remains relatively straightforward because we can use the multiperiod valuation model developed earlier.

Example 4•5   Stock Value with a Variable Dividend Growth Rate

To illustrate, Figure 4•2 contains information on Howser Corporation's dividends for the next four years, as well as the expected ending price. If an

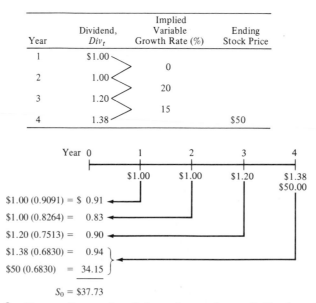

FIGURE 4•2   Howser Corporation: Information on future dividends and ending price.

investor's *RRR* is 10%, this implies a current stock price of

$$S_0 = \$1(PVF_{.10,1}) + \$1(PVF_{.10,2}) + \$1.20(PVF_{.10,3}) + \$1.38(PVF_{.10,4})$$
$$\qquad + \$50(PVF_{.10,4})$$
$$\quad = \$37.73$$

Case 4: The Constant Growth Model Adjusted for Changes in Growth Rates

In a situation such as this, the Gordon model can still be used, but certain other steps are necessary in our calculation. The trick is to recognize that the Gordon model applies from year 3 on because after year 3 the growth rate is a constant 5%.

Figure 4•3 illustrates how Pyrotech's stock price can be calculated, assuming a discount rate of 10%. Consider an investor who plans to hold the stock for three years. What are the cash flows to this investor? Clearly, the investor would get dividends of $1.20, $1.44, and $1.73 for the three years in addition to S_3, the price of the stock in year 3. If S_3 could be estimated, the current stock price (S_0) would simply be the sum of the present values of the dividends and S_3, discounted at the investor's required rate of return of 10%. To find S_3, the Gordon

Given: Current dividend (Div_0) = \$1.00
Required rate of return (k_s) = 10%
Growth rate: 20%/year for 3 years; 5%/year thereafter

Year	Dividend Div_t	Expected Stock Price
1	\$1.20[a]	
2	1.44[a]	
3	1.73[a]	$S_3 = \dfrac{Div_4}{k_s - g} = \dfrac{\$1.82}{0.10 - 0.05} = \$36.40$
4	1.82[b]	

[a] Dividend 20% more than previous dividend.
[b] Dividend 5% more than previous dividend.

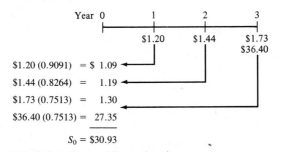

$1.20 (0.9091) = $ 1.09
$1.44 (0.8264) = 1.19
$1.73 (0.7513) = 1.30
$36.40 (0.7513) = 27.35

$S_0 = \$30.93$

FIGURE 4•3 Calculating Pyrotech's stock price.

valuation model can be used because, from that year, the constant growth rate of 5% per year is assumed to be sustained forever. As Figure 4•3 illustrates, S_3 equals $36.40 and the current stock price for Pyrotech is $30.93.

VALUE LIES IN THE EYES OF THE BEHOLDER

We have examined several different methods for calculating stock prices when the discount rate is given. How can these calculations help us?

For one thing, the formulas help us understand qualitatively the impact of various changes on stock prices. If the *RRR* goes up, formula (4-7), for example, clearly suggests that stock prices should fall. In fact, several other qualitative conclusions can be drawn from equation (4-7), when we examine the factors that determine k_s, the *RRR*.

For example, if an investor calculates the stock price to be $40 and her broker tells her that the stock is selling for $45, the stock is overvalued. By contrast, a market price of $36 would suggest that the stock is undervalued by the market. By recalling that the calculated stock price is based on an individual's personal estimate of k_s and g, it becomes clear why the labels *overvalued* and *undervalued* make sense only for the particular person making the calculations. Another person could take the opposite viewpoint, and both would be right. After all, both people define under- or overvalued stock in terms of their personal calculations of formula values. It makes no sense whatsoever for a broker to call a client's attention to an undervalued stock. Depending on the values of the discount rate used and the forecasted dividends, any undervalued stock can be converted into an overvalued stock, and vice versa. Thus, value lies in the eyes of the beholder. (See the highlight "A Tale of Two Rats.") It is precisely because two people disagree about values that they have an incentive to trade.

■ *HIGHLIGHT*

A TALE OF TWO RATS

Advice on "overvalued" and "undervalued" stocks has always been available to investors. Of course, the usefulness of acting on such advice in an efficient market is questionable. Taking a jab at "knowledgeable" stockbrokers, G.E. Hanson wrote the following amusing story in *Life* magazine (May 26, 1887):

An old rat, whose long residence in the city had given him great knowledge of the wiles of civilized life, observed one evening a tempting bit of cheese close by his favorite hole in the wall.

Instead of greedily rushing at it, he called a young friend, saying, "Whiskerando, some kind person has prepared a feast for us. Help yourself."

The guileless innocent rushed on the cheese, which he devoured voraciously: but, alas! in a few minutes he rolled over on his back, stone dead. The dainty was poisoned.

> "My experience in Wall Street has stood me in well," mused the old rat as he turned into his hole: "it is safer to give other folks pointers, and pocket your commission, than to risk your all on a wildcat investment."

For the preceding valuation models to be market valuations, not only must all investors agree on the future cash flows, but in addition, the *RRR* used in the valuation must be a market-determined rate. Unfortunately, it is not possible to say when these conditions will be satisfied in this framework.

DIVIDENDS AND STOCK PRICES

At first glance, it appears from equation (4-7) that dividends are a crucial determinant of stock prices. In fact, if a firm is not expected to pay any dividends, $Div_1 = 0$, and the implied stock price appears to be zero. However, this conclusion is incorrect. Table 4·6 presents a partial list of stocks that have not paid a dividend in years, and all of them have nonzero prices. Thus, actual economic experience indicates that it is not mandatory for a firm to pay dividends. How can one explain this paradox?

In deriving stock valuation equations such as equation (4-7), the price of the stock is calculated as the present value of an infinite series of dividends growing at a constant rate, *g*. By focusing on an infinite dividend series, the selling price of the stock at a future date does not enter the calculations. However, even if a company pays no dividends at all, an implicit dividend is still built in; some day, the firm will liquidate and pay a *liquidating dividend*. Thus, the stock that pays no cash dividends can be treated as a property right that is expected to yield the investor a fractional ownership in the firm when it liquidates. The present value of this liquidating dividend contributes to the value of the stock. Even if an investor cannot wait until the day of liquidation to get this reward, he or she may be willing to pay a price for the stock because this property right (stock) is readily tradeable. That is, when an investor needs cash, he or she can expect to

TABLE 4·6 Some Corporations That Pay No Dividends

Bio-Rad Labs	Photo Controls
Crown-Cork & Seal	Quotron Systems
Data General	SCI Systems
Digital Equipment	Teradyne, Inc.
Federal Express	Timesharing
Kevex Corporation	U.S. Surgical
LaQuinta Inns	Whitehall Corporation
May Petroleum	Xidex
Petroleum Equipment Tools	

sell the stock at a positive price to someone else. Others may be willing to buy the stock from this investor again for a similar reason: There is a value to holding property rights in the economy. As long as property rights are recognized and not threatened by major socioeconomic or political changes, an active secondary market can exist for stocks that pay no dividends. As seen in Chapter 1, property rights are a fundamental characteristic of the U.S. capitalist system. Hence dividend payments are not necessary as long as investors expect to be able to sell their property rights in the marketplace.

Learning Check for Section 4·3

Review Questions

4·14. What are some of the problems in applying the fundamental valuation equation of Chapter 3 to the valuation of common stock?

4·15. What are the three possible holding-period assumptions? Which is the most realistic for valuing common stock?

4·16. What is the relationship between the growth rate and the retention ratio?

4·17. If your *RRR* increases, what will happen to the stock price?

4·18. What are the crucial assumptions underlying the Gordon valuation model? How is the growth rate *g* estimated?

New Terms

Capital gains yield	Dividend yield	Multiperiod valuation
Dividend growth rate	Gordon valuation model	Retention ratio
Dividend payout ratio	Infinite-period valuation	Single-period valuation

SUMMARY

Equity Ownership

Equity is simply ownership and carries certain rights. Corporate ownership carries with it certain rights and privileges, such as electing a board of directors to oversee management. Some bylaws give shareholders cumulative voting and preemptive rights. Whatever the specific laws, the basic premise remains the same: In the event of bankruptcy, shareholders do not have a claim on the company, as lenders do, but they do share in the profits, with no limit, if the company does well. For assuming greater risks, equity holders can expect to receive a higher return on their capital than can debtors.

Sources of Equity Capital

Obtaining equity capital for a new corporation can begin as informally as trading a piece of the company to a relative for seed capital. When the business needs more capital, its original owners must either borrow or convince others to become owners of the firm. For a new company, these new owners may be venture capitalists. However, as the firm grows, its need for capital increases, and it may seek to go public and issue stock, which may be traded in the capital markets.

Common Stock Valuation

Valuing a stock using the fundamental valuation equation poses certain problems: The holding period must be specified, and an assumption must be made concerning the dividend growth. To get around the holding period problem, we can use an infinite-period model. In this model, it is unnecessary to estimate future stock prices. However, it becomes necessary to make assumptions about the future sequence of dividends. There are four assumptions concerning dividend payments that are commonly made: zero growth, constant growth, variable growth, and changing growth.

The Gordon valuation model is a widely used model that assumes that dividends grow forever at a constant rate. The growth rate can be estimated using the firm's *ROE* and the retention ratio. This model can be used in conjunction with other frameworks to recognize certain cases of variable growth rates.

PROBLEMS

4•1. The LeCompte Corporation's equity portion of its balance sheet has the following information.

LeCompte Corporation: Stockholders' Equity, December 31, 1990

Common Stock 500,000 shares, $1 par, 300,000 shares issued	$300,000
Additional Paid-in Capital	121,000
Retained Earnings	68,000
Total Stockholders' Equity	$489,000

However, you, as a recent business graduate, know that the firm has 60,000 shares of treasury stock which was purchased last year at a price of $2.42 per share. What is the correct total Stockholders' Equity for LeCompte Corporation?

4•2. Gravelle Research Corporation has the current balance sheet entries for its stockholders' equity.

Gravelle Corporation: Stockholders' Equity, December 31, 1990

Common Stock: 1,000,000 shares authorized, $2 par,	
500,000 shares issued	$1,000,000
Additional Paid-in Capital	450,000
Retained Earnings	5,840,000
Total Stockholders' Equity	$7,290,000

Gravelle's management has decided to issue 120,000 shares of stock. They feel that the stock can be sold for $45 per share. Change the above Equity accounts to reflect the sale of stock.

4•3. Atilla Industries is a publicly held company that has 1,500,000 shares outstanding with a market value of $23.2 million. The records show that the company has 6,805 shareholders, 4,200 of whom own 100 or more shares. Atilla's net tangible assets are worth $24 million. If Atilla had pretax earnings of $1.6 million this year, what other requirements must Atilla meet before it can consider being listed on the NYSE?

4•4. Bulls-Eye Stores, Inc., has 2,000,000 common shares outstanding. The share price is currently $20, and the annual dividend paid at the end of the year will be $0.75 per share. What is your expected rate of return on a share if you expect the share price to be $22.50 at the end of the year?

4•5. One year ago, you purchased 100 shares of Pacific Oil for $25 each. The annual dividend per share was $1, and the share price today is $27. On the same day you purchased your shares, your brother purchased 100 shares of Georgia Edison for $15 per share. The annual dividend per share was $2.30, and the share price today is $14.50. Who earned a greater rate of return, you or your brother?

4•6. Your broker told you that she expects Trans-Earth Airlines common shares to earn a 20% return during the coming year. The share price is currently $15, and the dividend is expected to be $0.50 per share. What does your broker expect the share price to be at the end of the year?

4•7. Sergeant Motors' common shares are trading for $30 each. You expect annual dividends (paid at the end of the year) to be constant at $1 for the next four years. If you expect a 15% return on your investment, what must you expect the share price to be in four years?

4•8. The TLL Corporation has announced that it will keep its annual dividend at $1.50 forever. If a share costs $10, what rate of return are you earning?

4•9. The Midwest Grain Company pays an annual dividend of $1.80 and is expected to do so permanently. If you require a 15% return on your investment, how much will you be willing to pay for a share?

4•10. The Libre Noir Referral Service is about to go public. You expect the end-of-the-year dividend to be $1.20, and you require an 18% return to buy the shares. How much will you be willing to pay for a share if you expect dividends to grow indefinitely at an annual rate of 10%?

4•11. Telstar, Inc., just paid a $1.60 dividend. They paid a dividend of $0.89 12 years ago. What has been the annual growth rate in dividends during this time? If the growth rate remains the same, how much will you be willing to pay for a share if you require a return of 12%?

4•12. C-Paul Restaurant has common shares outstanding that are currently trading for $12 each. You expect the end-of-the-year dividend to be $0.80 and for dividends to grow indefinitely at a rate of 6%. What rate of return do you anticipate on the stock?

4•13. A friend of yours is incorporating her business, the Office Box. She has promised to pay a $1 annual dividend at the end of each of the next three years, with dividends to grow at an annual rate of 8% thereafter. How much will you be willing to pay for a share if you require a 14% rate of return?

4•14. Compuchat, Inc., paid a dividend of $0.68 five years ago and has just paid an annual dividend of $1; you expect dividends to grow at the same annual rate for the next four years. After that, you expect dividends to grow at an annual rate of 12%. How much will you be willing to pay for a share if you require a 16% rate of return?

APPENDIX 4·A *Investment Banking*

If a company decides to go public, it will probably enlist the aid of **investment bankers.** Their services are sought by corporations due to the increasingly complex legal requirements and marketing aspects of going to the public for external funds. Investment bankers perform three roles: originating, underwriting, and selling.

Although this section of the chapter deals primarily with equity financing, the same principles and procedures generally hold true for raising capital in the debt market. Where applications to the bond and stock markets diverge, we point out the differences.

PRELIMINARY CORPORATE CONSIDERATIONS

Assuming that the company has decided to make a public offering, it must make some preliminary decisions before approaching the investment banker. Presumably, it has already ascertained its future financing needs and its optimum capital structure. Now it must decide whether the sale should be a privileged subscription, also called a **rights offering,** to its existing shareholders, or whether it should be a cash offering to the general public. The rights offering refers to the previously discussed preemptive rights owned by stockholders in some companies. Rights offerings generally are less expensive than cash offerings, but cash offerings are more often used.

The corporation must also choose either to arrange a **negotiated deal** with the investment banker or to request **competitive bids.** The latter requires the investment house to invest time and effort without any assurance of obtaining the bid. Thus, only the biggest, best-established companies use the competitive-bid process, since investment houses are reluctant to perform the preliminary work for smaller companies. Only about 3% of all public-equity offerings are done by competitive bid. Of all bond and preferred stock public offerings, about 15% are done by competitive bid. Public utility holding companies are the major exception. Under normal market conditions, they are required by the SEC to choose underwriters by competitive bid.

In seeking an investment banker, corporations consider several factors, including the banker's reputation for successfully marketing similar offerings. For example, Drexel Burnham Lambert has aggressively pursued the junk-bond market. Other houses may emphasize the sale of municipal bonds or smaller regional issues. Morgan Stanley & Company may be more receptive to older, established companies, since it prefers to represent them. The choice of the investment banker is important, since an association with a highly regarded one can enhance a company's credibility in the marketplace.

ORIGINATION ROLE

Once chosen, the investment banker reviews the preliminary decisions, such as the type of offering and its timing, in the light of current market conditions. The banker's role as adviser and consultant in originating the issue is important to its eventual sale.

The investment house also starts a routine due diligence investigation. Due diligence is important to the investment banker, particularly with new issues, since the investment house will be associating its reputation with the company. As noted in the discussion of penny stocks, due diligence is stricter and more important for some types of issues than others.

The investment banker's most critical function at this point is to recommend to the company what type of issue to pursue and with what timing, pricing, and issue characteristics. On an equity offering, for example, the corporation may be advised to raise less equity and more debt under current market conditions.

In addition, the investment house prepares other marketing and informational material. Since many of the potential buyers are customers of the firm (particularly institutional investors), it is relatively easy for the investment house to "test market" the proposed offering before completing all the required documents and filings.

UNDERWRITING ROLE

Investment bankers usually assume the risk of the issue, thereby **underwriting** the offering on a guaranteed basis. The guarantee provides that if investors fail to buy the entire offering, meaning that it is not fully subscribed, the underwriter is obligated to buy the remaining unsold lots at a previously specified price. Thus, once an underwriter has taken the issue on a guaranteed basis, the issuing company is guaranteed to receive a specified amount of capital. The risk of salability of the issue is borne by the investment house. As compensation for that additional risk, however, the underwriter receives a larger fee than if there were no guarantee.

When there is no guarantee, the underwriting is done with only a promise of best efforts, as is often the case with new, more speculative issues. Thus, if the issue fails to sell out, the issuing company bears the risk of failing to raise enough capital, despite the expenses incurred. Offerings are made on a best-efforts basis when either the investment house deems it too risky to guarantee or the issuer is confident of the salability of the issue and chooses to save the higher fee charge for the guarantee.

Investment bankers often form underwriting and selling **syndicates** with other underwriters to reduce the risk and increase marketing outlets. These syndicates may have as few as two or three members or as many as a few hundred with a very large offering. The hierarchy in an underwriting syndicate is clear from the so-called **tombstone announcements** of offerings in the business press. As shown in Figure 4A•1, the offering of the new issue of 4.6 million shares of Herman's Sporting Goods, Inc., shares was handled by 80 broker-dealers. The lead underwriters were Merrill Lynch Capital Markets and Bear, Stearns & Company. The size of the type indicates their greater importance compared with that of the other 78 members of the syndicate (listed alphabetically). Table 4A•1 lists the underwriters of the most issues in 1984.

NEW ISSUE

4,600,000 Shares

Herman's Sporting Goods, Inc.

Common Stock

Price $16.50 Per Share
The New York Stock Exchange symbol is HER

Copies of the Prospectus may be obtained in any State in which this announcement is circulated from only such of the undersigned or other dealers or brokers as may legally offer these securities in such State.

Merrill Lynch Capital Markets   Bear, Stearns & Co.

Alex. Brown & Sons   The First Boston Corporation   Dillon, Read & Co. Inc.   Donaldson, Lufkin & Jenrette
Incorporated   Securities Corporation
Drexel Burnham Lambert   Goldman, Sachs & Co.   Hambrecht & Quist   E.F. Hutton & Company Inc.
Incorporated   Incorporated
Kidder, Peabody & Co.   Lazard Freres & Co.   Montgomery Securities   Morgan Stanley & Co.
Incorporated   Incorporated
PaineWebber   Prudential–Bache   Robertson, Colman & Stephens
Incorporated   Securities
L.F. Rothschild, Unterberg, Towbin   Salomon Brothers Inc.   Shearson Lehman Brothers Inc.

Smith Barney, Harris Upham & Co.   Wertheim & Co., Inc.   Dean Witter Reynolds Inc.
Incorporated
F. Eberstadt & Co., Inc. A.G. Edwards & Sons, Inc. Oppenheimer & Co., Inc. Thomson McKinnon Securities Inc.

ABD Securities Corporation   Advest, Inc.   Allen & Company   Bacon Stifel Nicolaus
                                                       Incorporated   Stifel Nicolaus & Company Incorporated
Robert W. Baird & Co.   Bateman Eichler, Hill Richards   Sanford C. Bernstein & Co., Inc.
Incorporated   Incorporated
William Blair & Company   Blunt Ellis & Loewi   J.C. Bradford & Co.   Butcher & Singer Inc.
                                    Incorporated   Incorporated
Cowen & Co.   Dain Bosworth   Daiwa Securities America Inc.   Deutsche Bank Capital
                       Incorporated   Corporation
Dominion Securities Pitfield Inc.   Eppler, Guerin & Turner, Inc.   EuroPartners Securities Corporation

First of Michigan Corporation   Robert Fleming   Janney Montgomery Scott Inc.   Kleinwort, Benson
                                   Incorporated
Ladenburg, Thalmann & Co. Inc. Cyrus J. Lawrence McDonald & Company McLeod Young Weir Incorporated
                                   Incorporated   Securites
Moseley, Hallgarten, Estabrook & Weeden Inc.   Neuberger & Berman   The Nikko Securities Co.
                                                                                International, Inc.
Nomura Securities International, Inc.   Piper, Jaffray & Hopwood   Prescott, Ball & Turbep, Inc.
                                           Incorporated
The Robinson–Humphrey Company, Inc.   Rotan Mosle Inc.   Rothschild Inc.

Swiss Bank Corporation International   Tucker, Anthony & R.I. Day, Inc.   Underwood, Neuhaus & Co.
Securities, Inc.   Incorporated
Wheat, First Securities, Inc.   Wood Gundy Corp.   Yamaichi International (America) Inc.

Algemene Bank Nederland N.V.   Banque Bruxelles Lambert S.A.   Banque Nationale de Paris

Banque de Paris et des Pays–Bas   Bayerische Landesbank Girozentrale   Bayerische Vereinsbank
                                                                                 Aksengesellschaft
European Banking Company Limited   Handelsbank N.W. (Overseas) Limited   Morgan Grenfell & Co. Limited

Orion Royal Bank Limited   J. Henry Schroder Wagg & Co. Limited   Vereins–und Westbank
                                                                            Aksengesselschaft

FIGURE 4·A1   Example of a tombstone announcement for a common stock offering.

MARKETING ROLE

The marketing role entails several functions, including fulfilling legal requirements and determining the type, size, pricing, and other issuing characteristics.

TABLE 4A·1 Top 10 Underwriters[a]
(Volume in billions of dollars)

1.	Salomon Brothers	47.72
2.	First Boston	41.82
3.	Merrill Lynch	31.34
4.	Goldman Sachs	29.89
5.	Drexel Burnham Lambert	27.58
6.	Morgan Stanley	26.55
7.	Shearson Lehman Brothers	16.76
8.	Kidder, Peabody	10.87
9.	Bear Sterns	5.74
10.	Paine Webber	4.67

[a]Rankings are based on a double credit given to
the lead underwriter and include all taxable
underwritten debt or equity deals of $2 million
or more offered for all of 1986.

Source: *Institutional Investor*, March 1987,
p. 177.

SEC Procedures

Most public interstate offerings valued for more than $1.5 million must be registered with the SEC.[5] The SEC requires that a **registration statement,** consisting of the offering circular, or the **prospectus,** and other legal documents be filed before the actual sale. The circular or the prospectus gives investors the company's financial statements, management, history, projections, and intended use of the proceeds.

The SEC can withhold approval of the offering until its staff is satisfied that the disclosure in the prospectus is adequate and accurate. The agency does not pass judgment on the merits of the investment, only on the accuracy and adequacy of the information provided. SEC documents require that all risks be made clear to the investor. Thus, the typical prospectus is filled with warnings about any riskiness of the investment. The SEC will write a **deficiency memorandum** to the company about anything it wishes changed in the prospectus. The company files an amended statement in response and then must wait at least 20 days before actually making the offer.

During the 20-day waiting period, the issuer is permitted to distribute the prospectus without undue publicity as long as the prospectus carries a warning in red ink that it is not an offer to sell at that time. Thus, these preliminary prospectuses are known as **red herrings** and contain substantially the same information as the offering prospectus except the price of the offering.

The actual prospectus must be provided to all buyers. Most investors seek

---

[5]The SEC does not require registration in certain categories, including issues sold entirely intrastate; issues that are short term, usually 270 days or less; and issues already controlled by another agency, such as public utilities.

the counsel of lawyers or accountants in analyzing the prospectus. A registrar is usually appointed by the company to record issuance of stock to investors, and transfer agents are appointed to take care of the transfer of the new securities.

State Laws

Investment bankers must also be sure that their clients are complying with the laws of the states in which they are operating. Many states, such as Ohio, have stricter laws protecting stockholders than those set by the SEC. Companies that issue stock in relatively new, more speculative issues must be cognizant of the **blue-sky laws** of some states. These laws are intended to protect state residents from being misled by untrustworthy securities marketers.

Setting the Price

The ease in setting the price of an issue depends on the type of issue. For bonds or other fixed-rate debt, it is fairly straightforward: Bond interest rates are usually set so that the bond price will be close to its $1,000 par value. Bond interest rates, in turn, are sensitive to current market interest rates, as discussed in Chapter 6.

The pricing of cash offerings of new equity issues, however, by definition has no market basis. The costs of miscalculations can be substantial. If the price is set too low, the company is giving up funds it could have received from the offering. If the price is set too high, the company may have trouble selling out its offering and fail to obtain enough capital. Generally, underwriters prefer to err with a price that is too low rather than too high.

The pricing of seasoned issues, whether cash offerings or rights offerings, is based on market prices. However, investment bankers must balance the size of the offering against the potential dilutive effects on ownership and earnings. Recall the earlier discussion regarding a rights sale, where the increase in shares outstanding when net income does not change causes earnings per share to fall. In turn, the stock price falls, provided that the price-earnings multiple remains the same.

A dilutive effect drops the price of all the company's stock, not just of the new issue. Financial theorists, however, have debated the extent of this effect. The prospect of an influx of capital into a company, which could have promising intended uses, could alter the perception of the company and, as a result, affect its stock price. In general, however, new issues are generally sold at below-market prices.

RIGHTS OFFERINGS

In rights offerings, the new shares are offered to existing shareholders rather than to the general public. Each shareholder receives an instrument called a right that gives them the option to buy the shares. Recall that in some firms preemptive rights are stipulated in corporate bylaws. The purpose of these rights is to protect the interests of existing stockholders by requiring that any equity distributions, such as a new stock offering, be offered first to the owners of the outstanding shares. The procedure for such a distribution via a rights offering differs from that of a cash offering only slightly in preparation but substantially in the selling process.

FLOTATION COSTS

The costs of raising capital consist of the underwriters' spread and the administrative costs. Underwriters typically acquire their fee, expressed as a percentage of the whole deal, by buying the offering at a discount from the actual offering price. The **spread** between these two prices is their income. Administrative costs consist of legal and accounting fees, printing costs, and other expenses.

Fees vary according to the size of the offering, the underwriter, and the type of offering. The larger the offering, the smaller the underwriters' fees as a percentage of the gross proceeds. Administrative fees drop sharply as a percentage of transactions as they grow larger, reflecting economies of scale. Many administrative costs, such as attorneys' fees for due diligence, require a minimum number of hours of work, regardless of the size of the transaction. Printing costs, involving high front-end expenses, rise in small increments with the volume after reaching a certain level. For underwritten rights offerings there is often a two-fee arrangement: a **standby commitment fee** that is based on the total number of shares in the offering and a **take-up fee** that depends on the number of rights handled.

Investment house pricing policies differ. Morgan Stanley, for example, is known on Wall Street for charging higher fees than many of its counterparts. Its rationale is that its transaction/employee ratio is lower than that of other houses; thus customers pay for more personalized attention. Also, on new issues, some investment bankers receive additional compensation in the form of options for stock in the company at a future date. Suppose that an investment banker holds a three-year option to buy a new company's stock at its $20 IPO price. If the company's stock rises to $30 a share in the next three years, the banker may choose to exercise the option at $20 and thus make an instant $10 profit (on paper anyway, since the banker has not yet sold the stock), and thus reap an additional profit from underwriting the issue.

Equity cash issues are the most expensive offerings. Offerings of less than $2 million can cost the issuer 7 to 13% of gross proceeds for the underwriting cost and another 4 to 9% in administrative charges. Offerings of more than $10 million, however, are much less expensive, consisting of underwriter compensation of less than 5% and administrative costs of less than 1% of the total proceeds.

Rights issues are somewhat less expensive than general cash offerings for issues of up to $20 million. Beyond $20 million, the cost advantage largely disappears, and the fees are about the same as for general cash offers.

Except for the smallest offerings, bond issues are significantly less expensive than equity offerings, with underwriting costs falling below 2% of the gross proceeds for issues over $5 million. Administrative expenses are similar to those of general cash offerings.

Comparing private placements with public ones, private offerings are substantially cheaper, due to savings in SEC filings and other requirements. As a rule of thumb, private offerings cost about one-fourth to one-half of the amount of public offerings.

SHELF REGISTRATION

Because of the time-consuming preparation required for raising public funds, the SEC in 1982 decided that companies could, after going through the preparation process, wait for up to two years before actually bringing an issue to sale. This concept became known as **shelf registration,** since it permitted companies to leave the offering documents for fund raising "on the shelf" until they were needed.

Established companies that make issues fairly often are eligible for shelf registration. They file a master registration statement and then follow up on it with a short-form statement when they actually offer the securities. Shelf registration does not require the corporation to issue the registered securities all at once, but rather in any partial amounts and at any time it wishes within the two-year period.

Shelf registration immediately became extremely popular because of the timing and flexibility it permitted. The company could respond to a change in the market more quickly, since it had already filed all the required documents and had obtained approval. This permitted the company, then, to meet market needs not only when it believed the market would be most receptive but also in amounts the market would wish to buy.

Learning Check for Appendix 4·A

Review Questions

4A·1. What are some of the issues that a firm should address before approaching an investment banker?

4A·2. What are the various activities, or roles, of an underwriter?

4A·3. What is the difference between a guaranteed basis underwriting and a best efforts underwriting?

4A•4.   What is shelf registration? What are its advantages?

4A•5.   Distinguish between a standby commitment fee and a take-up fee.

New Terms

Blue-sky laws

Competitive bid

Deficiency memorandum

Flotation costs

Investment banker

Negotiated deal

Prospectus

Red-herring

Registration statement

Rights offerings

Shelf registration

Spread

Standby commitment fee

Syndicate

Take-up fee

Tombstone announcements

Underwriting

READINGS

BROSKY, JOHN J., *The Implicit Cost of Trade Credit and Theory of Optimal Terms of Sale* (New York: Credit Research Foundation, 1969).

GLADSTONE, DAVID, *Venture Capital Investing* (Englewood Cliffs, N.J.: Prentice Hall, Inc., 1988).

HANSEN, R. S., AND J. M. PINKERTON, "Direct Equity Financing: A Resolution of a Paradox," *Journal of Finance*, June 1982, 651–666.

HENDERSON, JAMES A., *Obtaining Venture Financing, Principles and Practices* (Lexington, Mass.: Lexington Books, 1988).

LOGUE, D. E., AND R. A. JARROW, "Negotiation vs. Competitive Bidding in the Sale of Securities by Public Utilities," *Financial Management,* Autumn 1978, 31–39.

SHAPIRO, E., AND C. R. WOLF, *The Role of Private Placements in Corporate Finance* (Boston: Division of Research, Graduate School of Business Administration, Harvard University, 1972).

SMITH, C. W., "Alternative Methods for Raising Capital: Rights versus Underwritten Offerings," *Journal of Financial Economics*, December 1977, 273–307.

5

Long-Term Debt and Preferred Stock

Long-term debt is the most popular method by which firms raise long-term capital. As seen in Table 5•1, it accounted for more than two-thirds of all new financing raised by corporations in the period 1978–1986. Life insurance companies' investments and pension funds dominate these corporate debt purchases.

Because we cover such a wide variety of topics in this chapter, it is useful at the outset to note the logic of the presentation. The chapter consists of four sections on debt, each of which is important in understanding the next section. Preferred stock, which combines characteristics of debt and stock, is discussed in a brief fifth section, which may be read independently.

TABLE 5•1 New Security Issues of Corporations (Billions of Dollars)

Type of Issue	1978	1979	1980	1981	1982	1983	1984	1985	1986[a]
All issues	47.2	51.5	73.7	70.4	84.6	120.0	132.5	201.3	195.3
Bonds	36.9	40.2	53.2	45.1	54.1	68.4	109.9	165.8	154.6
Stocks	10.4	11.3	20.5	25.3	30.6	51.6	22.6	35.5	40.7

[a]1986 figures are year-to-date August.

Source: *Federal Reserve Bulletin*, Board of Governors of the Federal Reserve System.

SECTION 5•1: *Debt Terminology and Characteristics.* Here we introduce basic bond terminology and then examine several characteristics that define a long-term debt issue. These characteristics include the maturity of the debt, the security of the debt, the provisions for the debt's repayment, the interest paid on it, and the denomination in which the debt is issued.

SECTION 5•2: *Debt Offerings.* Bonds may initially be issued through private placements or public offerings. We discuss each of these methods, as well as bond ratings.

SECTION 5•3: *Bond Valuation.* In this section, we explain the procedure for valuing bonds and then examine the relationship among a bond's coupon rate, market price, and *RRR*. We conclude by discussing the valuation of bonds with semiannual coupon payments.

SECTION 5•4: *Bond Values Over Time.* First, we examine the changes in a bond's price as it approaches its maturity date and then define the yield to maturity of a bond and review its uses and limitations.

SECTION 5•5: *Preferred Stock.* The chapter concludes with a discussion of preferred stock, which combines some of the characteristics of equity and debt.

SECTION 5•1 *Debt Terminology and Characteristics*

TERMINOLOGY

The length of time a bond will be outstanding is called its **maturity.** *Long-term debt* generally refers to debt that matures in one year or more. Bonds are a form of long-term debt that is usually secured by property.[1] Debentures, often called *debs,* are unsecured bonds.

The **par value** of a bond or **debenture,** also known as the *face value* or *maturity value,* is always $1,000, unless otherwise specified. This is the amount of principal to be repaid at maturity. The **coupon interest rate** is the stated annual rate of interest paid on the par value of the bond. Issuers typically seek to sell bonds as close to the par value as possible, so that the coupon rate on the bond is determined by current market interest rates, allowing the bond price to be set near $1,000. We will have much more to say on this subject later.

When the annual interest is stated in dollar terms, it is called the **coupon amount.** Figure 5•1 shows the March 1985 public announcement of Eastman Kodak Company's offering of $400 million worth of 30-year debentures. The coupon interest rate on this offering is $12\frac{1}{4}\%$, so the coupon amount is $122.50 a

---

[1] Technically, a bond is a security evidencing long-term debt. The distinction is sometimes made but is not of material consequence to the common use of the term.

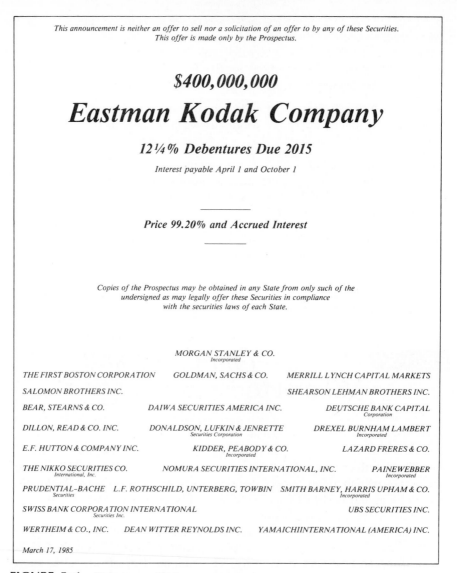

This announcement is neither an offer to sell nor a solicitation of an offer to by any of these Securities. This offer is made only by the Prospectus.

$400,000,000

Eastman Kodak Company

12¼% Debentures Due 2015

Interest payable April 1 and October 1

Price 99.20% and Accrued Interest

Copies of the Prospectus may be obtained in any State from only such of the undersigned as may legally offer these Securities in compliance with the securities laws of each State.

MORGAN STANLEY & CO.
Incorporated

THE FIRST BOSTON CORPORATION   GOLDMAN, SACHS & CO.   MERRILL LYNCH CAPITAL MARKETS

SALOMON BROTHERS INC.   SHEARSON LEHMAN BROTHERS INC.

BEAR, STEARNS & CO.   DAIWA SECURITIES AMERICA INC.   DEUTSCHE BANK CAPITAL
Corporation

DILLON, READ & CO. INC.   DONALDSON, LUFKIN & JENRETTE   DREXEL BURNHAM LAMBERT
Securities Corporation   Incorporated

E.F. HUTTON & COMPANY INC.   KIDDER, PEABODY & CO.   LAZARD FRERES & CO.
Incorporated

THE NIKKO SECURITIES CO.   NOMURA SECURITIES INTERNATIONAL, INC.   PAINEWEBBER
International, Inc.   Incorporated

PRUDENTIAL-BACHE   L.F. ROTHSCHILD, UNTERBERG, TOWBIN   SMITH BARNEY, HARRIS UPHAM & CO.
Securities   Incorporated

SWISS BANK CORPORATION INTERNATIONAL   UBS SECURITIES INC.
Securities Inc.

WERTHEIM & CO., INC.   DEAN WITTER REYNOLDS INC.   YAMAICHIINTERNATIONAL (AMERICA) INC.

March 17, 1985

FIGURE 5•1   Debenture-offering announcement.

year. The coupon amount is found by multiplying the annual interest rate by the face value (0.1225 × $1,000). Although the semiannual payments can be calculated easily, annual payments will be assumed for ease of discussion.

Coupons are literally attached to many types of bonds; bondholders tear off the dated coupons and redeem them at a local bank or the bond issuer's agent.

Bonds issued for the first time are called *new* or **unseasoned issues,** while those that have been on the market for more than a couple of weeks are called **seasoned** or *outstanding* **issues.** Unseasoned issues are generally considered more risky than seasoned ones because investors have less information about them.

Long-term debt may be sold publicly through an **underwriter,** who is usually an **investment banker,** or through private placement directly with institutions, which may number as few as 2 or as many as 20.

BASIC CHARACTERISTICS OF DEBT

Long-term debt comes in many forms. But all these debt instruments, despite some seemingly complex elements, possess five basic characteristics: maturity, security, repayment provisions, interest rates, and denomination.

Conventional debt simply consists of packages of characteristics that are commonly used. Small changes in the conventional elements can give rise to significantly different debt instruments. As a result, with a little creativity, the capital markets have developed new debt entities.

MATURITY

As discussed previously, short-term debt is generally considered to be debt maturing in a year or less. Any debt maturing after a year or more is often called *funded debt*. The word *funded* simply indicates that the maturity is a year or longer. Funded debt is sometimes divided into medium-term and long-term debt. *Medium-term* or *intermediate-term* debt refers to debt maturing in 1 to 10 years. In this usage, *long-term* debt encompasses anything longer, with most debt maturing in less than 30 years.

Term loans are borrowings on which fixed amounts of principal and interest are paid regularly over the life of the loan. Term loans run from three to seven years, although their maturities vary widely. Unlike bonds, term loans are borrowed from a bank or a group of banks, although insurance companies often get involved as well. Term loans are normally used by smaller companies.

Bonds may mature in 7 to 30 years from the date of issue. Traditionally, bonds have been issued for 20 to 30 years, but more recently, 7- to 10-year maturities have become more popular.

SECURITY

Security refers to the recourse of the debt holder in the event of default. Term loans are usually unsecured. When they are secured, it is usually by equipment to finance equipment purchases. They may also be used for other purposes, such as interim financing.

Bonds may also be secured by plant, equipment, and other securities. When they are secured by a mortgage, they are called, not surprisingly, **mortgage bonds.** When a company's stocks, notes, or bonds are pledged as security, or collateral, for a bond issue, they are called *collateral trust bonds*. There are first mortgage and second mortgage bonds, indicating priority of claims.

Debentures are riskier than even second mortgage bonds of the same issuer because debentures are unsecured, giving debenture holders only a general claim on the unmortgaged assets of the company. Debenture holders are second to bondholders in making claims on the mortgaged assets of the company. Debentures thus pay a higher return to investors for the higher risk. They are usually sold only by well-established companies with high credit ratings. Debentures may also be classified as *senior* or *subordinated*—another reference to their claim status in case of default. Subordinated debenture holders are paid after senior debenture holders. Unless specifically stated, all issues are senior issues.

REPAYMENT PROVISIONS

For term loans, repayment provisions vary widely, depending on a company's history, cash flows, age, profitability, management, and other factors. Repayment may be in the form of equal monthly or quarterly payments of interest and principal, or it may be minimal in the first few years, with a balloon on maturity. Term loans are often tailored for a company's expected needs; for example, the repayment schedule may be tied to projected cash flows.

Interest payments on bonds are usually semiannual. Principal repayments are contingent on the stipulations set forth in a legal document known as an **indenture,** which specifies all the requirements and conditions that must be met by bondholders and the corporation to protect both parties. To make sure that the company abides by the indenture, a trustee, usually a bank official, is specified to act on behalf of the bondholders who have the fiduciary responsibility. If the company fails to adhere to the indenture's requirements, the indenture gives the trustee, or some of the bondholders, the right to declare the entire issue due and payable immediately.

These requirements are important, not only because of the ramifications to the company if they are not met, but also because they greatly influence the risk and return of the bond, and thus its value. Therefore, we must examine the basic provisions of the indenture in detail. Although specific provisions vary across different types of offerings, we discuss each of these provisions in the indenture.

Basic Provisions of an Indenture

Sinking Fund Bonds that are publicly traded are usually repaid through a **sinking fund.** The sinking-fund provision usually requires the company to retire regularly a specified amount of outstanding bonds.[2] It may either buy back

---

[2] There are sinking funds that tie bond redemptions to profits, but these are atypical.

bonds in the marketplace or retire them by serial number, determined by a lottery, as set forth in the indenture. In any case, the effect is to require the company to make regular cash payments on its debt, not unlike regular payments on a term loan.

The term *sinking fund* originally referred to an actual money fund that was set aside, invested, and then used to retire bonds at maturity. But problems with this practice—where the fund was found to be insufficient to retire all the bonds—led to the current practice of retiring bonds before maturity. The prior funding method is now rarely used.

Note that although a bond's maturity date may be 20 years from the date of issue, very few of the bonds may actually be outstanding on that maturity date. This in fact characterizes the outcome of most bond issues. For example, in May 1985, the Jamesway Corporation made an offering of $25 million in 8% convertible subordinated debentures, due in 2005. The sinking fund of these 20-year debentures is to begin in May 1995, 10 years after the issue date. The company is required to redeem $2 million of its bonds annually; thus, the sinking fund is designed to retire 80% of the debentures before maturity. Thus, at maturity in May 2005, Jamesway will have no more than 20%, or $5 million, of the debentures outstanding.[3]

Call Provisions   When a company redeems bonds before maturity, it is said to *call* them. The company may call any or all of the bond issue as long as the indenture allows it under the sinking-fund provision or call provision, which usually specifies the call price at a particular time. In the Jamesway offering just discussed, Jamesway has the option to call, in part or as a whole, the offering according to the schedule shown in Figure 5•2. Note the pattern: The call price includes a call premium, an amount related to the coupon interest rate added to the par value.

When a company replaces an entire old issue with a new one, it is said to engage in a **refunding operation.** A refunding operation is attractive when interest rates have fallen since the date of the first issue. To carry out a refunding operation, the company must first be permitted to do so by the call provision, and then the company must consider the flotation costs and call premium involved, to determine whether refunding would be justified.

Call provisions give the issuer more flexibility but restrict a bondholder's potential earnings from the issue since, as noted previously, the issuer is likely to carry out a refunding operation when it is paying a higher rate than that found in the current market. As a result, investors never pay more than the call price for an issue, since they know that companies will call their bonds if they become

---

[3] Note that the $5 million represents the maximum principal amount of bonds left outstanding. It is not necessarily the actual amount expected to be outstanding. The sinking fund is a mandatory means of reducing the outstanding bonds, but there are other ways for the issue to be retired that are optional for both bondholders and the company. Bonds in this Jamesway issue may be converted by holders into stock at any time, thus reducing the outstanding bonds, or the company may simply call the entire issue. These alternatives are discussed elsewhere in this chapter.

20–YEAR CONVERTIBLE SUBORDINATED 8% DEBENTURE,
ISSUED MAY 15, 1985

Callable—As a whole or in part at any time, at the option of
company on at least 30 but not more than 60 days' notice to
each May 15 as follows:

1986	108.0	1991	104.0
1987	107.2	1992	103.2
1988	106.4	1993	102.4
1989	105.6	1994	101.6
1990	104.8	1995	100.8

and thereafter at 100 plus accrued interest. Not callable,
prior to Nov. 15, 1986, unless the closing price of company's
common stock on the New York Stock Exchange has been in
excess of 150% of the conversion price then in effect for at
least 20 trading days within the period of 30 consecutive
trading days ending no more than 5 days prior to the date of
the notice of redemption. Also callable for sinking fund at 100.

(*Moody's Industrial News Reports*, June 7, 1985, p. 3898.)

FIGURE 5•2 Jamesway Corporation's call provisions on a debenture issue.
(**Source:** *Moody's Industrial News Reports*, June 7, 1985, p. 3898.)

worth more than the call price. Thus, the callable bond has a ceiling on its price, whereas the noncallable bond does not.

When a call is prohibited for a certain initial period, say 10 years, the issue is said to carry a *deferred* **call provision.** Issues may also be *freely callable* or *noncallable*, terms that are self-explanatory. In practice, many 25- to 30-year industrial bonds are nonrefundable for 10 years. Medium-term bonds, maturing in 7 to 10 years, generally restrict the call option to the last 2 years, if one is permitted at all.

Restrictive Covenants The indenture also specifies **restrictive covenants,** which are conditions under which the company must operate to ensure that the bondholders' interests are protected. If these covenants are broken, the issue could become due immediately. Restrictive provisions include production investment, financing, and dividend covenants.

Generally, production and investment covenants can prohibit certain actions by the company, such as limiting its stake in other enterprises. They can also require certain actions, such as investing in particular projects, holding specified assets, and requiring maintenance of the firm's properties and of its working capital above a certain minimum level. Although enforcement may not be easy for some of the covenants, their violation is usually regarded as a signal that the company has problems. The violation of, say, the working capital requirement warns bondholders, lenders, and equity holders to investigate a probable cash flow problem.

Financing and dividend covenants are aimed at restricting the company from engaging in activities that can hurt the safety of the bondholders' position or benefit stockholders at the expense of the bondholders. For example, a covenant could preclude a firm from borrowing a large amount of additional funds that might effectively increase the risk of newly issued bonds.

Example 5•1:   A Financing Covenant

A typical financing covenant requires the net tangible assets of an industrial company to be at least 2.5 times the long-term debt before additional debt can be incurred. The dividend restrictions accompanying Federal Paper Board Company's June 1985 offering of 13% subordinated debentures specified that the company could not make any dividend distributions under two conditions. No dividends on common stock were allowed if "(1) at the time of such action, an event of default under the indenture has occurred and is continuing; or (2) immediately after giving effect to such action, the consolidated tangible common equity of the Company and its subsidiaries would be less than $150,000,000."[4]

Companies that break their covenants are considered to be in technical default, and the entire debt becomes due immediately. As with defaults on payments, though, lenders and trustees typically work closely with companies, allowing grace periods or renegotiation of debt agreements. The creditor may, for instance, grant waivers of the broken covenants, meaning that the violation is ignored for a time to give the company a chance to end the default. The highlight "What Happens When a Company Cannot Pay Its Debts" gives three examples of how creditors and firms have dealt with violations of restrictive covenants.

◼ HIGHLIGHT

WHAT HAPPENS WHEN A COMPANY CANNOT PAY ITS DEBTS?

Creditors have the right to call loans, attach the firm's assets, or take other actions if a company violates restrictive covenants or fails to make a payment. Typically, however, such drastic action can be avoided if it appears the company can work out of its problems.

A creditor may waive covenants, renegotiate loans, or "stand by" while the debtor tries to remedy its problems. The remedies, which include massive cost-cutting measures, sale of parts of the business, changing management, or finding a merger partner, run the gamut. Three examples of how companies handled their respective predicaments are presented below.

[4]*Moody's Industrial News Reports*, August 6, 1985, p. 3657.

Mansfield Tire & Rubber Company

When this tiny, Mansfield, Ohio-based tiremaker defaulted—for the second time in less than two years—on certain of its restrictive covenants, management knew that desperate measures were in store.

To its credit, Mansfield had not missed a single payment on its debts. But the covenant violations pointed to severe cash flow problems. Mansfield violated covenants covering its current ratio (cash and accounts receivable/current liabilities), limitations on the amounts past due to trade creditors, and working capital requirements. Mansfield received waivers the first time it defaulted, but this time, none were forthcoming. On October 1, 1979, Mansfield filed for bankruptcy under Chapter XI of the Bankruptcy Reform Act of 1978.

The company had been trying to turn around its Tupelo, Mississippi, tiremaking plant, having previously fired two sets of managers and set programs to improve production and revamp its marketing. Mansfield's remedy: get out of the tire-making business; sell the Tupelo plant, which accounted for 85% of its $77 million in 1978 sales, in hopes that sale proceeds would permit it to concentrate profitably on automotive instrument panels and other molded-wood products. Mansfield did succeed in its company restructuring plans.

Braniff, Inc.

Airline deregulation in 1978 was a boom for some airlines and a bust for others. For Braniff, then a full-service carrier based in Dallas, it was a bust.

The company filed under Chapter XI, which gives a company protection from creditors while it works out a plan of reorganization to pay its debts. Braniff *chose* to file under Chapter XI; although, in many instances, creditors can *force* a company to file for Chapter XI.

Braniff emerged from Chapter XI status in early 1984 and by late 1984 was showing the traveling public a new face: It cut back one-third of its 30-plane fleet and marketed itself as a low-cost, no-frills carrier. A year later, it reported its first profitable quarter since leaving Chapter XI status.

Wilson Freight Co.

Though on the ropes, in July 1980 this Cincinnati-based motor carrier was confident that it was mustering the financial strength to keep going.

Wilson Freight had been dealt some heavy blows. It had defaulted nine months before on $22.4 million owed to a Citibank-led group of banks. It had had $5.1 million in losses the last two fiscal years. And just when the company felt sure that it was to receive an influsion of cash from American Financial Corporation of Cincinnati, the financial-services company pulled out. Citibank, which had been standing by, was growing nervous.

But another effort to raise capital looked promising. Wilson appealed to its own employees to raise a minimum $9.5 million as the key to a survival plan that began with the restructuring of its loan agreements. By mid-July, Wilson employees had pledged to buy $10.7 million of Wilson common shares to recapitalize the company—and save their jobs. "We're buying time," one employee said.

In the end, though, time had already run out. Citibank lost faith. It would not restructure its loan agreements, despite the anticipated success of the offering. Wilson was forced to file under Chapter XI.

A deepening recession, Citibank believed, was too much for the company to withstand. "We hoped the scheme would work," a Citibank official said. "We had seen all sorts of improvements in its operations and it was probably on the road to recovery. But it was the economy that knocked off Wilson Freight."

Citibank also feared that it could be held responsible if the company plan failed. The plan was intended to keep Wilson going for about 18 months, but Citibank feared that if the plan actually "got under way, and the company had to go out of business after six or eight months, not only would the directors and officers be liable, it's conceivable the banks would have been liable as well," the Citibank official said.

Source: Adapted from "Ailing Wilson Freight Woos Small Investors—Its Workers." July 3, 1980. "On the Ropes, Wilson Freight Came Back Slugging, but Recession Dealt Knock-down," July 24, 1980, Sept. 25, 1979, by Margaret Yao; reprinted by permission of *The Wall Street Journal,* © Dow Jones & Company, Inc. (1979, 1980); all rights reserved. The author thanks Margaret Yao for her assistance.

INTEREST RATES

Interest on term loans may be *fixed* or *floating*. While a fixed interest rate is constant throughout the life of the loan, a **floating rate** varies with market conditions. Floating rates are meant to protect creditors from changes in market rates due to inflation. They are often tied to the **prime lending rate,** which is considered to be the rate that banks charge their most creditworthy customers.[5] Interest may also be tied to rates for commercial paper, Treasury bills, or the London Inter-Bank Offered Rate (LIBOR).

Bond rates are simply the coupon interest rate, regardless of changes in market interest rates. Recall, however, that prices reflect swings in market interest rates and that swings in the market interest rate expose corporate issuers to interest-rate risk.[6]

DENOMINATION

When a bond offering is made overseas in foreign currency, it is called a **Eurobond** offering. Unsecured debt offerings in Europe are called *Eurodollars.* Similarly, other countries issue debt in U.S. dollars. Chapter 24 provides a more detailed discussion of these issues.

Table 5•2 summarizes the five basic characteristics of long-term debt financing, giving the conventions that are typically used in each category.

---

[5] Although the prime lending rate is defined as the rate charged to the most creditworthy customers, some large, healthy companies pay a percentage point or two less than the prime rate. By contrast, small businesses are usually charged at least 1.5 to 2% above prime.

[6] Corporate managers have found that one way to protect corporate issues from exposure to that risk is through careful hedging in the financial futures market. We will not examine hedging in this textbook.

TABLE 5·2   Summary of Conventions in Term Loans and Bonds

	Term Loans	Bonds
Maturity	3–7 years	7–30 years *Medium-term bonds:* 7–10 years *Long-term bonds:* 10–30 years
Security	Unsecured or secured by equipment	*Most bonds:* secured by plant, equipment *Mortgage bonds:* mortgages *Debentures:* unsecured
Repayment provisions	Varies, ranging from equal monthly payments to those custom-designed for the company's needs	Usually semiannual interest payments; principal repaid based on sinking-fund, call, and refunding provisions
Interest rate	Usually floating, tied to the prime rate or another accepted rate; sometimes fixed	Fixed
Denomination	U.S. dollars usually	U.S. dollars usually; Eurobonds are next most common denomination

Learning Check for Section 5·1

Review Questions

5·1.   Why does a corporation issue debt?

5·2.   What is security for a bond?

5·3.   What is the purpose of a sinking fund?

5·4.   Why would a firm want a call provision for its bonds?

5·5.   What are the five characteristics of long-term debt?

5·6.   Why do bond issues often carry sinking-fund requirements, call provisions, and restrictive covenants?

5·7.   What are the advantages and disadvantages of callable bonds to the issuing company? To the bondholder?

New Terms

Call provision	Maturity	Seasoned issue
Coupon amount	Mortgage bond	Security
Coupon rate	Par value	Sinking fund

Debenture	Investment banker	Term loans
Eurobond	Prime lending rate	Underwriter·
Floating interest rate	Refunding operation	Unseasoned issue
Indenture	Restrictive covenant	

SECTION 5·2 *Debt Offerings*

Most of this chapter so far has focused on the different types of publicly traded, long-term bonds because these offerings comprise the majority of corporate debt. Publicly offered bonds are so voluminous that they have helped establish not only the investment-banking industry (discussed in Appendix 4·A) but also a ratings system for easier evaluation. The ratings procedures are discussed later in this section, but first, privately placed debt will be examined. Although small relative to public debt, this form of debt is important to small companies and is increasing in use by large companies.

PRIVATE PLACEMENTS

Term loans are privately arranged, but longer-term debt may be negotiated with a small group as well. Traditionally, **private placements** have been attractive to small and medium-sized companies that need to raise less than $5 million in capital. However, in recent years, larger companies' placements rising to the $100 million level have gained in popularity. Private placements account for roughly one-fourth of all long-term corporate debt securities.

The debt may be placed with two or three institutional investors or as many as two dozen. For example, in June 1985, ICN Pharmaceuticals, Inc., signed an underwriting agreement with 22 Swiss banks, covering the placement of the equivalent of $19.2 million in Swiss currency of 5 $\frac{3}{4}$% convertible bonds due in 1995.

Companies find private placements desirable because they are far less costly than **public placements.** They need not be registered with the SEC, and companies avoid large underwriting fees and other flotation costs. Companies generally pay only a finder's fee to the investment bank that helped arrange the private placement, if there was one. Speed and confidentiality are other important advantages of private placements.

Private placements typically are custom-made for a firm's needs, whereas offerings need to be more uniform to sell publicly. The investors are more willing to allow nonstandard terms, since they perform intensive due diligence, a legal term describing their investigation of all aspects of the firm's business, finances, management, projections, and so on, and thus are more familiar and more comfortable with the company.

Such special treatment, however, is not free. The savings over public placements are partially or wholly offset by increased interest costs due to the illiquidity of the private placement, the costs of research into the company, and the inherent risks of the debt.

PUBLIC PLACEMENTS AND RATINGS

We examined the procedures for bringing debt and equity issues to the public market in detail in Appendix 4•A. What is peculiar to bonds and not stocks, however, is the system of rating the bond issues. Investors rely on this system—which is intended to measure creditworthiness—so heavily that a ratings reduction generally results in a lower bond price, at least temporarily. In fact, the market often anticipates rating changes and depresses the value of the bond in question. The details of the bond rating system are contained in Appendix 5•C.

Learning Check for Section 5•2

Review Questions

5•8.   What are the differences between a public placement and a private placement?

5•9.   What are the advantages of a private debt placement?

New Terms

Private placement   Public placement

SECTION 5•3 *Bond Valuation*

Because the cash flows of a bond are a contractual payment of a fixed amount of interest over a certain number of years plus the face value at redemption, the fundamental valuation equation (4-1) can be easily applied to find a bond's current market value.

$$D_0 = \underbrace{I(PVFA_{k_d,n})}_{\substack{\text{Present value of an} \\ \text{annuity stream of} \\ \text{cash flows}}} + \underbrace{M_n(PVF_{k_d,n})}_{\substack{\text{Present value of} \\ \text{a future lump-} \\ \text{sum payment}}} \qquad (5\text{-}1)$$

where D_0 = current market price of the bond

I = periodic coupon interest paid

k_d = required rate of return on the debt instrument (bond)

n = number of periods remaining before the bond is redeemed

Example 5•2   Bond Value with Annual Interest

Suppose that a 20-year, $1,000 par value bond has an annual coupon rate of 10% (i.e., $0.10 \times \$1,000 = \$100$ in interest is paid every year). If the investor's RRR on the debt, k_d, is 12%, what is the bond's current price or market value? From equation (5-1),

$$D_0 = \$100(PVFA_{.12,20}) + \$1,000(PVF_{.12,20})$$
$$= \$100(7.4694) + \$1,000(0.1037)$$
$$= \$850.64$$

Note that the bond is selling for less than par value because the RRR on the bond (12%) is greater that the coupon rate the bond offers (10%). If investors want a 12% return and the company will pay a 10% rate, how can investors get their RRR? Clearly, by paying less than $1,000 for the bond. Bonds that sell at less than par value are said to sell at a *discount*.

It is instructive to examine what happens to this bond's value if the required rate of return is 8% instead of 12%. In this case, only k_d changes, so that

$$D_0 = \$100(PVFA_{.08,20}) + \$1,000(PVF_{.08,20})$$
$$= \$100(9.8181) + \$1,000(0.2145)$$
$$= \$1,196.31$$

That is, the bond's market value is greater than its par value. In this case, market interest rates are lower than when the bond was issued. Bonds that sell for more than par value are said to be selling at a *premium*.

PRICE–INTEREST RATE RELATIONSHIPS

The Relationship Between Bond Par Values and Market Values

A bond's coupon interest rate never changes. The Kodak offering (Figure 5•1) is set at $12\frac{1}{4}\%$, and it always pays $12\frac{1}{4}\%$ of the par value, regardless of changes in market interest rates. However, once issued, bonds trade in the market, and this price strongly reflects changes in the market.

An Intuitive Explanation of Premiums and Discounts

KEY CONCEPT: The fundamental principle in **bond price behavior** is that when market interest rates rise, bond prices fall. Conversely, when market interest rates fall, bond prices rise.

Intuitively, this makes sense. Suppose that the market rate jumped to 14%. Buyers are not going to pay the par value for Kodak's $12\frac{1}{4}\%$ bond when they can get a 14% return elsewhere—unless they can get the bond at a discount, which is a price less than the $1,000 par value. By paying less for the bond, the buyers are raising the effective rate of return to themselves, since the actual interest payment to them never changes.

Similarly, if market rates fell to 10%, sellers would not be willing to part with the bond unless they could obtain a premium price for it, a price more than the par value. Put differently, if buyers have a choice between paying $1,000 for this $12\frac{1}{4}\%$ bond and $1,000 for a 10% bond, they will naturally seek the $12\frac{1}{4}\%$ bond. They will then bid the price of the $12\frac{1}{4}\%$ bond up to the level at which they would be indifferent between the 10% bond and the $12\frac{1}{4}\%$ bond.

Table 5·3 summarizes the relationship among coupon rates, required rates of return, and the par value of bonds. For a more detailed discussion of yields and the term structure of interest rates, see Appendix 5·B.

What is the bond's (market) value? As just shown, it is simply the present value of the bond's future cash flows, the interest payments plus its principal repayment upon maturity. The appropriate discount rate at the time of purchase is the rate of return the investors are foregoing in order to lock in the bond's $12\frac{1}{4}\%$ rate, assuming equal levels of risk. This rate is the investors' opportunity cost of capital, the expected return from alternative investments that they are giving up to buy the bond.

TABLE 5·3   Relationship Between Required Rates of Return, Coupon Rates, and Bond Prices

If:[a]	Then:
k_d > coupon rate	Bond will sell at a discount
k_d = coupon rate	Bond will sell at par
k_d < coupon rate	Bond will sell at a premium

[a]$k_d = RRR$ on the bond.

SEMIANNUAL COUPON PAYMENTS

Up to this point, the examples for bond price calculations have assumed that interest is paid annually. Many bonds, however, pay interest on a semiannual basis. The procedure used to value bonds in this situation is similar to that described by the "Frequency of Compounding Periods" procedure covered in Chapter 2. The process involves three steps:

Step 1. Convert annual interest, I, to semiannual interest by dividing it by 2.

Step 2. Convert the remaining number of years to maturity, n, to the number of six-month periods to maturity by multiplying n by 2.

Step 3. Convert the required return from an annual rate, k_d, to a semiannual rate by dividing it by 2.

Substituting these changes into equation (5-1) yields

$$D_0 = (I/2)(PVFA_{k_d/2,2n}) + M_{2n}(PVFA_{k_d/2,2n}) \qquad (5\text{-}2)$$

Example 5·3 Bond Value with Semiannual Interest Payments

Take the earlier example of a 20-year, $1,000 par value bond with an annual coupon rate of 10% but a 12% required return. If this bond is now assumed to pay interest semiannually, application of equation (5-2) reveals that the current bond price should be

$$
\begin{aligned}
D_0 &= (\$100/2)(PVFA_{.12/2,2\times20}) + \$1,000(PVF_{2,2\times20}) \\
&= \$50(PVFA_{.06,40}) + \$1,000(PVF_{.06,40}) \\
&= \$50(15.0463) + \$1,000(0.0972) = \$849.52
\end{aligned}
$$

This price is slightly less than the $850.90 value found using annual compounding.

We have valued bonds using their total cash flows. However, it is sometimes possible to separate the interest cash flows from the bond's principal. This is discussed in the highlight "Stripping the Corpus."

■■■ *HIGHLIGHT*

STRIPPING THE CORPUS

While the discussion in the text suggests that bondholders can expect to get periodic coupon interest and the face value of a bond at maturity, this is not true of "coupon-stripped" bonds. **Coupon stripping** is becoming increasingly popular in the U.S. Treasury market, where investment houses are separating the coupon payments from the face value of the bond (the "corpus"). These separated financial claims can be traded separately by investors. Both the coupons and the corpus have separate market values. Recognize that the stripped coupons, in effect, represent a series of zero-coupon bonds.

Stripped coupons offer the individual investor or a corporation enormous flexibility in designing a series of investments to achieve specific investment goals. A proper choice of a stripped-coupon portfolio can provide known cash flows at future dates and can be invaluable to the financial manager. For example, the well-known corporate practice of "cash flow matching" (or hedging) calls for the matching of anticipated cash outflows (liabilities) with an investment in an asset. Stripped coupons can make an ideal choice for matching up known assets with known liabilities.

Learning Check for Section 5·3

Review Questions

5·10.   "The coupon rate on a bond only determines the interest payments on it. It does not determine the investor's true rate of return on the bond." True of false? Why?

5·11.   Review the logic for the inverse relationship between bond prices and interest rates.

5·12.   When would a bond be expected to sell for more than its par value?

5·13.   Is your answer to question 5·12 consistent with the inverse relationship between value and opportunity cost discussed in Chapter 3?

5·14.   Why do bond values approach their par values at maturity? Is this true for both premium and discount bonds?

New Term

Coupon stripping

SECTION 5·4   *Bond Values Over Time*

As bonds approach their maturity date, their value approaches their par value. Why does this happen? The answer lies in how bond values are calculated.

This process is best illustrated by looking at a 30-year, 8% bond due in 1990. Suppose that when this bond was issued in 1960, the market interest rate was 6%. Using equation (5-1), in 1960 an investor would have been willing to pay ($80 × 13.7648) + ($1,000 × 0.1741) = $1,275.28.

In 1970, 10 years later, with the same market rate of 6%, how much would the investor be willing to pay? Using the 20-year period remaining in the life of the bond, the amount is $1,229.39. Table 5·4 shows how the value approaches the par value as the years to maturity decrease. With just one year before the bond matures, the investor would be willing to pay only about $18 over the par value.

TABLE 5·4   Present Values on an 8% Bond, 6% Discount Rate, Approaching Maturity

Year (for 1960 Bond Issue)	Years Until Maturity	Present Values				
		Annuity	+	Principal	=	Total
1960	30	$1,101.18	+	$174.10	=	$1,275.28
1970	20	917.59	+	311.80	=	1,229.39
1980	10	588.81	+	558.40	=	1,147.21
1989	1	75.47	+	943.40	=	1,018.87
1990	0	0	+	1,000	=	1,000

Figure 5·3 depicts this principle graphically, not only for a **premium bond,** which was used in the Table 5·3 example, but also for a par value bond, where interest rates are assumed constant at 8%, and for a **discount bond,** where interest rates are assumed constant at 10%. Clearly, if rates are assumed to change, the bond values will fluctuate as well.

That fluctuation is much greater for long-term debt than for short-term debt. To understand why, reexamine Table 5·4. Think of the calculations given in the table as showing several bonds with different maturities rather than one bond at different stages in its life. Indeed, the table gives precisely the same calculations as if these were examples of a 30-year bond, a 20-year bond, a 10-year bond, and a 1-year bond.

Now suppose that interest rates changed from 8%, which is the coupon interest rate and for which investors would be willing to pay $1,000 for the bond, to 6%, the rate assumed in the calculations. It should be clear that the long-term bonds were much more responsive to the interest-rate change than was the short-term debt. For example, the 20-year bond's price moved $229 from the $1,000 level, whereas the 1-year debt, which would be called a *note,* moved only about $19.

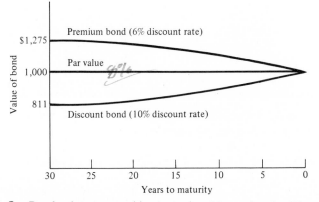

FIGURE 5·3   Bond values approaching maturity: 30-year bonds, 8% coupon interest rate, $1,000 par value.

For investors who intend to hold a bond until maturity, these fluctuations in interest rates are irrelevant as long as they choose to ignore opportunity costs. In other words, no matter what happens, they will still receive the interest payments and $1,000 upon maturity. They would be irrational, though, to ignore alternative investments if those could bring a higher return.

YIELD TO MATURITY (YTM) FOR A BOND

The Meaning of Yield to Maturity

In calculating the bond price as in Section 5•3, the investor's required rate of return (k_d) was taken as a given. In Example 5•2, at a discount rate of 8%, the bond's price was calculated as $1,196.31. If the market price of the bond were only $1,150, then for this investor the bond will be a good buy. Whether an investor finds an asset a good buy or a bad buy depends both on the cash flows provided by the asset and on the investor's required rate of return. Suppose, however, that the investor *knows* the price of a bond and its characteristics, he can then infer a rate of return called the yield to maturity.

The *yield to maturity* (*YTM*) is the expected rate of return on the bond *given* (1) its market price, (2) that the bond is held to maturity, and (3) that the interest payments on the bond are reinvested at the same rate (the *YTM*). This is another name for the bond's internal rate of return (*IRR*): the discount rate that equates the bond's market value with the present value of the future interest payments and repayment of principal. In general, *YTM* is different from the coupon rate on the bond. *YTM* equals the coupon interest rate if and only if the bond is purchased at its par value.

KEY CONCEPT: The yield to maturity (*YTM*) of a bond is that discount rate that equates the present value of the bond's cash flows to the market price. It is no different from the bond's internal rate of return (*IRR*).

Determining *YTM*

There are three methods by which the *YTM* for a bond can be obtained.

Method 1: Using a calculator. Most financial calculators are programmed to calculate the *IRR* for a project. Because *YTM* is no different from the *IRR*, the same function will provide the bond's *YTM*. This procedure is not only accurate, but less painful than the two methods discussed below.

Method 2: Using the approximation formula. This method provides a rough measure of YTM with a single computation.

$$YTM = \frac{I + (V - P)/T}{(V+P)/2} \qquad (5\text{-}3)$$

where I = annual coupon interest payment

V = par value

P = price of the bond

T = number of time periods involved

Example 5•4 YTM (Approximation Formula)

An investor wishes to find the YTM on a 12-year, 12% bond selling for 121.48% of its par value. Use the approximation formula.

$$YTM = \frac{\$120 + (\$1,000 - \$1,214.80)/12}{(\$1,000 + \$1,214.80)/2}$$
$$= 0.0921 \text{ or about } 9\%$$

Method 3: Using the trial-and-error procedure. Because YTM is no different from the IRR, the IRR trial-and-error method introduced in Chapter 2 can be used to calculate YTM.

Example 5•5   YTM (Trial and Error)

To illustrate, assume that a 10-year, $1,000 par value bond has an annual coupon rate of 8%. If this bond's current price is $935.80, what is the yield to maturity? From the valuation model, the bond price must satisfy

$$\$935.80 = \$80(PVFA_{x,10}) + \$1,000(PVF_{x,10})$$

where x is the (unknown) YTM.

Since the bond price is below the face value of the bond, the YTM must be more than the coupon rate. (See Table 5•3 to verify this statement.) Let us start the trial-and-error procedure by assuming that the YTM is 10%. Inserting 10% in place of x in the above equation, we obtain a bond value of $877.07. Since this is lower than the actual price of the bond ($935.80) we must lower our estimate of the YTM. Trying $x = 8\%$, we obtain a value of $1000.01 which is higher than the actual price of the bond. Thus, the correct YTM must lie between 8% and 10%. By improving our estimate of x, we can obtain a bond value which approximately equals the actual price of the bond. In this example, setting $x = 9\%$ gives us a bond price of approximately \$935.80. Hence, the *YTM* of the bond is 9%.

USING YTM

YTM must be interpreted carefully. It is the expected return for an investor over the life of the bond assuming that the coupon interest received is reinvested at the *YTM*. Examine Example 5•5 where the *IRR* was determined to be 9%. This calculation implicitly assumed that the \$80 coupon interest received by the investor will, in fact, be reinvested at 9%. This assumption may not be accurate if interest rates change over the life of the bond. Even though the \$80 interest payments are fixed, they may be reinvested at a higher or lower rate than 9%. In this case, the actual return to the investor from holding the bond may be higher or lower than the *YTM* of 9%.

It should be clearly understood that the *YTM* does not determine bond prices; rather, *YTM* can be determined only after the market value of the bond is known. The *RRR* of the bond determines its market value, which in turn *implies* a *YTM*.

Learning Check for Section 5•4

Review Questions

5•15.   How can an approximate *YTM* be calculated?

5•16.   What are the weaknesses of *YTM*?

5•17.   Which is likely to change over time: a bond's coupon rate or its *YTM*?

New Terms

Discount bond   Premium bond   Yield to maturity

SECTION 5•5   *Preferred Stock*

GENERAL CHARACTERISTICS OF PREFERRED STOCK

Preferred stock is often considered a hybrid of two securities: bonds and common stock. In terms of riskiness, preferred stock is always subordinate to bondholder claims but is superior to the claims of common stockholders. Thus, if a firm is faring poorly, it will first pay its bondholders their required interest and will then pay dividends to its preferred stockholders. Anything left over will go to the common stockholders. Unlike interest to bondholders, however, payments to preferred stockholders may be omitted. Although such an action hurts the company in the credit markets, it does not carry the dire consequences of default on bond payments.

Preferred stock is sold at par values of $25 or $100, with a given dividend rate. Preferreds have a fixed amount of dividend, which is usually expressed as a percentage of the par value (its dividend yield). This preferred dividend yield is set when the stock is issued and is paid on a certain date. For example, the 1982 issue of Crown Zellerbach Corporation's $3.05 cumulative preferred stock was issued at $20 a share, thus yielding a 15.25% annual rate. As with bonds, the $3.05 dividend is fixed, with the preferred's price on the market fluctuating to reflect current interest rates.

The **cumulative provision** on preferred stock stipulates that the company must pay all the preferred dividends that it has skipped, called *arrearages*, before it pays common stock dividends. In any case, a company can never pay a common stock dividend without paying a preferred one first. However, the preferred stockholders earn no interest on the arrearages.

The regular dividends paid to holders provide preferred stock with its fixed-income financing status in the credit markets. Also, since the late 1970s, preferred stock has usually carried with it a sinking fund or some type of retirement requirement similar to that of bonds.

Another bondlike aspect of preferred stock is that its holders usually do not have voting privileges, except under certain circumstances. Any matters affecting the seniority of their claim usually require a two-thirds approval of preferred holders. Also, after a preferred payout is omitted, most covenants provide that preferred stockholders obtain a minority position on the board to protect their interests.

Roughly half of preferred issues in recent years have been convertible into common stock. Like convertible bonds, convertible preferred stocks are more attractive to investors than comparable securities without convertibility. But the price also reflects that added flexibility for the investor. Thus, individual ownership is much higher among convertible than among nonconvertible preferreds.

PREFERRED STOCK VALUATION

In contrast to common stocks, preferred stocks are much easier to value because their cash benefits are regular, fixed dividends. Moreover, because preferreds usually do not have a maturity date, their constant dividends can be treated as a perpetual annuity stream of cash flows. From equation (2-9), which gives the value of a perpetuity, the value of a share of preferred stock is

$$P_0 = \frac{Div}{k_p} \tag{5-4}$$

where *Div* is the constant dividend per period and k_p is the investor's required rate of return. Note that this is an example of a perpetuity, which we discussed in Chapter 3. Also note that the rate of return earned on the preferred stock, k_p, will usually not be the stated dividend yield when the preferred stock was originally issued. The main reason is that preferred stocks are fixed-income securities. As investors' opportunity costs change, k_p will also change.

Example 5•6 Determination of Preferred Stock Value

Greyhound Corporation's $4.75 cumulative preferred was issued with a $100 par value. This implied a stated dividend yield of $4.75/$100 = 4.75%. Yet, if investors now require a 9% return, this stock's value would be only

$$P_0 = \frac{\$4.75}{0.09} = \$52.78$$

Learning Check for Section 5•5

Review Questions

5•18. Explain why a preferred stock has hybrid characteristics.

5•19. Review the essential features of preferred stock. Why does a discussion of preferred stock appear in a chapter on debt?

5•20. Compare preferred stocks with bonds and common stock.

New Terms

Cumulative provision   Preferred stock

SUMMARY

Basic Characteristics of Debt

Long-term debt is the dominant form of financing of corporations today, largely because of its relatively low cost and the flexibility it provides. Bonds and other types of debt come in many forms. A comparison of the different debt instruments can be based on the five attributes of debt: maturity, security, repayment provisions, interest rates, and denomination.

Debt Offerings

Long-term debt may be arranged privately or sold publicly. If sold publicly, bonds are graded for their creditworthiness, which translates into relatively higher or lower interest costs. Ratings firms consider a variety of factors, both financial and nonfinancial, in their gradings (see Appendix 5•C).

Bond Valuation

The valuation of bonds is relatively easier than that of stocks because the cash flows from these assets are predictable. Whenever the *RRR* on a bond is greater than the coupon rate, the bond will sell at a discount, and when the coupon rate exceeds the *RFRR*, it will sell at a premium. Bond prices reflect changes in market interest rates as well as the riskiness of the bond issue, as measured by bond rating services. *YTM* is useful as a rough measure of a bond's returns, but it can be dangerous to rely on this measure alone.

Bond Values Over Time

A bond's price, its coupon rate, and the market rate of return are all related. If the market rate on debt is above the coupon rate, the bond will sell at a discount. If the market rate is below the coupon rate, the bond will sell at a premium. As the bond approaches its maturity date, its price approaches its face value. A bond's *YTM* is its *IRR*.

Preferred Stock

Finally, preferred stock is a hybridized version of bonds and common equity and is attractive mainly to corporate purchasers for tax reasons.

PROBLEMS

5•1. Sam Malone, vice-president of AMI, Inc., wishes to find the *YTM* on his company's 10-year, 10% bond selling for 106.38% of the par value of $1,000. Calculate the *YTM*, using
(a) a financial calculator.
(b) the trial-and-error method.
(c) the approximation formula.

5•2.   An investor wants to know the *YTM* on an 8-year, 7% bond selling for 88.95% of its par value before investing in it. What is the bond's *YTM*, using the approximation formula?

5•3.   A 20-year, 10% coupon-interest-rate bond has a $1,000 par value. The market rate of interest is 8%. Compute the market price of this bond if it has 5 years to maturity. Assume that interest is paid annually.

5•4.   Is a bond selling at a discount or a premium if the coupon interest rate is 14% and the market requires a return of 12%? How much are you willing to pay for this bond if it matures in 15 years?

5•5.   A bond with six years left to maturity has a coupon rate of 9% and a par value of $1,000. How much will you be willing to pay for the bond if you require an annual rate of return of 12%?

5•6.   The Milan Corporation just issued a 5-year and a 10-year bond, each with a coupon rate of 10%. Both bonds have a par value of $1,000, and both were issued at par (consequently, each has a promised *YTM* of 10%). What will each bond be worth if interest rates rise to 14%?

5•7.   A bond pays interest annually and sells for $835. It has six years left to maturity and a par value of $1,000. What is its coupon if its promised *YTM* is 12%?

5•8.   A share of preferred stock has an annual dividend of $5. If you require a 12% return, how much are you willing to pay for a share of this stock?

5•9.   You have the opportunity to purchase a share of preferred stock for $42.00. If the stock pays an annual dividend of $5.88, what rate of return will you earn on the stock?

APPENDIX 5·A *Debt Innovations*

Drastic changes in the economy, such as fluctuating interest rates and inflation in recent years, have spurred innovative thinking in the bond community. Variations on conventional bond financing abound and probably will continue to proliferate in response to changes in the economic environment. Some have yet to prove themselves to be more than fads; nonetheless, they are worth discussing.

The first type of bond was created by statute to encourage development and pollution control as beneficial to the public interest. Other bonds were created in the marketplace in response to the economic environment and specific market needs.

GOVERNMENT-RELATED BONDS

Federal law provides for special financing treatment of corporate investments deemed to be in the public interest. These are development bonds, sometimes called **industrial-development bonds,** and pollution-control bonds. Their big advantage is their tax-exempt status. Bondholders' net interest is not taxable, thus giving the company a financing mechanism that costs about one-third less than conventional bond financing.

Here is how they work: The company qualifies for the use of proceeds from the bonds if its planned investment meets federal criteria. An example of this would be the building of a plant in an economically depressed area or the installation of federally mandated pollution-control devices. The company guarantees the bonds and agrees to meet retirement provisions and other requirements. The bonds are then issued through state or local industrial-development or pollution-control agencies.

CONVERTIBLE BONDS

Convertible bonds permit bondholders to change (at their option) their debt to equity at certain prespecified prices. *Converts*, as they are called, carry maturity dates, requiring conversion before maturity, and, like conventional bonds, are subject to sinking-fund and call provisions. At the time of issue, their conversion price is set at a premium over the stock price, usually ranging from 15 to 30%. The $1,000 par value of a bond divided by this price gives the **conversion ratio,** or the number of shares the bond is worth. Suppose that the conversion price is $25. The conversion ratio is $1,000/$25 = 40, meaning that each bond may be converted into 40 shares.

The attractiveness of convertible bonds to buyers lies in the prospect of receiving income while waiting to convert to stock. Of course, the flexibility of choosing to keep the bond rather than converting it is a big advantage. However, the benefit of flexibility reduces the risk, and thus the return, to the buyer.

This lower cost of capital, in turn, is one of the prime benefits of converts for issuers. Savings in interest-rate costs over a conventional nonconvertible bond may range between 300 and 600 basis points, equivalent to 3 to 6%, a significant difference in large offerings. Converts also provide issuers with, in effect, an equity offering for the future, assuming that the bonds are converted, and the chance to sell equity at prices higher than the current level.

For example, in August 1981, the MCI Communications Corporation sold $100 million of B-rated, $10\frac{1}{4}$% convertible debentures in less than an hour, and its shares were selling at a premium a month later. MCI would have had to pay 18% if it had offered straight debentures. The debentures gave the holders the right to trade their bonds for common stock at an 18% premium over the MCI share price of $21.75 on the day of issue. Conversion of all the shares would mean an issue of 3.9 million additional common shares. (MCI common shares were selling at between $6 and $11.375 in 1985; correspondingly, its debentures were selling at a discount.)

Bonds with warrants operate in a similar fashion, giving the bondholder the option to buy common stock at a given price. The warrant is an inducement for investors to pay a lower interest rate on the bonds.

INCOME BONDS

Interest on **income bonds** is paid only out of the company's income. The change in the repayment characteristic, then, means a higher risk to the bondholder, which in turn results in a higher coupon rate. If the company has no income, the bondholder does not receive interest. However, when the company again becomes profitable, income bondholders must generally receive the accrued interest owed to them before the company can pay preferred or common stock dividends. The advantage to the issuer, of course, is protection from default if earnings fall.

ZERO-COUPON BONDS

Zero-coupon bonds pay no interest (i.e., have no coupon rate). They made their debut in the early 1980s in response to high interest rates and were sold primarily to pension funds and other tax-exempt organizations. Essentially, they were bonds sold at deep (very big) discounts that paid nothing until maturity. These are another example of a change in the repayment provision.

The advantage to the corporate issuer is that since this instrument pays no interest until maturity, the corporation need not worry about making regular payments. At the same time, the company can take a tax deduction each year of an amount equal to the amortization of the discount (the difference between the $1,000 principal and the price paid for the bond). The disadvantages are the noncallability of the issue and the large payment at maturity, which is not deductible.

The advantages to the buyer are the bond's noncallability and a guarantee of the yield on the bond. The holder need not be concerned about the reinvestment risk, since there are no coupons to be reinvested. However, the holder is exposed to price risk, because the price of the bond will fluctuate with interest rate changes.

However, two recent developments have affected the appeal of zeros. First, in 1983 the IRS required that corporate issuers amortize the discount using an annuity, not the straight-line, method, effectively negating the bonds' tax advantages to the issuer.[7]

Second, brokerage houses introduced zero-discount bonds that were default free, and pension funds found these more attractive. These variations were a new type of security backed by Treasury securities. Merrill Lynch's first version of these securities were called *Treasury investment growth receipts*, known as *TIGRs* (pronounced "tigers").

Here is how *TIGRs* work: A pension fund manager buys from Merrill Lynch a series of *TIGRs* maturing at different times, say in 1995, 1996, and 1997, to match his expected cash outflows in pension annuities. He buys them today at a deep discount and receives nothing until 1995, 1996, and 1997, when he receives the face amount of each *TIGR*. The net effect is no different from that of zero-coupon bonds.

The difference, however, is that the *TIGRs* are default free. To establish the program, Merrill Lynch bought $500 million of 30-year Treasury bonds and literally "stripped" off the coupons from the bonds.[8]

PUT BONDS

The volatility in interest rates prompted the invention of **put bonds**— conventional bonds that the holder may redeem at par value at a specified time before maturity. This added feature has proven attractive to investors. Put bond issues soared to more than $10 billion in 1984 from $346 million in 1978, when they were first offered.

The big advantage to the bondholder is that the investor can "put" the bond back to the issuer if interest rates go up. For example, suppose that interest rates have risen sharply since the bonds were issued. Without the put feature, the bond would sell for, say $800 as a result. With the put, the investor can, at that time, receive the $1,000 par value of the bond from the issuer instead of receiving just $800 from selling the bond in the market. As might be expected, this safety feature results in a lower yield to the investor; this is the issuer's advantage. Chrysler Financial Corporation's 10-year put bond offering in October 1984, with a put option exercisable in the fifth year, cost Chrysler a 0.7% annual return, or $48 per $1,000 bond compounded.

---

[7] The problem arose in the required treatment of the amortization of the discount by an annuity method instead of a straight-line method, resulting in less favorable early-years tax treatment and an after-tax cost equal to that of a conventional bond.

[8] Refer back to the highlight "Stripping the Corpus."

PROJECT FINANCING

Project financing is a form of lending that has arisen in recent years, usually for large, complicated mineral extractive or processing operations. Such projects include offshore oil exploration, refineries, and nuclear-power plants. Typically, a large bank, or banks, lend to an entity specifically created for the project that is a joint venture or other affiliate of a large company. Since the lending is project specific, so is the timing of repayment.

Security varies considerably. It may be tied to the sale of the assets (e.g., the flow of oil), or it may be a comfort letter—assurances from the parent company that are not legally binding. Usually surrounding the comfort letter, however, are contractual obligations between the purchasers of the project's product and the project operator and other contractual arrangements. In addition, the lenders have claims against the project operators' equity in the project.

One advantage of project financing is said to be the segregation of high-risk projects from the rest of a company's balance sheet, although the true nature of such segregation is debatable. The segregation of the projects occurs because the lending is backed up by the project and is project specific. Some proponents believe that investment in politically unstable countries is better off being project financed, since those governments have more to lose by, say, expropriating a foreign subsidiary tied to major banks than one financed solely by its parent company.

Learning Check for Appendix 5·A

Review Questions

5A·1. What are the general characteristics of government-related bonds?

5A·2. How is a convertible bond different from a standard bond?

5A·3. Why would an investor want to purchase a zero coupon bond?

New Terms

Conversion ratio	Industrial development	Put bonds
Convertible bonds	bonds	Zero coupon bonds
Income bonds	Project financing	

APPENDIX 5·B *Term Structure of Interest Rates*

The term structure of interest rates is a relationship between the *YTM* on a number of *different* bonds and their maturities. Theories developed to explain this relationship have been the subject of considerable debate among economists, financial theorists, and practitioners for years. One reason for the ongoing debate is that each theory has some appeal, but no single theory explains everything satisfactorily. Term structure is important to both the corporate manager as a borrower and the investor as a lender, for an understanding of term structure helps these decision makers choose between long- and short-term forms of debt.

Until recently, the relationship between yield and maturity has generally been upward sloping (i.e., the longer the maturity of the investment, the higher the yield). Figure 5B·1 illustrates this historical relationship. Figure 5B·2 shows what the yields were for debt of varying maturities on particular days in 1983 and 1975. The diagram shows that on these days, rates on long-term debt were higher than those for short-term debt, inverting the slope of the line.

Note that the rates of the **yield curve** are the rates paid for new issues of varying maturities and are not expected rates of the future. The curve shows the current rate earned on a bond with a given maturity. It does not mean that this is the rate expected for 1990.

These rates can and do change at any time. Figure 5B·3, shows the downward-sloping relationship between yield and maturity in early 1980. This was the first time in history that rates for short-term debt were higher than rates for long-term debt. Although it did not last long, the inversion created a furor in investment circles. The slope of the yield curve, then, simply reflects the relationship between long-term and short-term rates. Changes in that relationship alter the slope of the curve.

In addition to slope changes, it is important to understand the implications of shifts in the yield curve, either upward or downward. Suppose that normal conditions, meaning an upward-sloping relationship, existed, as in Figure 5B·1, and a bond investor expected overall interest rates to fall. The investor, then, expected a shift of the entire curve downward, as shown in Figure 5B·3. The

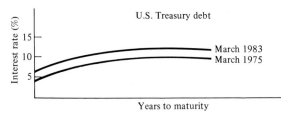

FIGURE 5B·1 Historical yield curve.

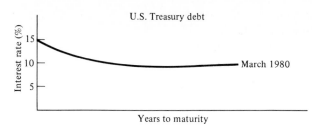

FIGURE 5B•2   Yield curve of early 1980.

investor would then want to invest long-term today to lock in the higher rate before the curve shifts downward, yielding a lower return.

Suppose that instead of an individual investor, a corporate borrower had the same expectation of lower interest rates. Assume that the same normal upward-sloping term structure existed. This borrower would take the opposite tack. Since it expects rates to fall, the company would rather wait, hoping to lock in the lower long-term rate that it is expecting rather than the higher long-term rate currently available. In the meantime, it would borrow short, raising enough funds for the short-term period while waiting for rates to fall.

Three theories explain the shape of the term structure and changes in the yield curve, and we will discuss each briefly.

THE EXPECTATIONS THEORY

The **expectations theory** postulates that current interest rates reflect expectations about future interest rates. Thus, under this theory, if interest rates are expected to rise, the yield curve should be upward sloping; if they are expected

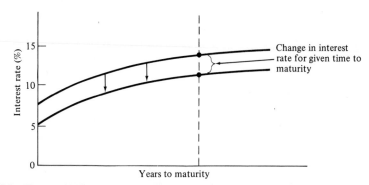

FIGURE 5B•3   Shift of the yield curve in response to lower expected interest rates.

to go down, it should be downward sloping; and if they are expected to remain flat, the curve will also be flat.

Expectations about future interest rates are dominated by expectations about inflation. Therefore, if inflation is expected to rise, interest rates will rise as well, and vice versa. The expected interest rate, according to proponents of this theory, can be obtained by adding the real, or inflation-free, rate to the expected rate of inflation. Forecasts of the expected level of inflation are published in the financial press.

THE LIQUIDITY PREFERENCE THEORY

As its name suggests, the liquidity theory postulates that investors prefer to make investment decisions for the short term, and therefore must be offered an inducement to invest for the longer term. The theory implies that long-term rates will be higher than short-term rates because of investors' preference for having the funds on hand, or being liquid.

Investors' preference for liquidity arises out of (among other things) reinvestment risk, which is the uncertainty about the rate of return that an investor can receive on funds from subsequent reinvesting. The **liquidity preference theory** asserts that investors prefer to lend short and borrowers prefer to borrow long. Therefore, the upward-sloping yield curve is the end result.

THE MARKET SEGMENTATION THEORY

The **market segmentation theory,** to which many practitioners on Wall Street subscribe, suggests that the marketplace for debt offerings is divided into three segments: short, intermediate, and long term. Each segment possesses its own unique demand and supply characteristics. For example, very generally, pension funds dominate the long-term market, corporations dominate the intermediate market, and individuals and nonprofit institutions' funds dominate the short-term market.

The theory thus suggests that each segment is a function of its own relatively unique characteristics and that rates among the three groups are less interactive than in the other two theories. However, there is little empirical support for this theory; the bulk of evidence points to the expectations and liquidity preference theories.

It should be recognized that the market segmentation theory is based on the self-imposed limitation of acting within a particular segment. If even one individual or institution is willing to go across segments, this theory loses its relevance. One could borrow at the lower-cost interest rate in one segment and lend at the higher interest rate in another segment, thereby earning excess returns. If this were possible, demand and supply considerations would affect bond prices, and consequently interest rates, until such opportunities for profit disappear.

Learning Check for Appendix 5·B

Review Questions

5B·1.   What is a yield curve? What does it show?

5B·2.   What are the different economic implications between an upward-sloping yield curve and a yield curve with an inverted slope?

5B·3.   What causes the yield curve to shift downward? To shift upward?

5B·4.   How does the liquidity preference theory differ from the market segmentation theory?

New Terms

Expectations theory	Liquidity preference theory	Market segmentation theory
		Yield curve

APPENDIX 5·C *Bond Rating Procedures*

In this appendix, we discuss the details of the bond rating system, including the firms that rate bonds and the rating criteria they use.

RATINGS FIRMS

Three major ratings firms in the United States—Standard & Poor's Corporation (or S&P), Moody's Investors Service, and Fitch Investor Services—*grade* bonds for their level of default risk. These debt ratings provide an easily recognizable yet simple measure that links a possibly unknown issuer of debt with a symbol of credit quality. Each debt rating becomes an indication of the creditworthiness of the firm with respect to a specific debt issue.

Ratings range from triple A to C or D, depending on the rating service.[9] Table 5C·1 shows Moody's definitions. For example, debts rated Aaa are judged to be of the "best quality" (i.e., to have the least degree of investment risk), while debts rated C are those with the lowest rating (i.e., "having extremely poor prospects of ever attaining any real investment standing").

The ratings, as measures of risk, are critical to the cost of debt. The lower the rating, the higher the cost. Dating back to the turn of the century, the ratings have become so well established that the bylaws of most pension funds prohibit investment in bonds below investment-grade level (i.e., below triple-B), thus restricting purchasers.

RATINGS CRITERIA

The procedure for assigning a debt rating begins with a formal request by a firm for such a service. After a request, the main ingredient that a rating agency uses to determine a firm's ability to make timely payments of principal and interest is a financial statement analysis, especially ratio analysis. Special emphasis is placed on ratios relating income and cash to debt service. Thus, coverage ratios are of considerable importance. For example, a company's issue will be rated AAA by Standard & Poor's (the equivalent of Moody's Aaa) if the after-tax coverage ratio is at least 5. It will get an AA rating if this multiple is 3 or 3.5, and so on. Rating agencies also examine such ratios as operating profit margins, return on capital, and return on total assets.

As for asset protection, the ratio most commonly used is long-term debt to

---

[9] In market jargon, D ratings stand for "desperate," and C- and D-rated offerings are known as *junk bonds* Junk-bond dealers argue, however, that the appellation is undeserved. In support of their argument, they quote a study by the Wharton School of the University of Pennsylvania for the period January 1980–June 1984 that showed that a diversified portfolio of low-grade bonds returned 13.5% annually, nearly twice the 7.2% return for AAA corporate bonds. Drexel Burnham Lambert, an investment house that has aggressively pushed low-grade bonds, brought out $14 billion of new issues of such bonds in 1984, up from about $900 million in 1977.

TABLE 5C•1 Moody's Bond Ratings[a]

Aaa. Bonds which are related Aaa are judged to be of the best quality. They carry the smallest degree of investment risk and are generally referred to as "gilt edge." Interest payments are protected by a large or by an exceptionally stable margin and principal is secure. While the various protective elements are likely to change, such changes as can be visualized are most unlikely to impair the fundamentally strong position of such issues.

Aa. Bonds which are rated Aa are judged to be of high quality by all standards. Together with the Aaa group they comprise what are generally known as high-grade bonds. They are rated lower than the best bonds because margins of protection may not be as large as in Aaa securities or fluctuation of protective elements may be of greater amplitude or there may be other elements present which make the long-term risks appear somewhat larger than in Aaa securities.

A. Bonds which are rated A possess many favorable investment attributes and are to be considered as upper medium grade obligations. Factors giving security to principal and interest are considered adequate but elements may be present which suggest a susceptibility to impairment sometime in the future.

Baa. Bonds which are rated Baa are considered as medium-grade obligations, i.e., they are neither highly protected nor poorly secured. Interest payments and principal security appear adequate for the present but certain protective elements may be lacking or may be characteristically unreliable over any great length of time. Such bonds lack outstanding investment characteristics and in fact have speculative characteristics as well.

Ba. Bonds which are rated Ba are judged to have speculative elements; their future cannot be considered as well assured. Often the protection of interest and principal payments may be very moderate and thereby not well safeguarded during both good and bad times over the future. Uncertainty of position characterizes bonds in this class.

B. Bonds which are rated B generally lack characteristics of the desirable investment. Assurance of interest and principal payments or of maintenance of other terms of the contract over any long period of time may be small.

Caa. Bonds which are rated Caa are of poor standing. Such issues may be in default or there may be present elements of danger with respect to principal or interest.

Ca. Bonds which are rated Ca represent obligations which are speculative in a high degree. Such issues are often in default or have other marked shortcomings.

C. Bonds which are rated C are the lowest-rated class of bonds and issues so rated can be regarded as having extremely poor prospects of ever attaining any real investment standing.

[a]Moody's applies numerical modifiers 1, 2, and 3 in each generic rating classification from Aa through B in its corporate bond rating system. Modifier 1 indicates that the security ranks in the higher end of its generic rating category; modifier 2 indicates a mid-range ranking; and modifier 3 indicates that the issue ranks in the lower end of its generic rating category.

Source: *Moody's Bond Record.*

assets. This figure helps assess how much book value in assets is available to pay off debt if the need arises. Another balance sheet measure of relative debt burden is the ratio of long-term debt to total capital.

Many other factors also come into play: industry risk, the issuer's market position in the industry, the issuer's operating efficiency, management, and accounting quality. Figure 5C•1 reproduces the ratings factors used by Standard & Poor's for industrial companies. The categories cover virtually every conceivable aspect of a business, although certain factors are much more important than others. For example, the ratings agency may pay special attention to energy costs in evaluating the "issuer's operating efficiency" if the company is an airline, but is less inclined to do so if the company makes shoes.

The ratings services say that they do not use any formulas, and statistical surveys bear out this contention. In any case, it would be difficult to quantify many of the qualitative judgments made. For instance, S&P lowered its ratings of Union Carbide Corporation's debt on January 8, 1985, following the December 3, 1984, gas-leak disaster at its Bhopal, India, plant, which killed more than 2,000 people. The downgradings, which included a reduction to BBB from A- of the company's subordinated long-term debt, was not because of liability but because of the accident's "potential negative spillover" to suppliers and customers, the diversion of management attention to defending itself against lawsuits, and the company's "constrained access to capital markets during a period of great uncertainty."[10]

DEBT INSURANCE AND BOND RATINGS

The importance of ratings in setting the cost of debt has prompted some companies to find new ways to keep debt costs down. One method is by purchasing what amounts to **debt insurance.** The firm purchases a surety bond from an insurance company for its entire debt issue. With such insurance, the investors now look to the rating of the insurance company rather than the issuing company. In one 1984 transaction, Samuel Montagu & Company and Morgan Guaranty, Ltd., sold a $100 million, seven-year Eurobond insured by the Aetna Casualty and Surety Company, where the issuer's identity was never revealed.

This anonymity is particularly attractive for private companies that wish to keep information private. In 1984 the secretive Rockefeller Group sold a $100 million Eurobond issue at nine points above Treasury rates, much less than conventional financing, and its balance sheet remained a private matter. The catch is that insurers are reluctant to insure the debt of companies whose ratings are less than investment grade. In addition, some insurers require collateral to back the surety bond.

---

[10] Union Carbide's response was that the downgrading was "an overreaction."

Rating

Profile Outlines

Industrial company rating methodology profile

I. Industry risk: Defined as the strength of the industry within the economy and relative to economic trends. This also includes the ease or difficulty of entering this industry, the importance of any diversity of the earnings base and the role of regulation and legislation.
- A. Importance in the economic cycle.
- B. Business cyclicality; earnings volatility, lead-lag and duration, diversity of earnings base, predictability and stability of revenues and earnings.
- C. Economic forces impacts; high inflation, energy costs and availability, international competitive position, social-political forces.
- D. Demand factors; real growth projections relative to GNP and basis for projections, maturity of markets.
- E. Basic financial characteristics of the business: fixed or working capital intensive; importance of credit as a sales tool.
- F. Supply factors: raw materials, labor, over/under utilized plant capacity.
- G. Federal, state, foreign regulation.
- H. Potential legislation.
- I. Fragmented or concentrated business.
- J. Barriers to entry/ease of entry.

II. Issuer's industry position—market position: The company's sales position in its major fields and its historical protection of its position and projected ability for the future.
- A. Ability to generate sales.
- B. Dominant and stable market shares.
- C. Marketing/distributing requirements of business—strengths, weaknesses, national, international, regional.
- D. R&D—degree of importance—degree of obsolescence—short or long product life.
- E. Support/service organization.
- F. Dependence on major customers/diversity of major customers.
- G. Long-term sales contracts/visibility of revenues/backlogs/prepayments (*e.g.*, subscriptions).
- H. Product diversity.

III. Issuer's industry position—operating efficiency: This covers the issuer's historical operating margins and assesses its ability to maintain or improve them based upon pricing or cost advantages.
- A. Ability to maintain or improve margins.
- B. Pricing leadership.
- C. Integration of manufacturing operations.
- D. Plant and equipment: modern and efficient or old and obsolete. Low or high cost producer.
- E. Supply of raw material.
- F. Level of capital and employee productivity.
- G. Labor; availability, cost, union relations.
- H. Pollution control requirements and impact on operating costs.
- I. Energy costs.

IV. Management evaluation:
- A. The record of achievement in operations and financial results.
- B. Planning—extent, integration and relationship to accomplishments. Both strategic and financial, Plan for growth—both internal and external.
- C. Controls—management, financial and internal auditing.
- D. Financing policies and practices.
- E. Commitment, consistency and credibility.
- F. Overall quality of management; line of succession—strength of middle management.
- G. Merger and acquisition considerations.
- H. Performance vs. peers.

V. Accounting quality: Overall accounting evaluation of the methods employed and the extent to which they overstate or understate financial performance and position.
- A. Auditor's qualifications.
- B. LIFO vs. FIFO inventory method.
- C. Goodwill and intangible assets.
- D. Recording of revenues.
- E. Depreciation policies.
- F. Nonconsolidated subsidiaries.
- G. Method of accounting and funding for pension liabilities. Basic posture of the pension plan assumptions.
- H. Undervalued assets such as LIFO reserve.

(continued on p. 171)

FIGURE 5C•1 Standard & Poor's rating criteria. (*Standard & Poor's Credit Overview*, pp. 90, 91. Reprinted with permission.)

VI. **Earnings protection:** Key measurements indicating the basic long-term earnings power of the company including:
   A. Returns on capital.
   B. Pretax coverage ratios.
   C. Profit margins.
   D. Earnings on asset/business segments.
   E. Sources of future earnings growth.
   F. Pension service coverage.
   G. Ability to finance growth internally.
   H. Inflation-adjusted earning capacity.

VII. **Financial leverage and asset protection:** Relative usage of debt, with due allowance for differences in debt usage appropriate to different types of businesses.
   A. Long-term debt and total debt to capital.
   B. Total liabilities to net tangible stockholders' equity.
   C. Preferred stock/capitalization.
   D. Leverage implicit in off-balance sheet financing arrangments, production payments, operating rentals of property, plant and equipment, nonconsolidated subsidiaries, unfunded pension liabilities, etc.
   E. Nature of assets.
   F. Working capital management—accounts receivable, inventory, and accounts payable turnover.
   G. Level, nature and value of intangible assets.
   H. Off-balance sheet assets such as undervalued natural resources or LIFO reserve.

VIII. **Cash flow adequacy:** Relationship of cash flow to leverage and ability to internally meet all business cash needs.
   A. Evaluation of size and scope of total capital requirements and capital spending flexibility.
   B. Evaluation of variability of future cash flow.
   C. Cash flow to fixed and working capital requirements.
   D. Cash flow to debt.
   E. Free cash flow to short-term debt and total debt.

IX. **Financial flexibility:** Evaluation of the company's financing needs, plans, and alternatives and its flexibility to accomplish its financing program under stress without damaging creditworthiness.
   A. Relative financing needs.
   B. Projected financing plan.
   C. Financing alternatives under stress—ability to attract capital.
   D. Capital spending flexibility.
   E. Asset redeployment potentials—nature of assets and undervalued liabilities.
   F. Nature and level of off-balance sheet assets or liabilities. This would include unfunded vested pension benefits and LIFO reserves.
   G. High level of short-term debt/high level of floating rate debt.
   H. Heavy or unwieldy debt service schedule (bullet maturities in future)—either of debt or sinking fund preferred stock.
   I. Heavy percentage of preferred stock as a percentage of total capital.
   J. Overall assessment of near-term sources of funds as compared to requirements for funds/internal financial self-sufficiency/need for external financing.
   K. Ownership/affiliation.

Learning Check for Appendix 5•C

Review Questions

5C•1.   What is the purpose of bond ratings?

5C•2.   What information do rating firms use in determining a corporation's bond rating?

5C•3.   How could debt insurance affect a firm's bond rating?

New Term

Debt insurance

READINGS

BARNEA A., R. HAUGEN, AND L. W. SENBET, "A Rationale for Debt Maturity Structure and Call Provisions in the Agency Theoretic Framework," *Journal of Finance*, December 1980, 1223–1234.

BIERMAN, H., JR., "The Bond Refunding Decision," *Financial Management*, Summer 1972, 27–29.

BOWLIN, O. D., "The Refunding Decision: Another Special Case in Capital Budgeting," *Journal of Finance*, March 1966, 55–69.

BROOKS, L. D., "Risk–Return Criteria and Optimal Inventory Stocks," *Engineering Economist*, Summer 1980, 275–299.

CAMPBELL, TIM S., "A Model of the Market for Lines of Credit," *Journal of Finance*, March 1978, 231–243.

DONALDSON, GORDON, "In Defense of Preferred Stock," *Harvard Business Review*, July–August 1962, 123–136.

PINCHES, GEORGE E., "Financing with Convertible Preferred Stock, 1960–1967," *Journal of Finance*, March 1970, 53–63.

WAKEMAN, L. MACDONALD, "The Real Function of Bond Rating Agencies," in *The Revolution in Corporate Finance*, Joel M. Stern and Donald H. Chew, Jr., (eds Basil Blackwell, 1986).

WEINSTEIN, MARK I., "The Seasoning Process of New Corporate Bond Issues," *Journal of Finance*, December 1978, 1343–1354.

APPENDIX 5•B

ROBINSON, RONALD I., AND DWAYNE WRIGHTSMAN, *Financial Markets: The Accumulation and Allocation of Wealth* (New York: McGraw-Hill Book Company, 1980).

VAN HORNE, JAMES C., *Financial Market Rates and Flows* (Englewood Cliffs, N.J.: Prentice-Hall, Inc., 1984).

PART III

The Analysis of Financial Statements

6

Financial Statement Analysis

The need to maintain financial records for an ongoing company cannot be overemphasized. Even though market-value considerations, as discussed in Chapter 3, should be the basis of financial decisions, many of these decisions cannot be followed through to completion if the financial manager disregards the books. Besides ensuring that the firm's cash flow position is not weakening, the manager has to rely on financial statements to assess the current condition and progress of the firm. In addition, outsiders—banks, other creditors, trade suppliers, tax authorities, customers, and other agencies—are all interested, for one reason or another, in different aspects of the firm's operations as reflected in the books of the company.

This chapter has two purposes: to explain book value and to familiarize the reader with financial statements and their interpretation. This chapter is divided into four sections.

SECTION 6•1: *Book Values in Finance.* In this section, we examine book values and discuss the book values of a physical asset and a financial asset. The role of book values in financial management concludes this section.

SECTION 6•2: *The Basic Financial Statements.* In this section, we analyze the basic financial statements of a company: the balance sheet, the income statement, and the statement of retained earnings. These statements are illustrated using the case of Byet Stores, Inc.

SECTION 6•3: *The Common-Size Statements.* Because the basic financial statements cannot provide certain useful detailed information, *derivative* financial statements are required. In this section, two derivative financial statements are developed: the common-size income statement and the common-size balance sheet.

SECTION 6•4: *The Cash Flow Statement.* After a discussion of the meaning and importance of cash flows in financial management, an additional derivative statement, the cash flow statement, is developed in this section. This statement shows how managerial, operational, financial, and investment decisions affect the cash flows of the firm.

SECTION 6•1 *Book Values in Finance*

WHY BOOK VALUE IS NOT REALLY "VALUE"

It is useful to examine what book value really is. As its name suggests, book value represents the value of an asset as recorded on the financial statements (books) of a company. Thus book values are the results of accounting procedures and reflect how the accountant is keeping track of a particular asset. Book values exist for all the assets and liabilities that a firm owns—plant and equipment, equity, bonds, short-term obligations, and so on.

We will review the concept of the book value of both a physical asset (machine) and a financial asset (stock).

Book Value of a Physical Asset[1]

Assume that a company bought a lathe 10 years ago at a cost of $10,000. Also assume that the lathe is being depreciated over a 15-year life, with a salvage value of $1,000. Assuming straight-line depreciation, we may use the procedures of Appendix 6•B to determine that the annual depreciation for the lathe is $600 per year.

The book value in any year t, represented by BV_t, is simply the original purchase price less the **accumulated depreciation** (equation 6-1):

$$BV_t = \text{purchase price} - \text{accumulated depreciation} \qquad (6\text{-}1)$$

Notice from Table 6•1 that the book value, BV_t, decreases systematically through time. Clearly, if the depreciation method chosen were different, the BV

---

[1] The terms *physical assets* and *real assets* are often used interchangeably.

TABLE 6·1 Book Value of a Physical Asset

End of Year t	Depreciation	Accumulated Depreciation	Book Value, BV_t
1	$600	$ 600	$10,000 − $600 = $9,400
2	600	1,200	$10,000 − $1,200 = $8,800
3	600	1,800	$10,000 − $1,800 = $8,200
4	600	2,400	$10,000 − $2,400 = $7,600
15	600	9,000	$10,000 − $9,000 = $1,000

would be different for any t. Several things should be clear from our simple example. Book value depends on

1. The original cost of the asset.

2. The depreciation method employed.

3. The expected life of the asset (strictly, the depreciable life).

4. The estimated salvage value.

5. The depreciable life (t) that has lapsed.

A change in any one of these items may result in a different book value. Once the asset has been purchased, the depreciation method is a decision of the accounting staff/management.[2] The depreciable life and salvage value estimates are also management decisions (the IRS prescribes guidelines, however). Thus book value depends on a variety of managerial decisions and has significance primarily to the company that owns the asset. Of course, the IRS is also interested, as will soon be seen.

Book Value of a Financial Asset (Common Stock)

Consider book value again, but this time focus on the book value per share of a company's common stock. Examine the balance sheet of Briloff, Inc., in Table 6·2. By dividing the $88 million in stockholders' equity by the 5 million shares outstanding, the book value per share turns out to be $17.60. What exactly does this mean? Does it mean that the Briloff's stock should sell for $17.60? No. Should the stock be worth more than $17.60? Not necessarily. What is the relationship between the stock price (market value) and its book

---

[2] For a detailed discussion of depreciation methods, see Appendix 6·B. The discussion here assumes straight-line depreciation. The situation is significantly different with the accelerated cost recovery system (ACRS), which the IRS uses to reduce the latitude managers have in making depreciation decisions.

TABLE 6·2 Balance Sheet of Briloff, Inc., December 31, 1988 (Million Dollars)

Assets		Claims	
		Total debt	$ 80
		Stockholders' equity	
		Common stock (5 million shares, $1 par)	5
		Additional paid-in capital	10
		Retained earnings	73
		Total net worth (stockholders' equity)	$ 88
Total assets	$168	Total claims on assets	$168

$$\text{Book value/share} = \frac{\text{stockholders' equity}}{\text{number of shares}} = \frac{\$88,000,000}{\$5,000,000} = \$17.60$$

value? Not much. For example, when Gulf Oil was acquired by Socal, the market value of Gulf's stock was approximately 60% of its book value.

BOOK VALUES REFLECT THE PAST

As is clear from the two previous examples, finding book values is a mechanical process. Book values are historical costs and reflect the costs on the accountant's books. Book values do not satisfy our two requirements of value (cash flow stream from the asset and sacrifice) and thus do not really measure value as defined in Chapter 3. Market values reflect the future income stream that an asset will produce, while book values reflect the past. There are no opportunities in the past, only in the future. Thus book values are not really useful in decision making, only in telling you where you have been. They simply represent decisions made in the past.

Consider an example. A firm has a computer with a zero book value. Will the firm sell it to the public for zero dollars? In general, no. As long as the computer can function (or has a salvage value), it has a market price greater than its book value.

The discussion so far should have made it clear that the book value of an asset has little to do with what one will pay for the asset. Thus, for decision-making purposes, managers should use market values. Yet no principles course in finance is complete without an understanding of several book-related concepts and procedures. This textbook is no exception; several chapters that follow rely heavily on book-value finance.

THE ROLE OF BOOK VALUE IN FINANCIAL DECISION MAKING

The question that one can ask now is: If book values really reflect the past, how are they of use to anyone? In other words, of what use is accounting information to the financial executive?

According to the Accounting Principles Board (APB):

Financial accounting information is produced for certain purposes by the use of conventional principles. The information they contain describes the past, while decision making is oriented toward the future. A record of past events and a knowledge of past position and changes in position, however, help users evaluate prior decisions and the information is also a starting point for users in predicting the future. Decision makers should not assume, however, that the conditions that produced past results will necessarily continue in the future.

Financial Accounting Standards, APB Statement Number 4, October 1970

Monitoring and Control

One reason why the financial manager has to be familiar with book value is that the operations of all firms, large or small, require careful monitoring and control. Managers can get a good idea of where the resources of the firm are coming from, where they are being used, where pockets of inefficiency exist, and so on, by looking at the book values of various accounts. This information enables the company to change some of its policies. In many instances, it may not be possible to estimate the market value of these items easily. These review and control procedures are especially important for working capital management.[3]

Working Capital Control

Although working capital management decisions should also be made while keeping in mind the ultimate wealth-maximizing objective of the firm, such considerations are sometimes very difficult to recognize. It may be virtually impossible for the manager to assess the market values of several working capital accounts. For this reason, most managers often seek to increase shareholder wealth through investments in long-term assets; working capital serves as "grease" that supports the working of these long-term plans. Managers often claim that their working capital policies are therefore not influenced so much by market values as they are by book values. Financial statements provide a wealth of information in this regard.

---

[3] *Working capital* refers to current assets and liabilities. Working capital management is covered in detail in Chapters 18 through 21.

Impact of Taxes on Cash Flows

Another very important consideration in financial decision making is the impact of taxes on cash flows. Again, a project that is attractive before tax considerations can be unattractive after the impact of taxes has been factored in.

In discussing book values and market values, it was stressed that, in general, there is no direct correspondence between these two concepts. However, the relationship between book and market values is of great interest to the IRS. This is because of the IRS's definition of gains and losses. Whenever a firm reports a gain, it has to pay a tax on that gain, and if there is a loss, it can be used to offset other income. In determining whether a firm has a gain (profit) on an investment (physical or financial assets), a firm must compare the market value of the asset to its book value. Whenever the market value of an asset is greater than its book value, the firm has a profit. When the book value of an asset is greater than its market value, the firm has a loss.

Go back to the company in Table 6•1, and look at the lathe it owns. Assume that the company is in the 25% tax bracket and that it decides to sell the lathe at the end of the third year for $9,000 (market value). Since the book value is $8,200, a profit of $800 is realized, and the IRS takes 25% of this profit ($200). Thus, when the lathe is sold, the firm really gets only $8,800. However, if the market value of the lathe had been $8,000, there would be a $200 loss. This loss would produce a tax-loss subsidy of $50 (25% of $200), and the company would, in effect, be getting $8,050.

Restrictive Covenants

A firm's activities are sometimes severely constrained by the suppliers of capital. To be specific, when a company raises debt capital, it often has to agree to satisfy certain performance conditions based on book values. For example, a company may agree not to raise any additional debt if the book value of the debt exceeds a certain fraction of the book value of its assets. The fact that such **restrictive covenants** exist forces the manager to monitor these book-value items carefully. In addition, the ability of a company to raise new debt capital is often influenced by a rating of the debt provided by certain rating agencies. These agencies rely heavily on the books of the company in assessing the rating of the debt, and the financial manager should be aware of this fact. Disregarding these realities can increase the cost of debt funds to the firm.

Regulated "Fair Rates of Return"

Regulated companies such as utilities are required to "make a case" for higher rates if they want to charge more for their products. Very often, a firm's rates are set to yield the firm a fair rate of return on the book value of its equity. While regulatory agencies are increasingly recognizing the opportunity cost concept and market value considerations in setting rates, an examination of most rate proceedings indicates that several aspects of book value still continue to play a crucial role in this process for a variety of reasons (state laws, precedent, etc.). Thus the managers of these companies have to tread a fine line between book values and market values. This is simply the reality of the situation.

Although market valuation provides the relevant framework for making value-maximizing decisions, in many instances it is not possible to ignore book values, either for working capital considerations or institutional reasons. In some instances, the information required may not be available. In cases where market-value rules are not readily implementable, the manager may be forced to emphasize book-value finance, that is, financial decisions based on book-value considerations. To do this, however, it is important to understand financial statements. This is the subject of the remainder of this chapter.

Learning Check for Section 6·1

Review Questions

6·1.   Why should book-value considerations be relevant to managers focusing on the market value of their company's stock?

6·2.   How does the depreciation method chosen by a firm affect the book value of an asset?

6·3.   What are the economic consequences of selling an asset for more than its book value? For less than its book value?

New Terms

Accumulated depreciation   Restrictive covenants

SECTION 6·2 *The Basic Financial Statements*

A firm's basic financial statements—the balance sheet and the income statement—are the most important sources of data on its actual performance or condition. This is because most activities are measured in dollars spent or received, and these two statements summarize the dollar flows through time, transaction by transaction. By reorganizing and restructuring the information in these reports in different ways, the manager can measure, for example, changes in the firm's liquidity position, profits earned during a time period, how assets were financed, and so on. Armed with this information, he or she can plan for uncertain future events by influencing current operating decisions and by making investment and financing decisions that can be supported by current book considerations.

THE BALANCE SHEET

A **balance sheet** is a summary of a firm's financial position at any point in time, although typically it is prepared for the last day of the year.

KEY CONCEPT: A **balance sheet** is a listing, at a specific point in time, of the book value of the assets of a firm and the claims on these assets.

Table 6•3 illustrates two recent balance sheets for Byet Stores, Inc., a chain of clothing stores, as of December 31, 1987, and December 31, 1988. First, the

TABLE 6•3 Byet Stores, Inc., Balance Sheets (Thousands of Dollars)

	December 31, 1988	December 31, 1987
Assets		
Current assets		
Cash	$ 40	$ 37
Marketable securities	3	3
Net accounts receivable	96	89
Inventories	111	92
Prepaid expenses	7	9
Total current assets	$257	$230
Long-term assets		
Gross plant and equipment	85	63
Less: Accumulated depreciation	(26)	(22)
Net plant and equipment	59	41
Total assets	$316	$271
Claims on assets		
Current liabilities		
Accounts payable	$ 77	$ 63
Notes payable—bank	31	46
Taxes payable	3	3
Other accruals	24	21
Total current liabilities	$135	$133
Long-term liabilities		
Bonds outstanding	49	33
Deferred taxes	12	10
Total long-term liabilities	$ 61	$ 43
Stockholders' equity		
Common stock		
(5 million shares, $5 par)	25	25
Additional paid-in capital	22	22
Retained earnings	73	48
Total shareholders' equity	$120	$ 95
Total claims	$316	$271

names of the assets and their respective dollar values are listed in descending order of liquidity, or "nearness to being cash."

As seen in Table 6•3, the assets are normally divided into two categories: current assets and noncurrent (long-term) assets. Current assets are those resources that will be converted into cash within one year or within the normal operating cycle of the firm.[4] Noncurrent or fixed assets represent longer-term commitments of funds (greater than one year).

The second major section of the balance sheet contains the claims on assets, which describes how the assets are financed by either liabilities or stockholders' equity. Liabilities represent the firm's financial obligations to outsiders—most importantly, its creditors. Like assets, liabilities can be either current or noncurrent. They are listed on the balance sheet roughly in order of increasing maturity. That is, current liabilities are followed on the balance sheet by long-term liabilities.

Current liabilities are obligations that must be paid within one year or within the normal operating cycle of the firm. Normally, accounts payable (credit extended by trade suppliers) is the largest item. Notes payable, however, can be sizable for firms that rely heavily on short-term credit from banks. Current liabilities and current assets are collectively referred to as **working capital.** The term **net working capital** refers to the *difference* between current assets and current liabilities. This figure indicates the extent to which current assets can be converted to cash to meet current obligations. The more working capital a firm has, the more liquidity it has.

Noncurrent liabilities, such as bonds and mortgages, are long-term debt payable in more than one year. They usually have fixed periodic interest (and principal) payments associated with them.

Stockholders' equity (net worth) is simply the residual difference between assets and liabilities. It follows from the accounting identity that assets must equal (balance) liabilities plus equity:

$$\begin{aligned} \text{Assets} \quad &- \text{ liabilities} = \text{stockholders' equity} \\ \$316{,}000 &- \$196{,}000 = \$120{,}000 \end{aligned} \tag{6-2}$$

This figure represents the net worth of the firm and indicates the wealth of the stockholders in book-value terms. This implies that the actual wealth of the shareholders (i.e., in market-value terms) may be higher or lower than $120,000. Stockholders' equity increases when retained earnings are added to the books (i.e., when the firm retains or "saves" part of its current earnings instead of paying them out as dividends).

---

[4]**Prepaid expenses** are an exception in that they represent cash expenditures made in advance of the use of the goods and services and are awaiting assignment to expenses. Other examples are unexpired insurance, rent, and subscriptions.

THE INCOME STATEMENT

Whereas a balance sheet summarizes a firm's financial position at a point in time:

KEY CONCEPT: An **income statement** reports a firm's performance by measuring the profits (losses) generated over a period of time—typically, a quarter or a fiscal year.

The **income statement** shows the extent to which revenues exceed the cost of producing and/or marketing a product. To facilitate a discussion of the income statement, Table 6•4 presents Byet's income statement in four distinct

TABLE 6•4   Byet Stores, Inc., Income Statements and Statement of Retained Earnings (Thousands of Dollars)

	December 31, 1988	December 31, 1987
a. Income Statements		
Part 1: Production activities		
Net sales	$801	$720
Less: Cost of goods sold	492	468
Gross profit	$309	$252
Part 2: Operating activities		
Less: Operating expenses		
Selling	$ 87	$ 63
Rent	40	30
General and administrative	126	115
Depreciation	4	3
Total expenses	$257	$211
Net operating income (*NOI*)	$ 52	$ 41
Part 3: Financial activities		
Less: Interest expense	$ 18	$ 21
Plus: Nonoperating income	4	5
Net profit before taxes (*NPBT*)	$ 38	$ 25
Part 4: Taxes		
Less: Income taxes (15%)	6	4
Net income (*NI*)	$ 32	$ 21
b. Statement of Retained Earnings		
Beginning balance	$ 48	$ 32
Add: Net income (*NI*)	32	21
Less dividends	7	5
Ending balance	$ 73	$ 48

sections so that the profit (loss) after each type of expense can be analyzed. These four sections result in the determination of the **gross profit, net operating income (NOI), net profit before taxes (NPBT)** (also called *taxable income*), and **net income (NI)** for Byet Stores, Inc.

Part 1 Production Activities

Gross profit recognizes the expense of producing (purchasing) a product by deducting the cost of goods sold from net sales (revenues).

Part 2 Operating Activities

Part 2 of the income statement subtracts out general and administrative, rent, and depreciation expenses from gross profits. These expenses collectively are called *operating expenses*; Thus

$$NOI = \text{gross profit} - \text{operating expenses}$$

Example 6·1   Determining a Firm's NOI

Standard Materials, Inc., had net sales during 1988 of $1,530,000. The firm has a cost of goods sold of $581,400 and operating expenses of $620,000. What is Standard's *NOI*?

First, we must determine Standard's gross profit. The gross profit is net sales less the cost of goods sold:

$$\$1,530,000 - \$581,400 = \$948,600$$

Second, operating expenses are subtracted from the gross profit to determine the *NOI*:

$$\$948,600 - \$620,000 = \$328,600$$

These calculations are summarized in the upper half of the income statement.

Sales revenue	$1,530,000
Less: Cost of goods sold	581,400
Gross profit	$948,600
Less: Operating expenses	$620,000
NOI	$328,600

Part 3 Financial Activities

Next, financial expenses such as interest payments and **nonoperating income** (or expenses) are netted against operating income to obtain *NPBT*. Nonoperating income includes income to the firm from activities not directly related to its day-to-day operations. Examples include income from royalties on patents and rental income from property. *NPBT* is also known as *taxable income* because this figure can be used as income for tax purposes. Thus

$$NPBT = NOI - \text{interest payments} + \text{nonoperating income} \qquad (6\text{-}3)$$

Part 4 Taxes

The bottom line of the income statement yields the net income (*NI*). This figure, also called **net income after taxes,** belongs to the stockholders of the firm. The firm may choose to pay out either part or all of the *NI* to stockholders as dividends. What remains goes into the firm's **retained earnings** account:

$$\text{Retained earnings} = NI - \text{dividends} \qquad (6\text{-}4)$$

The income statement satisfies a fundamental need for information that has characterized businesses for centuries. Its early use may be seen in the highlight "A Fourteenth-Century Income Statement."

■ HIGHLIGHT

A FOURTEENTH-CENTURY INCOME STATEMENT

Francesco di Marco Datini & Co. in Barcelona, Statement of Profit and Loss, July 11, 1397–January 31, 1399 (Barcelonese Currency)

	£	s.	d.
Profits on trade (*Pro di mercatantie*)	689	11	5
Profits on foreign exchange (*Pro di cambio*)	262	4	0
Credit balance of merchandise expense			
(*Spese di mercatantie*)	133	13	7
Total of gross profits	1,085	9	0

	£	s.	d.
Deduct expenses			
Rent for 18 months	60	0	0
Irrecoverable account	3	8	0
Convoy expenses (*guidaggio*)	67	12	0
Living expenses	106	1	5
Depreciation on office equipment	16	17	0

Reserve for unpaid taxes and other accruals (*riserbo di spese di lelde a pagare e altre spese*)	80 0 0		
Total expenses		333 18 5	
Net income		751 10 7	

Source: Datini Archives, Prato (Tuscany), No. 801, Barcelona, *Libro verde C.*

THE STATEMENT OF RETAINED EARNINGS

Table 6•4 also contains a statement of retained earnings.

KEY CONCEPT: A **statement of retained earnings** is a financial statement that reconciles the changes in the book value of equity between balance sheet dates.

The construction of this statement is straightforward: The retained earnings at any time is the retained earnings last year plus any new retained earnings from the current year. For Byet Stores, the beginning retained earnings balance for 1988 of $48,000 is the ending balance for 1987. The ending balance of $73,000 for 1988 is thus determined by the income earned and dividends paid during the year.

Two comments are necessary with regard to the change in retained earnings. First, this figure is a result of the interaction between the income statement and the balance sheet. Of all that happens within an income statement, interest expense and depreciation expense are perhaps the most important variables directly affecting the balance sheet. Second, earnings retention actually occurs over the entire year, and such earnings are usually reinvested in assets such as plant and equipment or accounts receivable, not in cash. Cash is an asset, whereas retained earnings are claims on assets. The existence of retained earnings simply means that past reported income has exceeded the payment of dividends from the cash account. That is, retained earnings have already been allocated to asset investments and may therefore not be available for distribution.

Learning Check for Section 6•2

Review Questions

6•4. Which basic statement reflects the flow concept of Chapter 2? Which basic statement reflects the stock concept?

6•5. How are the basic financial statements interrelated?

6•6. What information can be obtained from the income statement?

6•7.   If a manager needed to know the short-term liabilities of the firm, which statement would she examine?

New Terms

Balance sheet
Gross profit
Income statement
Net income (*NI*)
Net income after
   taxes

Net operating income
   (*NOI*)
Net profit before
   taxes (*NPBT*)
Net working capital

Nonoperating income
Prepaid expenses
Retained earnings
Statement of retained
   earnings
Working capital

SECTION 6•3 *The Common-Size Statements*

The basic financial statements cannot provide the financial manager and outsiders with information regarding several aspects of the firm's operations: How were the firm's profits used? Were long-term sources of financing adequate to support major investments and sales growth? Was there an overreliance on short-term funds? What do changes in working capital imply about the firm's ability to generate funds? And so on. To answer these and similar questions, **derivative financial statements** are needed. These provide additional information for interpreting the accounting data and establishing basic financial relationships. Three such statements will be studied. In this section, we will examine the common-size income statement and the common-size balance sheet. In Section 6•4, we will study the cash flow statement.

COMMON-SIZE STATEMENTS

So far, financial information has been expressed in absolute dollar amounts. However, another derivative statement, the common-size statement, converts these absolute amounts into more easily understood percentages of some base amount. As a result, certain insights not evident from a review of the raw figures themselves become more apparent. In addition, the different statements can be compared both over time and across companies within the firm's industry.

KEY CONCEPT: A **common-size statement** is either a balance sheet or an income statement in which each item is expressed as a percentage (rather than in dollars) of some amount.

Table 6•5 presents the **common-size balance sheets** for Byet Stores (1988 and 1989), and Table 6•6 shows the **common-size income statements** for the same company, again for the same years.

TABLE 6·5 Byet Stores, Inc., Common-Size Balance Sheet (Thousands of Dollars)

	December 31, 1988	Percent	December 31, 1987	Percent	Comparative Industry Averages (%)
Assets					
Current assets					
Cash and marketable securities	$ 43	13.6	$ 40	14.8	7.9
Net accounts receivables	96	30.4	89	32.8	14.5
Inventories	111	35.1	92	33.9	52.5
Prepaid expenses	7	2.2	9	3.3	1.1
Total current assets	$257	81.3	$230	84.8	76.1
Net fixed assets	59	18.7	41	15.2	23.9
Total assets	$316	100.0	$271	100.0	100.0
Claims on assets					
Current liabilities					
Accounts payable	$ 77	24.4	$ 63	23.3	14.6
Notes payable—bank	31	9.8	46	17.0	10.7
Taxes payable	3	1.0	3	1.1	3.7
Other accruals	24	7.6	21	7.7	7.4
Total current liabilities	$135	42.8	$133	49.1	36.4
Long-term liabilities					
Debenture bonds	$ 49	15.5	$ 33	12.2	16.3
Deferred taxes	12	3.8	10	3.7	2.0
Total long-term liabilities	$ 61	19.3	$ 43	15.9	18.3
Stockholders' equity					
Common stock	$ 38	12.0	$ 38	14.0	—[a]
Additional paid-in capital	9	2.8	9	3.3	—
Retained earnings	73	23.1	48	17.7	—
Total stockholders' equity	$120	37.9	$ 95	35.0	45.3
Total claims	$316	100.0	$271	100.0	100.0

[a] Not available.

THE COMMON-SIZE BALANCE SHEET

In a common-size balance sheet, each item is calculated as a percentage of total assets. This derivative statement has been in vogue for hundreds of years (see the highlight "A Fourteenth-Century Merchant's Common-Size Balance Sheet"). For Byet, the total assets of $316,000 represents 100%. For example,

TABLE 6•6   Byet Stores, Inc., Common-Size Income Statement (Thousands of Dollars)

	December 31, 1988	Percent	December 31, 1987	Percent	Comparative Industry Averages (%)
Net sales	$801	100.0	$720	100.0	100.0
Less: Cost of goods sold	492	61.4	468	65.0	64.0
Gross profit	$309	38.6	$252	35.0	36.0
Less: Operating expenses					
Selling	$ 87	10.9	$ 63	8.7	—[a]
Rent	40	5.0	30	4.2	—
General and administrative	126	15.7	115	16.0	—
Depreciation	4	0.5	3	0.4	—
Total expenses	$257	32.1	$211	29.3	32.6
Net operating income (*NOI*)	$ 52	6.5	$ 41	5.7	3.4
Less: Interest expense	$ 18	2.3	$ 21	2.9	—
Plus: Nonoperating income	4	0.5	5	0.7	—
Net profit before taxes (*NPBT*)	$ 38	4.7	$ 25	3.5	2.0
Less: Income taxes (15%)	6	0.7	4	0.6	—
Net income (*NI*)	$ 32	4.0	$ 21	2.9	—

[a] Not available.

Byet's $43,000 in cash amounts to $(43,000/316,000) = 13.6\%$. The other percentages are calculated similarly. From Table 6•5 we can observe that Byet invests heavily in current assets (over 80% of total assets), especially in accounts receivable and inventories. This is typical of a retailer such as Byet; the two main sources of financing used to support assets are short-term liabilities and equity. In terms of year-to-year comparisons, current assets have declined (from 84.8% to 81.3% of total assets between 1987 and 1988), while investments in fixed assets have gone up from 15.2% to 18.7% over the same time period.[5] This reflects Byet's (perhaps) recent aggressive expansion of new store openings. Byet has also increased its reliance on long-term debt from 15.9% to 19.3% relative to short-term liabilities, while equity has remained a stable source of financing. Although the discussion has focused on an arbitrary set of variables, virtually any two variables in the common-size statement can be compared to draw inferences.

[5] Another useful common-size statement for analyzing such behavior over time is one that relates statement items to a base year. For example, a base year such as 1980 could be selected, and all financial statement items for that year could be designated as 100.00. Items for all subsequent years would then be expressed as an index to that year.

A FOURTEENTH-CENTURY MERCHANT'S COMMON-SIZE BALANCE SHEET

It is interesting to note that common-size balance sheets were in vogue almost 600 years ago. Despite what some modern labor union leaders might claim, we no longer include labor under "fixtures" as was done with the slave Martha in the balance sheet of Datini & Co.

Francesco di Marco Datini & Co. in Barcelona, Balance Sheet on January 31, 1399

a. Assets

Explanation	Barcelonese Currency						Percent of Total
	£	s.	d.	£	s.	d.	
Cash at bank and in hand							
Cash in hand	18	17	2				0.1
Deposit accounts	1,242	9	8				8.2
Special account	440	0	0				2.9
				1,701	6	10	11.2
Receivables							
Local tradesmen for goods sold	4,841	14	10				31.9
Local customers for exchange	2,192	19	4				14.5
Local customers for insurance	99	17	11				.7
				7,134	12	1	47.1
Balances with foreign correspondents							
Venice	1,305	5	9				8.5
Genoa	9	7	7				.1
Avignon		6	0				.0
Montpellier	854	15	1				5.6
Paris	19	5	2				.1
Pisa	980	12	7				6.4
Bruges	1,036	2	7				6.5
Florence	520	10	10				3.8
Perpignan	118	18	5				.8
				4,845	4	0	31.8
Datini branches in other places							
Majorca	88	9	0				.6
Venice	224	16	10				1.4
Florence	211	16	0				1.4
				525	1	10	3.4
Inventories							
Goods in stock				288	0	9	1.9
Fixtures							
Office furniture	95	0	0				.6
Martha, our slave (*Marta, nostra schiava*)	30	0	0				.2
				125	0	0	.8
Miscellaneous							
Sundry deferred charges and supplies	112	1	10				.7
Drawing account Simone d'Andrea	25	0	2				.2
Shortage in cash	38	13	0				.3
Sundry adjustments for errors	17	18	6				.1
				193	13	6	1.3
Bad debts				384	7	3	2.5
Untraced error in casting the balance				11	9	1	.0
Total				15,208	15	4	100.0

b. Liabilities

Explanation	Barcelonese Currency						Percent of Total
	£	s.	d.	£	s.	d.	
Payables							
Local merchants (mostly acceptances)				1,951	2	9	12.8
Balances with foreign correspondents							
Majorca	586	5	6				3.8
Valencia	865	1	9				5.7
Perpignan	3	11	2				.0
Montpellier	91	0	10				.6
Paris	297	0	0				2.0
Bruges	2,848	18	9				18.7
Bologna	570	7	6				3.8
Florence	2,090	12	10				13.7
Genoa	666	12	11				4.4
Pisa	182	7	1				1.2
Venice	59	10	6				.4
				8,261	8	10	54.3
Datini branches in other places							
Florence	804	19	1				5.3
Genoa	1,037	13	11				6.8
Avignon	32	1	8				.2
Majorca	510	11	6				3.4
Valencia	171	11	3				1.1
				2,557	13	5	16.8
Consignment sales				828	7	9	5.5
Reserve for accrued taxes and contingencies				80	0	0	.5
Owner's equity							
Francesco di Marco Datini da Prato				768	6	8	5.1
Net profit on merchandise and exchange	751	10	7				4.9
Later adjustment	10	5	4				.1
				761	15	11	5.0
Total				15,208	15	4	100.0

Source: Datini Archives, Prato (Tuscany), No. 1165, Barcelona.

An astute financial manager should be aware of most of these general conclusions. While this analysis shows how Byet has been acting over time, there is no indication of whether it has been performing well or poorly. An additional step that can answer such questions involves a comparison of Byet's balance sheet percentages to its industry's average percentages. These industry averages are also presented in Table 6•5.

Such an analysis leads to a number of observations. First, Byet's current assets (as a percentage of total assets) are only slightly larger than those of the typical retailer. However, the mix between accounts receivables and inventories stands out in stark contrast. In 1988, Byet's accounts receivables and inventories amounted, respectively, to 30.4% and 35.1% of total assets. In contrast, the industry averages for these same ratios are 14.5% and 52.5%, respectively. Such pronounced deviations from the industry averages require further investigation to determine the underlying reasons. These deviations from the norm should encourage the analyst to ask several questions that can identify potential weaknesses and strengths within the company. For example, does Byet have a credit and collection policy consistent with its size? Is management overly proficient at controlling inventory levels, or are inventories too low, resulting in lost sales due to shortages?

Byet also tends to rely more heavily on current liabilities than do other firms in the industry. This is because of Byet's much higher level of accounts payable. Is Byet shrewdly using its trade suppliers to help carry its large investment in current assets? Or is Byet having trouble meeting its obligations on time, causing payables to build up? Again, this significant deviation warrants further attention. Finally, Byet is using debt to a greater extent than normal. This conclusion follows from the observation that its equity is only 37.9% of assets, whereas this ratio is 45.3% for the typical retailer. The financial manager needs to determine whether this mix of debt and equity is simply a temporary phenomenon or a stated policy objective.

THE COMMON-SIZE INCOME STATEMENT

As Table 6•6 shows, each item in the common-size income statement is calculated as a percentage of the sales (i.e., Byet's 1987 sales of $720,000 and its 1988 sales of $801,000 represent 100%). The industry averages are also presented. An analysis of Byet's common-size income statement shows that Byet's 1988 gross and operating profit percentages have improved significantly over the 1987 profit margins. This has resulted mainly from an improvement in the control of its cost of goods sold even while operating expenses were increasing as a percentage of sales. The primary cause of the latter result was a sharp increase in selling expenses. Nevertheless, Byet's overall profit picture compares quite favorably with the industry's. In fact, Byet's 1988 net profits before taxes were more than twice the industry's average of 2.0%.

Learning Check for Section 6·3

Review Questions

6·8. What are the insights gained by analyzing a company by means of common-size statements rather than the basic statements?

6·9. What information would you need to construct a common-size balance sheet?

New Terms

Common-size balance sheet	Common-size income statement	Derivative financial statement

SECTION 6·4 *The Cash Flow Statement*[6]

Corporate accounting deals with the determination of income or profits on an accrual, or book, basis, not with cash flows. The reason for this convention is that outsiders (and perhaps management) might be misled if they considered net cash flows to be the earnings (profits) for a given period.

As seen in Chapter 1, financial management decisions should be based on cash flows rather than on profits. This is especially important when analyzing capital projects (i.e., capital budgeting), for which estimates of future incremental cash flows are used to evaluate the attractiveness of the investments. For such financial decisions, it is necessary to convert profits (as determined in the income statement) to cash flows.

THE MEANING OF CASH FLOW

As seen earlier, profits less depreciation is taxed by the IRS. What is left after the IRS has taken its cut is net profits after taxes or **net income (*NI*)**. However, if it is recognized that depreciation was subtracted out purely for tax considerations (to determine tax payable) and is not really a dollar amount paid out, the actual cash flow to the firm can be defined as follows:

KEY CONCEPT: The **cash flow** to a company is the total dollar amount of funds available for the firm to put to productive uses.

---

[6]The cash flow statement has recently replaced a book-value–based statement called the *statement of changes in financial position*. This change, directed by the Financial Accounting Standards Board (FASB), demonstrates the increasing importance of cash-flow analysis in financial decision making.

The difference between cash flows and accounting net income for Roscoe Company is demonstrated in Figure 6•1. As seen in this figure cash flows are determined by adding depreciation to net income.

Focusing on profits alone does not capture the extent to which a firm has resources for alternative investments. In fact, a firm may show increased profits at the same time that its cash available for productive investments is decreasing.

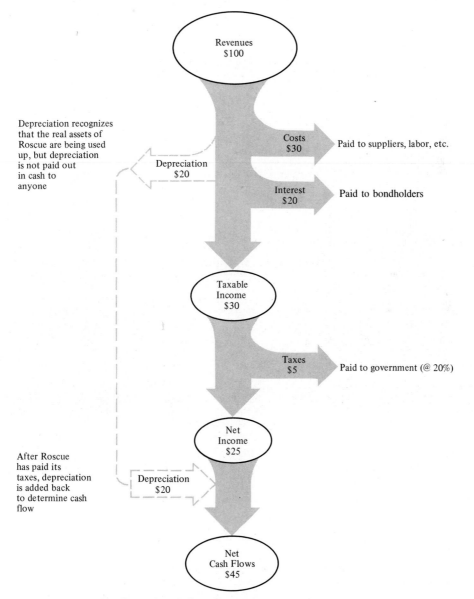

FIGURE 6•1   Profits and cash flow for a firm.

As demonstrated in Table 6•7, cash flow and accounting profits may differ for a firm. In fact, the accounting profits shown by a firm may improve at the same time that the firm's cash flow is decreasing! It is cash flow, not profit, that determines the value of assets.

Calculating a company's cash flow by adding its net income to its depreciation is a useful simplification. However, this method can be imprecise. Implicit in the cash flow calculation for Roscoe Company in Figure 6•1 is the assumption that the $100 in revenues represents cash sales and that the $30 in costs have been paid for in cash. This assumption may not reflect the actual cash available to the company. Roscoe, even though it has sales of $100, might have a portion of its revenues as credit sales. Similarly, it might have used credit to acquire some of its raw materials. To obtain a precise estimate of the firm's cash flow we develop the cash flow statement.

CONSTRUCTING THE CASH FLOW STATEMENT

The basic idea in developing the cash flow statement is to start with the income statement, adjust it for changes in the balance sheet, and then use the

TABLE 6•7 Differences Between Cash Flow and Accounting Profits

Company	Cash Flow		Net Income	
	$ Millions	% change vs. '83	$ Millions	% change vs. '83
1. Exxon	11,195	−9.36	5,528	11.05
2. Int'l. Business Machines	8,322	−25.22	6,582	20.00
3. General Motors	8,300	0.23	4,517	21.08
4. Ford Motor	6,708	34.12	2,907	55.70
5. Atlantic Richfield	4,873	18.67	1,129	−27.06
6. Mobil	4,832	24.18	1,268	−15.64
7. Amoco	4,782	9.27	2,183	16.86
8. Shell Oil	3,987	8.55	1,772	8.51
9. Texaco	3,795	19.91	306	−75.18
10. Du Pont (E.I.)	3,773	−10.87	1,431	26.97
11. Chevron	3,716	−15.66	1,534	−3.52
12. GTE	3,713	17.95	1,080	10.41
13. Standard Oil	3,512	32.58	1,488	−1.59
14. Chrysler	2,384	35.65	1,496	395.56
15. Phillips Petroleum	2,153	−7.68	810	12.34
16. Unocal	2,027	20.49	700	11.90
17. General Electric	2,006	−33.33	2,280	12.65
18. Burlington Northern	1,777	103.99	579	40.10
19. Sun Co.	1,728	−17.60	538	18.76
20. Reynolds (R.J.)	1,685	5.31	843	0.96

Source: Dunn's Business Month, July 1986.

results to explain the change in the cash balance. This new approach is more detailed but yields further information on the impact of funds flow from management's past decisions. To facilitate the analysis of these decisions, the cash flow statement is divided into areas examining the cash inflows and cash outflows due to managerial decisions concerning operations, finance, and investment.

Table 6•8 contains Byet Stores' cash flow statement for 1988. As shown, cash flow from operations amounted to $45,000. On the other hand, the financial decision produced a net outflow of $20,000 due to $25,000 in financial expenses, a $15,000 reduction in short-term debt, and only $20,000 in cash inflows. Finally, there was an investment outflow for $22,000 in new plant and equipment. Together, the three types of cash flows generated a positive cash flow of $3,000.

This $3,000 figure denotes the change in Byet's cash position, which increases from $37,000 to $40,000. The cash flow statement gives more detailed information for analyzing the different types of decisions made during the year.

A CONCLUDING COMMENT

Before concluding this chapter, it is important to recognize that none of the statements examined—basic or derived—produced any financial decisions per se. They merely provided some information that can be used by the financial manager to monitor the firm's ongoing activities, to be alerted to any current or impending problems, and to serve as a basis for making decisions that will be consistent with the firm's financial objectives. In the next chapter, an approach to garnering information on a firm's current and past cash flows will be studied. But again, a framework for making financial decisions will not be presented because financial statement analysis deals with the outcomes of past decisions. The techniques that will be discussed next simply provide an informational base for making better decisions about the future.

Learning Check for Section 6•4

Review Questions

6•10. Why do managers need the cash flow statement?

6•11. What is the general procedure for constructing a cash flow statement?

6•12. Distinguish between profits and cash flow. Explain why cash flow, in contrast to profits, has earnings potential.

6•13. What is the goal of financial management? Why?

6•14. How is cash flow defined?

TABLE 6·8   Byet Stores, Inc., Cash Flow Statement (Thousands of Dollars)

	Net Cash Flow December 31, 1988
Operating cash flows	
Net sales	$ 801
Less: Increase in receivables	7
Cash from sales	$ 794
Cost of sales	$ 492
Plus: Increase in inventories	19
Less: Increase in payables	14
Cash production costs	497
Gross cash margin	$ 297
Operating expenses (excluding depreciation)	$ 253
Less: Decrease in prepaid expenses	2
Less: Increase in accruals	3
Plus: Increase in other current assets	0
Cash operating expenses	$ 248
Cash from operations	$ 49
Less: Income taxes paid[a]	4
Net cash income from operations	$ 45
Financial cash flows	
Financial outflows	
Interest expenses	$ 18
Cash dividends paid	7
Decrease in notes payables	15
Total financial outflows	$−40
Financial inflows	
Nonoperating income	$ 4
Increase in long-term debt	16
Increase in new equity	0
Total financial inflows	$ 20
Net financial cash flows	$−20
Investment cash flows	
Investment outflows	
Less: Increase in marketable securities	$ 0
Less: Increase in gross P&E	22
Net investment cash flows	$−22
Net cash flow from operating, financing, and investment decisions (change in cash position)	$ 3
Plus beginning cash balance	$ 37
Ending cash balance[b]	$ 40

[a] Income taxes from income statement less increase in deferred taxes (i.e., $6,000 − $2,000 = $4,000).

[b] Note that this cash balance exactly matches the figure in Byet's 1988 balance sheet (Table 6·3).

6·15.   Is profit maximization consistent with maximizing the wealth of the stockholders? Why? ·

6·16.   Which depreciation method would a firm use in determining its income tax? What are the basic characteristics of this depreciation method?

6·17.   What is accumulated depreciation?

6·18.   What is the relationship between the net income and the cash flow of a firm?

6·19.   If a firm pays no taxes, what is the difference between its net income and its cash flow?

New Terms

Cash flow   Net income

SUMMARY

Book Values in Finance

Even though market values should be used for financial decision making, it is often impossible for managers to ignore book values. This happens for a variety of reasons—for internal control of operations, to recognize liquidity considerations, to recognize institutional realities, for rate hearings, and so on. In these cases, managers have to rely heavily on the books of the company. For this, an understanding of financial statement analysis is required.

The Basic Financial Statements

Even though market-value–related decisions cannot be made simply by looking at historical accounting information, it is important to understand the structure and interpretation of financial statements. A good financial manager will pay close attention to financial statements in order to ensure that the firm's operations are consistent with the company's objectives.

The balance sheet provides a statement of the firm's assets and liabilities at a particular time. An income statement summarizes the outcome of the firm's annual operations as they affect its net income. The statement of retained earnings shows the increased book value of the shareholders' equity.

The Common-Size Statements

Derivative financial statements provide more detailed information than do the basic statements. The common-size balance sheet and the common-size income statement express each item on the statement in percentage terms. The cash flow statement shows the inflows and outflows of cash during a given period.

The Cash Flow Statement

Cash flows are the total dollar amount of funds available for the firm to put to productive uses. The cash flow statement allows analysis of how managerial decisions have affected the firm's cash flow. The statement gives the cash inflows and cash outflows due to operational, financial, and investment decisions.

PROBLEMS

6•1. Four years ago, your firm purchased a printing press for $12,000. The press is being depreciated straight line to a salvage value of zero in six more years.
   (a) What is the annual depreciation of the press?
   (b) What is the book value of this asset today?

6•2. Three years ago, your firm purchased a forklift for $10,000. It is being depreciated straight line to a salvage value of zero in two more years. If your firm sells the forklift today for $5,000, it will receive only $4,600 after taxes.
   (a) What is the annual depreciation on the machine?
   (b) What is the current book value of the machine?
   (c) What is your firm's marginal tax rate?

6•3. The long-term liabilities and stockholders' equity portion of BT&T's balance sheet on December 31, 1987, is shown. During 1988, BT&T issued $5,000,000 of long-term debt, issued $10,000,000 of equity, earned $3,000,000, and paid $1,000,000 in dividends. Construct a new balance sheet for December 31, 1988, that reflects these changes.

Long-term debt	$ 60,000,000
Preferred stock	20,000,000
Common stock	60,000,000
Retained earnings	40,000,000
Total long-term liabilities and stockholders' equity	$180,000,000

6•4. The balance sheet of the Oliva Manufacturing Company on June 30, 1988, is shown. During the next quarter, Oliva has gross sales of $905,000, sells inventory valued at $600,000, and manufactures $620,000 of new inventory. They collect $780,000 of outstanding accounts receivable and extend new credit in the amount of $801,000. Net income for the period is $84,000, of which $63,000 is paid in dividends. None of the other accounts have changed (except cash).

Cash	$ 221,000	Accounts payable	$ 417,000
Accounts receivable	385,000	Notes payable	217,000
Inventory	526,000	Current liabilities	634,000
Current assets	1,132,000	Long-term debt	800,000
Net fixed assets	1,613,000	Common equity	1,311,000
Total assets	$2,745,000	Total liabilities and stockholders' equity	$2,745,000

(a) Construct a balance sheet as of September 30, 1988.
(b) What was the level of net working capital on June 30, 1988?

6•5. Following are parts of an income statement and two balance sheets of the O'Conner Broadcasting Company. Sheila O'Conner, station manager, has asked you to produce a statement of retained earnings. Do it.

1986 Balance Sheet		*1987 Balance Sheet*	
Long-term debt	$ 500,000	Long-term debt	$ 550,000
Common stock	600,000	Common stock	700,000
Retained earnings	750,000	Retained earnings	775,000
Total long-term liabilities and stockholders' equity	$1,850,000	Total long-term liabilities and stockholders' equity	$2,025,000

1987 Income Statement

Net operating income	$80,000
Less: Interest expense	25,000
Plus: Nonoperating income	15,000
Net profit before taxes	$70,000
Less: Taxes	32,000
Net income	$38,000

6•6. Last year, the Myers Entertainment Center was formed, with current assets of $50,000, fixed assets of $150,000, and stockholders' equity of $85,000. During the past year, current assets have increased in value by

$30,000, fixed assets have increased by $40,000, current liabilities have increased by $25,000, and long-term debt has increased by $37,000.

(a) What was the sum of current liabilities and long-term liabilities when the center was formed?

(b) What is the current level of stockholders' equity?

6·7. During 1988, Magee Auto Supply Outlets had gross sales of $900,000, cost of goods sold of $300,000, and general and selling expenses of $400,000. They also had outstanding $200,000 of 10% notes and $400,000 of 12% coupon bonds. Nonoperating income was zero, depreciation was $100,000, and dividends of $80,000 were paid.

(a) What was *NOI*?

(b) What was *NPBT*?

(c) What was *NI* if the average tax rate was 40%?

(d) If retained earnings were $240,000 on December 31, 1987, what are they on December 31, 1988?

6·8. Construct a December 31, 1988, common-size balance sheet for Jet Electro and compare it with the common-size balance sheet for the industry (shown here).

(a) What accounts are most different from the industry norm?

(b) Are these deviations necessarily undesirable?

(c) Why might these deviations have occurred?

	1988	1988 % Jet Electro	1988 % Industry
Cash	$ 10		4.5
Marketable securities	4		5.0
Net accounts receivable	11		3.2
Inventory	9		2.5
Prepaid expenses	1		.6
Total current assets	$ 35		15.8
Net plant and equipment	183		84.2
Total assets	$218		100.0
Accounts payable	$ 8		6.2
Wages payable	2		2.0
Notes payable	15		3.3
Taxes payable	2		.8
Other accruals	2		.9
Total current liabilities	$ 29		13.2
Long-term debt	$ 60		27.7
Deferred taxes	3		1.3
Total long-term liabilities	$ 63		29.0

Common stock	$ 42		18.1
Additional paid-in capital	38		19.1
Retained earnings	46		20.6
Total stockholders' equity	$126	57.8	57.8
Total liabilities and			
stockholders' equity	$218	100	100.0

6•9. Construct a common-size income statement for Jet Electro for 1988 and compare it with the common-size income statement for the industry.

	1988 % Jet Electro	1988 % Industry	1988 Jet Electro (Thousands)
Net sales		100.0	$162
Cost of goods sold		73.1	118
Gross profit		26.9	$ 44
Operating expenses			
Selling		4.1	$ 6
General and administrative		6.6	14
Depreciation		5.7	5
Total operating expenses		16.4	$ 25
Net operating income		10.5	$ 19
Interest		4.6	9
Taxable income		5.9	$ 10
Taxes		2.4	4
Net income		3.5	$ 6

6•10. Sparky's Seafood Restaurants in 1988 had a net cash flow from operations of $52,000, net financial cash outflows of $22,000, and net investment cash outflow of $26,000.
   (a) What was Sparky's net cash flow for 1988?
   (b) If Sparky's level of cash on the balance sheet for December 31, 1987, was $42,000, what is the level of cash on the balance sheet for December 31, 1988?

6•11. Wilfong Brothers, Inc., reported a net cash inflow from operations of $63,000 during the fourth quarter of 1988. In addition, Wilfong had a net financial cash inflow of $12,000 and a net investment cash outflow of $52,000.
   (a) What was Wilfong's net cash flow for the fourth quarter of 1988?
   (b) If Wilfong's level of cash was $55,000 on December 31, 1988, what was it on September 31, 1988?

6•12. The *Athens Banner-Herald* had a cash level of $96,000 on December 31, 1988, and a cash level of $92,000 on December 31, 1987. The net financial cash outflow for the year was $47,000, and the net investment cash outflow for the year was $62,000. Cash operating expenses were $265,000.

(a) Find the net cash income from operations.

(b) Find the *Banner-Herald*'s gross cash margin for 1988.

(c) Suppose that there was no change in current assets or liabilities and that the cost of goods sold (CGS) is always 70% of sales. Find the CGS and net sales.

(d) Suppose that inventory increased by $12,000 and receivables increased by $9,000, and that all other current accounts stayed the same during 1988. Find the CGS and net sales if the CGS is always 70% of net sales.

6•13. A summary of the Alps Clothiers cash flow statement for 1988 is provided. Fill in the blanks.

Operating cash flows

Net sales	$1,382,000
Decrease in receivables	26,000
Cash from sales	_____
Cost of goods sold	$ 857,000
Increase in inventory	12,000
Decrease in payables	16,000
Cash production costs	_____
Gross cash margin	
Operating expenses	357,000
Cash from operations	_____
Income taxes paid	62,000
Net CF from operations	_____

Financial cash flows

Outflows	
Interest expense	$ 28,000
Dividends paid	13,000
Total outflows	_____
Inflows	
Nonoperating income	6,000
Increase in new equity	10,000
Total inflows	_____
Net financial cash flows	_____

Investment cash flows

Decrease in marketable securities	8,000
Increase in gross plant and equipment	35,000
Net investment cash flows	

Net CF from operating, financing, and investment decisions	
Beginning cash balance	153,000
Ending cash balance	

READINGS

FOSTER, GEORGE, *Financial Statement Analysis* (Englewood Cliffs, N.J.: Prentice-Hall, Inc., 1978).

HELFERT, ERICH A., *Techniques of Financial Analysis* (Homewood, Ill.: Richard D. Irwin, Inc., 1977).

LEV, BARUCH, *Financial Statement Analysis: A New Approach* (Englewood Cliffs, N.J.: Prentice-Hall, Inc., 1974).

Tax Reform 1986, Analysis and Planning (Arthur Anderson and Co., 1986).

APPENDIX 6·A   *Taxes and Financial Management*[7]

It is often said that death and taxes are inevitable. However, there are a thousand different ways to die and at least an equal number of ways to be taxed. Financial decisions are invariably affected by tax considerations. An alternative that is attractive before taxes can become unacceptable after the tax ramifications have been incorporated into the analysis. However, it is almost impossible to include all relevant tax details in an introductory financial management textbook for several reasons. First, the tax code applies unevenly across industries, and generalizations across firms are broad simplifications. Second, a detailed tax analysis of alternatives takes us into a discussion of tax accounting, an area outside the intended scope of this book. Finally, tax rules are subject to frequent change, and current tax rules may not apply at a later point in time. For these reasons, a more useful approach to studying financial decision making involves the conceptual rather than the precise technical details of the tax code. It may therefore best serve the reader to be familiar with the broadest aspects of tax considerations in financial decision making and to seek expert tax advice for specific issues.

Any discussion of taxes is made difficult by the recent major changes in the U.S. tax code. The Tax Reform Act of 1986 changed tax practices that had been in place for decades; however, several politicians are already proposing the restoration of some tax rules changed by the 1986 act. There is a growing sentiment that the United States is losing its competitive edge in the world economy and that investment tax credits and other preferential tax treatment for investment in "real" assets are thus required. It is therefore best to present the tax system as it exists today but also to discuss elements of taxation that have traditionally been a part of the U.S. tax code.

After this discussion, the use of these tax rules in the remaining chapters of this book will be kept to a minimum so that we may concentrate on aspects of financial theory and practice.

CORPORATE INCOME TAXES

Corporate Ordinary Tax Rate

A corporation's taxable income is calculated by subtracting its business expenses from its revenues. As Table 6A·1 indicates, current corporate income tax rates are on a graduated scale and range from 15% on the first $50,000 to 34% on taxable income over $75,000, with a 5% surcharge on taxable income between $100,000 and $335,000. This system is called a **progressive tax system**

---

[7] I wish to thank Professor Stephen T. Limberg for his many helpful comments on tax issues.

because those firms that make greater profits pay a higher proportion of taxes. Note that the successively higher tax rates are applied only to the incremental income, or latest income received, and are called **marginal tax rates.** In contrast, the **average tax rate** is the average tax paid per dollar of taxable income; that is

$$\text{Average tax rate} = \frac{\text{total taxes paid}}{\text{total taxable income}} \qquad (6\text{A-1})$$

TABLE 6A•1   Tax Rates Specified by the Tax Reform Act of 1986

Tax Rates on Ordinary Income for Corporations	
Income	Tax Rate (%)
0–$50,000	15
$50,001–$75,000	25
$75,001–$100,000	34
$100,001–$335,000	39[a]
$335,001 and above	34

[a]Contains a 5% surcharge that offsets the tax savings derived from taxing the first $15,000 at rates below 34%.

Tax Rates on Ordinary Income for Single Individuals	
Income	Tax Rate (%)
0–$17,850	15
$17,851–$43,150	28
$43,151–$89,560	33[a]
$89,561 and above	28[b]

Example 6A•1   Calculating Marginal and Average Tax Rates

Mitus Corporation's taxable income in 1988 was $92,000. What were Mitus' tax liability, marginal tax rate, and average tax rate? Using the tax rates in Table 6A•1, Mitus had a tax liability of $19,530.

$$
\begin{aligned}
\$50,000(0.15) &= \$7,500 \\
[\$75,000 - \$50,000](0.25) &= \$6,250 \\
[\$92,000 - \$75,000](0.34) &= \underline{\$5,780} \\
& \$19,530
\end{aligned}
$$

[a]Contains a 5% surcharge that offsets the tax savings that resulted from taking the first $17,850 at 15% instead of 28%.
[b]In addition, the personal exemption(s) of a single taxpayer is (are) phased out by imposing a 5% surtax on taxable income above $89,560. The surcharge will not exceed $560 for each exemption claimed.

Mitus' marginal tax rate, the highest rate it paid, was 34%. Its average tax rate was 21.2%.

$$\text{Average tax rate} = \frac{\text{total taxes paid}}{\text{total taxable income}} = \frac{\$19,530}{\$92,000} = 0.212$$

Capital Gains

Corporations purchase assets that enable them to produce goods and services. These assets may be real assets, such as trucks or complete manufacturing facilities, or financial assets such as investments in the stock of other firms. Eventually, the firm may sell an asset. The difference between the sales price received from the asset and the original purchase price is either a gain or a loss. If the time elapsed between the sale and purchase exceeds a specified time period, traditionally six months, the gain (loss) on the sale becomes a capital gain (loss) and is taxed at a reduced rate. A capital loss is used to offset capital gains made on other assets.

It is widely believed that investment in assets held for a substantial period of time fosters economic growth more than speculative, short-term trading. To encourage such investment, the tax laws may specify that capital gains on long-term assets will be taxed at a lower rate than ordinary income. Investors will then plan their strategies to take advantage of these lower tax rates and thus produce economic growth.

Prior to the 1986 Tax Reform Act, special tax treatment was given to long-term capital gains, or those on assets held more than six months. The long-term capital gains tax rate was the lesser of the firm's marginal income tax rate or a flat 28%. On the other hand, short-term capital gains, or those on assets held for six months or less, were taxed at the same marginal tax rate as ordinary income. The Tax Reform Act eliminated the capital gains tax: under the current law; all income is taxed at the ordinary income tax rate. As before the 1986 act, a capital loss can be used only to offset capital gains on other assets. Unused capital losses can be carried back to offset capital gains in the prior three years and then carried forward to offset capital gains for five years in the future.

Tax Loss Carryback and Carryforward

A corporation incurring a net operating loss may offset this loss against taxable income in the prior three years (*loss* **carryback**) and as far as 15 years into the future (*loss* **carryforward**). The law requires any loss to be applied first to the earliest preceding year and then applied forward sequentially in time.

Example 6A•2   Illustration of a Tax Loss Carryback

The DeLaGatto Construction Company, Inc., sustained a $60,000 loss in 1988. Their accountant has taken the following actions to use this loss to reduce the firm's taxes.

The 1988 loss is used first to offset 1985's taxable income. The firm's taxable income was $25,000 in 1985, and the firm paid $4,000 in taxes. Its 1985 taxable income is now recomputed to show zero profits, and the firm receives a tax refund of $4,000. The remaining loss of $60,000 − $25,000 = $35,000 is then carried back to 1986. Any losses still remaining are carried back to 1987.

If the operating loss was greater than the operating income in all three prior years, the remaining amount will be carried forward and applied to 1989's income and sequentially to future profits thereafter.

Investment Tax Credit

In today's competitive world economy, governments are concerned with economic growth and employment. One strategy they follow is to identify asset investments that encourage economic growth and then grant tax credits to firms making these investments. These **investment tax credits (*ITCs*)** allow a firm to deduct a portion of its new investment from its tax liability. *ITCs* are powerful incentives for investment in that they are dollar-for-dollar reductions in the firm's taxes. The *ITC* was eliminated by the Tax Reform Act of 1986; however, its return is being considered by Congress.

Dividend Income

As explained in Chapter 1, dividends are payments made by a firm to its owners. Occasionally, a corporation may own another corporation's stock. This means that any cash dividends received from the stock of the other corporation must be reported as income. These intercompany dividends, however, are afforded special treatment in that 80% of the dividends are exempt from taxes.

Interest Expense

Interest paid on debt issued by a corporation is tax deductible. In effect, the government "pays" part of the interest expense and the firm's cash outflow for taxes is reduced. This gives a decided tax advantage to using debt capital rather than equity capital because dividends paid on stock are paid out of net income (after taxes) and are thus not a tax-deductible item.

KEY CONCEPT: The cost of debt is reduced by the tax deductibility of interest payments.

$$\text{After-tax cost of debt} = (\text{before-tax cost of debt})(1 - T) \qquad (6\text{A-}2)$$

This relationship holds true for both dollar amounts and interest rates. Throughout the book, this relationship will be used to determine the net cost of debt to the firm.

Example 6A•3   The Effect of Tax-Deductible Interest Payments

The treasurer of the DeLaGatto Construction Company, Inc., must raise $100,000 and wants to determine what the after-tax cost of debt will be if the firm is in the 15% marginal tax bracket.

THE AFTER-TAX COST OF DEBT EXPRESSED IN DOLLARS

The tax deductibility of interest payments will affect the dollar amount that DeLaGatto will pay for the $100,000 it needs to raise.

Debt: Given a borrowing rate of 10%, the annual interest charges on the debt will be $100,000(0.10) = $10,000

However, given the firm's marginal tax rate of 15%, the firm will receive a tax subsidy of 15% for every dollar of interest paid and will have a net after-tax outflow of

$$\text{After-tax interest charge} = (\text{before-tax interest charge})(1 - T)$$

where T is the marginal tax rate.

$$\$10,000(1 - 0.15) = \$8,500$$

Tax deductibility of interest expenses reduces DeLaGatto's tax liability by $1,500!

AFTER-TAX COST OF DEBT EXPRESSED AS AN INTEREST RATE

The after-tax rate of interest that DeLaGatto pays is clearly affected by the tax deductibility of interest on debt. Although DeLaGatto must make its full interest payments to its creditors, the net rate it pays will, when taxes are considered, be less.

$$\text{After-tax interest rate} = (\text{before-tax interest rate})(1 - T)$$
$$= 10\% \ (1 - 0.15)$$
$$= 8.5\%$$

Multiplying the borrowed amount by this net interest rate gives $100,000(0.085) = \$8,500$, which is the same answer obtained earlier when calculating the net dollar cost of the debt.

PERSONAL INCOME TAXES

Individuals must pay taxes on wages and salaries, investment income (interest, dividends, rents, etc.), and profits from proprietorships and partnerships. In a manner similar to corporate tax rates, individual tax rates are progressive and are summarized in Table 6A•1. Wages, salaries, and interest income are fully taxed at the individual's marginal tax rate.

Prior to the Tax Reform Act of 1986, long-term personal capital gains, gains made on assets held by an individual, were taxed at 40% of the individual's marginal tax rate. Since long-term capital gains were taxed at lower rates than dividends, a stockholder who did not desire current income might have preferred to receive capital gains through stock appreciation rather than receive cash dividends. As with corporate capital gains, the Tax Reform Act of 1986 eliminated special tax treatment for personal capital gains or losses. As before the act, capital losses may be used to offset an individual's capital gains. However, the deduction for capital losses in excess of capital gains cannot exceed $3,000 a year. Unused losses can be carried forward indefinitely to offset capital gains or be deducted up to $3,000 each year.

Learning Check for Appendix 6•A

Review Questions

6A•1. Are payments to equity holders and payments to debt holders tax deductible for the firm? What effect could the tax deductibility of such payments have on the firm's financing decisions?

6A•2. What is the difference between the average tax rate and the marginal tax rate?

6A•3. If you were a member of Congress and desired to encourage employment, what elements would you include in the nation's tax code?

6A•4. Would the capital gains tax rate be greater or less than the ordinary tax rate? Why?

6A•5. What is the common purpose of a capital gains tax rate and an investment tax credit?

6A•6. Why is the tax deductibility of interest paid on debt important for a firm?

New Terms

Average tax rate   Carryforward   Marginal tax rate
Capital gains (losses)   Investment tax credit   Progressive tax
Carryback   (*ITC*)   system

PROBLEMS

6A•1. The Harris Corporation has a taxable income of $128,000.
  (a) What is its total tax liability?
  (b) What is Harris' average tax rate?
  (c) What is Harris' marginal tax rate?

6A•2. As the financial manager for a small corporation, you are faced with a loss for fiscal year 1988 of $42,000. Your income for the previous three years was the following:

Year	Income
1987	$12,000
1986	$32,000
1985	$34,000

How will you use this current loss to reduce your taxes?

6A•3. Your firm must raise $150,000 in new capital. This capital may be raised by issuing new stock, which requires dividend payments of 9%, or by issuing new debt, which requires interest payments of 10%. The firm's tax rate is 25%.
  (a) What is the after-tax cost of acquiring the capital by issuing equity?
  (b) What is the after-tax cost of acquiring the capital by issuing debt in terms of dollars? In terms of the interest rate?
  (c) Based on these costs, which plan would you prefer?

APPENDIX 6·B *Depreciation*

DEPRECIATION

Assume that a firm buys a machine that will last for seven years. Initially, the firm spends a large sum of money to acquire the machine and will not have to spend any more on it until the end of year 7, when the machine has to be replaced. It is clearly foolish to assume that the company is making a handsome profit in years 1 to 6 and incurring a massive loss in year 7.

The truth is that the machine is not used up just in year 7; it is being used up all the time. Thus this usage has to be recognized every year, and depreciation laws stipulate the rules for calculating this usage. Profits less **depreciation** are taxable profits, and the IRS taxes the company on this amount.

KEY CONCEPT: **Depreciation** is an allocation of the historic cost of an asset over its economic life, the period over which it is expected to provide benefits to its owner.

It makes sense to allocate this cost over the estimated economic life of the asset; however, it is more than just common sense. While depreciation is an accounting expense that does not involve the payment of cash to anyone, it does affect the amount of cash paid out in the form of taxes, and thus is of great importance to the firm.

Several methods are used for depreciating assets. These methods are divided into two classes, depending on the reason for developing the information: those used for financial accounting and those used for tax reporting.

Financial Accounting Depreciation Methods

The firm faces numerous requirements for reporting information. Financial reports usually use one of three depreciation methods. **Straight-line depreciation** spreads the historic cost of the asset evenly over its economic life. The amount of depreciation taken each year using this method is given by the following formula:

$$\text{Annual depreciation} = \frac{\text{initial cost} - \text{salvage value}}{\text{economic life}} \qquad \text{(6B-1)}$$

The salvage value is the value of the asset at the end of its economic life.

The book value of the asset at any time is the original cost of the asset less the total amount of depreciation taken on the asset up to that time:

$$\text{Book value} = \text{original cost} - \text{accumulated depreciation} \qquad \text{(6B-2)}$$

Example 6B•1 Computing Depreciation Using the Straight-Line Method

J. T. Jacobs Instruments has purchased a new laser-guided lathe. The lathe, which cost $142,000, is expected to last for 10 years and then to be sold for $10,000. Using equation (6B-1), the depreciation to be taken each year is $13,200.

$$\frac{\$142,000 - \$10,000}{10} = \$13,200$$

Using equation (6B-2), the asset's value on the books of J. T. Jacobs four years into its life would be

$$\$142,000 - (\$13,200)(4) = \$89,200$$

In addition to the straight-line method, other procedures that allow the firm to claim larger annual depreciation amounts during the early part of the asset's life are sometimes used.

Tax Depreciation Methods

The government is naturally concerned with the amount of taxes it collects, and thus with the depreciation expenses claimed by firms. Because of the direct connection between depreciation and taxes, the IRS requires firms to use the accelerated cost recovery system (*ACRS*).

THE ACCELERATED COST RECOVERY SYSTEM (ACRS)

The **accelerated cost recovery system (ACRS)** provides detailed guidelines that the firm must follow when depreciating assets for tax purposes. The *ACRS* allows firms to claim a larger percentage of depreciation in the early life of an asset that is not real estate. This is often appropriate in that many assets suffer a greater proportional decrease in their market values early in their lives (e.g., a new automobile becomes a "used car" upon being driven off the showroom floor). However, the primary advantage of an accelerated depreciation method is that it reduces taxes now rather than later and thus increases the firm's immediate cash flow.

The *ACRS* method is fairly simple. First, firms identify an asset as belonging in one of eight asset classes. These classes, which are listed in Table 6B•1, reflect the tax life of the asset.

Second, once the asset class has been identified, the *ACRS* specifies the amount of the asset's value that may be claimed as depreciation in each year. The approximate percentages are given in Table 6B•2.

Example 6B•2 Using ACRS

Town Limos has just purchased a new limousine for $64,000 and must determine the amount of depreciation to claim over the vehicle's economic life. By consulting an IRS publication (or Table 6B•1), the firm's manager determines that the limo fits in the 5-year asset class. From IRS publications (or Table 6B•2), the manager then determines the *ACRS* percentages of allowable depreciation for each year of the asset's life.

TABLE 6B•1   ACRS Property Classes

Property Class[a]	Example
3 year	Special handling devices for the manufacture of food and beverages Special tools and devices for the manufacture of rubber products Breeding hogs Racehorses more than 2 years old when placed in service
5 year	Automobiles, light-duty trucks, heavy-duty general-purpose trucks Computers, typewriters, copiers, duplicating equipment Trailers, cargo containers, trailer-mounted containers
7 year	Office furniture, fixtures, and equipment Railroad tracks Single-purpose agricultural and horticultural structures
10 year	Assets used in petroleum refining and manufacture of tobacco products and certain food products
15 year	Municipal sewage treatment plants, telephone distribution plants
20 year	Some real estate with a life greater than 27.5 years Municipal sewers
Residential rental	Apartment complexes, duplexes, and vacation rental home (Recovery period is 27.5 years)
Nonresidential real estate	Office buildings and warehouses (Recovery period is 31.5 years)

[a]Property is classified by its tax life, also called its **recovery period.**

TABLE 6B·2   ACRS Depreciation Percentages

	If the Recovery Year is:		And the Recovery Period Is:			
	3 Year	5 Year	7 Year	10 Year	15 Year	20 Year
			The Depreciation Rate Is:			
1	33.33	20.00	14.29	10.00	5.00	3.750
2	44.45	32.00	24.49	18.00	9.50	7.219
3	14.81	19.20	17.49	14.40	8.55	6.677
4	7.41	11.52	12.49	11.52	7.70	6.177
5		11.52	8.93	9.22	6.93	5.713
6		5.76	8.92	7.37	6.23	5.285
7			8.93	6.55	5.90	4.888
8			4.46	6.55	5.90	4.522
9				6.56	5.91	4.462
10				6.55	5.90	4.461
11				3.28	5.91	4.462
12					5.90	4.461
13					5.91	4.462
14					5.90	4.461
15					5.91	4.462
16					2.95	4.461
17						4.462
18						4.461
19						4.462
20						4.461
21						2.231

Year	Base Amount × Percent	Annual Depreciation Claimed
1989	$64,000(0.20)	$12,800
1990	$64,000(0.32)	$20,480
1991	$64,000(0.192)	$12,288
1992	$64,000(0.1152)	$7,373
1993	$64,000(0.1152)	$7,373
1994	$64,000(0.0576)	$3,686
		$64,000

Thus, the *ACRS* allows Town Limo to claim more depreciation expense earlier in the vehicle's life than would be the case with straight-line depreciation.

It must be emphasized that our intent in this appendix is to present an overview of *ACRS* and not to make the reader an expert on depreciation or cost recovery procedures. Many of the details involved in the tax treatment of depreciation have not been covered, as they provide little additional understanding of the important concepts involved. In addition, the details of the tax laws are subject to constant change, and most textbooks that attempt to cover them are soon obsolete. Individuals who desire more detailed information should consult current IRS publications or an up-to-date accounting textbook.

Learning Check for Appendix 6•B

Review Questions

6B•1.   What is accumulated depreciation?

6B•2.   How does the allowable depreciatable life of an asset affect the cash flows of a firm?

6B•3.   Which depreciation method would a firm use in determining its income tax? What are the basic characteristics of this depreciation method?

New Terms

Accelerated cost
  recovery system

Accumulated
  depreciation

Annual depreciation
Recovery period
Straight-line depreciation

PROBLEMS

6B•1.   Clifton Industries has just purchased a metal press for $120,000 and will depreciate the press using straight-line depreciation over 10 years to a $5,000 salvage value.
(a)   How much is the annual depreciation claimed on the press?
(b)   What is the accumulated depreciation on the press after 4 years?

6B•2.   Big Tex Limo has just replaced their fleet of limos, and must for tax purposes determine the depreciation schedule for the fleet.
(a)   Which depreciation method should Big Tex use? Why?
(b)   What property class do the limos fall in?
(c)   What is the depreciation claimed for each year of the economic life of the limo fleet?

6B•3. Three years ago your firm purchased a forklift for $10,000. The forklift is being depreciated straight-line to a salvage value of zero in two more years. If your firm sells the forklift today for $5,000, it will receive only $4,750 after taxes.

(a) What is the annual depreciation on the machine?

(b) What is the current book value of the machine?

(c) What is your firm's marginal tax rate?

7

Financial Ratio Analysis

The previous chapter introduced the concepts underlying accounting, or book, values and examined the basic and derivative financial statements. These statements, while providing a substantial amount of information concerning the historical and current status of a firm, do not provide all the information required by managers and others.

Management must constantly ensure that the firm is using its resources efficiently. For example, are its assets being employed in the most profitable way? Is the company sufficiently liquid to meet its current obligations? Is the firm profitable enough to guarantee the interest and principal payments on its long-term debt? The financial statements per se may not be able to provide the answers. A common approach to answering such questions is to perform a financial ratio analysis.

In this chapter, we will examine the types of ratios, the strengths and weaknesses of each, and their use in financial management. This topic is divided into four sections.

SECTION 7•1: *The Types of Financial Ratios*. Four classes of ratios are defined: short-term solvency, long-term solvency, asset utilization, and profitability. Some important ratios in each class are introduced and their uses explained.

SECTION 7•2: *Uses of Ratio Analysis*. Ratios are useful in intrafirm analysis, where the performance of the firm is evaluated over time, or in interfirm analysis, where the performance of a firm is compared to that of other firms in the industry.

SECTION 7•3: *Limitations of Ratio Analysis.* Ratio analysis must be used carefully. This section reviews the limitations and problems inherent in ratio analysis.

SECTION 7•4: *Other Users and Applications of Ratio Analysis.* Whereas the previous section focused on management's use of ratios, this section discusses the use of ratio analysis by those who are not managers of the firm.

SECTION 7•1 *The Types of Financial Ratios*

KEY CONCEPT: **Financial ratio analysis** is the systematic use of ratios to interpret financial statements so that the existing strengths and weaknesses of a firm, as well as its historical performance and current financial condition, can be determined.

This is achieved by reducing the information from financial statements to a small set of indices or percentage values that then form the basis for measuring different aspects of a firm's activities.

Out of the possibly hundreds of ratios that could conceivably be developed from the financial statements, only a few are commonly used. These ratios can conveniently be grouped into four categories. In this section on ratio analysis, we first define the various ratios and then compute each ratio for Byet Stores for 1987 and 1988.

SHORT-TERM SOLVENCY RATIOS

Short-term solvency or liquidity ratios measure a firm's ability to meet its short-term obligations. They focus on the extent to which a firm has enough cash or assets readily convertible into cash to pay its current liabilities. If a firm has adequate cash, it should have no problem paying its bills on time (i.e., it is solvent). If it has insufficient cash, a short-term crisis called *insolvency* occurs. Insolvency can be disastrous for a firm: Banks become reluctant to loan money, suppliers balk at selling goods on credit, and an overall drop in creditworthiness occurs.

Two ratios are calculated to measure liquidity: the current ratio and the quick ratio.

Current Ratio

The **current ratio** is defined as current assets divided by current liabilities:

$$\text{Current ratio} = \frac{\text{current assets}}{\text{current liabilities}} \qquad (7\text{-}1)$$

$$1988: \frac{\$257}{\$135} = 1.90 \qquad 1987: \frac{\$230}{\$133} = 1.73$$

It measures the extent to which those assets closest to being cash cover those liabilities closest to being payable. Normally, larger values of this ratio are desirable.

Quick (Acid Test) Ratio

The current ratio assumes that all current assets are equally liquid. Inventories, however, are often quite illiquid compared to marketable securities or accounts receivable. The **quick ratio** considers only assets that can be readily converted to cash and is therefore a stricter test for liquidity.

$$\text{Quick ratio} = \frac{\text{current assets} - \text{inventories} - \text{prepaid expenses}}{\text{current liabilities}} \qquad (7\text{-}2)$$

$$1988: \frac{\$257 - \$111 - \$7}{\$135} = 1.03 \qquad 1987: \frac{\$230 - \$92 - \$9}{\$133} = 0.97$$

LONG-TERM SOLVENCY RATIOS

Long-term solvency ratios emphasize the longer-term commitments to creditors. Claims by creditors on a firm's income arise from a contractual agreement that must be honored before any income becomes available to stockholders. Further, the greater the amount of these claims, the greater the chances are that a firm will fail to satisfy them. Failure to meet these claims may result in legal action to force their fulfillment. This may force the company to liquidate (sell) part or all of its assets to satisfy these obligations. These ratios are of two types: debt utilization ratios and coverage ratios.

Debt Utilization Ratios

Debt utilization ratios measure a firm's degree of indebtedness. The term **degree of indebtedness** refers to the proportion of the firm's assets financed by debt relative to the proportion financed by equity. The information needed to compute this ratio is found in the balance sheet. One debt ratio will be discussed formally, and two others will be mentioned informally.

The *debt-equity ratio* is the value of total debt divided by the book value of equity:[1]

$$\text{Debt-equity ratio} = \frac{\text{current liabilities} + \text{long-term liabilities}}{\text{stockholders' equity}} \quad (7\text{-}3)$$

$$1988: \frac{\$135 + \$61}{\$105} = 1.87 \qquad 1987: \frac{\$133 + \$43}{\$89} = 1.98$$

Two variants of the debt–equity ratio may be used, depending on how debt and equity are defined. For example, only long-term debt may be included in the numerator of equation (7-3). This is done because only long-term debt involves a fixed obligation extending beyond one year and hence is more appropriate for long-term insolvency assessment. This obligation is usually in the form of interest payments and occasionally the periodic repayment of principal, and is called a **sinking-fund payment.**[2] Another type of debt ratio uses the book value of assets (debt plus equity) in the denominator and is called the **debt-to-assets ratio.** It is used to focus on the percentage of total funds contributed by debt.

Coverage Ratios

Coverage ratios measure the degree to which fixed payments are "covered" by operating profits. The emphasis here is on assessing a firm's ability to service its financial (nonoperating) expenses. Information for these ratios comes from the income statement. This type of solvency ratio looks at the servicing of fixed obligations rather than the extent to which debt is utilized.

The **times interest earned** (or interest coverage) **ratio** is the most common coverage ratio and measures how many times interest expenses are earned or covered by profits:

$$\text{Times interest earned} = \frac{\text{net profits before taxes} + \text{interest expense}}{\text{interest expense}} \quad (7\text{-}4)$$

$$1988: \frac{\$38 + \$18}{\$18} = 3.11 \text{ times} \qquad 1987: \frac{\$25 + \$21}{\$21} = 2.19 \text{ times}$$

[1]In those cases where the firm also has preferred stock, there are two versions of this debt-equity ratio. One version treats preferred stock as equity and adds it to the denominator in equation (7-3). The other version treats preferred stock as debt and adds it to the numerator.

[2]Sometimes firms may have mortgage payments on property. In this case, the periodic payments include both interest and principal.

The **fixed-charge coverage ratio** is a more meaningful ratio because it considers the extent to which all fixed financial charges (long-term leases, rental expenses, etc.) are covered:

Fixed-charge coverage =

$$\frac{\text{net profit before taxes} + \text{interest expenses} + \text{lease and rental payments}}{\text{interest expenses} + \text{lease and rental payments}}$$

(7-5)

$$1988: \frac{\$38 + \$18 + \$40}{\$18 + \$40} = 1.66 \qquad 1987: \frac{\$25 + \$21 + \$30}{\$21 + \$30} = 1.49$$

This ratio is especially relevant today because leasing is gaining in popularity as an alternative to debt financing.

ASSET UTILIZATION RATIOS

Asset utilization or turnover **ratios** indicate how efficiently management utilizes its assets in generating revenues by relating or comparing sales to different types of assets. The intent is to obtain an idea of the speed with which assets generate sales. The more rapidly assets are "turned over," the more efficient is their use.

An implicit assumption of any turnover ratio is that there is some optimal mix between sales and different asset investments. By analyzing these ratios, one can determine whether too many or too few resources are invested in a particular asset. It is possible, for example, that too much is invested in accounts receivable. This discovery may suggest that the firm's credit policy is too lax and that the inflated receivables hide an excessive amount of delinquent debts. All three of the most widely used asset utilization ratios relate sales to accounts receivable, inventories, and fixed assets.

Accounts Receivable

The **average collection period** is a measure of the efficiency of a firm's credit policy. It estimates the number of days it takes for a dollar in sales to be collected by the firm:[3]

---

[3]Often the level of sales and the investment in assets will fluctuate throughout the year, especially if the sales demand is seasonal. Therefore, asset utilization ratios should be computed throughout the fiscal year if they are to have any real meaning. Unfortunately, information on these asset accounts may not be available that often. An approximation using the average level of the current asset account is often employed. The average can be computed by adding the beginning and ending account values and dividing by 2. If, on the other hand, quarterly information is used, the average is computed by summing the four values and dividing by 4.

$$\text{Average collection period} = \frac{\text{accounts receivable}}{\text{net sales per day}} \qquad (7\text{-}6)$$

$$= \frac{\text{accounts receivable}}{\text{sales}/365 \text{ days}}$$

1988: $\dfrac{\$96}{(\$801/365)} = 43.7$ days   1987: $\dfrac{\$89}{(\$720/365)} = 45.1$ days

Accounts receivable reflect only credit sales. The numerator should therefore contain only credit sales. Often total sales are used because accurate information on the breakdown of revenues into cash and credit sales is not readily available. Sometimes this calculation is based on a 360-day calendar year. This practice grew out of the banking industry's simplifying practice of assuming a convenient 30 days in a month.

Inventory

The **inventory turnover ratio** is used to determine whether too much or too little is invested in inventories. Too much inventory may mean that resources are being employed unproductively; too little inventory may mean that sales, and hence profits, are being lost because of stockouts (shortages):

$$\text{Inventory turnover} = \frac{\text{cost of goods sold}}{\text{inventories}} \qquad (7\text{-}7)$$

1988: $\dfrac{\$492}{\$111} = 4.43$ 1987: $\dfrac{\$468}{\$92} = 5.09$

Note that cost of goods rather than sales is used in the numerator. Accounts receivable are carried at the prices at which the products are sold. The appropriate way to measure how efficiently the investment in this asset is used is to relate it to sales. Inventories, however, are carried at what it cost to produce or acquire them.[4] To be consistent, then, inventory utilization should be measured in terms of the cost of goods sold. Nevertheless, total sales is often used in practice because either the sales figure is easier to obtain or the firm provides a service, in which case, cost of goods sold has no meaning.

---

[4] Often, "average" inventories are used in the denominator of this ratio to account for fluctuations in inventory levels.

Fixed Assets

The **fixed-asset turnover ratio** indicates how well the investment in long-term (fixed) assets is being managed. Normally, the higher the turnover ratio, the more efficiently assets are being used to generate sales:

$$\text{Fixed-asset turnover ratio} = \frac{\text{net sales}}{\text{net fixed assets}} \qquad (7\text{-}8)$$

$$1988: \frac{\$801}{\$59} = 13.6 \qquad 1987: \frac{\$720}{\$41} = 17.6$$

A total asset turnover ratio (sales divided by total assets) may also be examined. This ratio signifies how efficiently total resources are being used. It is like a "summary" turnover ratio because all of the other turnover ratios are included in and hence affect its value.

PROFITABILITY RATIOS

Profitability ratios measure the overall record of management in producing profits. If a firm does not earn an adequate profit, its long-term survival will be threatened. If profits are too low, for example, investors will be reluctant to provide new capital, which, in turn, will stifle or even halt its growth.

How do we determine when profits are low or high? The level of profits alone does not answer this question. Profits must be converted into a measure of profitability, which then reveals how successful past decisions and policies have been in earning a return for its investors. Four profitability ratios will be examined. As with all ratios, it is important to note that profitability ratios can measure only past performance.[5] Too often, it is assumed that these figures will persist into the future. Little evidence can be found to show that past performance is repeated consistently in the future.

The Operating Profit Margin

The **operating profit margin** determines the percentage of each sales dollar that is represented by operating profits. It indicates how good a job management has done in controlling its costs and how effective its pricing policy has been.

---

[5]For example, the Dorchester Gas Corporation received considerable press in 1981 for being ranked number one (in the Fortune 500 list) in total return to investors over the previous 10 years—a respectable 43% per year. Because of a sharp dropoff in natural gas prices and demand, however, Dorchester's 1982 return plummeted to 13%.

$$\text{Operating profit margin} = \frac{\text{net operating income}}{\text{net sales}} \tag{7-9}$$

$$= \frac{\text{sales} - \text{cost of goods sold} - \text{operating expenses}}{\text{net sales}}$$

$$1988: \frac{\$801 - \$492 - \$257}{\$801} = 6.5\% \qquad 1987: \frac{\$720 - \$468 - \$211}{\$720} = 5.7\%$$

The Net Profit Margin

The **net profit margin** goes one step further and considers income after all costs (operating plus financial plus taxes) have been deducted. It is found by dividing net income after taxes by net sales:[6]

$$\text{Net profit margin} = \frac{\text{net income } (NI)}{\text{net sales}} \tag{7-10}$$

$$1988: \frac{\$32}{\$801} = 4.0\% \qquad 1987: \frac{\$21}{\$720} = 2.9\%$$

The Book Return on Assets

The book **return on assets (*ROA*)** is a guide to the overall profitability of a firm and measures the after-tax returns without regard to the manner in which the assets were financed. Very often, book *ROA* is computed by dividing net income by the book value of the assets. However, this definition overlooks the fact that *ROA* measures the rate of return to both the stockholders and the creditors, and should be a measure of productivity of the firm irrespective of the manner in which the assets are financed. For this reason, the definition that will be used in this and the next chapter will be[7]

$$\text{Book } ROA = \frac{\text{net operating income } (1 - T)}{\text{total assets}} \tag{7-11}$$

$$\text{where } T \text{ is the firm's tax rate.}$$

---

[6]For those firms that deal in merchandise—retailers, for example—another profitability ratio, called the **gross profit margin,** is often calculated. This ratio measures the percentage of each sales dollar that remains after the cost of goods sold has been deducted. The higher the margin, the more efficient management's control of the cost of its merchandise. The ratio is defined as

$$\text{Gross profit margin} = \frac{\text{net sales} - \text{cost of goods sold}}{\text{net sales}}$$

[7]Note that this is different from the standard accounting treatment of this ratio, calculated as net income divided by total assets.

$$1988: \frac{52(1 - 0.15)}{\$316} = 13.99\% \qquad 1987: \frac{\$41(1 - 0.15)}{\$271} = 12.86\%$$

The Book Return on Equity

Unlike book *ROA*, which measures the profitability of a firm without regard to the manner in which the assets are financed, book **return on equity** (***ROE***) recognizes both—the profitability of the underlying assets and the manner in which the assets are financed:

$$\text{Book } ROE = \frac{\text{net income } (NI)}{\text{stockholders' equity}} \qquad (7\text{-}12)$$

$$1988: \frac{\$32}{\$120} = 26.67\% \qquad 1987: \frac{\$21}{\$95} = 22.11\%$$

Stockholders are usually interested in the total return, net of all other considerations, on their equity investment; book *ROE* is useful for this purpose.

Learning Check for Section 7•1

Review Questions

7•1. What are the different categories of financial ratios? What is the primary purpose of computing ratios in each of these categories?

7•2. Does the quick ratio give a better measure of the firm's liquidity than the current ratio? Why or why not?

7•3. What is the primary purpose of coverage ratios?

7•4. Can you use sales as the denominator in the inventory turnover ratio? Explain.

7•5. If you, as a manager, wished to evaluate how well your firm is controlling its costs, what profitability ratio would you use?

New Terms

Asset utilization ratio	Fixed-asset turnover ratio	Operating profit margin
Average collection period	Fixed-charge coverage ratio	Profitability ratios
Coverage ratio	Gross profit margin	Quick ratio
Current ratio	Inventory turnover ratio	Return on assets (*ROA*)
Debt-equity ratio		Return on equity (*ROE*)
Debt-to-assets ratio	Long-term solvency ratio	Short-term solvency ratios
Debt utilization ratios		Sinking-fund payment
Degree of indebtness	Net profit margin	Times interest earned ratio
Financial ratio analysis		

SECTION 7•2 *Uses of Ratio Analysis*

Like the percentage values in the common-size statements, a ratio by itself normally has little meaning. For example, a firm with a current ratio of 1.0 may be cash rich, while another, with a 4.0 current ratio, may be struggling to pay its bills. In addition, higher values for some ratios are preferred to lower values; for others, the opposite is true. To illustrate this and other aspects of ratio analysis, two types of analyses can be done: an **interfirm** (industry) **analysis and an intrafirm (trend) analysis.**

INTERPRETING RATIOS WITH AN INTRAFIRM ANALYSIS

KEY CONCEPT: An **interfirm analysis** interprets ratio values by comparing a firm's financial ratios to related firms' comparable ratios at a point in time. Interfirm analysis involves no time dimension and can thus be considered a static ratio analysis.

An interfirm analysis uses industry-based ratio averages as standards of comparison or norms. These ratio standards represent the appropriate ratio values for the typical firm in the industry. The implication is that the ratios of companies in the same industry should be very close to each other. Industry ratios are available from a number of sources. The more important ones are listed in Table 7•1, and Table 7•2 provides an example from Dun & Bradstreet.[8]

---

[8]To estimate an industry average, Dun & Bradstreet draws the year-end financial statement for 400,000 firms from its computerized financial statement file and categorizes each firm into one of the 125 industries it follows. Then 14 ratios are calculated for each company. Next, the individual ratio values are arranged by size, from strongest to weakest. The value that falls exactly in the middle of this series becomes the median or average for that ratio in that line of business.

TABLE 7•1   Major Sources of Industry and Other Comparative Ratios

Dun & Bradstreet. Dun & Bradstreet, Inc., annually publishes a survey of 125 different types of retailing, wholesaling, manufacturing, and construction companies. From their financial statements, statistics on the median, upper quartile, and lower quartile values for 14 key ratios are reported.

Robert Morris Associates. This national association of bank loan and credit officers compiles statistics on the median, upper quartile, and lower quartile values for 16 key ratios for over 300 lines of business by firm size and publishes them in its *Annual Statement Studies.*

Financial and investor services. *Standard & Poor's Industry Survey and Analyst's Handbook,* Moody's *Manuals* and *Handbook of Common Stocks,* and the *Value Line Investment Survey,* to name a few of the more popular services, provide comparative ratios on the companies and industries they follow.

Governmental agencies. The Federal Trade Commission (FTC) and the SEC have a joint publication called the *Quarterly Financial Report for U.S. Manufacturing Corporations.* It contains quarterly financial data such as common-size and other financial statements by firm size and by industry. The Small Business Administration and the U.S. Department of Commerce also issue periodic financial statement studies.

Trade associations. Various trade associations, such as the American Paper Institute and the National Retail Merchants Association, have staffs that collect financial data and compute standards for their respective industry members. This information is usually available upon request.

Business periodicals. *Business Week, Forbes,* and *Fortune* magazines provide summary data on a limited number of financial ratios on a regular basis.

Corporations' annual and quarterly reports. Many corporations now present different financial ratios in summary statements in their published stockholders reports and SEC 10-K reports.

Miscellaneous sources. Major commercial banks and public accounting firms also compile financial ratio statistics on their clients and customers. For example, the Accounting Corporation of America publishes its semiannual *Barometer for Small Business,* in which financial data for firms by sales and by geographical location are covered. Computerized financial data bases, such as the Compustat Investor Service (a subsidiary of Standard & Poor Corporation), contain a wealth of financial data that can be used to form industry ratios with relatively simple "canned programs." In addition, a publishing house, Prentice-Hall, makes available annually its *Almanac of Business and Industrial Financial Ratios,* which includes 10 financial ratios grouped by asset size. This service is also one of the few sources for ratios on industries in finance insurance and real estate.

TABLE 7•2 Examples of Dun & Bradstreet's 14 Ratios for 10 Manufacturing Industries[a]

Ratios	SIC 01 Agr. Production (No Breakdown) 1984 (2206 Estab.)			SIC 01 Agr. Production Northeast 1984 (252 Estab.)			SIC 01 Agr. Production Central 1984 (711 Estab.)			SIC 01 Agr. Production South 1984 (652 Estab.)		
	UQ	Med.	LQ	UQ	Med.	LQ	UQ	Med.	LQ	UQ	Med.	LQ
Solvency												
Quick ratio (times)	1.6	0.6	0.2	1.3	0.6	0.2	1.3	0.4	0.1	2.0	0.8	0.3
Current ratio (times)	4.5	1.7	0.9	4.1	1.4	0.8	4.2	1.6	0.9	5.2	2.1	1.0
Current liabilities to NW (%)	7.5	22.2	64.2	9.6	27.5	79.7	7.5	22.9	61.0	6.4	17.8	55.0
Current liabilities to inventory (%)	43.8	111.3	238.2	46.6	116.8	263.3	52.8	106.6	235.6	26.6	91.7	218.3
Total liabilities to NW (%)	19.8	55.9	129.8	19.4	64.5	138.2	22.0	59.3	151.8	18.6	46.4	106.2
Fixed assets to NW (%)	49.0	88.9	134.1	59.9	101.4	149.2	58.4	96.4	143.8	43.6	77.8	123.3
Efficiency												
Collection period (days)	9.4	24.4	48.5	12.4	25.9	48.5	7.3	19.3	39.0	8.7	22.6	46.7
Sales to inventory (times)	19.5	7.0	3.0	15.1	7.6	3.3	21.9	7.6	3.1	19.5	7.4	2.7
Assets to sales (%)	54.4	100.7	207.5	50.5	84.2	166.0	51.1	96.0	216.0	58.8	100.2	214.9
Sales to NWC (times)	12.0	4.8	2.3	12.8	5.4	2.5	11.3	4.8	2.4	12.2	4.0	2.1
Accounts payable to sales (%)	1.3	3.4	7.4	1.8	4.8	8.7	1.0	2.8	5.8	1.4	3.8	7.5
Profitability												
Return on sales (%)	15.0	6.4	1.6	10.8	5.6	(0.1)	14.4	5.7	2.0	17.2	7.8	2.2
Return on assets (%)	12.6	5.9	1.2	12.7	6.1	0.1	11.6	6.0	2.1	13.3	6.2	1.2
Return on NW (%)	24.1	10.6	2.1	24.9	12.9	1.4	20.5	10.3	3.0	25.3	10.3	2.3

Ratios	SIC 01 Agr. Production West 1984 (591 Estab.)			SIC 01 Agr. Production Industry Assets Under $100,000 1984 (174 Estab.)			SIC 01 Agr. Production Industry Assets $100,000–$500,000 1984 (715 Estab.)			SIC 01 Agr. Production Industry Assets $500,000–$1,000,000 1984 (456 Estab.)		
	UQ	Med.	LQ	UQ	Med.	LQ	UQ	Med.	LQ	UQ	Med.	LQ
Solvency												
Quick ratio (times)	1.7	0.7	0.3	2.1	0.8	0.2	1.9	0.7	0.3	1.5	0.6	0.2
Current Ratio (times)	3.9	1.7	1.0	4.9	1.5	0.7	5.1	1.7	0.9	4.1	1.7	0.8
Current liabilities to NW (%)	8.4	26.2	68.8	7.4	30.8	94.4	7.2	23.7	65.5	8.0	21.1	57.9
Current liabilities to invest (%)	60.1	122.5	248.2	26.6	103.3	183.7	36.8	98.7	213.2	44.7	107.1	237.9
Total liabilities to NW(%)	21.5	57.3	127.8	11.6	45.1	112.6	18.2	50.4	130.2	20.2	54.8	109.3
Fixed assets to NW (%)	46.3	87.1	124.8	41.1	70.2	109.7	48.9	86.0	133.2	51.5	95.4	129.6
Efficiency												
Collection period (days)	14.2	30.8	64.9	5.1	15.3	24.6	7.6	19.7	37.9	11.6	26.2	58.0
Sales to inventory (times)	18.7	5.9	2.7	25.9	14.5	6.2	18.2	8.0	3.3	15.4	5.2	3.0
Assets to sales (%)	57.1	113.1	210.8	23.4	35.7	63.1	44.4	76.7	145.5	72.7	117.0	224.5
Sales to NWC (times)	11.1	5.1	2.3	15.6	8.2	5.4	18.7	6.3	2.6	9.0	4.8	2.0
Accounts payable to sales (%)	1.5	3.3	7.5	1.2	2.7	4.9	1.3	3.3	6.9	1.3	3.5	8.7
Profitability												
Return on sales (%)	14.0	5.7	1.3	15.5	7.6	(0.1)	14.8	5.8	1.7	16.7	7.2	1.8
Return on assets (%)	11.8	4.7	0.9	42.6	18.3	0.1	15.4	7.7	2.0	9.0	5.1	0.9
Return on NW (%)	24.3	10.6	1.7	68.0	33.1	0.3	32.7	13.9	3.9	16.1	7.8	3.3

[a] The *median* represents the ratio value that falls exactly in the middle of the series. The *upper quartile* represents the ratio value lying halfway between the median and the top of the series. The *lower quartile* is the ratio value lying halfway between the median and the bottom of the series.

Source: Dun & Bradstreet, Inc. *Selected Key Business Ratios in 125 Lines of Business,* 1981; reprinted with permission.

To interpret an individual ratio value, one compares it to the industry average and then classifies it as being either "good," "satisfactory," or "poor," depending on the direction and extent to which it deviates from the average. A "poor" rating is given to a current ratio that is too low. Poor ratios normally indicate weaknesses or potential trouble spots that require further investigation. This investigation should reveal whether any serious problems exist and suggest what action might be taken to improve the situation. "Good" ratios, of course, indicate areas of major strength. The difficult part is assigning a rating to a particular ratio value. There are no hard-and-fast rules to follow; thus judgment and experience are the final criteria.

A ratio analysis of Byet Stores' most recent financial statements is presented next. Table 7•3 contains a summary of its ratios by categories and the industry averages.

TABLE 7•3   Byet Stores, Inc., Summary of Financial Ratios and Industry Averages, 1988

Ratio	Formula	Byet (1988)	Industry Average	Evaluation
Short-Term Solvency				
Current ratio	$\dfrac{\text{Current assets}}{\text{Current liabilities}}$	1.9	2.4	Poor
Quick ratio	$\dfrac{\text{Current assets} - \text{inventory} - \text{prepaid expenses}}{\text{Current liabilities}}$	1.03	0.8	Satisfactory
Long-Term Solvency				
Debt-equity ratio	$\dfrac{\text{Liabilities}}{\text{Total equity}}$	1.63	1.2	Poor
Times interest earned	$\dfrac{\text{Net profit before tax} + \text{interest expense}}{\text{Interest expenses}}$	3.1	2.6	Good
Fixed-charge coverage	$\dfrac{\text{Net profit before taxes} + \text{interest payments} + \text{lease and rental payments}}{\text{Interest expense} + \text{lease and rental payments}}$	1.7	1.5	Good
Asset Utilization				
Average collection period	$\dfrac{\text{Accounts receivable}}{\text{Sales per day}}$	43.7 days	20.9 days	Poor
Inventory turnover	$\dfrac{\text{Cost of goods sold}}{\text{Inventory}}$	4.4	3.3	Good
Fixed-asset turnover	$\dfrac{\text{Sales}}{\text{Fixed assets}}$	13.6	14.1	Satisfactory
Profitability				
Operating profit margin	$\dfrac{\text{Net Operating income}}{\text{Net sales}}$	6.5%	3.5%	Good
Net profit margin	$\dfrac{\text{Net income}}{\text{Net sales}}$	4.0%	1.6%	Good
Book *ROA*	$\dfrac{\text{Net Operating income }(1 - T)}{\text{Total assets}}$	13.99%	5.1%	Good
Book *ROE*	$\dfrac{\text{Net income}}{\text{Stockholders' equity}}$	26.67%	10.0%	Good

Short-Term Solvency

Normally, the higher the liquidity ratios, the better. This generalization should be viewed cautiously, however, because these ratios can be too high. A high current ratio, for example, may mask an excessive investment in current assets that is nonproductive.

This is not the case with Byet. Its current ratio is rated "poor" in Table 7•3, while the quick ratio receives a "satisfactory" rating. The low current ratio normally implies that Byet may have problems meeting its current obligations. The favorable quick ratio, which reflects only very liquid assets, indicates that this is not the situation.

The common-size balance sheet in Table 6•5 shows that, for its size, Byet has a below-average holding of inventories and an above-average amount of accounts receivable and current liabilities. From the definitions of the two liquidity ratios in Table 7•3, note first that if current liabilities are larger than average, the current ratio will be less than the industry's. Second, since Byet has less inventory than usual and since inventories are excluded from the numerator in the quick ratio, the quick ratio will tend to be higher than it would be if Byet had an average amount of inventory.

Three additional comments on liquidity ratios are in order. First, a better measure of an ability to pay bills on time would be an analysis of a firm's cash flow pattern, since bills are paid with cash rather than with other assets. Second, low liquidity ratios may also mean that a firm is very efficient in managing its cash position and does not need to maintain as liquid a position as other firms. This is a case where "poor" may actually be good. Third, low liquidity ratios may be only temporary. An intrafirm analysis will help determine if this is indeed so.

Long-Term Solvency

Byet's long-term solvency ratios also reveal a mixed picture. Its debt–equity ratio of 1.63 is considerably higher than the industry norm of 1.2, and a ratio value over 1.0 simply indicates that a higher proportion of debt than equity is being used to finance assets. Although there are advantages to borrowed funds, the financial manager should be concerned about the reaction of the firm's present (and future) creditors and stockholders to this relatively high level of debt. A high debt burden makes creditors less certain of receiving all their payments, and they therefore become reluctant to lend more money to Byet. Additional funds then have to carry a higher rate of interest to entice creditors into lending more money.

Stockholders, however, should be concerned because a higher debt–equity ratio and the resulting higher interest expenses imply that less income may be available to them. On the other hand, higher levels of debt carry the potential advantage of *financial leverage*—a topic examined closely in Chapter 8. Thus increasing debt may or may not be to the advantage of the stockholders. The financial manager needs to establish whether the firm's debt–equity ratio is consistent with the firm's financial policy, taking these trade-offs into consideration.

The times interest earned ratio receives a "good" rating, somewhat reducing the concern over Byet's high debt–equity ratio. This is because this coverage ratio focuses on the ability to service periodic interest payments out of current income. That is, the level of debt may be low or high, but it is the ability to meet debt obligations that really matters. For example, Byet's ratio of 3.1 suggests that future profits before taxes could drop to zero before its ability to pay interest becomes impaired. To see this, note from the definition of the times interest earned ratio that when net profits before taxes equal zero, interest expenses are just met and the ratio value is 1.0. Thus it may be tentatively concluded that Byet has a relatively small chance of defaulting on its debt interest. Of course, before this conclusion can be totally accepted, the financial manager must check the extent to which other fixed charges must come out of profits. The fixed charge coverage ratio is useful for this determination. Byet's 1988 fixed charge coverage ratio is 1.7, much better than the average for the industry. Thus the conclusion that the company's chances of default are not too high appears to be reasonable.

Asset Utilization

Byet's average collection period of 43.7 days is over twice the industry average of 20.9 days and is clearly a potential trouble spot. The most obvious reason, as seen earlier, is the disproportionate investment in accounts receivable for a retailer of Byet's size. Management must determine whether this investment is consistent with a good credit policy. That is, Byet's policy may be too lenient, or its customers may be slow in making payments or may even be defaulting on their obligations.

Byet's inventory turnover brings a "good" rating (i.e., it is turning over its inventory at a faster rate than the average retailer). On the surface, this implies a good job of keeping inventories at a low level (the common-size statement also indicated that Byet had a below-average holding of inventory). But this may be a case of "good, but too high." The reason is that good inventory management attempts to optimize—not minimize—inventory. Too low a level of inventories may reflect lost sales due to shortages. Only a closer inspection of Byet's inventory controls can tell.

Byet's fixed-asset utilization is neither too low nor too high. However, the financial manager does need to consider several things before drawing any conclusions. First, the book value of fixed assets changes little from year to year. There is normally a continuous process of depreciation and replacement of fixed assets. Moreover, as sales increase, fixed assets tend to increase such that the fixed asset turnover ratio does not change much from year to year. For this reason, it is better to examine this ratio over time rather than at a point in time. What the analyst must look for is any significant deviation from a relatively constant ratio level. Second, the use of book values may disguise important information. Because book values depend on the original cost, age, and rate of depreciation, it is possible for two firms to have similar assets and sales, but very different turnover ratios. The major implication of this fact is that a high or rising (improving) turnover ratio may be deceptive. It may just mean that a firm is operating with old plant and equipment. A failure to make new investments in fixed assets may prove disastrous if this situation continues because the firm will begin to lag in its industry and lose market share (i.e., lose sales and thereby reduce profits).

Profitability

Profitability ratios provide a yardstick to measure the overall effectiveness of prior managerial decisions—and the higher they are, the better. Byet's management clearly distinguishes itself in this area. Returns on sales and investments are all well above average and deserve a "good" rating.

Nevertheless, a few additional observations are necessary. First, profitability on sales refers to the ability to generate revenues in excess of expenses. Because operating profits are determined by the difference between sales and operating expenses, Byet's good operating profit margin indicates that its pricing policy and/or its cost controls are very effective. The net profit margin supports this conclusion and indicates that interest expenses are not too high (this supports the earlier conclusion about the interest coverage ratio).

The second observation is that the net profit margin of 4.0% is much closer to the industry average than is the operating margin. Because net profits are operating profits less interest expenses and taxes, Byet's high debt burden is revealed once again through its disproportionate effect on the net profit margin.

Third, Byet's good profitability picture applies only to a point in time. Perhaps it just got lucky that year, or perhaps 1988 was an exceptionally good year for the economy as a whole. The true test is to look at profitability over time. This will indicate whether 1988s results were a fluke. This comment applies equally to returns on investment. The intrafirm (trend) analysis discussed in the next section is designed for this very purpose—to examine the patterns in a firm's ratios through time.

INTERPRETING RATIOS WITH AN INTRAFIRM ANALYSIS

While the preceding interfirm analysis is helpful in assessing Byet's current condition, a number of questions regarding the interpretation of certain ratios' values were left unanswered. Specifically, should the financial manager be concerned about Byet's low liquidity and high average collection period and about whether its high profitability was only happenstance? Were these situations just temporary or, for example, did the poor ratios reflect a deterioration in those areas of Byet's operations?

These questions arise because the analysis dealt with data for only one year. Moreover, reliance on a single set of ratio values can often be misleading. An intrafirm analysis is important because it examines the historical pattern of each ratio and identifies those ratios that are deteriorating or improving over time. For example, a ratio rated "poor" may actually have been improving steadily for the last few years. In such a case, no remedial action may be necessary.

KEY CONCEPT: An **intrafirm analysis** interprets ratio values by examining the behavior of a firm's ratios over time. Because of the time dimension, intrafirm analysis may be considered a dynamic ratio analysis.

By taking an additional step and combining this information with the historical performance of the industry averages, a more complete picture of a firm's overall condition and performance emerges. Furthermore, knowledge of developing trends is useful in monitoring management's past decisions and policies and in deciding whether any future changes are required.

Figure 7•1 is a graphic representation of a trend analysis of Byet's questionable financial ratios for the last five years. The behavior of Byet's liquidity ratios confirms some of the earlier suspicions. These ratios have been below average for the last three years and have been in a downward trend until recently. It is now evident that management needs to investigate the cause of this deterioration. On a positive note, the current ratio recorded a slight improvement, so perhaps this problem has been corrected.

The trend analysis also shows that Byet's use of debt has exceeded the industry average over the entire time period, with 1985 witnessing a sharp increase in the debt–equity ratio to above 2.0. While a small decrease in debt utilization is noticeable, Byet has apparently overrelied on debt to finance its investments. A reduction in debt would seem advisable because any slowdown in sales could shrink Byet's excellent net profit margin and book return on equity.

The trend in Byet's average collection period has been below the industry average ratio. This seems to imply that there is a good reason for Byet's high collection period. Byet's excellent profitability picture is no fluke, as the trends in the profit margin and *ROA* indicate. Byet has consistently turned in an above-average performance in this area. The slight deterioration in 1987 in the net profit margin and *ROA* was due to a sharp increase in debt, but even these two ratios appear to be improving more recently.

In conclusion, management has several issues to investigate involving information not given in the financial statements. The interfirm and intrafirm analyses have identified those areas where performance deviated from the industry norm. Byet's weaknesses appear to be a poor liquidity position and high debt utilization. The high average collection period does not appear to be as serious a problem as was first thought. Nevertheless, management should keep an eye on its accounts receivable in case any further deviation from the norm occurs. Finally, Byet's profitability is clearly its greatest strength. Management has apparently promoted good pricing and cost control policies. Moreover, this strength has helped to offset an otherwise high debt burden.

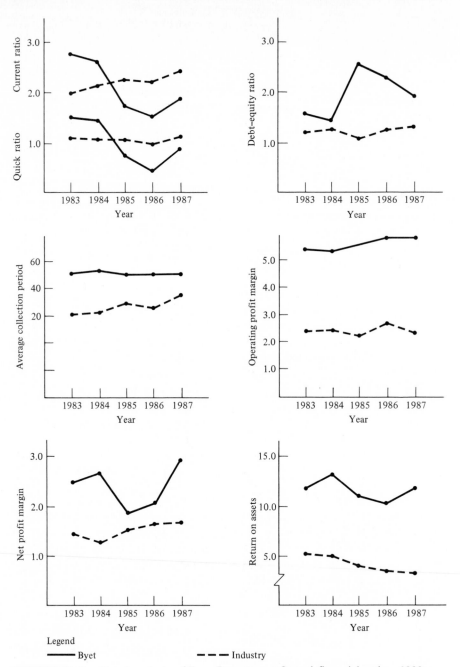

FIGURE 7·1 Trend analysis of Byet Department Stores' financial ratios, 1983–1987.

Learning Check for Section 7•2

Review Questions

7•6. A firm with a high net income is more profitable than a firm with a low net income. Is this statement true or false? Explain.

7•7. Can ratio analysis be used to evaluate the effectiveness of a firm's collections department? If it can, what kind of ratio analysis would be appropriate?

7•8. From a bondholder's perspective, which firm would be safer: one with a high or low fixed charge coverage ratio?

7•9. Comment on the following: A firm with very high liquidity ratios may not be using its assets effectively.

7•10. What is trend analysis? Is it interfirm or intrafirm analysis?

New Terms

Interfirm analysis   Intrafirm analysis   Trend analysis

SECTION 7•3   *Limitations of Ratio Analysis*

As seen during the analysis of Byet Stores, ratios indicate only good or poor performance; they do not provide an explanation for this performance. For this reason, ratios should be viewed only as a tool of analysis, not an end in itself. Unfortunately, some analysts lose sight of this fact and become too enamored of the mechanics of "number crunching." Moreover, there are several inherent limitations in any ratio study.

DIFFERENT ACCOUNTING PRACTICES

Ratios depend on accounting information and therefore are only as reliable as the accounting data. In addition, different firms in the same industry may follow different accounting practices for depreciation, inventory valuation, recognition of sales, and so on. This makes an interfirm analysis more difficult because the data must be adjusted for these differences in order to make the ratios comparable. To make matters worse, some managers are tempted to "smooth earnings" or to show continued growth in earnings by taking liberties with accounting practices.[9]

WHAT IS A GOOD OR A BAD RATIO?

It is not always easy to determine what a good or a bad ratio is. For example, a high quick ratio would seem to indicate a strong liquidity position, which is good, but in fact, this may be bad because excessive cash is a nonproductive asset that contributes little to profits. On the other hand, a low quick ratio may mean that management is very efficient in managing its cash flow. A high inventory turnover is often rated good but in fact, may be bad if the high turnover stems from inadequate inventory, resulting in lost sales and profits.

USE OF INDUSTRY AVERAGE RATIOS

An interfirm analysis of ratios resorts to **industry average ratios** as a standard of comparison in interpreting a firm's ratio levels. This approach assumes that all the companies falling into a particular industry produce the same product or service and thus have the same operating and financial characteristics. This is true in some cases but, in general, is not the rule.

Multiproduct Subsidiaries

Many products or services, especially those of large companies, cross industry lines. For example, Sears, Roebuck is classified as a "retailer-general merchandiser," yet Sears also has subsidiaries in insurance (Allstate), real estate (Coldwell Banker), and financial services (Dean Witter). Firms like this usually defy clear-cut industry identification. So, comparing the ratios of this type of firm with a single industry's average ratios may be mixing apples and oranges. In these cases, a company's activities must be broken up by lines of business (i.e., by industry) and separate sets of ratios calculated for each operation.

[9]In 1982 Datapoint Corporation, a one-time favorite among computer companies, saw its 10-year growth rate of 40% per year come to a screeching halt. Up to that point, management had apparently taken advantage of the accounting practice of recording revenues as soon as products were shipped in order to maintain its enviable growth record. This meant that at the end of the quarter, Datapoint employees were working overtime to get shipments out of the door in order to beef up quarterly results at the last minute. Eventually, Datapoint ended up choking on a glut of unwanted computers that were returned by distributors. The result: profits dropped, and the stock market rewarded Datapoint with an 80% plunge in stock price, from around $60 per share to a low of $12.

Industry Performance

Like individual companies, an industry may be growing or facing a decline in the demand for its products. Using industry average ratios implicitly assume the former case (i.e., performance is satisfactory on average). If, on the other hand, an industry has failing health, comparing a firm's ratios against the industry average simply shows that a firm is an average sick firm. A better practice is to compare a firm's ratios with the ratios of the industry's leaders.

Same Product

The use of industry ratios assumes that firms make or sell the same product and therefore have the same business characteristics. This is not always a valid conclusion. For example, The Limited is a retailer specializing in the sale of medium-priced fashion apparel for younger women. Pic'n'Save, on the other hand, specializes in the sale of close-out or discontinued lines of merchandise at 40 to 70% off the original retail price. Although these two firms are grouped in the same industry, they have very different operating characteristics. The Limited tends to have a high profit margin but low turnover ratios; Pic'n'Save tends to have a lower profit margin but high turnover ratios. Therefore, industry averages do not represent a target or norm that a firm must achieve to receive a satisfactory rating. Rather, industry averages provide only a general guideline as to what is good, satisfactory, or poor. Any ratio that departs from the "norm" should only be interpreted to mean that further investigation and analysis are necessary.

Learning Check for Section 7•3

Review Questions

7•11. What are the weaknesses inherent in ratio analysis?

7•12. How can different accounting practices affect ratio analysis?

7•13. What limitations must be considered when using industry average ratios? How might these factors affect the validity of your analysis?

New Term

Industry average ratios

SECTION 7·4 *Other Users and Applications of Ratio Analysis*

OTHER USERS OF RATIOS

Up to this point in the chapter, ratio analysis has been studied primarily from the perspective of management. However, a number of other parties are often just as interested in assessing a firm's operational performance and financial condition. For convenience, they can be classified into four groups: (1) short-term creditors, (2) long-term creditors, (3) stockholders, and (4) other interested parties. Each group has different objectives in mind when it looks at a firm's financial statement and, hence, each group tends to emphasize different types of ratios in its analysis.

Short-Term Creditors

Short-term creditors, such as a commercial bank or trade creditors, are most interested in liquidity ratios because their orientation is on the short-term performance of a firm. A bank wants to determine whether a firm holds an adequate amount of liquid assets because the bank wants assurance that its short-term loan will be repaid. A trade creditor seeks some guarantee that a firm is solvent enough to pay promptly for any goods or services that have been bought on credit.

Long-Term Creditors

On the other hand, long-term creditors or lenders, such as bondholders, look at long-term solvency and profitability ratios. They prefer, for example, a low debt–equity ratio because it affords more protection of their principal if the firm falls on troubled times and has to liquidate its assets. High coverage ratios are desirable because they indicate a margin of safety in that income can drop without inhibiting the scheduled payment of interest. Long-term creditors are also concerned about profitability because a healthy firm is one that will be around for a while. So, in a sense, lenders have two viewpoints. They have an interest both in investing in a successful, ongoing operation and in protecting themselves from the possibility of default and liquidation.

Stockholders

A firm's stockholders are interested in the returns on their share of the invested funds and in the effect of these results on the value of their investment.

Investment value is affected by all phases of a firm's operations and financing. Like management, stockholders want to examine all four types of ratios. Inadequate liquidity may lead to insolvency, excessive debt and interest may cause bankruptcy, and poor asset utilization and low profitability may discourage additional investments by investors. All of these problems decrease the value of equity.

Other Interested Parties

The final group is a catchall group containing a wide variety of individuals, each with his or her own objectives. For example, labor unions want to assess the firm's ability to pay wages, while the IRS needs to measure the reliability of tax receipts. Other interested groups include investment bankers, investment advisors, law firms, and regulatory and governmental agencies.

OTHER APPLICATIONS OF FINANCIAL RATIO ANALYSIS

Ratios find other applications in financial analysis: **credit scoring, debt ratings,** bankruptcy tests, and **security analysis.**

Credit Scoring

An important application of financial ratios is to the credit or loan decisions of commercial banks and other financial institutions. In fact, banks are perhaps the major user of financial analysis for purposes of credit evaluation. A credit decision involves many factors. When a bank receives a new loan application, decisions on whether a loan should be granted, the interest rate to be charged, the loan amount, and collateral for the loan must be made. Financial ratios are often used in this process, which is called a **numerical credit scoring model.**

Instead of examining each ratio individually, a credit scoring system combines ratios by assigning a predetermined weight to each ratio value and summing these weights to arrive at an overall credit rating. This credit rating is then used to distinguish good from bad loans. Which specific ratios are critical to the analysis usually depends on the past loan experience, with borrowers' characteristics and other variables representing industry and economic factors.

Debt Rating

Until recently, decisions to extend credit were based upon a close personal relationship, such as between a bank and its corporate client. But the enormous size of today's credit market for publicly held corporate debt makes necessary some type of impersonal credit judgment. Another **credit analysis** tool that relies heavily on financial ratios is the debt ratings assigned to the different issues of corporations. These debt ratings assist creditors and investors in making their investment decisions by providing an easily recognizable yet simple measure that links a possibly unknown issuer of debt with a symbol of credit quality. Each debt rating becomes an indication of the creditworthiness of the firm with respect to a specific debt issue.

The details of the rating process are found in Appendix 5•C. A main ingredient that a rating agency uses to determine a firm's ability to make timely payments of principal and interest is a financial statement analysis, especially ratio analysis. Special emphasis is placed on ratios relating income and cash flow to debt service. Thus, coverage ratios are of considerable importance. Rating agencies also examine such ratios as operating profit margins, return on capital, and *ROA*. The ultimate criterion for assigning a rating is difficult to state with precision because of its proprietary nature and because subjective judgment and experience enter into the final decision. Nevertheless, a significant part of debt rating involves analyzing the relationship between different financial items.

Financial Distress or Bankruptcy Tests

A firm that fails to make a scheduled payment of either interest or principal on a bank loan or on its bonds is said to be in *default* on that obligation. If payment is not forthcoming soon, litigation procedures will inevitably begin, which will force liquidation of the firm's assets. Any proceeds are then divided up among the various creditors—leaving the stockholders with what is left (if anything).

Clearly, creditors and investors want to avoid this messy situation so as to avert or minimize losses. So the question becomes: Can financial analysis allow you to forecast financial distress ahead of time? In other words, can an "early warning system" be devised to predict bankruptcy? There is considerable evidence that an analysis of a firm's financial ratios can do just this. For example, it has been shown that the financial ratios of firms that subsequently fail are significantly different (poorer) from those of firms that survive. The ratios of failed firms sometimes demonstrate a remarkable deterioration as many as five years before bankruptcy. Moreover, failed firms tend to have lower returns on sales and assets than nonfailed firms. They also have more debt, lower current ratios, and less cash.

Security Analysis of Common Stocks

Security analysis determines the value of different common stocks and the levels of risk and return associated with them. The objectives of security analysis are to find common stocks of quality corporations selling at undervalued prices and to monitor the current and expected performance of individual companies and their industries. The final product of this effort usually comes in the form of specific buy, sell, or hold recommendations on underpriced, overpriced, and fairly priced stocks, respectively.

A significant portion of a security analyst's job involves analyzing annual and interim stockholders' reports and performing ratio analyses of the financial statements. From this the analyst forms judgments and forecasts about a corporation's present strengths and past performance, which are then used as indications of what can be anticipated in the future. The primary focus is on assessing the earning power or profitability of the firm. While there are more than a dozen ways to compute the earning power of a corporation, every security analyst has a preferred method—usually some variation of our accounting return on investment.[10]

Moreover, like the owners of a firm, security analysts are also interested in the firm's liquidity position, its long-term solvency position, and the utilization of its assets. But security analysts go beyond ratio analysis. They evaluate a company's pricing policies, sales record, marketing success, research and development, competitive position, and industry's prospects; they appraise the quality of management; and they estimate future earnings and dividends.

Learning Check for Section 7·4

Review Questions

7·14. Which ratios would a labor union be interested in? Why?

7·15. How do the ratios used by short-term creditors differ from those of interest to long-term creditors?

7·16. What does credit scoring mean? How are ratios used in credit scoring?

7·17. If you were concerned with the bankruptcy risk of a specific firm, which ratio would you examine? What type of ratio analysis would you utilize?

New Terms

Credit analysis	Debt rating	Security analysis
Credit scoring	Numerical credit scoring model	

---

[10]For example, security analysts preparing the *Value Line Investment Survey* prefer what they call the *percentage earned on capital:*

$$\text{Percentage earned on capital} = \frac{\text{after-tax profit} + \frac{1}{2} \text{ interest on long-term debt}}{\text{stockholders' equity} + \text{long-term debt}}$$

SUMMARY

The Types of Financial Ratios

Ratio analysis is the study of financial statements through the computation of specific ratios that provide further information regarding specific aspects of the firm's operations. Ratios are classified into one of four categories: short-term solvency, long-term solvency, asset utilization, and profitability.

Uses of Ratio Analysis

The ratios computed are compared to a standard, typically one drawn from published sources. Depending on the nature of the information sought, either an interfirm or an intrafirm analysis can be performed. Interfirm analysis involves the comparison of a firm's ratios to those of other firms in its industry or to an industry average. Intrafirm analysis consists of examining the trends in a firm's ratios over time.

Limitations of Ratio Analysis

Ratio analysis should be viewed as a tool rather than as an end in itself. This is particularly true because of the several limitations of ratios derived from financial statements. Different accounting practices across firms, the difficulties in using industry averages, and the problems in determining good and bad ratios make ratio analysis an imperfect guide for decision making.

Other Users and Applications of Financial Ratios

Financial ratios, when properly employed, can be useful tools. Besides the firm's management, ratio analysis may be used by short-term creditors, long-term creditors, stockholders, and others. Ratio analysis has many applications besides managerial decision making, including credit scoring, debt ratings, bankruptcy tests, and security analysis.

PROBLEMS

7•1. The December 31, 1984, balance sheet and income statement for May-berry Cafeterias, Inc. are given.
   (a) Compute the specified ratios, and compare them to the industry average (better or worse).

(b) If you were appointed financial manager of the company, what decisions would you make based on your findings?

Balance Sheet

Cash	$ 17	Accounts payable	$ 7
Marketable securities	5	Notes payable	3
Accounts receivable	3	Taxes payable	2
Inventory	16	Other accruals	3
Prepaid expenses	6	Current liabilities	$ 15
Current assets	$ 47		
		Long-term debt	$ 35
Gross plant and equipment	$126	Preferred stock	10
Less: Accumulated		Common stock	20
depreciation	(57)	Capital contributed	
Net plant and equipment	69	in excess of par	10
		Retained earnings	26
Total assets	$116	Total liabilities and	
		stockholders' equity	$116

Income Statement

Net sales	$1,072
Cost of goods sold	921
Gross profit	151
Selling expense	86
General and administrative expense	26
Depreciation	6
Net operating income	$ 33
Interest expense	4
Profit before taxes	$ 29
Taxes	12
Net income	$ 17

Ratios to Compute	1984 Mayberry	Better or Worse	1984 Industry Average (%)
Current			2.86
Quick			2.31
Debt–equity			0.51
Times interest period			12.36
Average collection period			1.06
Inventory turnover			95.71
Fixed-asset turnover			16.15
Operating profit margin			0.036
Net profit margin			0.019
Book return on assets			0.192
Book return on equity			0.271

7•2. On January 1, 1982, you appointed Tanya Dawkins as financial planner and manager for your family-owned local chain of seafood restaurants. Using the company's balance sheets for the last three years (shown here), evaluate her performance in each of the following areas: improving the firm's short-term solvency, asset utilization, and profitability.

Balance Sheets		Dec. 31, 1982 (Thousands)		Dec. 31, 1983 (Thousands)		Dec. 31, 1984 (Thousands)
Cash		$ 27		$ 28		$ 32
Marketable securities		16		18		13
Accounts receivable		21		18		13
Inventory		13		17		18
Current assets		$ 77		$ 81		$ 76
Gross plant and equipment	$192		$198		$219	
Less accumulated depreciation	(61)		(66)		(74)	
Net plant and equipment		131		132		145
Total assets		$208		$213		$221
Accounts payable		$ 29		$ 26		$ 20
Wages payable		3		3		4
Notes payable		52		56		60
Total current liabilities		$ 84		$ 85		$ 84
Long-term debt		60		60		60
Common stock		20		20		20
Additional paid-in capital		20		20		20
Retained earnings		24		28		37
Total liabilities and stockholders' equity		$208		$213		$221

Income Statements	12/31/82 (Thousands)	12/31/83 (Thousands)	12/31/84 (Thousands)
Sales	$912	$921	$942
Cost of goods sold	827	833	851
Gross profit	$ 85	$ 88	$ 91
Selling expense	37	41	46
General and administrative	27	24	10
Depreciation	4	5	7
Net operating income	$ 17	$ 18	$ 28
Interest	12	11	10
Taxable income	$ 5	$ 7	$ 18
Taxes	2	3	7
Net income	$ 3	$ 4	$ 11

Ratios	1982	1983	1984	1984 Industry Average (%)
Current ratio			.905 w	1.36
Quick ratio			.69 w	1.21
Debt–equity		14½/7	1.87 w	1.03
Times interest earned			2.8 w	4.51
Average collection period			5.04 w	4.96
Inventory turnover			47.3 W	117.8
Fixed-asset turnover			6.497 w	7.61
Operating profit margin			.0297 w	0.036
Net profit margin			.0117 w	0.012
Book return on assets			.077 w	0.098
Book return on equity			.1143 B	0.113

7·3. Given the ratio values for the following firm, fill in the blanks in its balance sheet and income statement.

Cash	$ 100,000	Accounts payable	$ 150,000	
Marketable securities	50,000	Notes payable	50,000	
Accounts receivable	150,000	Long-term debt	300,000	
Inventory	100,000	Common stock	300,000	
Net plant and equipment	600,000	Retained earnings	200,000	stockholders
		Total liabilities and stockholders'		
Total assets	$1,000,000	equity	$1,000,000	TA = FA + CA
Sales	$1,200,000	Ratios:		1,000,000
Cost of goods sold	840,000	Current	2.0	
Gross profit	360,000	Quick	1.5	
Fixed costs	300,000	Times interest earned	6	
Net operating income	60000	Debt–equity	1	
Interest	10,000	Gross profit margin	0.30	
Taxes	40,000	Book return		
Net income	$ 10,000	on equity	0.02	

(handwritten notes in left margin:) gross profit margin = net sales − CGS / net sales

7·4. The balance sheet and income statement for Genco Olive Oil Co. as of December 31, 1984 are as follows:

Cash	$ 26	Accounts payable	$ 42
Marketable securities	3	Notes payable	31
Accounts receivable	13	Current liabilities	$ 73
Inventory	28	Long-term debt	43
Current assets	$ 70	Common stock	38
Net fixed assets	114	Retained earnings	30
Total assets	$184	Total liabilities and stockholders' equity	$184

Sales	$835
Cost of goods sold	631
Gross profit	$204
Fixed costs	187
Net operating income	$ 17
Interest	11
Earnings before taxes	$ 6
Taxes	3
Net income	$ 3

Genco is considering the purchase of some oil processors on credit from your firm. Mr. Jenkins of the collections department reports that another firm, Barzini Oil, is considered a marginal client because of its high credit risk and recommends that your firm not extend credit to any firm riskier than Barzini. Barzini's current ratio is 0.98, its quick ratio is 0.81, and its inventory turnover is 36.1. Compute these ratios for Genco and, on that basis, decide whether or not credit should be extended.

7•5. At the same time, Genco applies to a bank for a three-year loan. The bank had loaned money earlier to Barzini and, based on past experience, has decided not to lend money to any firm riskier than Barzini. However, the bank uses different ratios for making the decision—the debt–equity ratio and the times interest ratio. If these two ratios for Barzini are 1.32 and 2.56, respectively, would the bank loan money to Genco?

7•6. The common-size balance sheet and income statement (in percent) for Lyon Publications as of December 31, 1988 are given below. Lyon's level of cash on December 31, 1988 was $20,000 and interest paid during 1988 was $90,000.

Cash	5	Accounts payable	8
Marketable securities	3	Notes payable	5
Accounts receivable	9	Wages payable	2
Inventory	12	Current liabilities	15
Current assets	29	Long-term debt	30
Net fixed assets	71	Common stock	30
Total assets	100	Retained earnings	25
		Total liabilities and stockholders' equity	100

Sales	100
Cost of goods sold	65
Gross profit	35

General, selling, and administrative expense	21
Net operating income	14
Interest	6
Taxes	4
Net income	4

(a) Determine Lyon's balance sheet and income statement (in dollars) as of December 31, 1988.

(b) Calculate the following ratios for Lyon as of December 31, 1988.

Current ratio	Fixed-asset turnover
Quick ratio	Operating profit margin
Debt-equity ratio	Net profit margin
Times interest earned	Book return on assets
Average collection period	Book return on equity
Inventory turnover	

7·7. John Easterwood recently inherited a large sum of money and is considering the purchase of one of two family-owned companies for sale in his hometown of Eastaboga, Alabama. The two firms are the Ancel Grocery Store and Starks Furniture Store. The balance sheets and income statements for these firms are given below.

	Ancel Grocery	Starks Furniture
Income Statements		
Sales	$1,200	$200
Cost of goods sold	960	100
Gross profit	$ 240	$100
General, selling, and administrative expense	210	32
Net operating income	$ 30	$ 68
Interest	6	20
Taxes	12	24
Net Income	$ 12	$ 24
Balance Sheets		
Cash	$ 30	$ 15
Marketable securities	10	5
Accounts receivable	30	40
Inventory	20	60
Current assets	$ 90	$120
Net fixed assets	110	120
Total assets	$200	$240

	Ancel Grocery	Starks Furniture
Balance Sheets		
Accounts payable	$ 15	$ 20
Notes payable	15	40
Current liabilities	$ 30	$ 60
Long-term debt	25	30
Common stock	85	70
Retained earnings	60	80
Total liabilities and stockholders' equity	$200	$240

(a) Calculate the operating profit margin ratio, the net profit margin ratio, the book return on assets, and the book return on equity for each firm.

(b) What advice would you give Mr. Easterwood? What are the weaknesses of a recommendation to purchase either company using these data?

READINGS

ALTMAN, EDWARD I., "Financial Ratios, Discriminant Analysis and the Prediction of Corporate Bankruptcy," *Journal of Finance*, September 1968, 589–609.

FINDLAY, M. CHAPMAN III, AND EDWARD E. WILLIAMS, "Toward More Adequate Debt Service Coverage Ratios," *Financial Analysts Journal*, November–December 1975, 58–61.

Standard & Poor's Rating Guide (New York: McGraw-Hill Book Company, 1985).

8

The Impact of Operating and Financial Decisions on the Firm

Operating and financial decisions affect a firm's pattern of cash flows, and this is best seen through the concept of *leverage*. Leverage is an important concept that refers to the use of assets and liabilities bearing fixed costs. In particular, operating leverage results from the existence of fixed operating costs; financial leverage occurs when sources of financing have fixed costs (e.g., fixed-interest payments on debt).[1]

Through the judicious use of both types of leverage, a firm attempts to increase the returns to its stockholders. This occurs whenever the firm earns returns greater than the fixed costs associated with its assets and liabilities. This excess then flows through as an additional return to the owners. Leverage, however, increases the variability of these returns by magnifying stockholders' potential losses as well as potential gains. How and why this is true will be seen subsequently.

This chapter consists of four sections.

SECTION 8·1: *Linear Break-Even Analysis.* This section presents the concept of break-even analysis and shows how sales volume and operating costs affect profits.

---

[1] In this chapter the word *costs* refers to accounting rather than opportunity costs. In discussing profits and cash flow, accounting costs are relevant. It is in the context of *valuing* cash flows that opportunity costs are relevant.

SECTION 8·2: *Operating Leverage.* The role of fixed costs is explained in the context of operating leverage.

SECTION 8·3: *Financial Leverage.* Financial leverage is the primary subject of this section. The role of interest payments in magnifying a firm's profits and losses is discussed.

SECTION 8·4: *Combined or Total Leverage.* In this section, we introduce the concept of combined leverage and establish its relationship to operating and financial leverage.

SECTION 8·1 *Linear Break-Even Analysis*

The first important concept in this chapter is **break-even analysis.** What is it, and how does it help financial managers?

Break-even analysis tells the manager how profits will vary when production costs, sales volume, and selling price vary. This is why it is sometimes called *cost-volume-profit (CVP) analysis.*[2] As stressed in Chapter 1, it is cash flows, not profits, that affect the wealth of the stockholders. However, profit considerations cannot be ignored because profits are a component of cash flow.

To illustrate the relationship among cost, volume, and profits, consider the startup of a new manufacturing operation. Initially, production volume is low, sales revenues are insufficient to cover all costs, and therefore operating losses occur. As production and sales volume begin to pick up, losses decrease. So the immediate objective of the financial manager is to reach, as quickly as possible, the **break-even point,** where revenues exactly offset all operating costs. Break-even analysis is helpful in identifying this break-even point.

KEY CONCEPT: The **break-even point** or **break-even quantity** is that level of production and sales at which total revenues (or dollar sales) are exactly equal to total operating costs (*TC*). That is, the break-even point occurs at that production level at which the net operating income (*NOI*) is zero.

From this definition, the meaning of *net operating income* should be clear:

$$\text{Net operating income} = \text{dollar sales} - \text{total operating costs} \qquad (8\text{-}1)$$

$$NOI = S - TC$$

NOI, sometimes called *operating profits*, deals only with revenues and pro-

---

[2] It has been this author's experience that even some of the largest multidivisional U.S. companies require a *CVP* analysis from each division manager before budgets are prepared or before funds are allocated to that division.

duction costs. Nonoperating costs such as taxes and financial costs (e.g., interest expenses) are not included at this stage. Their role is described later.

It is useful to examine equation (8-1) more closely in order to focus on the terms *revenue* and *operating costs*.

REVENUES

Revenue refers to the total dollar amount that a firm derives from selling its goods and services. It is calculated by multiplying the selling price per unit (P) and the quantity of units sold (Q), that is, $S = P \times Q$. For example, if the Lumen Light Company wants to manufacture and sell the "eternal light bulb" for $10 per bulb, Figure 8·1 shows that the more bulbs Lumen sells, the larger are its revenues.

OPERATING COSTS

Operating costs are divided into three categories: fixed, variable, and semi-fixed or semivariable.

Fixed Operating Costs

Fixed operating expenses (e.g., depreciation and insurance) do not vary with the level of production (i.e., they are fixed). They are incurred whether the firm produces 100 or 100,000 units. Suppose the Lumen Light Company purchases a machine that can produce 300,000 bulbs per year and costs $200,000. This cost must be borne at any level of production up to 300,000 bulbs and is thus a fixed cost.

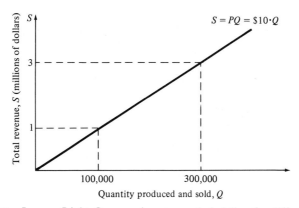

FIGURE 8·1 Lumen Light Company's revenue (sales) line for different levels of quantity sold. It is assumed here, as in the text, that the firm sells everything it produces.

But what if the company wants to make 400,000 light bulbs a year? In this case, another machine must be bought to increase plant capacity. This will result in an increase in fixed costs. Because even **fixed costs** change when a firm expands its plant capacity, a more precise definition of fixed costs is:

KEY CONCEPT: Fixed operating costs (F) are those costs that do not depend on the number of units produced *within a given range of production.*

The definition of fixed costs (F) reveals that in the long run, fixed costs typically do not remain fixed because ongoing companies continue to expand and grow, increasing their fixed costs along the way.

Because break-even analysis deals with fixed operating costs and because these costs are fixed only for a given plant capacity (or range of production), break-even analysis is valid only over the short run.

Variable Operating Costs

In contrast to fixed operating costs, variable operating costs have a close relationship to the level of production and sales. Items such as direct labor wages and the cost of raw materials fall into this category.

KEY CONCEPT: Variable operating costs are those expenses that vary directly with the level of production and sales.

Note that it is the total variable operating costs (TVC) that increase or decrease as the quantity produced increases or decreases. On the other hand, the variable cost per unit (V) is constant. Thus:

$$\text{Total variable costs} = \text{variable cost per unit} \times \text{quantity produced} \quad (8\text{-}2)$$

$$TVC = V \times Q$$

Equation (8-2) illustrates the significance of the words *varies directly with production.* If production increases by 5%, TVC will also increase by 5%. TOC can now be defined as

$$\text{Total operating costs} = \text{fixed operating costs} \quad\quad\quad (8\text{-}3)$$
$$+ \text{ total variable operating costs}$$

$$TOC = F + TVC$$

Semifixed or Semivariable Operating Costs

Semifixed or **semivariable** operating **costs** are "hybrids" because a portion of these costs is fixed, while another portion is variable. Semifixed costs are perhaps better explained with examples than through formal definitions. Table 8•1 contains examples of what accountants typically call fixed and variable costs. The footnoted items need a closer look.

Executive salaries are listed as a fixed expense because officers draw their salary regardless of how much a company produces and sells. But suppose that Lumen decides to pay its president $110,000 a year and an incentive bonus of $1,000 for each 1% increase over last year's production and sales. Is the president's salary a fixed or a variable cost to the company? It is fixed over a certain range of production but then becomes variable over another range. Energy costs may behave in a similar manner. Although one normally thinks of energy bills rising with the firm's production, energy bills often include a minimum or base charge (fixed cost) to which is added a variable portion for energy consumed above a certain amount.

It is not always easy to categorize operating costs as either fixed or variable because they may, in fact, be semifixed or semivariable. In those cases where a cost is semifixed, a portion of it must be carefully allocated to fixed costs and another portion to variable costs.

Developing Cost Lines

Once all operating costs have been classified, *cost lines* can be constructed in a graph. Assume that Lumen's fixed cost is $1 million and its variable cost is $5 per unit. At a production level of 300,000 bulbs, Lumen's total variable cost is $1.5 million. Equation (8-3) indicates that the total operating cost is the sum of the fixed and variable operating expenses, so it is convenient to add the fixed and variable operating costs to get the total operating costs, as shown in Figure 8•2. This diagram indicates more clearly that the total operating expenses are $2.5 million for 300,000 light bulbs. This diagram greatly facilitates the determination of the break-even point.

To find Lumen's break-even point, superimpose Figure 8•1 on Figure 8•2 to obtain Figure 8•3. The break-even point, $Q^\star$, is found at the intersection of the TC and total revenue lines. For Lumen, this occurs at a production and sales

TABLE 8•1 Common Examples of Fixed and Variable Costs

Fixed Costs	Variable Costs
Executive salaries[a]	Direct labor
Staff salaries	Raw materials
Insurance	Energy[a]
Property taxes	Packaging and shipping
Rentals	Sales commissions
Depreciation	Advertising[b]

[a]Items that typically have both fixed and variable cost components.
[b]Can also be a fixed cost.

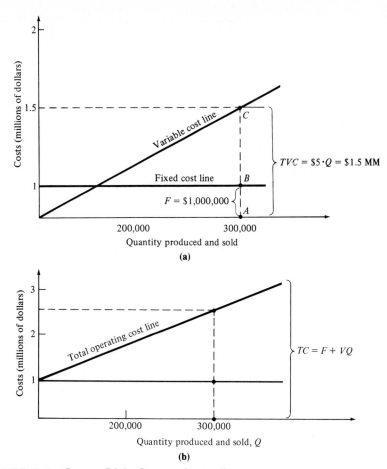

FIGURE 8•2   Lumen Light Company's cost line.

level of 200,000 units. Figure 8•3 also indicates that at levels of production to the right of $Q^\star$ (say, $Q = 300,000$), the firm realizes a profit, while to the left of $Q^\star$ (say, $Q_1 = 10,000$), the firm suffers a loss. To make things clearer, assume that Lumen produces and sells 300,000 units (i.e., a quantity greater than its break-even point). Then, using equation (8-1), we have

$$\text{Net operating income} = \text{total revenues} - \text{total operating costs} \quad (8\text{-}4)$$

$$
\begin{aligned}
NOI &= S - TC \\
&= PQ - (F + VQ) \\
&= \$10 \times 300{,}000 - (\$1{,}000{,}000 + \$5 \times 300{,}000) \\
&= \$500{,}000
\end{aligned}
$$

If Figure 8•3 were drawn to scale on graph paper, the break-even point could be found quickly. But there is an easier way. The following equation yields the answer directly:

254

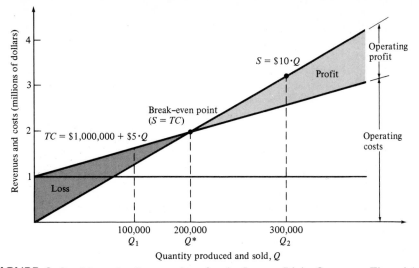

FIGURE 8·3   Linear break-even chart for the Lumen Light Company. Financial data: $F = \$1,000,000$; $V = \$5$; $P = \$10$.

$$Q^\star = \frac{F}{(P - V)} \tag{8-5}$$

where $Q^\star$ is the break-even point. Using the information on fixed costs, sales price per unit, and variable cost per unit yields

$$Q^\star = \frac{\$1,000,000}{(\$10 - \$5)} = 200{,}000 \text{ light bulbs}$$

the same result that was obtained using the graphic approach. $P - V$ in the denominator of equation (8-5), called the **contribution margin** *per unit*, denotes the dollar amount that each unit sold will contribute to meeting fixed costs. Once break even is attained, $P - V$ measures the amount that each unit will contribute to profits. For an example of contribution margin analysis, see the highlight "Contribution Margin in Action."

■■ *HIGHLIGHT*

CONTRIBUTION MARGIN IN ACTION:
CONTINENTAL AIRLINES

One measure of an airline's productivity, and hence potential profits, is its "load factor," which may be defined as the average percentage of its available passenger seats filled per flight. The national average is about 60 to 65% during normal economic periods. So if an airline's management finds that only 50% of its available seats are being filled, it would appear that by eliminating a few of its less popular flights (e.g., its 3:11 A.M. flight out of Steamboat Springs, Colorado) it should be able to raise its average load and thereby its profits. However, it does not work that way. Surprisingly, this is because the improved load factor would actually mean reduced profits. This conclusion stems from the concept of *contribution margin.*

Consider, the case of Continental Airlines, Inc., to see how Continental's economic planners translated contribution margin analysis into hard, dollar-and-cents decisions and how the old business adage "Nobody ever made a profit without meeting all costs" is misleading.

Put simply, contribution margin analysis suggests that a company should undertake any new activity that adds more to revenues than it does to "costs"— and not limit itself to those activities whose revenues equal "fully allocated" (or variable plus allocated fixed operating costs). It is important to recognize that in this context, the word "costs" refers to what we have been calling "variable operating expenses." Also, while we have discussed contribution margin on a "per unit" basis $(P - V)$, here we are referring to this margin on a "total dollar" basis (i.e., revenues minus variable costs).

Now, for Continental's approach: They first required that the entire schedule of flights return at least their fully allocated costs. Fixed costs such as overhead, depreciation, and insurance are real expenses and must be covered. The out-of-pocket costs come into play only *after* the basic schedule has been set. They then see if *adding* more flights will contribute to the corporate net income. Similarly, if they are thinking of *dropping* a flight with a disappointing record, they put it under the contribution margin microscope, and if the revenues will be more than their out-of-pocket costs, they keep the flight.

By "out-of-pocket costs" Continental means just that: the actual dollars that Continental has to pay out to run a flight (i.e., the variable operating expenses). They get this figure not by applying any hypothetical equations but by circulating a proposed schedule to every operating department concerned and finding out just what extra expenses it will entail. If a ground crew already on duty can service the plane, the flight is not charged a penny of their salary expense. There may even be some costs eliminated in running the flight: They will not need workers to roll an incoming plane to a hanger, for instance, or to rent an overnight hanger if it flies to another stop. The caption below illustrates how Continental's thinking might run with regard to a proposal for an additional flight to Mineral Wells, Texas.

Contribution Margin Analysis in a Nutshell

Problem: Should Continental Airlines add an extra daily flight from Houston to Mineral Wells?

The facts:

1. Fully allocated (total operating) costs of this flight: $4,500.

2. Out-of-pocket (variable) costs of this flight: $2,000.

3. Revenues generated by this flight: $3,100.

Decision: Run the flight. It will add $1,100 (contribution margin in total dollars) to net profit (and to covering fixed costs) because it will add $3,100 to revenues and only $2,000 to costs. Overhead and other fixed costs, totaling $2,500

($4,500 − $2,000), would be incurred whether or not the flight is run. Therefore, the fully allocated costs of $4,500 are not relevant to this business decision. It is the out-of-pocket (variable) costs that count.

Source: Adapted from information provided in various trade journals.

So far, the discussion has involved revenues, fixed and variable operating costs, and determination of the break-even point. Equation (8-5) can be used in other ways, too; it can provide a useful planning tool for decisions under "what if" conditions. For example, what if Lumen's fixed costs were increased by 40%, from $1.0 to $1.4 million, due to further automation of the production process? What would happen to the break-even point? It would increase to

$$Q^\star = \frac{\$1,400,000}{(\$10 - \$5)} = 280,000 \text{ light bulbs}$$

If Lumen's management decided to raise its selling price by 20% to $12 per unit to offset the higher fixed costs, what would be the effect on the break-even point? It would move back to

$$Q^\star = \frac{\$1,400,000}{(\$12 - \$5)} = 200,000 \text{ light bulbs}$$

As can be seen, break-even analysis is a valuable aid in assessing the impact of changes in sales price and operating costs on a firm's break-even point and profitability.

OTHER USES OF BREAK-EVEN ANALYSIS

With the rapid development of computer-based financial planning systems, break-even analysis has easily been extended to a variety of complex considerations. In addition to its standard use studied so far, break-even analysis has become useful in at least three other decision-making contexts. First, managers who are considering an expansion of operations use break-even analysis to determine whether the additional fixed costs can be justified in light of their projections of sales and other costs. Second, "go or no-go" decisions on new products are often based on break-even analysis. Using this information in conjunction with marketing surveys and other product analyses, the product's potential benefits and risks to the company can be assessed. Third, management is often confronted with a decision on a change in technology (usually involving higher fixed costs and lower variable costs). They need to know how break-even levels will change to enable them to evaluate the extent to which sales are sufficient to cover operating expenses.

LIMITATIONS OF BREAK-EVEN ANALYSIS

The method for finding the break-even quantity is fairly straightforward, thanks to several simplifying assumptions. What assumptions were made (implicitly or otherwise)? A closer examination will reveal which ones can be relaxed without making the problem too complex and which ones cannot. If nothing else, the decision maker must recognize the limitations inherent in any break-even analysis.

Linearity

Break-even analysis assumes that there is a constant selling price and variable cost per unit regardless of the production volume. Because they are constant, all lines in Figure 8·3 are straight (i.e., linear). This representation of the cost–volume–profit relationship is not entirely valid because usually the relationship between the number of units produced and the price at which the product can be sold is not a straight line. For example, if output were increased dramatically, the sales price might have to be reduced to stimulate demand. This implies that the total revenue line is a curve rather than a straight line. As production and sales increase, total revenues will increase but at a decreasing rate, because the contribution to revenue made by each unit gets progressively smaller (i.e., the sales price per unit declines).

Similarly, the variable cost line can be nonlinear, too. Take the labor cost component of total operating costs as an example. As a firm pushes its capacity to the limit, labor must work overtime at perhaps one-and-a-half times the hourly wage to keep the products flowing out the door. Therefore, wage (variable) costs per unit will increase rather than being a constant cost per unit. As a result, the total cost will begin increasing, but at an increasing rate, and the total operating cost line becomes nonlinear.

With nonlinearity, the break-even point cannot be determined with equation (8-5). This problem can be overcome, however, through nonlinear break-even analysis. If the nonlinear revenue and cost curves can be drawn (or the algebraic function between the sales price per unit and the quantity produced and between the variable cost per unit and the quantity produced), the break-even point can be found.[3]

Certainty

In developing the standard break-even point formula (8-5), the sales price and the variable cost per unit were assumed to be known (constant) at every level of output. That is, uncertainty about these factors' values was not allowed into the analysis. In reality, they may not be known with certainty. For example, cost estimates are often based on historical data, and there is no reason to

---

[3] The details of nonlinear break-even analysis are beyond the scope of this textbook.

expect past experience to be the same as the current situation. That is why a "what if" analysis, wherein a range of prices to costs is assumed, is normally done to get an idea of what can happen if the estimates are wrong.

Classification of Costs

Costs may defy being easily categorized as either fixed or variable; they may be both. As a practical matter, firms often resort to one of the following procedures to categorize the various cost components.

Categorizing Costs by Departments Some companies treat each department separately and arbitrarily classify all of its costs as fixed or variable. For example, all expenses incurred by the accounting, legal, and research and development departments are generally considered fixed because they do not depend directly on production levels. On the other hand, production-related costs and marketing expenses are more sensitive to changes in sales and are classified as variable.

Categorizing Costs from Engineering Studies Other companies have industrial engineers conduct cost studies of the manufacturing process. The results of these studies are then used to classify operating costs and to develop standard unit costs for each product. In addition, these engineers (or accountants) estimate overhead (fixed) expenses for different levels of activity.

Categorizing Costs Through Statistical Analysis For those firms whose technology and operating policies change little over time, fixed and variable costs can be approximated by simple statistical techniques.

Single Product

The simple break-even formula assumes that only one product or service is being sold by the firm. This is all right for the WD-40 Company, which sells a popular aerosol lubricant, as this is the only product the company produces. Realistically, though, few firms have only one product or service. How, then, does one find the break-even point in this case? If the product mix remains the same, the simple method for break-even analysis can still be used. On the other hand, if the product mix changes over time, each product's contribution to fixed and variable costs must be determined and a separate analysis conducted to identify each product's break-even point.

Relevant Range of Production

The simple form of break-even analysis is valid only over the short term or over a certain range of production. If plant capacity has to be expanded, for example, fixed costs will have to increase. Since the benefits of this expansion will not be realized until later, operating costs will increase and raise the break-even point without causing any noticeable change in revenues. Hence break-even analysis typically applies to only one year's operations.

Break-even analysis is a valuable technique for identifying the important relationships among costs, volume, and profits. While it is simple to apply, therein also lies its weakness. Break-even analysis, in its simplest forms, can serve only as a rough guide in financial analysis and thus is an incomplete decision-making tool.

THE FIXED VERSUS VARIABLE COST ISSUE

So far, several aspects of break-even analysis—its underlying assumptions, its strengths and weaknesses—have been discussed. What has not been addressed is the issue of whether or not a firm should have high fixed costs relative to its variable costs.

The mix of fixed and variable costs depends on the firm's choice of technology. For example, if a firm decides to automate its plant and reduce its direct labor, fixed costs will necessarily be high and variable costs will generally decrease. It is already clear that a high-fixed-cost firm must produce and sell more units to break even than a low-fixed-cost firm. Therefore, more capital-intensive companies must produce and sell more just to survive.

Ever since Henry Ford introduced the assembly-line process, auto companies have moved increasingly toward mechanization (higher fixed costs). Using the break-even formula, this implies that firms with high fixed costs must generate more revenues than firms with low fixed costs to break even. This means that the Big Three—General Motors, Ford, and Chrysler—depend heavily on vigorous sales. If the economy weakens and car sales fall, these companies can easily move from the profit region to the loss region depicted in Figure 8·3. In fact, this is exactly what happened in the late 1970s, when fierce Japanese competition began to cut into domestic auto demand, followed by a recession in 1981–1982. Tremendous losses were suffered by the Big Three. For example, Chrysler ran up nearly $3.5 billion in operating losses during this period and had to resort to a $1 billion bailout through federal loan guarantees. As Chrysler's chairman, Lee Iacocca, stated, most of his energy had to be spent getting Chrysler's break-even point down from 2.4 million vehicles to less than 1 million through a massive cost-reduction program by increasing automation and slashing labor costs.

How, then, can a heavy investment in fixed assets be rationalized? Are companies not better off staying with low fixed costs and minimizing their exposure to heavy losses? These issues are examined in greater detail in the following section.

Learning Check for Section 8·1

Review Questions

8·1.   What is the purpose of break-even analysis?

8·2.   What are the limitations of break-even analysis?

8·3.   What is the significance of the contribution margin?

8·4.   What are the two major decision areas that affect a firm's NI?

8·5.   When would you expect the fixed costs of a firm to change?

8·6.   What is the difference between linear and nonlinear break-even analysis? How would this difference affect your decision process?

8·7.   What procedures can a firm use to classify its costs as fixed or variable?

New Terms

Break-even analysis   Fixed costs   Semivariable costs
Break-even point   Semifixed costs   Variable costs
Contribution margin

SECTION 8·2 *Operating Leverage*

The discussion so far has focused on how the financial manager estimates the break-even point. In the case of a recently established firm, reaching this level of production is a major milestone in the company's growth. Once the firm's revenues cover the total costs, the next logical step is to continue to increase production and sales. This is because, given linear costs and revenues, any production level greater than the break-even quantity will put the firm in the profit region. Figure 8·3 illustrates this fact. It is also clear from this figure that as the quantity produced and sold increases, profits increase. Any business operating to the right of the break-even point knows that it will make a profit.

This raises an interesting question. If a firm is to make a profit, it should produce at least the break-even quantity. From equation (8-5), the lower the firm's fixed costs, the lower the break-even quantity. Then why not minimize fixed costs? That way, the firm can enter the profit zone very quickly.

Something is wrong with this argument because we know that Ford and Exxon have very high fixed costs. Obviously, these highly capital-intensive firms have high fixed costs for a specific reason that must somehow be to their advantage. Indeed, as will be seen shortly, fixed costs provide operating leverage, or first-stage leverage, for the firm, and businesses with high fixed costs hope to "lever up" or magnify their earnings for small increases in sales by using operating leverage. Before understanding how **operating leverage** works, a formal definition is useful:

KEY CONCEPT: Operating leverage measures the extent to which a firm uses fixed production costs in its operations. The higher the ratio of fixed costs to net operating income, the higher the operating leverage of the firm.

This key concept provides a general idea of operating leverage. However, it is better to develop a more useful measure called the **degree of operating leverage (DOL)** for a fixed production level Q, DOL_Q, and use this to measure the operating leverage for a firm. This concept permits the financial manager to compute and evaluate the effects of operating leverage more easily. DOL_Q is called *first-stage leverage* because it is used to examine the first, or operating, part of the income statement. If firm B has a lower DOL than firm A at a certain production level, we can conclude that firm B has less operating leverage at that production level than firm A. To simplify the notation, the subscript Q will henceforth be omitted from DOL_Q.

KEY CONCEPT: The **degree of operating leverage (DOL)** at a particular production level Q measures the percentage change in NOI (% ΔNOI) for a given percentage change in sales (% ΔS). In other words:

$$DOL = \frac{\text{percentage change in } NOI}{\text{percentage change in sales}}$$

and can be written as[4]

$$DOL = \frac{Q(P - V)}{Q(P - V) - F} \qquad (8\text{-}6)$$

Example 8•1   Using DOL

Lumen makes "eternal" light bulbs and has $F = \$1,000,000$. $V = \$5$ and $P = \$10$ at $Q = 250,000$ units. Its DOL at a production level of 250,000 bulbs is given by equation (8-6) as

---

[4] Derivations for the formulas used in this chapter are contained in the derivation appendix at the end of this book. Note that $Q(P - V)$ is *not* the percent change in NOI, and $Q(P - V) - F$ is *not* the percent change in sales.

$$DOL = \frac{250,000(10 - 5)}{250,000(10 - 5) - 1,000,000} = 5.0$$

From the definition of *DOL*, this means that if Lumen's sales go up by 5%, its *NOI* will go up by 25%. This is because

$$DOL = \% \Delta NOI / \% \Delta S \quad \text{or} \quad \% \Delta NOI = DOL \times \% \Delta S$$
$$= 5 \times 5\%$$
$$= 25\%$$

Notice from the example that the *DOL* is a *magnification factor*. A 5% sales increase is magnified to a 25% *NOI* increase. This magnification is achieved by the use of fixed costs. To see why, assume that a firm has zero fixed costs. Then equation (8-6) would suggest that the magnification factor for this firm is 1.0. In other words, there is no real magnification when there are no fixed costs.

Operating leverage exists because of fixed costs, and fixed costs amplify changes in *NOI* for small changes in sales. So it appears that to have maximum magnification in *NOI*, the firm must have the maximum degree of operating leverage. But it is imprudent to increase operating leverage indiscriminately. Just as operating leverage magnifies increases in sales, it can magnify decreases in sales as well. If a firm has a high operating leverage, a substantial drop in sales may cause substantial financial distress. Estimates of *DOL* for various industries are contained in Table 8•2.

Figure 8•4 is a useful diagram to remember. It shows that the percentage change in *NOI* is found by multiplying the percentage change in sales by the *DOL*.

Consider the following examples.

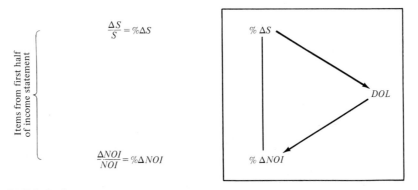

FIGURE 8•4 Relationship between sales, *NOI*, and the degree of operating leverage. In algebraic terms, we know that $DOL = \% \Delta NOI / \% \Delta S$, so, rearranging terms slightly, we have $\% \Delta NOI = \% \Delta S \cdot DOL$.

Example 8·2   Inferring DOL

A small fur company in Mashpee, Massachusetts, has a current *NOI* of $200,000. Next year's *NOI* is expected to be $300,000, as sales are expected to go up by 25%. What does this imply about its *DOL?*

$$\% \ \Delta S = 25\% \qquad \% \ \Delta NOI = \frac{\$300,000 - \$200,000}{\$200,000} = 50\%$$

From Figure 8·4, % $\Delta S \times DOL = \% \ \Delta NOI$, or

$$DOL = \% \ \Delta NOI / \% \ \Delta S = \frac{50\%}{25\%} = 2.0$$

TABLE 8·2   *DOL* Estimates by Industry

Industry	Estimated *DOL*
Food	0.42
Tobacco	0.73
Waste	0.96
Chemicals	1.01
Broadcasting	1.14
Petroleum	1.34
Packaging (containers)	1.49
Trucking	1.66
Plumbing and valves	1.80
Distillers	1.87
Metals (minor)	1.96
Herbicides	1.97
Steel	2.21
Fiberglass	2.43
Building materials	3.03
Paper and lumber	3.21

Estimated *DOL*s are averages for various firms in each industry. This information was compiled from T. J. O'Brien and P. A. Vanderheiden, "Empirical Measurement of Operating Leverage for Growing Firms," *Financial Management,* Summer 1987.

Example 8·3   Using DOL to Find Fixed Costs

Zee-Zee Tops, Inc., manufactures plaid vinyl and chenille cartops for convertibles. These roofs sell for $200 each and have an associated variable cost per unit of $120. Management fully expects next year's sales and *NOI* to drop sharply, by 20% and 50%, respectively, due to a lack of demand (i.e., "consumer resistance"). If Zee-Zee's current level of production and sales is 112 cartops, what is its level of fixed costs?

$$\% \Delta S = -20\% \quad \text{and} \quad \% \Delta NOI = -50\%$$

From Figure 8·5,

$$DOL = \frac{\% \Delta NOI}{\% \Delta S} = \frac{-50\%}{-20\%} = 2.5$$

and from equation (8-6),

$$DOL = \frac{Q(P - V)}{Q(P - V) - F}$$

$$2.5 = \frac{112(\$200 - \$120)}{112(\$200 - \$120) - F}$$

or

$$F = \$5,376$$

Learning Check for Section 8·2

Review Questions

8·8.   What are the determinants of operating leverage?

8·9.   What is the relationship between operating leverage and fixed costs? Why does this relationship exist?

8·10.   Why must we specify Q when computing DOL_Q?

8·11.   What are the advantages and disadvantages of operating leverage?

8·12.   "Technological considerations determine a firm's *DOL*." Explain.

New Terms

Degree of operating leverage (*DOL*)   Operating leverage

SECTION 8·3 *Financial Leverage*

The next logical question becomes: If financial managers can use fixed operating costs to magnify the sensitivity of changes in *NOI* to changes in sales in the first half of the income statement, can they also do something to magnify the sensitivity of net income (*NI*) to changes in *NOI* in the second half of the income statement? Recall from Chapter 7 that the progression from *NOI* to *NI* occurs in the second half of the income statement.

This can, in fact, be done by financing a firm's assets with debt. Because this method of financing carries a fixed obligation or cost in the form of interest, and because this fixed obligation arises from a financial rather than an operating decision, it is called **financial leverage.** Financial leverage, or *second-stage leverage*, is the ability of the firm to magnify the sensitivity of *NI* to changes in *NOI*. In contrast to operating leverage, where the concern is fixed and variable costs, financial leverage is concerned with the mix of debt and stockholders' equity used to finance a firm's activities. As the proportion of debt to equity increases, financial leverage increases. This results in greater fluctuations in *NI* with changes in *NOI*.

Investors and creditors often view financial leverage and financial risk as one and the same. Financial risk, however, is defined in market-value terms, while the formula for the **degree of financial leverage** is calculated using book-value information (book values of debt and equity). Since market-value measures have not been discussed, financial leverage will temporarily serve as the relevant risk measure.

KEY CONCEPT: The **degree of financial leverage (*DFL*)** measures the percentage change in net income (% ΔNI) for a given percentage change in *NOI* (% ΔNOI).

DFL is expressed as $DFL = \% \Delta NI / \% \Delta NOI$ and can be shown to be equal to[5]

$$DFL = \frac{Q(P - V) - F}{Q(P - V) - F - I} \tag{8-7}$$

where *I* is the dollar amount of interest expenses. From the preceding formulas, it is easy to see why financial leverage exists because of debt financing. Notice

---

[5] Notice that taxes do not enter the formula. Why? Because taxes affect both the numerator and the denominator in the derivation of equation (8-7) and thus cancel out.

that for a firm that uses no debt (called an *unlevered firm*), I is zero and DFL equals 1.0. Therefore, there will be no magnification effect in the second half of the income statement in this case.

THE IMPACT OF ALTERNATIVE FINANCING PLANS ON NI

The Lumen Light Company is considering two alternative schemes for financing a $1.2 million production facility. Plan A would finance the facility with equity; Plan B would borrow 40% of the capital needed. The details of the plans are given in Table 8•4.

Management wishes to analyze these two financing plans in terms of their effect on reported earnings available to common stockholders (i.e., *NI*). *NOI* will be the same for both plans because it is unaffected by the mode of financing. However, *NI* under plan A is almost twice that under plan B. This would seem

TABLE 8•4 Effect of the Two Alternative Financing Plans on Lumen Light Company's *NI*[a]

	Plan A All Equity	Plan B 40% Debt, 60% Equity
Profitability		
Revenues	$2,500,000	$2,500,000
Less: Variable operating costs	(750,000)	(750,000)
Less: Fixed operating costs	(1,540,000)	(1,540,000)
Net operating income (*NOI*)	$ 210,000	$ 210,000
Less: Interest expenses	0	(100,800)[b]
Net profits before taxes	$ 210,000	$ 109,200
Less: Taxes (39%)	(81,900)	(42,588)
Net income (*NI*)	$ 128,100	$ 66,612

(Using Equation 8-7)

$$DFL = \frac{QP - QV - F}{QP - QV - F - I} \qquad \frac{QP - QV - F}{QP - QV - F - I}$$

$$= \frac{\$2,500,000 - \$750,000 - \$1,540,000}{2,500,000 - 750,000 - 1,540,000 - 0} \qquad \frac{\$2,500,000 - \$750,000 - 1,540,000}{\$2,500,000 - \$750,000 - \$1,540,000 - \$100,800}$$

$$= \frac{\$210,000}{\$210,000} \qquad \frac{\$210,000}{\$109,200}$$

$$1.00 \qquad 1.92$$

[a]Production level = 250,000 light bulbs.
[b]Interest expenses are $720,000 × 0.14 = $100,800.

to indicate that the equity plan is superior (i.e., why not always use equity and avoid fixed financial charges?). What is missing is that the debt–equity financing plan has a *DFL* of 1.92, while the all-equity plan has a *DFL* of only 1.0 (i.e., no magnification effect). This means that if management can expect a production and sales level greater than the current 250,000 units, the *percentage change* in *NI* under plan B will be nearly twice that of plan A. In other words, as long as fixed financial charges are covered, stockholders receive a magnification of their earnings.

As with *DOL*, this outcome can be portrayed graphically, as in Figure 8•5. From this diagram, the exact percentage change in *NI* can be determined by multiplying the percentage change in *NOI* by the *DFL*. A change in *NOI* will be magnified into an even greater change in *NI*.

However, it should not be forgotten that financial leverage, like operating leverage is a two-way street. If the firm's production falls, appealing results would switch signs and produce a disastrous outcome for the firm.

Before concluding the discussion of financial leverage, consider two more examples. The first focuses on financial leverage. The second deals with both operating and financial leverage.

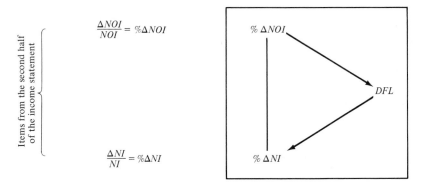

FIGURE 8•5 Relationship between *NOI*, *NI*, and the degree of financial leverage. In algebraic terms, we know that $DFL = \% \Delta NI/\% \Delta NOI$, so, rearranging terms yields $\% \Delta NI = \% \Delta NOI \cdot DFL$.

Example 8•4 Computing DFL

The Mercedes Company expects that next year its *NOI* will fall by 10%, and because of this its *NI* will fall by 33%. If these estimates are correct, what *DFL* does Mercedes have?

From Figure 8•5,

$$\% \Delta NOI \times DFL = \% \Delta NI$$
$$10\% \times DFL = 33\%$$

Therefore, $DFL = \dfrac{33\%}{10\%} = 3.3.$

Example 8•5   Using DOL and DFL Simultaneously

Assume that Mercedes has a *DOL* of 2.0 at the current level of production. If sales are expected to go up by 12%, how much will *NOI* and *NI* increase?
From Figure 8•4,

$$
\begin{aligned}
\% \, \Delta NOI &= \% \, \Delta S \times DOL \\
&= 12\% \times 2.0 \\
&= 24\% \\
\% \, \Delta NI &= \% \, \Delta NOI \times DFL \\
&= 24\% \times 3.3 \\
&= 79.2\%
\end{aligned}
$$

Learning Check for Section 8•3

Review Questions

8•13.   What are the determinants of financial leverage?

8•14.   What are the advantages and disadvantages of financial leverage?

8•15.   "Financial policies determine a firm's *DFL*." Explain.

8•16.   In increasing *DFL*, what is a financial manager seeking to magnify? What does this increase indicate about the manager's expectations concerning the future prospects of the firm?

New Terms

Degree of financial leverage (*DFL*)   Financial leverage

SECTION 8•4   *Combined or Total Leverage*

Two distinct concepts of leverage have been developed so far: *DOL* is first-stage leverage, and *DFL* is second-stage leverage. These two leverage effects can be combined into an overall measure of leverage called **combined** or **total leverage.**

KEY CONCEPT: **Combined leverage** measures the overall sensitivity of *NI* to change in sales, and the **degree of combined leverage (DCL)** is defined as the percentage change in *NI* for a given change in sales.

It can be shown that

$$DCL = \frac{Q(P - V)}{Q(P - V) - F - I} \qquad (8\text{-}8)$$

To calculate *DCL*, one can use equation (8-8) or compute it indirectly by multiplying the *DOL* by the *DFL*; that is,

$$DCL = DOL \times DFL \qquad (8\text{-}9)$$

For a given change in sales, *DCL* measures the combined magnification of *NI* created by fixed operating costs and interest payments. If sales change, operating leverage magnifies *NOI*, and this change in *NOI* is translated into a magnification of *NI* by financial leverage. Instead of this two-step magnification procedure, combined leverage directly magnifies sales changes into changes in *NI*.

Example 8•6 Using DCL

If the Ajax Appliance Corporation has a *DOL* of 2.0 at a production level of 10,000 refrigerators and its *DFL* is 1.5, its *DCL = DOL × DFL* = 2 × 1.5 = 3.0. If Ajax's sales increase by 10%, it can be concluded directly that its *NI* will increase by % $\Delta S \times DCL$ = 10% × 3.0 = 30%.

Example 8•7 Finding Fixed Costs Using DCL

Meditech Products is a small electronics firm making digital thermometers. Management feels that if sales go up by 10%, *NI* will increase by 40%. Meditech has a *DFL* of 2.0. What is the level of fixed costs (F) for Meditech at a production level of 1,000 thermometers if the contribution margin per unit = $5? Since

$$\% \ \Delta S \times DCL = \% \ \Delta NI$$
$$10\% \times DCL = 40\%$$

Therefore, $DCL = 4.0$.
Since it is also true that

$$DCL = DFL \times DOL$$
$$4.0 = 2.0 \times DOL$$
$$DOL = 2.0$$

From equation (8-6),

$$DOL = \frac{Q(P - V)}{Q(P - V) - F}$$

Recognizing that $Q = 1,000$, $P - V = \$5$, and $DOL = 2.0$, we have

$$2.0 = \frac{1,000 \times 5}{(1,000 \times 5) - F} \quad \text{or} \quad F = \$2,500$$

As an aid to consolidating the concepts of operating and financial leverage, see the highlight "Chrysler Corporation." Notice from the discussion in the highlight that both technological and financial changes were used to obtain the combined leverage effect.

■■ *HIGHLIGHT*

CHRYSLER CORPORATION: BREAK-EVEN ANALYSIS AND LEVERAGE

For the first time in decades, U.S. automakers began in 1978 to restructure and streamline their operations to meet customer demand for smaller, more economical cars. Traditionally a highly capital intensive (high-fixed-cost) industry that had relied on strong market growth and sales volume to remain profitable, auto firms were forced to instigate a retailing effort to lower their break-even point. The added motivation: three years of depression-level sales coupled with fierce competition from the Japanese. The strategy: a five-year $70 billion switch to more efficient manufacturing operations that used such new technology as robotics and computer-assisted design and manufacturing (CAD/CAM). The result: lots of red ink, amounting to over $7 billion in losses.

One of the more notable non-break-even victims was Chrysler Corp., which alone accounted for half of the $7 billion in losses. Because of its weakened financial stamina, Chrysler had to make the most drastic transformation. That is, its dramatic overhaul was powered by the threat of financial collapse rather than the need to reposition for a changing auto market. "We didn't do it because we were smart, we did it to survive," admitted Chrysler's Chairman Lee A. Iacocca.

What were the dimensions of this transformation? Let us look at several steps that Chrysler took to improve its position.

1. Management either closed or consolidated 20 obsolete plants and pared overhead expenses by cutting its 40,000-white-collar force in half. The result was a reduction in fixed costs of $2 billion a year.

2. To enhance the effectiveness of the lowered break-even point, Chrysler greatly improved its contribution margin $(P - V)$ by chopping its blue-collar employment by 41,800 and gaining "givebacks" from the United Auto Workers in terms of reduced wages and benefits.

After lowering Chrysler's break-even point by reducing fixed costs and improving contribution margin, Chrysler's Lee Iacocca did something that puzzled people—he completely revamped the production process and introduced robots and other computer-assisted manufacturing processes. Chrysler obtained massive loan guarantees from the U.S. government to achieve the "New Chrysler Corporation" status.

Can Iacocca's actions be justified? By revamping the production process he only increased the break-even point! Iacocca knew that with the loan guarantees, Chrysler *had to* make it—it would not get another chance. By increased automation of its production process, Chrysler was in fact increasing its *operating leverage*, hoping to magnify its earnings for a small increase in sales. The loans Chrysler took out increased its *financial leverage* and the *combined leverage* for Chrysler increased drastically.

We already know that leverage can be a great advantage to a company only if it has sufficient sales to overcome these added costs. So for this highly levered situation to benefit Chrysler, Iacocca took two steps to increase sales:

1. Chrysler embarked on a massive advertising campaign touting its new quality control standards, made feasible by increased robotics and computer-assisted design. In addition, Chrysler offered an innovative quality assurance program to spur sales.

2. To provide an additional incentive for customers, Chrysler offered cash rebates (of as much as $1,000) payable directly to customers.

Thus with added leverage and a strong sales push, Chrysler was poised to fare very well *if* the company did in fact succeed in increasing its sales dramatically. If, on the other hand, Chrysler's sales do not rise or if they fall, the company would be in dire straights. As it turned out, the U.S. economy and the entire automobile industry did very well subsequently. However, Chrysler showed the most dramatic increases in profits.

LEVERAGE EFFECTS: PUTTING IT ALL TOGETHER

Figure 8•6 connects the concepts of operating leverage, financial leverage, and combined leverage. It also connects the leverage concepts presented in this

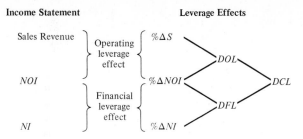

FIGURE 8·6 The concept of leverage: a composite picture.

chapter with the income statement. As described previously, operating leverage reflects the operating decisions determined in the first part of the income statement. Financial leverage reflects the financing decisions of the firm, which are detailed in the second part of the income statement. The *DOL*, *DFL*, and *DCL* allow the manager to see quickly the impact of investment and financing decisions on the two major earnings indicators of the firm: *NOI* and *NI*.

LEVERAGE AND CASH FLOWS

The discussion of leverage in this chapter has been conducted with profits rather than cash flows. The concept of leverage—measuring the impact of investment and financing decisions on the firm—can also be applied to the cash flows of the firm. Cash flow leverage formulas are slightly different from the formulas in this chapter, and instead of *NOI* and *NI*, we would be examining operating cash flows and net cash flows.[6]

Learning Check for Section 8·4

Review Questions

8·17. How are *DOL* and *DFL* integrated with the notion of *DCL*?

8·18. Is it correct to say that a firm's *DCL* is determined by both its operating and financial policies? If it is, what aspects of its operating and financial policies are involved?

8·19. What is the difference between *DCL* and *(DOL)(DFL)*?

New Terms

Combined leverage   Degree of combined leverage (*DCL*)

[6] Interested students are referred to Rao, *Financial Management: Concepts and Applications* (New York: Macmillan Co., 1987), for a detailed view of leverage and cash flows.

SUMMARY

Linear Break-Even Analysis

Managers must be concerned with the interaction of revenues and costs, which determines whether the firm is profitable or not. After a firm reaches its break-even level of sales, the manager typically makes several operating and financial decisions to magnify profits. This can be done via the use of leverage. In this chapter, we have introduced the ideas of operating and financial leverage. These are magnification effects that exist because of fixed costs.

Operating Leverage

Operating leverage, also called *first-stage leverage*, works in the first half of the income statement and exists because of fixed operating costs. Technological considerations are the prime determinant of operating leverage. A simple *DOL* can be used to assess the effect of changes in, say, sales projections on changes in *NOI*. Because operating leverage magnifies both profits and losses, it can be considered a measure of business risk. Managers must weigh carefully the risk aspects of increasing leverage.

Financial Leverage

Financial leverage, or *second-stage leverage*, works in the second half of the income statement and arises with debt financing, which imposes on the firm a fixed-interest obligation. In a manner similar to operating leverage, changes in *NOI* can be translated into changes in *NI* by using the *DFL* formula.

Combined Leverage

Operating and financial leverage can be combined to give the total leverage of the firm. The *DCL* allows managers to evaluate the effects of a change in the level of sales on the firm's *NI*.

PROBLEMS

8•1. David Willis is considering opening up a new copy center store near a large university. If he does, he will rent six machines for $1,200 per month for each machine. Rent, utilities, and wages will total $2,000 per month. David's cost of paper and ink is $0.01 per copy, and he plans to charge $0.05 per copy.

(a) What is his break-even point?

(b) Suppose that David thinks he can get by with only four machines. What will his break-even point fall to?

(c) Suppose that David rents four machines and sells 200,000 copies in one month. What is his *NOI* for that month?

(d) David is considering placing in the student newspaper a $200 ad with a coupon for $0.04 per copy for orders of 50 copies or more. He estimates that if he places the ad, he will sell 250,000 copies and that about 50% of his customers will use the coupon. If he places the ad, what will his break-even point and his *NOI* be?

8·2. Jim Korp designs game cartridges for home computers. His total fixed cost for designing a game package is $4,000. The cartridges the game is programmed into cost $4 each, and he sells them for $20 each. He currently sells 300 cartridges for each game he designs.

(a) What are his break-even point, *NOI*, and *DOL* now?

(b) If the cost of a cartridge rises to $6 and he keeps the sales price constant at $20, what will the new break-even point, *NOI*, and *DOL* be?

(c) If the price of a cartridge rises to $6 and he simultaneously raises the sales price to $22, what will the new break-even point, *NOI*, and *DOL* be?

(d) Same question as part (c), expect that fixed costs also increase to $4,500.

8·3. The C&D TV store currently has fixed costs of $6,000 per month and $400 per TV set. Their sales price for the TV sets is $700 each, and their current volume is 25 sets per month.

(a) Find C&D's break-even point and their *NOI* and *DOL* at the current level of sales.

(b) Find C&D's break-even point and their *NOI* and *DOL* if fixed costs decrease to $4,750 and at the same time the cost of the TV sets rises to $450.

8·4. The Mobile Shoe Company's weekly fixed costs (rent, utilities, etc.) have just increased to $42,000. Their variable costs for producing shoes include $5 per pair for raw materials and $\frac{1}{6}$ labor hour. Mobile has a labor force of 100 employees, who are paid $24 per hour of labor and $27 per hour for overtime (more than 40 hours per week).

(a) Suppose that Mobile sells shoes for $12 per pair. What is their break-even point?

(b) Suppose that Mobile sells shoes for $10 per pair. What is their break-even point?

(c) What is the break-even point if overtime labor costs $30 instead of $27 per hour?

8•5. The Newcastle Utility Company has fixed costs of $20,000 per month and sells electricity for $0.015 per kilowatt-hour. It costs them $0.005 per kilowatt-hour to produce the electricity.
(a) What is Newcastle's break-even point?
(b) What is Newcastle's *DOL* at a sales level of 2,750,000 kilowatt-hours?

8•6. The W. V. Scott Company had sales last year of $600,000, a *NOI* of $20,000, and a *DOL* of 4. Assume that fixed costs are the same this year as last year.
(a) Suppose that next year's sales are $630,000. What will next year's *NOI* be?
(b) Suppose that next year's sales are $550,000. What will next year's *NOI* be?
(c) Next year's *NOI* is $25,000. What must sales be for that year?

8•7. The Magee Publishing Company last year had sales of $800,000, an *NOI* of $20,000, and a *DOL* of 6. What will its *NOI* be if sales increase to $900,000?

8•8. Klinger's Clothiers is considering expanding the production of a new line of women's clothing and is examining two different financing plans to raise the requisite $4,000,000. The first plan (all equity) involves the sale of 200,000 new shares at $20 each. The second plan (50% equity, 50% debt) involves the sale of 100,000 new shares at $20 each and 2,000 12% coupon, 20-year bonds at par. In either case, annual fixed costs will be $2,000,000, the average cost per unit produced will be $15, and the average price per unit produced will be $50. Klinger currently has 400,000 shares outstanding and has a 25% tax rate.
(a) Find net profit after taxes, earnings per share, and *DFL* if the expected sales level is 70,000 units.
(b) At what level of sales (in units) will earnings per share be equal under either plan?

READINGS

O'BRIEN, THOMAS J., AND PAUL A. VANDERHEIDEN, "Empirical Measurement of Operating Leverage for Growing Firms," *Financial Management*, Summer 1987, 45–53.
PREZAS, ALEXANDER P., "Effects of Debt on the Degrees of Operating and Financial Leverage," *Financial Management*, Summer 1987, 39–44.

9

A Framework for Financial Planning

In an economy that is constantly changing, financial managers must, at all times, attempt to anticipate future trends in the economy, in the industry, and in their own firms. Most successful firms have a mission statement—a goals and objectives statement that specifies the company's operating philosophy, primary and secondary objectives, and so on. This mission statement is developed by the board of directors, and the management of the company follows it to the greatest extent possible in light of changing circumstances. To ensure that the company's operating and financial policies are compatible with the corporate mission and to ensure that the firm will be on financially firm ground in the future, the company requires a systematic financial planning framework. Moreover, the firm's objective of maximizing the wealth of the stockholders cannot be fully achieved without proper financial planning.

The term **financial planning** means different things to different managers, depending on the nature of the business, the firm's size and organizational structure, and so on. However, in the most general terms, financial planning involves primarily anticipating the impact of operating and financial policies on the future financial position of the firm and instituting remedial measures as needed. *Short-term financial planning* refers to the planning function as it applies to, say, a one-year period, while *long term* in this context usually refers to three, four, or even five years.

The basic and derivative financial statements examined in Chapter 6 are used primarily to analyze past performance and to provide some indication of the future financial position of the firm. However, these financial statements are not financial forecasts. To develop forecasted financial statements, much more information is necessary—information that the various functional and divisional managers must provide to the planner. These projected financial statements form the basic financial planning tools and are the subject of this chapter.

KEY CONCEPT: A **pro forma statement** is a projected or forecasted report on a firm's financial condition over a specified time interval.

Pro forma literally means "for the sake of form." Firms often project future financial statements using existing financial statements as a form for the analysis. The use, construction, and interpretation of these pro forma financial statements are discussed in this chapter. In understanding the use of the projected statements, several aspects of financial planning will become clear. The tools used for financial planning are examined in two sections.

SECTION 9·1: *Short-Term Financial Planning.* In this section, we see how a firm can project its cash flows based on certain assumptions about the firm's operating and financial policies and sales. With this projection of future cash flows, we can then prepare a forecasted income statement and a forecasted balance sheet. The uses of these projected statements are also examined.

SECTION 9·2: *Long-Term Financial Planning.* Long-term planning, which focuses on planning horizons of more than a year, is normally accomplished using only the pro forma balance sheet. The percent-of-sales approach to developing this statement is examined.

SECTION 9·1 *Short-Term Financial Planning*

Table 9·1 illustrates the short-term financial planning process. As can be seen, short-term financial planning involves the development of three pro forma statements, as mentioned earlier. The dependence of the various decisions made in other divisions in the firm is highlighted in Table 9·1. Note how the forecasted cash flows originate from sales, operational activities, and financial activities. Typically, each of these forecasts is prepared separately by different individuals, although certain estimates require an interdivision cooperative effort. This basic information is then used by the financial manager to prepare an overall cash budget and forecast of the firm's ending cash position at different points during the planning period. Finally, the financial manager combines these data with other financial information to determine how the income statement and balance sheet will appear at the end of the planning period. Despite their close interrelationship, each report provides a different perspective and different information to the financial decision maker. These various reports can

278

also be compared against each other as a check on the internal accuracy and consistency of the forecasts.[1]

TABLE 9•1 The Three Pro Forma Statements for Short-Term Financial Planning

MARKETING: Sales Cash Flows	PRODUCTION: Operating Cash Flows	FINANCE: Financial Cash Flows
1. Cash sales	1. Wages	1. Short- and long-term investments
2. Collections of accts receivable (credit policy)	2. Purchase of materials or merchandise	2. Issuance and retirement of debt
	3. Selling and advertising costs	3. Interest payments and income
	4. General administrative expenses	4. Rent or lease payments
	5. Capital expenditures	5. Dividend payment
		6. Income tax payments
		7. Issuance of new common stock

Cash Flow Budget
1. Operating cash flows
2. Financial cash flows
3. Net cash position

Pro Forma Income Statement
1. Sales
2. Operating expenses
3. Financial expenses
4. Net profit (loss)

Pro Forma Balance Sheet
1. Projected asset balances
2. Projected liabilities and equity balances
3. Net funding required

FINANCIAL PLANNING WITH THE CASH FLOW BUDGET

Most firms can be organizationally divided into three different activities along functional areas lines: marketing, production (or purchasing), and fi-

---

[1] One way to increase internal accuracy and consistency is to prepare the pro forma income statement and the balance sheet independently of the cash flow budget information.

nance.[2] Carrying out the marketing and production decisions involves substantial outlays of cash. As a result, an extremely important job for the financial manager is to anticipate the cash flow implications of these two activities and to anticipate the timing and magnitude of future cash flows in order to aid the internal planning of the firm and to maintain control over the firm's cash position.

This task is accomplished through the preparation of a cash flow budget (or just **cash budget**).

KEY CONCEPT: A **cash flow budget** is a detailed estimated schedule of future cash inflows (receipts), outflows (expenditures), and cash balances at different points in time over a specific time interval.

This statement describes how a firm's cash will be spent on wages, merchandise, overhead, and so on, and on how much funding and investment will be required. Normally, the time interval covered by a cash flow budget is less than one year, with the forecasts being made on a weekly or monthly basis. Many large firms have also implemented computerized financial models that perform most of the forecasting work for short- and long-term planning. With the widespread use of microcomputers, most firms, regardless of their size, can now easily afford these resources. Larger firms also use daily cash forecasts for the following week or two so as to plan for any potential problems that may affect their liquidity position. Failure to anticipate cash flows properly can lead to idle cash balances, lower profits, cash shortages, and possibly even a liquidity crisis.

Besides facilitating the short-term planning function, a cash budget is useful for control purposes. That is, forecasted cash flows can be used as a standard against which actual cash flows may be compared. This helps in monitoring planned receipts and disbursements. Any significant deviations between planned and actual cash flows require further investigation by management to evaluate the reasons for such deviations.

Constructing a Cash Flow Budget

A cash flow budget is the result of a rather involved and time-consuming process because it represents a number of individual budgets prepared by the entire management team. As already mentioned, management requires different departments (and divisions) to prepare their own cash budgets. Examples of these budgets are sales, production or purchasing, advertising, administrative expenses, and capital expenditures. The starting point is a forecast of expected sales by the marketing manager. Given this sales forecast, the production department then develops a budget that estimates the costs for meeting the pro-

---

[2] Production often does not properly describe the activities of certain types of firms, such as airlines or retailers. Therefore, the word *production* is also used to mean *purchase, merchandise,* or *cost of goods.*

jected sales figures and for providing an adequate level of inventory. Next, the financial manager is responsible for combining the sales, production, and other expense information into a summary of the operating cash inflows and outflows. Finally, this summary is combined with the projected financial cash flows, such as interest expenses, dividends, and repayment of long-term debt (which are usually known in advance). The end result of this process is the cash flow budget.

Before examining the cash flow budget in detail, certain preliminary calculations are necessary. To discuss these calculations and to facilitate a discussion of the financial planning implications of a cash budget, it is useful to develop a three-stage approach to cash budgeting. Stages 1, 2, and 3, when combined into a single statement, yield the desired cash budget.

Stage 1: Estimating the Operating Cash Flows The first stage of the cash budget for Byet Stores, Inc., is presented in Table 9•2. The major sources of operating cash inflows are cash sales and collections of account receivables. "Cash sales" is self-explanatory, but "collections of accounts receivables" deserves some discussion. Most corporations extend credit to their customers and

TABLE 9•2 Byet Stores, Inc., Summary of Projected Operating Cash Flows, Fourth Quarter, 1989[a] (Thousands of Dollars)

	Aug.	Sept.	Oct.	Nov.	Dec.
Operating cash inflows					
Total sales	$51	$66	$ 59	$ 158	$208
Cash sales (30%)			18	47	62
Collections of accounts receivable[b] (68%)					
One month later (60%)			40	35	95
Two months later (8%)			4	5	5
Total operating cash inflows			$ 62	$ 87	$162
Operating cash outflows					
Purchases	$90	$ 72	$ 62	$ 39	
Payment of payables[c]			90	72	62
Wages and salaries			12	19	24
Selling and advertising			9	14	21
General and administrative			5	7	7
Capital expenditures			9	3	4
Total operating cash outflows			$ 125	$ 115	$118
Net operating cash flows			$−63	$−28	$ 44

[a] All numbers are rounded to the nearest whole number. Circled numbers do not directly enter the calculation of the totals.
[b] Two percent of total sales is assumed eventually to prove to be uncollectible and will subsequently be written off as a bad-debt expense.
[c] All merchandise is assumed to be purchased on credit and is then paid off one month later. For example, the October payment figure is $90,000, which represents purchases made in September.

carry them as an accounts receivable. Credit sales become cash only after a lapse of time as customers begin to pay off their accounts. An assumption must therefore be made about the payment pattern or rate at which credit sales will become cash. This assumed rate is usually based on an analysis of the firm's past sales and collection experience. One reason for this intermediate step (Table 9•2) in developing the cash budget is to recognize that actual cash collections are not the same as sales. In effect, stage 1 of the cash budget (i.e., Table 9•2) adjusts for the fact that the cash collections in any particular month depend on the firm's sales performance in previous months and on its collection policy.

To be specific, for the fourth quarter, Byet's monthly operating cash flow budget in Table 9•2 indicates that 30% of sales is assumed to be for cash and that 68% of sales is on credit. The remaining 2% is assumed to be uncollectible and will be charged against sales as a bad-debt expense. Furthermore, 60% of sales will be realized as cash one month later (i.e., after the customers are billed and have paid for their purchases). Another 8% will become cash only after a two-month lag. For example, October collections will be $(0.60 \times \$66) + (0.08 \times \$51) = \$44,000$. The $51,000 and $66,000 figures are the total sales figures for August and September, respectively.

In estimating operating cash outflows, the list of cash uses could be a long one—cash purchases, payments of payables, wages, utilities, capital expenditures, and so on. Nevertheless, Table 9•2 summarizes Byet's major operating expenses. The most important item is the payment of payables, which represents prior purchases made by Byet. Most firms have well-defined credit arrangements with their suppliers, and the items bought on credit are reflected as accounts payable *(payables)*. Note that the payment of payables may also be treated like credit sales in that just like their customers, firms pay back their suppliers slowly. Most purchases made in a particular month are paid for in a subsequent month.[3] To simplify the situation, Byet's purchases are assumed to be paid for after a one-month delay.

Stage 2: Estimating the Financial Cash Flows[4]   The financial manager is responsible for forecasting the expected cash inflows and outflows associated with a firm's financial activities. Table 9•3 contains these forecasts for Byet's fourth quarter. In contrast to operating cash flows, financial flows are scheduled well ahead of time and generally occur at known points in time. In fact, interest and dividend payments are made at around the same time every year. Significant cash flows expected for Byet are a scheduled new issue of long-term debt of $30,000 to finance new store openings and repayment of short-term debt amounting to $28,000.

---

[3] Like accounts receivable, this does not imply that the level of accounts payable is reduced to zero at some point. Purchases (receivable) occur continually, so that a certain amount of existing payables (receivables) is paid off each month. Current purchases (sales) serve to build the account back up.

[4] To keep matters simple, the discussion of the second stage does not involve delayed collections or disbursements of cash, as in stage 1. Thus Table 9•2 is identical to stage 2 in the completed cash budget presented in Table 9•3. It is entirely conceivable that financial cash flows may also require adjustments, as in Table 9•2.

TABLE 9•3 Byet Stores, Inc., Summary of Projected Financial Cash Flows, Fourth Quarter, 1989 (Thousands of Dollars)

	Oct.	Nov.	Dec.
Financial cash inflows			
Maturing marketable securities	$ 2	$ 1	—
Issuance of long-term debt	—	30	—
Other financial receipts	—	2	1
Total financial cash inflows	$ 2	$33	$ 1
Financial cash outflows			
Rent[a]	$ 2	$ 2	$ 3
Interest payments	—	5	—
Income taxes	—	—	4
Dividends	—		6
Repayment of short-term debt	8	8	12
Total financial cash outflows	$ 10	$15	$ 25
Net financial cash flows	$−8	$18	$−24

[a]Rental or lease payments normally appear as an operating expense in the income statement. In finance, these expenses are viewed as *financial* expenses because long-term leases serve to reduce outlays on fixed assets.

Stage 3: Calculating the "Bottom Line" Examine Table 9•4, which shows the final statement, the cash flow budget. Notice that stages 1 and 2 are reproductions of Tables 9•2 and 9•3, respectively. The third stage of the cash flow budget, however, is new and warrants discussion.

Line 20 in the cash budget calculates the net cash flow from all activities—operating and financial. Now focus on line 21 in October. The starting cash balance for Byet for this month, $48, is based on information that is obtained from outside the table—the starting cash balance in any month is the ending cash balance for the previous month. Thus September must have ended with a cash balance of $48,000. The cash at the beginning of the month plus the cash actually generated in that month yields the cash at the end of the month (line 22). From line 22 is subtracted a "minimum cash balance" figure of $14,000. This minimum cash balance is the result of a management decision and represents the amount of cash the company wishes to hold as a safety margin. Remember that nearly all items in the cash flow budget are estimates, and this safety or buffer of cash can compensate for some errors in estimation. Subtracting the $14,000 minimum cash balance from the negative $23,000 cash position at the end of October yields the cumulative cash position in line 24. In October, Byet will have a cash shortage of $37,000. By following the same procedure, the November and December cumulative cash positions are deficits of $47,000 and $27,000, respectively. For obvious reasons, line 24 in the cash budget is often called the *bottom line*, a line that takes on a very special significance in financial planning.

TABLE 9•4 Byet Stores, Inc., Cash Flow Budget, Fourth Quarter, 1989 (Thousands of Dollars)

	Oct.	Nov.	Dec.
Stage 1			
Operating cash inflows			
1. Cash sales	$ 18	$ 47	$ 62
2. Collection of accounts receivable	44	40	100
3. Total operating cash inflows	$ 62	$ 87	$162
Operating cash outflows			
4. Payment of payables	$ 90	$ 72	$ 62
5. Wages and salaries	12	19	24
6. Selling and advertising	9	14	21
7. General and administrative	5	7	7
8. Capital expenditures	9	3	4
9. Total operating cash outflows	$125	$115	$118
Stage 2			
Financial cash inflows			
10. Maturing marketable securities	$ 2	$ 1	$ 0
11. Issuance of long-term debt	0	30	0
12. Other financial receipts	0	2	1
13. Total financial cash inflows	$ 2	$ 33	$ 1
Financial cash outflows			
14. Rent	$ 2	$ 2	$ 3
15. Industrial payments	0	5	0
16. Income taxes	0	0	4
17. Dividends	0	0	6
18. Repayment of short-term debt	8	8	12
19. Total financial cash outflows	$ 10	$ 15	$ 25
Stage 3			
20. Net cash flow from all activities (lines 3 less 9 plus 13 less 19)	($ 71)	($ 10)	$ 20
21. Plus: Cash at the beginning of the month	$ 48	($ 23)	($ 33)
22. Cash at the end of month	(23)	(33)	(13)
23. Less: Minimum cash balance	14	14	14
24. Cumulative cash position (surplus/deficit)	($ 37)	($ 47)	($ 27)

[a]All numbers in parentheses are negative numbers.

Uses of the Cash Flow Budget in Financial Planning

Having developed the cash budget, the financial manager can use this pro forma statement in a variety of ways. Some of the more obvious uses of cash budgets in financial planning considerations are now detailed.

Monitoring and Control of Operations The cash flow budget can shed light on several aspects of the firm's operations for perhaps a closer scrutiny by management. Any undesirable patterns or trends observed can be remedied, if necessary, by taking the appropriate action. An examination of the cash budget clearly indicates the seasonal nature of Byet's cash flow pattern. Most retailers realize the majority of their sales in the fourth quarter because of the Christmas season. Note that Byet will experience a sharp increase in sales and operating cash inflow during December. Operating outflows, on the other hand, remain fairly stable from month to month because the decrease in purchases is offset by the increase in wage and selling expenses as Christmas approaches. The net result is a net cash outflow in October–November and a sizable net inflow in December. In contrast, the expected financial flows have a more erratic pattern, but this is due to the large debt offering in November. If this issuance were not planned, the financial cash flows would have been negative throughout the quarter. This implication of the proposed debt issuance, for example, would not have been obvious without a cash budget.

Solvency Considerations Byet's cash budget indicates that it will have serious liquidity problems for the last quarter of 1989 if it does not take remedial action to cover the cash deficits. The bottom line thus alerts management to both the timing and the magnitude of the firm's cash surplus or deficit. If a company has a surplus, it should make plans to invest it in short-term interest-bearing securities (marketable securities), and to use this surplus, it must make additional investment plans. A firm cannot pursue its objective of maximizing the wealth of the shareholders if its cash flow cannot sustain its operations. If the cash flows from operations (i.e., internally generated cash flows) are not adequate, management must make arrangements to generate cash flows from outside. However, a firm cannot continue indefinitely without positive operating cash flows. Negative operating cash flows for an extended period of time can spell disaster. The highlight illustrates the case of W.T. Grant and Company's bankruptcy, which resulted from poor operating cash flows.

■ *HIGHLIGHT*

CASH FLOWS FROM OPERATIONS: W.T. GRANT COMPANY BANKRUPTCY

The importance of monitoring cash flows has been stressed repeatedly. While a firm can generate cash in a variety of ways from external sources, it is extremely important that it have the potential to generate cash flows from its day-to-day operations (i.e., operating cash flows). Operating cash flow should be monitored carefully because it can convey information not conveyed by net income. Consider an extreme example: Assume that a company has only credit sales and that total sales exceed total expenses. This firm will show profits but there may be a significant time lag before any cash is actually received by the company. Since profits cannot pay the bills, these delayed cash flows cannot be delayed forever without endangering the survival of the company. If a company cannot generate cash flows from operations for an extended period, its probability of bankruptcy rises.

The case of W.T. Grant Company provides a good illustration of this possibility. W.T. Grant was the biggest retailer in the United States prior to its bankruptcy in 1975. Figures 1 and 2 are an intrafirm analysis of W.T. Grant and show the firm's profitability ratios and liquidity ratios. Figure 3 shows the company's net income and operating cash flows.

Over the period 1966–1975 the intrafirm analysis shows that the book *ROA* and *ROE* were steadily declining. Yet although they are a cause for concern, they are not alarming; the returns are still positive in 1975. Similarly, the liquidity ratios show a gradual decline without cause for alarm. In fact, the quick ratio has been fairly stable over the entire nine-year period.

Figure 3, which focuses on the cash flows from operations, tells an entirely different story. Notice that except over approximately two years (1968–1970) W.T. Grant was unable to generate cash flows from operations. Yet an investor looking at net income would not have recognized the gradually worsening health of the firm. After 1972 the cash flows become extremely poor, and in 1972 the net income became negative. In 1975, W.T. Grant was bankrupt—it could not sustain operations.

It is not unusual for a firm to report losses in any particular year; one bad year does not usually spell disaster. However, W.T. Grant became bankrupt not because it had losses in 1974 but because it was suffering from severe cash flow problems—a hidden "cancer" that could not have been detected with basic financial statement analysis.

Moral: Even if net income is heading north, if operating cash flows head south for an extended period—watch out!

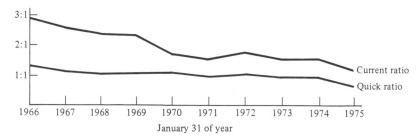

FIGURE 1 Liquidity ratios.

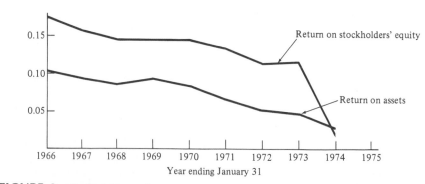

FIGURE 2 Profitability ratios.

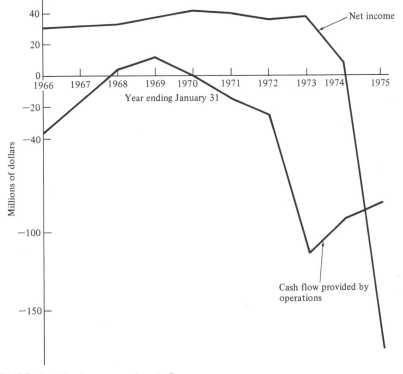

FIGURE 3   Net income and cash flow.

Source: Adapted from information provided in J. A. Largay III and C. P. Stickney, "Cash Flows, Ratio Analysis and the W.T. Grant Company Bankruptcy," *Financial Analysts Journal*, July–August 1980, pp. 51–54.

The simplest way to cope with the deficits would be to establish a line of credit with a bank for the maximum deficit shown on the bottom line—$47,000 in Table 9•4. A line of credit for $47,000 is an arrangement that allows the company to borrow up to $47,000 over the specified period of the agreement. That is, Byet would borrow $37,000 in October, borrow another $10,000 in November, and then in December repay $20,000 of the $47,000 loan outstanding. It is important to recognize that these conclusions follow from the bottom line. Remember that the bottom line is a cumulative statement and reflects the borrowing decisions of the previous months.

Note that a monthly cash budget does not describe the timing of the cash flows within the month. Daily cash flows are often quite variable, and therefore a monthly budget may mask a mismatch in cash flows. For example, Table 9•4 indicates a net inflow from all activities in December. If the outflows occur at the beginning of the month and the inflows toward the end, Byet may be "cash short" during December. A daily or weekly cash budget will help anticipate such an occurrence and may provide a different picture of the firm's financing needs. Thus, whereas the preparation of a cash budget is straightforward, the management of cash is quite complicated. Cash management is studied in greater detail in Chapter 19.

It would be prudent to arrange for additional financing in case the cash budget understates Byet's actual needs. Forecasts are estimates, and the further into the future the forecast period is, the greater the uncertainty associated with these estimates. One way a prudent financial manager could handle this situation is to prepare three forecasts for each estimate: a pessimistic, an optimistic, and a most likely estimate (Table 9•4 would be considered the most likely case). This procedure produces a range of ending cash balances and allows an examination of the impact of alternative assumptions on sales, expenses, and financial inflows.[5] With the recent proliferation of spreadsheet software, such detailed financial analyses of pro forma statements are becoming more and more feasible.

Debt Policy/Dividend Policy Planning Other potential ways to balance the cash budget would be to postpone the projected repayment of short-term debt or delay payment on accounts payable. In addition, management can look at the cash budget and draw inferences about the feasibility of planned dividend payments. However, such analyses require further scrutiny. Because these debt- and dividend-related decisions alter the firm's cash flow pattern, a revised budget becomes necessary. For example, if a seasonal bank loan is taken out, this loan would generate an additional cash inflow and its interest expenses would produce an outflow. New cash budgets may be required to try out several "what if" scenarios. The feasibility of such alternatives cannot even be explored without a cash budget.

Credit Establishment In discussing solvency considerations earlier, a line of credit was identified as a possible solution to the deficit problem. Interestingly, the cash budget not only helps the manager identify the cash needs of the company but may also be required by the bank in deciding whether to grant the loan. No bank lends money to a company without the expectation of being repaid. To assess the ability of the company to repay the debt, banks often examine the cash budget carefully to be sure that they are not subsidizing a lost cause. If the bottom line of the cash budget has no hope of showing a surplus, this information will jeopardize the approval of the company's loan request. Of course, companies realize that banks are influenced by the cash budget, and banks, in turn, are aware of the propensity of companies to present the rosiest cash budget possible. For this reason, banks often prepare their own pro forma cash budget for the firm, using more stringent assumptions. Alternatively, a bank may ask the company to prepare several revised cash flow budgets with

---

[5] A more sophisticated approach to assessing cash flow uncertainty is to stimulate the cash flows with the use of a computer. This technique considers more information and allows a probability assessment to be made about the ending cash flows. This provides a better measure of the cash flow estimates by quantifying the degree to which deviations may occur. Simulation is examined in greater detail in Chapter 14.

certain specific assumptions imposed by the bank. The basic purpose of these exercises is to provide a conservative picture of the firm's cash flow pattern. See the highlight "Quoth the Banker, 'Watch Cash Flow,'" for a humorous statement of the importance of cash flow.

■ *HIGHLIGHT*

QUOTH THE BANKER, "WATCH CASH FLOW"

Once upon a midnight dreary as I pondered weak and weary
Over many a quaint and curious volume of accounting lore,
Seeking gimmicks (without scruple) to squeeze through some new tax loophole,
Suddenly I heard a knock upon my door,
    Only this, and nothing more.

Then I felt a queasy tingling and I heard the cash a-jingling
As a fearsome banker entered whom I'd often seen before
His face was money-green and in his eyes there could be seen
Dollar-signs that seemed to glitter as he reckoned up the score.
    "Cash flow," the banker said, and nothing more.

I had always thought it fine to show a jet black bottom line.
But the banker sounded a resounding, "No.
Your receivables are high, mounting upward toward the sky;
Write-offs loom. What matters is cash flow."
    He repeated, "Watch cash flow."

Then I tried to tell the story of our lovely inventory
Which, though large, is full of most delightful stuff.
But the banker saw its growth, and with a mighty oath
He waved his arms and shouted, "Stop! Enough!
    Pay the interest, and don't give me any gruff!"

Next I looked for non-cash items which could add ad infinitum
To replace the ever-outward flow of cash,
But to keep my statement black I'd held depreciation back,
And my banker said that I'd done something rash.
    He quivered, and his teeth began to gnash.

When I asked him for a loan, he responded, with a groan,
That the interest rate would be just prime plus eight,
And to guarantee my purity he'd insist on some security—
All my assets plus the scalp upon my pate.
    Only this, a standard rate.

Though my bottom line is black, I am flat upon my back,
My cash flows out and customers pay slow.

The growth of my receivables is almost unbelievable;
The result is certain—unremitting woe!
And I hear the banker utter an ominous low mutter,
   "Watch cash flow."

Herbert S. Bailery, Jr.

Source: Reprinted from *Publishers Weekly*, January 13, 1975, published by R. R. Bowker Company. Copyright © 1975 by Xerox Corporation; reprinted with the permission of the author.

Raising Equity Capital When firms raise equity capital, the suppliers of the equity capital, even more than the firm's creditors, base their decisions on the future prospects of the company. Although this is true of all companies, it is especially important in the case of young startup or developmental-stage companies—new companies that typically have severe shortages of capital. As was seen in Chapter 4, many of these firms raise equity capital through venture capitalists. Venture capitalists supply capital to the company in return for a percentage ownership in the firm. Often these capital suppliers base their decisions on whether to take an equity position in the firm by evaluating the projected financial statements prepared by the company in a proposal called the *business plan*. Although venture capitalists come up with their own versions of the firm's future financial statements, most rely heavily on the firm's cash budget and the projected balance sheets. Cash budgets usually provide information for a "go–no-go" decision, while the projected balance sheets and income statements over, say, the next four years form the basis of the negotiation regarding the percentage of the firm's ownership that must be given up for the equity capital being provided.

FINANCIAL PLANNING WITH THE PRO FORMA INCOME STATEMENT

Cash forecasts are limited to cash flows and thus provide no information on expected profits or performance. One way to gain this information is to prepare a **pro forma income statement**.

KEY CONCEPT: A **pro forma income statement** is simply a forecast of the expected revenue, expense, and profit situation over some planning period.

Because this statement represents a summary of all projected transactions over a planning period, the information in the cash budget serves as a vital input into its construction.[6] Projected financial relationships such as ratios are also often used.

Constructing a Pro Forma Income Statement

Table 9•5 is Byet's pro forma income statement. As with the cash budget, the sales forecast is the key variable in a pro forma income statement. In Table 9•5, the $425,000 sales figure was obtained by summing the three monthly sales estimates in the operating cash flow budget (Table 9•2): $59 + $158 + $208 = $425,000. Moreover, the descriptions in the "Information Source" column reveal that all items except the cost of goods sold, income taxes, and depreciation are derived from the cash budgets. The cost of goods sold figure is based on a historical percentage-of-sales average (from the common-size statements) because a portion of the merchandise expected to be sold was purchased earlier in the year. If the "payment of payables" figure has been used instead, the cost of goods sold, and hence profits, would be misstated. Similarly, the quarterly income tax estimate of $4,000 (Table 9•3) understates Byet's estimated tax lia-

TABLE 9•5   Byet Stores, Inc., Pro Forma Income Statement, December 31, 1989

	(Thousands)	Information Source	Table
Net sales	$425	Operating cash budget	9•2
Less: Cost of goods sold	268	63% of expected sales	
Gross profit	$157		
Less: Operating expenses[a]			
Selling	$ 44	Operating cash budget	9•2
Rent	7	Financial cash budget	9•3
General and administrative	74	Operating cash budget	9•2
Depreciation	2	Depreciation schedule	
Net operating income (*NOI*)	$ 30		
Less: Interest expense	$ 5	Financial cash budget	9•2
Plus: Nonoperating income	3	Other receipts from	
		financial cash budget	9•2
Taxable income	$ 28		
Less: Income taxes (15%)	4	Historical average (%)	
Net income (*NI*)	$ 24		

[a]Operating expenses are expected to be paid as incurred rather than carried over as accruals into the first quarter of 1990.

[6]Often, in practice, a pro forma income statement may be developed before a cash budget. The primary reason is to derive an income tax estimate for the cash budget.

bility of $9,000.[7] Only $4,000 is actually paid in cash this quarter; the remainder is deferred to a subsequent quarter. These two items once again point out the differences between accrual and cash accounting. Finally, depreciation is a non-cash expense and therefore does not appear in the cash budget. This figure is derived from the existing depreciation schedule, with adjustments for new investments in fixed assets included.

Uses of the Pro Forma Income Statement in Financial Planning

Monitoring and Control Like the cash budget, the pro forma income statement can be used to coordinate and control policy decisions. If the cash budgets have been accurately forecasted, the actual income statement should be similar to the pro forma income statement. If not, significant deviations warrant an investigation to determine their cause. From an analysis of the pro forma income statement, the financial manager has a basis for assessing the expected profitability and performance of the company. In addition, since this statement depends heavily on operating cash forecasts, the financial manager has the added responsibility of coordinating and advising other officers on the development and implications of their forecasts. In fact, the financial manager in most large corporations heads a planning staff that performs coordination and consulting in the development of the operating cash forecasts. For example, if the gross profit margin is too low, the marketing and purchasing decisions need to be reexamined if this potential problem is to be eliminated. If the operating profit margin is unacceptable, operating expenses may be too high. In this case, the operations manager will be consulted and cost-cutting actions will be taken if needed.

News Releases It is common business practice, at least for large companies, to provide, say, quarterly news releases to the business press, the investment bankers, and industry specialists. These announcements center on projections of the company's realized earnings. However, announcements are often based on projections of the company's future performance, and companies generally recognize that large deviations from these projections can adversely affect the stock price. Quarterly pro forma income statements are the basis for these announcements.

Another common practice in large corporations is an annual stockholders' meeting, at which the chairman of the board usually makes projections on the firm's expected profits for that year. These estimates are typically based on the projected income statements.

---

[7] The $4,000 figure is obtained instead of the $9,000 figure because accelerated depreciation is used for taxes in this example.

Wage Negotiations In 1985, the United Auto Workers met with the management of General Motors to renegotiate salaries, benefits, and job security considerations. In such negotiations between labor and management, both parties typically use their own versions of pro forma statements to make their respective cases. Clearly, the more profitable the company is expected to be, the stronger is labor's negotiating power. Another example involves Chrysler's labor force, which in 1985 demanded compensation for wage concessions they had granted during the company's less profitable years. Their new demands stemmed from the high profits projected by auto industry experts.

Tax Planning The tax consequences of several decisions require careful analysis before a manager can make an intelligent decision. In particular, the company must know its cash flow situation and its projected income statement to assess the magnitude and nature of the impact. Accountants use the projected income statement in conjunction with other financial statements to suggest policy changes to management that can lower the firm's tax liability.

Another use of projected income statements is for estimation of the firm's marginal tax rate. While the example in Table 9•5 used a historical average tax rate, management may require more precise estimates for certain decisions. For example, capital budgeting decisions (examined in later chapters) depend on estimates of the after-tax cash flow from an investment, and the precision of these estimates depends on the accuracy of the tax rate estimation. Pro forma income statements generated with computer programs can address several "what if" questions in estimating the tax rate more accurately.

FINANCIAL PLANNING USING THE PRO FORMA BALANCE SHEET

Unlike a cash budget, a **pro forma balance sheet** gives only the cumulative funds required over a period of time rather than when (within the period) the funds will be needed. In addition, cash budgets are directly related only to a few balance sheet items, such as cash, while a pro forma balance sheet forecasts all assets and claims on assets. Moreover, based on this projected statement, additional information on the company's future financial condition and performance can be obtained by performing a ratio analysis of the pro forma statements and by constructing pro forma derivative statements such as a common-size statement.

KEY CONCEPT: A **pro forma balance sheet** is a direct estimate of the expected ending values for all asset, liability, and equity accounts for a future planning period.

Because a cash flow forecast is normally prepared first, and because most approaches to constructing a pro forma balance sheet depend on cash flow estimates, this statement is not only a supplementary source of information but also a check on the consistency of the two forecasts. Besides cash flow estimates, the construction of a pro forma balance sheet relies on the current period's ending balance sheet and the pro forma income statement.

Constructing the Pro Forma Balance Sheet

The starting point for the creation of this projected statement is the latest period's ending (actual) balance sheet, which serves as the forecasted balance sheet's beginning figures. The following general rule is then applied to each balance sheet item:

$$
\left.
\begin{array}{l}
\text{Beginning (actual) balance} \\
+ \text{ Inflows} \\
- \text{ Outflows} \\
\hline
\quad\text{Ending (forecasted) balance}
\end{array}
\right\}
\begin{array}{l}
\text{Net change in} \\
\text{the balance}
\end{array}
$$

To illustrate this rule, the major sections of Byet Stores' pro forma balance sheet in Table 9•6 will now be considered to describe how the forecasted changes and ending balances were derived, using the supporting worksheet information (Table 9•7). To facilitate the discussion that follows, the reader is urged to examine Table 9•6 constantly together with Table 9•7. The calculations involved in obtaining the numbers in the "Net Change" column in Table 9•6 are then discussed sequentially.

Assets

Cash Management's desired cash balance is $14,000 (Table 9•4). This implies that cash should decline by $34,000 during the fourth quarter.

Accounts Receivable From Table 9•2, credit sales amount to $297,500. This is because credit sales are expected to be 70% of total sales or $0.70 \times \$425,000 = \$297,500$. But management expects that 2% of total sales will prove to be uncollectible and to be charged against sales as a bad-debt expense. Net credit sales are therefore $0.68 \times \$425,000 = \$289,000$. However, the actual collection of accounts receivable is $184,000, producing an ending level of receivables of $151,000. The change in receivables is therefore the ending value of $151,000 less the beginning value of $46,000, or an increase of $105,000. This is shown in the worksheet in Table 9•7.

Inventory The ending inventory balance requires that the difference between purchases and the cost of goods sold be added to the beginning inventory figure. Purchases represent the sum of the monthly purchase in Table 9•2. While purchases increase inventories, the costs of goods sold from the pro forma income

TABLE 9•6 Byet Stores, Inc., Pro Forma Balance Sheet, December 31, 1989 (Thousands of Dollars)

	Starting Balance Sheet: Actual Value Sept. 30, 1989	Net Change +/−[a]	Pro Forma Balance Sheet: Ending Value Dec. 31, 1989
Assets			
1. Current assets			
Cash	$ 48	($ 34)	$ 14
Net accounts receivable	46	105	151
Inventories	191	(95)	96
Prepaid expenses	6	0	6
Total current assets	$291	($ 24)	$267
2. Net fixed assets	72	14	86
Total assets	$363	($ 10)	$353
Claims on Assets			
3. Current liabilities			
Accounts payable	$ 90	($ 51)	$ 39
Notes payable—bank	73	(28)	45
Accrued taxes	5	0	5
Other accruals	20	0	20
Total current liabilities	$188	($ 79)	$109
4. Long-term liabilities			
Debenture bonds	$ 49	$ 30	$ 79
Deferred taxes	14	0	14
Total long-term liabilities	$ 63	$ 30	$ 93
5. Stockholders' equity			
Common stock	$ 25	$ 0	$ 25
Paid-in capital	22	0	22
Retained earnings	65	18	83
Total stockholders' equity	$112	$ 18	$130
Total claims	$363	($ 31)	$332
Total funds required			$ 21

[a]Detailed calculations of net change (+/−) provided in Table 9•7.

statement represent how much inventories are expected to decrease. The result: a net decrease of $95,000 to an ending balance of $96,000.

Net Fixed Assets The change in net fixed assets depends on the budgeted expenditures on plant and equipment less the expected depreciation expense. Capital expenditures are found by summing the monthly estimates in the financial cash flow budget, while the $2,000 depreciation expense comes from the pro forma income statement. The net effect is an increase of $14,000 to $86,000.

TABLE 9•7 Worksheet for Pro Forma Balance Sheet

		Change	
Cash		($ 34)	
Beginning cash	$ 48		
Ending cash	14		
Accounts Receivables		$105	
Beginning accounts receivable	$ 46		
+ Net credit sales	289		
− Accounts receivable collected	184		
Ending accounts receivable	$151		
Inventory		($ 95)	
Beginning inventory	$191		
+ Purchases	173		(Table 9•2)
− Cost of goods sold	268		(Table 9•5)
Ending inventory	$ 96		
Long-term fixed assets		$ 14	
Beginning net fixed assets	$ 72		
+ Capital expenditures	16		(Table 9•2)
− Depreciation expense	2		(Table 9•5)
Ending net fixed assets	$ 86		
Accounts payables		($ 51)	
Beginning accounts payables	$ 90		
+ Purchases	173		(Table 9•2)
− Payment of payables	224		(Table 9•2)
Ending accounts payables	$ 39		
Notes payables		($ 28)	
Beginning notes payables	$ 73		
+ New borrowing	0		
− Repayment of bank debt	28		(Table 9•3)
Ending notes payables	$ 45		
Accrued taxes		$ 0	
Beginning accrued taxes	$ 5		
+ Income tax liability	4		(Table 9•5)
− Income taxes paid	4		(Table 9•3)
Ending accrued taxes	$ 5		
Debenture bonds		$ 30	
Beginning debenture bonds	$ 49		
+ Issuance of new bonds	30		
− Retirement of existing bonds	0		
Ending debenture bonds	$ 79		
Stockholders' equity		$ 18	
Beginning retained earnings	$ 65		
+ Net income	24		(Table 9•5)
− Dividend payments	6		
Ending retained earnings	$ 83		

Liabilities

Current and Long-Term Liabilities The net decrease of $51 million in accounts payable is derived by subtracting the summed monthly estimates for the payment of payables (Table 9•2) from planned purchases. This will reduce accounts payable to an ending balance of $39,000. A scheduled $8,000 repayment of bank debt in November (Table 9•3) produces an ending notes payable balance of $45,000. Ending accrued taxes are obtained by subtracting the estimated cash tax payments in December (Table 9•3) from the tax liability incurred (but not paid) on fourth-quarter profits (Table 9•3) and adding this figure to the beginning balance. Finally, Byet Stores has arranged for the issuance of new bonds in November (Table 9•3). No retirement (repayment) of existing bond is scheduled, and therefore this account will increase by $30,000 to $79,000.

Stockholders' Equity Common stock and paid-in capital are normally assumed to remain unchanged because any changes are made at the discretion of management. The only change in equity thus occurs with regard to the retention of earnings. From the pro forma income statement (Table 9•5), net income after taxes is expected to be $24,000. However, Byet will pay a $6,000 dividend in December (Table 9•3). The difference between these two figures implies that retained earnings should rise to $83,000.

Using the Pro Forma Balance Sheet for Planning

Funds Planning Byet's pro forma balance sheet provides certain insights for funds planning. First, the "Total Funds Required" line acts as a "plug figure" to balance the assets against the claims on assets in Table 9•6.[8] This figure indicates that Byet will experience a $21,000 financing shortfall if the projected total asset investment of $353,000 holds true. This result is consistent with the negative cash flow forecasted in the cash budget and reinforces the fact that additional financing needs to be prearranged to meet the projected deficit. Moreover, the financial manager must decide what mix of short- and long-term financing is best, as well as the type of financing.

Performance Evaluation The financial manager could also analyze Byet's projected financial condition and performance through the use of common-size statements, sources-and-uses-of-funds statements, and financial ratios. These results could be compared with its past performance and with industry averages. If any weaknesses or serious deviations are discovered, management would be forewarned to take corrective measures. For example, accounts receivable is expected to balloon to approximately 42% of assets ($151/$353) from about 13% ($46/$363) ending September 30, 1989 (refer to Table 9•6). Byet's credit and

---

[8]Alternative approaches to estimating financing requirements use cash or notes payable as the plug figure. Management must them determine whether or not these accounts' balances are reasonable and take corrective action if they are out of line.

collection policy might bear closer scrutiny to determine the reason for this situation.

Ensuring Compliance with Indenture Agreements When firms raise debt capital, they are often required to agree to certain conditions spelled out in a document called the *indenture agreement*. For example, management might have agreed not to allow the long-term debt–equity ratio to fall below a certain value. Similarly, banks may require a company to maintain, say, a current ratio of at least 0.6 until the loan is paid off. Because a variety of financial decisions affect these ratios, the manager needs to try out several potential plans in order to make sure that proposed policies do not violate any of these agreements.

Bond-Rating Considerations The debt levels raised by companies have different risks, and bond-rating agencies assign a letter grade to each bond based on a variety of considerations, which rely to a great extent on the financial statements of the company. Managers generally regard major deviations in certain key ratios as having an adverse impact on their debt rating, and therefore carefully examine the effects of several decisions on future balance sheet ratios. Pro forma balance sheets and income statements offer a convenient vehicle for such analyses.

INTERRELATIONSHIP OF THE VARIOUS PRO FORMA STATEMENTS

The pro forma balance sheet and the pro forma income statement are linked together in that the balance sheet cannot be prepared without the income statement. This is because the level of retained earnings in the projected balance sheet will depend on the net income projected in the income statement. Byet's projected net income is $24,000, and with the planned dividend of $6,000, the increase in retained earnings in the projected balance sheet is therefore $18,000. However, the pro forma balance sheet provides information on the required total borrowings, and the interest on these borrowings affects the pro forma income statement. This complication can be overcome by using a computer to prepare the two statements simultaneously, recognizing this interrelationship.

Financial managers often gain more information by looking at more than one pro forma statement at a time. For example, note that the cash flow estimate in Table 9•4 indicates a substantial negative cash position. Yet the pro forma income statement indicates a profit. If financial managers relied strictly on this pro forma statement, they would see a rosy picture of Byet's financial performance. The cash budget tells them, on the other hand, that substantial short-term financing must be arranged to meet Byet's obligations. Remember: Profits do not pay bills.

Finally, note that both the pro forma income statement and the balance sheet were based on the most likely cash flow estimates. Financial managers may want to develop additional sets of these statements by using the most pessimistic and most optimistic cash forecasts or by varying the different assumptions underlying the various forecasts. This additional information would provide a range of estimates, and thus a range of financial conditions and performances that would better help them gauge the seriousness of any financing requirements or deviations from the desired results. This procedure can be used with an interactive computer spreadsheet to do this, recognizing the interrelationship between the various statements.

Learning Check for Section 9•1

Review Questions

9•1. What are the different stages or steps involved in developing a cash budget?

9•2. What are the uses of a cash budget?

9•3. How are pro forma balance sheets and income statements constructed?

9•4. What are the uses of pro forma balance sheets and pro forma income statements?

9•5. What are the differences between the cash flow budget seen in this chapter and the cash flow statement seen in Chapter 7?

9•6. What is financial planning?

9•7. What are the primary differences between short-term and long-term planning? What concerns are relevant for each?

9•8. How is the cash flow budget related to the pro forma balance sheet and the pro forma income statement?

9•9. What is the bottom line of the cash budget? What does it tell the financial manager?

9•10. What are some of the uses of the cash budget? Why is the cash flow budget important to the firm?

9•11. How can a financial manager use the pro forma income statement?

New Terms

Cash budget	Pro forma balance	Pro forma income
Financial planning	sheet	statement

SECTION 9·2 # *Long-Term Financial Planning*

The pro forma statements developed thus far are short term; they usually deal with projections for no more than one year. Longer-term forecasts are often needed by management to provide information for decisions on asset investments and long-term financing requirements. Although very tentative, they are usually an integral part of management's overall strategic planning, by which it attempts to modify its policies in order to take advantage of broad changes in its industry and its operating environment. Besides financial needs, other considerations, such as forecasts of economic, political, and social trends, are normally included. In this section, one approach to forecasting long-range financing needs is presented. This is followed by a discussion of forecasting long-range investment needs.

LONG-TERM FORECASTS OF FINANCING REQUIREMENTS

For several reasons, long-range forecasts of financing requirements are often made with only a set of pro forma balance sheets. First, the detail required and the difficulty of forecasting cash flows beyond one year preclude a cash budget approach. Moreover, the degree of forecast error increases markedly as the time span increases. Second, financial managers usually seek only a broad view of the firm's financial needs, because a three- to five-year period normally provides adequate time to adjust to new information and to work around unforeseen circumstances. Finally, the primary objective of a long-range financial forecast is to determine the amount of financing not covered by short-term liabilities—existing long-term debt and equity, as well as expected earnings retentions. This information is most easily obtained from a forecast of a firm's pro forma balance sheets. If a significant deficit in resources is expected, for example, plans must be formulated to raise additional outside financing, reduce dividend payments (retain more earnings), or adjust expected sales and assets growth to be more consistent with available financing.

Rather than go through an elaborate budgeting process, a manager may construct a pro forma balance sheet by using a much simpler approach called the **percent-of-sales** *forecasting* **method.**

KEY CONCEPT: The **percent-of-sales forecasting method** forecasts certain key balance sheet items as percentages of sales and then uses these percentages together with a forecasted sales estimate to construct a pro forma balance sheet.

This technique is simply a modified common-size statement, as discussed in Chapter 6. By assuming that balance sheet items bear a constant percentage relationship to sales, this approach, in effect, assumes that the firm's major economic characteristics will remain unchanged. For example, it is assumed that the firm's existing credit policy and its payable policy will not change. A primary difference between a pro forma balance sheet derived via the percentage-of-sales method and a common-size balance sheet statement is that values in the balance sheet are figured as a percentage of sales in the first statement, while the ratios are calculated as percentages of assets in the common-size statement.

CONSTRUCTING THE PRO FORMA BALANCE SHEET USING THE PERCENT-OF-SALES METHOD

The underlying logic of the percent-of-sales long-range forecasting method is that most balance sheet items tend to be highly correlated with sales. Therefore, the first step is to identify those items that vary directly with sales. For example, if sales are expected to increase, receivables and inventory will increase to support this change. Similarly, current liabilities, such as payables and accruals, will also increase spontaneously as larger purchases and more labor are needed to accommodate higher sales. Certain balance sheet items, such as direct sources of financing (notes payable and common stock), however, do not change proportionately with sales and are held constant. Changes in these accounts do not occur automatically because they require negotiations and deliberate action by management.

The next step involves taking the appropriate balance sheet variables and expressing them as a percentage of last year's sales. Alternatively, each percentage can be based on its average historical relationship with sales. These percentage values can then be adjusted for conditions not reflected in the historical statements.

Next, a sales forecast is derived for each future period. Long-range sales forecasts normally involve projections of past sales, the forecasts developed with varying degrees of sophistication. The simplest method, and the one used here, consists of three steps:

1. Determine the year-to-year sales growth rates over the last few years.

2. Average these rates.

3. Use this average to estimate the sales for each future period.

More elaborate methods employ statistical techniques to establish a relationship between sales and certain predictive economic or industry variables. Most of these methods, however, are beyond the scope of this book. Finally, the balance sheet percentages are applied to the expected sales estimate to obtain each balance sheet value.

To illustrate, Table 9•8 contains an abbreviated version of Byet's latest balance sheet on December 31, 1988, as well as the percent-of-sales estimates for

TABLE 9•8 Byet Stores, Inc., Forecasting Financial Requirements for Three Years with the Percent-of-Sales Method (Assumed Growth Rate = 12% per Year)

	Actual Balance Sheet on December 31, 1988 as Percentage of Sales (Actual Sales = $801,000)		Pro Forma Balance Sheet Ending December 31		
			1989	1990	1991
Expected sales			$897	$1,005	$1,125
Assets					
Total current assets	$257	32.1%	$267	$ 304	$ 340
Net fixed assets	59	7.4%	86	74	83
Total assets	$316	39.5%	$353	$ 378	$ 423
Claims on assets					
Notes payable—bank[a]	$ 31	[b]	$ 45	$ 31	$ 31
Other current liabilities	104	13.0%	64	131	146
Long-term liabilities[a]	61	[b]	93	61	61
Common stock[a]	47	[b]	47	47	47
Retained earnings	73	9.1%	83	72	81
Total claims	$316	22.1%	$332	$ 342	$ 366
Total assets − total claims					
Required financing			$ 21	$ 36	$ 57
Cumulative financial needs			$ 21	$ 57	$ 114

[a]The 1989, 1990, and 1991 projections are based on the ending balance on December 31, 1988.
[b]Assumed not to vary directly with sales.

those items assumed to vary directly with sales. For example, total current assets were $242/$801 = 0.302, or 30.2% of 1988 sales. To construct the pro forma balance sheets, the ending account balances are found by multiplying the estimated annual sales by their percentage relationships. For example, assume that the marketing manager expects sales to increase 12% per year over the next three years. In this case, 1989 sales will be 1.12 × $801 = $897,000. This implies that total current assets will be 0.302 × $897 = $271,000. This same process is then applied to the remaining accounts that vary with sales. Next, simply substitute those figures from the 1988 balance sheet for the accounts not assumed to change with sales: notes payable, long-term liabilities, and common stock.

LONG-TERM PLANNING IMPLICATIONS

Funds Requirement Analysis

The asset accounts in Table 9•8 are then summed to obtain the projected asset investments (e.g., $337,000 in 1989). Similarly, the claims on assets are totaled to arrive at the available funds figure (e.g., $320,000 in 1989). The difference between these two figures is a "balancing" amount that tells management what additional funds will be required each year.

Growth Planning

Byet will need to secure $21,000 in additional external financing during 1989 to support its projected sales and asset investment of $897,000 and $353,000, respectively. This projected shortfall will further increase annually by an additional $20,000 (approximately) during the subsequent years. Moreover, the cumulative external funds requirement will come to $114,000. This should also point out the crucial importance of the sales forecasts. A small change in sales growth will have a disproportionate change in future financial needs because the faster sales are expected to grow, the greater will be the demand for additional financing. If Byet's financial manager believes that this amount will be difficult to raise, a slower sales growth or a less rapid buildup of assets must be planned. Growing companies seldom grow by accident; they are the result of careful planning on the part of management. Without **growth planning,** even the company with a product in great demand may be unable to sustain the level of operations required to get the product to the stores and into the hands of the consumer. In addition, long-range forecasts can be useful for planning and control.

Learning Check for Section 9•2

Review Questions

9•12.   What is the fundamental assumption underlying the percent-of-sales method of forecasting?

9•13.   What are the uses of a pro forma statement generated using the percent-of-sales method?

9•14.   Can the percent-of-sales method be used for all accounts in the pro forma balance sheet? What characterizes the accounts for which this procedure cannot be used?

9•15.   What are the steps in developing the pro forma balance using the percent-of-sales method?

New Terms

Growth planning   Percent-of-sales method

■ *HIGHLIGHT*

MICROCOMPUTERS AND FINANCIAL PLANNING

Microcomputers offer ways to improve the efficiency of planning processes. Application software for micros fall in four main areas: word processing, spreadsheet/graphics, database management, and telecommunications. Integrated software packages combine all these features into one program.

Spreadsheet software is particularly useful for financial planning. A spreadsheet program displays a row-columnar screen on the terminal. Each cell in this "spreadsheet" represents a variable. Text, numbers, or formulas (which refer to different cells within the spreadsheet) may be entered into the cells. The screen will always display text or numbers (which may be a result of a formula entered into that cell).

Every time the contents of a cell are changed, the entire spreadsheet is recalculated. This provides a powerful tool to perform "what if" analysis for any set of financial statements. For example, one may set up pro forma financial statements (income statement, balance sheet, etc.), with appropriate relationships between them to compute successive statements, by using figures from the preceding statements. It is then possible to change any one (or more) numbers in one statement and see the effects ripple into the other pro forma statements, thereby improving the productivity of the financial manager.

What makes the micros and spreadsheet programs more useful are the capabilities of these tools to transfer data from one user to another user. First, data from one spreadsheet may be incorporated into another spreadsheet at the press of a button. The numbers transferred may be simply copied, or they may be added to (or subtracted from) the numbers in the receiving spreadsheet. This operation allows for consolidation of divisional budgets/forecasts/statements into one statement at the touch of a button. Second, the data may be sent over telephone lines using a telecommunication program. This allows fast communication between physically distant units of the organization.

Implications for Financial Planning

The interactive nature of the financial statements allows a company to set up what may be called a *distributed planning system* between the various functional areas of the company. Marketing managers and the production department, for example, can directly provide input into the financial manager's pro forma statements. To set up such a distributed planning system the firm must first develop models of divisional cash flow statements and then tie them into a consolidated model for the financial manager. Second, managers must be trained (or provided with staff) to work with the micros. The advantages for the planning process are as follows:

1. Planning is done with a reduced set of assumptions. Financial managers need not make assumptions as to how marketing or operations managers plan for their functions. Financial managers need only be concerned with the results of their plans.

2. The numbers have greater validity. There are not only fewer assumptions underlying the plans, but they are also based on the intimate

knowledge of functional managers for their own departments, thus injecting greater competency in the planning process.

3. It is possible to iterate through the planning process a number of times within a short interval. Managerial time is a premium resource for the firm. Planning sessions between departmental managers are often difficult due to scheduling conflicts. Physical distances compound the situation. These problems are overcome by having managers perform planning in their departments and (tele)communicate the results to be consolidated by the financial manager.

4. Increased iterations provide opportunities for improved problem solving by allowing examination of a greater number of alternatives by functional experts. Microcomputers and distributed planning systems do not by themselves guarantee better problem solving, but they increase the likelihood of producing better financial plans. To the extent that financial planning is facilitated, it will cease to be a rote exercise; instead, it will prepare the firm to deal with future operational and financial obstacles.

The assistance of R. P. Khandekar in the preparation of this Highlight is gratefully acknowledged.

A Concluding Observation

Several of the chapters that follow develop rules for analyzing investments that increase the value of the company. This increase in value is brought about by investing in projects that increase the value of the firm. It is important to keep in mind that firm-value maximization is not guaranteed solely by picking the best projects. Management must constantly engage in financial planning analyses to ensure that the various operational details and institutional realities are not ignored. Even the best investment in the world is of little value to a firm with inadequate planning. If the company's basic financial stability is threatened, the full benefits provided by even the best project may never be realized.

Techniques of financial planning have been improved in the last decade by the introduction of the microcomputer. The microcomputer's use in financial planning is examined in the highlight "Microcomputers and Financial Planning."

SUMMARY

Short-Term Financial Planning

Pro forma statements are projected financial statements that provide the financial manager with useful information. A cash budget enables the manager to anticipate both the magnitude and timing of cash deficits and surpluses in the future. This information can provide ample time to arrange for lines of credit or to plan for the investment of future cash surpluses. Cash budgets are also required by banks and other lenders of funds. In addition, for startup companies, even suppliers of equity capital may require cash budgets. Cash budgets also facilitate monitoring and control functions. If the actual receipts or expenditures are significantly different from the projected values, management will be alerted to a potential problem and will be able to take immediate corrective action.

Pro forma balance sheets and income statements provide information on the future expected profits and net worth of a company, among other things. These statements enable the manager to estimate future retained earnings, future ratio values from the financial statements, and so on. This can be extremely useful to the manager and can facilitate the adherence to certain financial policies that management has decided to follow. For example, in borrowing money, the company may have agreed to maintain a current ratio of 2.0 at all times. By examining the projected financial statements, the manager can anticipate any serious violations of this requirement and take corrective action. Finally, all of the projected financial statements are used extensively in negotiations between the firm and potential suppliers of equity capital.

Long-Term Financial Planning

Long-range (greater than one year) balance sheet forecasts can be made with the percent-of-sales method. This method assumes that all balance sheet items vary as a constant percentage of sales and can be a reasonable approach over a two- or three-year period for a firm that is not expected to undergo major changes.

PROBLEMS

9•1. Nater, Inc., expects sales of $4,000 in March, $6,000 in April, $5,000 in May, $4,000 in June, and $5,500 in July. On average, they collect 35% of their monthly sales in cash, 45% in one month, and 19% in two months (the remaining 1% is bad-debt expense and is never collected). Find Nater's expected cash inflows during the months of May, June, and July.

9•2. Bilch's Fried Chicken is a fast-food chain. Although its expenses depend primarily on sales, these expenses are not necessarily paid in cash in the month of the sale. For example, wage expense amounts to 25% of a month's sales but is paid on the first day of the next month (the wage expense incurred in January is not actually paid until February). Chicken is purchased for the current month (its cost represents 20% of the sales volume) and is paid for in cash. Frozen french fries, oil, and other supplies cost 30% of a given month's sales. They are purchased with cash one month prior to the sale. Finally, Bilch has rent expenses totaling $220,000 per month; their expected sales (in dollars) are as follows:

Month	Aug.	Sept.	Oct.	Nov.	Dec.	Jan.
Expected Sales	1,000,000	1,200,000	1,100,000	850,000	700,000	950,000

(a) Find Bilch's operating expenses for September, October, November, and December.
(b) Bilch's is currently experiencing cash flow problems and is considering an offer by the chicken supplier to take 60 days' credit with a credit charge of $2\frac{1}{2}$% for this two-month period. Find Bilch's expected outflows for September, October, November, and December if they take advantage of this offer.

9·3. Koufand's Jeweler's has expected cash inflows, variable cash outflows (outflows that depend on sales), and fixed cash outflows as follows:

	Jan.	Feb.	Mar.	Apr.
Inflows	$600,000	$700,000	$620,000	$500,000
Variable outflows	290,000	330,000	270,000	235,000
Fixed outflows	320,000	320,000	320,000	320,000

Koufand's has a cash balance of $50,000 as of January 1 and a minimum desired balance of $40,000. Find Koufand's expected net cash flow for each of the four months listed, and construct a monthly cash budget for the four months.

9·4. Following is the cash flow budget for the Baxter Corporation, a retailing firm, for the last quarter of 1985.

	Aug.	Sept.	Oct.	Nov.	Dec.
Total sales	$720	$760	$840	$920	$ 900
Cash sales (35%)			294	322	315
Collections from previous month (35%)			266	294	322
Collections from 2nd previous month (30%)			216	228	252
Total operating cash inflows			$776	$844	$ 889

	Aug.	Sept.	Oct.	Nov.	Dec.
Cash outflows					
Payment of accounts payable			$172	$197	$ 225
Wages and salaries			152	165	182
Selling			145	151	154
General and administrative			153	159	157
Capital expenditures			18	9	18
Rent			120	120	120
Taxes			0	0	52
Interest			17	17	17
Total cash outflows			$777	$818	$ 925
Net cash flow			$ −1	$ 26	$−36
Beginning cash balance			300	299	325
Ending cash balance			$299	$325	$ 289
Minimum desired			250	250	250
Surplus (deficit)			$ 49	$ 75	$ 39

Depreciation for the quarter will be $164, and the cost of goods sold generally averages about 20% of sales. Baxter's tax rate is 34%. Baxter pays its accounts receivable one month after its purchase of inventory; December purchases will be 30% of sales. Construct a pro forma income statement for the last quarter of 1985.

9•5. Following is the balance sheet of the Baxter Corporation as of September 31, 1985. Construct a pro forma balance sheet for December 31, 1985. (Refer to the data in Problem 9•4 if necessary.)

Cash	$ 300	Accounts payable	$ 169
Accounts receivable	512	Notes payable	142
Marketable securities	36	Taxes payable	44
Inventory	421	Total current	
Current assets	$1,269	liabilities	$ 355
Net fixed assets	5,208	Long-term debt	2,900
Total assets	$6,477	Common stock	1,700
		Capital contributed	
		in excess of par	721
		Retained earnings	801
		Total liabilities and	
		stockholders' equity	$6,477

9•6. Which of the following balance sheet items would ordinarily be expected to increase spontaneously with sales?

Cash	Accounts payable
Marketable securities	Wages payable
Accounts receivable	Notes payable
Inventory	Long-term debt

9•7. Following is the balance sheet of Krivaco, Inc., on December 31, 1984. Sales during 1984 were $12,000,000 but are expected to increase to $13,800,000 during 1985. Krivaco's net profit margin ratio is expected to remain constant at 2%, and they pay out 40% of their earnings in the form of dividends. Using the percent-of-sales method, construct a pro forma balance sheet for December 31, 1985.

Cash	$ 495,000	Accounts payable	$ 524,000
Marketable securities	257,000	Wages payable	57,000
Accounts receivable	620,000	Notes payable	316,000
Inventory	512,000	Current liabilities	$ 897,000
Current assets	$1,884,000	Long-term debt	1,500,000
		Common stock	2,300,000
Gross fixed assets	6,168,000	Retained earnings	1,503,000
Less: Accumulated		Total liabilities and	
depreciation	−1,852,000	stockholders' equity	$6,200,000
Net fixed assets	$4,316,000		
Total assets	$6,200,000		

Krivaco will spend $200,000 for the construction of a new plant during 1985, and depreciation during the year will be $162,000.

9•8. Following are the current accounts of the Frederick Corporation as of December 31, 1985.

Cash	$ 60	Accounts payable	$60
Marketable securities	10	Wages payable	10
Accounts receivable	120	Notes payable	20
Inventory	80	Current liabilities	$90
Current assets	$270		

Sales during 1985 were $1,200 and are expected to grow to $1,500 during 1988. Frederick desires to maintain its current ratio of 3.0. Using the percent-of-sales method and assuming that marketable securities remains at $10, determine what notes payable must be to maintain this current ratio.

READINGS

ANTHONY, R. N., *Planning and Control Systems: A Framework for Analysis* (Boston: Division of Research, Graduate School of Business, Harvard University, 1965).

DRUCKER, P., "Long-Range Planning: Challenge to Management Science," *Management Science*, April 1959, 238–249.

FRANCIS, JACK CLARK, AND DEXTER R. ROWELL, "A Simultaneous Equation Model of the Firm for Financial Analysis and Planning," *Financial Management*, Spring 1978, 29–44.

GRINYER, P. H., AND J. WOOLLER, *Corporate Models Today—A New Tool for Financial Management* (London: Institute of Chartered Accountants, 1978).

PAN, JUDY, DONALD R. NICHOLS, AND O. MAURICE JOY, "Sales Forecasting Practices of Large U.S. Industrial Firms," *Financial Management*, Fall 1977, 72–77.

TRAENKLE, J. W., E. B. COX, AND J. A. BULLARD, *The Use of Financial Models in Business* (New York: Financial Executives' Research Foundation, 1975).

The Firm's Investment Decisions

10

The Investment Decision: Determining Cash Flows

Each year, American businesses invest hundreds of billions of dollars in new fixed assets—plant, equipment, pollution control devices, cars, trucks, and storage facilities. Unlike current assets, which have a short life, these longer-term investments in fixed assets involve cash outlays that are expected to result in benefits to the firm over several years. Such expenditures, which are expected to generate future cash benefits lasting longer than one year, are classified as **capital expenditures.** Cash outlays that are expected to result in benefits for a short (less than one year) horizon only are classified as **operating expenditures.** Capital expenditures are usually incurred to obtain capital assets, which are used by the company in the actual production of goods and services. Capital assets can include, for example, plant facilities, bulldozers, computers, and even other companies. In most cases, the dollar volume involved in acquiring these capital assets is very large, and firms must plan carefully before committing scarce resources to them. The plans for capital expenditures are summarized in a **capital budget,** and the process of determining exactly which assets to invest in and how much to invest is called **capital budgeting.**

The capital budgeting decision is a complex process that involves several activities: searching for new profitable investments, marketing and production analyses to determine economic attractiveness, careful cash flow estimation, preparation of cash budgets, evaluation of proposals, and the control and monitoring of past projects. Several types of capital expenditures lend themselves to capital budgeting analysis:

1. The purchase of new machinery, real estate, or patent rights.

2. Expansion of product lines.

3. Replacement of existing capital assets.

4. Credit policy decisions.

5. Bond refunding.

6. Lease-versus-buy analysis.

7. Merger-acquisition analysis.

Capital budgeting decisions are made frequently within a business organization, and these decisions exert considerable influence on the profitability of the company and on the company's stock price. This is because companies undertake new activities to increase the wealth of the stockholders. Thus, with good capital budgeting decisions, a company maximizes its stockholders' wealth, and such benefits accrue not only to the individual stockholder but to society as a whole.

Two parallel considerations are required for proper capital budgeting analysis, and a company is not likely to serve the best interests of the owners if either of them is ignored. First, there are **strategic considerations**—items that involve the company's objectives and long-term plans, **intangible considerations** (e.g., corporate philosophy), and **financial and operational feasibility considerations.** Second, and just as important, are **economic considerations.** Detailed analyses are necessary to ensure that a capital investment is, in fact, to the firm's advantage. The qualitative and computational aspects of capital budgeting are the subject of this chapter.

The systematic development of capital budgeting principles is covered in two chapters. This chapter provides an overview of the capital budgeting process and explains how the relevant cash flows used in capital budgeting decisions are obtained. Chapter 11 discusses five methods commonly used to evaluate these cash flows, and compares their strengths and weaknesses. In this and the next chapter, all cash flows and discount rates are known. In Chapters 13 and 14 we will discuss how the appropriate discount rate is determined.

The discussion of the capital budgeting process and the determination of relevant cash flows is divided into two sections.

SECTION 10•1: *An Overview of the Capital Budgeting Process.* In the first section, the stages of the capital budgeting process are discussed. Managers must determine their long-term goals, identify prospective investment proposals, evaluate the profitability of those proposals, implement and control the projects accepted, and, upon completion of a project, evaluate its success or failure.

SECTION 10•2: *The Relevant Cash Flows for Capital Budgeting.* In this section, the cash flows relevant to capital budgeting are identified and a systematic procedure for classifying the cash flows is provided. Cash flows are characterized as initial, operating, and terminal, depending on where in the life of the project

313

they occur. Two examples are worked out in detail to provide a detailed understanding of how these cash flows are determined.

SECTION 10•1 *An Overview of the Capital Budgeting Process*

The capital budgeting process involves several activities, and the entire process may be viewed conveniently in terms of six phases. In some companies, the various activities are done on a companywide basis by a centralized planning group that performs the capital budgeting analysis. In other firms, it is done at a divisional level. For example, the electronic typewriter division of an office products manufacturing company may prepare the entire project analysis, using its own staff, and submit a written proposal to top management. In most cases, however, the capital budgeting process involves the joint efforts of various individuals at different levels within the company.

IDENTIFYING THE IMPACT ON LONG-TERM GOALS

The first step in evaluating investment decisions is to formulate long-term goals. Regardless of the project being considered, the firm's ultimate objective is to maximize the stock price and, consequently, the shareholders' wealth. Although this overriding objective does not change from project to project, many projects cannot be completely evaluated in terms of their impact on stock price. For example, the decision of a firm to spend millions of dollars on environmental improvement may lower its profits and cash flows in the short run. However, management might feel that it is consistent with another of the company's long-term goals—being of service to the community. Alcoa's commitment to land restoration and beautification in areas close to its strip-mining operations is an example of this type of consideration. Thus intangible benefits that are consistent with a firm's long-term goals should be identified with each project, and these benefits and costs should be considered together with other economic analyses. These intangibles are often labeled strategic considerations. Other examples of strategic considerations are timing related (e.g., Apple Computer's decision to develop the Macintosh computer after evaluating IBM's competing product) or marketing related (e.g., Polaroid's strategy of selling cameras at giveaway prices, expecting to benefit from the sale of expensive film). These decisions are extremely difficult to make because they involve a variety of factors that simply cannot be generalized, and therefore they are not addressed in this chapter.

SCREENING PHASE

Before an objective analysis can be performed, the company must identify potential investment proposals. These **proposals** can originate in a variety of ways. Large companies have entire project analysis divisions that actively search for new ideas, projects, and ventures. Divisional managers and product managers usually take their proposals to a planning committee or even to the board of directors. Managers use the input from a variety of sources: engineers, market analysts, sales personnel, and so on. Virtually every employee of the company is a potential source of ideas, and many companies encourage their employees to develop new concepts for evaluation by the investment division.

Management must first evaluate in qualitative terms its ability to exploit the investment opportunities and gauge, in crude terms, the potential impact of these investments on the firm's revenues and costs. If a proposal passes this initial screening, it is subjected to more detailed analysis. In this **screening phase,** it is useful to categorize potential proposals into three groups.

KEY CONCEPT: A **cost-reduction proposal** is one that will lower the firm's operating costs if accepted.

A firm may choose to replace its inefficient old lathe with a newer version that reduces waste and consumes less energy. Buying the new lathe, in this case, would be a **cost-reduction proposal.**

KEY CONCEPT: A **vertical revenue expansion proposal** is one that increases the revenues of the company if output is increased.

For example, a company producing 5,000 barrels of formaldehyde contemplates doubling the output to 10,000 barrels.

KEY CONCEPT: A **horizontal revenue expansion proposal** is one that is unrelated to the company's existing activity.

For example, a small printing company plans to invest in real estate.

Proposals in each category are characterized by similar objectives and operating characteristics. Classifying proposals into these categories simplifies the analysis and enables management to address and answer key questions such as the following: Can the existing plant be used to achieve the new production levels? Does management have the knowledge and skill to take on this new investment? Does the new proposal warrant the recruitment of new technical personnel? The advantage of having answers to these questions is that it helps the firm screen out certain proposals if, for example, they warrant a drastic change in personnel or subject the firm to new risks that management finds unacceptable. When the screening process has eliminated certain proposals based on, for example, qualitative considerations, the capital budgeting process enters the third phase. Often, financial planning considerations can suggest that certain proposals are not feasible. As seen in Chapter 9, the financial manager must ensure that the firm will not face liquidity crises and that accepting a proposal does not jeopardize the feasibility of the firm's other operations. Again, it is important to realize that the objective capital budgeting decisions are meaningless if subjective and institutional considerations suggest that the company's day-to-day operations will be hampered by funds flow problems.

EVALUATION PHASE

The **evaluation phase** consists of three distinct activities: estimating the cash flows from the various proposals, identifying projects, and applying objective criteria before making an accept/reject decision. First, it is necessary to identify any dependencies between the cash flows of various proposals. To understand the significance of the last sentence, it is necessary to distinguish between proposals and projects.

KEY CONCEPT: Any idea under consideration is a **proposal.**

For example, a plan to introduce a new product line, discussions on increasing the advertising budget, a plan to buy a vineyard, and a plan to cease credit sales are all capital budgeting proposals. Of the many proposals being considered by a firm, several may be related to one another in terms of after-tax cash flows $(CFAT)$.[1] It is important that all of these related cash flows be identified and properly handled in the capital budgeting process. As will be explained, all proposals whose cash flows are economically dependent on one another must be evaluated together as a **project.** Thus:

KEY CONCEPT: A **project** is either a single proposal or a collection of dependent proposals that is economically independent of all other proposals.

Why Distinguish Between Proposals and Projects?

The rationale for grouping proposals into projects for capital budgeting analysis is fairly easy to understand. Consider an example. Assume that a soft-drink company manufacturing a cola drink plans to introduce a new orange drink (a new proposal). Based on casual capital budgeting analysis, management has decided that the orange drink (proposal) will be a good addition to the firm because it will increase the value of the company's equity.

Although it is tempting to conclude that management should accept this new proposal, a little reflection will suggest that this is true only if acceptance

---

[1] The question of how after-tax cash flows are estimated is addressed in Section 10•2.

does not affect the cash flows of other projects. For example, if management has to channel the advertising dollars it has set aside for the cola market into the orange drink's advertising budget, the sales and consequently the cash flows from the cola drink can fall. In this case, while the cash flows from the orange drink can increase the wealth of the shareholders, the decreased sales of the cola drink can lower it. Thus it is not clear that the orange drink proposal is a good idea. The cola and the orange drink should be evaluated together as a project. Only if the cash flows from the orange drink have no impact on the cash flows from the cola project would management be justified in accepting the orange drink without worrying about its impact on the cola market.[2]

Thus it is important to group all proposals with cash flow dependencies together into a project and then subject the project to capital budgeting analyses.

Complementary Proposals

Assume that the acceptance of proposal X increases the cash flow from proposal Y. Then X and Y are **complementary proposals.** In other words, X and Y are complementary proposals if the cash flows from these projects together exceed the sum of the cash flows that would be generated from either project individually.

As an example, consider a company evaluating two proposals: the canning of peaches (proposal X) and the growing of peach trees (proposal Y). Clearly, if the firm did both activities itself, it could expect to realize substantial cost savings because middlemen are ruled out. In this case, X and Y could be complements.[3]

Substitute Proposals

If the acceptance of proposal X reduces the cash flows from proposal Y, then X and Y are **substitutes.** That is, the cash flows from taking on two substitute proposals are less than the sum of the cash flows generated by the two projects individually.

An example of substitute proposals would be a proposal to repair and remodel an existing warehouse (proposal X) and a proposal to build a new warehouse (proposal Y) next to the existing facility. If both are accepted, the firm

[2] Another example relates to an American car manufacturer that established manufacturing plants in Europe. After the new plants were set up, management was surprised to find that its performance in the domestic market suffered. Since cars were being made overseas, it had become unnecessary for domestic plants to produce as many cars as before. For these plants, the overseas export market virtually disappeared. The overseas plants and the domestic plants are substitute proposals and should have been evaluated simultaneously in any capital budgeting analysis.

[3] If the company can undertake a project only if another project is undertaken, the two projects are called *purely complementary projects.* This is an extreme form of complementarity.

will have one warehouse too many, and this inefficient utilization of resources will lower cash flows overall.

An extreme case of substitution is **mutual exclusivity.** Proposals X and Y are mutually exclusive when the acceptance of X implies the rejection of Y. In the warehouse example, X and Y would be mutually exclusive proposals if, for example, Y involves building a new warehouse where the old warehouse now stands. If building the new warehouse generates the larger cash flow and if the old warehouse is discarded when the new one is built, the situation is one of mutual exclusivity.

Independent Proposals

If the acceptance of proposal X has no effect whatsoever on the cash flows of proposal Y, then X and Y are **independent proposals.** In this situation, the two cash flows are additive; there is neither a gain nor a loss in cash flows from accepting both X and Y.

For example, the proposal to get into peach farming and the proposal to repair a company automobile may be completely independent. Economic independence is of special significance to capital budgeting, and this concept is crucial in identifying projects.

To reiterate, only proposals that are economically independent of each other (i.e., projects) can be evaluated separately. Otherwise, the evaluation of a particular proposal will have to consider the side effects of the proposal on all other proposals of the firm. This can be extremely difficult.

Once the projects have been identified, objective capital budgeting criteria are applied to analyze the cash flow from each project, and the project is determined to be acceptable or unacceptable. These quantitative procedures are discussed later in the chapter.

IMPLEMENTATION PHASE

In the **implementation phase,** the company makes the required arrangements to take on the new project. In particular, the firm must ensure that the capital required to get the project started is readily available. This initial startup capital is often called **capital outlay.** Assuming that the capital outlay can be raised by the firm without serious problems, the implementation phase is fairly straightforward. The firm can proceed with the necessary changes to get the project going: training personnel, altering floor design configuration, designing new procedure manuals, and so on.

CONTROL PHASE

Once the project has been implemented, the firm must constantly monitor the costs and revenues generated by the project and assess the extent to which the actual figures deviate from the forecasted values used in making the capital budgeting decision. There are several advantages in doing this analysis. For one thing, any unnecessary inefficiencies can easily be corrected. If some cash flow figures deviate drastically from planned (projected) values, this could mean one of several things. The forecast might have been bad, and the firm can learn from this experience and correct for potential forecast errors in making future capital budgeting decisions. On the other hand, the forecast might have been good, but unpredictable events (war, tax-law changes, etc.) might have changed the situation drastically, and the firm may have no way of controlling the new cash flows. In any event, by observing the deviation between planned and actual cash flows, the firm gains valuable experience and can apply it to future capital investment analyses. If the deviations are too large, the firm may even decide to abandon the project.

AUDIT PHASE

The **audit phase,** often called the *postcompletion audit,* is one stage of capital budgeting that is often ignored. Strictly speaking, the postaudit is not part of the capital budgeting decision process, since it deals only with completed projects. When a project is completed, the extent of its success or failure should be studied carefully. In addition, firms must attempt to identify the reasons for success or failure. The audit phase, like the control phase, provides valuable information for the firm. Consistent errors can be rectified, overlooked areas of concern can be identified, and personnel and administrative changes may be required to increase the efficacy of future project performance.

Table 10·1 summarizes the results of a survey concerning the relative importance of the various phases of capital budgeting. The importance of each activity was determined by the amount of time managers spent on it. As the table shows, analyzing and selecting projects consumes the largest amount of time, while project follow-up and review (the audit phase) consumes the least.

TABLE 10·1 Relative Importance of Capital Expenditure Activities

Capital Expenditure Activity	Weighted-Average of Time Spent on Activity
Analyzing and selecting projects (screening phase)	24.4%
Implementing projects (implementation and control phases)	22.4
Capital expenditure planning (identifying impact on long-term goals)	20.3
Defining and estimating project cash flows (evaluating phase)	19.3
Project follow-up and review (audit phase)	13.6
	100.0%

Source: Adapted from Lawrence J. Gitman and Charles E. Maxwell, "Financial Activities of Major U.S. Firms: Survey and Analysis of Fortune's 1000," *Financial Management* (Winter 1985), 57–65.

Learning Check for Section 10·1

Review Questions

10·1. Outline the important features of each stage of the capital budgeting process.

10·2. What are the various long-term objectives of a firm? Does maximizing the value of the firm always fulfill these objectives?

10·3. Define *capital budgeting* in your own words.

10·4. "A proper capital budgeting analysis requires grouping proposals into projects." Explain the logic underlying this statement.

10·5. What are the different kinds of economic dependence between projects?

New Terms

Audit phase
Capital budget
Capital budgeting
Capital expenditures
Capital outlay
Complementary proposals
Control phase
Cost-reduction proposal
Economic
    considerations

Evaluation phase
Financial and
    operational feasibility
    considerations
Horizontal revenue
    expansion
    proposal
Implementation phase
Independent proposals
Intangible considerations

Mutual exclusivity
Operating
    expenditures
Project
Proposal
Screening phase
Strategic considerations
Substitute proposals
Vertical revenue
    expansion proposal

SECTION 10·2 *The Relevant Cash Flows for Capital Budgeting*

To determine the overall attractiveness of an investment opportunity, its benefits and costs must first be estimated. The benefits provided by a project are its net cash flows, which incorporate all cash inflows and outflows of the project, including the **initial cash outflow** normally necessary to begin the project. The costs of an investment opportunity are opportunity costs, which reflect the risk of the project. In this section, only the net cash flows are analyzed. The question of how one determines the appropriate opportunity cost, or discount rate, is the subject of Chapters 13 and 14.

Not all cash flows are relevant in capital budgeting. The only relevant cash flows are the **incremental cash flows after taxes**, denoted as $\Delta CFAT$.

KEY CONCEPT: Incremental cash flows after taxes ($\Delta CFAT$) are those periodic cash outflows and inflows that occur if and only if an investment project is accepted.

This concept is extremely important, and a detailed examination is warranted.

Incremental Only those cash flows that affect a firm's existing total cash flows should be considered. That is, only changes in the flow of revenues, expenses, and taxes caused by a project's acceptance are relevant. All other cash flows are irrelevant for decision-making purposes. Consider a proposal to build a new warehouse. All construction expenditures are considered incremental because these cash outflows will not arise unless the warehouse is built. On the other hand, the allocation of certain overhead expenses to the project, such as corporate staff salaries, is not considered incremental because these outlays would be incurred even if the warehouse were not built.[4]

An important concept for the determination of incremental cash flows is the idea of **sunk costs.** While this term is a common buzz word in business, its specific meaning is sometimes not fully appreciated. The highlight "Sunk Costs Are Irrelevant" clarifies the use of sunk costs in capital budgeting problems.

■ *HIGHLIGHT*

SUNK COSTS ARE IRRELEVANT

In making economically justifiable decisions, managers must focus only on incremental net cash flows—inflows and outflows that will exist *only* if the decision is adopted. All other costs are irrelevant.

A common mistake is to include historical or sunk costs in the analysis. Consider an example: A company spends $500,000 in research on two drugs, X and Y. Only Y is eventually approved for sale in the United States by the Food and Drug Administration (FDA). Before Y is produced, the company will want to conduct a capital budgeting analysis of Y. How should the $500,000 already spent be factored into the capital budgeting analysis? Should it be included in the initial cash flows, or should it be spread out evenly over the assumed life of the project?

Neither. The $500,000 is irrelevant for the analysis because it is a sunk cost. That is, it has already been spent and is not incremental to project Y. Sensible economic decisions are not made by looking at the past; only future cash flows are relevant.

The implications of sunk costs for capital budgeting decisions are often misunderstood. Some thought should convince you that if the money has already been

---

[4]While allocating a portion of general overhead to a new project should generally not be done, occasionally overhead expenses such as indirect labor and energy costs may increase because a project is accepted. In those cases, it is appropriate to include such expenses in the project's cash flow estimates.

spent, it cannot be affected by your decision. You should devote your efforts to examining only those cash flows that will be affected by your decision. Determining the best course of action is based only on the incremental cash flows. The old saying "It's no use crying over spilled milk" is most appropriate in capital budgeting.

Cash Flow Once again, the relevant measure of dollar benefits is cash flow rather than accounting income and expenses. As noted in Chapter 6, cash flows are generally not the same as income or profits. Accountants deduct current expenses to calculate profits. However, accrual accounting recognizes these expenses when they are incurred, not when they are paid. Therefore, an increase in after-tax expenses does not necessarily translate into a cash outflow. Moreover, for accounting purposes, the initial cost of an asset is depreciated over its useful life. This means that different sets of income figures for the same investment can be derived simply by changing depreciation methods. An income approach also ignores the fact that cash is needed initially to purchase the asset, thus distorting the actual cash outflows in future periods. For example, a cash flow analysis would take into account the first year an initial $100,000 outlay for a bulldozer. An accountant, on the other hand, would spread the cost over the machine's depreciable life (e.g., deduct an annual depreciation expense of $20,000 for five years). These two approaches would clearly produce different results, and are equivalent only if the discount rate is zero—a most unlikely situation.

After-Tax All cash flows must be estimated consistently on an after-tax basis for several reasons. First, the initial cash flows are normally investment outlays of after-tax dollars. Second, most investments affect a firm's tax payments. It is easier, therefore, to measure cash flows after accounting for taxes. Take the case where a new project will generate additional revenues and expenses. These incremental cash flows are first determined without any tax considerations. Next, taxes are estimated and deducted to produce the cash flow after taxes.

A Special Note on Tax Laws and Depreciation Rules

Tax laws can be incredibly complex when applied to capital investment decisions and are subject to legislative changes from year to year. Moreover, these laws apply unevenly across different industries. For example, oil and gas companies can take depletion allowances, whereas companies in most other industries cannot. Such diversity forces us to treat tax effects at a very general level. In this book, we assume a simplified tax structure. The only detailed tax analysis in this chapter will arise in the context of the replacement of an old asset with a new asset.

In the examples given in this chapter, we use straight-line depreciation. Depreciation per year will be calculated as the asset's purchase price less its salvage value divided by its useful life. By simplifying the treatment of depreciation, we can concentrate on the important aspects of capital budgeting. Several problems at the end of this chapter involve the more complex, but realistic, accelerated cost recovery system, ACRS.

It is important to remember that the details of the tax code are not the subject of study here. What we are attempting to understand is the general approach to making capital budgeting decisions. The ideas developed in this chapter will hold irrespective of the tax laws in effect. The various aspects of the present (or future) tax code can easily be incorporated into the capital budgeting analysis, with appropriate adjustments to the appropriate cash flows.[5]

CLASSIFICATION OF CASH FLOWS AFTER TAX

In analyzing cash flows, the number of different cash flows can be large, and it is easy to overlook some of them. For a systematic estimation of all cash flows, it is useful to break up the periodic—say, annual—stream of expenses and benefits into three categories:

1. Initial $\Delta CFAT$.

2. Operating $\Delta CFAT$.

3. Terminal $\Delta CFAT$.

Each category has its own types of cash flows, which will be examined in greater detail.

Initial Cash Flows[6]

The initial investments are the one-time expenditures to acquire property, plant, and equipment when the project begins. Within this category, cash flows can conveniently be divided into the following:

Direct Cash Flows	Indirect Cash Flows
Capital expenditures	After-tax proceeds of old assets sold
Operating expenditures	Change in net working capital

---

[5] In conformance with the Tax Reform Act of 1986, the examples of capital budgeting in this chapter do not include either the investment tax credit (ITC) or the capital gains tax rate. ITCs and capital gains tax rates can be easily incorporated into capital budgeting problems if these tax aspects are reintroduced into the tax code.

[6] While cash flows associated with the initial investment usually occur at the beginning of a project's life, certain outflows that are nonrecurring may not take place until after the first year. If this is the case, these outflows are simply lumped together with the other annual cash flows in the year they occur.

A particular investment proposal may involve a few or all of these types of cash flows. A proposal to replace an existing manual spot welder with a computer-driven welder may involve all of these cash flows. A new welder might even affect net working capital if it produced fewer defects, because then the number of parts in inventory might be reduced. On the other hand, a decision to buy a fleet of delivery trucks rather than use a third-party trucking service might include only direct cash flow considerations.

Direct Cash Flows For accounting purposes, all cash expenditures for the acquisition of an asset must be classified as either capital or operating expenditures. Most initial outlays involve **capital expenditures** on fixed assets such as property, plant, and equipment. Although this term was utilized earlier, it is useful to provide a formal definition in order to contrast it with **operating expenditures.**

KEY CONCEPT: **Capital expenditures** are those cash outflows that are expected to produce future benefits extending beyond one year.

For this reason, they are treated as an asset on the balance sheet. Other expenditures besides the purchase price may also be incurred to make an asset operational. Cash expenses for freight, preparation or installation costs, removal of old assets, or building modifications are properly treated as part of the asset's cost. Together, these outlays determine the gross investment for depreciation purposes. (If land is purchased, its cost is included as an initial cash outflow but is not included in the project's depreciation base.)
In contrast:

KEY CONCEPT: **Operating expenditures** are those cash outlays that provide no benefits beyond the current period.

They are expensed (charged against current revenues) rather than being treated as an asset on the balance sheet. Hence they do not become part of an investment's depreciation base. An example would be training costs required to familiarize employees with the new computerized welder's operations. Moreover, because these outlays are tax deductible, the "true" expenditure is less because the firm, in effect, gets a "rebate" from the government. In general, the after-tax or effective cost of a tax-deductible item is the before-tax cost multiplied by $(1 - T)$, where T is the firm's marginal tax rate in percent. Thus

$$\text{After-tax cost} = (\text{before-tax cost}) \times (1 - \text{tax rate})$$

If, for example, the company purchasing the welder is in the 15% tax bracket and the personnel training costs are $5,000, the net or after-tax cost is only $5,000 \times (1 - 0.15) = \$5,000 \times 0.85 = \$4,250$. In effect, the government picks up the other $750 in training costs.

Indirect Cash Flows If an older asset is sold, to be replaced by a new asset, tax considerations become important. Any time an asset is sold, depending on whether there is a gain or a loss, the company may pay taxes or may be entitled to a tax credit. These tax considerations affect the cash flows from the project and must be recognized in any capital budgeting decision. Two potential situations may arise, depending on where the selling price or market value (MV) of the asset falls in relationship to the book value (BV) of the asset.

Case 1: $MV < BV$. Market value (MV) is less than book value (BV). The firm has a loss, which will be "subsidized" by the tax code.

Case 2: $MV > BV$. Market value is greater than book value. The firm has a taxable profit.

Example 10•1 Computing Indirect Cash Flows

To illustrate each case, assume that the asset's book value is as follows:

Original purchase price	$50,000
Less: Accumulated depreciation	30,000
Book value (BV)	$20,000

CASE 1: A Loss on the Sale of the Old Asset

If the old asset was sold for $5,000 ($MV$), a loss of $15,000 ($5,000 − $20,000) is produced. This loss helps to reduce current taxes. The net effect when the firm's tax rate $T = 15\%$ is a $CFAT$ given by

$$\begin{aligned} CFAT &= \text{market value} - (\text{loss on sale})(\text{tax rate}) \\ &= MV - (MV - BV)(T) \\ &= \$5,000 - (\$5,000 - \$20,000)(0.15) \\ &= \$7,250 \end{aligned}$$

Thus, even though the firm can sell the asset for only $5,000, the tax "subsidy" increases its total cash flows to $7,250.

CASE 2: A Profit on the Sale of the Old Asset

If the old asset was sold for $35,000 ($MV$), the difference between its sales proceeds and book value is taxed at the firm's ordinary income tax rate. The net effect in this case becomes

$$\begin{aligned} CFAT &= \text{market value} - (\text{profit on sale})(\text{tax rate}) \\ &= MV - (MV - BV)(T) \\ &= \$35,000 - (\$35,000 - \$20,000)(0.15) = \$32,750 \end{aligned}$$

It is important to remember that this (tax) analysis becomes necessary only if the firm is making a replacement decision.

Another indirect cash flow that may affect an investment proposal is a change in net working capital. If the project increases a firm's revenues, for example, there will be an increased need for funds to support the higher level of operations. The appropriate estimate of these additional funds should be the increase in net working capital, which is the difference between current assets and current liabilities. For example, consider the case of a firm planning a new product line. It has to procure inventories (a current asset) for $35,000. If the firm had to pay for this in cash, it will require $35,000 in extra cash. However, the firm can finance these inventories via a $35,000 increase in accounts payable (a current liability) by buying on credit. This will involve no cash. Although changes in net working capital may not reflect cash inflows/outflows and may occur throughout the life of the project, for simplicity we will treat a project's required increase in net working capital as a cash flow occurring when the project is adopted. Thus the increased net working capital is treated as one initial cash outflow that is unaffected until the end of the investment, when it is recovered.

Operating Cash Flows

An appropriate capital budgeting analysis, as developed in this chapter, requires that the investment and financing decisions be separated. That is, management should evaluate the project without explicit recognition of the manner in which the capital to finance the project is being raised. This implies, among other things, that the interest payments on debt should not be included in the computation of a project's cash flows. The cost of debt will enter indirectly via the required rate of return (RRR) used to discount these cash flows.

The logic of this approach follows from the logic of Chapter 3. The value of an asset is equivalent to the cash flows generated by the asset discounted at the appropriate RRR. The cash flows generated by an asset are the **operating cash flows,** which do not depend on the amount of debt or interest payments being made by the company. The financing (i.e., debt) considerations are implicit in the RRR. This will be seen more clearly in later chapters.

In contrast to the initial investment cash flows, the operating cash flows normally represent the net benefits (incremental cash flows after taxes) received over a project's economic life. These $CFAT$ values are calculated easily once the estimates of future sales, fixed and variable costs, and depreciation are determined. From Chapter 6 we know that $CFAT$ is net income (NI) plus depreciation (D). From the income statement, taxable income is sales revenues (S) less costs (C) less depreciation (D). Net income is what remains after taxes have been paid. Therefore,

$$CFAT = (S - C - D)(1 - T) + D \qquad (10\text{-}1)$$

or, in terms of incremental (Δ) cash flows,

$$\Delta CFAT = (\Delta S - \Delta C - \Delta D)(1 - T) + \Delta D \qquad (10\text{-}2)$$

where ΔS = incremental sales

ΔC = incremental expenditures (costs)

ΔD = incremental depreciation

For example, if the adoption of a project will increase a firm's revenues from $50,000 to $54,000 per year, ΔS = $4,000 per year. If the adoption of new manufacturing techniques will lower the operating expenses from $4,000 to $3,000 per year, the incremental expenditures ΔC = $-1,000. Note the negative sign in this case because the incremental expenses are really savings. To avoid confusion, it is useful to remember that all incremental values are "new value" minus "old value." Suppose also that the new project will lower the company's total depreciation from $5,000 to $4,500 per year. Then ΔD = $-$500 per year (new depreciation minus old depreciation). For this example, assuming that the firm is in the 15% tax bracket, the incremental cash flows after taxes will be

$$\begin{aligned}\Delta CFAT &= (\Delta S - \Delta C - \Delta D)(1 - T) + \Delta D \\ &= [\$4,000 - (\$-1,000) - (\$-500)](1 - 0.15) + (\$-500) \\ &= \$4,175\end{aligned}$$

▉ HIGHLIGHT
THE LOGIC UNDERLYING THE ΔCFAT FORMULA

Consider the formula for calculating the incremental operating cash flows for a project.

$$\Delta CFAT = (\Delta S - \Delta C - \Delta D)(1 - T) + \Delta D \qquad (10\text{-}2)$$

How is this equation derived? Notice that equation (10-2) is essentially derived from the income statement:

Sales revenue	S
Less: Costs	C
Less: Depreciation	D
Net operating income	$S - C - D$
Less: Taxes	T
Operating income after taxes	$(S - C - D)(1 - T)$
Operating cash flows ($CFAT$)	$(S - C - D)(1 - T) + D$

Recognizing only incremental items yields

$$\Delta CFAT = (\Delta S - \Delta C - \Delta D)(1 - T) + \Delta D$$

Notice that we ignored interest on debt in determining $\Delta CFAT$. This is because our capital budgeting analysis here is concerned only with the incremental *operating* cash flows. The interest on debt will enter indirectly through the discount rate, as will be seen later.

Also note that the $\Delta CFAT$ formula implicitly assumes that the sales (S) and costs (C) are cash items.

Equation (10-2) is extremely convenient for the calculation of the intermediate cash flows. Typically, the $\Delta CFAT$s will be calculated for every month for project analysis. By examining the formula for $\Delta CFAT$, notice that if the incremental sales, costs, and depreciation are constant for every month, the project's $\Delta CFAT$s will be an annuity. If this condition is not satisfied, the $\Delta CFAT$ for each month will have to be calculated separately, thereby increasing the computational complexity of the analysis. The examples and problems in Chapter 11 will make this point even clearer.

Terminal Cash Flows

The cash flows that are expected to occur at the point when a project's useful life ends are the **terminal cash flows.** Two types of cash inflows influence the capital budgeting decision:

1. Salvage value of the asset(s).

2. Recovery of net working capital.

Salvage Value Often a project's fixed assets will have some resale value even though their usefulness has ended (i.e., someone else may be able to use them). For instance, a firm's existing computer may be too small due to expanding operations. Even though the computer is of little value to this firm, another company might find it perfectly suitable for its needs. If the computer is sold, a terminal cash inflow is generated. Even if the computer is technologically obsolete, it may still have some scrap value. In practice, the depreciated or book value of an asset is normally assumed to be the best estimate of its salvage value.

For example, if an asset was purchased for $50,000 and is expected to have a salvage value of $10,000 at the end of five years, the straight-line depreciation per year is ($50,000 − $10,000)/5 = $8,000 per year. In five years, the book value of the asset will be $10,000 (the purchase price of $50,000 less the accumulated depreciation of $40,000). One reason for making this assumption is to avoid additional tax considerations. As seen earlier, selling an asset for other than its book value requires adjusting the sales proceeds for its tax consequences. So if an asset is expected to have a salvage value different from its estimated book value, the $CFAT$ estimate must be determined by using the tax rules discussed earlier.[7]

---

[7] Similar tax adjustments may be required if this is a replacement decision. The salvage value of the old asset becomes important in determining the tax implication for the firm.

Net Working Capital If a project's initial investment outlays call for an initial increase in net working capital, this investment in net working capital is converted back into cash when the project terminates. Consider the earlier example involving the introduction of a new product line. Acceptance of this project will cause a net increase in inventories and accounts payable in order to support new sales. Assume that the increase in net working capital because of the new product is $10,000. Once the product line is dropped, the funds tied up in these noncash current items are no longer needed. The inventories can be sold and the accounts payable reduced. This can result in a net cash inflow to the firm, which must be captured in the analysis.[8]

The preceding discussion identified the three categories of cash flows: the initial, operating, and terminal cash flows. In addition, the procedures for computing the three cash flows were outlined. With this understanding, it is now possible to perform an overall *CFAT* analysis that involves all these cash flows. Capital budgeting decisions require this overall *CFAT* analysis of an investment proposal, and the following section provides examples of applying *CFAT* analysis to two different types of capital budgeting proposals. (See the highlight "Cash Flow Classification and Capital Budgeting for Some Space Shuttle Operations.")

■■ *HIGHLIGHT*

CASH FLOW CLASSIFICATION AND CAPITAL BUDGETING FOR SOME SPACE SHUTTLE OPERATIONS

The U.S. Air Force (USAF) and the Environmental Protection Agency (EPA) contracted with Radian Corporation to evaluate the economic feasibility of the on-site production of electricity to support space shuttle launch activities at Vandenburg Air Force Base. Radian conducted a comprehensive capital budgeting analysis of this project, and it is interesting to outline briefly the procedure used by Radian. It will be observed that the cash flow classification used by Radian is illustrative of the scheme suggested in the text.

In making its final recommendation, Radian used the *NPV* criterion. A 22-year project life and a 11.75% discount rate were assumed based on other analyses. All *initial cash flows* were divided into two categories: direct and indirect costs. Following is a summary of these initial cash flows.

1. Direct costs
   Delivered equipment cost.
   Equipment installation. Instruments, piping, foundations and supports, insulation, erection and handling, painting, site development, electrical, and buildings.

---

[8] It must be pointed out that this treatment of working capital is a simplification. In reality, working capital cannot be treated as an investment made when the project is adopted and recovered when the project ceases to exist. Working capital can change from period to period, and additional inflows/outflows may be necessary during the life of the investment. To keep the analysis manageable, however, these considerations are ignored in the examples developed in this chapter and in the problem set at the end of the chapter.

2. Indirect costs
Engineering and supervision. Construction and engineering, travel, drafting, cost engineering, purchasing, home office expenses, and accounting.
Contractor's fee.
Startup and modifications.
Working capital.

In calculating the *operating cash flows* over the project's life, Radian identified the following incremental revenues and incremental costs (expenses).

1. Revenues
Liquid hydrogen, liquid oxygen, liquid nitrogen, gaseous nitrogen, and electricity.

2. Expenses
Nonfuel. Operating materials, off-site waste disposal, operating labor, process water, supervising labor, cooling water, maintenance materials and replacement parts, and plant and labor overhead.
Fuel. Electricity, natural gas, No. 2 fuel oil, No. 6 fuel oil, and coal.

Assuming that the *terminal cash flows* would be zero, the project was found to have a negative *NPV*. Based on this cash flow analysis, Radian recommended that the shuttle program abandon the project and instead, buy electricity from electric utilities.

Note that the capital budgeting analysis above involved no depreciation or tax considerations. This is because the USAF does not have to pay any taxes to the federal government.

Source: Information compiled from "Feasibility of Producing Commodities and Electricity for Space Shuttle Operations at Vandenburg Air Force Base," *Report EPA-600/7-84-100,* November 1984, prepared by the Radian Corporation. The assistance of P. J. Murin, one of the authors of this report, is gratefully acknowledged.

APPLICATIONS OF CFAT ANALYSES

As seen earlier in this chapter, capital budgeting proposals are normally grouped into one of two categories during the screening phase: cost-reduction (savings) proposals or revenue expansion proposals.[9]

[9] As seen earlier, investments are also made to satisfy social, legal, or environmental requirements. Investments in new athletic facilities for employees or safety and pollution control devices are difficult to evaluate in this framework because they usually involve only cash outflows. That is, no (dollar) benefits can be directly measured. Such decisions are largely discretionary. For example, a decision to install scrubbers in a smelting plant may be made to forestall an even bigger cash outflow that might result from federal lawsuits. Such projects, however, fall outside the scope of this book.

Cost-Reduction Proposals

A **replacement proposal** is often a cost-savings proposal. For example, a company's decision to substitute its fuel-fired kilns with electric-arc kilns can provide both additional revenues and lower costs. However, the focus in this section is on a pure cost-reduction project. A pure cost-savings proposal provides no direct benefit in the form of increased sales; instead, the benefits come through higher future income because of cost reductions. The most common example of this type of investment is the replacement of existing equipment or facilities with more efficient ones. Over time, plant, equipment, and production facilities wear out or become obsolete. Older equipment eventually becomes too expensive to operate because of increased maintenance and repair (downtime) costs. Moreover, even well-functioning equipment may become obsolete due to technological advances. Decisions to increase automation to reduce labor costs also fall into this category. These potential cost-reduction situations may offer the company opportunities to reduce variable operating costs by replacing employees or old, obsolete plant and equipment.

Example 10•2   A Cost-Saving Proposal

Assume that Mylanta Diversified Products wants to upgrade its present computer system by purchasing a new computer. Thus, Mylanta is making a replacement decision and must take into account the $\Delta CFAT$ created by the purchase of the new computer and also the $\Delta CFAT$ produced by the disposal of the old computer. To analyze these $\Delta CFAT$s, it is necessary to identify the relevant information with regard to the proposed situation and the existing situation.

The proposed situation. The new computer costs $75,000 plus another $5,000 for installation. Its expected economic life is five years, after which it could be sold for $20,000. Its variable and fixed operating expenses are expected to be $10,000 and $5,000 per year, respectively. No change in working capital is anticipated. The company plans to depreciate the new computer over its five-year life, using straight-line depreciation, toward a salvage value of $20,000.

The existing situation. The existing computer originally cost $48,000 three years ago, at which time it was assumed to have a zero salvage value after eight years. The firm now expects that its salvage value (future market value) will be $5,000 in five years. It could be sold today, however, for $28,000 (i.e., its current market value is $28,000). Its annual depreciation expense is $6,000 on a straight-line depreciation basis, and variable and fixed operating expenses are estimated to be $26,000 and $7,000 per year, respectively. The firm's marginal income tax rate is 15%.

From this information, the $\Delta CFAT$s can be calculated as in Table 10•2. Each category of cash flows will be dealt with individually.

TABLE 10·2 $\Delta CFAT$ Analysis for a Cost Saving Proposal

Initial Cash Flows

    Direct cash flows (from purchase of new computer)

Purchase price of computer	$75,000 (O)
Installation costs	5,000 (O)
Depreciable base	$80,000

    Indirect cash flows (from sale of old computer)

Sale of old computer	$28,000 (I)
Tax paid	
($28,000 − $30,000)(0.15)	300 (I)
Total indirect cash flows	$28,300 (I)

    Total initial cash flows

        = direct cash flows + indirect cash flows

        = $80,000 (O) + $28,300 (I)

        = $51,700 (O)

Operating cash flows

    $\Delta CFAT = (\Delta S - \Delta C - \Delta D)(1 - T) + \Delta D$

        $= [0 - (\$18,000) - \$6,000](1 - 0.15) + \$6,000$

        $= \$16,200$ (I)

Terminal cash flows

Salvage value of new computer	$20,000 (I)

INITIAL CASH FLOWS

Because this example involves the sale of the existing computer, both direct and indirect cash flows are involved. In $\Delta CFAT$ analysis it is often convenient to label cash outflows as "(O)" and cash inflows as "(I)." This will avoid potential errors that can arise because of confusion as to whether a cash flow increases or decreases cash to the firm.

Direct cash flows. As can be seen in Table 10·2, the purchase of the new computer will require a cash outflow of $75,000 (O) and the additional installation cost of $5,000 (O) raises the depreciable base of the new computer to $80,000. The term *depreciable base* refers to the total amount that the IRS will recognize as being depreciable.

Indirect cash flows. The indirect cash flows to Mylanta include the proceeds from the sale of the old computer of $28,000 (I) and any other cash flow that may arise from tax considerations.

To anticipate the tax consequences of this sale, it is necessary first to calculate the book value of the old computer. The original purchase price of the computer is $48,000, and since it is being depreciated (straight line) toward a zero salvage value over eight years, the depreciation per year is ($48,000 − $0)/8 = $6,000 per year. Thus the book value of the machine when it is sold is given by the original purchase price ($48,000) less the accumulated depreciation of $18,000 ($6,000 per year for three years), or $30,000. Since the market value of the computer ($28,000) is less than the book value ($30,000), the sale yields a loss of $2,000 and the ordinary tax loss treatment (Case 1) applies. Since Mylanta is in the 15% tax bracket, it can expect a tax credit of $2,000 × 0.15 = $300 (I) as a cash inflow.

The total indirect cash flows are therefore the proceeds of $28,000 from the sale of the computer plus the tax credit of $300, yielding a total indirect cash flow to Mylanta of $28,300.

The total initial $\Delta CFAT$ is therefore the sum of the direct [$80,000 (O)] and indirect cash flows [$28,300 (I)], a total of $51,700 (O) (as verified by Table 10·2).[10]

It is stressed that the indirect cash flows appear in this example because we are dealing with a replacement decision requiring the disposal of the old computer. If the project was not a replacement decision, the total initial $\Delta CFAT$ would consist of only the direct cash flows.

OPERATING CASH FLOWS

The operating cash flows for Mylanta can be calculated using equation (10-2) as follows:

$$\Delta CFAT = (\Delta S - \Delta C - \Delta D)(1 - T) + \Delta D$$

For Mylanta, since this is a pure cost-reduction project, the incremental sales are zero, or $\Delta S = 0$.

However, the variable and fixed costs change for this cost-reduction project. The fixed costs are expected to decrease from $7,000 to $5,000 per year, thereby changing fixed costs by $-2,000. Similarly, the variable costs are expected to go down from $26,000 to $10,000 per year, a change in variable costs of $-16,000. Thus $\Delta C = (\$-2,000) + (\$-16,000) = \$-18,000$.

The depreciation for the old machine is $6,000 per year, as calculated earlier. The depreciation of the new machine is $12,000 per year. This is calculated as follows: The depreciable base for the new computer includes the price of the computer ($75,000) plus the installation costs ($5,000), a total of $80,000. Since it is being depreciated straight-line over five years toward a salvage value of $20,000, the depreciation is ($80,000 − $20,000)/5 = $12,000 per year. The incremental depreciation, ΔD, is therefore the new depreciation of $12,000 per year less the old depreciation of $6,000 per year; thus $\Delta D = \$6,000$ per year.

The operating cash flows per period from this project are therefore calculated using equation (10-2) as follows:

$$\begin{aligned}
\Delta CFAT &= [0 - (\$-18,000) - \$6,000](1 - 0.15) + \$6,000 \\
&= (\$12,000 \times 0.85) + \$6,000 \\
&= \$16,200 \ (I)
\end{aligned}$$

---

[10] When computing initial cash flows, the identity of each cash flow—an inflow (I) or an outflow (O)—must be kept in mind!

Thus the effect on the operating cash flows from taking on the new computer is an increase in $\Delta CFAT$ of \$16,200 per year for the next five years.

TERMINAL CASH FLOWS

The final category of cash flows, terminal cash flows, are easy to compute in this example. When the new machine is sold for \$20,000 at the end of five years, Mylanta realizes a cash inflow of \$20,000 (I). No tax consequences arise in this case because we assume that the asset will be sold for its book value. In cases where a tax loss/gain arise, the same tax rules discussed earlier should be applied.

THE COMPOSITE $\Delta CFAT$ PICTURE

To help visualize the overall cash flow pattern, summarizing the analysis of the three categories of cash flows, a $\Delta CFAT$ time line would appear as follows:

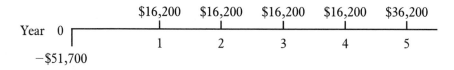

where the last year's $\Delta CFAT$ represents a combination of the operating cash flow of \$16,200 and the terminal cash flow of \$20,000.

Revenue Expansion Proposals

The revenue expansion proposal, the second type of capital budgeting investment, is the result of either expanding current operations or introducing a new product line. The primary purpose of this type of investment is to increase revenues rather than to decrease costs. If a firm expects future demand for its products to push plant capacity beyond its limits, proposals designed to expand operations should be considered. On the other hand, competition and changing consumer tastes require a constant reassessment of existing products' market appeal. Decisions must be made about the elimination of obsolete or unpopular products and the introduction of new ones.

When a proposal expands revenue through the sale of additional goods or services, it may also reduce some costs. However, for simplicity the example that will be developed ignores cost reductions. A project that only increases revenues and has no effect on costs is a pure revenue expansion project. The next example is different from Example 10•2 because it is not a replacement problem, net working capital considerations are required, and the operating $\Delta CFAT$ sequence is not an annuity.

Example 10·3 A Revenue-Expanding Project

Suppose that a food-processing company is considering the introduction of a new line of yogurt. Based on marketing research studies, the products are expected to have a life cycle of eight years. The 1989 sales of $29.5 million are expected to grow to $55 million in 1990 and to $80.5 million for each of the years 1991 to 1995. The final year's (1996) sales are expected to taper off to $35 million. An additional $9.1 million in net working capital will be needed to support these sales projections. Engineering and accounting cost studies forecast variable and fixed costs to be 40% and 18% of sales, respectively. The firm is in the 25% tax bracket. The projected incremental sales, fixed costs, and variable costs are presented in Table 10·3b for the years 1989–1996.

The firm's engineers estimate that a new processing plant will be required, involving a capital outlay of $42.2 million (see Table 10·3a). The salvage value of the building and equipment is expected to be $4.0 million. Since this plant will not replace an existing one, no cash flows from the disposal of old assets will occur. Other initial costs for training and relocation and for marketing research will run $2.4 million and $2.0 million, respectively.

As in Example 10·2, the three categories of cash flows will be examined separately. Table 10·3 summarizes the calculations involved for the three cash flow categories.

INITIAL CASH FLOWS

Direct cash flows. As shown in Table 10·3a, the total capital expenditures amount to $42.20 million in 1988. The firm's marketing and training expenses are $2.00 and $2.40 million, respectively. However, we must use after-tax figures in capital budgeting analysis. The after-tax marketing and training costs are therefore ($2 million)(1 − 0.25) = $1.50 million and ($2.4 million)(1 − 0.25) = $1.80 million, respectively. The *after-tax* operating expenditures in Table 10·3a therefore total $3.30 million in 1988.

Indirect cash flows. Since the sale of old machinery is not involved, tax effects do not enter. Instead, this project requires additional working capital of $9.10 million in 1988. Again, it is important to stress that changes in working capital occur over the life of the project rather than as a one-shot increase, as portrayed in this example.

OPERATING CASH FLOWS

The calculations for the operating $\Delta CFAT$ are presented in Table 10·3b. Once the relevant estimates are generated, these cash flows can be determined using equation (10-2). Notice that in this example the $\Delta CFAT$s are not an annuity because of varying sales and costs through the years. Thus equation (10-2) has to be applied to every year individually. Assuming straight-line depreciation and a salvage value of $4.00 million for items in place at the end of 1988, the

TABLE 10·3 Cash Flows for a New Line of Yogurt (Millions of Dollars)

a. Initial cash flows
   Direct cash flows
      Capital expenditures
         Land $ 7.40 (O)
         Building and equipment $34.80 (O)
            Total $42.20 (O)

      After-tax operating expenditures
         Training [2.4(1 − 0.25)] $1.80 (O)
         Marketing [2.0(1 − 0.25)] $1.50 (O)
            Total $3.30 (O)

      Total direct cash flows $45.50 (O)

   Indirect cash flows
      Changes in *NWC* $9.10 (O)

   Total initial ΔCFAT $54.60 (O)

b. Operating cash flows (millions of dollars)

	1989	1990	1991	1992	1993	1994	1995	1996
Sales (ΔS)	29.50	55.00	80.50	80.50	80.50	80.50	80.50	35.00
ΔVC	11.80	22.00	32.20	32.20	32.20	32.20	32.20	14.00
ΔFC	5.31	9.90	14.49	14.49	14.49	14.49	14.49	6.30
Total costs (ΔC)	17.11	31.90	46.69	46.69	46.69	46.69	46.69	20.30
Depreciation (ΔD)	3.85	3.85	3.85	3.85	3.85	3.85	3.85	3.85
$\Delta CFAT$	10.26	18.29	26.32	26.32	26.32	26.32	26.32	11.99

$$\Delta \text{Depreciation:} \quad \frac{\$34.80 - \$4.00}{8} = \frac{\$30.80}{8} = \$3.85$$

c. Terminal cash flows
   Salvage value $4.00 (I)
   Recovery of *NWC* $9.10 (I)
   Sale of land $8.67 (I)
   Tax on profit $0.32 (O)
      Total $21.45

Notes
Out of the $42.2 million in direct cash outflows, only $34.8 million is depreciable. Land is never depreciated.
The value of the land is assumed to grow at a rate of 2% per year, resulting in a terminal value of $8.67 million. Thus, upon the sale of the land, the firm makes a profit of $1.27 million ($8.67 million − 7.40 million). The firm must pay tax of $0.32 million on this profit ($1.27 million × 0.25).

annual depreciation is $3.85 million [($34.80 million − $4.0 million)/8]. Note from these computations that of the initial capital expenditures, land is not depreciable. The final values of $\Delta CFAT$ calculated using equation (10-2) are on the bottom line of Table 10·3b.

TERMINAL CASH FLOWS

Table 10·3c summarizes the terminal cash flow calculations. The salvage value and the book value of the equipment are identical, thereby resulting in no tax consequences. Thus this cash inflow of $4 million, together with the recapture of net working capital of $9.1 million, the sale of land, and the tax paid on the profit made on the sale of land total $21.45 million (I) for 1996.

THE COMPOSITE $\Delta CFAT$ PICTURE

The three categories of cash flows are summarized in the following time line. The cash inflow in 1996 of $33.44 million is the sum of the terminal cash flows of $21.45 million plus the operating $\Delta CFAT$ of $11.99 million.

	$10.26	$18.29	$26.32	$26.32	$26.32	$26.32	$26.32	$33.44
1988	1989	1990	1991	1992	1993	1994	1995	1996

−$54.60   Year

This time line provides a substantial amount of information; however, it does not indicate whether the firm should introduce the new line of yogurt.

Determining the cash flows of a project does not indicate whether the project should be undertaken. Our next step is to develop methods of evaluating these cash flows to determine if the projects associated with them will increase wealth. This topic will be addressed in the next chapter.

Learning Check for Section 10·2

Review Questions

10·6. What is the meaning of the term *incremental* in *incremental CFAT*?

10·7. Explain the three categories of $\Delta CFAT$ for a capital budgeting analysis.

10·8. What types of expenditures can be considered operating expenditures?

10•9. Why is an increase in required net working capital considered a cash outflow when evaluating a project?

10•10. When evaluating a cost-reducing proposal, would you expect operating cash flows to increase or decrease?

10•11. Discuss some of the tax consequences of the sale of an asset.

New Terms

Capital expenditures
Direct cash flows
Incremental cash flows
  after tax ($\Delta CFAT$)

Indirect cash flows
Initial cash flows
Operating cash flows

Operating
  expenditures
Replacement proposal
Sunk costs
Terminal cash flows

SUMMARY

An Overview of the Capital Budgeting Process

In this chapter we have presented a systematic approach to capital budgeting decisions. In analyzing these decisions, both strategic, or qualitative, considerations and objective, or quantitative, considerations are important. The capital budgeting process consists of several phases, and each of these phases, in a different way, affects the final capital budgeting decision. The firm must identify its long-term objectives. It must then identify the proposals available to it. Generally, these proposals will involve cost savings, horizontal expansion, or vertical expansion. Once the proposals have been identified, they must be evaluated. This evaluation consists of determining the cash flows of projects, which are single proposals or collections of dependent proposals that are economically independent of all other proposals examined. Projects identified as wealth increasing are then implemented. Firm managers monitor and control the project during its life and audit the project after its completion.

The Relevant Cash Flows for Capital Budgeting

The fundamental requirement in any capital budgeting analysis is proper estimation of the various cash flows. Only those after-tax cash flows that are incremental to the project are relevant. To analyze these $\Delta CFATs$, it is often convenient to divide the cash flows from any project into three categories based on when in the life of the project they occur. The initial cash flows consist of the cash flows necessary to start the project. Initial cash flows may also include indirect cash flows from the disposal of old assets and changes in working capital. Operating cash flows consist of the incremental changes in sales, costs, and depreciation resulting from the project. Terminal cash flows, consisting of salvage value and changes in working capital, occur at the termination of the project. Estimating cash flows is only the first part of evaluating projects. These cash flows must then be evaluated, using the techniques introduced in Chapter 11.

PROBLEMS

10·1. Five years ago, the Van de Graaf Electric Company purchased a generator for $180,000. At that time, the generator was estimated to have a salvage value of $30,000 in 15 years (i.e., 10 years from today). Van de Graaf has a marginal tax rate of 25% and uses straight-line depreciation.
   (a) What is the book value of the generator today?
   (b) What will Van de Graaf's initial cash flows be if it sells the generator today for $100,000?
   (c) What will Van de Graaf's initial cash flows be if it sells the generator today for $150,000?

10·2. The Maxey Printing Company purchased a wet press for $120,000 two years ago and has been depreciating it (using the straight-line method) to a salvage value of $30,000 three years from today. The manager, Glen Maxey, is considering selling the old press today and buying a more modern one. The company's marginal tax rate is 25%.
   (a) What is the book value of the old press today?
   (b) What will be the net cash flow from selling the press if it is sold for $50,000?
   (c) What will be the net cash flow from selling the press if it is sold for $90,000?

10·3. Gamma Rayco is planning to replace an old cathode ray tube (CRT) (book value: $15,000) with a newer model, which costs $30,000. If it decides to replace the old CRT, it can be sold for $10,000. Furthermore, the new CRT has installation costs of $1,000 and an anticipated salvage value of $5,000 in 10 years. Gamma Rayco has a marginal tax rate of 25%. What will be the net cash outflow associated with the purchase of the new CRT (and the sale of the old one)?

10·4. The Lloyd Paint Company currently manufactures paint with a machine that cost $1.1 million five years ago and was being depreciated (straight-line) to a salvage value of $200,000 10 years from today. The raw materials for a gallon of paint cost $2.00, and the sales price is $3.50 per gallon. Lloyd sells 25,000 gallons per year. Beverly Reeves, Lloyd's new manager, estimates that Lloyd can sell 20% more paint if she replaces the current machine with a new one that produces a higher-quality paint at the same cost. The new machine costs $1.5 million and will be depreciated (straight-line) to a value of $500,000 10 years from today. Lloyd's marginal tax rate is 25%.

(a) What is Lloyd's annual operating cash flow from operations from the current machine?

(b) What will be Lloyd's annual operating cash flow from operations from the new machine?

(c) Find the incremental change in annual cash flow from operations from replacing the old machine with the new one.

(d) Your accountant has recommended using ACRS to provide a more accurate estimate of incremental cash flows. Assuming that the paint manufacturing machines are in the five-year ACRS class, use ACRS instead of straight-line depreciation to compute the incremental change in annual cash flow from operations from replacing the old machine with the new one.

10•5. The Godfrey Vending Company plans to replace 10 of its vending machines with newer models. The current machines were purchased three years ago for $8,000 each and are being depreciated (straight-line) to a salvage value of $2,000 five years from now. The machines collectively generate annual revenues of $30,000 and annual expenses of $12,000. New machines can be purchased for $12,000 each and will be depreciated (straight-line) to a salvage value of $7,000 five years from now. The new machine will generate annual sales of $40,000 because of less downtime than the old machines and annual expenses of $8,000 (smaller repair bills than the old machines).

(a) If Godfrey's marginal tax rate is 25%, what will be the incremental change in its annual cash flow if the old machines are replaced?

(b) Use ACRS instead of straight-line depreciation to compute the annual incremental changes in operating cash flows from replacing the old vending machines with new ones. Assume that the vending machines are in the five-year ACRS class.

10•6. The Hart Medical Supplies Company is thinking of replacing a machine that presently produces the pacemakers they sell. The existing machine cost $150,000 three years ago and is being depreciated (straight-line) to a salvage value of $40,000 seven years from now. It could be sold today for $100,000. The new machine would cost $200,000 and would be depreciated (straight-line) to a salvage value of $60,000 10 years from now. The cost of training employees to use the new machine would be $5,000, and installation costs for the new machine would be $3,000. Finally, the new machine would necessitate an increase in working capital of $10,000. Hart's marginal tax rate is 25%. Find the net initial outlay associated with the replacement of the old machine.

10·7. Victoria Korchnoi is thinking of importing caviar to sell to restaurants and specialty stores. She estimates that this venture will require an initial outlay of $300,000 to buy a refrigerated storage unit, which can be depreciated (straight-line) to a salvage value of $50,000 in eight years. In addition, Ms. Korchnoi estimates that she will need $40,000 in working capital during the eight years of the project. Annual sales are estimated to be $110,000 and annual expenses $20,000. Ms. Korchnoi estimates that the marginal tax rate will be 25% during the lifetime of the project.
   (a) What is the initial outlay associated with starting the business?
   (b) What is the annual cash flow from operations?
   (c) What will be the terminal cash flow in year 8?
   (d) Assuming that the refrigerated storage unit is in the five-year ACRS class, use ACRS instead of straight-line depreciation to compute the annual cash flow from operations.

10·8. Universal Farm Supply's management has observed that it can sell as much fertilizer as it can stock and is considering the possibility of purchasing a forklift and expanding its warehouse space in order to be able to handle and stock more fertilizer (both are necessary to expand sales). The forklift costs $42,000 and would be depreciated to a salvage value of zero in 7 years, even though it is expected to last for 10 years. The warehouse expansion would cost $100,000 and would be depreciated to a salvage value of $60,000 in 10 years. The expansion would allow Universal to sell 1,000,000 more pounds per year at $0.20 per pound (the fertilizer actually costs Universal $0.17 per pound to manufacture). Universal's marginal tax rate is 34%, and its required rate of return is 12%.
   (a) Find the net initial outlay associated with the expansion.
   (b) Find the annual cash flow from operations during years 1 to 7.
   (c) Find the annual cash flow from operations during years 8 to 10.
   (d) Find the value of the terminal cash flows.

10·9. Joley's department store has recently received the results of a study that suggests that potential sales are being lost because many customers dislike having to use the elevator in Joley's and prefer to go across the street to Foske's department store, which has an escalator. Consequently, Joley's is considering the replacement of the elevator with a new escalator. The elevator was purchased 10 years ago for $140,000 and is being depreciated (straight-line) to a salvage value of $40,000 10 years from now. It can be sold today for $80,000. The escalator can be purchased for $300,000 and would be depreciated (straight-line) to a salvage value of $100,000 in 10 years. In addition, Joley's anticipates that having an escalator rather than an elevator will increase sales by $20,000 annually and decrease operating expenses by $5,000 annually. Joley's has a marginal tax rate of 25%.
   (a) What is the present book value of the elevator?

(b) What is the initial cash outflow associated with the replacement of the elevator?

(c) What will the incremental change in annual cash flow be if Joley's replaces the elevator?

(d) What will the terminal cash flows be if Joley's replaces the elevator?

READINGS

ALCHIAN, A. A., "The Rate of Interest, Fisher's Rate of Return Over Cost and Keynes' Internal Rate of Return," *American Economic Review*, December 1955, 938–942.

BIERMAN, HAROLD, JR., AND SEYMOUR SMIDT, *The Capital Budgeting Decision* (New York: Macmillan Publishing Company, 1984).

BLUME, M., E. FRIEND, AND R. WESTERFIELD, *Impediments to Capital Formation* (Philadelphia: Rodney L. White Center for Financial Research Monograph, The Wharton School, University of Pennsylvania, 1980).

BOWER, J. L., *Managing the Resource Allocation Process* (Boston: Division of Research, Graduate School of Business Administration, Harvard University, 1970).

GRANT, EUGENE L., WILLIAM G. IRESON, AND RICHARD S. LEAVENWORTH, *Principles of Engineering Economy* (New York: Ronald Press Company, 1976).

KLAMMER, T., "Empirical Evidence of the Adoption of Sophisticated Capital Budgeting Techniques," *Journal of Business*, July 1972, 387–397.

LEVY, HAIM, AND MARSHALL SARNAT, *Capital Investment and Financial Decisions* (Englewood Cliffs, N.J.: Prentice-Hall, Inc., 1982).

REINHARDT, U. E., "Break-Even Analysis for Lockheed's TriStar: An Application of Financial Theory," *Journal of Finance*, September 1973, 821–838.

SCHALL, L. D., G. L. SUNDEM, AND W. R. GEIJSBEEK, "Survey and Analysis of Capital Budgeting Methods," *Journal of Finance*, March 1978, 218–287.

SCHWAB, B., AND P. LUSZTIG, "A Comparative Analysis of the Net Present Value and the Benefit-Cost Ratios as Measures of the Economic Desirability of Investment," *Journal of Finance*, June 1969, 507–516.

11

The Investment Decision: Evaluating Cash Flows

In Chapter 10 we saw that capital budgeting analysis requires the separation of investment and financing decisions. The manager must evaluate a project independently of how the money to implement the project is obtained. We examined the six phases of the capital budgeting process and showed how the cash flows of the project are estimated. The incremental cash flows after tax ($\Delta CFAT$) were divided into three categories—initial, operating, and terminal—depending on where in the life of the project they occur.

This chapter continues the discussion of capital budgeting by examining several methods of evaluating the cash flows of the project. Once these methods are introduced, we will compare their strengths and weaknesses and then identify the best method to use in making capital budgeting decisions. As in Chapter 10, we consider all cash flows and discount rates to be known with certainty. Once this chapter is completed, we will begin our discussion of risk and show how risk can be managed in the capital budgeting framework.

This chapter is divided into four sections.

SECTION 11•1: *Criteria for Capital Budgeting.* In this section, we present two incorrect but popular criteria for capital budgeting and then examine in detail the *NPV* and *IRR* concepts introduced in Chapter 2 and a new evaluation measure called the *profitability index*. These methods are discussed here because only through an examination of their weaknesses can we understand why they are incorrect.

SECTION 11•2: *Applying the Project Selection Criteria.* This section shows how the time-value capital budgeting criteria discussed in Section 11•1 can be applied to a project's cash flows. The two example projects of Chapter 10 are examined, using *NPV* and *IRR*, to determine whether they are acceptable.

SECTION 11•3: *The NPV Profile.* We examine a graphic method, called the *NPV profile,* which is a representation of the *NPV*s for a project corresponding to different discount rates. This approach is particularly useful in understanding several aspects of *NPV* and *IRR*. The *NPV* profile may also be used to determine the *IRR* of a project.

SECTION 11•4: *Problems with the IRR and PI as Decision Criteria.* Although the *IRR* is widely used, it has several limitations. For some projects, more than one *IRR* may exist; for others, there may be no *IRR* at all. After examining these cases, we discuss the conflicts that can arise between (1) *IRR* and *NPV* and (2) *NPV* and *PI*. The *NPV* method is shown to be best for evaluating the cash flows of a project.

SECTION 11•1 *Criteria for Capital Budgeting*

To decide whether a particular project should be adopted, a criterion or rule is needed to form the basis for decision making. The best criterion is one that is consistent with the goal of financial management (i.e., one that leads to the selection of investments that will increase current shareholders' wealth). As seen earlier, a preferred investment will adequately compensate its owner for the time value of money and for risk.

Historically, practitioners have relied on two criteria for investment decisions: the payback period and accounting rate-of-return methods. After studying these criteria, it should become obvious that they are incompatible with the financial manager's objective of stockholder wealth maximization. Yet it is necessary to review them because of their widespread popularity. Then two conceptually sound criteria—the net present value (*NPV*) and internal rate of return (*IRR*)—are reexamined in the context of capital budgeting.

THE PAYBACK PERIOD CRITERION

The **payback period** for a project measures the number of years required to recover the initial investment. Consider a project with an initial investment of $500,000 and an expected cash inflow of $100,000 per year for 10 years. The payback period for this project is given by

$$\text{Payback period} = \frac{\text{initial investment outlay}}{\text{annual cash inflows}} \qquad (11\text{-}1)$$

$$= \frac{\$500,000}{\$100,000} = 5 \text{ years}$$

Thus, in five years, the initial investment is recovered. Even if cash flows are not uniform, the payback period can be calculated easily by summing the cash flows until the initial outlay is recovered.

Table 11•1 summarizes the cash flows from two projects, A and B. Both require a $500,000 outlay; however, their respective cash inflow patterns are different. As can easily be seen, the payback period for project A is five years, while that of project B is just three years. Since decisions involving the payback period require choosing the project with the shorter payback period, project B will be chosen over project A.[1] Although the payback criterion is quite simple, there are several problems in using it for capital budgeting.

Cash Flows Beyond the Payback Period Ignored

Even if project A's cash flows in years 6 and 7 were $1,000,000 each, it would not make any difference. Project B will still be preferred to project A simply because of its shorter payback period. This aspect of the payback criterion is clearly disturbing.

TABLE 11•1 Initial Outlays and Cash Inflows for Projects A and B

Year	Project A	Project B
Initial outlay		
0	$500,000	$500,000
Net cash inflow		
1	$100,000	$200,000
2	100,000	200,000
3	100,000	100,000
4	100,000	5,000
5	100,000	2,000
6	100,000	0
7	100,000	0

[1]Firms that use the payback period method sometimes establish a minimum or required payback period to make accept/reject decisions. In this case, projects with expected payback periods greater than this standard are rejected, and those with payback periods less than this standard are accepted.

Opportunity Cost Considerations Ignored

Suppose that project B's cash flows were zero for the first two years and $500,000 for the third year. This would still leave the payback period unaltered, and B would still be preferred to A. The pattern of cash flows within the payback period is treated as totally irrelevant. In addition, the risks of the two projects—factors that affect the opportunity costs of investing in them—are completely ignored.[2]

Despite these weaknesses, the payback period is popular, perhaps because it is easy to use. Another reason for its use is that it emphasizes the liquidity objective of managers. That is, the shorter the payback period, the quicker the project generates cash inflows. Nevertheless, the fact that stockholders want companies to take on projects with the highest market values is completely ignored.

THE ACCOUNTING RATE-OF-RETURN CRITERION

The **accounting rate-of-return (*AROR*)** criterion relates the after-tax profits provided by a project to its average investment.

$$AROR = \frac{\text{average annual profit}}{\text{average investment}} \tag{11-2}$$

Average investment can be calculated in a variety of ways; however, we will approximate it by adding the beginning and ending values of the investment and dividing this result by 2. For example, if an investment in a lathe costing $5,000 depreciates to a value of $1,000 in four years, the average investment in the lathe is $3,000 [($5,000 + $1,000)/2]. If two projects, X and Y, have *AROR*s of 15% and 20%, respectively, it is concluded that Y is better than X.

The weaknesses of *AROR* should be obvious. By using profits rather than cash flows and by ignoring the time value of money, *AROR* has no relationship to market-determined return measures. Choosing the project with the highest *AROR* does not mean, therefore, that the firm is choosing the project with the highest market value.[3]

The three capital budgeting techniques discussed next all have one thing in

---

[2]Sometimes a **discounted payback rule** is used. The discounted payback period is the number of years it takes for the discounted cash flows to yield the initial investment. Although this rule is somewhat better than the standard payback rule, which completely ignores the time value of money, it still suffers from a serious weakness—it, too, ignores all cash flows beyond the discounted payback period.

[3]A related rate-of-return criterion is the *average return on investment (AROI)*. This measure uses the average annual cash flow after taxes instead of the average annual profit. Although the *AROI* corrects one of the flaws inherent in the *AROR* criterion, it still ignores the time value of money.

common: they use the time-value methods concepts developed in Chapter 2. In fact, *NPV* and *IRR*, which were introduced in that chapter, will be used extensively to evaluate the cash flows of capital budgeting projects.

NPV CRITERION

In Chapter 3 the market value (present value) of any asset was found to be a function of the magnitude and timing of the cash flows received from the ownership of the asset. By focusing on all cash flows generated by a project and by capitalizing them at a market-determined discount rate, the *NPV* does exactly this and thereby overcomes all the weaknesses of the payback period and *AROR* methods. Formally,

$$NPV = PV_{\text{inflows}} - PV_{\text{outflows}} \qquad (11\text{-}3)$$

where the present values are after-tax cash inflows and outflows, respectively, which are determined by discounting the cash flows at a market-determined opportunity cost of capital. In calculating *NPV*s as in equation (11-3), it is implicitly assumed that the intermediate cash flows from a project are reinvested at the opportunity cost of capital.

The opportunity cost of capital, especially in the context of capital budgeting, is often referred to as the **required rate of return (RRR)**.

KEY CONCEPT: The **required rate of return (RRR)** for a project is the minimum rate of return that the project must yield to justify its acceptance.[4]

If *NPV* is positive, the project produces excess market value, as discussed in Chapter 4; if *NPV* is negative, the project produces negative excess market value, or economic losses. *NPV* is therefore the net or excess market value accruing to the firm on acceptance of the project. Thus we have the following *NPV* rule:

KEY CONCEPT: The *NPV* **rule** accepts projects with positive *NPV*s and rejects projects with negative *NPV*s.

THE IRR CRITERION

Unlike the *AROR* method, which ignores the time value of money and is based on profits, the *IRR* is a discounted rate-of-return measure derived directly from knowledge of a project's cash flow pattern.

---

[4]The *RRR* is the same as the opportunity cost discussed in Chapter 3. The reason for calling the discount rate used in capital budgeting the *RRR* will be made clear when we begin our discussion of risk in the next chapter.

KEY CONCEPT: The **internal rate of return (IRR)** is that discount rate that makes the present value of the cash inflows equal to the present value of the cash outflows.

Alternatively, as seen in Chapter 2, the *IRR* is that discount rate that makes the present value of an investment's cash inflows (PV_{inflows}) equal to the present value of its cash outflows (PV_{outflows}). Stated algebraically, *IRR* is that discount rate that causes

$$NPV = PV_{\text{inflows}} - PV_{\text{outflows}} = 0 \qquad (11\text{-}4)$$

An implicit assumption in all *IRR* calculations is that the intermediate cash flows from the project are also reinvested at the *IRR*. A project is accepted or rejected by comparing its *IRR* to its *RRR*, which is the opportunity cost of capital.

KEY CONCEPT: The **IRR rule** accepts a project if its *IRR* > *RRR*, and rejects a project if its *IRR* < *RRR*.

Technically speaking, if *IRR* = *RRR*, the project is marginally acceptable; however, it may not make much economic sense to accept a project when the firm simply expects to recover its opportunity cost.

Because the *IRR* criterion explicitly considers the timing of the *CFAT*s, it satisfies the requirement that capital budgeting decisions criteria must account for the time value of money. However, the *IRR* is not a market-determined rate of return. The assumption that the cash flows are reinvested at the *IRR* rather than at the opportunity cost of capital makes this a nonmarket-value-based criterion. What this implies is that the *IRR* criterion will not necessarily be consistent with the goal of shareholder wealth maximization.[5] Thus *NPV* is superior to *IRR* in making correct capital budgeting decisions.

THE PROFITABILITY INDEX CRITERION

Another discounted cash flow criterion used for evaluating capital budgeting projects is the **profitability index (PI)** or benefit–cost ratio.

KEY CONCEPT: The **profitability index (PI)** is the present value of the cash inflows divided by the present value of the cash outflows.

The *PI* is simply a different way of presenting the same information that *NPV* provides. *NPV* is the difference between the *PV* of the cash inflows and cash outflows, while *PI* is the ratio of these two values:

$$PI = \frac{PV_{\text{inflows}}}{PV_{\text{outflows}}} \qquad (11\text{-}5)$$

[5]This and related problems with the *IRR* are addressed in greater detail in Section 11•4.

KEY CONCEPT: The *PI* **rule** accepts projects if *PI* > 1 and rejects projects if *PI* < 1.[6]

Because the present value of the cash outflows represents the true, time-adjusted investment in the project, the *PI* is a relative measure in that it measures the benefits per dollar of investment adjusted for time value. The *NPV* criterion, on the other hand, is an absolute measure. This has some interesting implications.

When should the *PI* criterion be used to select capital budgeting projects? Since both the *NPV* and the *PI* criterion are essentially the same, they yield identical accept/reject decisions. That is, a project that is acceptable with the *NPV* rule will also be found to be acceptable with the *PI* rule. However, the *PI* and the *NPV* can lead to conflicting decisions when one of two projects has to be chosen. However, since this chapter is concerned with accept/reject rather than ranking decisions, *PI* and *NPV* will lead to identical conclusions.[7]

Learning Check for Section 11•1

Review Questions

11•1.   What are the weaknesses of the payback period and the *AROR*?

11•2.   Explain why the *AROR* cannot, in general, lead to wealth-maximizing decisions.

11•3.   If a project has a *PI* greater than 1.0, then its *NPV* must be greater than zero. True or false? Why?

New Terms

Accounting rate of return (*AROR*)	*NPV* Rule	Profitability index (*PI*)
Discounted payback	Payback Period	Required rate of
IRR Rule	*PI* Rule	return (*RRR*)

SECTION 11•2 *Applying the Project Selection Criteria*

With an understanding of the *NPV*, *PI*, and *IRR* criteria, it is now possible to decide whether the two projects presented in Chapter 10 (Example 10•2, the cost-reducing computer project, and Example 10•3, the revenue-expanding yogurt project) should be accepted or rejected. Only the *NPV* and *IRR* criteria are used here because conceptually they are perhaps most defensible. As seen

---

[6]The reader is encouraged to verify that this rule follows from the *NPV* rule.

[7]The conflicts between *NPV* and *PI* in ranking projects are examined in Section 11•4.

earlier, accept/reject decisions using *PI* and *NPV* will be the same. Thus *PI* will not be addressed in the following discussion. *PI* will be addressed in greater detail in Section 11•4.

Assume that both projects being evaluated have an *RRR* (i.e., opportunity cost or discount rate) of 11%. Using equation (11-3), the *NPV* for each project is calculated as shown in the following example.

Example 11•1   A Computer Replacement Project

Examine the composite *CFAT* picture, which gives the cash flows for the capital budgeting problem developed in Example 10•2 (Chapter 10).

$$
\begin{array}{cccccc}
 & \$16{,}200 & \$16{,}200 & \$16{,}200 & \$16{,}200 & \$36{,}200 \\
\text{Year} \quad 0 & \vrule & & & & \\
 & 1 & 2 & 3 & 4 & 5 \\
\$-51{,}700 & & & & &
\end{array}
$$

$NPV = PV_{\text{inflows}} - PV_{\text{outflows}}$
$= \$-51{,}700 + \$16{,}200(PVF_{.12,1}) + \$16{,}200(PVF_{.12,2}) + \$16{,}200(PV_{.12,3})$
$\quad + \$16{,}200(PVF_{.12,4}) + \$36{,}200(PVF_{.12,5})$
$= \$-51{,}700 + \$16{,}200(0.8929) + \$16{,}200(0.7972) + \$16{,}200(0.7118)$
$\quad + \$16{,}200(0.6355) + \$36{,}200(0.5674)$
$= \$18{,}046$

Using the *NPV* rule (i.e., accept if *NPV* is positive), the computer should be replaced because, by doing so, the market value of the firm will increase by $18,046.

Example 11•2   A New Brand of Yogurt

The composite *CFAT* picture developed for Mylanta in Example 10•3 (Chapter 10) is as follows:

$$
\begin{array}{ccccccccc}
\$10.26 & \$18.29 & \$26.32 & \$26.32 & \$26.32 & \$26.32 & \$26.32 & \$33.44 \\
1989 & 1990 & 1991 & 1992 & 1993 & 1994 & 1995 & 1996 \\
\end{array}
$$

$\$-54.60$

Year

The *NPV* (in millions) for this revenue expansion project is:

$$NPV = \$-54.60 + \$10.26(PVF_{.12,1}) + \$18.29(PVF_{.12,2}) + \$26.32(PVF_{.12,3})$$
$$+ \$26.32(PVF_{.12,4}) + \$26.32(PVF_{.12,5}) + \$26.32(PVF_{.12,6})$$
$$+ \$26.32(PVF_{.12,7}) + \$33.44(PVF_{.12,8})$$

Upon substitution of the appropriate present value factors, it can be seen that $NPV = \$58.28$

Expanding the yogurt line is thus a productive endeavor because the market value of the firm will go up by $58.28 million.

IRR COMPUTATIONS

The procedure for computing the *IRR* was described in Chapter 2. With the aid of a financial calculator, it is extremely easy. However, one could also determine the *IRR* for a project using the methods described in Chapter 2. In the interest of brevity the *IRR* calculations are not provided here. The reader can verify the *IRR*s provided in the following discussion as an exercise.

Computer Replacement   The *IRR* for the computer replacement project is approximately 24%. Using the *IRR* rule, this project should be accepted. This is because the *IRR* for this project is greater than the *RRR* of 12%.

New Brand of Yogurt   The *IRR* for this project is 33.7%. Since the *RRR* for this project is only 12%, the *IRR* rule would accept this project.

Thus, as expected, the *NPV* rule and the *IRR* rule agree; both suggest that the projects should be accepted. A manager who follows this recommendation will, in fact, be acting in the best interests of the owners of the company.

The framework developed here can help determine whether an individual project should be accepted or rejected. However, there are several complications that can arise when one has to choose between mutually exclusive projects. Mutual exclusivity exists when the acceptance of one project automatically rules out the acceptance of another project. For instance, a manager needing a truck must choose between two projects. She could lease the truck (project *A*) or purchase it outright, (project *B*). She could not do both. As we will see, *NPV* and *IRR* may provide conflicting conclusions when ranking mutually exclusive projects. The same is true when both *PI* and *NPV* are used in ranking situations. When such conflicts exist, the *NPV* criteria should be used. As long as the manager uses the *NPV* rule, he or she will make the right decision.

In the next section, we will examine in more detail the different methods of evaluating cash flows. Before doing this, however, it is useful to examine some evidence on whether choosing projects using *NPV* actually affects the value of the firm. The highlight "Capital Budgeting Decisions: Do They Really Increase Firm Values?" presents the results of some recent research on this issue.

■ *HIGHLIGHT*

CAPITAL BUDGETING DECISIONS: DO THEY REALLY INCREASE FIRM VALUES?

The entire justification for the use of the *NPV* criteria is that the *NPV* of an investment measures the increase in wealth to the firm adopting that investment. This concept was first explored in Chapter 3, and the present chapter relies on the *NPV* rule in making capital budgeting decisions.

How does the theory carry over to practice? Is there any evidence that capital budgeting decisions *actually* affect the value of the firm or the wealth of stockholders? That is, when managers announce their capital budgeting decisions, does the market respond by revaluing the companies' stock? According to the theory, we know that it should.

Two researchers examined precisely this issue.* They analyzed what happened to the stock prices of 658 corporations when managers announced unexpected increases in capital expenditures. Over the period 1975–1981, the evidence indicated that increases in planned corporate capital expenditures resulted in increases in stock prices (increase in excess returns, to be precise). The data also indicated the opposite effect when these firms reduced capital expenditures.

This is forceful evidence that stockholder wealth does indeed increase for those firms whose capital expenditure decisions are motivated by firm value maximization.

*John J. McConnell and Chris J. Muscarella, "Corporate Capital Expenditure Decisions and the Market Value of the Firm," *Journal of Financial Economics*, September 1985, pp. 399–422.

Learning Check for Section 11•2

Review Question

11•4. What are the various criteria used to evaluate a project? List their strengths and weaknesses.

New Term

Mutual exclusivity

SECTION 11•3 *The NPV Profile*

Three methods for finding the *IRR* of a project were presented in Chapter 2. A fourth method, the **NPV profile,** will now be discussed. The

NPV profile is especially useful for achieving some of the objectives of this chapter—for cataloging the weaknesses of the *IRR* criterion and for highlighting the potential for conflict between *NPV* and *IRR* when projects are ranked.

KEY CONCEPT: For a given set of project cash flows, the **NPV profile** is a graph that for every possible discount rate plots the corresponding NPV.

The *NPV* profile provides an easy way to see how a change in the discount rate will affect the *NPV* of a project. Because *IRR* is defined as the discount rate that causes the *NPV* to be zero, the *NPV* profile is also a graphic approach to the determination of the *IRR* for a project. This method involves identifying a project's *NPV*s for different discount rates and then fitting a curve through these points. Figure 11•1 is the *NPV* profile for a project. The first step is to calculate the *NPV* of the project, using a zero discount rate. For this example, the *NPV* turns out to be $39,900.[8] Next, a low and a very high discount rate, say 5% and 35%, are arbitrarily selected, and their implied *NPV*s are calculated and plotted. Figure 11•1 calculates the *NPV*s for the different discount rates. With this information, a curve can now be fitted through these points, and in this case the curve cuts the horizontal axis. Of course, the more rates selected, the more precise the profile will be.

Notice that in Figure 11•1 the intercept on the horizontal axis corresponds to the discount rate at which the *NPV* is zero. Since, from the definition, this discount rate has to be the project's *IRR*, the *IRR* for this project can be read off from the *NPV* profile as approximately 21%.

The *NPV* profile also illustrates the correspondence between the *NPV* and *IRR* criteria. Consider point *A* in Figure 11•1. If the *RRR* is 12%, the computer project should be accepted using both criteria because *NPV* is positive and the project's 21% *IRR* is greater than the *RRR* of 12%. In fact, as long as the *RRR* is less than the *IRR* (i.e., all points to the left of the *IRR*), the *NPV* will always be positive. Thus both the *NPV* and *IRR* criteria will accept this project when the *RRR* is less than the *IRR*. Similarly, both criteria will reject this project if the *RRR* is greater than the *IRR*.[9]

For projects such as the one depicted in Figure 11•1, a manager using the *NPV* or *IRR* criterion will arrive at the same accept/reject decision irrespective of the criterion used. If the project is acceptable with the *NPV*, it will also be acceptable with the *IRR*; similarly, if it is rejected with the *NPV*, it will also be rejected with the *IRR*. Thus, in this case, there is no conflict between the recommendations of either criterion. However, this result cannot be generalized to all projects or to situations when project ranking is required.

---

[8]Recognize that when the discount rate is zero, the cash flows can simply be summed, carefully distinguishing between inflows and outflows.

[9]The *NPV* profile will be of assistance later when we examine how *NPV* and *IRR* may give conflicting recommendations concerning the acceptance of a capital budgeting project.

RRR	NPV
0	$39,900
5	26,719
10	16,357
15	8,092
20	1,413
25	(4048)
30	(8564)

IRR → (between 20 and 25)

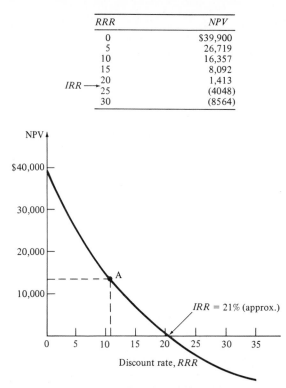

FIGURE 11•1 Using the *NPV* profile to find the *IRR* for a project.

Learning Check for Section 11•3

Review Questions

11•5. What information is required to generate an *NPV* profile for a project?

11•6. How can the correspondence between the *NPV* and *IRR* criteria for an accept/reject decision be illustrated using an *NPV* profile?

New Term

NPV profile

SECTION 11•4 *Problems with the IRR and PI as Decision Criteria*

In Section 11•2 we stated that the *NPV* should be used if there is a conflict between it and the *IRR* in ranking mutually exclusive projects. The reader may wonder why a detailed discussion of *IRR* is even necessary. If *NPV* is better than *IRR*, why not disregard *IRR* altogether?

One cannot ignore the *IRR* criterion for a variety of reasons. *In practice*, the *RRR* used to perform an *NPV* analysis is not generally known at lower levels of management in large corporations (e.g., at the divisional or production level). In these cases, projects are initially ranked by their *IRRs*, and then the better projects are forwarded to upper-level management. It is at this upper level that a formal *NPV* analysis is conducted. Also, corporations have historically viewed investments in terms of their profitability, and the *IRR* does just this by measuring the *return per dollar invested*. Many managers have trouble evaluating the attractiveness of an investment using *NPV*. For example, while a rate of return of 68% makes a project appear very attractive, an *NPV* of $45,000 does not communicate the level of "performance." Because of the widespread appeal of this rate-of-return measure, it is helpful to understand the extent of its usefulness and its limitations.

However, before proceeding, we must introduce the notions of **conventional** and **nonconventional projects**.

CONVENTIONAL AND NONCONVENTIONAL PROJECTS

If net cash outflows are identified with a minus sign and net cash inflows with a plus sign, Mylanta's computer replacement project (Example 10•2), for example, can be represented as

That is, Mylanta's proposed project involves a net annual cash flow pattern: $(-, +, +, +, +, +)$. In this example, notice that the sign changes only once, from $-$ to $+$ in year 1.

KEY CONCEPT: A project with a $\Delta CFAT$ pattern $(-, +, +)$ is known as a **conventional** project; a project with any other cash flow pattern is called a **nonconventional** project.

In many situations, large capital outlays are required initially when a new project is implemented, and once the project becomes operational, the $\Delta CFATs$ are positive over the life of the project. Unlike these conventional projects, in many other situations a project may require a large cash outlay (e.g., for maintenance and repairs) periodically over its life, and thus future net cash flows may become negative. As an example, consider a strip-mining operation. Strip mining typically involves very large cash outflows at both the beginning and end of the project. Initially, capital and revenue expenditures cause large outflows, while at the end, when the project is terminated, land restoration costs cause large net cash outflows. The intermediate $\Delta CFAT$s, however, are net inflows as revenues from the sale of the ore are generated. Nonconventional projects like this can pose special problems for the financial manager using the IRR criterion.

The several problems that can be encountered with the IRR criterion will now be examined, using the NPV profile.

Multiple *IRR*s for a Project

A conventional project will have only one positive IRR. In contrast, a nonconventional project may have as many positive IRRs as there are sign changes in its cash flow pattern.[10] For example, if a project's cash flow pattern is $(-, +, -, +, +)$, there are three sign changes and possibly three positive IRRs.

To illustrate, suppose that Walker Plastics is considering a two-year project that has the following cash flow pattern:

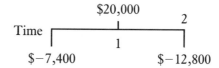

This project's cash flow pattern $(-, +, -)$ indicates that two possible IRR solutions may exist. Solving for the IRR yields

$$NPV = \$-7,400 + \$20,000(PVF_{IRR,1}) - \$12,800(PVF_{IRR,2}) = 0$$

Walker would find that the IRRs for its project equal 4.08% and 66.19%.

If Walker's RRR for this project is 15%, should Walker accept or reject the project? The answer is not obvious. To see why, examine Figure 11•2, which contains the NPV profile for this project. First, notice that the NPV is positive over the range 4.08 to 66.19% and is negative otherwise. If the RRR is 15% and the IRR is really 4.08%, the project should be rejected because $IRR < RRR$. If the IRR is really 66.19%, the project should be accepted because $IRR > RRR$.

Next, notice that this dilemma is highlighted by the nonconventional NPV profile of this project. The NPV profile in Figure 11•2 begins with a negative

[10]Because finding an IRR is equivalent mathematically to solving a polynomial of the nth degree, there are n possible solutions. In the case of a conventional project, there is only one (unique) positive IRR. The other $n - 1$ solutions are either negative or imaginary and therefore make no economic sense. With a nonconventional project, however, more than one possible solution (IRR) may result, one for each change in signs.

Assumed Discount Rate (%)	NPV
0	$-200
4.08	0
5	38
10	203
15	313
20	378
25	408
30	411
35	392
40	355
45	305
50	244
55	175
60	100
65	20
66.19	0
70	−64

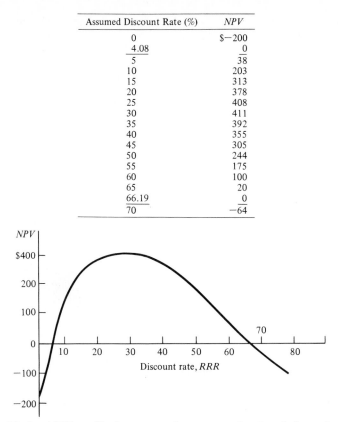

FIGURE 11·2 *NPV* profile for a type of nonconventional cash flow where multiple *IRR*s exist.

NPV, which increases slowly, then becomes positive for a range of discount rates, and then returns to a negative value.[11]

When multiple *IRR*s exist, which *IRR* is correct? The answer is, all are correct. Each *IRR* causes *NPV* to equal zero, and from the definition of *IRR*,

[11]For the sake of completeness, it should be noted that a nonconventional project's *NPV* profile may take on any number of forms. That is, depending on the number as well as the magnitude and timing of the future net cash outflows, the *NPV* profile may take on any shape. For example, the following are just two possible profiles. As an exercise, the interested reader might want to think about what pattern of cash flows could produce these *NPV* profiles.

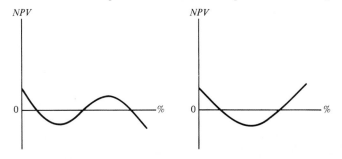

any discount rate that satisfies this condition is an *IRR*. Although multiple *IRRs* may be the mathematically correct rates of return for a set of cash flows, managers, understandably, have difficulty interpreting the economic significance of such a result. They must then turn to the *NPV* criterion. Fortunately, cash flow patterns that have multiple *IRRs* are uncommon. Nevertheless, they do occur. To avoid the multiple-*IRR* problem, decisions should be based on a project's *NPV*.

NO IRR MAY EXIST FOR A PROJECT

For certain projects it might be impossible to find a discount rate that makes the project's *NPV* equal to zero (i.e., some projects might have no *IRR*). This is because the *NPV* for these projects does not decline smoothly with higher discount rates.

Figure 11•3 shows the *NPV* profile for such a project. As this graph indicates, there is no discount rate for which *NPV* = 0, even though two sign changes occur. In fact, at discount rates greater than 50%, *NPV* actually rises.

Discount Rate (%)	NPV	Discount Rate (%)	NPV
0	$500	40	$337
5	456	45	334
10	421	50	333
15	395	55	334
20	375	60	335
25	360	65	339
30	349	70	342
35	341		

The *NPV* profile shows that there is no point where the *IRR* is determined.

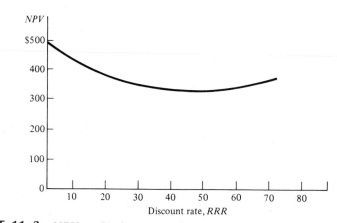

FIGURE 11•3 *NPV* profile for a type of nonconventional cash flow where no *IRR* exists.

358

This situation may occur in cases where the initial cash flow is positive, for example, when a firm initially borrows funds but does not invest the money until later.

CONFLICTS IN USING THE IRR AND NPV CRITERIA

If capital budgeting projects were evaluated one at a time, one would not normally encounter a problem with using either the *NPV* or the *IRR*. The accept/reject decisions would be identical by both criteria. (Of course, this observation does not apply to cases where multiple *IRR*s exist or where an *IRR* cannot be determined.) However, when two or more projects must be ranked because they are *mutually exclusive,* the ranking based on their *IRR*s may differ from the ranking based on their *NPV*s.

To illustrate these points more clearly, consider Figure 11•4, which provides the *NPV* profiles for two mutually exclusive projects—*K* and *L*. The *NPV*s of these projects intersect at a discount rate of 14%. At this *RRR*, they have identical *NPV*s and thus are equally attractive to the firm considering them. Moreover, from the profiles of *K* and *L*, their respective *IRR*s are $IRR_K = 17\%$ and $IRR_L = 20\%$. Now consider two separate problems.

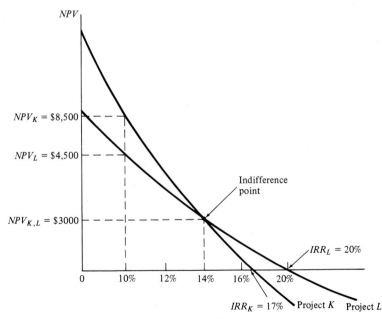

FIGURE 11•4   Conflicts in ranking between the NPV and IRR criteria.

Independent[12] Projects:
An Accept/Reject Decision

Assume that a manager is interested in evaluating projects K and L independently (i.e., each one separately) by using the *NPV* and *IRR* criteria and that the *RRR* is 10% for both projects. At this discount rate, $NPV_K = \$8,500$ and $NPV_L = \$4,500$. Since both have positive *NPV*s, both are acceptable projects, using the *NPV* criterion.

Now use the *IRR* criterion to evaluate acceptability. Since $IRR_K = 17\%$ and $IRR_L = 20\%$, both projects have *IRR*s greater than the *RRR* of 10%. Hence both K and L are acceptable projects. Therefore:

KEY CONCEPT: For independent projects, both *NPV* and *IRR* lead to identical accept/reject project decisions. If a project is acceptable by the *NPV* criterion, it will be acceptable by the *IRR* criterion. Similarly, if a project is rejected by the *NPV* criterion, it will be rejected by the *IRR* criterion.

Mutually Exclusive Projects:
A Ranking Decision

The ranking of projects is important when choosing among a number of alternative or competing investments. If only one is to be chosen, the projects need to be ranked in descending order by their *NPV* and *IRR* values, and the project with the highest (best) value is chosen. Returning to Figure 11•4, assume that the *RRR* for projects K and L is again 10%. Using the *NPV* criterion, the ranking of K and L is as follows:

$RRR = 10\%$

Project	Criterion: NPV	Rank
K	\$8,500	1
L	4,500	2

On the other hand, using the *IRR* criterion, project L's *IRR* is 20%, which is clearly superior to K's *IRR* of 17%. In this case, the ranking of K and L is reversed:

[12]Here independent means that we may evaluate each project separately because an accept/reject decision for one project has no influence on an accept/reject decision for the other project.

$$RRR = 10\%$$

Project	Criterion: *IRR* (%)	Rank
K	17	2
L	20	1

Thus, with $RRR = 10\%$, there is a conflict in the project ranking. *NPV* ranks project L over K, while *IRR* ranks project K over L. Since the *NPV* rule is the preferred method, selecting the investment with the higher *IRR* leads to accepting the less lucrative project. Notice, however, that *this ranking conflict disappears to the right of the indifference (crossover) point.* That is, if $IRR = 17\%$, both *NPV* and *IRR* rank project L over project K. It can therefore be concluded that:

KEY CONCEPT: In ranking mutually exclusive projects, *NPV* and *IRR* can lead to conflicting decisions. Whether or not a conflict occurs depends on the *RRR* being used.

Conflicts Between *NPV* and *PI* in Project Ranking

Just as *IRR* and *NPV* can lead to ranking conflicts, *NPV* and *PI* can lead to different project selections. Because *PI* is a relative measure of profitability, it ignores the size of the initial investment. For example, which of the following projects should be selected if *only one* can be accepted?

Project	*NPV*	Initial Investment	*PI*
A	$400	$ 800	1.50
B	800	1,400	1.44

First, recognize that both *NPV* and *PI* indicate that both A and B are acceptable. But since only one project can be chosen, they must be ranked. The *NPV* criterion will choose project B over project A, while the *PI* criterion will prefer project A over project B. However, project B will lead to the greater increase in firm value, since it has the higher *NPV*, and should be the one selected.[13]

---

[13]The *PI* criterion is useful for capital budgeting decisions in special situations of capital rationing. This issue is addressed in Appendix 11·A.

A FINAL WORD

In evaluating capital budgeting projects, both the *NPV* and *IRR* criteria are preferable to criteria that ignore the time value of money. Yet because there can be ranking conflicts between *NPV* and *IRR*, and because there can be more than one *IRR* for some projects, it is advisable to use the *NPV* criterion. *The NPV criterion is always consistent with the goal of shareholder wealth maximization*, and a properly determined discount rate for *NPV* calculations allows the financial manager to make decisions that increase the market value of the company and, consequently, the stock price.

Learning Check for Section 11·4

Review Questions

11·7. What is the difference between conventional and nonconventional projects? What is the practical significance of this distinction?

11·8. When a project has more than one *IRR*, which one is correct?

11·9. Explain the distinction between a ranking decision and an accept/reject decision. For what type of decision can there be a conflict between *NPV* and *IRR*?

11·10. Why can't *PI* always be used to rank projects? In what situations is it reasonable to use *PI*?

New Terms

Conventional project   Nonconventional project

SUMMARY

Criteria for Capital Budgeting

Once the incremental cash flows for a project are estimated, a composite *CFAT* time line can be drawn to summarize the *CFAT*s from a project. There are several criteria for determining whether the project will lead to an increase in wealth. Two criteria, payback and accounting rate of return (*AROR*), have been widely used in capital budgeting analysis; however, they do not recognize the time value of money and are not based on market value considerations. *IRR*, while recognizing the time value of money, does not reflect market values. Only *NPV* and *PI* reflect both the time value of money and market values.

Applying the Project Selection Criteria

To arrive at an accept/reject decision using these cash flows, the *NPV* criterion is most appropriate. Accepting a project with a positive *NPV* will increase the market value of the company by an amount equal to the *NPV* of the project because of the value-additivity property. The *IRR* method will also provide an accept/reject recommendation and, for independent projects, will give the same recommendation as the *NPV*.

The NPV Profile

The *NPV* profile is a useful tool for examining several aspects of popular capital budgeting criteria. The *NPV* profile is simply a graph, with the *NPV* of a project on the vertical axis and the various discount rates on the horizontal axis. The *IRR* for a project can be read off directly from the *NPV* profile at the point where the curve cuts the horizontal axis.

Problems with the IRR and PI as Decision Criteria

Using the *IRR* for capital budgeting can sometimes lead to several problems. In some cases, projects can have several *IRR*s, all of them correct. In others, a project may have no *IRR* at all. To avoid these situations, the financial manager is better off using the *NPV* criterion.

To decide between mutually exclusive projects, a manager must rank the projects and pick the highest one. In these situations, *NPV* and *IRR* can sometimes lead to conflicting recommendations. Whether a conflict will occur depends on the *RRR* being used. To solve the conflict, the manager is well advised to follow the *NPV* criterion simply because the *NPV* is consistent with the manager's objective of stockholder wealth maximization. The *IRR* may not be consistent with this objective because it is a relative measure that ignores the net addition in wealth to a company from taking on a project. The *PI* criterion can conflict with the *NPV* in ranking decisions. Again, this problem can be overcome by using the *NPV* rather than the *PI* in such situations.

PROBLEMS

11•1. Barbarian Pizza is analyzing the prospect of purchasing an additional firebrick oven. The oven costs $200,000 and would be depreciated (straight-line) to a salvage value of $120,000 in 10 years. The extra oven would increase annual revenues by $120,000 and annual operating expenses by $90,000. Barbarian's marginal tax rate is 25%.

(a) What would be the initial, operating, and terminal cash flows generated by the new oven?

(b) What is the payback period for the additional oven?

(c) What is the *AROR* for the additional oven?

(d) Barbarian Pizza's *RRR* is 12%. What is the *NPV* of the additional oven?

(e) What is the *PI* for the additional oven?

(f) What is the *IRR* of the additional oven?

11·2. Chin Jen Lie is considering the expansion of his chain of Chinese restaurants by opening a new restaurant in Duluth, Minnesota. If he does, he estimates that the restaurant will require a net initial outlay of $500,000. Furthermore, he estimates that the restaurant will generate annual cash flows of $20,000 and that he can sell it for $1,000,000 in 10 years.

(a) If Mr. Lie's *RRR* is 10%, what is the *NPV* of opening the restaurant? Should he open the retaurant?

(b) If Mr. Lie's *RRR* is 14%, what is the *NPV* of opening the restaurant? Should he open the restaurant?

11·3. Victoria Korchnoi is thinking of importing caviar to sell to restaurants and specialty stores. She estimates that this venture will require an initial outlay of $300,000 to buy a refrigerated storage unit, which can be depreciated (straight-line) to a salvage value of $50,000 in eight years. In addition, Ms. Korchnoi estimates that she will need $40,000 in working capital during the eight years of the project. Annual sales are estimated to be $110,000 and annual expenses $20,000. Ms. Korchnoi estimates that the marginal tax rate will be 25% during the lifetime of the project. [Parts (a), (b), and (c) are the same as Question 10·7. If you have already worked them out, you may use your solutions to answer parts (d) through (g) of this problem.]

(a) What is the initial outlay associated with starting the business?

(b) What is the annual cash flow from operations?

(c) What will be the terminal cash flow in year 8?

(d) What is the payback period for this project?

(e) What is the *AROR* of this project?

(f) If Ms. Korchnoi requires a 16% *RRR* to make this investment, what is the project's *NPV*? What is its *PI*?

(g) What is the project's *IRR*?

11·4 Universal Farm Supply's management has observed that it can sell as much fertilizer as it can stock and is considering the possibility of purchasing a forklift and expanding its warehouse space in order to be able to handle and stock more fertilizer (both are necessary to expand sales). The forklift costs $42,000 and would be depreciated to a salvage value of zero in 7 years, even though it is expected to last for 10 years. The warehouse expansion would cost $100,000 and would be depreciated to a salvage value of $60,000 in 10 years. The expansion would allow Universal to sell 1,000,000 more pounds per year at $0.20 per pound (the fertilizer actually costs Universal $0.17 per pound to manufacture). Universal's marginal tax rate is 25% and its *RRR* is 12%. [Parts (a), (b), and (c) are the same as Question 10•8. If you have already worked them out, you may use your solutions to answer parts (d) through (f) of this problem.]

(a) Find the net initial outlay associated with the expansion.
(b) Find the annual cash flow from operations during years 1 to 7.
(c) Find the annual cash flow from operations during years 8 to 10.
(d) Find the *NPV* of the expansion project. Should Universal expand to sell the extra fertilizer?
(e) Find the *NPV* of the expansion project if Universal's discount rate is 20%. What is the profitability index?
(f) Based solely on your answers to parts (d) and (e), what can you say about the expansion project's *IRR*?

11•5. Joley's department store has recently received the results of a study that suggests that potential sales are being lost because many customers dislike having to use the elevator in Joley's and prefer to go across the street to Foske's department store, which has an escalator. Consequently, Joley's is considering the replacement of the elevator with a new escalator. The elevator was purchased 10 years ago for $140,000 and is being depreciated (straight-line) to a salvage value of $40,000 10 years from now. It can be sold today for $80,000. The escalator can be purchased for $300,000 and would be depreciated (straight-line) to a salvage value of $100,000 in 10 years. In addition, Joley's anticipates that having an escalator rather than an elevator will increase sales by $20,000 annually and decrease operating expenses by $5,000 annually. Joley's has a marginal tax rate of 25%. [Parts (a), (b), and (c) are the same as Question 10•9. If you have already worked them out, you may use your solutions to answer parts (d) through (g) of this problem.]

(a) What is the present book value of the elevator?
(b) What is the initial cash outflow associated with the replacement of the elevator? Be sure to include any required changes in working capital.
(c) What will be Joley's incremental change in annual cash flow if they replace the elevator?
(d) What is the payback period for the replacement decision?
(e) If Joley's uses a 12% discount rate to value projects, what is the *NPV* of the replacement decision? What is the *PI* at 12%?
(f) If Joley's uses a 16% discount rate to value projects, what is the *NPV* of the replacement decision? What is the *PI* at 16%?
(g) What is the *IRR* of the replacement decision?

11•6.   Catherine Mauzy cannot decide between two machines that manufacture umbrellas. Both machines cost $100,000 and can produce 10,000 umbrellas annually (the umbrellas can be sold for $4 each). Machine *A* can be depreciated straight-line to a salvage value of zero in 10 years, and the annual expense of producing 10,000 umbrellas is $13,350. Machine *B* can be depreciated to a salvage value of $90,000 in 10 years, and the annual expense of producing 10,000 umbrellas is $15,650. Ms. Mauzy's corporation has a marginal tax rate of 25%.
   (a)   Find the *NPV* of each machine if the relevant discount rate is 10%. If Ms. Mauzy uses the *NPV* method to rank the machines, which will she choose?
   (b)   Find the *IRR* of each machine. If Ms. Mauzy uses the *IRR* to rank the machines, which will she choose?

11•7.   Dinesh Vaswami of the Dutch League Importing Company is considering a project that will require an initial outlay of $1,250,000 for a freighter plus $500,000 working capital. The freighter will be depreciated (straight-line) to a salvage value of $250,000 in 10 years. This project is expected to produce sales of $850,000 and require expenses of $425,000 annually for the next 10 years. Dutch League Importing has a marginal tax rate of 25%.
   (a)   Calculate the incremental cash flow from operations for this project.
   (b)   Calculate the *NPV* of this project for the following discount rates: 6%, 8%, 10%, 12%, 14%, and 16%. Draw a graph with the *NPV* on the vertical axis and the discount rate on the horizontal axis. Where will the *NPV* curve cross the horizontal axis? Is there any special significance to the point at which the graph crosses the horizontal axis?

11•8.   The Anthracite Coal Company is considering a strip-mining project that requires a $230,000 initial outlay and will generate cash inflows from operations of $100,000 at the end of each of the next 10 years. At the end of the 10th year, a $1,000,000 expenditure will be necessary to restore the land environmentally.
   (a)   What can be said about the uniqueness of the *IRR* of this project?
   (b)   Would you accept this project if the *RRR* were 5%? 20%? 40%?

11•9.   Plot an *NPV* profile for Barbarian Pizza in Problem 11•1. Use discount rates of 0%, 5%, 10%, 15%, 20%, and 25% in drawing the graph. What is the approximate *IRR* for the additional oven?

11•10.   Your first task as financial manager of the Reginald Corporation is to choose between two alternative projects for producing and marketing video cassettes. Project *A* requires an initial outlay of $100,000 and will generate annual cash flows of $16,000 during its 12-year life. At that time, its salvage value will be $48,000. Project B also requires an initial outlay of $100,000, but will generate annual cash flows of $17,500 during its 12-year life. Its salvage value at the end of year 12 is estimated to be $10,000. Your firm will use a 12% discount rate to value both projects.

(a) Find the *NPV* of project A.

(b) Find the *IRR* of project A to the nearest tenth of a percent.

(c) Find the *NPV* of project B.

(d) Find the *IRR* of project B to the nearest tenth of a percent (using a calculator).

(e) Which project should you choose, and why?

(f) A cohort of yours argues that since project B has the higher *IRR*, it should be adopted. Show that comparing the two projects using the *IRR* method correctly implies that project A should be chosen.

APPENDIX 11·A *Capital Rationing: A Ranking Decision*

The development of the capital budgeting procedures in Chapter 11 has centered on maximizing stockholders' wealth. By applying the *RRR* to each project's expected cash flows and then accepting every project that had a positive *NPV*, the firm ultimately determines the amount of funds needed for investments (the size of the capital budget).

For one reason or another, firms often reverse this process, in effect, by imposing a limitation on capital expenditures during a particular year and then deciding which projects to accept. It is important to note that this approach is inconsistent with the goal of value maximization. Rather than accepting all attractive investment opportunities, the firm attempts to select that combination of projects that will provide the greatest increment in the firm's value, subject to the budget size constraint. This behavior may involve, for example, accepting smaller, less profitable projects that completely use up the constrained budget rather than accepting a few larger projects that result in less than a 100% commitment of the funds available. In these situations, where capital expenditures are subject to a constraint, the firm is described as facing **capital rationing.**

KEY CONCEPT: **Capital rationing** is the process whereby a firm allocates a limited amount of capital to wealth-maximizing projects.

REASONS FOR SEEMINGLY IRRATIONAL FUNDING

To Constrain Organizational Units' Growth

A company that feels that its divisional managers are overenthusiastic in their budget requests might choose to impose a capital expenditure limit for a particular division. Moreover, divisions may have few acceptable projects but will undertake undesirable projects simply to allocate all their funds.

To Constrain the Firm's Overall Growth

Management may think that it will be extremely difficult to control operations if projects beyond a certain level are accepted. This may be true especially when the size of the project's investments is large relative to the firm's present size.[14] Lack of sufficient managerial skills and other dislocation costs are usually given as reasons for this limitation of growth. An example of how uncontrolled growth can cause serious managerial problems is presented in the highlight "A Case for Capital Rationing."

■■■ *HIGHLIGHT*

A CASE FOR CAPITAL RATIONING

In December 1983, American Express Company shocked investors when it announced that its 35-year string of annual earnings gain had been broken by a 10% drop in 1983 profits. American Express had often been cited as a prototype of the conglomerates that someday might dominate financial services. Its businesses included charge cards and traveler's checks, securities brokerage, insurance, and international banking. Most of its recent growth had come from acquisitions, but the acquisitions apparently continued despite signs of indigestion. Interviews with company insiders and outside observers revealed that American Express had acquired so many companies so quickly that it had lost managerial control over some of them. An overextended management allegedly had difficulty integrating the various subsidiaries, and internal rivalries undermined efforts to coordinate the various units.

The consensus is that three to five years will be needed to iron out all the wrinkles. American Express is a classic example of what can happen to a firm that grows too quickly. It may sometimes be advisable for a firm to limit its internal growth to a level it can absorb, rather than expand as quickly as the available capital will allow.

Source: D. B. Hilder and T. Metz, "A Spate of Acquisitions Puts American Express in a Management Bind," *Wall Street Journal*, August 15, 1984, pp. 1+.

To Constrain Financing to Internally Generated Funds

Management (especially in closely held firms) may sometimes prefer to avoid the use of long-term debt or new equity issues to fund projects. This attitude usually stems from an aversion to the risks of debt or the fear of losing ownership control if new shares of common stock are sold to outsiders. In such cases, the size of the capital budget becomes restricted to the availability of "excess" cash inflows from operations (cash, marketable securities, and retained

---

[14]A good example was the 1983 acquisition of Qualicare by Universal Health Services, a rapidly growing hospital management company. This investment effectively doubled Universal's size but heavily penalized its earnings growth and stock price (which traded at less than one-half of its 1983 high) for several years before this major investment was assimilated into its existing operations.

earnings). Management must weigh (be held accountable for) the loss of incremental wealth from rejecting acceptable projects due to any capital constraint against the "benefits" gained by being debt free or retaining control.

PROJECT SELECTION UNDER CAPITAL RATIONING

Before examining the process of selecting investment projects under capital rationing, it is necessary to understand that some projects are indivisible, whereas others are divisible. Projects that must be accepted or rejected in their entirety are called **indivisible.** For example, if a project involves the purchase of a corporate jet, it is either accepted (i.e., buy the jet) or rejected. It makes no sense to think about accepting half of the project.

On the other hand, projects may be **divisible.** For instance, if a rental car company is considering the replacement of all tires on its fleet of cars, we can think of one-half or one-third of the project. That is, the company can replace the tires on just part of its fleet.

Indivisible Projects

Consider the Thibbadeaux Company, which has decided to invest a maximum of $30,000 in new projects this year. Thibbadeaux's *RRR* is 15% and it has identified four potential (independent) investments with the following information:

Capital budget = $30,000

Project	Initial Investment	*NPV*
A	$15,000	$1,970
B	8,000	1,130
C	12,000	6,840
D	30,000	6,900

Which projects should be accepted if all projects are indivisible? At first glance, it is tempting to conclude that project *D* is the best investment because it has the highest *NPV* and because its initial investment just satisfies the capital budget. However, this conclusion is incorrect. Why? Because it may be possible to identify a combination of other, smaller projects that can lead to higher *NPV*s. To choose the projects correctly in this case, the following rule should be used:

KEY CONCEPT: With **capital rationing,** maximizing value requires that managers choose that combination of projects that maximizes the sum of their *NPVs* without exceeding the capital constraint.

To see how this rule can be made operational, consider the information in Table 11A•1. First, identify all feasible project combinations and the associated *NPV* for each combination. By feasible, we mean that the combination does not exceed the capital constraint. From Table 11A•1, the combination $A + C$ is the best because Thibbadeaux will receive an *NPV* of $8,810 with a $27,000 investment. All other projects must be rejected, including project D, which appeared to be the best initially.

Note that under capital rationing, the firm attempts to maximize shareholder wealth subject to the constraint that the allocated funds are not exceeded. Clearly, this constrained *NPV* maximization behavior will lead to less incremental wealth ($8,810) than following the more desirous unconstrained *NPV* maximization $(A + B + C + D = \$16,840)$.

Moreover, although the method just outlined is quite straightforward, it is tedious and can be quite involved when the number of combinations is large. A more efficient procedure requires the use of a computer, and mathematical programming techniques may be used to simplify the problem. This book will not delve further into mathematical programming.

Divisible Projects

What if Thibbadeaux's four projects were divisible? The method suggested in Case 1 will no longer lead to the correct decision. When projects are divisible, the *PI* can be used to make the right decision. Recall from Section 11•1 that

TABLE 11A•1 Selecting Capital Budgeting Projects Under Capital Rationing When Projects Are Indivisible

Capital budget = $30,000

Feasible Project Combination*	Size of Capital Budget	NPV ($RRR = 15\%$)
A	$15,000	$1,970
B	8,000	1,130
C	12,000	6,840
D	30,000	6,900
A + B	23,000	3,100
A + C	27,000	8,810
B + C	20,000	7,970

*All other combinations exceed the $30,000 capital budget constraint.

$$PI = \frac{PV_{\text{inflows}}}{PV_{\text{outflows}}}$$

Using PI, the problem of choosing the right divisible projects with capital rationing is operationalized as follows:[15]

KEY CONCEPT: If projects are divisible and a capital constraint exists, rank projects by their *PI* value from highest to lowest, and then select all the highest-ranked projects that do not exceed the imposed capital budget.

Table 11A·2 summarizes the relevant information required for this analysis. Based on the *PI*s, the projects are ranked in descending order as C, D, B, and A. As the table indicates, C, requiring a \$12,000 investment, should be accepted first. That leaves \$18,000 for further investing. Project D should be picked next; however, this requires \$30,000, and only \$18,000 remains. There-

TABLE 11A·2 Selecting Capital Budgeting Projects Under Capital Rationing When Projects Are Divisible

Capital budget = \$30,000

Project	Initial Investment	NPV (*RRR* = 15%)	Profitability Index (*PI*)	Rank
A	\$15,000	\$1,970	1.13	4
B	8,000	1,130	1.14	3
C	12,000	6,840	1.57	1
D	30,000	6,900	1.23	2

Step 1. Accept project C first, with $PI_C = 1.57$. Since $C = \$12,000 < \$30,000$, all funds have not been allocated, so proceed to step 2.

Step 2. Accept project D next, with $PI = 1.23$. However, $C + D = \$12,000 + \$30,000 > \$30,000$; therefore, solve the following equation to determine what portion of D (x_C) to accept:

$$\$12,000 + \$30,000 x_D = \$30,000$$

or

$$x_D = \frac{\$30,000 - \$12,000}{\$30,000} = 0.60$$

[15]The simplicity of the PI method for a one-year analysis is somewhat deceptive in that this approach fails whenever more than one year's capital budget is rationed. Moreover, difficulties arise whenever there are other constraints on projection selection. For example, the PI method cannot handle cases in which projects are mutually exclusive.

fore, as shown in Table 11A•2, only 60% of project *D* can be undertaken. Because fractional projects are allowed, Thibbadeaux's capital budget would be composed of project *C* and 60% of project *D*. Notice that this budget is completely different from that found in Case 1, where projects were indivisible.

WHY THE PI CRITERION APPLIES WHEN CAPITAL IS RATIONED

When the *PI* criterion was examined in Section 11•4, the reader was warned that ranking projects by their *PI*s could be misleading because the *PI* ignores the scale of investment. Yet, as has just been shown, *PI* can be useful in capital rationing situations when projects are divisible.

Why does the *PI* criterion apply in this case? Without capital rationing, decisions are based on *NPV* because the ultimate objective is to pick all projects that increase wealth ($NPV > 0$). However, with capital rationing, funds are not available to finance all projects that increase wealth. Our objective now becomes the maximization of the increment in wealth per dollar invested. That is, a financial manager faced with capital rationing must pick projects such that the present value of benefits for every dollar invested is as high as possible. This is exactly what the *PI* will do.

Learning Check for Appendix 11•A

Review Questions

11A•1. What are some common reasons for capital rationing?

11A•2. Explain why the *PI* criterion is applicable for choosing between divisible projects under capital constraints.

New Terms

Capital rationing   Divisible projects   Indivisible projects

PROBLEMS

11A•1. Merlin Pet Stores, Inc., is planning to open up stores in shopping malls in each of several cities and has estimated the required initial outlay, *NPV*, *IRR*, and *PI* for each of the stores. The results are tabulated as follows:

City	Net Initial Outlay	NPV	IRR (%)	PI
San Francisco	$300,000	$40,000	18	1.133
Phoenix	250,000	30,000	16	1.12
Austin	250,000	35,000	17	1.14
Baton Rouge	150,000	22,000	19	1.146
Atlanta	100,000	15,000	18	1.15
Richmond	50,000	10,000	16	1.2

Merlin is subject to capital rationing and has decided to spend no more than $600,000. In which cities should Merlin open new stores?

11A·2. The Bruce Construction Company specializes in building hospitals and has requests from a number of companies in various cities to contract to build hospitals. The cities making the requests, together with the initial outlay required, the number of labor hours required for construction, and the *NPV* of the projects are as follows:

City	Initial Outlay	Labor Hours (Thousands)	NPV
Los Angeles	$200,000	80	$30,000
San Diego	150,000	70	26,000
Santa Fe	150,000	60	25,000
El Paso	100,000	60	23,000
Kansas City	100,000	50	20,000
Pittsburgh	50,000	50	12,000
Miami	50,000	40	10,000

The financial manager of Bruce Construction is subject not only to capital rationing (he is not allowed to have initial outlays exceeding $400,000) but also to rationing of labor hours (only 200,000 hours of labor are available). Which contract offers should be accepted? (*Hint*: Find all the feasible combinations that satisfy the capital rationing constraint, and then exclude from this list those that exceed the 200,000 labor hours available and proceed from there.)

11A·3. Webster's Discount Store has recently experienced many stockouts. To alleviate this problem, management has decided to increase the storage areas in their regional warehouses. This will cost $4 per square foot of warehouse area. The maximum area by which each regional warehouse might be expanded, together with the *NPV* of future benefits from this maximum expansion, are shown in the following table:

City	Maximum Addition Possible (Square Feet)	NPV of Maximum Addition
Los Angeles	100,000	$50,000
Dallas	80,000	45,000
Atlanta	75,000	40,000
St. Louis	60,000	35,000
Chicago	50,000	30,000
Philadelphia	40,000	20,000
Baltimore	30,000	18,000
New York	25,000	15,000

These projects are divisible, and the *NPV* of an addition smaller than the maximum is proportional to the *NPV* of the maximum addition; for example, if the Los Angeles facility is increased by 75,000 square feet, the *NPV* of this addition will be $37,500.

(a)   Find the initial outlay and the *PI* for the expansion projects for each of the eight cities.

(b)   If Webster's can allocate only $1.5 million to the expansion project this year, how should this money be spent?

READINGS

BACON, P. W., "The Evaluation of Mutually Exclusive Investments," *Financial Management*, Summer 1977, 55–58.

BAUMOL, W., AND R. QUANDT, "Investment and Discount Rates Under Capital Rationing—A Programming Approach," *Economic Journal*, June 1965, 317–329.

BERNHARD, RICHARD H., "Mathematical Programming Models for Capital Budgeting—A Survey, Generalization, and Critique." *Journal of Financial and Quantitative Analysis*, June 1969, 111–158.

FORSYTH, J. D., AND D. C. OWEN, "Capital Rationing Methods," in *Capital Budgeting Under Conditions of Uncertainty*, ed. R. L. Crum and F. G. J. Derkinderen (Hingham, Mass.: Martinus Nijhoff Publishers, 1981), pp. 213–235.

HIRSHLEIFER, J., "On the Theory of Optimal Investment," *Journal of Political Economy*, August 1958, 329–352.

LORIE, J. H., AND L. J. SAVAGE, "Three Problems in Rationing Capital," *Journal of Business*, October 1955, 229–239.

MYERS, STEWART C., AND GERALD A. POGUE, "A Programming Approach to Corporate Financial Management," *Journal of Finance*, May 1974, 579–599.

PART V

Uncertainty in the Investment Decision

12

The Meaning of Return and Risk

Whether we like it or not, risk and uncertainty are real. Everyone encounters uncertainty in everyday life—uncertainty about the weather, uncertainty about the performance of one's investments, and uncertainty about one's health. Although few would argue with this statement, nearly everyone would have trouble explaining the difference between risk and uncertainty. *Uncertainty* exists when a decision maker knows all potential future outcomes of a certain act but, for one reason or another, cannot assign probabilities to the various outcomes. *Risk,* on the other hand, exists when the decision maker knows not only the various future outcomes but also the probability associated with each potential outcome. In other words, risk is quantifiable uncertainty.[1] This chapter focuses on the analysis of the risk of an investment (stock, capital investment, etc.), and therefore, it is important to see how uncertainty can be quantified. In spite of this technical distinction between risk and uncertainty, in many practical situations the two terms are often used interchangeably.

Assume that the Metal Box Company is contemplating the purchase of a new sheet metal printer. Before it proceeds with this new project, management would presumably go through the various stages of capital budgeting described

---

[1] For example, if the weatherman says that "it might rain tomorrow," he is explaining that uncertainty exists about the weather tomorrow. However, if he says that "there is a 60% chance of rain tomorrow," he has quantified the uncertainty, and this becomes a risk situation.

in Chapter 10. Only if the project will potentially increase the value of the company will it be adopted. To evaluate this project, management must first estimate the potential benefits from the project and then discount these benefits at the opportunity cost (or *RRR*). However, as seen in Chapter 3, to identify the appropriate opportunity cost, it is necessary to assess the risk of the investment.

In this chapter we begin an analysis of this issue—the estimation of project/investment risks and potential returns. We develop concepts of risk and return and see that the manner in which we combine assets into portfolios (a collection of assets) affects the amount of risk we must bear. This chapter is thus a necessary first step toward understanding how the *RRR* of an investment is estimated. Chapter 13 builds on this concept and provides a usable structure for analyzing financial risk.

First, Metal Box must somehow estimate the future benefits to the company from buying the printer. (If there are no expected benefits, the company would not even consider this project.) Since the benefits are usually uncertain, Metal Box has to quantify the uncertainty associated with these future benefits in order to make a decision. Four distinct questions emerge:

1. How does one quantify the benefits? And incidentally, what are the benefits?

2. How does one define risk formally, and how is risk measured?

3. How does one use risk and return measures in comparing risky alternatives?

4. Are there any strategies for reducing risk?

To answer these questions, this chapter is presented in four sections.

SECTION 12•1: *Basic Return and Risk Concepts.* In this section, we introduce the reader to some fundamental concepts required for quantifying risk. First, we contrast book and market measures of return and explain why return measures based on market values are needed. We then develop the concepts of ex ante and ex post returns and conclude with the idea that we can represent the uncertainty about future returns via discrete and continuous probability distributions.

SECTION 12•2: *Summarizing and Interpreting the Information from a Probability Distribution.* The probability distributions introduced in Section 12•1 often contain an overwhelming amount of information. This section shows how this information can be conveniently summarized into measures of location (the most likely or expected value) and measures of variability (how widely the observations may be expected to vary from this expected value). We also provide an explanation of these measures' practical significance.

SECTION 12•3: *Comparing the Risk and Expected Return of Two Distributions.* Here we explain the process of choosing between two probability distributions by examining the summary statistics introduced in the previous section. An investor or manager compares the expected returns and risks of various projects and chooses the project that offers the best risk–return tradeoff. We then introduce a new statistic, the coefficient of variation, which is sometimes used to examine the risk–return tradeoffs of different projects.

SECTION 12·4: *Diversification and Portfolio Risk.* This section shows that, under certain conditions, the risk of a portfolio (a collection of assets) can be reduced by diversification. We first demonstrate how the expected return of a portfolio is calculated. We then examine relationships that exist among assets and develop statistical measures of these relationships. These statistical measures are then used to calculate the risk of a portfolio of assets and to show formally how some combinations of assets are less risky than others.

SECTION 12·1   *Basic Return and Risk Concepts*

In Chapter 7 we introduced two measures of return: the book return on assets (*ROA*) and the book return on equity (*ROE*). Although these are legitimate measures of accounting return, these returns are calculated from the books of the company and reflect historical accounting information. Because the corporate manager making decisions has the goal of market value maximization, these return measures offer little guidance. Instead, *return measures based on market values* are needed. As already seen, profit-based decision making should be replaced with an analysis of cash flows. In other words, the return from any transaction should be measured in terms of the returns provided by the cash flows from the transaction. It is the uncertainty associated with these returns that introduces risk into an investment. This idea will be pursued in greater detail.

Most transactions can be viewed as a series of cash flows. This is true irrespective of whether the transaction involves the purchase of a machine, an act of consumption, or an investment in securities. For example, if Ms. Trueval purchases a security (say, ACR stock), this transaction involves a (negative) cash flow (i.e., an outflow at first) because she has to pay a seller the market price of the ACR stock to acquire it. But why does she buy the stock? If her answer is "for investment purposes" or "because I expect high returns," she is really saying "for its future cash flows (benefits)."

To see this, recognize that the purchase of a stock entitles Ms. Trueval to receive future dividends declared by the company. Of course, these dividends are uncertain. Nevertheless, they are cash inflows that Ms. Trueval expects to receive. In addition to dividends, when the stock is sold, she will get another cash inflow—the selling price of the stock.

To estimate the benefits from an investment such as this, the decision maker, Ms. Trueval in this case, must calculate the returns from this investment.[2] The cash flow that she receives obviously depends on how long she owns the investment. Thus, to speak of returns in a meaningful way, it is important to specify clearly the period over which the return is computed.[3] The rest of this chapter deals with one-period returns. That is, the assumption will be that the asset is held for one year (or one month or week) and that the return is computed over this time period. Two different types of returns will be identified.

EX ANTE AND EX POST RETURNS

Ex ante simply means "before the fact," while *ex post* means "after the fact." When we speak of returns, it is important to distinguish between these two return measures because there is no assurance that they will be the same.

KEY CONCEPT: An **ex ante return** is the (uncertain) return that one expects to get from an investment.

If Ms. Trueval plans to hold her shares of ACR for one year, how would the return be computed? Obviously, she has to estimate the dividends to be received from ownership of the stock and the selling price the following year. Thus the ex ante return that she would compute is an estimate. There is no guarantee that she will, in fact, get this rate of return. On the other hand, what if at the end of the year she computes the actual (or realized) return from ACR? Since a computation of the return after the fact involves no uncertainty, we have:

KEY CONCEPT: An **ex post** or **realized return** is the (certain) return that one actually obtains from an investment.

The symbol $\tilde{R}_i$ will be used to represent the uncertain return on an asset *i*. The tilde (˜) over the R_i denotes that it is an uncertain variable. R_i without the tilde will represent an ex post or realized return. In the remainder of this chapter, the subscript *i* is omitted, except where confusion can result.

Calculating Ex Ante and Ex Post Returns[4]

The formulas for calculating $\tilde{R}$ and R for Ms. Trueval's investment in ACR stock, for the period over which the stock is held, are now provided.

---

[2] Returns can be measured in absolute (dollar) terms or in relative (percentage) terms. Often, *rate of return* is used to refer to percentage returns. Unless specified, returns will be in percentage terms.

[3] Because these returns are sensitive to the time period for which the asset is held, they are sometimes called **holding-period returns**.

[4] Whether the asset in question is a lathe, a sales outlet, or a share of common stock, the analysis is similar. The definition of returns may have to be changed slightly for different situations. This chapter focuses on common stock since it is easier to relate to this asset. In a later chapter, the returns from owning a physical asset (e.g., a machine) are calculated.

$$\tilde{R} = \frac{\text{forecasted dividend} + \text{forecasted end-of-period stock price}}{\text{initial investment (i.e., market price of stock)}} - 1 \quad (12\text{-}1)$$

or, equivalently, equation (12-1) can be written as

$$\tilde{R} = \frac{\text{forecasted dividend} + \text{forecasted change in stock price}}{\text{initial investment (i.e., market price of stock)}} \quad (12\text{-}1)'$$

Since equations (12-1) and (12-1)' are equivalent, either can be used in computing the ex ante return from an investment.

In contrast, the ex post or realized return is calculated using the formula

$$R = \frac{\text{actual dividend} + \text{actual end-of-period stock price}}{\text{initial investment (i.e., market price of stock)}} - 1 \quad (12\text{-}2)$$

or, in terms of stock price changes, as

$$R = \frac{\text{actual dividend} + \text{actual change in stock price}}{\text{initial investment (i.e., market price of stock)}} \quad (12\text{-}2)'$$

Example 12•1 Calculating Ex Ante and Ex Post Returns

Suppose that John Tritt bought a share of York, Inc., stock on January 1, 1988 for $52. At the end of the year he expects to sell it for $68. He also expects to receive $4 in dividends over this period. Assume that, for some reason, York paid only $2 in dividends, and by year end the stock was selling for only $40. John's ex ante return, using equation (12-1), is

$$\tilde{R}_{\text{York}} = \frac{\$4 + \$68}{\$52} - 1 = 38.46\%$$

while his ex post or realized return, using equation (12-2), is

$$R_{\text{York}} = \frac{\$2 + \$40}{\$52} - 1 = -19.23\%$$

The reader should verify that equations (12-1)' and (12-2)' would also yield the same results.

Notice in this example that while Mr. Tritt expected to realize a high positive return, he in fact had a negative return. We therefore make an important observation that holds whether the investment in question is a financial asset or a physical asset (capital investment):

KEY CONCEPT: Ex ante returns, in general, do not bear any direct relationship to ex post returns for individual transactions.[5]

In other words, while investors make decisions based on the benefits they expect on an investment, the actual outcomes may not correspond to their expectations. If realizations corresponded to expectations exactly, there would be no risk.

EXPECTED RETURNS AND RISK

Consider an investor or a company planning the purchase of an asset. The asset in question can be a *physical asset* such as the sheet metal plant considered by Metal Box, a lathe, or a new sales outlet. Alternatively, it can be a *financial asset*, as, for example, Ms. Trueval's purchase of a share of ACR stock. Consider the purchase of ACR stock. For simplicity, it will be assumed that ACR pays no dividends and that the stock's current price is $50. It will also be assumed, as before, that Ms. Trueval plans to sell the stock next year at whatever price ACR commands in the market at that time.

Now what can be said about the return from owning ACR stock for one year? Not much at this stage. If it were known, for example, that ACR stock could be sold next year for $75, then, using equation (12-1), the return can safely be computed as ($75/$50) − 1 = 50%. However, this is an unrealistic situation because no one knows the future price of ACR stock. If economic conditions improve to a great extent, ACR's price might rise considerably by year end. If, on the other hand, the United States goes through a recession, one can expect ACR stock to fall in value.

Although such general statements are acceptable descriptions of the future, they do not help individuals decide on what the return from owning ACR stock will be. Nor does the discussion so far shed any light on whether or not ACR is a risky stock. To say anything specific about the returns from ACR stock, one has to quantify the risk of owning it. This is done by means of a probability distribution.

---

[5] The words *for individual transactions* are used advisedly. The significance of these words is not important at this point and will therefore not be addressed until later in this chapter. This footnote is intended simply to *alert* the reader that the statement applies to individual transactions.

KEY CONCEPT: A **probability distribution** is a statement of the different potential outcomes for an uncertain variable together with the probability of each potential outcome.[6]

DISCRETE PROBABILITY DISTRIBUTIONS

Assume that ACR's performance depends on how well the U.S. economy is performing. This is a reasonable assumption because however effective a company's management is, its performance is better if general economic conditions are good and is not as good when general economic conditions are poor. Assume that a good measure of the state of the economy is the Dow Jones Industrial Average (DJIA). Assume that the information in Table 12•1 is representative of Ms. Trueval's beliefs about the future.

Thus the returns on ACR stock range between +40% and −20%, depending on which state of the economy actually materializes next year. Notice that the stock can take on three distinct values ($70, $50, or $40) with specific probabilities (0.3, 0.5, and 0.2). By specifying probabilities, Ms. Trueval has converted an uncertain situation to a risk situation. The probability distribution in Table 12•1 is said to be a **discrete distribution,** since the variables of interest (returns or stock prices) can take on only discrete values, with a probability assigned to each value.

By plotting the probability distribution in Table 12•1, we get the distribution in Figure 12•1. Figure 12•1a represents the probability distribution for the stock price, and Figure 12•1b represents the probability distribution for returns.

Although such probability distributions can be drawn for either future stock price or future returns, it is more useful to work in terms of returns. This is because returns recognize the total reward that an investor gets from investing. The future stock price is only one element in the return computation.

In the example of ACR's stock, we used the DJIA as a measure of the state of the economy. The DJIA is probably the best-known and most widely quoted

TABLE 12•1 Probability Distribution of ACR's Returns

State of the Economy	Probability	ACR Stock Price	Return[a] (%)
DJIA > 1,600 (boom)	0.3	$70	40
1,600 > DJIA > 1,000 (normal)	0.5	50	0
DJIA < 1,000 (recession)	0.2	40	−20

[a] Returns computed using equation (12-2). ACR pays no dividends and its current market price = $50. Thus, in the boom state, for example, the return is ($70 − $50)/$50 = 40%.

[6] A probability distribution must use all possible alternatives. That is, it must include the full probability set. This implies that the probabilities must always sum to 1.

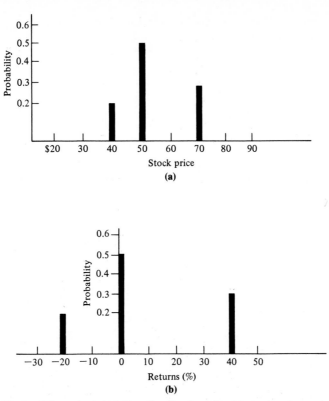

FIGURE 12·1 Discrete probability distributions for (a) stock price and (b) stock return.

indicator of stock market performance. The highlight "The Dow Jones Averages: Getting a Handle on the Market" provides a brief overview of the history and uses of this and other averages.

■ *HIGHLIGHT*

THE DOW JONES AVERAGES: GETTING A HANDLE ON THE MARKET

When people ask, "How is the market doing?", they usually mean, "How is the Dow Jones industrial average (DJIA) doing"? In 1884 Charles Dow added together the prices of 11 important stocks and divided the total by 11. The answer he obtained was the beginning value for his index. The performance of this index (i.e., the returns on this index) is often a rough measure of the performance of the U.S. economy as a whole. In 1928 the average was broadened to include 30 stocks, and the composition has been updated again over the years.

Today, the DJIA consists of 30 stocks and is price weighted; that is, the component stock prices are added together and the result is divided by another figure called the *divisor*. This means that a high-priced stock has a greater effect on the index than a low-priced one. Market value is the price of a stock multiplied by the number of shares outstanding. This system gives greater significance to larger companies with a large number of shares outstanding than to smaller companies. To compensate for stock splits, stock dividends, and other factors, the divisor has been changed frequently and is no longer equal to the number of stocks in the index. As this book goes to press, the current divisor for the DJIA is 0.703 and the index is around 2100.

The industrial average continues to be the most widely watched of the Dow Jones stock averages, although there are other Dow Jones indexes covering 20 transportation-company stocks (the transportation index) and 15 utility-company stocks (utility index), as well as a composite index of the 65 stocks in the three indexes (composite index). Some publications, such as *Barron's*, provide hourly averages for these different indexes.

Not withstanding the historical prominence of the DJIA, several researchers and analysts today focus on Standard and Poor's 500 index (the S&P 500), which is a similar stock index consisting of 500 stocks. Like the Dow Jones indexes, Standard and Poor's provides separate industrial, transportation, and utilities indexes. In addition, S&P has a separate financial index.

Irrespective of the index under consideration, the purpose of the indexes is the same: their ups and downs provide a rough measure of the performance of the U.S. economy.

CONTINUOUS PROBABILITY DISTRIBUTIONS

In Figure 12•1b the returns on the stock can take on only three distinct values, each with a specific probability. But what if the returns on the stock can take on infinitely different values? Clearly, this is a more realistic case, since the returns can fall anywhere between −100% and infinity.[7] In this case, the uncertainty about the returns can be represented using a continuous distribution.

In a **continuous distribution** the required probability of a range of outcomes is given by the area under the curve over the appropriate range. For example, the probability of a return falling between 27 and 30% is given by the shaded area in Figure 12•2. For a continuous distribution, the probability of a return taking on a particular value is zero. For example, the probability of a return being exactly 28% is zero.

Although continuous distributions are more realistic descriptions of future outcomes, in most practical applications one deals with discrete distributions as a simplification. Typically, probability distributions of returns are estimated using actual historical data. By studying the behavior of stock returns over the recent past, it is possible to come up with a subjective probability assessment for future returns. But in observing historical (or ex post) data, we are observing a finite number of historical returns, each with a specific frequency. Thus it is possible to develop discrete probability distributions only by looking at the

---

[7]The worst possible outcome is −100% because of the limited-liability feature of stocks. One cannot lose more than the price of the stock.

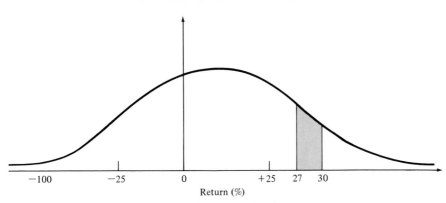

FIGURE 12·2   A continuous probability distribution.
Normal distribution: Mean = 16%, σ = 4%.

stock's past performance record. In this chapter, we will therefore deal only with discrete probability distributions in providing examples and illustrations.

Learning Check for Section 12·1

Review Questions

12·1.   What is the difference between book and market measures of return?

12·2.   What is the difference between ex ante and ex post returns? How can each of these returns be computed?

12·3.   Distinguish between discrete and continuous probability distributions. What type of distribution is a more realistic description of historical returns? Of future returns?

New Terms

Continuous distribution   Ex ante return   Holding period
Discrete distribution   Ex post return   return

SECTION 12·2   *Summarizing and Interpreting the Information from a Probability Distribution*

Assuming that Ms. Trueval has identified the probability distribution for ACR stock, it is necessary to reduce the information contained in the distribution to two simple measures in order to simplify decision making. One measure should indicate the potential benefits from the investment, and the other measure should capture the riskiness of these benefits. In this manner, by developing two measures that summarize the information in the distribution, Ms. Trueval can effectively throw aside the entire distribution and, instead, base her decision on these two **summary statistics**.[8]

SUMMARIZING THE INFORMATION ABOUT RETURNS

Consider Figure 12•1a. How could Ms. Trueval use this information? Should she assume that the return on the stock is 0%, or should she assume that it is 40%? Each of these returns is an uncertain variable that can occur with a different probability. It is therefore necessary to come up with an expected return that summarizes these possible outcomes by taking into consideration each potential return and its associated probability in Figure 12•1a.

The **average return** from the stock should be a basis of Ms. Trueval's estimate of potential returns. This is provided by calculating the expected return from owning the stock.

KEY CONCEPT: The **expected return** from an investment is the average return from the investment and is calculated as the probability-weighted sum of all potential returns.[9]

$$E(\tilde{R}) = \sum [p(\text{return}) \times \text{return}] \tag{12-3}$$

In the preceding definition, $p(\text{return})$ is the probability of a particular value of return and Σ represents the summation notation with the summation carried over all possible outcomes. In words, equation (12-3) requires that each potential return be multiplied by its probability of occurrence and then that all these products to be added together.

Refer to the information provided in Figure 12•1b or Table 12•1 and calculate the expected return of the distribution. Since Figure 12•1b deals with ACR stock returns, the answer will yield the expected return on this stock. Table 12•2 illustrates the procedure for calculating the expected return on ACR stock. As seen in the table, the expected return on ACR stock is 8%. In evaluating this stock, Ms. Trueval can focus on this one return—the expected return of 8%.

---

[8] In the discussion that follows, two summary statistics—the expected return and variance of returns—will be developed. The discussion of probability measures revolves around returns only because it facilitates the development of the required concepts. These two measures can be calculated not only for returns but for any random variable. For example, from a probability distribution of male life expectancy, one could calculate the expected life expectancy and the variance associated with life expectancy.

[9] The reader should note that this is like the calculation of an arithmetic average, except that the outcomes are uncertain. When no risk is involved, the same expected return calculation, with an assigned probability of 1.0 to each outcome, gives the average. Thus the expected value is a *probabilistic average*.

TABLE 12·2   Expected Return on ACR Stock

Return (%)	Probability	Return × Probability (%)
40	0.3	12
0	0.5	0
−20	0.2	−4

Expected return = $\Sigma[p(\text{return}) \times (\text{return})] = 8$

SUMMARIZING INFORMATION ABOUT THE VARIABILITY OF RETURNS

So far, Ms. Trueval cannot draw any detailed inferences about the attractiveness of ACR stock by looking at either the probability distribution in Figure 12·1a or the expected return. In particular, Ms. Trueval cannot, simply on the basis of the expected return of 8% for ACR, make any decision regarding the stock. Expected returns alone are not sufficient for decision making for any person who is averse to **risk.**[10] The risk aspect should be explicitly recognized. How risky is ACR stock?

To answer this question, a definition of risk has to be developed. There are several different ways of defining risk, but the most popular and convenient way to define it is in terms of variability. In finance, an investment whose returns are fairly stable is considered a relatively low-risk investment, whereas one whose returns fluctuate significantly is considered to possess greater risk. For example, U.S. Treasury bills (T bills) are obligations of the U.S. government, and because investors' returns are guaranteed if they hold a bill to maturity, T bills are characterized as *risk-free assets*. On the other hand, stocks are risky investments because the potential return has variability. Other investments, such as options (which we have not yet seen in this book), are considered even more risky because the potential variability in returns from options is greater than that from stocks. Thus, loosely defined, *risk* is the potential for variability in returns. Of course, it is necessary to introduce probabilities into the calculations in order to recognize the likelihood of these variable returns.

The most popular measure of risk is the **variance,** or the standard deviation of a distribution. First, the definition of variance will be provided; then variance of returns of ACR stock will be calculated. The meaning and the calculation of the standard deviation are easy after variance is examined.

KEY CONCEPT: The **variance** of returns from an investment is the sum of the probability-weighted squared deviations from the mean.

---

[10] Recall that the expected return is really an average. A risk-averse investor making decisions using the expected return alone is like a nonswimmer planning to cross a river because the average depth is only 5 feet. Ignoring variability can be very costly.

Variance is usually denoted by σ^2:

$$\sigma^2 = \sum \{p(\text{return}) \times [\text{return} - E(\tilde{R})]^2\} \qquad (12\text{-}4)$$

In this definition, $E(\tilde{R})$ represents the expected return, and all other variables have been defined earlier. In words, variance is calculated first by finding the expected return, finding the difference between each potential return and the expected return, squaring this value, multiplying it by the probability of that occurrence, and summing this resulting value over all possible occurrences.

The variance of ACR stock can be calculated easily, using the information in Table 12·1. Table 12·3 illustrates how this is done. While the calculations in Table 12·3 show that the variance (σ^2) of returns for ACR stock is 496, the table does not provide any *meaning* for variance. To understand the practical significance of variance, it is useful to define another risk measure called **standard deviation.**

KEY CONCEPT: The **standard deviation** (σ) of returns is the square root of the variance of the distribution:

$$\text{Standard deviation } (\sigma) = \sqrt{\sigma^2} \qquad (12\text{-}5)$$

While variance is expressed in squared terms, standard deviation is expressed in the same units as the mean and is thus easier to interpret, since $\sigma = \sqrt{496} = 22.3\%$.

SUMMARY INFORMATION ON ACR STOCK

Having calculated the expected return and variance of returns for ACR stock, it is now possible to draw some inferences about this investment, assuming that the returns on ACR are normally distributed:[11]

TABLE 12·3 Calculating the Variance of ACR's Returns

Return (%)	Probability	Deviation from Expected Return[a]	Squared Deviation	Probability × Squared Deviation
40	0.3	32	1,024	307
0	0.5	− 8	64	32
−20	0.2	−28	784	157
	1.0			

$$\sigma^2 = \Sigma[p(\text{return}) \times (\text{return} - \text{expected return})^2] = \overline{496}$$

[a] Expected return of 8%.

[11] The reader may find it surprising that the discrete probability distribution for ACR stock returns is now assumed to be normal—a continuous distribution. This approximation is necessary to quantify the ranges of potential future returns and their associated probabilities.

Summary Information from Probability Distribution

Expected return from holding ACR = 8%

Variance of returns on ACR = 496

Standard deviation of returns = 22.3%

    Knowledge of probability distributions can aid a manager in understanding and using these summary measures in financial decision making. A discussion of one widely known probability distribution, the **normal distribution,** and its application to ACR is contained in the highlight "The Practical Significance of Variability Measures."

◼ HIGHLIGHT

THE PRACTICAL SIGNIFICANCE OF THE VARIABILITY MEASURES

    To understand the practical implications of the standard deviation, it is necessary to use a theoretical result. Assume that a normal distribution has a mean of 16% and a standard deviation of 4%.* Then, as Figure 12•3 shows, one can say that with 68.26% probability the *actual future return* will fall between 16% + 1σ = 16% + 4% = 20% and 16% − 1σ = 12%, that is, between 12% and 20%. Similarly, with 95.46% probability, the *actual* return will lie between 8% and 24%. With 99.74% certainty, the *actual* return for the stock will be between 4% and 28%.

    Note that the probability ranges apply to any normal distribution, regardless of its mean or standard deviation. For instance, consider another normal distribution with an expected value of 10% and a standard deviation of 5%. The range of $+1\sigma$ and -1σ from the mean is 5% (10% − 5%) and 15% (10% + 5%). The probability of a return falling within this range is exactly the same as that given in the accompanying figure, 68.26%.

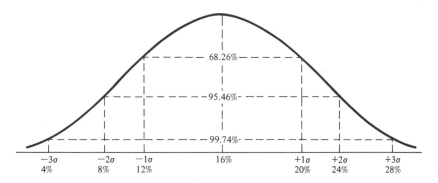

−3σ		−2σ	−1σ	16%		+1σ	+2σ	+3σ
4%		8%	12%			20%	24%	28%

    Thus, by using standard deviations in conjunction with the mean, it is possible to say something more specific about the actual return. Of course, the uncertainty about the future return is still not removed. But this process has helped to quantify the uncertainty by saying that the actual return will lie somewhere between two values with a certain probability.

Notice that the preceding numbers are correct only for a normal distribution. For arbitrary (nonnormal) distributions, the confidence intervals have different values. However, many theoretical results are based on the assumption that returns are normal, and so, the figure is allowed to take on a special significance.†

Interpretation of the Summary Measures of ACR Stock

The average return is 8%. There is a 0.6826 probability that the actual (ex post) returns from ACR will lie between −14.3% and 30.3%. There is a 0.9546 probability that the actual returns will fall between −36.6% and 52.6%. There is a 0.9974 probability (a virtually certain outcome) that the actual return from ACR will be between −58.9% and 74.9%.

*The normal distribution occurs frequently in nature, and a variety of random variables can be characterized by the normal. In fact, stock returns can be approximated with normal distributions. The details, however, are beyond the scope of this book. Almost any statistics textbook contains an exposition on the normal distribution.

†The returns on many financial assets are approximately normally distributed. Hence the normality assumption appears reasonable.

Learning Check for Section 12•2

Review Questions

12•4. What statistics are used in summarizing information from a probability distribution? What is the practical significance of these measures?

12•5. Why do we assume that the returns on financial assets are normally distributed in order to explain the practical significance of the standard deviation measure? Does it not have any practical meaning if returns are not normal?

New Terms

Expected return   Standard deviation   Variance
Normal   Summary statistics
    distribution

SECTION 12•3 *Comparing the Risk and Expected Return of Two Distributions*

Having seen how the detailed information provided by a probability distribution can be simplified to two measures that can be used to make definitive statements about actual future outcomes, it is now possible to address the question of how two different probability distributions can be compared using these summary measures.

It is fairly safe to assume that most people are risk averse. Risk only complicates matters, and most people try constantly to avoid risk. That explains why insurance is so popular. It also explains why investors do not like to invest all their wealth in risky ventures. Of course, people do not avoid all risk. Investing in a stock amounts to taking on a certain amount of risk, but if one has two stocks with identical expected returns, the stock with the lower risk will be preferred. Similarly, in comparing two stocks with identical risks, the one with the higher expected return will be preferred by a risk-averse investor.

This simple observation can help rank-order risky alternatives that are represented in terms of their associated probability distributions. Consider, for purposes of illustration, four different stocks also being examined by Ms. Trueval. Their expected returns and standard deviations have been computed, using the procedure outlined earlier. Table 12•4 summarizes these statistics for the four stocks. Faced with a choice between stocks W and X, which would Ms. Trueval (a risk-averse investor) prefer? The answer is easy. Both W and X have the same expected return, but X has a lower risk. Hence X is clearly better than W, and X would be ranked higher than W.

KEY CONCEPT: In choosing between two alternatives with the same expected return, the alternative with the lower risk is preferred.

Now compare X and Y. Both have the same standard deviation, but Y has a higher expected return. Y therefore would rank higher than X because the alternative with the higher expected return for a given level of risk is preferred.

KEY CONCEPT: In choosing between two alternatives with the same level of risk, the alternative with the higher expected return is preferred.

As a last example, how would Ms. Trueval rank Y and Z? Y has both a lower risk and a lower expected return than Z, and it is difficult to decide immediately which one is better. To get around this problem, several authors incorrectly advocate the use of another risk measure called the **coefficient of variation (CV)**.

TABLE 12•4   Expected Returns and Risks
for Four Stocks

Stock	Expected Return (%)	Standard Deviation (%)
W	12	15
X	12	12
Y	15	12
Z	18	18

KEY CONCEPT: The **coefficient of variation (CV)** for a return distribution is the ratio of the standard deviation of returns to the expected return:

$$CV = \frac{\sigma}{E(\tilde{R})} \tag{12-6}$$

CV is a relative measure of risk. It is a pure number that is useful for comparing one investment with another. How does one use CV? From the definition of CV, observe that CV measures the risk associated with each unit of expected return. A risk-averse person will want to minimize the risk taken for each unit of expected return. Therefore, the distribution with the lower coefficient of variation is preferred.

KEY CONCEPT: The CV may be used to rank securities represented by probability distributions. The distribution with the smallest CV has the lowest risk per unit of return, and thus the highest rank.

Referring to Table 12•4, the CV for stock Y is given by $CV = 12/15 = 0.8$, while for stock Z, $CV = 18/18 = 1.0$. Similarly, the CVs for W and X are 1.25 and 1.0, respectively. Applying the preceding rule, the stock with the lower coefficient of variation would be chosen. Therefore, Y is preferred to Z. Thus Ms. Trueval's ranking of the four stocks by their CV would be:

Rank 1: Stock Y.

Rank 2: Stocks X and Z.

Rank 3: Stock W.

The CV is a relative measure that shows the amount of risk per unit of expected return. This procedure is useful for ranking probability distributions; however, the CV does not show which stock will be the most wealth maximizing. That is, if stock A is ranked higher than stock B using CV, there is still no guarantee that the investor's *wealth* will increase more with stock A than with stock B. This is because the measure of risk (σ) used in calculating the CV is *not* the risk relevant for making wealth-maximizing decisions. The *relevant risk*, that is, the risk that is relevant for determining the market value of the asset, is an extremely important concept and is introduced carefully in this and the next chapter.

KEY CONCEPT: Choices based on CV rankings may not be consistent with wealth maximization.

Learning Check for Section 12•3

Review Questions

12•6. Explain the logic of the *CV* rule in ranking two alternatives.

12•7. Explain why *CV* may not be useful in making wealth-maximizing decisions.

New Term

Coefficient of variation (*CV*)

SECTION 12•4 *Diversification and Portfolio Risk*

The discussion so far has pointed out that people are, for the most part, risk averse. So, how would investors like Ms. Trueval, who are considering investing in securities such as stocks, go about reducing their risk? Is there a strategy that can be followed that will help the investor reduce the risk (variance) of his or her investment returns? Indeed, such a strategy does exist: it consists of forming a diversified portfolio.

KEY CONCEPT: A **portfolio** is simply a collection of two or more assets.

Thus, if Ms. Trueval bought two stocks—IBM and Teledyne—she would have a two-stock portfolio. It is important to realize that the investments included in a portfolio need not be restricted to stocks; a portfolio can consist of stocks, bonds, gold, paintings, call options, or real estate. However, to keep the presentation at a fairly simple level, the discussion will focus on stock portfolios.

As alluded to earlier, the formation of certain portfolios can lower the investor's overall risk. This is because of **diversification.**

KEY CONCEPT: **Diversification** is the process of reducing risk by forming portfolios of securities with imperfectly correlated returns.

Thus, to reduce risk, it is not sufficient simply to form portfolios. Another condition must be met: the portfolio should consist of imperfectly correlated securities. Unfortunately, this explanation is not very satisfactory for two reasons. First, the term **imperfectly correlated returns** has not yet been explained; second, it is not clear why diversification should reduce risk. To remedy these shortcomings, an intuitive explanation of **correlation** and diversification is presented, with a minimum of mathematical detail.

AN INTUITIVE LOOK AT DIVERSIFICATION

Assume that Ms. Trueval is evaluating two stocks—Procyc, Inc., and Countersyc, Inc. Procyc's returns are high when the economy as a whole is doing well and suffer badly when the economy is in a recession. Countersyc, on the other hand, has the opposite characteristics; it performs well during bad economic times and does poorly when the economy is booming. If Ms. Trueval invests in Procyc alone, her returns will have a high variability between economic booms and busts. With high returns in good times and low returns in bad times, the range of outcomes (returns) is large. Since risk in finance is measured by variability, this would be a high-risk investment. Similarly, an investment in Countersyc alone would also expose Ms. Trueval to high risk.

Now assume that instead of investing in only one asset, Ms. Trueval forms a portfolio consisting of both Procyc and Countersyc in equal amounts. In good times, Procyc will result in high returns, but Countersyc will underperform, pulling down the total return on the portfolio. In bad times, Procyc will yield very low returns, but the total return on the portfolio will not be that low because Countersyc will pull the returns up. Thus, by forming this portfolio, high returns get pulled down and low returns get pulled up. In other words, the range of potential outcomes is lessened by this "dampening" effect. Figure 12•3 illustrates the dampening effect of diversification. Because variability in returns is lowered, the risk of the portfolio becomes lower.

The two-stock portfolio reduced risk because of the nature of the relationship between Procyc and Countersyc. Recognize that if they both reacted the same way to economic conditions, the dampening effect would disappear. Diversification helped to reduce risk in this example because the two stocks are *imperfectly correlated*, a term that will be defined more precisely subsequently.

MEASURING THE RELATIONSHIP BETWEEN ASSETS

Consider three securities, A, B, and C, and assume four states of the world, recession, slow growth, moderate growth, and boom. If the probabilities associ-

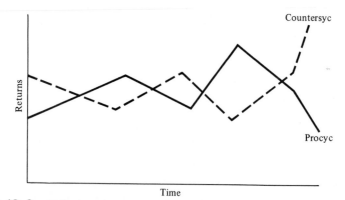

FIGURE 12•3   Behavior of Procyc, Inc., and Countersyc, Inc.

ated with each state and the returns on the three stocks were given, we could calculate the expected returns and variances for A, B, and C, using the procedures discussed earlier. While the expected returns and variances would summarize the individual returns and the risk for each of the stocks, they would not convey any information about the interrelationships between the stocks. To examine this relationship, the following concept is crucial:

KEY CONCEPT: The relationship between two assets is explained by the correlation between their returns and is measured by the **correlation coefficient.**

Unfortunately, it is difficult to provide a precise explanation of the **correlation coefficient** without getting into its statistical definition. Here we give only a casual explanation.

The correlation coefficient between two securities, A and B, is denoted as ρ_{AB} and measures the strength of the association between them. It measures the degree to which the returns on the two securities move together. The correlation coefficient can lie between -1.0 and $+1.0$ (both values inclusive).

If the correlation coefficient between two securities is $+1$, the securities are said to be *perfectly positively correlated.* This, in turn, implies that the returns on these two securities move in perfect lock step. That is, when the returns on one stock are high, so are the returns on the other. On the other hand, a correlation coefficient of -1.0 implies that the two assets are *perfectly negatively correlated.* In this case, the returns on the two securities move in exactly opposite directions.

The term *imperfectly correlated*, used earlier in the context of diversification, can now be more precisely explained as follows:

KEY CONCEPT: **Imperfectly correlated** refers to the absence of perfect positive correlation.

Thus, as alluded to earlier, it is not necessary for assets to be negatively correlated for diversification to work. All that is required is **imperfect correlation.** Figure 12•4 shows the returns on each stock for each state of the world.

Conclusions Drawn from Figure 12•4

Correlation of A and B   First, notice that whenever security A's return is high, B's is also high. When A's returns are low, so are B's. Thus A and B appear to behave alike, although not exactly alike. A and B are said to be *positively correlated. Positively* simply means that when A's returns change in a particular way (say, decreasing during a recession), B's returns also change in the same direction. The correlation coefficient between A and B, ρ_{AB}, in this case will be greater than 0 but less than $+1.00$.

Correlation of A, B, and C   Security C's returns behave in a manner opposite to that of A or B. When A or B has high returns, C has low returns, and vice

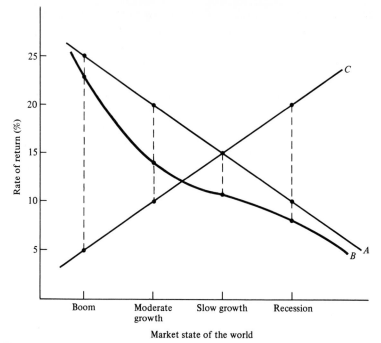

FIGURE 12•4 Returns on each stock for each state of the world.

versa. Thus *C*'s returns are *negatively correlated* with the returns of *A* and *B*. *Negatively* simply means that when *A*'s or *B*'s returns change in a particular way, *C*'s returns change in the opposite direction. However, as Figure 12•4 illustrates, the returns on *A* and *C* are perfectly negatively correlated, implying that the correlation coefficient $\rho_{AC} = -1.0$. The correlation coefficient between *B* and *C*, ρ_{BC}, although negative, is not -1.0. It will lie somewhere between 0 and -1.

Thus the sign of the correlation coefficient (positive/negative) permits a characterization of the nature of the interdependence between securities. The returns of positively correlated securities move in the same direction; the returns of negatively correlated securities move in the opposite direction. The extent of this association is provided by the magnitude of the correlation coefficient.

The correlation coefficient is an important determinant of the risk of a portfolio—an idea that will be explored in the next section.

CALCULATING THE EXPECTED RETURN AND RISK OF PORTFOLIOS

Armed with the notion of the correlation coefficient, it is now possible to gain a deeper appreciation of the diversification concept. That is, it is now possible to see how an investor's risk can be reduced by forming a portfolio of imperfectly correlated assets. The discussion that follows deals only with two-asset portfolios. This analysis can be extended to deal with any portfolio, irrespective of whether there are 2 or 20 assets.

The first step is to determine the expected return and risk of the portfolio. These items depend on the amount invested in each asset, the expected return and variance of each asset, and the nature of the relationship between the assets in the portfolio. We will examine each of these in turn.

The Amount Invested in Each Asset

Let the proportion of wealth invested in A be represented by X_A. Then the proportion invested in B must be the remainder, $1 - X_A$, since the sum of the proportions invested in each asset must be 1. For example, if 20% of an investment is made up of A, then $X_A = 0.2$ and therefore $X_B = (1 - 0.2) = 0.8$ represents the proportion invested in B.

The Expected Return of a Portfolio

The expected return of a two-asset portfolio, $E(\tilde{R}_P)$, is given as

$$E(\tilde{R}_P) = X_A E(\tilde{R}_A) + X_B E(\tilde{R}_B) \qquad (12\text{-}7)$$

where $E(\tilde{R}_A)$ and $E(\tilde{R}_B)$ represent the expected returns on assets A and B, respectively. X_A and X_B represent the proportion of the total investment devoted to assets A and B, respectively.

The expected return $E(\tilde{R}_P)$ for a portfolio containing stocks A and B can be calculated easily. Suppose that Ms. Trueval's portfolio consists of a 15% investment in stock A. Then $X_A = 0.15$ and $X_B = 0.85$ is the proportion of the portfolio investment in B. The actual dollar amount invested in each is irrelevant. Only the proportions matter. For example, Ms. Trueval might have invested a total of $100 ($15 in A and $85 in B) or a total of $5,000 ($750 in A and $4,250 in B). The expected returns will be the same for both alternatives.

Table 12•5a summarizes the returns on stocks A, B, and C, and Table 12•5b calculates the expected returns and the variance of these returns. Consider a portfolio of only two stocks, A and B. Since $E(\tilde{R}_A) = 17.5\%$ and $E(\tilde{R}_B) = 14\%$ using formula (12-7), the expected return on Ms. Trueval's portfolio is

$$E(\tilde{R}_P) = (0.15)(0.175) + (0.85)(0.14) = 14.53\%$$

The Variance of a Portfolio

The next step is to measure the risk of a two-asset portfolio. The variance of a two-asset portfolio is calculated as

TABLE 12·5 Information for Analyzing the Relationship Between Assets

a. Returns on Stocks

State of the World	Probability	A	B	C
			Security Returns (%)	
Boom	0.2	25	23	5
Moderate growth	0.3	20	14	10
Slow growth	0.3	15	12	15
Recession	0.2	10	8	20
	1.0			

b. Expected Returns (%) and Variances

	A	B	C
Expected return	17.5	14	12.5
Variance of returns	26.25	24.60	26.25

c. Correlation Coefficients

$\rho_{AB} = 0.94$
$\rho_{AC} = -1.00$
$\rho_{BC} = -0.94$

$$\sigma_P^2 = X_A^2\sigma_A^2 + X_B^2\sigma_B^2 + 2X_AX_B\rho_{AB}\sigma_A\sigma_B \qquad (12\text{-}8)$$

where σ_A^2, σ_B^2, and ρ_{AB} represent the variance of security A, the variance of security B, and the correlation coefficient between A and B, respectively.

Again, the portfolio variance for the two-asset portfolio (σ_P^2) can be readily determined, using equation (12-8). $\sigma_A^2 = 26.25$, $\sigma_B^2 = 24.60$ (Table 12·5b), $X_A = 0.15$, and $X_B = 0.85$. The correlations between the securities is summarized in Table 12·5c. Therefore:

$$\sigma_P^2 = (0.15)^2(26.25) + (0.85)^2(24.60) + 2(0.15)(0.85)(0.94)(\sqrt{26.25})(\sqrt{24.60})$$
$$= 24.46$$

It is worthwhile examining this result carefully because it illustrates an important point. If Ms. Trueval puts all her wealth in A, the variance of her returns would be 26.25 (σ_A^2). Similarly, by investing only in B, her investment would have a risk of 24.60 (σ_B^2). But by forming a portfolio consisting of both A and B, she can reduce the overall risk to 24.48 (σ_P^2). She is able to achieve this because A and B are imperfectly correlated securities (see Table 12·5c to check this).

However, this does not imply that Ms. Trueval should prefer this portfolio over an investment in security A or B. However, we need a better measure of risk, which will be developed in the next chapter.

The Relationships Between the Assets in the Portfolio

The variance of the portfolio σ_P^2 depends critically on the correlation coefficient. The portfolio variance reaches a minimum if $\rho_{AB} = -1$ (i.e., when A and B are perfectly negatively correlated) and reaches a maximum when $\rho_{AB} = +1$ (perfectly positively correlated securities).

Thus the lowest achievable portfolio variance occurs when $\rho_{AB} = -1$. However, it is not necessary to have $\rho_{AB} = -1$ for diversification. As long as the two securities are not perfectly positively correlated, diversification reduces the risk of the portfolio.

Example 12•2   How Changes in the Correlation Coefficient Affect Variance

Assume that a portfolio consists of two securities, A and B. Let the proportion of the portfolio invested in A be 60% (i.e., $X_A = 0.60$) and in B be 40% ($X_B = 1 - X_A = 0.40$). Table 12•6 summarizes the information about the securities and calculates the variance of the portfolio for different values of the correlation coefficient (ρ_{AB}) between A and B. As can be seen, the variance of the portfolio is sensitive to the magnitude and sign of the correlation coefficient. It is also clear from Table 12•6 that the greatest benefits from diversification are attained when the two securities are perfectly negatively correlated.

TABLE 12•6   How the Correlation Coefficient Affects Portfolio Risk[a]

ρ_{AB}	+1	0.6	0.3	0	−0.5	−1
Portfolio Variance σ_P^2	25.54	20.66	17.00	13.35	7.26	1.16

[a] The portfolio variances are calculated using equation (12-8); $\sigma_A = 5.12$; $\sigma_B = 4.96$; $X_A = 0.6$.

A CONCLUDING COMMENT

In this chapter we introduced several statistical measures, which were then used to show how diversification can reduce risk. The statistical measures presented thus far do not allow us to make wealth-maximizing decisions. However, they do provide a necessary foundation for the next chapter. We are now ready to extend the concept of diversification to develop a measure of relevant risk—the risk that affects opportunity costs and hence market values. By combining the statistical measures from this chapter with the concepts of economic value and the market valuation process from Chapter 3, we will have a powerful framework for financial decision making. The construction of this framework is the objective of the next chapter.

Learning Check for Section 12•4

Review Questions

12•6. What does *imperfect correlation* mean? Why is this concept important for diversification?

12•7. How are the expected return and variance of a portfolio determined? Can the *CV* rule be used to rank portfolios?

12•8. Explain how diversification reduces risk in two different ways: first by using intuitive arguments and then by using mathematical arguments.

New Terms

Correlation	Diversification	Portfolio
Correlation coefficient	Imperfect correlation	

SUMMARY

Basic Return and Risk Concepts

This chapter has dealt with the concepts of measuring benefits (in terms of returns) and the risk associated with these benefits. It is useful to define benefits in terms of one-period returns. Although one evaluates an investment in terms of an uncertain (ex ante) return, the actual return obtained, the ex post return, may be quite different. Formulas for calculating the ex ante return and the ex post return were developed.

Since decision making involves ex ante returns, it becomes necessary to quantify the uncertainty associated with these returns. In this regard, it is necessary to look at the entire probability distribution of returns. Although continuous probability distributions are perhaps more realistic, discrete distributions are typically used to make the analysis more tractable. The actual data available to an individual can provide only a discrete distribution.

Summarizing and Interpreting the Information from a Probability Distribution

The central tendency of the distribution is captured through the expected value of the distribution. The variability, or risk, of the distribution is summarized by its variance. An equivalent risk measure is the standard deviation of the distribution, which is the square root of the variance. For the special case of a normal distribution, the standard deviation takes on a special significance; it is possible to provide more precise statements about the potential future returns.

Comparing the Risk and Expected Return of Two Distributions

In making a choice between two distributions, risk-averse individuals should focus on both the expected return and the variance of the distribution. In choosing between two alternatives with the same expected return, the alternative with the lower risk is preferred. In choosing between two alternatives with the same level of risk, the alternative with the higher expected return is preferred. The coefficient of variation (*CV*) can be used to compare two or more distributions when neither risk nor expected return match. The alternative with the lowest *CV* is best. However, the *CV* cannot indicate which distribution is optimal for wealth maximization because it does not reflect the risk, which is relevant in determining the market value of the assets.

Diversification and Portfolio Risk

Risk can be reduced by forming portfolios of assets. The assets must be chosen so that their returns are not all perfectly correlated. The concepts of correlation are useful in measuring the extent and nature of the interrelationships between assets. Once the expected return and variance of a portfolio are computed, investors can choose between portfolios, using a method similar to the procedure used for choosing between two assets.

PROBLEMS

12•1.   An investment will have a return of 30% if economic conditions improve, 20% if they stay the same, and −5% if they get worse. The probability that conditions will improve is 20%, that they will stay the same is 40%, and that they will get worse is 40%. What is the expected return from this investment?

12•2.   TPI is considering marketing a new games cartridge for their popular TPI 3000 computer. Preliminary marketing reports suggest that the probability that the project will do very well is 30%, that it will do about average (for a new cartridge) is 30%, and that it will do poorly is 40%. You know that the project will have a 20% return if it does about average and a −10% return if it does poorly, but a coffee stain on your report makes illegible the project's return if it does well. However, you do know that the expected return on the project is 12.5%. What is the illegible figure?

12•3. The DJIA is a number that reflects the value of a portfolio of shares of the 30 DJIA stocks. Suppose that the stocks in this portfolio have the same return as the market, and that this return is expected to be 15%. The DJIA is currently 1,150, and you expect it to be 1,270 at the end of the year. What dividend yield (dividends paid/initial value of the portfolio) do you expect on this portfolio of 30 DJIA stocks?

12•4. The range is a simple measure of risk that consists of the best possible outcome minus the worst possible outcome. Suppose that you are considering the following two investment opportunities:

	Probability	Return (%)
Stock *A*		
Does well	0.10	30
Does average	0.80	15
Does poorly	0.10	0
Stock *B*		
Does well	0.30	25
Does average	0.40	15
Does poorly	0.30	5

(a) What is the range of stock *A*? Of stock *B*?
(b) What is the expected return on stock *A*? On stock *B*?
(c) What is the standard deviation of the return on stock *A*? Of stock *B*?
(d) If you had to select *A* or *B*, which would you select if you were using ranges as a measure of risk? If you were using standard deviation as a measure or risk?
(e) Why is the range a poor measure of risk?

12•5. Given the following investment opportunities, only one of which you can select, which ones (if any) can you exclude from consideration
(a) if you are risk averse?
(b) if you are risk averse and use the *CV* rule?

Opportunity	Expected Return (%)	Standard Deviation of Returns
Build new restaurant	30	20
Purchase existing restaurant	20	10
Build new convenience store	20	10
Purchase existing convenience store	15	10
Build new adhesive-tape store	5	10

12·6. Given the following information for two stocks, X and Y, calculate:
(a) The expected return of X and Y.
(b) The standard deviation of returns of X and Y.
(c) The standard deviation of a portfolio of half X and half Y, given that the correlation coefficient between the returns on X and Y is 0.7549.

State of the Market	Probability	Return on X (%)	Return on Y (%)
Large boom	0.10	15	35
Small boom	0.20	15	27
Little or no change	0.35	15	18
Small downturn	0.20	15	8
Large downturn	0.15	15	8

12·7. Two companies respond to the economy in the following manner:

Event	Probability	Return on Vulcan Tire Recapping Co. Shares (%)	Return on Goodwealth Tire Co. Shares (%)
Economic upturn	0.3	12	24
No change in the economy	0.4	18	18
Economic downturn	0.3	24	12

One of your friends argues that since both shares have the same expected return and the same risk (as measured by the standard deviation of returns), investors will be indifferent to buying shares of either company. Is this true?

12·8. Lorn Hanks is considering an investment in the hardware business. He has narrowed his decision down to the following two stocks:

Return on Handy Ed (%)	Return on Quick Bob (%)	Probability
10	10	0.3
12	11	0.3
14	15	0.3
17	17	0.1

(a) What is the expected return on the two securities?
(b) What is the variance of the rate of return on the two securities?
(c) Given these rates of return and variances, which stock should Lorn choose?

12·9. Given the following information on two stocks, A and B, answer the following questions:

Return on Stock A	Return on Stock B	Probability
10%	8%	0.3
11%	10%	0.4
12%	12%	0.3

(a) What is the expected return on stocks A and B?
(b) What are the variances of the rates of return on stocks A and B?
(c) What is the variance of the rates of return on a portfolio consisting of 20% invested in stock A and 80% invested in stock B, given that the two stocks are perfectly positively correlated?

12·10. Bob Jacobs, an avid golfer, is thinking of investing in the shares of two golf equipment manufacturers. He has obtained the following information. In addition, he has determined that the correlation coefficient between the securities is 0.6.

Return on Golf Clubbers (%)	Return on Longflite (%)	Probability
3	5	0.3
8	9	0.4
13	13	0.3

(a) What is the expected return and variance of returns of a portfolio composed of 50% in each stock?
(b) What is the expected return and variance of returns of a portfolio composed of 30% in Golf Clubbers and 70% in Longflite?
(c) Using the CV, which portfolio would you prefer?

APPENDIX 12·A *Correlation and Covariance*

Although Chapter 12 explained the concept of correlation in simple, intuitive terms, it did not provide a precise definition of the correlation coefficient. As a result, the chapter provided no explanation of how the correlation coefficient figures in Table 12·6 were derived. This appendix will remedy this shortcoming, first by providing a mathematical definition of the correlation coefficient and then by providing a sample calculation of the correlation coefficient calculations used in Table 12·6.

Unfortunately, even at this stage, it is difficult to provide a direct explanation of the correlation coefficient. It is easier first to study the measure of relationship between two securities called **covariance**. Knowing the covariance between two securities, it is easy to find the correlation coefficient.

COVARIANCE

KEY CONCEPT: The **covariance** between the returns of two securities, A and B, Cov_{AB}, is given by

$$Cov_{AB} = \sum P_i \times [R_{Ai} - E(\tilde{R}_A)][R_{Bi} - E(\tilde{R}_B)] \qquad \text{(12A-1)}$$

where, as before, Σ represents the fact that all possible values should be added together. P_i is the probability of the ith outcome. Cov_{AB} is often represented as σ_{AB}.

Covariance is very similar to variance. The variance of returns for a particular asset is computed by subtracting the expected value of the return from each of the possible outcomes and then squaring that difference. The covariance between two assets is computed in a very similar way, except that the deviations of the possible outcomes from their expected values for two probability distributions are multiplied together. Table 12A·1 provides a sample calculation of covariance. The covariance between stocks A and B seen in Table 12·5a is calculated to be 24.

TABLE 12A·1   Calculating Covariance Between A and B[a]

P_i	$R_A(\%)$	$R_A(\%) - E(R_A)$	$R_B(\%)$	$R_B - E(R_B)$	$P_i(R_A - ER_A)(R_B - ER_B)$
0.2	25	7.5	23	9	13.5
0.3	20	2.5	14	0	0.0
0.3	15	−2.5	12	−2	1.5
0.2	10	−7.5	8	−6	9.0
					$Cov_{AB} = 24$

[a]The expected returns on A and B have been calculated in Table 12·5b. $E(R_A) = 17.5\%$; $E(R_B) = 14\%$.

CORRELATION COEFFICIENT

Even though covariances can be computed, as shown in Table 12A•1, the magnitude of the covariance is not very meaningful in assessing the strength of the relationship between two securities. Instead, a standardized measure called the *correlation coefficient* is used to assess this relationship. The correlation coefficient between A and B is often denoted by ρ_{AB} and can be calculated from the covariance, as the next definition shows.

KEY CONCEPT: The **correlation coefficient** between the returns of A and B measures the magnitude of the relationship between A and B and is calculated as[12]

$$\rho_{AB} = \frac{Cov_{AB}}{\sigma_A \times \sigma_B} \tag{12A-2}$$

where σ_A and σ_B, as before, represent the standard deviation of returns for securities A *and* B, respectively. ρ_{AB} will always lie between -1.0 and $+1.0$ (both values inclusive).

Since the covariance between A and B was shown in Table 12A•1 to be 24, and since the variances of the returns of A and B are 0.2625 and 0.246, respectively (see Table 12•5b), we can use equation (12A-2) to calculate ρ_{AB}:

$$\rho_{AB} = \frac{Cov_{AB}}{\sigma_A \times \sigma_B} = \frac{24}{(\sqrt{26.25})(\sqrt{24.60})} = 0.94$$

Using the same approach, the correlation coefficients ρ_{AC} and ρ_{BC} can be calculated to be -1.00 and -0.94, respectively. These calculations are left to the interested reader as an exercise.

Learning Check for Appendix 12•A

Review Question

12A•1. If the correlation coefficient is positive, does it necessarily imply that the covariance is positive? Why?

New Term

Covariance

---

[12] Notice that this definition suggests another way to calculate the covariance: $Cov_{AB} = \rho_{AB} \times \sigma_A \times \sigma_B$.

PROBLEMS

12A·1. Being a sharp analyst, you have narrowed the possible outcomes for two potential investments as follows (also included is your estimate of the returns on the market):

State of the Economy	Probability	Return (%)		
		Stock A	Stock B	Market
1 (great)	0.30	25	20	18
2 (good)	0.50	16	14	16
3 (mediocre)	0.20	8	12	14

(a) Calculate the expected returns for stocks A and B and the market.

(b) Calculate the standard deviation of returns for stocks A and B and the market.

(c) Find the covariance between stock A and the market, and between stock B and the market.

(d) Find the correlation coefficients between stock A and the market and between stock B and the market.

12A·2. Estimates of standard deviations and correlation coefficients for three stocks are as follows:

Stock	Standard Deviation (%)	Correlation With:		
		A	B	C
A	10	1.0		
B	12	0.5	1.0	
C	14	0.7	0	1.0

(a) If equal investments are made in stocks A and C, what is the standard deviation of the portfolio?

(b) If 50% of the investment is distributed equally between stocks A and B and the remaining 50% in stock C, what is the standard deviation of the portfolio?

READINGS

BOYLE, GLENN W., AND RAMESH K. S. RAO, "The Mean-Generalized Coefficient of Variation Selection Rule and Expected Utility Maximization," *Southern Economic Journal* July 1988.

BREALEY, R. A., *An Introduction to Risk and Return from Common Stocks*, 2nd ed. (Cambridge, Mass.: MIT Press, 1983).

BROWN, S. J., AND MARK P. KRITZMAN, ed., *Quantitative Methods for Financial Analysis* (Homewood, Ill.: Dow Jones-Irwin, 1987).

ELTON, E. J., AND M. J. GRUBER, *Modern Portfolio Theory and Investment Analysis* (New York: John Wiley & Sons, Inc., 1981).

HAUGEN, R. A., *Modern Investment Theory*, (Englewood Cliffs, N.J.: Prentice-Hall, Inc., 1986).

HAYS, WILLIAM L., AND ROBERT L. WINKLER, *Statistics: Probability, Inference and Decisions*, (New York: Holt, Rinehart and Winston, 1971).

13

Relevant Risk, Opportunity Cost, and Market Value

In Chapter 12 the discussion revolved around the definitions of returns and risk. It should be clear by now that even though individuals are risk averse, they should not ignore high-risk assets as long as the expected returns are handsome enough to compensate them for the risk they bear. Thus the attractiveness of any risky asset depends on both the expected return on the asset and its risk. Understanding the nature of the relationship between expected returns and risk in equilibrium is a major objective of this chapter.

It is important to understand this relationship between risk and return because it forms the basis for determining opportunity costs (RRR). Recall that all discounting and market valuation considerations require an explicit assessment of the RRR. It is therefore not an exaggeration to say that the subject of this chapter forms the basis of modern market-value finance.

Although the material in this chapter may appear abstract at times, ironically, many of the applications discussed so far have little practical significance without the theoretical basis that is presented here. The theoretical developments addressed in this chapter form the basis for a financial manager's practical decisions that pertain to market-value maximization. Without this logical framework for determining opportunity costs, managers have no way of knowing how to maximize the wealth of the shareholders.

This chapter is divided into five sections:

SECTION 13·1: *The Limits of Diversification.* This section extends the diversification idea introduced in Chapter 12 to demonstrate that diversification cannot eliminate all risks. The total risk (variance) of an asset is broken into two components. The *relevant* risk for an asset, the risk relevant for the determination of opportunity costs, and consequently its market value, is not the variance; rather it is related to the risk that cannot be eliminated by diversification.

SECTION 13·2: *The Beta of an Asset.* The relevant risk measure of an asset, called its *beta*, is a measure of the variability of the asset relative to the variability of the market as a whole. Betas can be determined for a single asset or for a portfolio of assets. They may be calculated directly or may be obtained from published sources.

SECTION 13·3: *The Relationship Between Relevant Risk and Opportunity Costs.* In Chapter 3 the concept of a market valuation model was introduced. In this section, we introduce a popular market valuation model called the *capital asset pricing model (CAPM)*. The CAPM is a simple equation that, given the beta (risk) of an asset, provides the appropriate opportunity cost for investing in that asset. Through examples, we show how to use the CAPM to price an asset. We also introduce a graphic representation of the CAPM, called the *security market line,* which makes it easy to see if an asset is overvalued, undervalued, or fairly priced.

SECTION 13·4: *Implications for Corporate Financial Management.* The CAPM has several implications for financial management. If the CAPM is a valid theory, it will affect the determination of discount rates and market values, the separation of relevant and irrelevant risks, the making of wealth-increasing decisions, and the management of regulated companies.

SECTION 13·5: *Criticism of the CAPM.* The final section focuses on criticisms of the CAPM. These criticisms revolve around the several restrictive assumptions made to derive the CAPM. We conclude the section with a discussion of the empirical tests of the CAPM. While not absolutely precise, several major elements of the CAPM have been supported by empirical tests.

SECTION 13·1 *The Limits of Diversification*

When a portfolio of two imperfectly correlated securities is formed, the overall risk of the portfolio will usually go down because of diversification. As the number of securities in the portfolio increases, the reduction in risk increases. Although the benefits of diversification increase as more and more securities are added to a portfolio, there is a limit to the amount of risk reduction that is attainable.

Figure 13·1 illustrates the results of several studies. The total risk of a portfolio is plotted on the vertical axis and the number of securities in the portfolio on the horizontal axis. As can be seen, the total risk decreases at a

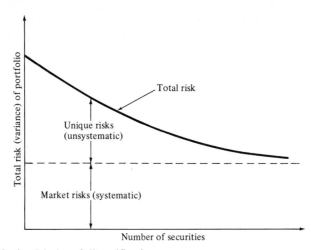

FIGURE 13•1   Limits of diversification.

decreasing rate as the number of securities in the portfolio increases. A substantial amount of risk can be diversified away by even as few as 25 or 30 securities. At this level of diversification, nearly all of the risk of the asset is the market risk (risk that cannot be eliminated). Notice that the total risk line approaches the horizontal line representing the minimum-risk line slowly. From the figure, one can infer that the total risk line will, in fact, touch the minimum-risk line if all stocks in the economy are included in the portfolio. Indeed, such a portfolio will be fully diversified. That is, a completely diversified portfolio will possess the minimum level of risk attainable; no more reduction in risk can be achieved through diversification.

A completely diversified portfolio, as noted, contains virtually every asset in the economy. This would make the behavior of the portfolio more and more similar to the behavior of the economy as a whole. Since the stock market is very often used to assess the behavior of the economy, this portfolio should behave very much like the market as a whole.[1]

THE COMPONENTS OF TOTAL RISK

Figure 13•1 suggests that the **total risk** of an asset (or a portfolio) can readily be divided into two components: the portion of the asset's risk that cannot be eliminated by diversification and the portion that disappears with diversification. That is,

Total risk = **undiversifiable risk** + **diversifiable risk**
(variance of returns)

---

[1] The terms *market* and *economy* will be used interchangeably in this context.

Although the figure demonstrates the limits of diversification benefits, it communicates nothing about the nature or the magnitudes of **diversifiable** and **undiversifiable risks.** That is, what are diversifiable and undiversifiable risks? How can they be measured for an individual security?

THE NATURE OF THE RISK COMPONENTS

Undiversifiable risks are market risks, while diversifiable risks are **unique risks.** Market risks represent the component of total risk that is systematically dependent on the vagaries of the U.S. economy. All American firms are affected, to varying degrees, by economic conditions in the United States. If the U.S. economy thrives, most companies do well, whereas if the United States is going through a recession, even the best-managed company with the best products or services will not be able to reach its peak performance level. In addition to the overall performance of the economy, there are several other factors that affect nearly all companies: tax changes instituted by Congress, the uncertainty associated with OPEC oil prices, the threat of war, and so on. These are factors outside the control of a corporation's management, and all corporations are subject to these uncertainties. Of course, different companies (stocks) display different sensitivities to market conditions. Companies that are very sensitive to changes in the economy have high market risks, while those that are less sensitive have low market risks.

Because all companies are affected systematically by market risks, this component of risk is also known as **systematic risk.** To summarize:

KEY CONCEPT: **Market risk** is risk that cannot be eliminated by diversification. Market risk is systematically related to the risk of the economy as a whole and is therefore also known as **systematic risk.**

Unique risks, unlike market risks, are risks specific to the company in question. The risk of technological obsolescence, the risk of reduced revenues due to increasing competition, and the risks associated with patent approval, antitrust legislation, labor contracts, management styles, and geographic location are all examples of unique risks. These are risks that can be diversified away by forming a large portfolio. The contributions of each of these risks for each company included in the portfolio effectively "wash out" and are thus eliminated.

Because these risks are firm-specific risks, this component of risk is also known as **unsystematic risk.** To summarize:

KEY CONCEPT: **Unique risk** is the diversifiable component of total risk that exists because of company-specific factors. Since this risk can be eliminated, it is also known as **unsystematic risk.**

IMPLICATIONS FOR THE DETERMINATION OF OPPORTUNITY COSTS

In Chapter 3 it was stated that the opportunity cost for an investment (i.e., its *RRR*) depends on, among other things, the risk of the investment. The main objective of this section is to show that while the variance of an asset measures the total risk of an asset, the *relevant* risk, the risk that affects opportunity costs, is the asset's beta.

KEY CONCEPT: The **relevant risk** of an asset is that portion of the asset's total risk that is relevant for the determination of opportunity costs (*RRRs*). In other words, it is the risk that affects the market price of an asset.

As seen already, investors can reduce their overall risk through diversification by forming portfolios of assets with imperfectly correlated returns. Because of the reduction of unique risk, the risk of a collection of assets becomes less than the sum of each asset's risk. Although this statement comes as no surprise, consider this result from another perspective: when held in a portfolio, each asset contributes to the risk of the portfolio an amount less than its own risk. This observation has profound implications for financial management, as it sets the stage for determining the relevant risk of an asset. The following simple example will illustrate the point.

Example 13•1 Total Risk and Relevant Risk

Assume that an investor plans to purchase a stock with a risk of 5 units. For the purpose of this example, it is not important what the "unit" of risk really is. Assume also that if this stock is added to his current portfolio, which has a risk of 10 units, the resulting risk of the portfolio is 13 units. Notice that in this case, because of diversification, the risk of the portfolio is *not* $10 + 5 = 15$ units. In this situation, it is as if the investor is really buying a stock with a risk of 3 units. Two units of the stock's risk can be diversified away by including it in a portfolio. Since investors are rewarded only for the risks that they bear, this investor can expect to be compensated only for the 3 units of risk.

KEY CONCEPT: Investors can expect to be rewarded only for the risks that cannot be diversified away (market risks).

Using this concept, financial models develop a relationship between the relevant risk of an asset and the opportunity cost of investing in that asset. One of these financial models is examined in Section 13•3. However, before introducing this financial model, we must develop a measure of the relevant risk of an asset, which, as we will see in the next section, is measured by a term called *beta*. Beta is a better measure of the risk of the asset than the variance.

Learning Check for Section 13•1

Review Questions

13•1. What are the components of an asset's risk? What are market risk, systematic risk, unsystematic risk, diversifiable risk, and undiversifiable risk?

13•2. What does *relevant risk* mean? What is the practical significance of this concept?

New Terms

Diversifiable risk   Total risk   Unique risk
Systematic risk   Undiversifiable risk   Unsystematic risk

SECTION 13•2   *The Beta of an Asset*

The **beta** of an asset, β_i, is a market-sensitivity measure.

KEY CONCEPT: The **beta** of an asset, β, is a measure of the variability of that asset relative to the variability of the market as a whole. Beta is an index of the systematic risk of an asset.

In this section, we explain the practical significance of betas and the calculation of individual asset and portfolio betas.

WHAT DOES BETA MEASURE?

Beta is a statistical concept that measures the sensitivity of a security's returns to changes in the returns on the market. In this sense, it is like the leverage factor seen in earlier chapters, except that in this case, it provides the relationship between the changes in an asset's returns in response to expected changes in the market's returns. This idea is presented pictorially as follows:

416

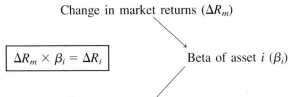

Change in market returns (ΔR_m)

$$\boxed{\Delta R_m \times \beta_i = \Delta R_i}$$

Beta of asset i (β_i)

Average change in asset i's returns (ΔR_i)

Thus beta measures the volatility of an asset's returns relative to the market. The larger the beta, the more volatile the asset is. A beta of 1.0 indicates an asset of average risk. A stock with a beta greater than 1.0 has an above-average risk; its returns are more volatile than those of the market. Similarly, a stock with a beta of less than 1.0 has a below-average risk. Beta can also be negative, implying that the stock moves in the opposite direction from the market.

Example 13•2   The Leverage Effect of Beta

Consider the Addison Company's stock, with a beta of 1.5. This beta value suggests that if the market returns increase by 2%, Addison's return would, on average, increase by 2% × 1.5 = 3%. On the other hand, consider Wormley, Inc.'s, stock, with a beta of 2.0. What happens if the market returns are expected to go down by 10%? Using the same line of reasoning, Wormley's stock would go down, on average, by 10% × 2.0 = 20%. Since beta is a form of leverage, it retains the familiar property of leverage: leverage magnifies the good and the bad.

How much riskier than Addison is Wormley? By comparing the magnitudes of their betas (2.00/1.5 = 1.33), we see that Wormley is 33% more volatile than Addison.

Suppose that Addison had a beta of −1.5. What would this imply? In this case, Addison's returns would, on average, go down by 3% if the market returns are expected to go up by 2%.[2]

PORTFOLIO BETAS

Just as a single asset has a beta coefficient, so does a portfolio of several assets. The beta coefficient for a portfolio depends not only on the betas of the assets held in the portfolio but also on the proportion of each asset in the portfolio. The formula for computing the beta for a portfolio is

---

[2] An Addison beta of −1.5 is an example of what is commonly called a *negative-beta asset*. Most assets are positively related to market returns: if market returns rise, so do those of the asset. However, there are some assets, such as gold, which generally move opposite to the market. From the discussion of diversification and correlation in Chapter 12, we can see that these negative-beta assets are highly prized for their diversification effect.

$$\beta_P = \sum X_i \beta_i \qquad (13\text{-}1)$$

where β_i is the beta of the ith asset and x_i is the proportion of the ith asset in the portfolio. Equation (13-1) says, in effect:

KEY CONCEPT: The beta for a portfolio is a **value-weighted average** of the betas of the assets included in the portfolio.

Example 13•3   Calculating the Beta for a Portfolio

A portfolio, P, consists of equal-dollar investments in three assets: asset 1, asset 2, and asset 3, with beta coefficients of -0.4, 1.2, and 1.8, respectively. Since there are equal amounts of each asset in the portfolio, $X_i = 1/3$ ($i = 1, 2, 3$), and using equation (13-1), the portfolio beta is given by

$$\beta_P = \sum X_i \beta_i = \frac{1}{3}(-0.4) + \frac{1}{3}(1.2) + \frac{1}{3}(1.8) = 0.87$$

This portfolio is therefore 87% sensitive to the market. That is, for every percentage change in the market's expected return, this portfolio is expected to change by only 0.87% in the same direction.

HOW ARE BETAS CALCULATED?

There are two different ways that betas can be calculated:

1. Using the characteristic line for the stock.
2. Using the statistical formula for beta.

The Characteristic Line Approach

The **characteristic line** is simply a regression line showing the average relationship between the returns on a stock and the returns on the market. Suppose it is felt that returns over the past 60 months are a good proxy for the future. Then the historical returns for each of the last 60 months would be computed for both the individual stock and the market portfolio, as represented by the S&P 500 index.[3] These historical returns are plotted on a graph to obtain a

---

[3] Recognize that these returns would be ex post returns and would be calculated using equation (12-2). The market index can be treated as if it were another stock. The availability of extensive data tapes with information on stock prices, dividends, and so on make this task easier.

scattergram, and a best-fit line showing the average straight-line relationship between the security and the market is drawn, using regression methods.[4] Figure 13•2 shows the characteristic lines for two hypothetical stocks, Poloflex and Soloroid. The slopes of the characteristic lines in the figure are the betas for the respective stocks. Notice that Poloflex has a greater slope than Soloroid. The greater the slope of the characteristic line, the greater the beta and, consequently, the greater the volatility of the stock. As can be seen from Figure 13•2, Poloflex is much more volatile than Soloroid.

Using the Statistical Formula for Beta

Betas can also be calculated analytically by using the statistical formula. That is, it is not always necessary to run a regression in order to find an asset's beta, as in the characteristic line approach. Using the formula for the slope of the characteristic line, the beta of an asset can be computed directly using historical data.[5]

PUBLISHED SOURCES OF BETAS

Betas are also available from many published sources. There are several investment houses that compute betas for various stocks periodically. Table 13•1 provides some estimates of stock betas from a published source. If these betas are used, it becomes unnecessary to compute them. Yet it is important to know the procedure for beta computations. The published beta sources are typically for stock (equity) betas. However, any asset can have a beta— machines, bonds, real estate, and so on. Since published sources for the betas of many assets may not be available, the procedures outlined earlier can sometimes become necessary.

---

[4] Standard regression packages for use on computers make this task fairly straightforward.
[5] The beta for asset i is given by:

$$\beta_i = \frac{\rho_{im}\sigma_i\sigma_m}{\sigma_m^2}$$

where ρ_{im} represents the correlation coefficient between the returns on stock i and the returns on the market portfolio, σ_i and σ_m are the standard deviation of returns on asset i and the market portfolio, respectively, and σ_m^2 is the variance of market returns.

The statistical definition of beta is extremely useful because it sheds additional light on the determinants of beta. First, an asset can have betas that are positive or negative or zero because betas depend on the correlation coefficient. In Chapter 12 it was seen that the correlation coefficient can vary between -1.0 and $+1.0$. If the correlation coefficient is zero, the asset is independent of market influences and its market risk is zero. A positive correlation coefficient implies a positive beta and consequently a positive market risk. A negative correlation coefficient suggests that the asset has a negative beta.

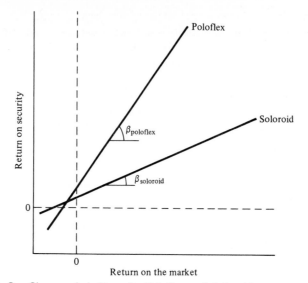

FIGURE 13·2   Characteristic lines for Poloflex and Soloroid.

With an estimate of an asset's beta, we can compute an investor's *RRR* on the stock if the relationship between betas and opportunity costs can be established. This is the subject of the next section.

In the next section, we will see how an asset's beta is used in a popular financial valuation model. Before moving on, however, a word of caution concerning betas is in order. Beta, as seen from the manner in which it is calculated,

TABLE 13·1   Selected Stock Betas

Amoco Corporation	0.85
Exxon Corporation	0.75
Pan American Airlines	1.15
Canadian Pacific	1.10
McDonalds	1.00
American Brands	1.05
Phillip Morris	1.05
CBS Inc.	1.10
Boeing Corporation	0.95
Lockheed	1.25
Rockwell International	1.10
Dow Jones & Co.	1.20
Federal Express	1.15
Xerox Corporation	1.20
Wal-Mart Stores	1.30

Source: Various issues of the *Value Line Investment Survey*, 1988.

420

is a *historical* measure of asset risk. In using beta, we implicitly assume that the relationship between asset variability and market variability will remain similar in the future to what it was in the past.

Learning Check for Section 13•2

Review Questions

13•3. Beta is a leverage measure for market returns. Why? How is beta calculated?

13•4. What are portfolio betas? How are they calculated?

New Terms

Beta   Characteristic line   Scattergram   Value-weighted average

SECTION 13•3 *The Relationship Between Relevant Risk and Opportunity Costs*

One of the most widely known market valuation models is the **capital asset pricing model (CAPM)**. Until recently, the CAPM has been the predominant theory of risk and return in **equilibrium** and has been the subject of hundreds of empirical tests. The CAPM has been extremely popular because of its intuitive appeal. The essential principle underlying the CAPM is this: risk-averse investors will not hold risky assets unless they are adequately compensated for the risks that they bear. In other words, the greater the risk of an asset, the greater should be its expected return. This would then provide investors with an incentive to invest in high-risk securities. Without additional rewards for bearing risk, investors would prefer to invest in riskless securities such as U.S. T bills.

Examine Figure 13•3, which is essentially a reproduction of Figure 13•1. An investor requires a *market discount rate* to find the market value of an asset. Once this market discount rate is estimated, market valuation consists of the mechanical process of *capitalizing* the estimated cash flows provided by the asset. However, as the figure indicates, a theory linking the risk-free interest rate, the asset's risk, and the market discount rate is required. The CAPM is such a market valuation theory.

The CAPM is a theory that makes several assumptions that have the net effect of forcing all investors to hold the same fully diversified portfolio. In this framework this fully diversified portfolio, common to all investors, is called the **market portfolio.** The market portfolio in the CAPM world contains all assets in

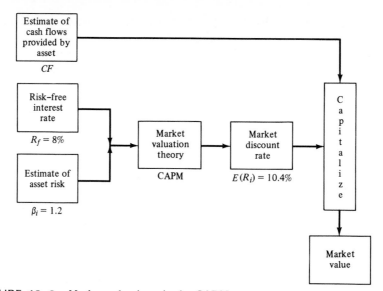

FIGURE 13·3   Market valuation via the CAPM.

the economy properly weighted to represent their proportionate market values. However, for most practical purposes, this portfolio is approximated by another portfolio, such as Standard and Poor's 500 index, which is a widely used index of 500 stocks. The performance of this index is considered to be indicative of the performance of the U.S. economy. Thus the return on the S&P 500 index represents the variance of the market's returns, σ_m^2.

The earlier discussion identified the relevant risk for an asset as the asset's beta. Once an asset's beta has been estimated, the CAPM provides a simple equation that links the beta of the asset to the appropriate opportunity cost for investing in that asset. In other words, given the risk of an asset, the CAPM provides the "premium" that investors can expect in terms of rate of return, which will induce them to purchase the asset.

CAPM

According to the CAPM, the expected return on an asset, i, is related to the risk of the asset as follows:

$$E(\tilde{R}_i) = R_f + \beta_i[E(\tilde{R}_m) - R_f] \qquad (13\text{-}2)$$

where $E(\tilde{R}_i)$ = expected rate of return on asset i, or the asset's *RRR*

$\quad R_f$ = risk-free rate of return

$\quad \beta_i$ = beta coefficient of stock i

$E(\tilde{R}_m)$ = expected return on the market portfolio (S&P 500)

The term $[E(\tilde{R}_m) - R_f]$ is the risk premium for bearing 1 unit of market risk. The expected return will equal the *RRR* in equilibrium. The terms *expected return* and *required rate of return* are sometimes not clear to readers. The highlight "Some Common Sources of Confusion: Expected Return and Required Rate of Return" clarifies the use of these terms.

■ *HIGHLIGHT*

SOME COMMON SOURCES OF CONFUSION: EXPECTED RETURN AND REQUIRED RATE OF RETURN:

The terms *expected rate of return* and *required rate of return* are often confusing to students. Their intuitive meaning is often obscured, and the usage of *expected return* in two different contexts in finance only increases the potential for confusion.

Section 12•2 first introduced the idea of an expected return. This expected return is a mathematical result that involves very little economic reasoning. The expected return as used in equation (12-3) is the result of multiplying each potential return by its associated probability and then adding these numbers together. Here the expected return on an asset simply represents the mean of the probability distribution of the returns and is, as explained in the text, a "probabilistic average."

The expected return on a security provided by the CAPM (equation 13-2) is an altogether different idea. It is the rate of return one could expect in an efficient market, given the risk of the security. In other words, equation (13-2) tells us that if a security is correctly priced in the market, an investor purchasing that security can expect to get the "expected (rate of) return." There are no guarantees, however. Notice that, unlike the expected return provided by equation (12-3), the expected return in equation (13-2) is the result of a theory of equilibrium pricing of assets.

Having understood the distinction between the two different notions of an expected return, it is now easy to see how the required rate of return (*RRR*) is related to the expected return given by the CAPM. The *RRR* is the opportunity cost of investing in an asset and is used as a discount rate in calculating the maximum price that one should pay for an asset. Yet, it has been suggested in the text that the expected returns from the CAPM should be used as a discount rate. This leads to the inference that the expected return provided by the CAPM and the *RRR* must be the same. Indeed, this conclusion is entirely correct. The $E(\tilde{R}_i)$ in equation (13-2) is the *RRR* for that investment.

A little reflection will convince you why this makes sense. The CAPM suggests that in equilibrium you can expect to earn $E(\tilde{R}_i)$ on an asset with a risk of β_i. Then what is the *RRR* (or the discount rate) for evaluating any other asset with a similar amount of risk? If the *RRR* is to represent an opportunity cost, it *has* to be the same as the equilibrium rate provided by the CAPM.

Because the CAPM is a model that provides an estimate of the appropriate *RRR* for calculating the fair price of an asset, the required returns and expected returns must be the same and all assets plot on the security market line (*SML*). When the expected return on an asset is greater than the *RRR*, the asset will plot above the SML and investing in this asset will generate positive excessive returns. Similarly, when the expected return is smaller than the *RRR*, the asset will plot below the SML and investing in this asset will produce negative excess returns.

Note that $RRR = E(\tilde{R}_i)$ only in an equilibrium situation.* If they are not the same, excess returns (negative or positive) are possible and one can lose or make money in the market. Again, in the long run, all assets will plot on the SML if markets are efficient, hence the justification for using $E(\tilde{R}_i)$ from the CAPM as an *RRR*. A numerical example later in this chapter illustrates why all assets must plot on the SML.

*This line of reasoning is explored again in the context of Figure 13·4.

Example 13·4 Calculating the Expected Return of a Stock

Suppose that the risk-free interest rate (yield on U.S. T bills) is 8%. If the market return is expected to be 10%, the expected return on stock j with a beta of 1.2 is

$$E(\tilde{R}_j) = 0.08 + 1.2(0.10 - 0.08) = 0.104 \text{ or } 10.4\%$$

Recognize in the example that the risk premium for bearing 1 unit of market risk (the market risk premium) is 2%. The investor who buys this asset is taking on 1.2 units of market risk and should therefore expect a risk premium of $1.2 \times 2\% = 2.4\%$. If the risk-free interest rate is 8% and the risk premium is 2.4%, the total return this investor should expect is 10.4%.

This example illustrates the basic principle that opportunity costs increase when the returns on other alternatives (here, the returns on the market) improve.[6] Because the premium per unit of market risk increases, the total risk premium for investing in any asset will therefore increase in proportion to its market risk (beta).

It is perhaps instructive to restate the CAPM as follows:

Expected return = risk-free rate + risk premium

= risk-free rate + (number of units risk borne ×
premium for bearing 1 unit of risk)

[6]This observation actually follows from the definition of opportunity costs.

Several interesting issues pertaining to the CAPM are addressed in a question-and-answer format:

Is the premium per unit of risk always positive? The risk premium per unit of risk, $E(\tilde{R}_m) - R_f$, can be negative only if the expected return on the market is less than the risk-free interest rate. However, this cannot happen. If the returns from a risk-free investment are greater than the expected returns from a risky investment, rational investors would cease to invest in the market and the market would collapse. Hence $E(\tilde{R}_m)$ must be greater than the risk-free rate.

But during economic downswings, isn't the return on the market less than the risk-free rate? There have been instances in recent years when the market returns were negative at a time when the risk-free rate was positive. Although this appears to contradict the point made earlier, this conclusion would be incorrect. The CAPM deals with *expected* returns, which are, by definition, ex ante returns. Of course, after an investment has been made (i.e., ex post), it might turn out to have yielded negative returns. The risk premium per unit of risk (an ex ante concept) is still positive.

What is the RRR on a negative-beta asset? Since the market premium per unit of risk is positive, a negative-beta stock, in effect, adds a negative risk premium. This can lower the *RRR* to below the risk-free interest rate. For example, assume that the risk premium $E(\tilde{R}_m) - R_f$ is 10% and a stock has a beta of -0.5. If the risk-free interest rate is 6%, an investor's *RRR* on this investment would be $6\% - 0.5(10\%) = 1\%$. Investors require a smaller *RRR* from negative-beta stocks because they provide "insurance": they can pay off handsomely when all other investments are doing poorly.

Why is the CAPM called a pricing model *when it only yields the expected return on an asset?* As seen as early as Chapter 3, it is impossible to find the value of an asset (i.e., the market price) without an appropriate discount rate. By providing a framework for identifying the proper discount rate (*RRR*), the CAPM can readily be used to price an asset.

The procedure for finding the market value of an asset via the CAPM is explained next.

Asset Pricing via the CAPM

The CAPM equation that provides the relationship between expected return and risk can be used to value assets that have a single risky cash flow at the end of the period. One approach, called the *required rate-of-return (RRR) method,* is now described.

Consider the pricing of an asset (say, a stock) in a one-period world. That is, we are interested in finding the value of the stock today (P_0), assuming that it will be sold at the end of the period. Denote the stock's expected selling price at the end of the period as $E(\tilde{P}_1)$. Then the total cash flow expected next period is $E(\tilde{P}_1)$, assuming no dividends. The current price of this cash flow should therefore be

$$P_0 = \frac{\text{expected cash flow}}{1 + RRR}$$

$$= \frac{\text{expected cash flow}}{1 + E(\tilde{R}_i)} \tag{13-3}$$

$$= \frac{E(\tilde{P}_1)}{1 + [R_f + \beta_i(E(\tilde{R}_m) - R_f)]}$$

where β_i, $E(\tilde{R}_m)$, and R_f, as before, represent the beta coefficient of the stock, the expected return on the market portfolio, and the risk-free interest rate, respectively. Recognize that the cash flows that are risky are not adjusted for risk. The risk adjustment is implicit in the *RRR* being used.

Example 13·5 Using the CAPM to Determine the Price of B&G Stock

If the current one-period U.S. T-bill rate is 8%, the expected return on the market is 12%, the beta for B&G stock is 1.5, and the expected price of B&G at the end of the period is $68, find its current price, using the *RRR* approach. B&G does not pay any dividends.[7]
Using equation (13-3) yields

$$P_0 = \frac{\$68}{1 + [0.08 + 1.5(0.12 - 0.08)]}$$
$$= \$59.65$$

When the market price of the stock is exactly $59.65, this stock will be considered to be **fairly priced.** This is because, at this price, the asset reflects the correct opportunity cost (*RRR*) of investing in it. Recall from Chapter 3 that cost is measured as opportunity costs and that, in general, price and costs may not be the same. When the price of an asset reflects its true cost, the market is said to be *efficient*. We can therefore conclude that:

KEY CONCEPT: In an efficient market, the price of an asset reflects its true cost.

---

[7] If the company is expected to pay, say, $2 in dividends at the end of the period, a minor adjustment is all that is required. The numerator of the relationship would be the sum of the future expected stock price and the expected dividend, or $70.

THE SECURITY MARKET LINE

Equation (13-2) can be represented graphically as in Figure 13•4. The straight line in the figure is called the **security market line (SML),** and all assets should plot exactly on the line.[8] This is not to suggest that temporary deviations from this line cannot occur. Such deviations from the SML, either below or above it, are a temporary phenomenon; they cannot occur for an extended period of time.

Why Should all Assets Plot on the SML?

Assume that there is an asset that does not plot on the SML. For purposes of illustration, say that stock k has a beta coefficient of 1.1. Then from the CAPM it follows that

$$E(\tilde{R}_k) = R_f + \beta_k[E(\tilde{R}_m) - R_f]$$

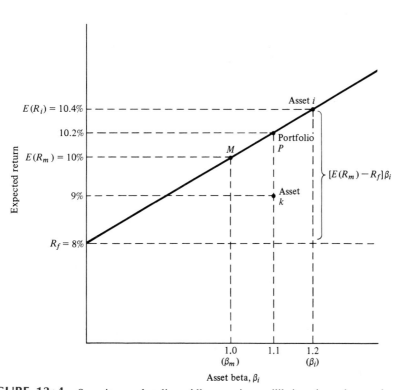

FIGURE 13•4 Security market line. All assets in equilibrium just plot on the SML. M represents the market portfolio.

---

[8] The CAPM and the SML are the same; the former concept represents the relationship between relevant risk and expected return in equation form, while the latter represents the same idea graphically.

If the risk-free rate is at 8% and the expected return on the market is 10%, stock k should have an expected return of

$$E(\tilde{R}_k) = 0.08 + 1.1(0.10 - 0.08)$$
$$= 0.102 \text{ or } 10.2\%$$

However, suppose stock k does not plot on the SML and the expected return on k is in fact 9%. With a 9% expected return, stock k plots below the SML. This situation cannot persist, given the assumptions underlying the CAPM (no transaction costs, taxes, etc.).

An investor will note that stock k is not providing a sufficient return to reward her for its risk and will sell the stock. Other investors will note this unfavorable relationship between stock k's return and risk and will also sell their shares. The selling pressure on the stock will cause its price to drop and its rate of return to rise.[9] As the price of stock k falls, it becomes more and more attractive for purchase because the potential returns from owning it increase; that is, $E(\tilde{R}_k)$ rises. These adjustments (the selling of asset k) will continue until stock k plots exactly on the SML. When this happens, the expected return on asset k will be 10.2%. Investors will then recognize that the return on stock k is sufficient to reward them for taking on its risk. A similar set of arguments can be used to show that an asset that plots above the SML will also be forced to plot on the SML.

OVERVALUED, UNDERVALUED, AND FAIRLY PRICED ASSETS

B&G stock, seen earlier, is priced fairly if the market price is equal to the equilibrium price provided by the CAPM. The term *fair* suggests that the asset's current price incorporates all information available on the asset's benefits and costs. If the price of the stock is, say, $65, B&G is **overvalued,** while if the price is $50, it is **undervalued** in this framework. Whenever a stock is overvalued, it will fall below the SML; whenever it is undervalued, it will fall above the SML. It is easy to see why these statements are true by comparing the expected benefits (the expected returns) from the stock with the economic cost (the *RRR*) of investing in the stock.

Learning Check for Section 13•3

Review Questions

13•5.   What is the *RRR* on a T bill?

---

[9]This inverse relationship between stock price and rate of return was covered from a time value viewpoint in Chapter 2 and a stock value viewpoint in Chapter 4.

13•6. What is the *RRR* on a stock with a variance of 25%?

13•7. The CAPM is a theory for estimating opportunity costs. Explain.

13•8. What is the difference between the CAPM and the SML?

13•9. Assets that fall above the SML are undervalued investments. Why?

13•10. Eventually, all assets should plot on the SML. Explain why this observation allows managers to use $E(R_i)$ from the CAPM as the discount rate.

New Terms

Capital asset pricing
  model (CAPM)
Equilibrium

Fairly priced asset
Market Portfolio
Overvalued asset

Security market line
  (SML)
Undervalued asset

SECTION 13•4 *Implications for Corporate Financial Management*

Although the discussion so far has developed several new concepts and ideas, the natural question that arises pertains to the relevance of these ideas for financial management. How does the CAPM help financial decision making? How do the concepts developed here relate to the various issues addressed in earlier chapters?

The contribution of the CAPM to financial management can be summarized in one sentence: the CAPM provides a framework for estimating the appropriate opportunity cost to be used in evaluating an investment. The implications of this statement are fairly strong and will now be discussed in greater detail.

DISCOUNT RATE CALCULATIONS

In Chapter 2 we introduced the notion of the *time value* of money. For this reason, there is an opportunity cost incurred in delaying cash flows. To compensate for this, future cash flows have to be discounted at the appropriate opportunity cost or *RRR* to find present values. In Chapter 2 we explained only the mechanical procedure for finding the present and future value of cash flows. We said nothing about how the appropriate discount rate is estimated. By providing a framework for estimating the proper discount rate to be used, the CAPM thus makes the methodology suggested in Chapter 2 operational.

MARKET VALUE CALCULATIONS

Since we argued in Chapter 1 that the goal of financial management is to maximize the market value of a firm's assets, a financial manager must, at the very least, know what determines market values. The CAPM provides the *market valuation theory*, which (as Chapter 3 has emphasized) is required for calculating market values. By using the CAPM in value-maximizing decisions, corporate managers do not have to worry about the potentially different discount rates that the owners of the firm may have. The market theory provides an *average discount rate* that the manager can use in an objective way.

SEPARATION OF RELEVANT AND IRRELEVANT RISKS

In making day-to-day decisions, managers are confronted with several alternatives, each with choices involving perhaps different returns and risks. The CAPM theory, in a sense, simplifies their decisions; it identifies those risks that they should recognize in making value-increasing investments and those risks that have no impact whatsoever in the market value of the project being undertaken. The only relevant risk is the systematic risk of the project, as measured by its beta.

The notion of *relevant* and *irrelevant* risks is often misunderstood. The threat of strikes, management changes, and potential illiquidity are all examples of risks that the manager cannot afford to ignore. Yet they are irrelevant in the sense that they will not affect the *RRR* on the project and, consequently, its market value.[10]

MAKING MONEY FOR THE COMPANY

In Chapter 3 we defined the notion of making money as used in finance. To make money, it is necessary to generate excess returns. Yet Chapter 3 provided no practical guidelines for calculating the excess returns on a project. As demonstrated here in Example 13•6, the CAPM provides a means of examining these excess returns. This example also illustrates that the CAPM is applicable not only to stocks but to all assets and thus has a prominent place in capital budgeting.[11]

---

[10] These other risks can, of course, affect the future cash flows that the project will generate, but not the required rate of return.

[11] The discussion in this chapter is set for an all-equity firm. The use of the CAPM in capital budgeting for a levered firm will be covered in Chapter 14.

Example 13•6   Making Money and the CAPM

Assume that asset k in Figure 13•4 is a one-year project. Like stocks, projects have expected returns and market risks.[12] Should project k be accepted or rejected? Since *NPV* should be the basis for the decision, it is necessary to calculate the project's *NPV*.

Assume, for simplicity, that this one-year project requires an initial outlay of $100. No further cash flows can be expected until the end of the year. Figure 13•4 shows that the project's beta is 1.1 and that the expected return is 9%. If there is only one cash flow at the end and this is expected to produce a 9% return, the expected cash flow at the end must be $109 ($100 × 1.09). The *NPV* of this project is obtained by discounting this future cash flow to the present by using a market discount rate (*RRR*), which according to Figure 13•4 is 10.2%. Therefore,

$$NPV = \text{present value of inflows} - \text{present value of outflows}$$
$$= \$109(PVF_{.102,1}) - \$100$$
$$= \$98.91 - \$100 = \$-1.09$$

Using the *NPV* rule, this project would be rejected.

Project k, which falls below the SML, is rejected because it has a negative *NPV*. Similarly, it can be shown that any project that falls above the SML will have a positive *NPV*. A project that falls on the SML will have zero *NPV*.

Example 13•6 suggests that the *NPV* rule developed in earlier chapters may be stated alternatively as:

KEY CONCEPT: The *NPV* rule accepts all projects that fall above the SML line and rejects all projects that fall below it.

However, just as in the case of a stock, no project can fall above the line for an extended period. Thus "good" projects will eventually lose their appeal and "bad" projects may eventually become good. To borrow the words of a poet,

Many shall be restored that now are fallen and many shall fall that now are in honor.

Horace, Ars Poetica

---

[12] This issue is addressed in greater detail in Chapter 14.

Regulated Companies

Regulated companies such as utilities cannot change the rates charged to customers without the approval of the appropriate regulatory agency. The companies have to justify their rate requests in order to obtain permission to hike the rates for products or services. It is becoming a widespread practice to use opportunity costs instead of accounting costs in calculating the appropriate rates that the company can charge consumers. By estimating a **fair rate of return,** the regulatory authority can determine the appropriate rates that consumers should pay. The CAPM can be used to calculate a company's fair rate of return on equity. The highlight "The CAPM in Action: Rate Regulation for Southern Bell" explains how this can be done in the context of a regulated company.[13]

■■ *HIGHLIGHT*

THE CAPM IN ACTION: RATE REGULATION FOR SOUTHERN BELL

The CAPM has been used to estimate the fair rate of return on equity for rate regulation. For regulated companies (e.g., utilities) the revenues are often set as stated in the *Hope* decision:

> From the investor or company point of view it is important that there be enough revenue not only for operating expenses but also for capital costs of the business. These include service on the debt and dividends on the stock. By that standard the rate to the equity owner should be commensurate with the returns on investments in other enterprises having corresponding risks. That return, moreover, should be sufficient to assure confidence of the financial integrity of the enterprise, so as to maintain its ability to attract capital.
>
> [*Federal Power Commission v. Hope Natural Gas Company, 320 U.S.*
> *591 (1944), p. 603*].

It is apparent from the preceding paragraph that the courts recognize the opportunity cost principle.

James Bicksler has used the CAPM to estimate the maximum required rate of return allowable for Southern Bell. The following information can be obtained from the Testimony of James L. Bicksler Before the South Carolina Public Service Commision (Docket No. 76-352-C):

1. Risk-free rate (R_f). The 30-day Treasury bill rate on November 12, 1976 was 4.65%

2. Beta. By regressing the monthly returns on Southern Bell on a value-weighted index of all NYSE stocks over January 1971–December

---

[13] The highlight motivates the use of the CAPM in a regulatory context. Understanding the theory of regulation is not a prerequisite for an understanding of the highlight.

1975, the beta was estimated to be 0.779 (upper value of the 95% confidence interval).

3. Risk premium of the market $[E(\tilde{R}_m) - R_f]$. Estimated using historical data to be 7.44%.

Given these estimates, the maximum required rate of return for Southern Bell was calculated as

$$E(R) = R_f + \beta[E(\tilde{R}_m) - R_f]$$
$$= 4.65\% + (0.779 \times 7.44\%)$$
$$= 10.45\%$$

Source: Compiled from information provided in George Foster, *Financial Statement Analysis* (Englewood Cliffs, N.J.: Prentice-Hall, Inc., 1978); adapted with the author's permission.

Learning Check for Section 13•4

Review Questions

13•11. What are the uses of the CAPM for the corporate financial manager?

13•12. Explain why an asset that plots above the SML is a positive-*NPV* investment.

New Terms

Fair rate of return   Regulated companies

SECTION 13•5   *Criticism of the CAPM*

In this chapter, we have not derived the CAPM in order to keep the discussion relatively simple. However, a derivation of the CAPM would have forced us to spell out clearly the several assumptions that underlie the model. Some of the required assumptions have already been introduced in the discussion (no transactions costs, no taxes, etc.). In addition, all investors are required to have identical expectations and assessments of an asset's risk. Although most of the restrictive assumptions can be removed to develop modified versions of the CAPM, there are still some aspects of the CAPM that are restrictive. For example, the CAPM theory implies that all investors invest in a combination of riskless U.S. T bills and the market portfolio, which is a conglomeration of all assets that exist. Only then can the expected return on any asset be expressed in terms of the returns on these two assets. To ensure this result, assumptions regarding either the distribution of asset returns or on the tastes of investors become necessary. Some of these assumptions are not entirely palatable.

In the absence of a complete understanding of how risk and return are related, we have to work with a simplification of reality. This simplification is achieved via convenient assumptions made to get a tractable model. The CAPM is an intuitively appealing statement: To earn higher returns, one must bear higher risks. What is nonintuitive (at least initially) is the notion of beta being the relevant risk.

A further discussion of the theoretical aspects of the CAPM will not be attempted at this point. The presentation of this "criticism section" was intended simply to convey to the reader that the model has been the subject of much debate in recent years. Yet, because of its intuitive appeal and relative ease of application, the CAPM is viewed by many as the best framework available for facilitating financial decision making. More elaborate models, although theoretically more elegant, become increasingly difficult to implement.

EMPIRICAL TESTS OF THE CAPM

A theory is perhaps best judged not in terms of the assumptions it makes but in terms of how well the theory conforms to empirical data. That is, whether or not the CAPM is a useful theory, the results of the empirical tests conducted on the CAPM with actual data must be analyzed.

There are five testable implications for the CAPM:

1. A security's return should increase with its relevant risk (beta).

2. The relationship between return and risk, as measured by the standard deviation, should be linear.

3. Nonsystematic risk should not affect returns.

4. On average, the slope of the SML should equal $[E(\tilde{R}_m) - R_f]$.

5. On average, the intercept of the SML should equal the risk-free rate, R_f.

Most academicians would agree that the first three implications have been verified by empirical tests. The major problems have arisen with the last two implications. Much of the empirical work done finds a smaller slope and a larger intercept than the CAPM would call for. In other words, the empirically observed SML is "flatter" than that of the theoretical model. This does not mean that the CAPM is not correct. It is simply not perfect. The important insights provided by the CAPM—that the relevant risk of an asset is its systematic risk and that the expected return is linearly related to this risk—are still extremely useful.

Learning Check for Section 13•5

Review Questions

13•13. What are some of the weaknesses of the CAPM?

13•14. What are the testable implications of the CAPM? What have the empirical results indicated?

SUMMARY

The Limits of Diversification

The primary objective of this chapter has been to explain the relationship between expected returns and risk in equilibrium. This relationship is important because it is the basis for determining opportunity costs. The total risk of an asset consists of two parts: unique risk and market risk. Unique risk is diversifiable risk that can be eliminated through diversification. However, even when unique risk is completely diversified away, systematic risk remains. This systematic risk represents the component of total risk that is systematically dependent on general economic conditions. Thus, systematic risk is the relevant risk for determining opportunity cost.

The Beta of an Asset

The beta of an asset is an index of its relevant risk. Beta is a statistical concept that measures the sensitivity of a security's return to changes in the return on the market, and exists for both individual assets and portfolios of assets. Betas can be calculated from historical data or, in the case of stocks, can readily be obtained from published sources.

The Relationship Between Relevant Risk and Opportunity Costs

The capital asset pricing model (CAPM) is a theory that explicitly identifies this relationship in the form of a simple equation. The CAPM is consistent with a market that rewards investors for bearing risks that cannot be diversified away. When the CAPM is represented graphically, it is called the *security market line (SML)*. All assets should eventually plot on the SML. Although temporary deviations from the line can occur, investors seeking economic profits will force the assets back on to the SML. Assets that plot above the SML are positive-*NPV* investments (i.e., they generate excess returns), while assets that plot below the SML are negative-*NPV* investments that managers must avoid.

Implications for Corporate Financial Management

The CAPM is a very relevant theory for financial decision making. The financial manager maximizing market values can use the CAPM to determine the market value of different investments. The CAPM identifies those risks that are relevant for value-increasing decisions and links those risks to opportunity costs. The CAPM is also useful for determining whether a project will produce excess returns and for estimating fair rates of return for regulated companies.

Criticism of the CAPM

The CAPM is derived via several restrictive assumptions. These assumptions, by providing a simplified view of the real world, allow us to develop a model that has intuitive appeal and is easy to apply. The CAPM is not entirely supported by empirical evidence. However, its major results—that a security's returns should increase with its relevant risk, that the relationship between risk and return is linear, and that nonsystematic risk should not affect returns—have been empirically verified and provide important guidance for financial decision making. The CAPM is the simplest and most easily applied valuation model available.

PROBLEMS

13•1. A stock has a beta of 1.5, and the risk-free rate is 10%. What is the expected return on the stock if
(a) the expected return on the market is 14%?
(b) the expected return on the market is 16%?
(c) the expected return on the market is 18%?

13•2. A year ago, you purchased some stock with a beta of 1.5. You have not noticed how well your stock has done during the year, but you do know that the T-bill rate has remained at 10% throughout the year. As you are driving down the road, you hear on the radio that the market return was 20% during the year. Given only this information, what do you expect the return on your stock to have been?

13•3. A stock has a beta of 1.2 and an expected return of 15% when the market's expected return is 14%. What must the risk-free rate be?

13·4.   Stock A has a beta of 1.2 and stock B has a beta of 1.5. You invest 40% of your money in stock A and the rest in stock B.
(a) What is the beta of your portfolio?
(b) If the expected market return is 16% and the risk-free rate is 10%, what is the expected return on your portfolio?

13·5.   Stock X has a beta of 0.5, stock Y has a beta of 1.0, and stock Z has a beta of 1.25. The risk-free rate is 10%, and the expected market return is 18%.
(a) Find the expected return on stock X.
(b) Find the expected return on stock Y.
(c) Find the expected return on stock Z.
(d) Suppose that you construct a portfolio consisting of 40% X, 20% Y, and 40% Z. Using your answers to parts (a), (b), and (c), find the expected return of this portfolio.
(e) What is the beta of the portfolio specified in part (d)?
(f) Using the information in the body of the problem and your answer to part (e), find the expected return on your portfolio.

13·6.   A stock with a beta of 1.5 has an expected return of 18% if the market has an expected return of 15%. If your estimate of the expected return of the market suddenly improves to 21% (from 15%), find the expected return on the stock.

13·7.   Suppose that the risk-free rate is 12% and the expected market return is 20%. The FM Corporation has a beta of 0.75 and the Gord Corporation has a beta of 1.25.
(a) Find the expected return on the FM Corporation.
(b) Find the expected return on the Gord Corporation.
(c) Suppose that because of a suddenly unanticipated increase in inflation, the risk-free rate rises to 16% and the market risk premium remains at 8%. Find the expected return of FM and Gord.

13·8.   Saldco shares have a beta of 1.2, are currently selling for $80 each, and pay no dividends. The risk-free rate is 10%, and the expected market return is 16%.
(a) What do you expect Saldco shares to trade for one year from today?
(b) If the expected market return is 20% (rather than 16%), what do you expect Saldco shares to trade for one year from today?

13·9.   The Baldwin-Mills Corporation has a beta of 1.25 and pays no dividends. The expected market return is 20%, and the T-bill rate is expected to remain constant at 10%. You expect Baldwin-Mills shares to be worth $50 in one year. Using the CAPM, find the value of a share today.

13·10. Shares of the Mullet Corporation have a beta of 1.2 and an expected return of 22%. The T-bill rate is 10%.

   (a) What is the expected return of another company with a beta of 0.6?

   (b) What is the expected return of a portfolio with a beta of 1.0?

13·11. You invest $10,000 in the Jaguar Vitamin Company (which has a beta of 1.5) and $20,000 in the Laverty Game Corporation (which has a beta of 1.2). The risk-free rate is 10% and the expected market return is 16%. What are the beta and the expected return of your portfolio?

13·12. Your next-door neighbor, a security analyst, has confided in you that his research (which does not involve the CAPM) causes him to think that the Johnston Glass Company will have a return of 18%, the Theil Flooring Corporation will have a return of 20%, and Kmenta Foods, Inc., will have a return of 22%. You have found that the betas of these three firms are 0.9, 1.15, and 1.4, respectively. If your neighbor is right, which stocks are underpriced (will have a higher return than the market estimates) if

   (a) the T-bill rate is 11% and the expected market return is 19%?

   (b) the T-bill rate is 14% and the expected market return is 19%?

13·13. You are considering the purchase of 100 shares of the Mead Beverage Company. The shares pay an annual dividend of $1 (which you expect to remain constant for the next several years) and have a beta of 1.25. Although you expect the T-bill rate to remain at 10% for the next three years, you believe that the market return will be 16%, 14%, and 12%, respectively. If you think that the share price will be $25 immediately after paying the dividend three years from today, how much are you willing to pay for a share today?

READINGS

Beaver, William H., Paul Kettler, and Myron Scholes, "The Association Between Market Determined and Accounting Determined Risk Measures," *Accounting Review*, October 1970, 654.

Brown, S. J., and Mark P. Kritzman, ed., *Quantitative Methods for Financial Analysis*, (Homewood, Ill.: Dow Jones-Irwin, 1987).

Elton, E. J., and M. Gruber, *Modern Portfolio Theory and Investment Analysis*, 3rd ed. (New York: John Wiley & Sons, Inc., 1986).

Haugen, R. A., *Modern Investment Theory* (Englewood Cliffs, N.J.: Prentice-Hall, Inc., 1986).

Ibbotson, R. G., and R. A. Sinquefield, *Stocks, Bonds, Bills and Inflation: The Past and the Future* (Charlottesville, Va.: Financial Analysts Research Foundation, 1982).

MODIGLIANI, FRANCO, AND GERALD A. POGUE, "An Introduction to Risk and
  Return," *Financial Analysts' Journal*, March–April 1974, 68–80, and May–June
  1974, 68–86.
ROLL, RICHARD, "A Critique of the Asset Pricing Theory's Tests," *Journal of
  Financial Economics*, March 1977, 129–176.
ROSENBERG, BARR, AND JAMES GUY, "Beta and Investment Fundamentals,"
  Financial Analysts' Journal, May–June 1976, 60–72.
SHARPE, WILLIAM F., "Capital Asset Prices: A Theory of Market Equilibrium
  Under Conditions of Risk," *Journal of Finance*, September 1964, 425–442.
WAGNER, W. H., AND S. C. LAU, "The Effect of Diversification on Risk," *Financial
  Analysts' Journal* 27, November–December 1971).

14

Adjusting for Uncertainty in Capital Budgeting Decisions

In Chapters 12 and 13, we outlined the qualitative and quantitative considerations in capital budgeting. The general rule is to evaluate the project's *NPV* and adopt the project if its *NPV* is positive. By following this rule, the firm can increase the wealth of the stockholders.

Unfortunately, this rule reduces the entire capital budgeting problem to a mechanical procedure. Following this rule mechanically would be relatively easy for a manager—assign some members of the staff to provide the expected cash flows, assign another team to compute the appropriate discount rate, and delegate others to the computation of *NPV*s.

Why, then, is the decision maker called a manager? Managing involves more than a simple analysis of numbers. A good manager will ask several questions while evaluating a project. Most of these questions involve uncertainty in cash flows and/or in the discount rate. For example:

1. How confident can the company be about the projected cash flows?

2. How are the uncertainties in the cash flow forecasts being factored into the analysis?

3. Where is the greatest risk in the future cash flow estimates? Is it from the production department? Or is it the uncertainty in future sales that makes the project risky?

4. What type of corrective action can the company take to reduce these uncertainties?

5. What is the appropriate discount rate that must be used for the project?

The purpose of this chapter is to develop procedures for incorporating uncertainty into the capital budgeting process. To do this in a systematic way, this chapter is divided into three sections. The first section is designed to provide managers with some guidance in answering the first four questions posed. The fifth question is addressed in the second section of the chapter.

To make the concepts of this chapter easier to understand, we provide the betas necessary to determine the discount rates. The methods for estimating beta are provided in Appendix 14B. Also, for most of the chapter, we will examine uncertainty in the framework of an all-equity firm. The complications arising from using debt to finance a project are discussed in the third section of the chapter.

SECTION 14•1: *Assessing the Impact of Uncertain Cash Flows.* In this section, the methods of coping with uncertainty in the cash flow forecasts developed by management are addressed. Two comprehensive methods are presented, and their advantages and weaknesses are discussed. Sensitivity analysis shows how sensitive *NPV* is to changes in *one* variable. Computer simulation, on the other hand, evaluates the sensitivity of *NPV* to changes in *several* variables simultaneously.

SECTION 14•2: *Two Approaches to Estimating the RRR for a Risky Project.* This section begins the discussion of how uncertainty affects the discount rate of *NPV* calculations. To understand this link, we join together the concepts developed in Chapters 3, 12, and 13. Two commonly used but unsatisfactory procedures—the weighted average cost of capital and the ad hoc method—are presented and their weaknesses discussed.

SECTION 14•3: *Using the CAPM to Estimate the RRR for a Risky Project.* The CAPM provides a viable means of estimating the *RRR*. The meaning of expected return and of a project's beta are explained. The relevant risk of the project—its beta—is determined and then inserted into the CAPM, which gives the proper discount rate for finding the *NPV* of a project's cash flows. The section concludes with a discussion of how leverage affects the beta used in the CAPM.

SECTION 14•1   *Assessing the Impact of Uncertain Cash Flows*

The capital budgeting methods presented in the earlier chapters did not directly address the issue of uncertainty associated with future cash flow estimates. How did the managers of Mylanta Diversified Products (in Chapter 10) estimate the cash flows for their computer project? Chapter 10 provided a framework for calculating the cash flows, given the future revenue, depreciation, and cost figures.

In most situations, the future cash flows from an investment are seldom known precisely. Managers have to rely on estimates, and these uncertain estimates are clearly the more realistic case that must be considered. Decision makers must acknowledge that these forecasts of future cash flows are uncertain, and they should make appropriate adjustments in their analyses of projects.

Consider the operating cash flows for Baxter, Inc.'s proposed new drug project. The relevant information is presented in Table 14•1. Baxter estimates that an initial investment of $150,000 is required to get the project off the ground. However, the cash flow picture looks promising; positive cash flows of $55,500 per year are expected over the life of the project (which Baxter expects to be five years). These cash flow numbers assume that the entire $150,000 investment is depreciated straight-line over the five years toward a $100,000 salvage value. Thus the annual depreciation amounts to $10,000. In addition, Baxter's calculations assume that the company will be in the 30% tax bracket over the life of the project. As can be seen, if Baxter's opportunity cost is 10%, the *NPV* of the project is $60,389 and Baxter is justified in accepting this project.

However, Baxter's management feels uneasy about this project because there are too many uncertain elements it has not considered in its analysis. Baxter's expected cash flows in Table 14•1 are merely expected; there is no guarantee that these cash flows will indeed materialize. For one thing, the company is not very confident about its revenue forecasts. Management believes that if competing firms enter the market, Baxter will lose a substantial portion of the projected revenues. Baxter simply does not have the established marketing network that many of its larger competitors have. Also, the production manager is unwilling to commit to the cost figures; he is not certain about the variable and fixed costs. Recognizing these uncertainties, management wants to assess the various potential future outcomes and then make an "executive decision" as to whether or not to accept this project.

What are the various ways in which Baxter can approach this problem of

TABLE 14•1   Baxter, Inc.'s Drug Project

Initial outlay	$150,000
Life of the project	5 years
Opportunity cost (*RRR*)	10%
Expected cash flow	$55,500/year

$$NPV \text{ at } 10\% = \$ - 150,000 + \$55,500(PVFA_{10.5})$$
$$= \$ - 150,000 + \$55,500(3.7908)$$
$$= \$60,389$$

uncertainty in the future cash flows? Two methods can be used, each with advantages and disadvantages.[1] These methods will now be examined briefly.

SENSITIVITY ANALYSIS

What if sales should fall to $190,000 because the drug does not gain market acceptance? What would happen to the *NPV* if, instead, the drug becomes an instant success, with revenues of $220,000? What if labor and distribution costs (variable costs) increase after the product is introduced? Will the project's *NPV* become negative? Or will it still be positive? How much of an increase in fixed costs can Baxter absorb before the project becomes unattractive (i.e., becomes a negative-*NPV* project)?

An innumerable list of such questions arise, and one way to answer these "what if" questions is by **sensitivity analysis** (sometimes casually referred to as *what-if analysis*).

Sensitivity analysis, as the name implies, involves an examination of the sensitivity of some variable to changes in another variable. In the Baxter, Inc., case, management is extremely interested in understanding the impact on *NPV* of changes in sales revenues, fixed costs, and variable costs. Thus it is useful to get an idea of how sensitive *NPV* is to changes in each of these variables.

Based on inputs from the marketing and production departments of the company, Baxter has assembled information on the expected, pessimistic, and optimistic estimates of the variables affecting the cash flows from this project. As Table 14•2a shows, the marketing staff believes that in a pessimistic "worst-case" scenario the revenues from the drug will fall to $170,000 per year, while in the optimistic "best-case" scenario the revenues will be $240,000 per year. Along the same lines, the production department has provided its optimistic and pessimistic estimates for fixed and variable costs.

Table 14•2b provides the results of Baxter's sensitivity analysis. There are three variables, which we think could change: revenues, variable costs, and fixed costs. Each of the numbers in Table 14•2b represents Baxter's *NPV*, given the appropriate changing variable. Consider the *NPV* of $166,532 in the table. What is the significance of this number, and how was it determined?[2]

Assuming that the optimistic revenue figure of $240,000 per year is the actual revenue, and holding all other numbers (fixed and variable costs, etc.) to be the same as the expected values, the *NPV* is $166,532. In other words, the

---

[1] A third approach to dealing with cash flow uncertainty involves *decision trees*. When a particular decision today depends on the outcome of some variable in the future, this eventuality must be recognized. Decision trees are extremely tedious to work with. This approach is not examined in this book.

[2] Readers should be careful in their interpretation of Table 14•2b. The *NPV*s in this table are the result of the expected values for all variables *except* the variable that we wish to examine (revenues, variable costs, or fixed costs) under the varying states of nature (pessimistic, expected, or optimistic). Read the interpretation comment at the end of this table carefully.

TABLE 14·2 Sensitivity Analysis for Baxter, Inc.'s Drug Project

a. Estimates

	Year 0	Years 1–5		
		Pessimistic	Expected	Optimistic
1. Initial Investment	$150,000			
2. Revenue $(Q \times P)$		$170,000	$200,000	$240,000
3. Variable costs		120,000	100,000	90,000
4. Fixed costs		30,000	25,000	21,000
5. Depreciation		10,000	10,000	10,000
6. Net operating income $(2 - 3 - 4 - 5)$		10,000	65,000	119,000
7. Taxes at 30%		3,000	19,500	35,700
8. Net income $(6 - 7)$		7,000	45,500	83,300
9. Operating cash flow $(8 + 5)$		17,000	55,500	93,300

b. Results of *NPV* Analysis[a] (opportunity cost = 10%)

	Pessimistic	Expected	Optimistic
Revenues	$-19,217	$60,389	$166,532
Variable costs	+7,318	60,389	86,925
Fixed costs	+47,122	60,389	71,004

[a] Interpretation: For example, consider the *NPV* of $47,122. This *NPV* is calculated assuming a pessimistic outcome for fixed costs [$30,000 from part (a)] while all other cash flows are the expected cash flows from part (a). In other words, the *NPV* of $47,122 will result if all cash flows except fixed costs are as expected and fixed costs are $30,000.

project has an *NPV* of $166,532 if the optimistic sales figures materialize and all other numbers are those expected to occur. To consider another case, if the drug sales are not encouraging, then under the pessimistic scenario (with the pessimistic value for sales and the expected values for the other variables), the project would have an *NPV* of −$19,217, which would clearly be a bad situation for Baxter. Notice from the analysis that the uncertainty in the fixed and variable costs is not as crucial as the uncertainty associated with the sales revenues. Even with the pessimistic fixed and variable numbers, Baxter's project will have positive *NPV*s.

So, what is Baxter's management to conclude? All in all, the project appears to be a good one. Except for one case, the *NPV*s are all positive. Baxter need not worry too much about its production manager's uncertainty. However, Baxter should examine its sales revenue forecasts more carefully. What can the company do to increase sales? After all, this is the main factor in determining the project's attractiveness for Baxter. Perhaps a lower selling price can lower the probability of the worst-case scenario. Perhaps management should employ an aggressive marketing agency to target the pharmaceutical market audience.

If management is reasonably confident that it can avoid this pessimistic sales forecast by, say, a change in pricing policies or advertising, it may choose to proceed with the project. However, any proposed changes must be examined again in a what-if analysis. It is virtually impossible to anticipate all the questions that management can ask and to catalog the myriad possibilities for corrective action. Each situation must be addressed on a case-by-case basis. A detailed knowledge of the business, the company, and the firm's management philosophy will be required.

Weaknesses of Sensitivity Analysis

Although sensitivity analysis can be a useful tool for alerting management to its potential for error, it is at best an aid in the decision process and, like other tools, should not be used in isolation. There are several aspects of sensitivity analysis that must be noted.

First, what do *optimistic* and *pessimistic* mean? Different decision makers can have different definitions for these words. In fact, even within the same company, a consensus may be lacking. For example, Baxter's marketing department might consider $170,000 in sales to be pessimistic, while the production department might define it as a reasonable measure of success.

Unfortunately, this problem cannot be resolved simply by management's telling all departments how *optimistic* and *pessimistic* are to be defined. The number and types of variables that affect the sales of the product are very different from the number and types of factors that production departments consider. For example, rising costs can be a favorable signal to the marketing manager concerned with sales revenues, while this is an unfavorable outcome for the cost-conscious production manager.

Second, what happens if the variables under consideration are related to one another? An optimistic variable cost estimate can arise, for example, because most of the costs become fixed. Such relationships between the variables cannot be handled easily in a sensitivity analysis.

Finally, would it not be more meaningful to assess the various what-if scenarios by evaluating the impact of changes in a few variables simultaneously? Sensitivity analysis allowed Baxter to evaluate the effects on *NPV* of changes in certain variables taken one at a time. What if Baxter wanted to evaluate the joint effects of, say, pessimistic sales and optimistic cost figures simultaneously?

COMPUTER SIMULATION

Unlike sensitivity analysis, **computer simulation** allows one to evaluate the impact of changes in several variables simultaneously. The computer simulation method, in fact, allows one to examine the impact of changes in all possible combinations of variables. Elaborate computer programs exist to conduct the analysis that provides the entire distribution of potential outcomes.

Baxter's Procedure for a Computer Simulation of Its Capital Budgeting Project

Step 1: Model the Problem. Baxter will first have to tell the computer what the problem is. This involves inputting the equation for the determination of cash flows, the equation to calculate the *NPV*, and, of course, the appropriate opportunity cost that the computer must use to discount the cash flows.

Step 2: Characterize the Uncertainty. In this stage, the computer is provided the information on the uncertainty associated with each variable. This uncertainty is characterized as a probability distribution of forecasting errors for each variable. A sample probability distribution (a triangular distribution) is provided in Figure 14•1. This distribution suggests that the mean forecast error is zero, but the error could be, say, as large as ±15% for sales or ±10% for variable costs. Management must come up with these numbers based on the confidence it attaches to its forecasted expected values.

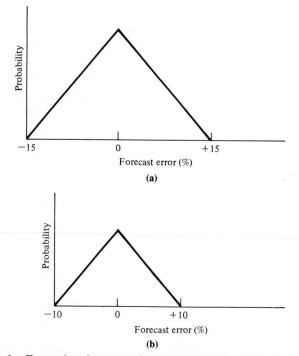

FIGURE 14•1 Expressing the uncertainty associated with (a) sales and (b) variable costs for Baxter's drug project in a simulation. Triangular distribution of forecast errors with a mean-zero forecast error. Management has more confidence in its ability to forecast variable costs than in its sales forecasting skills.

Step 3: Provide Data. The expected cash flow information is then provided to the computer.

Step 4: Run the Simulation. This stage is simply a series of computations performed by the computer. The computer first samples from the distributions of forecast errors, forecasts each variable, and then calculates the cash flows. This sequence of calculations is known as an *iteration*. After several iterations, the computer can provide the probability distribution of cash flows. Hypothetical computer outputs for Baxter's cash flow simulation for the first two years are presented in Figure 14•2.

Step 5: Analyze the Cash Flows. With the distribution of cash flows in hand, Baxter can evaluate the cash flows. The output of the simulation provides the mean cash flow, the range of potential outcomes, and the probability that the actual cash flows will fall between a particular range (say, between $14,000 and $21,000) for each year. In addition, management can ask questions such as: What is the probability that the cash flows will exceed $17,000 per year? By

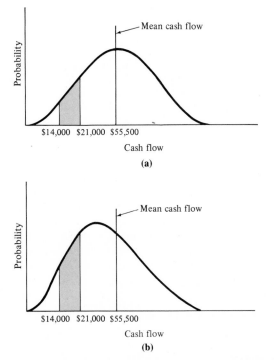

FIGURE 14•2 Hypothetical output for Baxter, Inc.'s simulations. The hatched area is the probability that the cash flows will be between $14,000 and $21,000. (a) Year 1; (b) year 2.

obtaining answers to such questions, management is in a better position to assess the impact of cash flow changes on the project's *NPV*. (The procedure for computing such probabilities is explained in Chapter 13.)

Disadvantages of Simulation

The major disadvantage of simulation is that it may be too expensive and time-consuming for small projects. Thus, while oil and aircraft manufacturing companies have been known to use simulation extensively, most smaller companies find it either too tedious or too expensive. Even though computing-time cost considerations are not as important in these days of efficient, high-speed computers, a proper simulation model is extremely difficult to build and requires specialized technical skills. In addition to these problems of designing the model, the output of computer simulations is often misinterpreted. (See the highlight "Misusing Simulation.") If the management of a company does not have experience in interpreting the output of a simulation analysis, the laborious analysis may simply not be worthwhile.

▮ *HIGHLIGHT*

MISUSING SIMULATION

The procedure for incorporating uncertainty into capital budgeting decisions is not always easy. Several different approaches have been advocated in the literature. In this search for better risk-adjustment techniques, several authors have been unjustifiably impressed with simulation in its various forms.

Consider the following approach to simulation suggested by some early authors: Instead of obtaining a probability distribution of cash flows as in the example considered in the text, obtain a probability distribution of *NPV*s. That is, let the computer calculate several potential values of the *NPV*s and provide the investigator with a distribution of *NPV*s directly. To avoid double counting the risk, discount the cash flows using the risk-free interest rate. The simulation output will provide the expected *NPV* and the variance of *NPV*s. This distribution of *NPV*s should be the basis for decision making. Unfortunately, this approach cannot be defended because it is inconsistent with the *NPV* concept. Why?

Opportunity Costs Ignored

Notice from the preceding procedure that in finding the *NPV*s, the risk-free interest rate is used. What does *NPV* then mean? From Chapter 3 we know that for *NPV* to be meaningful, the discount rate used should be the opportunity cost.

Relevant Risk Ignored

Even if the company uses a higher discount rate, the question is: How does management assess the project's risk? Recall that it is only the undiversifiable risk of a project that affects the discount rate.

Market Values Ignored

This is a direct consequence of the previous two objections. Because the relevant risk of the project cannot be determined in this procedure and because the discount rate used has no relationship to opportunity costs, it is extremely unlikely that a project's *NPV* computed in this manner has any relationship to market values.

Why is management conducting the complicated analysis in the first place? Presumably, to see whether the project in question will increase stockholder wealth. However, it may not be achieving its objectives by using this analysis. Suppose that the expected "*NPV*" from a simulation along the lines just described is $40,000. Management simply has no basis for expecting the wealth of its stockholders to increase by $40,000 upon acceptance of the project. In fact, using this procedure, one has no way of determining whether this is a good project.

Learning Check for Section 14•1

Review Questions

14•1. What are the advantages and disadvantages of sensitivity analysis?

14•2. How does simulation overcome certain weaknesses of sensitivity analysis? What are the weaknesses of sensitivity analysis?

New Terms

Computer simulation   Sensitivity analysis

SECTION 14•2 *Two Approaches to Estimating the RRR for a Risky Project*

No one will disagree with the idea that an investment's expected benefits should provide some minimum *RRR*. However, putting this basic concept into practice is another matter. The major problem revolves around how a firm should determine what this minimum *RRR* for an individual capital budgeting project will be.

Several new issues and concepts are introduced in this and the next section. To keep things in perspective, a visual outline of these sections may be useful. Three approaches that have been developed over time to solve this problem will be outlined. In fact, it might be helpful to think of the following discussion as an evolutionary development from the earliest attempts to wrestle with the *RRR* issue (the WACC approach) to the newer method (CAPM) for estimating a risky project's *RRR*. Figure 14•3 summarizes pictorially the various procedures for determining the opportunity cost (*RRR*) for evaluating an investment. The WACC and ad hoc methods are covered in this section. The use of the CAPM in capital budgeting will be examined in Section 14•3.

THE WEIGHTED-AVERAGE COST OF CAPITAL APPROACH

Until the 1960s, financial managers had to rely on what is known as the traditional **weighted-average cost of capital *(WACC)*** approach to estimating a firm's cost of capital. This cost of capital then served as the discount rate for evaluating potential projects.

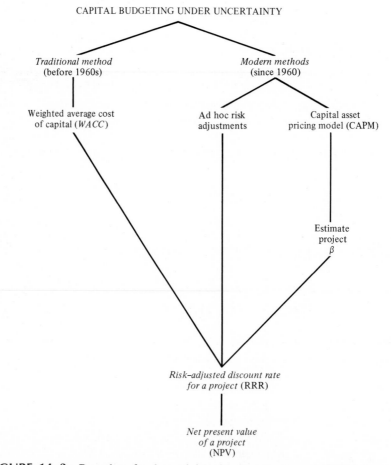

FIGURE 14•3 Procedure for determining the opportunity cost (*RRR*) for evaluating an investment.

At first glance, this procedure may seem extremely appealing. Consider the following school of thought. First, a firm relies on different sources of capital to finance its asset investments. In fact, each dollar invested can be viewed as being provided by a mix of debt and equity. For instance, if a firm uses 20% debt and 80% equity in its capital structure, an invested dollar is supported by 20 cents in debt and 80 cents in equity. Second, the firm pays the different owners of these capital sources their *RRR*. From this, the firm's average cost of capital (as a percentage) is simply a weighted average of all these costs, with the weights depending on the proportion of each component in the firm's capital structure. Finally, as logic would seem to conclude, any attractive investment opportunity should then return at least the average cost of the financing required for the investment.

What are these costs of capital incurred by firms? Recall from Chapter 1 that all investors, irrespective of whether they are stockholders or bondholders, invest with the expectation of rewards. For example, stockholders expect dividend payments and bondholders expect interest payments. If the firm does not, in fact, provide these expected benefits, investors will sell the securities, thereby depressing their market price. Thus, even if a firm is not really paying out dividends, there is an implicit cost associated with this retention of funds; they are not free in an opportunity cost sense.

If a firm's cost of capital calculated in this manner is 11%, a project whose *NPV* is positive at a discount rate of 11% is a good project because this can happen only if the project's *IRR* is greater than 11%. (This was seen in Chapter 11.) Thus this procedure appears quite reasonable; it ensures that only projects with *IRR*s greater than the cost of the investment will be undertaken. Yet despite its apparently straightforward logic, the WACC method cannot generally be used to estimate a project's discount rate. It is necessary to look at the WACC a bit more closely via an example to see why this approach may not be appropriate in many cases.[3]

Example 14•1   The WACC Approach

Suppose that the Iota Corporation is financed with two components of capital: $400,000 in debt and $600,000 in equity.[4] Since the company will incur a cost in raising this capital, it is necessary to estimate these component costs of capital. It is not important to discuss the procedures for finding these component costs. For now, it will simply be assumed that the costs of debt and equity are 6% and 16%, respectively.[5] From this, Iota's WACC is computed as follows:

[3] One reason why we study this method is that it is fairly widely practiced and is still used rather routinely without, in many instances, a recognition of its limitations.

[4] A company can have other components in its capital structure as well (say, preferred stock). The procedure for calculating the WACC is the same; the only difference is that there are more components and more component costs.

[5] For now, the question of how the cost of each component is determined will not be addressed. We examine this issue in Appendix 14•A.

(1) Capital Component	(2) Dollar Amount	(3) Weight	(4) Component Cost	(5) Weighted Component Cost (3) × (4)
Debt	$400,000	0.40	0.06	0.024
Equity	600,000	0.60	0.16	0.096
	$1,000,000			WACC = 0.120

Now, how would Iota decide which projects are acceptable if it used the WACC approach? Any project that offered a rate of return greater than its 12% cost of capital would be accepted. On the other hand, Iota would reject any project whose return was less than 12%; otherwise, it would be raising capital with a 12% cost and investing this capital in projects with returns lower than this cost.

Figure 14•4 graphically represents the accept/reject criterion for Iota. First, note that the WACC is a single-point estimate (i.e., it is constant regardless of how risky a project is). For purposes of illustration only, beta is used as a measure of risk in this figure, even though the WACC does not consider risk explicitly. Notice that projects B, D, and E would be acceptable, whereas A would be clearly undesirable. Iota would be indifferent to project C.

Project	IRR (%)	Decision
A	10	Reject
B	15	Accept
C	12	Indifferent
D	18	Accept
E	16	Accept

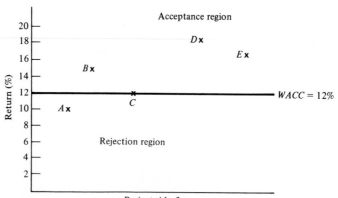

FIGURE 14•4   Using the WACC provides a single risk-adjusted discount rate for all the firm's projects.

Weaknesses of the WACC Approach

The WACC approach suggests that any project with an *IRR* greater than the WACC (i.e., any project that lies above the WACC line) is acceptable. Moreover, risk considerations need not be explicitly recognized. Why? Because the risks of a firm's projects are assumed to be implicitly recognized in the WACC, since the costs (required returns) of debt and equity should reflect these assets' risk; at least, this has been the (erroneous) reasoning.

Therein lies a major conceptual flaw. The WACC only reflects the risk of the firm's existing assets as a whole, and not necessarily that of the project under consideration. Therefore, the WACC is not a useful measure of the *RRR* for each individual project. For the traditional WACC approach to be valid, projects must be exact replicas of the firm's existing assets in terms of risk. In other words, if projects B, D, and E are accepted, we are implicitly assuming that they have the same average risk as the firm. This may or may not be a reasonable assumption.

In most instances, a firm does not necessarily take on only projects that are carbon copies of itself. In fact, as seen in Chapter 13, there is often an incentive to reduce risk by taking on projects with substantially different characteristics from those of the firm in order to benefit from diversification. In such situations, the WACC fails. Stated a bit differently, by using 12% as the discount rate, the company is implicitly requiring all projects to earn at least 12% regardless of their risks. This means that the WACC is company specific, not project specific.

Some other disturbing implications become apparent. The WACC approach implies that all projects should meet the same test to be acceptable. This is unrealistic. A very-low-risk (or risk-free) investment can never be expected to earn the 12% rate if interest rates are much lower. Even more important, the WACC criterion is biased in favor of accepting high-risk projects. The reason, of course, is that high-risk investments tend to have higher expected returns than lower-risk projects. Moreover, a low-risk division within a firm may be unable to get capital even if it can find projects that offer returns in excess of those required for the risk involved. These implications all lead to a lower stock price if the WACC is used.

The WACC can lead to erroneous decisions because it is often inconsistent with the opportunity cost principle.[6] Recall from Chapter 3 that the *RRR* on an investment is measured by the opportunity cost. Consider an example. Assume that the Boeing Corporation is considering a $50 million investment in a medical electronics business. How would this capital budgeting decision be made? The principles developed in Chapters 3, 9, and 13 would require that Boeing assess the risk of this new investment and then estimate the appropriate market-determined discount rate to calculate the project's *NPV*. Notice that this procedure does not involve consideration of the components of Boeing's capital structure

---

[6]It is sometimes erroneously argued that many of the weaknesses of the WACC approach can be overcome by using the *marginal weighted-average cost of capital*. However, even this approach is not entirely consistent with the opportunity cost principle.

or the individual costs of each type of capital. The WACC simply does not enter the picture. The appropriate market-determined *RRR* for this investment should be the same regardless of whether the project is being analyzed by Boeing, Lockheed, Kodak, or Southland Oil.[7]

KEY CONCEPT: Projects should be evaluated on the basis of a market-determined opportunity cost because only then will the accepted projects lead to an increase in firm value.

This observation should come as no surprise to the reader after the extensive discussion in previous chapters on the determinants of market value. Yet this principle is commonly forgotten by decision makers. (See the highlight "A Common Fallacy.")

■ HIGHLIGHT

A COMMON FALLACY

Consider the following scenario, which illustrates a common misconception. John Brenner simply cannot see the logic of his company's financial policies. His company, Grumman Electronics, has both debt and equity in its current capital structure. The board of directors, in its last meeting, has decided that all projects this year will be financed by debt. Grumman can raise debt capital at 8%, and since it is in the 15% tax bracket, its after-tax cost of debt is $8\% \times (1 - 0.15) = 6.8\%$.

Recently, John had brought one of his new inventions to the attention of management and requested funds for product development. In fact, he had calculated the *IRR* for this project to be 9%. He was perplexed that management had turned down his request.

Since the company was to raise debt capital at a cost of only 6.8% and his project would yield 9%, John cannot understand the wisdom of management's decisions. He is convinced that his project, because it offers a 2.2% return in excess of the cost of funds, is a clear winner.

John has fallen prey to a common misconception. He does not recognize that the relevant cost in finance is the *opportunity cost* of capital. By increasing debt, the equity of the firm becomes riskier and investors' *RRR* on equity (and thus the WACC) becomes higher. By focusing only on the cost of debt, the company cannot evaluate the impact of its decision on the wealth of its stockholders. Thus a proper analysis will require an assessment of the risk of John's project and its *RRR*.

Perhaps management has concluded that the returns from the proposed project may have a negative *NPV*.

---

[7]This is not to suggest, however, that all these firms will estimate the same *NPV* for the project.

THE AD HOC APPROACH[8]

The **ad hoc approach** to estimating the risk-adjusted discount rate provides an approximation to the conceptually correct method. It is discussed here only because some financial managers and regulatory agencies still use this approach.[9]

Often, companies have project classifications based on the level of perceived risk. For example, a firm using the ad hoc approach might have three project risk categories:[10]

Risk Category	Subjective Risk Level
1	Low risk (e.g., a cost-savings project)
2	Average risk (e.g., a project to expand current operations)
3	High risk (e.g., a new-product project)

Using this method, management estimates the *RRR* for a project by first classifying the project under one of these categories and then by deciding on an appropriate risk premium for each category. For example:

Risk Category	Risk Premium (%)
1	2
2	5
3	10

The *RRR* for a particular project is estimated by adding the management-determined risk premium to the risk-free interest rate as follows:

$$\underset{\text{(market-determined)}}{RRR} = \text{risk-free rate} + \underset{\text{(management determined)}}{\text{risk premium}} \qquad (14\text{-}1)$$

---

[8] Although there must be several ad hoc methods in use, one method is explained in detail here. The term *ad hoc method* is used in reference to this particular ad hoc procedure.

[9] In terms of evolution, it is interesting that the notion of using an *RRR* was first developed in the 1950s by regulatory agencies in their governing of monopolistic industries such as electric utilities and telephone companies. The law allowed a regulated company to cover its operating costs plus a fair rate of return on its invested capital. Since the objective of regulation is to ensure that the company, as a whole, earns a rate of return just sufficient to compensate investors who provide capital, this fair return came to be defined as a company's WACC. However, as the use of the WACC spread to nonregulated businesses, a major obstacle was encountered. Most utility companies provide a single service, and hence their asset investments are similar in risk characteristics. But this is not the case for the typical nonregulated firm. Therefore, the use of a single *RRR* was jettisoned, and the idea of using risk categories and different risk premiums for the evaluation of investments with different risk characteristics was developed.

[10] Category 2, "average risk," describes asset investments that are similar to or typical of the firm's existing assets.

For instance, if the T-bill rate is 8% and if Iota's project C from the earlier example falls into category 2, this average-risk project would have an *RRR* given by equation (14-1) as

$$RRR = 8\% + 5\% = 13\%$$

Since this project has an *IRR* of 12%, it will have a negative *NPV* with a 13% discount rate. This project should therefore be rejected.[11] To illustrate further, Figure 14•5 presents a graphic contrast of Iota's accept/reject decisions for proj-

Project	Level	RRR (%)	IRR (%)	Decision
A	Low	10	10	Indifferent
B	Low	10	15	Accept
C	Average	13	12	Reject
D	Average	13	18	Accept
E	High	18	16	Reject

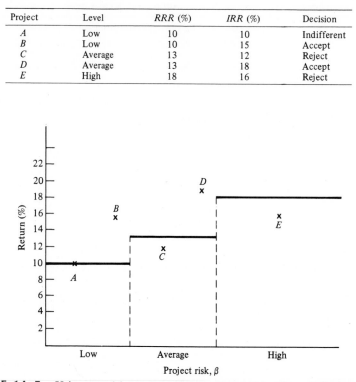

FIGURE 14•5 Using an ad hoc approach to estimate risk-adjusted discount rates for risky projects.

[11] A related ad hoc approach involves adjusting the WACC by subtracting or adding an arbitrary risk premium if a project has a lower or higher risk than the firm's average asset investment. For example, the risk premium adjustments might be:

RISK CATEGORY	RISK LEVEL	RISK PREMIUM (%)
1	Low	−4
2	Average	0
3	High	+6

Thus, if the WACC = 12%, a high-risk project's *RRR* would be 12% + 6% = 18%. Nevertheless, this approach suffers from the same shortcomings as those of the ad hoc method just discussed.

ects A to E with the ad hoc versus WACC methods. In contrast to Figure 14•4, notice that the ad hoc approach results in a stair-step rather than a horizontal *RRR* line. Also, by making an explicit, albeit arbitrary, adjustment for risk, the ad hoc method reverses three of the decisions made with the WACC approach:

1. Project A becomes an indifferent project rather than a rejected one.

2. Projects C and E are now rejected.

Weaknesses of the Ad Hoc Method

Although the ad hoc method described here captures the essential idea behind the *RRR* approach, it has a number of serious shortcomings.

Definition of Risk How does management define risk? Is it total variability (variance) of cash flows? If variance is used to measure risk, this ignores the fact that the opportunity cost (discount rate) does not depend on total variability; only a project's systematic risk is relevant. On the other hand, if management claims that its project categories were somehow based on systematic risk (beta), how were these betas determined?

Arbitrary Risk Adjustment The classification of project categories and their associated risk premiums is purely arbitrary. Why should the risk premium for a category 2 project be 5% instead of 8%? Or is 7% more realistic? No easy answers to such questions exist.

Company-Specific Risk If the *RRR* for a project is set by management, this *RRR* becomes company specific rather than project specific. This, in turn, implies that a project is good, or bad depending solely on management's evaluation of it. That is, its *RRR* is not related to market opportunities and thus is unrelated to the opportunity cost principle.

Inconsistent with Market-Value Maximization Firms using this ad hoc approach may not be maximizing their stock price because their decisions totally ignore the market-determined *RRR*. In the language of Chapter 4, the values calculated using the ad hoc method are personal values, not market values. These two valuations will not necessarily be the same.

Because of these inherent weaknesses, we do not advocate this approach either. Yet the alternatives, although more conceptually sound, are neither simple nor entirely satisfactory. The CAPM, for example, is a more sophisticated approach that can be used to arrive at an estimate of the *RRR* for an investment. Even though the CAPM is derived from some restrictive assumptions, it is still perhaps the most justifiable and operational approach available. Managers who dismiss the CAPM approach on the grounds that it is unrealistic have the responsibility of providing alternative procedures compatible with the concept of market-valuation principles. This, however, may not be easy.

Learning Check for Section 14•2

Review Questions

14•3. Why is the WACC a company-specific rather than a project-specific discount rate?

14•4. "The WACC is often inconsistent with the opportunity cost principle." Explain.

14•5. In what sense is the ad hoc method an improvement over the WACC method?

New Terms

Ad hoc method   Weighted average cost of capital (WACC)

SECTION 14•3 *Using the CAPM to Estimate the RRR for a Risky Project*

The CAPM approach to the determination of an investment's *RRR* follows directly from the development in Chapter 13. Recognize that the CAPM holds for all assets: financial securities and physical assets. Thus the use of the CAPM for the determination of a project's *RRR* follows exactly the same procedure used in Chapter 13 for determining the *RRR* on stocks:

1. The relevant risk of the project (β_{proj}) must be estimated.

2. This β_{proj} must then be substituted into the CAPM equation to estimate its *RRR*.

This is the basic idea involved. After first explaining this idea via an example, we address several issues related to this procedure. The technical aspects of computing beta are fairly advanced and are not covered here; we will simply assume for purposes of this discussion that β_{proj} is known.

Example 14•2 Determining Project Discount Rates for an All-Equity Firm

If the risk-free interest rate is 8%, and $E(\tilde{R}_M)$, the expected rate of return on the market is 12%, the *RRR* on a project whose $\beta_{\text{proj}} = 1.4$ is given by the CAPM as

$$E(R_{\text{proj}}) = R_f + \beta_{\text{proj}}[E(R_m) - R_f] \qquad (14\text{-}2)$$
$$= 0.08 + (1.4)(0.12 - 0.08)$$
$$= 0.08 + 0.056$$
$$= 0.136 \qquad \text{or } 13.6\%$$

The logic of this approach to finding *RRR*s should be clear: For taking 1 unit of market risk (since the beta of the market is 1.0), an investor can expect a risk premium of $[E(R_m) - R_f] = 4\%$. Therefore, for investing in a project with a market risk equal to β_{proj}, the project's risk premium should be $\beta_{\text{proj}}[E(R_m) - R_f] = 1.4 \times 4\% = 5.6\%$. Thus the total *RRR* should be the risk-free interest rate of 8% plus the project's risk premium of 5.6%, or 13.6%.

LEVERAGE AND PROJECT BETA

Example 14•2 implicitly assumed that the project is being evaluated by an all-equity firm. The general procedure is the same if a levered firm—one that uses debt—makes the decision. The beta used, however, must be adjusted for increased risk.

Recall from the discussion in Chapter 8 that a firm faces two kinds of risk. Operating risk reflects the operating leverage of the firm. This operating risk is captured in the project beta used thus far in this section. For a levered firm, there is also financial risk. This risk is reflected in the equity beta (of the firm making the decision), which reflects not only the operating risk of the firm but also its financial risk.

If the project is to be financed with debt, the equity beta is the proper beta to use in determining the appropriate discount rate. The relationship between the project beta and the equity beta for a levered firm is:

$$\beta_E = \beta_{\text{proj}}\left[1 + \frac{D}{E}(1 - T)\right] \qquad (14\text{-}3)$$

where D, E = market values of debt and equity, respectively

T = corporate tax rate

Example 14•3   Determining the Project Discount Rate for a Levered Firm

Consider the situation in Example 14•2, but in this case we are interested in determining the discount rate for a firm that has a mix of debt and equity. The risk-free rate of interest is 8%, the expected return on the market is 12%, and the beta of the project is 1.4. However, we must use equation (14-3) to determine the beta of the asset when the firm adopting it uses both debt and equity. If the firm has \$400,000 in debt and \$600,000 in equity, equation (14-3) gives the beta that reflects the risk of the project and its financing.

$$\beta_E = \beta_{\text{proj}}\left[1 + \frac{D}{E}(1 - T)\right]$$

$$= 1.4\left[1 + \frac{\$400,000}{\$600,000}(1 - .25)\right]$$

$$= 1.4[1.5] = 2.1$$

The reader can readily see that this beta is higher than the one used in Example 14•2. The higher beta reflects the increased risk of the project when it is financed partly by debt.

The final step in determining the discount rate is to insert beta into the CAPM.

$$\begin{aligned}
E(R_{\text{proj}}) &= R_f + \beta_{\text{proj}}[E(R_m) - R_f] \\
&= 0.08 + (2.1)(0.12 - 0.08) \\
&= 0.08 + 0.0840 \\
&= 0.1640 \qquad \text{or } 16.4\%
\end{aligned}$$

The higher beta will cause the discount rate for the project to increase from 13.6% to 16.4%.

Learning Check for Section 14•3

Review Questions

14•6. How does the use of the CAPM for finding discount rates overcome the criticisms implicit in the use of the WACC and ad hoc methods?

14•7. Why is the discount rate for an all-equity firm's projects different from that of a levered firm's projects?

New Term

Project beta

CONCLUDING COMMENTS

Given the market risk of an investment, finding its *RRR* is relatively easy. It is important to bear in mind, however, that the procedures for finding project betas may not be easy or exact. The methodology discussed in this chapter is a theoretically justifiable approximation; the extent to which these procedures are reasonable is not yet known. Although this thought is somewhat disconcerting, the alternative methods of finding a project's *RRR* (the WACC and ad hoc approaches) seem even less desirable.

Many other ad hoc methods commonly used lack the economic rationale implicit in this procedure. In particular, these methods are usually not entirely consistent with the fundamental notion of opportunity costs. Logical shortcomings are much harder to overlook than the potential estimation problems that the procedures suggested in this chapter may cause.

SUMMARY

Assessing the Impact of Uncertain Cash Flows

Any meaningful capital budgeting analysis should address the complications introduced by risk. In this regard, the uncertainty associated with future cash flows can be handled either via sensitivity analysis or by means of more complicated simulation methods. The advantage of explicitly focusing on the uncertainty of cash flows is that the techniques of analysis used can give the analyst very useful information for management strategy. With an idea of potential dangers and strengths, management can take corrective action in many cases. In other instances, the information may result in the company's abandoning a project altogether. Each situation should be handled individually, and it is extremely dangerous to make generalizations regarding how a company should react to its cash flow analysis or to suggest what measures it should then institute. To make these recommendations, familiarity with the company, its market, and its management philosophy is required.

Two Approaches to Estimating the RRR for a Risky Project

An investment's expected benefits should provide some minimum *RRR*. This *RRR* should also reflect the risk of the investment being examined. The WACC and ad hoc approaches do not provide a valid estimate of the *RRR*. The WACC, while popular in the past, reflects the risk of the firm's existing assets, and not necessarily the risk of the project under consideration. The WACC is thus inconsistent with the principle of opportunity costs. The ad hoc method, while attempting to adjust the discount rate to reflect a project's risk, is not a market-based measure of opportunity cost.

Using the CAPM to Estimate the RRR for a Risky Project

The CAPM provides a market-determined *RRR* that is specific to the project being evaluated and not to the firm or individual evaluating it. The relevant risk that must be recognized is the market risk of the investment, as reflected in the asset's beta. Unfortunately, it may not be easy in many instances to estimate this risk measure. The CAPM may be used for an all-equity firm or for a firm that uses debt to finance its projects.

PROBLEMS

14•1. The Yorkshire Shrubbery Company uses the WACC approach for determining the *RRR* for new projects. Yorkshire's financial manager, Steve Smith, has determined that the relevant cost of equity is 18% and the relevant cost of debt is 12%. Further, he wishes to maintain Yorkshire's current mix of 70% equity, 30% debt.
   (a) What is Yorkshire's WACC for the coming year?
   (b) Suppose that next year Yorkshire's relevant cost of equity is 19% and their WACC is 17.5%. If Steve has maintained the same capital structure (70% equity, 30% debt), what must the relevant cost of debt have been?

14•2. The Swamp Kasle Ice Cream Company classifies projects as having one of five possible risk levels (determined by the coefficient of variation of cash flows), and then adds a corresponding risk premium to the T-bill rate to determine an *RRR*. The categories and risk premiums are summarized in the following table:

Risk Class	Coefficient of Variation of Annual Cash Flows	Risk Premium
1	Up to 0.050	0.03
2	0.050–0.299	0.05
3	0.300–0.599	0.07
4	0.600–0.999	0.09
5	1.00 and up	0.12

Swamp Kasle is considering expanding to four locations, with the following expected annual cash flows and standard deviation of cash flow:

462

Location	Initial Outlay	Expected Annual Cash Flow	Standard Deviation
A	$120,000	$30,000	$ 5,000
B	160,000	40,000	10,000
C	240,000	55,000	30,000
D	320,000	75,000	60,000

(a) Suppose that the risk-free rate is 11%. What discount rates should Swamp Kasle use for each of the four possible locations?

(b) Suppose that each of the projects (A, B, C, and D) is a 10-year project. If the projects are independent, which project(s), if any, should they adopt?

(c) Suppose that the projects are mutually exclusive. Which project (if any) should they adopt?

14•3. The Helms Tobacco Company evaluates projects by using a discount rate that is equal to the T-bill rate plus the estimated standard deviation of returns (standard deviation of the *IRR*) of the project. They are evaluating the following 10-year projects:

Project	Initial Outlay	Expected Cash Flow	Expected Salvage Value	Expected Standard Deviation of Returns
W	$150,000	$30,000	$ 20,000	0.04
X	140,000	25,000	75,000	0.06
Y	170,000	35,000	125,000	0.08
Z	230,000	50,000	200,000	0.12

(a) Find the *NPV* of each project if the T-bill rate is 8%. If the projects are independent, which one(s) should they adopt? If the projects are mutually exclusive, which one (if any) should they adopt?

(b) Find the *NPV* of each project if the T-bill rate is 12%. If the projects are independent, which one(s) should they adopt? If the projects are mutually exclusive, which one (if any) should they adopt?

(c) Is the "*NPV*" in part (b) really an *NPV*? Why or why not?

14•4. The Multiple Interests Company (MIC) has a number of investments under consideration. Assuming that MIC will use a mix of $2 million of debt and $8 million of equity to finance these projects, estimate the return that each project would need for acceptance. Assume that the risk-free rate is 7% and the expected market return is 16%.

(a) An insurance company (asset beta of 2.1)

(b) A tobacco plantation (asset beta of 0.75)

(d) A gold mine (asset beta of −0.4)

14•5. The Blow Fast Company has determined that its after-tax costs of equity and debt are 16% and 10%, respectively. Its total capital is $2 million and the firm has $666,667 of equity.
  (a) What is Blow Fast's WACC?
  (b) What would Blow Fast's WACC be if its capital structure contained $1 million in equity?

14•6. Nervus, Inc., is considering two mutually exclusive projects. Their cash flows are as follows:

Cash Flows

Project	0	1	2	3	4	5
X	$-20,000	$7,000	$7,000	$7,000	$7,000	$7,000
Y	$-40,000	$12,000	$12,000	$12,000	$12,000	$12,000

The after-tax returns on Nervus' debt and equity are 8% and 14%, respectively. Nervus has a capital structure of 66.6% debt and 33.3% equity.
  (a) If Nervus used the WACC approach to evaluate its projects, which project would it select?
  (b) Which project would Nervus select if its capital structure contained 80% debt?

14•7. Assume that Nervus, Inc., is faced with the same decision as in problem 14•6, but now has decided to use the CAPM to make its decision. It has determined that the betas of the two projects, X and Y, are 1.5 and 1, respectively.
  (a) If the expected rate of return on the market is 14% and the risk-free rate is 8%, what is the *RRR* on the two projects?
  (b) Which project should Nervus select?

14•8. Big Catch Fisheries is considering investing in the canning industry. It has determined that the average betas of the assets of firms in the canning and fishing industries are 1.2 and 1.4, respectively.
  (a) If the risk-free rate of return is 8% and the expected return on the market portfolio is 12%, what is the *RRR* on Big Catch's investment?
  (b) Big Catch's management estimates that an investment of $6 million can earn it an annual return of $8 million for the indefinite future. Should it invest in the canning industry?

14•9. Consider the situation of Big Catch Fisheries in the previous problem. Big Catch attempted to raise the full amount of capital needed to start its canning factory with equity. It failed. Big Catch's managers have come up with a revised financing plan that would entail raising $3 million in equity and $3 million in debt to finance the venture. Given this new financing plan and the information from the previous problem, should Big Catch invest in the canning industry?

APPENDIX 14•A *Calculating the WACC*

Although the WACC has been discredited as a means of determining the opportunity cost of capital, it is nevertheless of interest to many managers. For a variety of reasons, the WACC has been used widely by corporate managers, regulatory authorities, and investment bankers. Although several managers acknowledge the weaknesses of the WACC, many argue that the theoretically justifiable procedures advanced in the financial literature (the CAPM) are often very difficult to implement. This is compounded by the fact that the theoretical models themselves are the subject of controversy. In addition, even the theoretically defensible procedures for finding opportunity costs yield only estimated values, and these estimates depend crucially on the financial model used.

Because many companies still use the WACC, we believe that the reader should know how it is calculated. It is difficult to sensitize management to problems with the WACC without knowing how it is computed. It is in this spirit that we outline here the various steps involved.

THE NOTION OF A WEIGHTED AVERAGE

Suppose that you wish to calculate the cost per pound to make a recipe for Molina's famous mixed nuts. The recipe calls for 3 pounds of peanuts, 2 pounds of cashews, and 1 pound of brazil nuts. The peanuts cost $1 per pound, the cashews cost $2.50 per pound, and the brazil nuts cost $4 per pound. What is the (weighted) average cost per pound of the mixed nuts?

We begin by adding up the cost of making a batch of mixed nuts. The 3 pounds of peanuts cost a total of $3. The 2 pounds of cashews cost a total of $5, and the 1 pound of brazil nuts costs $4. Thus the total cost is $12. Since the recipe makes a total of 6 pounds of mixed nuts, the price per pound is $2.

Instead of just adding up the cost of the ingredients and dividing by the amount of mixed nuts we get from the recipe, we could use the formula for a weighted average, and calculate the WACMN (the weighted-average cost of mixed nuts). We would have to calculate the proportion (or *weight*) of each ingredient in the mix. The 3 pounds of peanuts account for half of the 6-pound batch of mixed nuts, so the weight for peanuts would be 0.5. Since the 2 pounds of cashews represent one-third of the ingredients, the weight for cashews would be $\frac{1}{3}$, or 0.3333. Finally, the weight for the brazil nuts would be $\frac{1}{6}$, or 0.1667. To calculate the WACMN, we would multiply the price of each ingredient by its weight and sum the results. The WACMN would be computed as follows:

$$(0.5 \times \$1) + (0.3333 \times \$2.50) + (0.1667 \times \$4) = \$2$$

THE WACC

The same procedure can be followed to calculate the weighted average cost of capital instead of mixed nuts. Suppose that the Fleener Corporation raises $10 million in order to start out in business. The first $5 million comes from common equity, which has an estimated cost of capital of 21.7%. Preferred stock, which has an estimated cost of 10.64%, provides $1 million. The remaining $4 million comes from debt, which has an estimated after-tax cost of 9.01%.

To calculate the WACC, we must first determine the weight of each component. Common equity accounts for half of the capital raised, so its weight is 0.5. Preferred stock accounts for one-tenth of the capital, so its weight is 0.1. Debt accounts for four-tenths of the total, so its weight is 0.4. To calculate the WACC, we multiply the weights by the costs and sum, as follows:

$$\text{WACC} = (0.5 \times 21.7\%) + (0.1 \times 10.64\%) + (0.4 \times 9.01\%) = 15.52\%$$

CALCULATING THE COMPONENT COSTS OF CAPITAL

In the previous examples, we took the component costs for retained earnings, new equity, and so on as a given. How did Fleener determine its equity cost of capital to be 21.7? Why are the costs of debt and preferred stock 9.01 and 10.64%, respectively? We will now illustrate the process of calculating the cost of each component of capital. We will examine each component of capital separately because each requires a different procedure for analysis. However, despite the apparent differences, all of these procedures have the same basic foundation. Each procedure requires two basic steps:

Step 1. Examine the terms under which each capital component is raised in order to determine exactly how much the company will receive, how much it will have to pay out, and when. The company's net receipts are the proceeds from the financing.

Step 2. Compute the rate of return being paid by the company on that component. Adjust this pretax cost of the component for taxes (where relevant) to find the after-tax cost of the capital component.

These two steps will now be followed in calculating the cost of each component of capital for Fleener.

Bonds

A company often issues bonds through an investment bank. The investment bank charges its fees, called **flotation costs,** at the time the bonds are issued. To find the net proceeds to a company from an issue of bonds, we subtract the flotation costs from the price of the bonds. To calculate the firm's pretax cost of debt, we use the net proceeds from the bond issue and substitute the proceeds in place of the price in the yield-to-maturity (*YTM*) calculation.

Example 14A·1   Calculating the Cost of Debt

Suppose that the Fleener Corporation issues a new series of coupon bonds with a face value of $1,000, a coupon rate of 10% annually (to be paid in equal semiannual installments), and 20 years to maturity. The investment bank that underwrites (sells) the issue guarantees to sell the bonds at face value and charges a 5% underwriting fee. The underwriting fee amounts to $50 per bond, so that the net proceeds to Fleener are $950 per bond. Fleener will subsequently be obligated to pay the coupon payment of $50 every six months for each bond outstanding, plus $1,000 per outstanding bond to be paid on the maturity date.

If the *YTM* on the bond is *X*%, then *X* is the solution to the following equation:

$$\$950 = \$50(PVFA_{X/2\%,40}) + \$1,000(PVF_{X/2\%,40})$$

Solving this equation, the *YTM* of Fleener's bonds is seen to be 10.60% compounded semiannually. This is Fleener's pretax cost of debt.

All that needs to be done to find the after-tax cost of debt to Fleener is to multiply the pretax cost by 1 minus the tax rate. Suppose that Fleener is in the 15% marginal income tax bracket. Since the before-tax cost of the bonds to Fleener is 10.60%, the after-tax cost of capital for the bonds would be 10.6% × $(1 - 0.15) = 9.01\%$.

Preferred Stock

The valuation of preferred stock was first examined in Chapter 5. In equation (5-4) it was seen that the price of a preferred stock issue is calculated by dividing the preferred dividend by the investors' *RRR* (k_p). Recognize that the investors' *RRR* has to be paid by Fleener. This rate and the additional costs of flotation will determine Fleener's cost of preferred stock.

Example 14A·2   Calculating the Cost of Preferred Stock

Suppose that Fleener issued preferred stock with a par value of $100 per share and a dividend rate of 10%. The investment banker guarantees to sell the stock at par and charges a flotation fee of 6%. Fleener will therefore receive $100 − $6 = $94 per share in proceeds and will be obligated to pay $10 per share in perpetuity.

All we have to do is substitute the $94 proceeds in place of the price of the preferred stock in equation (5-4). The cost of the preferred stock will thus be

$$k_p = \frac{Div}{P(\text{net})} = \frac{\$10}{\$94} = 10.64\%$$

The dividends are not tax deductible and thus a tax adjustment becomes unnecessary.

Retained Earnings[12]

Retained earnings represent funds that could be paid out in dividends to common stockholders and are thus equity funds. WACC calculations therefore apply the cost of equity to retained earnings. The cost of equity in WACC calculations can be estimated using the Gordon model (equation 4-7):

$$k_s = \frac{Div_1}{S_0} + g$$

where k_s = cost of equity capital

Div_1 = dividend expected at the end of time period 1

S_0 = price per share of common stock

g = expected growth rate of dividends for the indefinite future

Example 14A•3 Calculating the Cost of Retained Earnings

Suppose that Fleener's stock is selling for $100 per share and that it just paid a dividend of $10 per share. Furthermore, the expectation is that the dividend will grow at the rate of 10% annually for the indefinite future. Therefore, the expected dividend at the end of the year (next year's dividend, in other words) is $10 × (1 + 0.1) = $11. Substituting this information into the Gordon model provides the following estimate of the cost of retained earnings:

---

[12] Notice that the Fleener Corporation had no retained earnings in the example. Nevertheless, it is important to see how the cost of retained earnings is calculated in order to allow for more general situations.

$$k_s = \frac{\$11}{\$100} + 0.1 = 0.21 \text{ or } 21\%$$

Since dividends are not tax deductible, the cost of capital for retained earnings is 21%. Notice that flotation costs are zero for retained earnings.

New Issues of Common Stock

The difference between using retained earnings and issuing new shares of common stock is that a new issue involves flotation costs. All that needs to be done to adjust the Gordon model for flotation costs is to subtract the flotation costs from the price of the common stock to find the proceeds per share, and substitute the proceeds in place of the price in the calculation.

Example 14A·4   Calculating the Cost of New Common Stock

Suppose that Fleener issued new shares of common stock at the current market value of $100, and that the investment bank charged a flotation fee of 6% per share. The proceeds from the sale would be $100 − $6 = $94, and the cost of the new equity would be

$$k_s = \frac{\$11}{\$94} + 0.1 = 0.217 \text{ or } 21.7\%$$

THE CONCEPT OF INCREMENTAL COST OF CAPITAL

In the previous example, we looked at a company that was just starting out, and calculated the WACC for its total capitalization. More frequently, managers are concerned with the cost of an increment of capital that is being raised to finance a set of projects. The calculation of Zentex, Inc.'s incremental cost of capital will now be illustrated.

Example 14A·5   Incremental Cost of Capital

Suppose that Zentex, Inc., has decided to invest $50 million in new projects this year and intends to raise the money as follows:

$25 million from retained earnings

$10 million from new equity

$15 million from new debt

Assume that the component costs are as follows:

20% for retained earnings

22% for new equity

8% after taxes for debt

Then the WACC for this $50 million increment of capital would be $(0.5 \times 20\%) + (0.2 \times 22\%) + (0.3 \times 8\%) = 16.8\%$.

Of course, the new projects might change the riskiness of an investment in Zentex, Inc., and the new debt and equity would change its capital structure, so we would not really be done with our analysis until we estimated how the implementation of these new projects affects the rate of return the market will require for an equity investment in Zentex. Doing so would lead us to what is called the **marginal cost of capital.** To calculate it, we would have to estimate the riskiness of the projects in which Zentex intends to invest and compute the effect of the new financing on the riskiness of Zentex's stock. That is precisely what we do when we estimate the opportunity cost of capital for a proposal, and that is what the most sophisticated financial managers now use when they evaluate a proposal.[13]

Learning Check for Appendix 14•A

Review Questions

14A•1. Why is the notion of a weighted average appropriate for the WACC?

14A•2. What is the WACC composed of ?

14A•3. Why is the after-tax cost of debt used in the WACC?

14A•4. What is the marginal cost of capital? Why would managers be concerned with determining it?

---

[13] Some authors suggest the use of a different definition of the marginal cost of capital for making investment decisions. Assume that a company is raising only debt capital to finance a new project. Under this alternative definition, the marginal cost of capital would be a firm's WACC, calculated using the cost of new debt as the relevant cost of debt. Unfortunately, this approach ignores the fact that the new project (because of its risk) may alter the cost of all the other components of capital.

New Terms

Flotation costs   Marginal cost of capital

PROBLEMS

14A•1. The Fleener Corporation raised $90 million from a bond issue. The issue of $1,000 face value, 9.5% bonds (semiannual interest payments) maturing in 25 years sold at par, with a 6% flotation fee. Fleener is in the 25% marginal tax bracket. What is the *YTM*, adjusted for flotation costs?

14A•2. Fleener raised an additional $50 million through an issue of $100 par value, 12% preferred stock, which sold for $95 per share, with flotation costs of $5 per share. What was the cost of capital for this issue, adjusted for flotation costs?

14A•3. Fleener is retaining $10 million of earnings this year for reinvestment in the company. This year's dividend is $2 per share, and it is estimated that investors expect a dividend growth rate of 6% for the indefinite future. The stock is now selling for $25 per share. What is the cost of capital for the retained earnings?

14A•4. Fleener is also issuing $50 million of new common stock at a market price of $25 per share. The investment bank that is underwriting the issue is charging a flotation fee of 5%. This year's dividend is $2 per share, and investors expect a dividend growth rate of 6% annually for the indefinite future. After adjusting for flotation costs, calculate the cost of capital for this new issue.

14A•5. Calculate the WACC of the $200 million raised by Fleener from the sources described in Problems 14A•1 to 14A•4.

14A•6. Megalithic Iron Works raised $1 billion of new capital from the following sources. Calculate the WACC for this increment of funding.
$500 million from bonds with an after-tax cost of capital of 7%.
$200 million from an issue of preferred stock, which costs 15%.
$200 million from retained earnings, which costs 20%.
$100 million from new common stock, which costs 21%.

14A•7. The Horizon Products Company raised $2 billion of new capital from the following sources. Calculate the WACC for this increment of funding.

$800 million from bonds with an after-tax cost of capital of 6%.
$400 million from an issue of preferred stock, which costs 14%.
$500 million from retained earnings, which costs 19%.
$300 million from new common stock, which costs 20%.

READINGS

ANG, JAMES S., AND WILBUR G. LEWELLEN, "Risk Adjustment in Capital Investment Project Evaluations," *Financial Management*, Summer 1982, 5–14.

BOWER, RICHARD S., AND JEFFREY M. JENKS, "Divisional Screening Rates," *Financial Management*, Autumn 1975, 42–49.

BRENNAN, M. J., "A New Look at the Weighted-Average Cost of Capital," *Journal of Business Finance*, No. 5, 1973, 24–30.

HERTZ, D. B., "Investment Policies That Pay Off," *Harvard Business Review*, January–February 1968, 96–108.

HERTZ, D. B., "Risk Analysis in Capital Investment," *Harvard Business Review*, January–February 1964, 95–106.

LESSARD, DONALD R., AND RICHARD S. BOWER, "An Operational Approach to Risk Screening," *Journal of Finance*, May 1973, 321–338.

LORIE, J. H., AND R. A. BREALEY, eds., *Modern Developments in Investment Management*, 2nd ed. (New York: Praeger Publishers, 1978).

LORIE, J. H., P. DODD, AND M. H. HAMILTON, *The Stock Market Theories and Evidence*, 2nd ed. (Homewood, Ill.: Richard D. Irwin, Inc., 1983).

MERTON, R. C., "On Estimating the Expected Return on the Market: An Exploratory Investigation," *Journal of Financial Economics*, December 1980, 323–361.

MYERS, STEWART C., "Procedures for Capital Budgeting Under Uncertainty," *Industrial Management Review*, Spring 1968, 1–20.

MYERS, STEWART C., AND SAMUEL M. TURNBULL, "Capital Budgeting and the Capital Asset Pricing Model: Good News and Bad News," *Journal of Finance*, May 1977, 321–333.

SHARPE, W. F., "Capital Asset Prices: A Theory of Market Equilibrium Under Conditions of Risk," *Journal of Finance*, September 1964, 425–442.

STAPLETON, R. C., "Portfolio Analysis, Stock Valuation and Capital Budgeting Decision Rules for Risky Projects," *Journal of Finance*, March 1971, 95–117.

WAGNER, W. H., AND S. C. LAU, "The Effect of Diversification on Risk," *Financial Analysts' Journal*, November–December 1971, 48–53.

PART VI

The Firm's Financing Decisions

15

Capital Structure Theory

All businesses need capital to keep their operations alive. Capital is required to finance investments in inventory, accounts receivables, plant and equipment, and so on. Financial managers must decide how their companies should raise capital. There are various capital sources for a company, for example, short-term bank debt, long-term publicly issued debt, common stock, and preferred stock. For the sake of simplicity, the discussion that follows is confined to two capital components: debt (bonds) and equity (stock).

Most firms rely on both debt and equity capital, and the proportion of each component of capital used by a firm characterizes the firm's capital structure. For example, if a company has $2 million in debt (market value) and $4 million in equity (market value), its capital structure can be characterized by its debt-equity ratio of 0.5 ($2 million/$4 million). A firm that has zero debt in its capital structure is called an **unlevered firm,** and a firm that has debt in its capital structure is called a **levered firm.**

An important decision that a company must make relates to the relative amounts of debt and equity that it should use in its capital structure. That is, in what proportions should the debt and equity be raised? Or, putting it another way, how levered should the firm be? Should a firm raise $0.40 in debt for every dollar in equity? Or would a debt–equity ratio of 30% be better? Is there any rule that the financial manager can follow in determining the optimal debt–equity ratio? Addressing such questions is the main purpose of this chapter.

To come up with an optimal capital structure, it is necessary to focus on the word *optimal*. Optimal in what sense? The answer should be consistent with the goal of the firm developed in Chapter 1. We now state a very important idea:

KEY CONCEPT: The **optimal capital structure** of a firm is the debt–equity ratio that maximizes the value of the firm.

This concept raises some interesting questions. We know from Chapter 1 that a firm's decisions should increase the welfare of its owners. Owners' welfare is maximized when the market value of their stock is maximized. So, why did we not state that the optimal capital structure is the debt–equity ratio that maximizes the value of the firm's equity? What is meant by *firm value*, and why did we define optimality in terms of firm value rather than equity value? In Section 15•1 we provide answers to these questions. In doing so, we show that under certain conditions both definitions of optimality will be equivalent.

To develop a framework for analyzing capital structure decisions, therefore, it is necessary to develop a framework for analyzing the relationship between a firm's debt–equity ratio and its market value. If it can be shown that there is a particular debt–equity ratio that yields the highest firm value, the optimal capital structure problem will have been solved. On the other hand, if there is no direct link between capital structure and firm value, the optimal capital structure is irrelevant and the manager need not worry about how his or her decision will affect the owners of the firm. To establish this link between capital structure and firm value in market-value terms, it is necessary to develop capital structure theories. As will be seen, capital structure is irrelevant under certain conditions (theories) but becomes relevant when certain other considerations are recognized.

It is important to understand the distinction between the subject matter of this chapter, the theory of capital structure, and that of the next chapter, capital structure decision making. By the *theory of capital structure* we mean the study of the relationship between capital structure and the market value of the firm. Such an analysis is useful in that it can provide the manager with guidelines for maximizing the owners' wealth.

As suggested in Chapter 6, in addition to market-value considerations, managers also have to be concerned with book values in day-to-day decision making. Decisions based on market-value considerations alone can be meaningless if day-to-day operations cannot be conducted effectively. For example, suppose that a company finds that a very heavy usage of debt will be in the best interests of the stockholders. It makes sense to raise this additional debt only if the company is confident that its cash flows from operations can pay the interest on this debt periodically. In developing theories of capital structure, several considerations, such as liquidity, financial flexibility, and legal and institutional constraints, cannot be explicitly modeled in a market context. Such qualitative considerations, which many managers recognize in making capital structure decisions, are discussed in Chapter 16. Unlike this chapter, Chapter 16 is not concerned directly with the relationship between capital structure and market values. In this sense, the present chapter may be viewed as a discussion of the conceptual aspects of capital structure, while Chapter 16 considers its operational aspects. The former requires explicit recognition of market-value considerations, while the latter focuses on other qualitative considerations.

This chapter is organized as follows:

SECTION 15•1: *Maximizing Firm Value.* In this section, we examine the notion of *firm value* and explain that firm-value maximization is equivalent to stock price maximization only if increases in firm value do not accrue primarily to bondholders. If this condition is met, an increase in the value of the firm will lead directly to an increase in equity value.

SECTION 15•2: *Capital Structure Irrelevance.* In this section, we examine conditions under which capital structure decisions do not affect firm value. When we assume that the firm is operating in a *perfect* market, one with no taxes or bankruptcy, changes in the firm's capital structure do not affect the firm's cash flows and thus have no effect on firm value. We introduce a concept called *homemade leverage* and conclude the section with an introduction to factors that might affect the firm's value.

SECTION 15•3: *Taxes and Capital Structure.* The impact of corporate and personal taxes on firm value is explored. The concept of a *tax shield* is used to develop the main result: that, with the existence of taxes, the more debt a firm takes on, the greater its value: a firm's optimal capital structure is 100% debt!

SECTION 15•4: *Bankruptcy Considerations.* In this section, bankruptcy and bankruptcy cost considerations are addressed in the context of optimal capital structure. The more debt a firm takes on, the greater the probability it has of going bankrupt. This increased risk of bankruptcy will cause the firm's optimal capital structure to be less than 100% debt.

SECTION 15•5: *Agency Costs.* The notion of *agency costs* is introduced, and its impact on capital structure decisions is outlined. Agency costs, like bankruptcy costs, reduce the amount of debt that a firm will assume. The section concludes with some general comments concerning capital structure theory.

SECTION 15•1 *Maximizing Firm Value*

WHAT IS FIRM VALUE?

KEY CONCEPT: The **value of a firm** is the *market* value of the firm's debt and equity.

In other words, firm value is the *market* value of the right-hand side of the balance sheet. Thus[1]

Firm value = market value of debt + market value of equity

or

$$V = D + E \qquad (15\text{-}1)$$

It is useful to approach capital structure theory from the perspective of firm values instead of stock (equity) values for two reasons:

1. By focusing exclusively on stock values, the role of the bondholders is obscured. By examining firm values, the role of bonds can be brought out more clearly.

2. In the earlier chapters, we made it clear that accepting positive-*NPV* projects will increase the value of the firm and, consequently, the value of the equity (stock). However, there is another condition that must be satisfied for this statement to be valid. To appreciate this, it is necessary to distinguish between firm value and stock value.

The second observation will be dealt with in more detail in the following discussion.

WHEN FIRM-VALUE MAXIMIZATION IS IN THE BEST INTEREST OF STOCKHOLDERS

Consider Ajax Cement, Inc., which has the following market-value balance sheet (in millions of dollars):

Assets = $70 M	Debt = $20 M
	Equity = $50 M
$70 M	$70 M

Since $V = D + E$, as seen earlier, the value of equity may be written as

$$\underset{\text{(value of equity)}}{E} = \underset{\text{(value of firm)}}{V} - \underset{\text{(value of debt)}}{D}$$

[1]Warning: It is tempting to fall into the following trap: "Since the market value of the left-hand side of the balance sheet (assets) must equal the market value of the right-hand side of the balance sheet, the value of the firm is the value of the assets held by the firm." This reasoning is valid only if the firm pays no taxes. As will be seen later in this chapter, the market value of the left-hand side of the balance sheet will not equal that of the right-hand side of the balance sheet when the firm pays taxes.

Assume that Ajax changes its capital structure by issuing $5 million in new debt and uses the proceeds to purchase $5 million of its own shares. Assuming that the new debt has not increased the riskiness of the old bondholders, the total value of the debt will be $25 million ($20 + $5). But what is the value of the equity now? That depends on the new value of the firm. For example:

Market Value of Firm	−	Market Value of Debt	=	Market Value of Equity
$60 million		$25 million		$35 million
$65 million		$25 million		$40 million
$70 million		$25 million		$45 million
$75 million		$25 million		$50 million
$80 million		$25 million		$55 million

Notice that since the value of debt remains constant, any change in firm value affects the shareholders directly.[2] Thus, the greater the value of the firm, the better off stockholders are.

In this example, the risk of debt has not changed. That is why the value of the total debt is $20 + $5 = $25 million. If the new debt increased the risk of the old bonds, however, the value of the old bonds would fall. If the value of the old bonds fell to, say, $18 million, the total debt for Ajax would be worth $18 + $5 = $23 million, and the value of the equity would now be higher for any given value of the assets. With this alteration in capital structure, Ajax's stockholders have gained at the expense of the bondholders. To prevent such adverse effects, bondholders typically insist that certain conditions (called *restrictive covenants*) be agreed upon before the debt is raised. Similarly, if the firm makes any decision that lowers the risk of the bonds, the value of the bonds will rise, as will the value of the firm. In this case, the stockholders will not benefit from an increase in the value of the firm.

The point illustrated here is that maximizing firm value is, in general, optimal for stockholders as long as the increase in the value of the firm does not accrue mostly to the bondholders. This is not to imply that bondholders' wealth should not increase; it only suggests that a larger proportion of the increase in firm value should go to the stockholders. Only if this possibility is precluded can increases in firm value be translated into increases in stock value. Thus the optimal capital structure can be defined as that debt–equity ratio that maximizes the market value of the firm under conditions that preclude a disproportionate increase in the wealth of the bondholders. Since management, working in the interests of the owners, will avoid such **wealth transfers,** it appears justifiable to talk of an optimal capital structure in terms of firm value instead of stock values.

---

[2]We do not consider how these changes in market value come about. Rather, these calculations demonstrate that by holding the value of debt constant, any change in the firm's market value will accrue to equity (the stockholders).

To avoid confusion, it is important to recognize that we are not being inconsistent with our earlier goal of equity-value maximization. We are simply adding to that objective. Since wealth transfers are precluded with appropriate restrictive covenants, equity-value maximization and firm-value maximization are equivalent objectives.

Learning Check for Section 15•1

Review Question

15•1. Under what conditions is firm-value maximization equivalent to stock price maximization?

New Terms

Firm-value maximization	Optimal capital structure	Unlevered firm
Levered firm		Wealth transfers

SECTION 15•2 *Capital Structure Irrelevance*

THE ANALYSIS OF CAPITAL STRUCTURE

Since the market value of an asset depends on its expected return and its market risk (beta), an analysis of the market values of stock, debt, and the firm as a whole can be conducted in the risk-return framework employed in earlier chapters. In addition, using this framework, it is possible to see explicitly how changes in the risk and the expected returns of the firm's assets affect the expected return and risk of the firm's equity. Because many of the analytical details are beyond the scope of this book, we discuss the general issues of capital structure theory and their implications.

We begin the analysis by making some rather restrictive assumptions. In financial analysis, we often begin with an ideal world and examine the actions of the firm and its managers. After drawing conclusions, we add more realistic details (real-world factors) and see how the decisions of the managers are affected. If managerial decisions differ from those made prior to the addition of the factors, we know that the factors are important. This is the approach we will follow in the remainder of this chapter.

The Perfect Capital Markets Assumption

We begin with the assumption of perfect capital markets. This assumption means that there are no imperfections such as taxes, brokerage fees, bankruptcy costs, or other frictions that would affect economic transactions. Is the assumption of no transactions costs reasonable? Although transactions costs are definitely not zero, they can be relatively small for certain market participants. For example, with a large dollar volume of transactions, institutions have surprisingly small transactions costs, and the assumption appears to be reasonable. However, taxes and bankruptcy costs may not be overlooked, and these imperfections are dealt with later in the chapter.

CAPITAL STRUCTURE IRRELEVANCE

The value of the firm is determined by its cash flows. These cash flows are themselves a product of the productive assets of the firm. To change the value of the firm, we must change the magnitude or the risk of the firm's cash flows. Using the CAPM in a world characterized by the preceding assumptions, it can be shown that the expected return on the assets of the firm is not changed by introducing debt into the capital structure of the firm. Using debt in the capital structure may produce leverage effects that increase the return to the equity holders, but it will also increase their risk. More important, the expected return on the assets of the firm is not changed by introducing debt into the capital structure. Since the operating cash flows are not changed and the return on the firm's assets remains unchanged, the value of the firm will not be affected.

KEY CONCEPT: If changes in capital structure do not affect a firm's operating cash flows, the amount of debt used by the firm has no impact on firm value.

Since the debt–equity ratio has no effect on firm value, it follows that capital structure is irrelevant in this framework. The irrelevancy argument was first expounded by Modigliani and Miller, and this result is known as the **M&M hypothesis.**[3]

AN INTUITIVE EXPLANATION FOR CAPITAL STRUCTURE IRRELEVANCE

This irrelevance result can be seen more directly using the concepts in Chapter 3. The value of any asset is the present value (*PV*) of the cash flows generated by the asset discounted at the appropriate *RRR*. The value of a firm's assets should therefore be the cash flows generated by the assets (operating cash flows) discounted at the *RRR* for those assets. Since the debt–equity ratio does not affect either the operating cash flows or the *RRR* for those assets, the value

---

[3]Franco Modigliani and Merton Miller published an article, "The Cost of Capital, Corporation Finance and the Theory of Investment," which contained this result. This article is considered one of the seminal works in modern financial theory.

of the assets should be unaffected by changes in debt. If the value of the firm's assets is unaffected, the value of the firm is unaffected.

Another way to understand this result is to recognize that individuals and businesses invest in companies only because the companies provide risk-return possibilities that they cannot find elsewhere. Given our perfect market assumptions, by altering the capital structure the firm does not do anything for investors that they could not have done themselves. An investor who borrows money and buys the stock of an unlevered firm can, in effect, replicate the leverage of the firm. As long as the assumptions are met, this **homemade leverage** is a perfect substitute for firm leverage and the firm has created nothing new for the investor by borrowing. Therefore, the market will attach no additional value to leverage.

However, it is important to understand precisely the context in which this irrelevance result holds. To do this, it is necessary to examine briefly the assumptions that are crucial for this framework.

A CLOSER LOOK AT THE M&M HYPOTHESIS

Homemade Leverage

In the M&M analysis, **homemade leverage** and corporate leverage are perfect substitutes. That is, it is assumed that investors can borrow on their own account what the corporation can, and on the same terms. The first question that arises is whether an individual can, in fact, borrow on the same terms as a corporation. Should not corporations be able to borrow money at a lower rate than that for individuals? The evidence is not clear. It appears that corporate borrowing is not very different from individual borrowing.[4]

Another difference between homemade leverage and corporate leverage relates to limited liability. When a corporation borrows money, it borrows with limited liability. If the borrowing corporation goes broke, the investors' losses are limited to the value of their stock. On the other hand, when individuals take out a loan and default, their personal assets can be seized to pay off the loan. In addition, individuals borrowing from their stock broker on margin are subject to margin calls. Thus it appears that homemade leverage is much riskier than corporate leverage and that borrowing by corporations must have some special value. This argument also seems to invalidate the M&M proposition. However, why should we restrict homemade leverage to individuals? Other corporations and financial institutions with limited liability can engage in this process, and the capital structure irrelevance result should hold. There is nothing sacrosanct

---

[4]High-grade corporate debt carries interest rates very close to those of home mortgages. Also, the rates banks pay on term loans (short-term bank debt) are very close to the rates that individuals pay on margin debt (the debt investors incur when they borrow from a stockholder, with securities as collateral). In addition, institutional investors may be able to borrow at the same rate as the corporation in question.

in the example provided earlier about individuals engaging in homemade leverage. The "individual" could just as well have been another company, and the M&M result would have survived this criticism.

Institutional Restrictions

Another factor that can reduce the effectiveness of the M&M argument is institutional restrictions. We have argued that institutions, and not necessarily individuals, can engage in homemade leverage. But what if institutional restrictions forbid institutions from engaging in such transactions? Life insurance companies and many pension funds, for example, are not allowed to engage in certain transactions. However, this does not really affect the M&M result. As long as there are some individuals or institutions that can engage in homemade leverage, the M&M theory cannot be dismissed altogether, at least on this count. Capital structure does not affect firm value.

Thus the M&M irrelevance proposition appears to be far more robust than it appears at first glance. It is extremely general and argues that both the composition (the proportion of debt, equity, and other instruments) and the structure (long-term or short-term debt, common or preferred stock, class A or class B stock, etc.) of the right-hand side of the balance sheet are immaterial. What matters is the value of the assets of the firm. That is the only truly productive component of a firm's possessions. The financial instruments issued by the firm do not affect the firm's productivity and thereby its value.

WHEN DO CAPITAL STRUCTURE DECISIONS AFFECT FIRM VALUE?

As just seen, the M&M proposition implies that managers really do not need to worry about capital structure in perfect markets and, in many instances, even when the perfect market assumptions do not strictly hold. The more severe the imperfections (the more restrictive real-world considerations) are, the stronger the case for the relevance of the financing decision. Generalizations, though, can be extremely difficult. Only a case-by-case analysis can determine the role of capital structure under nonmarket (institutional) conditions.

One generalization can be made, however. As long as capital structure decisions intended to benefit security holders can be replicated by investors, these decisions provide nothing new and thus should provide no new value. If, however, a financing decision can offer something new or valuable that is not available to investors elsewhere, capital structure will be relevant. For example, if the financial manager can identify the needs of a particular type of investor (e.g., a high-tax-bracket investor) and offer a new security that he or she desires but cannot find elsewhere, this security, when added to the firm's capital structure, will affect the firm's value if it is issued. Nevertheless, given the myriad securities available in the marketplace, the creation and issuance of a new type of security, although not impossible, may not be easy. As will be seen, when corporate taxes are recognized, the firm can provide a risk-return possibility that investors cannot find on their own.

Learning Check for Section 15•2

Review Questions

15•2. Capital structure is irrelevant when a firm's operating cash flows are unaffected by changes in the firm's debt level. Why? What does *irrelevant* mean in this context?

15•3. What are the assumptions underlying the M&M hypothesis? Why is it not easy to dismiss them as being unrealistic?

New Terms

Capital structure   Homemade   M&M hypothesis
  irrelevance   leverage   Perfect capital markets

SECTION 15•3   *Taxes and Capital Structure*

What happens to the M&M argument if one imperfection, corporate taxes, is introduced? Is capital structure still irrelevant? Surprisingly, the recognition of corporate taxes implies that a firm should be totally debt financed. The reason is that debt provides valuable **tax shields.**

To understand what these tax shields are, consider two firms with identical operating incomes but different capital structures. Table 15•1 shows that the unlevered firm has $65,000 in equity, while the levered firm has $40,000 in equity and $25,000 in debt with a coupon interest rate of 8%. Assuming a 25% marginal tax rate, notice that the total income available to security holders in firm L is higher than that of firm U by $500.

The reason for this is that interest expenses are tax deductible, which lowers the levered firm's taxable income and, consequently, its taxes. Debt-financed firms are, in effect, "subsidized" by the federal government because the levered firm pays lower taxes than the unlevered firm. In effect, the government is picking up the $500 of interest payments, which is as if the levered firm has received a "bonus" of $500. This bonus is called a *tax shield* and is computed as

$$\text{Tax shield} = T \times I$$

where T is the corporation's tax rate and I is the dollar amount in interest paid by the firm. In the case of the levered company, L:

TABLE 15·1 Income Available to Stockholders and Bondholders with Different Capital Structures

	Firm *U* (Unlevered)	Firm *L* (Levered)
Capital Structure (Market Values)		
Debt (8%)	$ 0	$25,000
Equity	65,000	40,000
Total	$65,000	$65,000
Income Statement		
Net operating income	$ 5,000	$ 5,000
Less: Interest (8%)		2,000
Taxable income	$ 5,000	$ 3,000
Less: Taxes (25%)	1,250	750
Net income	$ 3,750	$ 2,250
Income to Security Holders		
Income to		
Bondholders (interest)	$ 0	$ 2,000
Stockholders (net income)	3,750	2,250
Total income to bondholders and stockholders	$ 3,750	$ 4,250

$$\text{Tax shield} = 0.25 \times \$2{,}000 = \$500$$

Notice from Table 15·1 that the difference in total income to bondholders and stockholders is greater for the levered firm by an amount exactly equal to the tax shield. Thus, because of taxes, it is as if every time an investment is financed with debt, the government is "throwing in" another project with a cash saving equal to the tax shield. Since this "project" generates savings, it is valuable. Tax shields should therefore increase firm value, and this increase in value should eventually accrue to the stockholders. If a levered firm can generate tax shields into the future, the value of these tax shields is given by their discounted values (present values). Consider the balance sheets (market values) of the levered and unlevered companies.

Unlevered Firm				**Levered Firm without Taxes**			
Assets	$65,000	Equity	$65,000	Assets	$65,000	Equity	$40,000
		Debt	0			Debt	25,000

Levered Firm with Corporate Taxes			
Assets	$65,000 + *PV* of tax shields	Equity	$40,000 + *PV* of tax shields
		Debt	$25,000

Recognize the following from these balance sheets:

KEY CONCEPT: Because of corporate taxes, the value of a levered firm is greater than the value of an unlevered firm by the present value of the tax shields.[5]

$$\begin{matrix} \text{Value of} \\ \text{levered firm} \end{matrix} = \begin{matrix} \text{Value of} \\ \text{unlevered firm} \end{matrix} + \begin{matrix} \text{Present value of} \\ \text{tax shields} \end{matrix} \qquad (15\text{-}2)$$

To calculate the increase in firm value, one must calculate the *PV* value of these tax shields. The interest payments that a firm makes are fairly predictable. It also appears reasonable to assume that the tax rate does not change much from period to period or year to year. Thus the magnitude of the tax shields becomes fairly predictable. However, to find their *PV*, these tax shields must be discounted at the appropriate discount rate. What is the appropriate market-determined discount rate that must be applied? The answer depends on the riskiness of these projected tax shields. Although this may not be easy to determine precisely, as a practical matter, tax shields are about as risky as the debt that the firm has issued, so that the appropriate discount rate is the *RRR* on debt. The process of valuing the tax shields along these lines will now be demonstrated.

Example 15•1 Calculating the Value of the Tax Shields

Assume that the Goodfly Corporation has $500,000 in debt, with a 10% coupon rate. If the debt matures in four years and debt holders *RRR* is 12%, what is the *PV* of the tax shields if the company is in the 25% tax bracket?

$$\begin{aligned} PV \text{ (tax shields)} &= PV(T \times I) \\ &= (0.25 \times 0.10 \times \$500{,}000)(PVFA_{.12,4}) \\ &= (0.25 \times 0.10 \times \$500{,}000)(3.0373) \\ &= \$37{,}966 \end{aligned}$$

That is, Goodfly's value is $37,966 higher than that of a comparable unlevered firm.

---

[5]Notice that equation (15-2) implies that with taxes, the market value of the right-hand side of the balance sheet will be greater than the market value of the left-hand side of the balance sheet. In other words, the value of the firm's securities will exceed the total value of the firm's assets.

PERMANENT DEBT: A SPECIAL CASE

The calculation of the *PV* of tax shields becomes easier when permanent debt is assumed. When debt matures, if the firm refinances the debt and continues to "roll it over" on the same terms, the tax shields become a perpetual benefit. The value of this **perpetual tax shield** can be calculated by multiplying the amount of interest by the tax rate to determine the tax shield for a single period and then, using the procedures from Chapter 2 for a perpetuity, dividing this single-period amount by the *RRR* on debt.

$$PV = \frac{T \times I}{RRR}$$

This formula may be simplified to give the *PV* of the tax shield of perpetual debt.

$$\text{Value of perpetual tax shield} = T \times D \qquad (15\text{-}3)$$

where $D = I/(RRR$ on debt) is the market value of the debt. Thus:

KEY CONCEPT: With permanent debt, corporate taxes will imply that:

$$
\begin{array}{ccccc}
\text{Value of} & = & \text{Value of} & + & \text{Value of} \\
\text{levered firm} & & \text{unlevered firm} & & \text{tax shield} \\
D + E & = & A & + & TD
\end{array}
\qquad (15\text{-}4)
$$

where *A*, the market value of the unlevered firm's assets, equals the market value of the unlevered firm's assets.

Equation (15-4) is M&M's original proposition adjusted for corporate taxes. It states that a firm with debt is more valuable than a similar firm with no debt. Referring to Figure 15•1, a levered firm and an unlevered firm can have equal values only when either (1) $D = 0$, or (2) the corporate tax rate is zero.

THE OPTIMAL CAPITAL STRUCTURE WITH CORPORATE TAXES

Examine Figure 15•1, which depicts the relationship between the value of a firm and the debt–equity ratio. This figure is bothersome because it implies that a firm can increase its value simply by increasing its debt–equity ratio. The maximum value of the firm occurs when the firm is entirely debt financed. That is, with corporate taxes, the optimal capital structure consists of 100% debt. But this is a meaningless conclusion. What is the practical significance of 100% debt financing? When all of the capital is raised via debt, the debt holders become the owners of the firm and the situation reverts to a 100% equity situation! Thus this situation is not possible, even in theory.

The capital structures of U.S. corporations show that all corporations have some amount of equity. Since the M&M result is logically consistent, the only explanation for this bizarre implication that 100% debt is optimal must be that some other factors, not yet considered, must restrain firms from moving toward a 100% debt structure. For example, we have ignored an analysis of what happens to the firm that engages in such heavy borrowing. Perhaps the default risk increases, and the firm becomes vulnerable to bankruptcy and its associated costs. If this conjecture is true, the expected bankruptcy costs should offset the benefits from increased tax shields.

Learning Check for Section 15•3

Review Questions

15•4. With corporate taxes, the market value of a levered firm will exceed the market value of a similar but unlevered firm. Why?

15•5. How is the value of tax shields measured?

15•7. What is the optimal capital structure implied by corporate tax considerations? How do personal taxes affect this result?

New Terms

Perpetual tax shield   Tax shield

SECTION 15•4 *Bankruptcy Considerations*

As the amount of debt increases, the probability that the firm will be unable to meet its financial obligations also increases. If this situation worsens, **financial distress** may result. For instance, the firm may be unable to pay dividends to preferred stockholders, suppliers or banks may stop extending credit, and so on.[6] Such restrictions ultimately may or may not have any effect on the firm. If this state of affairs continues over an extended period, the firm may be forced to forgo attractive investment opportunities, thereby adversely affecting its profitability. At an extreme, financial distress may lead to **bankruptcy.** The highlight "Bankruptcy" contains a brief discussion of the various types of bankruptcy.

---

[6]In some instances, financial distress is defined to include only the situation where the firm fails to meet its contractual obligations.

■ *HIGHLIGHT*

BANKRUPTCY

A capitalist society is characterized by the freedom to create profit-seeking businesses. However, this freedom to pursue profit is accompanied by the freedom to fail. When a corporation is not able to meet its obligations, informal agreements may be worked out with its creditors to allow the firm to regroup its resources and attempt a comeback. If the firm cannot reach a voluntary agreement with its creditors, legal procedures exist to settle the firms accounts and either liquidate its assets or formally reorganize the firm and allow it to continue operations.

The federal government has special bankruptcy courts, with judges who preside over only bankruptcy cases, in every federal judiciary district. These courts enforce the federal bankruptcy laws, which were primarily created by the Bankruptcy Acts of 1898 and 1978. While these laws have many provisions, there are two main parts that affect businesses.

Chapter 7: Liquidation

If there is no practical way for the firm to recover, it may file for Chapter 7 bankruptcy. Under the provisions of this chapter of the bankruptcy code, the court will appoint, with the consent of the creditors, a trustee who will work to liquidate the assets of the firm and pay off the creditors. How much a creditor is paid will depend on the type of claim the creditor has, whether he has a claim, or lien, against specific assets of the firm and the liquidation value of these assets.

Chapter 11: Reorganization

In some cases, the best course of action for the firm and its creditors may be to reorganize the firm rather than liquidate it. The firm is placed under the protection of the bankruptcy court, and one or more plans of reorganization are filed. Plans of reorganization may be filed by the firm or by one or more of the creditors. The plans are submitted to the court, which will judge if they are fair, equitable to all concerned, and feasible. The creditors and stockholders then vote on the plans. The court will confirm the plan approved by the claim holders of the firm or, if the claim holders cannot agree on an acceptable plan, confirm what it feels to be the best plan. All claim holders, including those who did not vote for the plan, are then bound by the plan.

Even before bankruptcy occurs, however, financial distress costs can begin to mount. Nevertheless, the tax advantages of tax shields may outweigh these costs, making debt still an attractive source of funds. However, when the firm is declared bankrupt, the picture changes drastically.

In bankruptcy, stockholders, in effect, elect to surrender the firm's assets to the creditors. Stockholders can simply walk away, letting the creditors fight over the remains. Stockholders will do this only if the value of the firm's assets is below the value of the bondholders' claims. Thus, with bankruptcy possible, bondholders are always taking the risk of getting back less than what is due to them. To make matters worse, bankruptcy costs, such as lawyers' and accountants' fees or reorganization costs, can jeopardize the bondholders' position even further. Thus two interesting questions arise:

1. Does the threat of costly bankruptcy affect firm value?

2. Are bankruptcy costs significant, or can they safely be ignored?

Each of these questions will be addressed separately in examining whether or not firm value is affected by capital structure considerations.

DOES THE THREAT OF COSTLY BANKRUPTCY AFFECT FIRM VALUE?

To focus only on the influence of bankruptcy, assume initially that corporate and personal tax rates are again zero. If creditors face the possibility of not recovering their total claims as the debt-equity ratio increases, it appears that firm value should depend on the probability of bankruptcy. As it turns out, the threat of **costless bankruptcy** alters the value of the firm's debt and equity, but the value of the firm as a whole is unchanged. However, this result does not follow for **costly bankruptcy.**

As a practical matter, bankruptcy has two costs: direct and indirect. Direct costs include legal and accounting fees, reorganization costs, and other administrative expenses. Indirect costs are less tangible. For instance, in dealing with bankruptcy (even imminent bankruptcy), management's efforts and resources are diverted from maximizing firm value to halting a deteriorating situation.[7] How much these indirect costs affect firm values is not clear, but both direct and indirect bankruptcy costs will affect the returns to security holders if a firm is in default. We will now state an important result:

KEY CONCEPT: With **costly bankruptcy,** a levered firm's value is lower by the *PV* of expected bankruptcy costs.

That is, equation (15-4) becomes

$$\begin{pmatrix} \text{Market value} \\ \text{of} \\ \text{levered firm} \end{pmatrix} = \begin{pmatrix} \text{Market value} \\ \text{of} \\ \text{unlevered firm} \end{pmatrix} + \begin{pmatrix} \text{Present value} \\ \text{of} \\ \text{tax shields} \end{pmatrix} - \begin{pmatrix} \text{Present value} \\ \text{of} \\ \text{bankruptcy costs} \end{pmatrix}$$

$$V_L = V_U + TD - PV(c)$$

(15-5)

where c is the expected bankruptcy costs.

---

[7] For example, Chrysler Corporation's near bankruptcy caused management to devote a great deal of time and expense to rebuilding the public's confidence in its ability to continue operations. Other examples of indirect but difficult to measure costs are lost sales, lost profits, higher costs of credit, and the inability to invest in profitable opportunities because external financing sources are unavailable.

Now take Figure 15•1 and modify it for the presence of bankruptcy costs in order to illustrate the joint effect of corporate taxes and costly bankruptcy on firm value. In Figure 15•2, line I is the original case, in which the levered and unlevered firms' values are equal under a perfect market setting. Line II represents the case of M&M with corporate taxes wherein firm value increases with the D/E ratio until a maximum is reached at 100% debt. In contrast, line III indicates that with costly bankruptcy, firm value increases initially, reaches a maximum, and then decreases with leverage. In other words, at low levels of debt, the probability of bankruptcy is very low and firm value will increase with leverage because the tax advantages of debt will predominate. After a reasonable amount of debt is incurred, though, the probability of bankruptcy, and hence the present value of expected bankruptcy costs, become significant. Even though the tax shield benefits continue to increase with relatively more debt, the presence of bankruptcy costs begins to affect firm value adversely. This trade-off between the potential benefits and the associated disadvantages of increased debt will result in an optimal debt-equity ratio. At this unique point, firm value is maximized (i.e., there is an optimal capital structure), and we have made the first clear-cut case for capital structure relevancy for an individual firm.

ARE BANKRUPTCY COSTS SIGNIFICANT?

What if bankruptcy costs are so small or insignificant that they can be ignored? Our exercise in search of an optimal capital structure will have been in vain. If the *PV* of expected bankruptcy costs is zero (or immaterial), equation (15-5) reduces to the M&M proposition with corporate taxes, and 100% debt would be optimal.

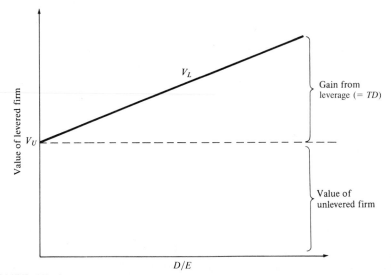

FIGURE 15•1 Value of the firm as the debt–equity ratio changes.

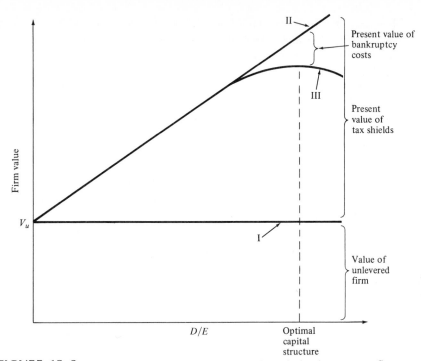

FIGURE 15·2   Joint effect of corporate taxes and costly bankruptcy on firm value. I, capital structure decisions in perfect markets (M&M proposition without taxes): capital structure is irrelevant; II, capital structure decisions with corporate taxes (M&M proposition with taxes): optimal capital structure is 100% debt financing; III, capital structure decisions with both corporate taxes and costly bankruptcy: optimal capital structure is between zero and 100% debt financing.

In a study of 11 railroad bankruptcies, Jerold Warner attempted to measure the magnitude of bankruptcy costs. He found that direct costs were small, ranging from about 1 to 5% of the firms' market values up to seven years prior to and just before bankruptcy.[8] Moreover, there were "economies of scale" in going bankrupt; as a percentage of firm value, bankruptcy costs were smaller for larger firms than for smaller firms. This implies that the capital structure decisions of smaller firms should be more strongly influenced by bankruptcy considerations than the decisions of larger firms.

Warner's study indicated that bankruptcy costs were trivial. However, it must be noted that indirect costs were not included. Using a measure of both direct and indirect bankruptcy costs, Edward Altman found that for 19 bankrupt industrial firms, the *PV*s of bankruptcy costs were not trivial, ranging from 11 to 17% of firm value up to three years prior to bankruptcy.[9] In fact, he found

---

[8]Jerold B. Warner, "Bankruptcy Costs: Some Evidence," *Journal of Finance*, May 1977, 337–348. Since railroad bankruptcies are invariably reorganizations, one must expect a downward bias in these estimates of bankruptcy costs.

[9]Edward I. Altman, "A Further Investigation of the Bankruptcy Cost Question," *Journal of Finance*, September 1984, 1067–1089.

that the *PV* of bankruptcy costs often exceeded the *PV* of the tax benefits from leverage, implying that firms were overleveraged.

Some researchers have provided very persuasive theoretical arguments to suggest why bankruptcy cost considerations should be entirely irrelevant in determining firm value. According to this line of reasoning, these costs are of no concern to anyone other than the firm's stockholders and bondholders. Bankruptcy costs have no bearing on the relationships between the firm and its suppliers, the firm and its customers, and so on. The presence of bankruptcy costs will affect only the relative values of equity and debt, not the firm as a whole.

So, what is the final word on the magnitude of bankruptcy costs? We do not know for sure. We must wait for the results of further studies before we can provide a definitive answer.

Learning Check for Section 15•4

Review Questions

15•8. Why is costless bankruptcy irrelevant in determining firm value? What if bankruptcy becomes costly? Why?

15•9. What are the direct and indirect costs of bankruptcy? Are these costs significant?

New Terms

Bankruptcy	Costly bankruptcy	Liquidation
Costless bankruptcy	Financial distress	Reorganization

SECTION 15•5 *Agency Costs*

In Chapter 1 we saw that in a corporation the managers and owners may not be the same. Managers, elected by a firm's owners, are expected to act in the best interest of the owners. In this sense, managers may be viewed as agents for the owners. The question that arises is this: Does this *agency relationship* really work? That is, do managers really make decisions based solely on the impact they will have on the owners, or do they also let personal considerations influence them? For example, will they give themselves excessively high salaries and perquisites? Will they hide information from the owners so that their own jobs are not threatened? (See the highlight "Unocal versus Mesa Petroleum: Capital Structure Theory in Action" for another perspective on managerial inefficiencies.) These and other situations in which there is a potential for managers to make decisions that are not in the owners' best interests result in **agency costs.**

■ *HIGHLIGHT*

UNOCAL VERSUS MESA PETROLEUM: CAPITAL STRUCTURE THEORY IN ACTION

Union Oil Company of California's (Unocal) management erected an interesting defense against the company's attempted takeover by Boone Pickens of Mesa Petroleum in 1985. One of Unocal's tactics was to sue Mesa for attempting to "monopolize the U.S. petroleum industry." Their argument was not that Mesa possessed predominant economic powers (Mesa's share of the U.S. petroleum market is in the neighborhood of 1%) but rather that Mesa engaged in "dirty tricks" in attempting to cripple major competitors within the industry. The alleged dirty tricks consisted of attempting to saddle objects of takeover with onerous levels of debt.

Since most takeover attempts are funded by debt rather than equity, it is true that "takeover artists" increase the ratios of debt financing in firms that are successfully acquired. Is there a basis in financial theory for higher debt levels to have pernicious effects on the firm? We know that higher debt levels increase the financial risk of the firm.

Stephen P. Magee, professor of finance at the University of Texas, testified on behalf of Mesa Petroleum in the case.* He pointed out that any increase in the risk of the firm due to the additional debt would be compensated for by the greater expected returns to both stockholders and bondholders. In other words, he used the familiar M&M argument that greater debt levels should have no effect on firm value in a perfect market (no taxes). Second, Magee argued that with corporate taxes, firm value would, in fact, have the advantage of corporate tax shields and that as long as debt was not excessive, this would lower the cost of capital to the firm. In Unocal's case, he argued that since Unocal's debt–equity ratio was below the industry mean, there was no basis for concluding that the debt was excessive.

Magee then went on to argue that in industries suffering from poor profitability (such as the oil industry in the 1980s), the competition for managerial jobs increases and managers must attempt to economize all inputs. Increased competition for managerial jobs is reflected in the increase in takeover activity as weak/inefficient managers are replaced by stronger ones.

Thus, in addition to arguing that debt can, up to a point, increase firm value, Magee suggested that theoretically, takeovers may increase firm value by weeding out another market imperfection—the costs arising out of managerial inefficiencies.

*Unocal vs. Mesa Petroleum, Civil Action No: 85-1004, Pretrial Hearing, U.S. District Court, Lafayette, La., April 30, 1985. (The judge ruled in favor of Mesa.)

Agency costs also arise with the use of debt in the firm's capital structure. When a firm uses debt, the potential for conflict between the stockholders and bondholders creates agency costs. Acting in the interests of stockholders, management may take on very risky projects or make other decisions that can hurt bondholders. To minimize this potential for conflict, bondholders and stockholders usually insist on several measures (restrictive covenants) to monitor and control the firm's activities. These measures are costly because the presence of the agency costs will affect the value of the firm adversely. That is, firm value decreases with agency costs.

While a firm's tax shield increases with debt, the default (bankruptcy) probability also increases, as do the monitoring costs. Thus it may not be optimal for a firm to continue borrowing beyond some point. In other words, monitoring costs in the form of higher interest charged by bondholders may dictate an optimal debt–equity ratio. Figure 15•3 depicts this effect on firm value in conjunction with corporate taxes and bankruptcy costs. Notice that monitoring costs will cause the optimal capital structure to occur at a debt–equity ratio somewhat less than that which occurs with corporate taxes and bankruptcy costs alone.

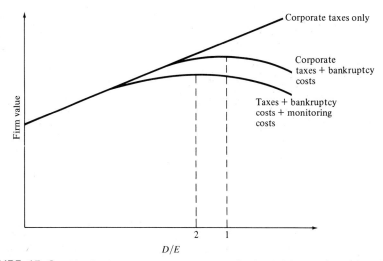

FIGURE 15•3   Monitoring and agency costs. 1, Optimal debt–equity ratio with taxes and bankruptcy costs; 2, optimal debt–equity ratio with taxes, bankruptcy, and monitoring costs.

Learning Check for Section 15•5

Review Question

15•10.   Explain the notion of agency costs. What impact do agency costs have on the optimal capital structure of the firm?

New Term

Agency costs

496

SOME CONCLUDING COMMENTS

It should be clear to the reader that the optimal capital structure issue is far from resolved. The nature of the relationship between the debt–equity ratio and the value of the firm is still not fully known. However, one directive for decision makers emerges clearly: in making capital structure decisions, management must keep in mind that the best way to make such decisions is to focus on firm-value considerations instead of other criteria, such as earnings maximization. This observation, coupled with a knowledge of the potential for agency costs, can help management take a more educated approach when making capital structure decisions. As we have seen, in spite of the tax advantages of debt financing, it may not be in the firm's best interests to borrow excessively. Of course, at this level of generality, it is impossible to define *excessive*. The manager of a company must make this decision based on a strong understanding of the company itself and the theoretical arguments advanced in this chapter.

In spite of the detailed examination of capital structure issues, the discussion in this chapter has completely ignored several practical considerations that managers must recognize in deciding on the appropriate level of debt. In addressing these practical issues, managers may not always be able to make capital structure decisions in a firm-value-maximizing framework. Some of the practical aspects of capital structure decisions are addressed in Chapter 16.

SUMMARY

Maximizing Firm Value

The value of a firm is the market value of the securities held by a firm. In making decisions in the interests of the owners, managers must bear in mind their objective of maximizing shareholder wealth. If adequate protection exists to prevent increases in firm value from accruing to bondholders, then maximizing firm value and maximizing owners' wealth are equivalent.

Capital Structure Irrelevance

As long as a firm's operating cash flows are unaffected by the amount of debt used by the firm, capital structure has no influence on firm value and thus the issue of an optimal capital structure is irrelevant. In markets without taxes, transactions costs, and other imperfections, this result holds. As long as investors can replicate by themselves what the firm proposes to achieve by changing its capital structure, these changes will not affect the market value of the firm.

Taxes and Capital Structure

When corporate taxes are recognized, however, investors cannot replicate what firms can do for them, and the amount of debt held by the firm affects market value. In fact, the optimal amount of debt becomes 100%. In reality, however, firms are not (and cannot be) 100% debt financed, so we must look for additional factors that explain the capital structures of American companies.

Bankruptcy Considerations

The potential for costly bankruptcy has a negative effect on firm value. As debt increases, the increase in firm value because of increasing tax shields must be weighed against the increasing present value of expected bankruptcy costs. In this framework, an optimal capital structure will exist, although it is not easy to characterize the optimal debt–equity ratio. However, several studies seem to indicate that the magnitude of bankruptcy costs is very small, thereby limiting the significance of an optimal debt–equity ratio.

Agency Costs

Agency costs can exist because of the potential for managers guided by their own interests to make decisions that are not necessarily in the best interests of the stockholders. Another source of agency costs is the potential conflicts that can arise between bondholders and stockholders. To protect themselves, bond-holders and stockholders insist on restrictive covenants in their lending agreements. However, since these covenants cannot protect bondholders from every possible management decision, bondholders must monitor the firm, and these agency costs are reflected in higher required rates of return to bondholders as the firm's debt load increases. These monitoring costs lower the tax advantages of debt and can ultimately lead to an optimal debt–equity ratio.

PROBLEMS

15•1. The Dooley Company is in the 25% marginal tax bracket. The current market value of the firm is $10 million. If there are no costs to bankruptcy:
   (a) What will Dooley's annual tax savings from interest deductions be if it issues $2 million of five-year bonds at a 12% interest rate? What will be the value of the firm?
   (b) What will Dooley's annual tax savings from interest deductions be if it issues $2 million of perpetual bonds at a 12% interest rate? What will be the value of the firm?

15•2.   Linda Dubberly is trying to determine whether or not there is an optimal capital structure for her new firm. She needs to raise a total of $2 million, and she expects the firm's tax rate to be 25%. Any debt financing will be with perpetuities. She has estimated the *PV* of the costs of bankruptcy to be $500,000, and she has estimated the probability of bankruptcy under the following possible capital structures:

Debt/Assets (%)	0	10	20	30	40	50	60
Probability of Bankruptcy	0.01	0.03	0.08	0.15	0.25	0.40	0.60

(a)   What is the value of Linda's firm under each of the capital structures if bankruptcy costs are ignored?

(b)   What is the value of Linda's firm under each of the capital structures if bankruptcy costs are included?

15•3.   The Geraci Corporation issued $50 million in equity and invested the entire proceeds in rental property. The Pollard Corporation, on the other hand, invested in similar property by issuing $25 million in equity and $25 million in debt. The market value of the property ($25 million) is the same for both companies. Because the Pollard Corporation plans to continuously refinance (roll over) the debt at maturity, its debt is effectively perpetual. If Pollard is in the 15% tax bracket and its debt carries a coupon interest rate of 10%, by how much will the value of Pollard exceed the value of Geraci?

15•4.   Ajax Cement is considering a $50 million investment. The project has an *NPV* of $20 million.

(a)   If Ajax raises $10 million by issuing debt (leaving the risk of the existing debt unchanged) and the rest by issuing equity, what is the net gain to equity holders from the project?

(b)   What would the benefit to equity holders be if all the funds were raised through a debt issue?

15•5.   Linguistics International has just issued perpetual bonds with a face value of $6 million, paying 10% per year.

(a)   If Linguistics is in the 25% tax bracket, what are its annual tax savings on interest payments?

(b)   What is the value of the tax saving on interest? (Assume that the bonds were sold at face value.)

15•6.   Corporations *A* and *B* are identical, except for the differences in their capital structure. *A* is totally equity financed, while *B* has a capital structure composed of equal proportions of debt and equity. The ex-

499

pected *PV* of *B*'s bankruptcy costs is 5% of its value. Assume that *B* has $60,000 in debt.

(a) If both firms are in the 25% tax bracket, what is the difference in their value?

(b) What is the difference in their value if the tax rate is 34%?

READINGS

HARRIS, JOHN M., JR., RODNEY L. ROENFELDT, AND PHILIP L. COOLEY, "Evidence of Financial Leverage Clienteles," *Journal of Finance*, September 1983, 1125–1132.

MILLER, MERTON H., "Debt and Taxes," *Journal of Finance*, May 1977, 261–275.

MODIGLIANI, FRANCO, AND MERTON H. MILLER, "The Cost of Capital, Corporation Finance and the Theory of Investment," *American Economic Review*, June 1958, 261–297.

MODIGLIANI, FRANCO, AND MERTON H. MILLER, "The Cost of Capital, Corporation Finance and the Theory of Investment: Reply," *American Economic Review*, September 1958, 655–669; "Taxes and the Cost of Capital: A Correction," *American Economic Review*, June 1963, 433–443; "Reply," *American Economic Review*, June 1965, 524–527.

SCHNELLER, MEIR I., "Taxes and the Optimal Capital Structure in an Incomplete Market," *Journal of Finance*, March 1980, 119–127.

16

Capital Structure Decision Making

In Chapter 15 the theory of capital structure was addressed by examining the impact of capital structure on the value of the firm. The role of taxes, bankruptcy, and monitoring costs was addressed, and it was concluded that capital structure can affect firm value under certain conditions. The extent to which firms face these conditions varies from firm to firm. Thus the analysis in Chapter 15 was unable to provide any policy recommendations for financial managers.

As a practical matter, firms make capital structure decisions constantly. The majority of financial managers believe that there is an optimal debt–equity ratio, but they are unable to say exactly what it is. It must be pointed out that although the theory outlined in Chapter 15 provides a starting point, actual capital structure decisions involve a host of other factors that have been completely ignored in our discussions so far.

To encompass these factors in capital structure decision making, a multifaceted approach is used. Rather than using a single tool or approach, managers examine the results of several types of analyses and develop a composite view of how the firm would be affected by their capital structure decisions. Because of these varied, sometimes unquantifiable factors, capital structure decision making becomes as much an art as a science. Thus it may be fruitless to search for an analytical procedure to find the optimal capital structure. A manager may, at most, be able to decide on a range of acceptable debt-equity ratios after studying both the quantifiable and nonquantifiable aspects of the firm's capital structure.

The considerations and tools for making capital structure decisions are covered in the three sections of this chapter.

SECTION 16·1: *Qualitative Considerations*. In this section, we examine the implications of several qualitative considerations that are relevant in making capital structure decisions. These considerations are important factors that managers should keep in mind as they make capital budgeting decisions. These factors include the presence or absence of taxable income, earnings stability, future flexibility and timing of equity and debt issues, and maintenance of control over the firm.

SECTION 16·2: *Some Basic Tools*. Some of the basic tools used by managers in evaluating capital structure changes are reviewed. *NOI-EPS* analysis, bankruptcy risk, ratio analysis, downside risk, and cash insolvency considerations all play a part in capital structure decision making.

SECTION 16·3: *Some Other Comprehensive Approaches*. Additional comprehensive procedures to facilitate capital structure decision making are outlined here. Funds flow analysis, computer simulation, and inventory of resources provide still other means for managers to evaluate a firm's capital structure.

SECTION 16·1 *Qualitative Considerations*

In this section, we introduce some qualitative considerations that managers should examine when making capital structure decisions. These considerations do not fit into a formula, nor do they give the manager a number that is "good" or "bad," as we saw in ratio analysis. Rather, they provide general guidance that helps the manager make better decisions.

TAXES

Because the tax deductibility of interest payments increases the total cash flows available to bondholders and stockholders, a firm that is paying taxes should consider financing with debt. Whether the company will pay taxes depends on its future profitability. If the company expects to incur large losses in the future, or if it has large tax-loss carryforwards, it may not pay taxes, and debt is not that attractive.

Consider a firm that expects losses over the next few years but eventually expects to make a profit. Even if the firm feels that it can carry the tax losses forward to offset its eventual profits, debt may not be very attractive. This is because the present value of these future tax shields may be very small.

STABILITY OF EARNINGS

Companies that expect to have stable earnings are best served by debt. Unstable earnings can subject a firm to financial distress. As a firm takes on more debt, it increases its fixed obligations (interest payments) to service the debt. If a firm's cash flows fluctuate widely, perhaps because the firm's business is cyclical, the possibility of financial distress increases. Firms with risky cash flows should therefore take on less debt. It does not make much sense to get into a situation of financial distress with the hope of capturing tax shields from debt financing. The tax shields may not be worth much if financial distress eventually leads to bankruptcy.

NATURE OF ASSETS

Another general observation that one can make about capital structure relates to the nature of the assets held by the firm. Assets can generally be classified into two categories: tangible and intangible. Tangible assets include land, inventory, patents, warehouses, machinery, and so on, that the firm owns, while intangible assets include goodwill, technical know-how, and management skills. Tangible assets can usually be sold easily because there are active secondary markets for them. On the other hand, it may not be easy to sell management skills or know-how. These items of "human capital" are more difficult to market. Further, how does one estimate what they might be worth if the firm goes bankrupt? No clear-cut answer exists. For these reasons, firms with tangible assets generally use more debt than those without such assets. Bondholders do not feel very comfortable extending much debt to, say, consulting firms.

FLEXIBILITY AND TIMING

There are two other factors—timing and flexibility—that are considered very important in the debt-equity decision. These factors have been ignored so far simply because they do not fit into the theory developed in Chapter 15. However, the realities of capital structure decision making warrant a closer look at these considerations.

Flexibility

Flexibility refers to the extent to which firms have some freedom in choosing the type of financing—debt or equity—they will employ in the future. So far, the debt–equity decision has been treated as if it were a one-dimensional decision. In reality, matters are not so straightforward or easy. When firms raise capital, they do so in *blocks*. That is, a firm may sell a large block of equity first, followed by a large block of debt, and so on, instead of issuing both debt and equity contemporaneously in a fixed proportion.

Large blocks of capital are cheaper to raise than small ones. There are economies of scale even in raising capital. Investment advisor fees, investment bankers' commissions, administrative fees, and so on, are lower (proportionally) with larger issues. Because of this, the actual process of reaching a target debt-equity ratio may extend over a long period—several months or even years. This situation is complicated by the fact that firms may sometimes be unable to raise additional debt unless they have a larger equity base. However, for one reason or another, the firm may be unable to increase its equity. Thus, acquiring new capital can be extremely difficult, and the firm may be forced to cut dividends or abandon several investment projects—clearly an undesirable state of affairs. For this reason, the company should have some **equity buffer**—equity that will give it the flexibility to raise additional debt in the future. An equity buffer will exist as long as the firm has not reached that debt-equity ratio which makes it very risky. Thus the advantage provided by the tax shield from debt should be weighed against this loss of flexibility.

One must also not forget the fact that stock and bond markets are volatile. Since raising capital takes time, the firm that makes a decision to raise equity, for example, is susceptible to developments in the equity market before new stock is actually sold. Typically, it takes about three to four months to sell equity in a public market, and during this period the firm's future is riding uncontrollably on the marketplace. If economic conditions worsen, the company may find it impossible to sell its stock, and this bodes ill for the firm. The bond market is also volatile, but not as much as the stock market. It is precisely for this reason that the debt alternative reduces flexibility. With increased debt, the firm may be forced to raise equity and thus face the volatile conditions in the equity market.

Timing

Added to the flexibility consideration is the timing issue. If the company's management has some flexibility, it may be able to **time the issue.** This means that the firm may be able to raise capital at the most opportune time. For debt capital, the firm would like to sell bonds when interest rates are low. For equity capital, the firm would like to sell stock when its stock price is high. If a company timed its issues correctly, it would have raised capital under the best possible terms. Whether a firm can time the issue depends on how much flexibility the firm has. For example, assume that a firm needs to raise funds to finance a new project, and that management has decided that it is best to issue equity. If the stock market is at an all-time low, the firm will have to issue a very large amount of stock, thereby diluting existing stockholders' ownership. If, on the other hand, the firm has some flexibility, it can get by with more debt and issue its equity when the stock market recovers.

Market-timing considerations raise interesting questions from the standpoint of market efficiency. Can management really time an issue? If markets are efficient and managers do not have any superior skills in forecasting, they will be unable to outguess the market, and the question of market timing becomes irrelevant. In efficient markets, managers are as likely to be right as wrong. However, if management has superior information about the firm's future prospects and this information is not available to the average investor, the market-timing issue may merit further consideration. Since it is reasonable to assume that managers know more about their company than outsiders do, market timing may be possible. Of course, the firm should not have issued so much debt that it does not have the flexibility to take advantage of market-timing opportunities.

CONTROL

Control is another consideration in the debt-equity ratio decision, especially for small, closely held companies. Suppose that a company's management has 51% of the voting shares outstanding. Any further equity issues that reduce its ownership to, say, 48% will imply a loss of control for the managers. In such a situation, a firm may find debt more attractive.

Having identified some of the qualitative factors that should be taken into account in determining the optimal amount of debt, let us turn to some standard tools that financial managers use in making decisions regarding debt policy.

Learning Check for Section 16•1

Review Question

16•1. What are some of the important nonquantifiable factors that a manager must evaluate in making a debt-equity financing decision?

New Terms

Control   Equity buffer   "Timing and issue"

SECTION 16•2 *Some Basic Tools*

Several surveys of corporate managers indicate that they focus on the following variables in making their capital structure plans:

1. Variability of net operating income (*NOI*).

2. Impact of changes in *NOI* on a firm's earnings per share (*EPS*).

3. Downside-risk considerations: the probability that *NOI* will fall below the dollar amount required to service the debt.

4. Cash flow analysis for a worst-case situation.

In the remainder of this chapter, we examine some analytical tools involving these variables to aid the manager's decision-making process.

NOI-EPS ANALYSIS

An **NOI-EPS analysis** chart helps the financial manager evaluate the impact of various plans over a range of net operating income levels. An example is perhaps most instructive in helping us to understand this tool. The Wembly Electronics Company, an all-equity firm (150,000 shares outstanding), has $15 million in common stock on its books. To finance its new product—the Wembly Wam—it plans to raise an additional $5 million. Two potential financing plans have been identified by management:

Plan A: Raise $5 million in common stock financing. Common stock can be sold for $50 per share. Thus 100,000 new shares have to be sold.

Plan B: Raise $5 million in debt. The interest rate will be 10%

Wembly Electronics is in the 34% tax bracket, and its current *NOI* is $2 million.

The effect of the two financing plans on Wembly's *EPS* can be seen in Table 16•1. The *EPS* is calculated at an assumed *NOI* of $2 million. Notice that only interest on debt is deducted before taxes. While the net income (*NI*) is much higher with equity financing ($1,320,000) than with debt ($990,000), the *EPS* under plan *A* is lower than that under plan *B*. This is because there are more shares outstanding under the all-equity plan—the original 150,000 shares plus the new 100,000 shares.

Since Table 16•1 provides the calculations for *EPS* under the two plans at an assumed *NOI* level of $2 million, it has a limited amount of information to convey. A more useful tool is the *NOI-EPS* chart, which provides the *EPS* for the two plans under various *NOI* levels.

Figure 16•1 is an *NOI-EPS* chart for Wembly Electronics. The horizontal axis plots *NOI* in millions of dollars, and the vertical axis yields the corresponding values of *EPS*. How was Figure 16•1 drawn? The procedure is very simple. Since the relationship between *NOI* and *EPS* is linear, only two points on the graph are needed to draw a straight line showing the *NOI-EPS* relationship.

For the common stock plan, one point for the graph is already available. In Table 16•1 it is seen that for an *NOI* of $2 million, the *EPS* will be $5.28. To

TABLE 16•1 Effect of Various Financial Plans on Wembly's *EPS*

	Plan *A*: All Common Stock	Plan *B*: All Debt
Net operating income (*NOI*)	$2,000,000	$2,000,000
Less: Interest on debt (10% on $5 mill.)	0	500,000
Earnings before taxes	$2,000,000	$1,500,000
Taxes (34%)	680,000	510,000
Net income (*NI*)	$1,320,000	$ 990,000
Number of shares outstanding	250,000	150,000
Earnings per share (*EPS*)	$5.28	$6.60

506

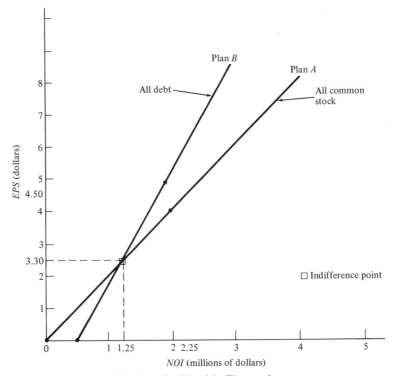

FIGURE 16•1 *NOI-EPS* chart for Wembly Electronics.

get the second point, we ask what the *EPS* will be if the *NOI* is zero. The answer is simple—when *NOI* is zero, *EPS* is also zero. This gives us the second point, and as seen in Figure 16•1, the line representing plan *A* passes through the origin.

For the debt plan, Table 16•1 again yields one point—at an *NOI* of $2 million, the *EPS* will be $6.60 for Wembly. To get the second point for the *NOI-EPS* line for plan *B*, we ask, when will the *EPS* be zero under plan *B*? The earnings to stockholders represent the amount available after all interest and tax payments have been made. Thus *EPS* will be zero when *NOI* is exactly equal to the interest obligations of Wembly. That is, *NOI* = $500,000 implies a zero *EPS*.

With a completed *NOI-EPS* chart, as in Figure 16•1, one can ask several "what if" questions: What if *NOI* were only $200,000? What if *NOI* soared to $4 million? In each of these cases, the *EPS* under the various financing plans can be obtained from Figure 16•1. It is precisely for this reason that some authors refer to Figure 16•1 as a **range-of-earnings chart.**

A CLOSER LOOK AT THE NOI-EPS CHART

Several interesting conclusions can be drawn from Figure 16•1. At low levels of *NOI*, plan *A* is superior to plan *B* because *EPS* is higher under plan *A*.

507

As *NOI* increases, *EPS* under plan *B* becomes positive after all interest obligations are met. At an *NOI* of $1,250,000, plans *B* and *A* have identical *EPS* values. The point at which the lines for plans *A* and *B* intersect yields the **debt-equity indifference point.** It is at this level of *NOI* that the *EPS* of both plans is identical. From Figure 16•1 it can be seen that the debt-equity indifference point occurs at an *NOI* of $1,250,000. At this *NOI*, plans *A* and *B* both produce an *EPS* of $3.30. If the manager expects *NOI* to be to the right of this indifference point (i.e., *NOI* greater than $1,250,000), she will prefer debt over equity because debt provides a higher *EPS*. To the left of the indifference point, the debt alternative will have a lower *EPS* than the equity plan.

This result should come as no surprise. It is entirely consistent with our discussions of financial leverage in Chapter 8. When the firm does well in terms of *NOI*, financial leverage (debt) works in the firm's favor. When the firm fails to reach its indifference point *NOI*, debt works to the firm's detriment.

ANALYTICAL DETERMINATION OF INDIFFERENCE POINTS

While a visual presentation of the *NOI-EPS* line has its own appeal, the computation of the indifference points under the different financing plans is cumbersome with this graphic method. An easier way to find the level of *NOI* at which *EPS* is identical can be obtained easily by equating the *EPS* formulas under the two different plans.

Indifference Between Debt and Common Stock

Let the indifference point *NOI* be represented as *NOI*★. Then, if *EPS* is the same under both plans at this level of *NOI*, we have[1]

$$EPS \text{ under debt plan} = EPS \text{ under equity plan}$$

$$\frac{(NOI^\star - I)(1 - T)}{N_D} = \frac{NOI^\star(1 - T)}{N_E}$$

or

$$NOI^\star = \frac{N_E}{N_E - N_D}(I) \qquad (16\text{-}1)$$

where N_D and N_E represent the number of shares of common stock outstanding under each plan after the new financing and I is the interest paid in dollars.

---

[1] Note that in computing *EPS* under the equity plan, our equation holds as long as the firm is initially an all-equity firm. If Wembly had some debt or preferred stock initially, *EPS* under the equity financing plan would be different. Equation (16-1) would have to be modified.

In the case of Wembly Electronics, the indifference point between debt and equity financing can be computed using equation (16-1):

$$NOI^\star = \frac{250,000}{250,000 - 150,000}(\$500,000) = \$1,250,000$$

which is verified by Figure 16•1.

WEAKNESSES OF NOI-EPS ANALYSIS

The *NOI-EPS* chart provides some useful information about potential *EPS* values for different possible *NOI*s. Of course, managers are not interested solely in maximizing *EPS*. Although leverage can give a high *EPS*, the risk involved is also higher. *NOI-EPS* analysis focuses primarily on the level of *EPS* rather than on its variability. Although variability might be undesirable, it might be in the firm's best interest to take on a more variable *EPS* stream by increasing its leverage. Of course, the optimal amount of debt will balance the disadvantages of greater risk with the advantages of greater earnings. To assess more clearly the nature of the risk–return trade-off, a theory of market values rather than a theory of book values is needed. *NOI-EPS* analysis thus appears to be an operational tool to aid in making financing decisions, but it does not let the manager decide whether the choice is in the best interests of the stockholders.

Perhaps the most significant weakness of *NOI-EPS* analysis is that it disregards the implicit cost of debt capital. In addition, the effect of a firm's financing decision on the cost of equity is ignored.

BANKRUPTCY RISK AND RATIO ANALYSIS

In making capital structure decisions, the manager must consider the ability of the firm's cash flows to cover all fixed charges. Fixed charges include the principal and interest payments on debt, preferred stock dividends, sinking-fund requirements, and lease payments. If the firm has debt maturing soon, its fixed charges will be considerably higher at that time. If the firm's cash flows are inadequate to meet these fixed charges, the firm may be forced into insolvency. Given that cash flows are uncertain, their variability becomes crucial in assessing whether the firm will be able to meet its fixed obligations. If, for example, the risk of bankruptcy is very great, the firm might not want to issue additional debt at this point. Instead, an equity issue might be more attractive. If the probability of bankruptcy is low, debt, with its potential tax shield, may look more attractive.

A crude way to assess the ability of a firm to handle its fixed obligations is through the use of balance sheet ratios and coverage ratios.

Balance Sheet Ratios

The essential feature of a balance sheet ratio is that it supposedly evaluates a firm's debt obligation in light of the collateral provided by the firm's assets. For example, the ratios

$$\frac{\text{Long-term debt}}{\text{Net worth}} \quad \text{and} \quad \frac{\text{Long-term debt}}{\text{Total assets}}$$

evaluate the debt obligation of the firm in terms of net worth and total assets. If a firm has a (long-term debt/total assets) ratio of 0.3, every dollar in long-term debt is supported by about $3 in assets in book-value terms.[2]

How useful are these balance sheet ratios in evaluating a firm's debt capacity? The answer depends on whether the firm's assets are good collateral. The book value of a firm's assets may be substantially higher (or lower) than the market value of its assets. If the book values are higher than the market values, the creditors do not have the collateral that the ratio implies. In addition, if the firm's debt is long term, this ratio is even less meaningful because of the greater potential discrepancy between the book and market values of the firm's assets.

Interest and principal payments on debt are typically made out of the cash flows generated by the firm rather than by liquidating productive assets. Hence a set of ratios using cash flows would be more meaningful.

Coverage Ratios

Unlike balance sheet ratios, coverage ratios relate a firm's cash flow available to service debt to some measure of the firm's annual fixed obligations. Typically, *NOI* is the relevant operating cash flow used in calculating these ratios. Some commonly used coverage ratios will now be examined.

Times Interest Earned (*TIE*)

$$TIE = \frac{NOI}{\text{total interest expense}}$$

TIE is perhaps the most commonly used coverage ratio. Assuming that a firm's expected *NOI* is $8 million and its total interest payments on debt are $2 million, the *TIE* ratio is 4.0. This suggests that every dollar in interest payments is supported by $4 in *NOI*. *NOI* can fall by as much as 75%, and the firm will still be able to meet its interest obligations.

Although it is clear that the lower the coverage ratio, the greater the risk of default on interest payments, the appropriate *TIE* ratio for a firm will depend

---

[2] This statement is obtained by examining the long-term debt/total asset ratio: 0.3 = long term debt/total assets = $1/$3.

on the nature of the industry the firm is in. If the industry is fairly stable, the firm can get by with a fairly low *TIE* ratio. If, on the other hand, *NOI* undergoes wide fluctuations with the business cycle, a higher *TIE* ratio might be desirable.

Recognize from the definition of *TIE* that the ratio in no way evaluates a firm's ability to make its principal payments. Thus the *TIE* ratio may not be appropriate, especially if the firm has debt that is to mature soon.

Debt-Service Coverage (*DSC*)

$$DSC = \frac{NOI}{\text{interest} + \dfrac{\text{principal}}{(1 - \text{tax rate})}}$$

If debt is maturing immediately, or if the firm has established a sinking fund, setting aside funds to retire some of the debt each year, this formula becomes

$$DSC = \frac{NOI}{\text{interest} + \dfrac{\text{sinking-fund payments}}{(1 - \text{tax rate})}}$$

DSC overcomes the weakness of *TIE* in recognizing principal payments. Notice that the principal or sinking-fund payments are divided by (1 − tax rate). The reason for this procedure is that these payments must be adjusted upward for the tax effect. Principal payments and sinking-fund payments must be made out of after-tax dollars, whereas *NOI* represents before-tax dollars. To ensure that we are comparing apples with apples, we convert all variables to their pretax values.

Extending the previous example of the firm with an *NOI* of $8 million and interest payments of $2 million, assume that sinking-fund payments are $2 million a year and that the firm is in the 34% tax bracket. Then

$$DSC = \frac{\$8 \text{ million}}{\$2 \text{ million} + \dfrac{\$2 \text{ million}}{(1 - 0.34)}} = 1.59$$

Clearly, the larger the *DSC* ratio, the more secure is the firm's position.

Since all ratios are merely numbers, a more meaningful way to evaluate them is by comparing them to industry standards. In that way, one can recognize that different industries have different characteristics, and any particular firm can be judged with respect to the average for the industry. Another technique used is trend analysis to evaluate the improvement/deterioration of a firm's position through time. Since these aspects of ratio analysis have also been discussed in Chapter 7, there is no need to elaborate further.

DOWNSIDE-RISK CONSIDERATIONS

Even if two companies have identical coverage ratios, their risks may be different because the probability distributions of their *NOIs* can differ. Coverage ratios as we have defined them are incapable of recognizing this feature.

To illustrate, consider two firms with identical interest payments, principal payments, and tax rates. Then the denominator in the *DSC* equation is the same for both companies. However, the two companies are in two different industries, and the probability distributions of the *NOIs* are different. For simplicity, we assume that the expected *NOI* is the same for both. Figure 16•2 illustrates the probability distributions. Firms *X* and *Y* both have an expected *NOI* of $2 million and a debt burden of $1 million.

Notice that firm *X* is riskier than firm *Y* in terms of the variability of *NOI*.[3] If creditors calculate the *DSC* ratio for both these firms, they will be identical. Yet, most business managers would consider firm *Y* to be riskier than firm *X*. Why? This is because the probability that *NOI* will fall below the debt-service burden is larger for *Y* (shaded area in Figure 16•2) than for *X*. Thus, in terms of **downside risk,** firm *Y* will be perceived as having less debt capacity than firm *X* even though the overall variability of *NOI* is larger for firm *X*.[4]

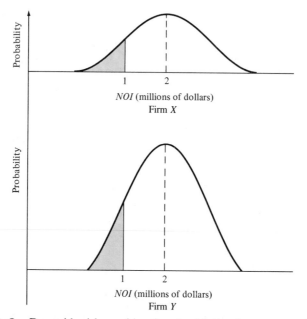

FIGURE 16•2 Downside-risk considerations in debt-service coverage. The crosshatched area shows the probability of *NOI* falling below the debt-service burden. 1, debt-service burden; 2, expected *NOI*.

---

[3] We define risk in terms of the variability of *NOI* rather than in terms of the variability of returns from the firm. The latter definition is necessary for equity valuation purposes.

[4] Notice that we are not comparing the variances of the probability distributions.

Thus coverage ratios, used in isolation without explicit recognition of probabilities, may not be appropriate. The nature of the firm's business as it affects the variability of the firm's *NOI* is important. Measuring these probabilities is easy if it can be assumed that the *NOI* for a firm has a particular probability distribution.

CASH INSOLVENCY CONSIDERATIONS

The tools just discussed focus primarily on *NOI* and the probability that it will fall below the debt-service burden. However, when it actually comes to paying the debt, there is no reason why the firm should use *NOI* alone. There may be other sources of funds to the firm: cash, the sale of fixed assets, new financing plans, and so on. Thus, by looking at coverage ratios, either alone or in conjunction with the probability of nonserviceability, one is ignoring cash flow considerations and the probability of insolvency. A firm is in a state of insolvency when its cash flows (rather than just its *NOI*) are unable to service the debt.

It is fairly easy to see why the probability of insolvency is a more useful measure than the probability of *NOI* falling below the debt-service burden. By focusing on cash flows and insolvency possibilities, the manager is effectively considering a variety of new variables—seasonal sales patterns, committed investment outlays, dividend payments, changing labor costs, and so on—virtually any variable that affects cash flows.

The probability of cash insolvency can be calculated in a manner similar to the calculation of the probability of nonserviceability of debt. Of course, the probability distribution that is relevant here is the distribution of cash flows rather than the distribution of *NOI*. Again, if management is willing to accept the maximum probability of insolvency, it is possible to evaluate whether a particular financing plan is feasible. (See the highlight "Factors Affecting Managers' Financial Policies.")

■ HIGHLIGHT

FACTORS AFFECTING MANAGERS' FINANCIAL POLICIES

After reviewing the theory (Chapter 15) and practical aspects of the capital structure decision (this chapter), it is interesting to examine managers' responses to a recent survey of 212 large U.S. corporations.

Are managers' beliefs consistent with the optimal capital structure theory of Chapter 15? Apparently so. Over 90% of the managers who participated in this survey believed that the use of debt would increase the value of their firms up to a point; beyond this point, increasing financial leverage would lower firm value. This belief suggests that managers subscribed to the notion of an optimal capital structure. Managers seemed to believe that as long as the debt was not excessive, financial leverage would be advantageous, although they might be unable to say exactly what debt–equity ratio would be optimal.

In identifying the most important influences on the choice of debt employed in their companies, managers brought up several factors. The analysis of their own staffs and management was rated as the most important factor. Investment bankers (who help the firm raise capital) were identified as the second strongest influence. Commercial bankers, creditors, security analysts, and comparative industry ratios were cited as the other most important factors influencing their decisions on the use of debt.

Source: Information from D. F. Scott and D. J. Johnson, "Financing Policies and Practices in Large Corporations," *Financial Management*, Summer 1982.

Learning Check for Section 16•2

Review Questions

16•2. How is an *NOI-EPS* chart created? What are the uses of this chart?

16•3. What are the weaknesses of the *NOI-EPS* chart? In particular, what implications does this chart have for maximizing the market value of the firm?

16•4. What ratios are commonly used in making capital structure decisions? What are the limitations of using such ratios in making these decisions?

16•5. How would a manager calculate the probability that a debt-financing plan will not be serviced?

New Terms

Downside risk   *NOI-EPS* analysis   Range of earnings chart

Debt-equity indifference point

SECTION 16•3 *Some Other Comprehensive Approaches*

It should be clear that cash flow analysis is superior to an analysis of *NOI* alone. Focusing on cash flows allows the financing manager to look at various other factors specific to the firm and to general economic conditions. In this section, two fairly comprehensive approaches to capital structure decision making are presented. These methods take into account the operations of the firm as a whole and management's assessment of the firm's future financial operations. Because they are more elaborate, they require considerably more time and effort than does *NOI-EPS* analysis or the calculation of the probability of insolvency.

Yet, because they are so comprehensive, these methods can be very useful to the decision maker.

FUNDS FLOW ANALYSIS

Funds flow analysis is simply the process of looking at all funds flowing into and out of the company over an extended period. Funds flow analysis will be explained via the example of Raytime, Inc.

Example 16•1   Funds Flow Analysis for Raytime, Inc.

Raytime, Inc., is a fairly large midwestern company manufacturing cable TV hookup kits. Since the demand for pay-TV tends to pick up during economic recoveries and slack off during recessions, Raytime's revenues are strongly dependent on the state of the economy. Currently, Raytime is an all-equity firm, but management is considering the issuance of $80 million in debt at an interest rate of 10%. In addition, Raytime agrees to make a sinking-fund payment of $10 million per year. Raytime's management would like to evaluate the impact of its debt issue on its cash flows over the next four years.

One reason why the next four years are especially relevant for Raytime is that management expects the next three years to be recessionary, with recovery beginning in year 4. Ray Sharpe, president of Raytime, likes to make decisions while expecting the worst to happen; hence "recession planning" seems especially appropriate to him.

Table 16•2 shows how Raytime estimates its cash position over the next four years. Most of the entries in the table are easily understood. In fact, this table is very similar to the cash budgeting tables seen in Chapter 9. However, an explicit recognition of different capital structure decisions can be made in items 14 to 18 in the table. Raytime could develop several alternative funds flowcharts by varying the inputs to items 17 to 23.

The basic question, however, is this: Can Raytime manage to cover the $37 million cash deficit in year 1 and the $58 million deficit in year 2? Perhaps Raytime can arrange some short-term bank credit for year 1. If this is not possible, is there any other way to avoid the deficit? Can Raytime renegotiate the terms with its suppliers? If that is not possible, should Raytime plan on declaring but not actually paying preferred dividends for year 1? What about postponing the payment of common stock dividends? Indeed, myriad questions come to mind. If Raytime thinks that its deficits can be covered one way or another, the proposed financial plan is feasible.[5] By carefully studying such funds flow projections in the light of other available contingency plans, Raytime can make a careful assessment of the pros and cons of its proposed strategy.

---

[5] Again, we stress that, though feasible, this may not be optimal.

515

TABLE 16·2 Funds Flow Analysis for Raytime, Inc. (Millions of Dollars)

		Year			
		1	2	3	4
	1. Revenues	120	110	120	200
	2. Variable costs of production	60	55	60	95
	3. Taxes	(5)	(5)	(10)	15
(1) − (2) − (3)	4. Net funds from operations	65	60	70	90
	Change in Noncash Working Capital Items				
	5. Accounts receivable	(15)	(20)	10	25
	6. Inventory	(10)	(15)	10	20
	7. Accounts payable	(5)	(5)	5	10
(5) + (6) − (7)	8. Funds from working capital	(20)	(30)	15	35
	Nonoperating Expenses				
	9. New investment	20	30	10	40
	10. Fixed costs of operation	10	20	8	15
	11. Other	5	5	2	5
(9) + (10) + (11)	12. Total	35	55	20	60
(4) + (8) − (12)	13. Net funds available for other payments	10	(25)	65	65
	Debt Service				
	14. Interest	8	7	6	5
	15. Sinking-fund payment	10	10	10	10
	16. Preferred dividends	4	4	4	4
	17. Dividends on common stock	6	5	4	7
(14) + (15) + (16) + (17)	18. Total disbursements to providers of capital	28	26	24	26
	Funds Position				
(13) − (18)	19. Net increase in funds	(18)	(51)	41	39
	20. Beginning funds	1	13	22	33
	21. Ending funds position	(17)	(38)	63	72
	22. Minimum funds required	20	20	20	20
	23. Surplus (deficit) funds	(37)	(58)	43	52

INVENTORY OF RESOURCES[6]

To aid managers in determining whether their firms can cover anticipated cash deficits, Gordon Donaldson has suggested another tool, known as **inventory of resources.** An inventory of resources is a statement of a firm's future

[6] This section draws from Gordon Donaldson, "Strategies for Financial Emergencies," *Harvard Business Review*, November–December 1969, 67–79.

purchasing power. The idea behind taking stock of a firm's inventory of resources is that in the event that an unexpected cash drain occurs, a firm with resources will be in a position to handle it.

In Donaldson's framework, a firm's resources consist of three categories: uncommitted reserves, reduction in planned outflows, and liquidation of assets. Table 16•3 reproduces Donaldson's scheme for assessing a firm's resources. Uncommitted reserves include those reserves that will not be required in the future, given current plans. These reserves can be used as a buffer or safety cushion by the company to cover unanticipated cash drains. Notice in Table 16•3 that uncommitted reserves include unused lines of credit and additional long-term debt. Of course, the more levered the company already is, the less the potential benefits from these sources. The second category represents reductions in dividends and cuts in operating expenditures. These resources are not as readily available to the firm as are the resources in the first category. Firms are usually hesitant to cut dividends (we shall see why in a later chapter), and

TABLE 16•3 Inventory of Resources

Resources	Available for Use Within:		
	One Quarter	**One Year**	**Three Years**
Uncommitted reserves			
Instant reserves			
Surplus cash	$		
Unused line of credit	$		
Negotiable reserves			
Additional bank loans			
Unsecured	$		
Secured	$		
Additional long-term debt		$	
Issue of new equity		$	
Reduction of planned outflows			
Volume-related			
Change in production schedule	$		
Scale-related			
Marketing program		$	
R&D budget		$	
Administrative overhead		$	
Capital expenditures		$	
Value-related			
Dividend payments		$	
Liquidation of assets			
Shutdown		$	
Sale of unit			$
		$	$
Total resources	$	$	$

Source: Gordon Donaldson, "Strategy for Financial Emergencies," *Harvard Business Review*, November–December 1969, 72. Copyright 1969 by the President and Fellows of Harvard College; all rights reserved.

sudden reductions in operating expenses can adversely affect firm profitability. The final category of resources is the least favorable option for a company; selling existing assets or shutting down operations are pretty drastic measures.

A firm using an inventory of resources chart must first forecast cash deficits along the lines of Table 16•3. These deficits must then be examined, together with the firm's inventory of resources, to see whether the firm can cover these deficits by tapping its existing resources. Two relevant questions emerge. First, can these deficits be covered from within the firm? Second, will the firm have sufficient warning to plan for sudden changes in its cash needs? For example, even if a firm has the resources to handle a sudden increase in cash needs, it may not be able to use them. This is true, for example, if the firm knows that it will have a major cash outflow next month but most of its resources consist of specialized plant and equipment (third category) that cannot be sold quickly. If the company, after careful study of its needs and resources, has sufficient excess resources, it may want to take on additional debt.

COMPUTER SIMULATION

When one analyzes capital structure decisions using funds flow analysis, it is necessary to fix the values of the different variables that go into the computational scheme. For example, Raytime, Inc., has revenue estimates of $120, $110, $120, and $200 million, respectively, for years 1 through 4. Obviously, these point estimates are "best guess" numbers for future revenues, and there is no guarantee that these revenues will, in fact, be realized. Consequently, the cash surplus/deficit figures obtained will depend on the accuracy of the assumed revenues and other variables that were inputs into the analysis. There is no way to measure the riskiness or uncertainty associated with the cash deficit/surplus forecasts obtained in this manner.

One way to recognize that nearly all the variables that are inputs into the funds flow analysis are uncertain is to use simulation analysis. **Simulation** can then be used to recognize explicitly the uncertainty associated with each of these input variables. The steps of simulation analysis are as follows:

Step 1. Management assesses the most likely probability distribution for each uncertain variable in the funds flow analysis.

Step 2. Management's future policies are identified. Is the company going to pay common dividends? Preferred dividends? Or will preferred dividends be declared but not paid? How much debt does management plan to have next year (capital structure decisions)? At what rate can the debt be borrowed? Will there be a sinking fund? And so on. Once management has answers to these questions, several numbers required for the simulation of funds flows (e.g., interest, dividends, cash outflows for repayment of principal, etc.) are input into the analysis.

Step 3. With the inputs completed by company officials, the computer then simulates the company's cash position by drawing random numbers from the probability distribution for each input that is uncertain and takes management's values for policy variables.

Step 4. The computer then proceeds to calculate the firm's cash surplus/deficit in a manner exactly similar to that done earlier for Raytime. However, one value of cash balances obtained by this method is not too meaningful. The computer repeats steps 3 and 4 again and again until perhaps 100 different cash balance figures are generated.

Step 5. Finally, a probability distribution is constructed using the (say) 100 values of cash balance.

Figure 16•3 shows, for example, the output for two different capital structures for a company. Capital structure II has more debt than I and, as can readily be seen, is more risky. It is risky both in terms of total variability (variance) and in terms of downside risk. That is, the probability of deficits is greater under capital structure II. Of course, this is not to imply that the firm should not adopt capital structure II. All that the results of simulation provide is a more comprehensive picture of potential outcomes with regard to its cash surpluses and the associated probabilities. If management feels that the risks of capital structure II can be handled easily, it may choose to abandon capital structure I. Again, like all other tools for capital structure decision making, simulation alone should not be used to make a decision. Nevertheless, it is a useful tool in making ultimately subjective capital structure decisions.

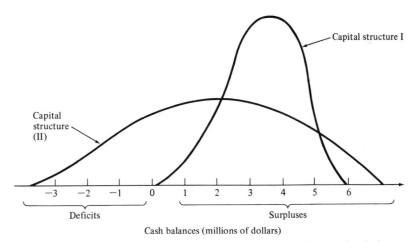

FIGURE 16•3 Cash surplus distributions generated by computer simulation.

Learning Check for Section 16•3

Review Questions

16•6. Explain why funds flow analysis and inventory of resources can be more useful to the manager than *NOI-EPS* analysis.

16·7. What are the advantages offered by simulation over funds flow analysis and inventory of resources?

New Terms

Computer simulation	Funds flow analysis	Inventory of resources

SUMMARY

Some Qualitative Considerations

In making capital structure decisions, there are several subjective considerations that cannot be quantified in any meaningful way. Yet the manager cannot afford to ignore these aspects of corporate financial management. For example, the tax advantages of increased debt levels should be weighed against the increased likelihood of financial distress. In addition to tax considerations, the manager should factor in several other considerations—the nature of the assets held by the firm, flexibility, timing, and control. To aid in this complex process, managers often use several tools.

Some Basic Tools

NOI-EPS analysis can be employed to help identify the nature of the impact on *EPS* of several potential financing plans being contemplated. In this framework, the manager can identify the various indifference points—the levels of *NOI* at which the *EPS* under various financial alternatives is the same.

Balance sheet ratios can be used to assess crude measures of a firm's bankruptcy possibilities. Although coverage ratios can aid in this regard, they do not actually provide an opportunity to quantify the probability of bankruptcy.

Other Comprehensive Approaches

Funds flow analysis, an inventory of resources, and computer simulation are more comprehensive techniques that management can employ. However, these methods are more time-consuming, since more detailed analyses are required. Nevertheless, these three methods, in conjunction with the simpler tools, can be valuable aids to the financial manager in dealing with the risks that must be recognized when confronting a capital structure decision—variability in *EPS*, decreased flexibility, and increased chance of bankruptcy. The final decision that management makes is a qualitative balancing of the benefits of (typically) increased *EPS* that accompanies debt and the risks identified earlier. It must be emphasized, however, that no single tool should be used in isolation.

PROBLEMS

16•1. The Hamilton Federal Paper Company is planning to open a new mill near Madison, Wisconsin. This project will require an initial outlay of $20 million during the coming year, and Hamilton is trying to decide whether to raise the money with common stock or with bonds. Hamilton currently has 6 million shares outstanding, and the shares are trading for $10 each. Hamilton currently has no long-term debt in its capital structure, but if bonds are issued, they can be sold at a 12% interest rate. The company has a marginal tax rate of 25%.

(a) If Hamilton raises the money by selling new shares, how many new shares must be issued?

(b) If Hamilton issues new shares, what will *EPS* be if *NOI* is $8 million next year? If *NOI* is $12 million next year?

(c) If Hamilton issues bonds, what will its annual interest payments be?

(d) If Hamilton issues bonds, what will *EPS* be if *NOI* is $8 million next year? If *NOI* is $12 million next year?

(e) Your answers to parts (b) and (d) should be that the equity plan has higher *EPS* than the debt plan if *NOI* is $8 million but that lower *EPS* will result if *NOI* is $12 million. Will it always be true that issuing equity is more favorable (i.e., has a higher *EPS* than debt) if *NOI* is low and debt is more favorable if *NOI* is high?

(f) At what level of *NOI* will *EPS* be the same for either plan?

16•2. The market-value capital structure of Zimmer Room Service, a hotel restaurant chain, is as follows:

Long-term debt (10% coupon)	$ 400,000,000
Common stock (10 million shares)	600,000,000
	$1,000,000,000

Zimmer is considering an offer to contract for providing food services for Jefferson Hotels. Such a venture will require a capital expenditure of $24 million; Zimmer is trying to decide between raising the money by issuing new common stock or new bonds. (New bonds will have a 12% coupon.) Zimmer's marginal tax rate is 25%.

(a) How many new shares must be issued at $60 each to raise enough money for the expansion?

(b) What will *EPS* be if Zimmer raises the money by issuing new shares and *NOI* is $100 million? If *NOI* is $120 million?

(c) What would be Zimmer's interest payments for the new bonds? What would be total interest payments if the new capital expenditure is financed by 12% coupon debt?

(d) What will *EPS* be if Zimmer raises the money by issuing new bonds and *NOI* is $100 million? If *NOI* is $120 million?

(e)   At what level of *NOI* will *EPS* be the same for the equity financing and the debt financing?

16•3.   The McGovern Bakery Chain manufactures French breads and pastries and is considering expansion into the West Coast area. Such a move would necessitate a capital expenditure of $200 million. McGovern is considering raising this money through one of two plans: (1) sell 20 million new shares of stock at $10 each or (2) sell 10 million new shares of stock at $10 each and sell $100 million of 13.7% coupon bonds. McGovern currently has outstanding 100 million common shares and $500 million face value of 12% coupon bonds. McGovern's marginal tax rate is 25%.

(a)   What will *EPS* be if McGovern adopts plan 2 and *NOI* is $200 million? If *NOI* is $250 million?

(b)   What will *EPS* be if McGovern adopts plan 1 and *NOI* is $200 million? If *NOI* is $250 million?

(c)   At what level of *NOI* will the two plans have the same *EPS*?

16•4.   The Corleone Importing Company is thinking of extending its market to the area surrounding Atlantic City, New Jersey. The expansion will require an initial outlay of $10 million. Corleone's board of directors is considering three financing plans: (1) issuing 250,000 new shares at $40 each; (2) issuing 125,000 new shares at $40 each and selling $5 million of new 12% coupon bonds; or (3) issuing $10 million of new 12% coupon bonds. Corleone currently has outstanding 2.5 million common shares, $25 million face value of 10% coupon bonds, and $15 million face value of 8% coupon bonds. Corleone's marginal tax rate is 25%. Calculate the answers to parts (a), (b), and (c) to the nearest tenth of a cent.

(a)   If *NOI* is $16 million, what will be *EPS* for plan 1? For plan 2? For plan 3?

(b)   If *NOI* is $17 million, what will be *EPS* for plan 1? For plan 2? For plan 3?

(c)   If *NOI* is $18 million, what will be *EPS* for plan 1? For plan 2? For plan 3?

(d)   At what level of *NOI* would plans 1 and 2 have the same *EPS*?

(e)   At what level of *NOI* would plans 2 and 3 have the same *EPS*?

(f)   Plot on a graph (with *NOI* on the *x*-axis and *EPS* on the *y*-axis) the relationship between *EPS* and *NOI* for each of the three plans. Notice that plan 2 does not result in the highest *EPS* for any level of *NOI*. Why can't plan 2 necessarily be excluded from further considerations?

16•5.   The Zapata Mexican Food Company needs $25 million to produce and market its new frozen dinner, the "Zapata Supreme." Zapata will raise the money either by selling 500,000 new common shares at $50 each or by selling 625,000 shares of $5 dividend preferred stock at $40 each.

Zapata currently has outstanding 4.5 million shares of common stock and no preferred stock. Their marginal tax rate is 25%.

(a) If Zapata issues preferred shares, what is the required annual dividend? What must *NOI* be to cover this dividend?

(b) What will *EPS* be under each of the two plans if *NOI* is $45 million? If *NOI* is $55 million?

(c) At what level of *NOI* will *EPS* be the same under either plan?

16•6. You have just accepted a position in the finance department of the Rotary Bicycle Company. Rotary needs to raise $15 million for capital expenditures during the coming year. They are considering three plans for raising the money:

1. *Equity:* Sell 1.25 million new shares at $12 each.
2. *Debt:* Sell $15 million of 12% coupon bonds.
3. *Preferred stock:* Sell 500,000 shares of $4 dividend preferred stock at $30 each.

Rotary currently has outstanding 5 million shares of common stock, $48 million face value of 12.5% coupon bonds, and 400,000 shares of preferred stock with a $4 dividend. Rotary's marginal tax rate is 25%.

(a) The financial manager has assigned you the task of calculating *EPS* and *TIE* for each plan for each of the following levels of *NOI*:

	Equity		Debt		Preferred Stock	
NOI	*EPS*	*TIE*	*EPS*	*TIE*	*EPS*	*TIE*
$12 million						
14 million						
16 million						
18 million						
20 million						

(b) At what level of *NOI* will the equity plan and the debt plan have the same *EPS*? At what level of *NOI* will the equity plan and the preferred stock plan have the same *EPS*? At what level of *NOI* will the debt plan and the preferred stock plan have the same *NOI*?

(c) If the financial manager tells you that *EPS* is the relevant measure of return and *TIE* is the relevant measure of risk, can you make any recommendations about financing plans if the only possible levels of *NOI* are the five that he specified to you? What if the only possible levels are $14, $16, or $18 million? What if the only possible levels are $12 and $14 million? What if the only possible levels are $16 and $18 million?

16•7. Harris Services is analyzing a proposal to change its capital structure from 100% equity to 80% equity/20% debt. The financial vice-president has presented you with the following information and requests that you determine whether the proposal is viable. More specifically, will Harris have a surplus or deficit of funds in each of the next four years if the plan is adopted? What would your recommendation be in either case?

	Year			
	1	2	3	4
Operating Revenues				
Net funds from operations	$25	$35	$60	$55
Change in Non-Cash Working Capital Items				
Funds from working capital	($2)	($1)	($3)	($1)
Non-Operating Expenses				
Total non-operating expenses	$20	$18	$15	$20
Disbursements to Providers of Capital				
Total disbursements to providers of capital	$20	$22	$19	$22
Beginning funds	$3	$2	$2	$1

READING

JAEDICKE, ROBERT K., AND A. A. ROBICHEK, "Cost-Volume-Profit Analysis Under Conditions of Uncertainty," *The Accounting Review*, October 1964, 917–926.

17

The Dividend Policy Decision

The issue of how much a company should pay its stockholders as dividends is one that has concerned managers for a long time. All firms operate with a view to generating earnings. Stockholders supply equity capital, hoping to share in these earnings either directly or indirectly. When a company pays out a portion of its earnings to stockholders in the form of a dividend, stockholders benefit directly. If instead of paying dividends the firm retains the funds to exploit other growth opportunities, stockholders can expect to benefit indirectly via future increases in the stock price. Thus shareholder wealth can be increased through either dividends or capital gains. Since the amount of dividends paid to stockholders is a decision that management must make, management needs guidance on how to evaluate the effect of its dividend policy decision on shareholder wealth.

A firm's optimal dividend policy may be defined as the best dividend payout ratio the firm can adopt.[1] But what does "best" mean in this context? Since the objective of the firm is to increase the wealth of its stockholders, the best dividend policy is one that increases shareholder wealth by the greatest amount. It is therefore necessary, first, to understand the nature of the relationship between dividends and value.

---

[1]Dividend payout ratio = dividend paid/net income.

There are two sections in this chapter.[2]

SECTION 17•1: *Do Dividends Affect Firm Value?* In this section, the relationship between dividend policy and stock prices is examined. The residual theory of dividends, which holds that dividend policy is irrelevant to the value of the firm, is examined. The conditions necessary for the dividend irrelevance argument to hold are examined, as are factors that may cause the dividend payment decision to affect the firm's value. After various arguments on whether or not dividends affect value are presented, managerial considerations in setting dividend policy are examined.

SECTION 17•2: *Dividend Payment Policies and Procedures.* The procedural aspects of dividend policy are the focus of this section. Three possible dividend payment patterns are discussed, and the importance of dividend stability is examined. Managers often exhibit a strong inclination to show stability in their dividend payments. Possible reasons for the need for stability are examined. The section concludes with an analysis of stock dividends and stock splits.

SECTION 17•1 *Do Dividends Affect Firm Value?*

THE RESIDUAL THEORY OF DIVIDENDS

Dividend policy can be viewed as being determined by a firm's investment decisions. Consider a firm planning to pay out dividends from its current earnings. Management's choice of the size of the dividend is determined by the amount of the firm's investment in acceptable projects. If the amount required to accept all available projects is less than the total earnings and other internally available funds, the residual or surplus sums are paid out to stockholders in the form of dividends. If, on the other hand, the firm's earnings are insufficient to accept all good investments available, the firm pays out no dividends. In fact, management will raise additional capital to finance all of its investments. The firm is treating dividend policy strictly as a financing decision. In this framework, dividend policy is a residual decision.

A firm that behaves in the manner just described is said to believe in the **residual theory of dividends.** According to this theory, dividend policy is a residual from investment policy. Whether or not a company pays dividends depends on its investment policy.

How is the residual theory made operational? After an examination of all the investment alternatives, the firm first estimates its dollar investment requirement. Next, the funds available from internal sources (earnings and deprecia-

---

[2]Our discussion of dividend policy will generally follow the approach used in studying capital structure earlier—theory first, followed by managerial considerations. However, unlike capital structure, which was covered in two chapters, we confine dividend policy to a single chapter.

tion) are estimated. The firm decides on a long-run target debt–equity ratio and then on whether any residual funds will be available for dividend payments. If a residual exists, the ratio of these residual funds to total earnings becomes the firm's long-run target payout ratio. If no residual funds are expected, the firm adopts a zero payout ratio (i.e., it pays no dividends).

The dividends themselves are irrelevant to the stockholder. If the firm can use the funds to earn a return greater than the investor's *RRR*, the investor will not resist the firm's retention of earnings. If the return from the firm's investment opportunities is below his or her *RRR*, the investor would like the firm to pay dividends. Thus there is no need for management to waste time analyzing the role of dividends on value; the company need merely analyze its investment opportunities carefully. Dividend policy is thus no more than a policy for the disbursement of surplus funds.

The residual theory of dividends appears to make further analysis of dividend policy unnecessary. However, empirical studies show that firms act as if dividends do affect their stock value. It is therefore necessary to take a closer look at the relationship between dividends and value. In studying this issue, it will be assumed that the firm's dividend policy decision is made after its investment decisions are made and that no further borrowing is done. By holding these variables constant, we can examine whether dividends are relevant by investigating the effect of a change in cash dividends on the wealth of shareholders. Notice that if the firm does not wish to borrow any more money, any plans to increase dividend payments must be financed by issuing new stock.

THE DIVIDEND IRRELEVANCE ARGUMENT

In the simplified world of perfect markets, dividends will have no impact on stock prices.[3] A stockholder may create **homemade dividends** if she desires cash by either obtaining an extra cash dividend or selling some of her stock. As her wealth is unaffected by these transactions, the value of the firm will be unaffected. This situation is depicted in Figure 17•1 and described in more detail here.

Alternative 1: Getting an Extra Cash Dividend

If the firm pays an extra cash dividend, it must raise new capital if it still wants to take on investments. Since borrowing is precluded, the firm sells new stock after paying the extra dividend to its existing stockholders. But the value of the firm will not change, since firm value depends on the return provided by

---

[3]Perfect markets are an idealized version of the capital markets in that there are no transactions costs or taxes, all investors have identical beliefs, and so on. It is very instructive for managers to understand the dividend policy implications even in this simplified scenario because it provides some powerful insights into the basic conditions under which dividends can affect stock prices.

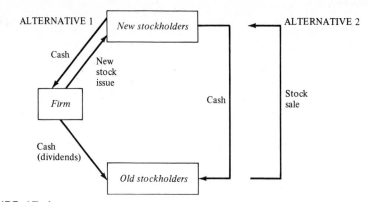

FIGURE 17·1 Irrelevance of dividends in perfect markets. The old stockholders can achieve the same effect (cash) without any action on the part of the firm. Thus any dividend policy decisions have no impact on stockholders' wealth.

the firm's assets, the investments have already been chosen, and no more borrowing will be done.[4]

If firm value is not changing and new stockholders buy stock, the old stockholders must suffer a loss of wealth because firm value has to be shared with the new stockholders. What is the value of this capital loss? It is equal to the part of the firm's value that belongs to the new stockholders. But if the new stockholders paid a fair price for their stock, the value of their equity must equal the extra dividends paid to the old owners. Thus the old stockholders suffer a capital loss exactly equal to the dividends they have received, and their total wealth is unchanged. After the extra dividends have been paid, old stockholders own the same number of shares, each worth less than before.

Alternative 2: Sale of Stock

Now consider the stockholder's second alternative. If she sells some of her stock to someone else, she has fewer shares of stock, but each share is worth exactly the same amount as before the sale. Clearly, the investor's realized cash (effectively, a dividend) equals the loss in her equity ownership of the firm.

Recognize that these alternatives are equivalent. If the firm pays a dividend, it does what the stockholder can do by herself. To be more specific, there is no difference between alternative 1, where the firm pays a dividend and lowers the stockholder's equity position, and alternative 2, where the stockholder sells some of her equity by herself. Stockholders can, in effect, create homemade dividends, and the act of paying dividends by the firm should have no effect on value.[5] In other words, dividend policy is irrelevant. Figure 17·1 depicts this

---

[4] Recall from earlier chapters that the value of the firm is determined by the operating cash flows generated by the firm and the appropriate opportunity cost of capital.

[5] As in the capital structure decision, the firm is not creating any new security by paying dividends. Shareholders have no new opportunities because of the firm's extra cash dividend.

discussion. Notice that the benefits from a dividend payment can be replicated by stockholders without any action on the part of the firm. Why, then, should dividends increase stock values?

KEY CONCEPT: In perfect capital markets, dividends have no impact on stock price.

WHAT HAPPENS WHEN A COMPANY CUTS ITS DIVIDENDS?

The discussion so far has considered the case of a firm increasing its dividend. But what if the firm plans to reduce dividends? Since investment and borrowing policies are assumed to be fixed, the reduction in dividends must be matched by a reduction in the number of shares of stock to be issued or by a repurchase of existing stock. This is the exact opposite of the previous situation, where a firm issued stock. By repurchasing stock, the firm decreases the number of shares outstanding, and since firm value is unchanged, each share is worth more. As far as the stockholder is concerned, the reduction in dividends is matched by an increase in the value of his shares, and repurchase has no net impact on his wealth.

A CLOSER LOOK AT THE IRRELEVANCE ARGUMENT

Having considered dividend irrelevance in perfect markets, it is now important to examine more closely some issues that are crucial for this result.

The most important requirement for dividend irrelevance is that markets be efficient. When a company issues new stock to finance its increased dividend, dividend policy is irrelevant if the new stock is sold for a fair price. Since efficient markets ensure that all assets are fairly priced, the dividend irrelevance argument requires that markets be efficient. This is crucial for the validity of the irrelevance result.

Regularity of Dividends

A common criticism of the dividend irrelevance argument is the "bird-in-the-hand" argument. An investor's return from stock comes from dividend yield and capital gains yield. It is generally accepted that high-dividend-yield stocks provide smaller capital gains. Even if an increase in dividend yields is exactly offset by a decrease in capital gains, one cannot choose between the two without looking explicitly at risk. Since managers like to follow a stable dividend policy, and because the vagaries of the stock market are not controllable by managers, the bird-in-the-handers argue that dividend payments are less risky and should therefore be preferred by risk-averse investors. However, this argument is fallacious. This is because the value of the firm, as seen in Chapter 15, is determined by the overall cash flow generated by the assets—and this does not depend on dividend policy.[6] (Remember that borrowing and investment decisions have already been made.)

MARKET IMPERFECTIONS AND TAXES

As just seen, the irrelevence of dividend policy rests on the crucial assumption of perfect and efficient markets. However, the real world has several imperfections, and it is interesting to look at the impact of some of these imperfections on dividend policy. In this regard, flotation costs, transactions costs, institutional constraints, and, finally (and most important), taxes warrant a closer look.

Flotation Costs

The dividend irrelevance discussion earlier assumed that if a company chooses to pay an extra dividend, it can finance this costlessly by issuing new equity. As a practical matter, however, flotation costs—the costs associated with issuing a new security (e.g., brokers' commissions)—make retained earnings more attractive to the firm than a new stock issue. If dividends and new equity are essentially the same, it does not make economic sense to pay out dividends and then to replace the lost funds with more costly new equity. Thus **flotation costs** tend to favor lower dividend payouts.

Transactions Costs

Whenever investors sell or buy a financial asset, they incur **transactions costs** in the form of brokerage commissions. Consider the case of a stockholder who wishes to increase his current consumption or to invest in another stock issued by another company. Because of transactions costs, this investor will prefer higher dividends on his current stock. With higher dividends, the sale of the stock may become unnecessary and the investor may avoid the transactions costs entirely. This shareholder will therefore prefer that the company pay higher dividends.[7]

However, this does not necessarily favor higher dividend payouts. There may be other investors who do not need the dividend to increase their current consumption; they may want to increase their capital gains instead. For such investors, a firm's dividend payment may not be an attractive feature, since the dividends have to be reinvested in another financial asset. Because of brokerage

---

[6]We are really saying that *NOI* is unaffected by a firm's dividend payout.

[7]Tax considerations are ignored temporarily.

commissions, these investors are forced to incur additional expenses. On the other hand, if the firm retained the dividend and invested it on behalf of the stockholder, the investor would receive an eventual capital gain without incurring any transactions costs in the meantime.

The Clientele Effect

Thus, given the different preferences among investors for dividends and capital gains, there is no unambiguous implication for a firm's dividend policy. Firms that have high dividend payout ratios will attract investors with a preference for current income, while low-payout firms will attract stockholders who prefer capital gains. This is the **clientele effect**—a firm will attract the clientele that approves of its dividend policies. As a result, companies have an incentive to publicize their dividend policies. This is done by maintaining a stable, predictable dividend policy. Potential shareholders can then know beforehand whether a particular firm's dividend policy is in their best interest. A sudden change in dividend policy will cause some rearrangement in the firm's ownership; disapproving stockholders may sell out, thereby putting downward pressure on stock prices. Because of this, managers favor a "sticky" (stable) dividend policy. Table 17•1 presents a partial list of companies that have consistently paid dividends for over 50 years.

Institutional Constraints

Contractual Constraints When a firm borrows money (debt capital), the contract between the firm and the creditors may include some constraints to protect the bondholders. For example, firms are sometimes allowed to declare dividends only out of earnings generated after the debt contract goes into effect. Similarly, a firm issuing preferred stock may also be constrained in some ways to protect the preferred stockholders. In addition, preferred stock contracts usually stipulate that common stockholders cannot be paid any new dividends unless all preferred dividends in arrears have been paid.

Legal Constraints Many institutions are not allowed by law to invest in securities that have not had a long record of stable dividends. Perhaps these legal requirements are the result of historical beliefs that dividends indicate the well-being of a firm. Such restrictions force these institutions to prefer liberal-dividend-payout firms.

Several universities and trusts are forbidden by law to use the capital gain on their investments. They rely heavily on the cash "throw-off" from their stock (i.e., dividends) to fund scholarships, endowments, and so on. These institutions, too, have a logical preference for high-dividend-payout stocks. The dividend income is used to service other fixed obligations.[8]

---

[8]Dividends become all the more attractive because most universities do not pay taxes.

TABLE 17·1 Some Consistent
Dividend-Paying Companies

Name of Company	Dividends Since:
Affiliated Publications	1882
Allied-Signal	1887
American Express	1870
AT&T	1881
Bank of Boston	1784
Bank of New England	1830
Bank of New York	1785
Bay State Gas	1853
Bell Canada	1881
Chase Manhattan	1848
Chemical New York	1827
CIGNA	1867
Cincinnati Bell	1879
Cincinnati	1853
CITICORP	1813
CON ED	1885
Continental Corp	1854
Corning Glass	1881
EXXON	1882
Eli Lilly	1885
Pennwalt	1863
Providence Energy	1849
Security Pacific	1881
Singer	1863
Stanley Works	1877
Travelers	1864
UGI Corp.	1885
U.S. Trust	1854

Source: Excerpted with permission from
CHANGING TIMES Magazine, (©) 1987
Kiplinger Washington Editors, Inc., June
1987. This reprint is not to be altered in any
way, except with permission from
CHANGING TIMES.

State laws can also affect dividend policy, at least to the extent that insolvent firms are not allowed to pay dividends. A firm is declared insolvent when the value of its liabilities exceeds the value of its assets. Zero payout is a legal requirement for insolvent firms.

Corporate Taxes

Corporate taxes have no impact whatsoever on the dividend decision, since dividends are paid only out of net income (*NI*). Corporate taxes enter the picture before the dividend issue needs to be addressed by management. Thus corporate tax effects should not influence a firm's optimal dividend policy.[9]

Personal Taxes

Personal taxes have in the past had a definite implication for dividend policy. In general, prior to the Tax Reform Act of 1986, the tax law favored low payout by firms. This is because shareholders had to pay ordinary income tax on dividend income and lower capital gains tax on long-term gains. Under the present tax code, the tax rate on capital gains is no different than the ordinary income tax rate, so that tax implications do not affect the dividend decision, as in the past. However, it is important to keep this tax bias in mind; serious efforts are already being made to restore the capital gains tax rate.

THEN WHY DO COMPANIES PAY DIVIDENDS?

If under some conditions dividends are irrelevent, why do so many companies pay them? And why are some dividends so large? There is some evidence that dividend policy does not affect firm value. Other researchers have found a positive relationship between dividend yield and expected before-tax stock returns, indicating that dividend policy does, in fact, affect stock prices. The issue has not been resolved satisfactorily. Further study is required before we can draw unambiguous conclusions about the relationship between dividend policy and value.

MANAGERIAL CONSIDERATIONS

In addition to the market imperfections that can affect a firm's dividend policy—transactions costs, flotation costs, institutional restrictions, and so on—there are a few other firm-specific factors that must be considered in making dividend decisions.

The Firm's Financial Reserves

The amount of dividends paid by a company is strongly influenced by a firm's financial reserves. Cash, other liquid assets, and unused borrowing capacity are examples of financial reserves. Consider the case of a company that has an unexpected but temporary reduction in earnings. Rather than lower the amount

---

[9]There is one exception, however. If a company retains an excessive amount of earnings without paying dividends, the IRS will penalize the firm for its "improper accumulation." The IRS interprets this to be a tax dodge unless the firm is able to justify its need for internally generated funds. Such justification is not, however, a difficult task for most companies.

of dividends paid, the company could draw on its financial reserves to keep the dividends at their originally planned level.

Flexibility

If a firm has the ability to postpone some new investments, this flexibility may help the manager keep a stable dividend policy. Temporary decreases in earnings need not lead to dividend decreases; management may choose to postpone some new investments to a later date. The funds hitherto earmarked for specific investments can be used to pay dividends.

Access to Equity Capital

Access to new equity capital plays a major role in influencing a manager's decision to pursue a residual or nonresidual dividend policy. Recall that a residual policy implies that the firm first uses its earnings to accept new investments; then the surpluses, if any, are paid out as dividends. However, if equity capital is easily available at a reasonable cost, the company may find it advantageous to deviate from its residual policy. If the stockholders want a larger dividend, the company can go ahead and issue new stock to finance the extra disbursement. All firms may not be able to do this. Needless to say, larger, more established firms have better access to new equity capital than do smaller, developmental-stage companies.

Control Considerations

With a liberal dividend policy, a company increases the probability of raising fresh capital at some future date. If the present shareholders cannot (or do not) subscribe to the new shares, new stockholders can dilute their controlling interest in the firm. Thus stockholders who are very sensitive to potential loss of control will prefer a low-dividend-payout policy.

Ability to Borrow

There is no reason why a company should finance future needs with equity only; debt, the other obvious alternative, need not be ruled out. However, management may often be unwilling to increase its debt for one reason or another; for example, the firm might already have excessive financial leverage, or the debt may be too expensive. In such cases, the company may not be able to make generous dividend payments.

Inflation

During periods of inflation, it is entirely possible that the funds generated from depreciation will be insufficient to replace outdated or unusable plant and machinery. Replacement costs may be so high that companies may have to acquire new equipment with a fresh influx of capital. In situations such as this, a company may want to reduce its payout ratio to ensure that it will have a sufficient amount of internally generated funds to finance necessary replacements or even new expansion.

The previous paragraphs have highlighted some of the factors that must be taken into account before setting dividend policy. Unfortunately, no clear-cut formula or decision-theoretic methodology for setting dividend policy exists. Part of the problem is that the link between dividends and firm value is not altogether clear. Even if dividends affect a firm's value, unless the manager knows exactly *how* they affect value, there is not much that can be done to increase the wealth of the stockholders. It is somewhat ironic that after so much research into the dividend policy of a firm, we still have no prescriptions for management. To conclude, we quote Fischer Black:[10] "What should corporations do about dividend policy? We don't know."

Learning Check for Section 17·1

Review Questions

17·1.   What is the residual theory of dividends? What are the implications of this theory?

17·2.   Explain why dividends are irrelevant in perfect capital markets. What does *irrelevant* mean?

17·3.   Since stockholders can create homemade dividends, corporate dividends should not affect firm value. Explain this argument.

17·4.   What are the implications for a firm's dividend policy of the various imperfections in the marketplace?

17·5.   What is the clientele effect? What should a manager do to cope with the diversity of the firm's owners?

17·6.   Explain the significance of various managerial considerations affecting dividend policy.

New Terms

Clientele effect	Flotation costs	Residual theory of
Contractual constraints	Homemade dividends	dividends

[10]See Fischer Black, "The Dividend Puzzle," *The Journal of Portfolio Management,* Winter 1976, 5–8; reprinted in *The Modern Theory of Corporate Finance,* M. C. Jensen and C. W. Smith, Jr. (eds.) (New York: McGraw-Hill Book Company, 1984), pp. 634–639.

SECTION 17•2 *Dividend Payment Policies and Procedures*

Although different corporations have different dividend payment procedures, we can identify three broad payment procedures that most companies follow.

CONSTANT DIVIDEND PER SHARE

Many corporations decide on a fixed dollar amount of annual dividends per share and pay out this dividend regularly. Sudden increases in earnings for a company that is following this procedure will have no effect on dividend payments. Management is unlikely to increase dividends unless they are perceived to be a permanent increase in the firm's future earnings stream. Similarly, these companies are very hesitant to cut dividends because of a temporary dip in the firm's earnings. Figure 17•2 illustrates this dividend payment procedure for a hypothetical furniture company—Bates, Inc.

Notice that Bates' dividend in 1960 was $1 out of an earnings per share (*EPS*) of $3. The 1960 dividend payout ratio was therefore $1/$3 = 0.33, or 33%. Bates continued to pay out $1 until 1980 even though earnings did jump earlier (1970). Management did not alter its dividends in 1970 because it did not expect the sudden increase in earnings to become permanent. Similarly, management did not cut dividends in 1982 in spite of a drastic decrease in earnings. Apparently, the company knew that the decrease was only temporary. In fact, in 1980, management actually raised the dividend $1.20. This is because a more

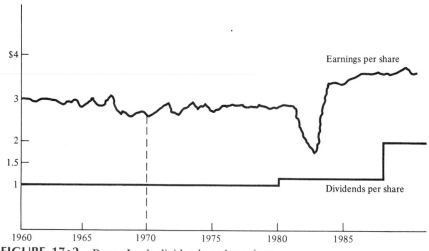

FIGURE 17•2   Bates, Inc.'s dividends and earnings.

sustained higher level of earnings was anticipated and management's dividend payments were influenced primarily by long-term permanent earnings trends.

If it is reasonable to assume that the earnings of a company will increase through time, the constant-dividend-payout procedure can be more accurately characterized as a *gradually increasing dividend payment policy.*

Another variant of this approach to dividend payments is the *stable growth* policy. Companies espousing this practice decide to maintain a constant growth rate in dividends. For example, a firm can plan to pay out dividends such that the growth rate in dividends over an extended period is 5%. For this procedure to be feasible, earnings must increase at a fairly reasonable rate. In inflationary periods, this requirement is more reasonably met. Perhaps this explains why this stable growth policy was especially popular in the mid-1970s.

CONSTANT PAYOUT RATIO

Some firms decide on a certain dividend payout ratio and stick to it through time. For example, if Bates chooses to follow a 20% payout policy, it would pay out $0.20, $0.80, and $0.40 in annual dividends per share if its earnings were, say, $1.00, $4.00, and $2.00 per share over the next three years. However, since earnings invariably fluctuate over time, a constant-payout-ratio procedure will yield an uneven stream of dividend payments. Managers in general prefer to hold the dollar amount of dividends stable, so the constant-payout-ratio policy is not pervasive.

REGULAR PLUS EXTRA DIVIDENDS

Certain corporations find a policy of a low, regular dividend plus an annual "extra" dividend plan attractive. Clearly, management has more flexibility with this approach than with the constant-dividend procedure. With fluctuating earnings, a company may find this policy especially attractive. If earnings are high, the company can issue an extra annual dividend. If earnings are below expectations, the extra dividend can be reduced or eliminated completely. Notice that this policy attempts to maintain a form of stability in dividend payments.

WHY STABILITY?

It is generally accepted without much argument that managers like to follow a stable dividend payment procedure. The three procedures just outlined all have one form of stability or another. Why this focus on stability? If it can be argued successfully that stable dividend payments increase stock price, this insistence on stability on the part of managers is justified. By contrast, if stability of dividends is irrelevant in terms of stock price, this preference for stability is hard to understand. Although formal valuation models have not been able to demonstrate satisfactorily the link between dividend stability and value, it is generally agreed that there may be a positive impact on stock prices resulting from a stable dividend policy. Some potential reasons for this link between stability of dividends and value are explored next.

The Informational Content of Dividends

It has often been pointed out that a company that raises its dividends often experiences an increase in its stock price and that a company that lowers its dividends has a falling stock price. This seems to suggest that dividends do matter in that they affect stock price. However, this causal relationship has been explained away by several researchers on the grounds that dividends per se are irrelevant; rather, it is the **informational content of dividends** that affects stock prices.

Recall that managers have a propensity to follow a stable dividend policy. In light of this, it is argued that any change in dividends is a signal from managers to stockholders about the future prospects of the firm. A dividend increase, for example, may suggest that management expects future earning prospects to improve. For temporary earnings increases, managers do not increase dividends. Similarly, given management's reluctance to cut dividends, dividend decreases suggest to stockholders that future earnings are expected to be lower. Of course, a company may succeed in fooling stockholders in the short run by not reducing dividends even if a permanent decline in earnings is expected. However, sooner or later, the stockholders will be able to see through this ploy. Miller and Modigliani, the proponents of this informational content of dividends theory, argue that this, too, is only a temporary phenomenon. Although a dividend increase may be perceived by stockholders as a harbinger of good news, stockholders can soon verify whether their interpretation of the dividend increase was justified. Thus there should be no direct link between dividends and stock prices. If any, there may be a short-term link between dividend changes and stock prices because of the informational content.

Legal History

Several fiduciary institutions are restricted in their equity investments in that they can only buy the stock of companies on their "legal list." **Legal listings** refer to the process of being included in a list of potential investment candidates. Firms like to be included on the legal list of institutions because this increases the demand for their stock. Although different institutions use different criteria in deciding whether a company should be included in this list, a common requirement is that the company's record reflect a stable, nondecreasing dividend policy. For this reason, stability of dividends is deemed important by managers. Since the purchase of their stock by these large institutional investors can put upward pressure on the stock price, corporate managers offer stability in dividends to institutional managers.

Two possible explanations for managers' preferences for a stable dividend policy have been identified. As noted earlier, the effect of a stable dividend policy on stock prices is not fully understood. What is lacking is a detailed study of this issue involving a large number of stocks. However, until this is done, the general belief that a stable dividend policy has a favorable effect on a company's stock price cannot easily be verified.

DIVIDEND PAYMENT PROCEDURES

Most U.S. corporations pay dividends quarterly. In addition, about 10% of them also declare an extra annual dividend. There are several dates involved in the payment of dividends. These dates are shown in Figure 17•3. All dividend payments must be declared by the board of directors. The date on which the board declares the dividend for the next quarter is quite appropriately known as the **declaration date.** The board also specifies a **date of record.** All stockholders on the date of record are eligible to receive the cash dividend. It is therefore on this date that the registrar of the company "closes" the books to mail out the dividend checks to the shareholders "on record."

Another date that has a special significance is the **ex-dividend date,** which is the fourth business day preceding the date of record.[11] Whereas the company paying the dividend decides on the date of record, the ex-dividend date is established by the securities industry. Consider a typical NYSE corporation with thousands of traded shares every day. Trading takes place even on the record date, and it takes some time before the company's books reflect these ownership changes. The ex-dividend date is set purely to ensure that the right owners get the dividend check.

All investors who own shares before the ex-dividend date are entitled to receive the cash dividend. If Mr. X buys the stock from Ms. Y on or after the ex-dividend date, Mr. X is not entitled to the dividend because the company's books will list Ms. Y as the owner. When the stock goes ex-dividend, its price falls by an amount approximately equal to the dividend declared.[12] The **payment date** is the date on which the firm actually mails out the dividend checks.

| Declaration date | Ex-dividend date | Date of record | Payment date |

Time

FIGURE 17•3 Dividend payment dates.

---

[11]Very often a weekend will be involved. Thus the ex-dividend date is usually six days prior to the record date.

[12]The stock price decline is not exactly equal to the dividend declared because of tax considerations.

Dividend Reinvestment Plans

Dividend reinvestment plans (DRPs) are a recent phenomenon. Many corporations allow shareholders to reinvest their cash dividends in additional shares of the firm's stock. Two standard DRP plans are currently in vogue.

The first arrangement involves a trustee (usually a bank), which collects the dividends from all stockholders opting for automatic reinvestment and buys the company's shares in the open market. Because the volume of transactions is usually large, the brokerage fees are relatively small.

The second arrangement calls for the purchase of newly issued stock. To encourage this practice, the company typically offers a 5 to 10% discount from the current market price of the stock. Allied Corporation, Chase Manhattan, Merchantile Texas, Union Carbide, and Wells Fargo are examples of companies that offer a 5% discount. Using this plan, a company can raise new equity capital without incurring additional flotation costs. In recent years, approximately one-fourth of all new common stock issued by corporations has been sold via DRPs. One factor that detracts from the broad appeal of DRPs is that shareholders must pay ordinary income taxes on the dividends even though they do not actually receive them when they participate in a DRP plan.

STOCK DIVIDENDS AND STOCK SPLITS

Sometimes, instead of paying a cash dividend, companies pay **stock dividends** or announce a **stock split**. Stock dividends and stock splits, except for some accounting differences, are very similar. Table 17•2 provides a partial list of companies that have had stock dividends or stock splits extensively over the last decade.

Stock Dividends

Table 17•3 illustrates the net worth accounts for the Gamma Ray Company before and after a stock dividend. Gamma currently has 500,000 shares outstanding ($10 par), and the stock's current market price is $30. Gamma's net

TABLE 17•2 Some Companies That Frequently Split Their Stock or Pay Stock Dividends

Alaska Airlines	Hewlett-Packard
Boeing	Luby Cafeterias
Church's Fried Chicken	Mesa Petroleum
Federal Express	Parker Pen Company
General Tire and Rubber	Southwest Airlines
Heinz	Wendy's International

TABLE 17·3 Stock Dividends, Gamma Ray Company[a]

a. Before Stock Dividend		b. After Stock Dividend	
Common stock		Common stock	
($10 par, 500,000 shares)	$5,000,000	($10 par, 550,000 shares)	$5,500,000
Paid-in capital	2,000,000	Paid-in capital	3,000,000
Retained earnings	8,000,000	Retained earnings	6,500,000
Net worth	$15,000,000	Net worth	$15,000,000

$$EPS = \frac{\$750,000}{500,000} = \$1.50 \qquad\qquad EPS = \frac{\$750,000}{550,000} = \$1.37$$

[a]Stocks dividend = 10% or 50,000 shares; net income = $750,000; current stock price = $30.

income is $750,000. Assume that Gamma declares a 10% stock dividend. Table 17·3b shows what happens.

With a 10% stock dividend, 50,000 new shares are created and shareholders receive 1 new share for every 10 shares they own. Since the stock price is $30 in the marketplace, Gamma has effectively created $30 \times 50,000 = \$1,500,000$ that must be accounted for somehow. Since the stock dividend does not really increase the firm's net worth, a few accounting changes are made to reflect the effects of this dividend. The $1,500,000 is removed from the retained earnings account and transferred to the common stock and paid-in capital accounts. Since Gamma's par value is unchanged, the common stock account increases by $10 \times 50,000$ shares, or $500,000. The remaining $1,000,000 from retained earnings goes into the paid-in capital account.

Notice that the net worth of the Gamma Ray Company and the par value of Gamma's stock are unchanged. It is only the number of shares and the various components of net worth that have changed. Because the number of shares has increased while the net profits after tax are the same, *EPS* has fallen from $1.50 to $1.37. However, the total earnings to a stockholder remain unaffected. To see this, note that a stockholder with 10 shares before the stock dividend would have $1.50 \times 10 = \$15$ in earnings. After the stock dividend, his earnings would be $1.37 \times 11 = \$15$. The stockholder now has more shares, but each share is capable of earning proportionately less. Thus the stock dividend does not increase the wealth of the shareholder; it is purely an accounting change.[13]

Then why do companies issue stock dividends? There must be some benefit, either to the company or to the stockholders. The majority of the arguments advanced rely on some sort of psychological impact on investors receiving stock dividends. For example, it has been argued that an investor who wishes to liquidate some stock may be more comfortable liquidating the stock dividend

---

[13]In fact, stock dividends are not taxable because the IRS itself does not recognize them as a thing of value.

because he does not view this as dipping into the principal. Another argument for stock dividends is that they (like cash dividends) convey some information. If a company in a growth phase wishes to pay dividends but at the same time needs to conserve cash, stock dividends convey the same signal as cash dividends. Perhaps this is why most growth companies issue stock dividends. Although these explanations are far from entirely satisfactory, there is one situation in which stock dividends do result in an actual dividend increase. This happens when management chooses to maintain the same cash dividends per share even after the stock dividends are paid. Stockholders receive the same dollar amount in cash dividends for each share they own, but now they own more shares. Finally, stock dividends may be used by firms to keep their stock's market price below a prespecified limit.[14] The disadvantage of stock dividends is that they are much more expensive to administer than cash dividends. Thus, when used instead of cash dividends, stock dividends can conceivably work against the best interests of the firm.

Stock Splits

A stock split is very similar to a stock dividend.[15] The fundamental difference between a stock dividend and a stock split is that unlike a stock dividend, where the stock's par value is unaffected, a stock split lowers the stock's par value.

Table 17·4 shows the net worth accounts for the Beta Scan Corporation before and after a two-for-one stock split. A two-for-one stock split implies that every share held by stockholders before the split is two shares after the split. Notice from Table 17·4 that just as with the stock dividend, the company's net worth is unaffected by the stock split. However, for a two-for-one stock split, the par value is halved and the number of shares is doubled. Neither the common stock account nor the paid-in capital account is otherwise affected.

Stock splits, like stock dividends, do not transmit any extra value to the stockholder. They are accounting rearrangements. Companies announce stock

TABLE 17·4 Two-for-One Stock Split: Beta Scan Corporation

a. Before Stock Split		b. After Stock Split	
Common stock		Common stock	
($10 par, 200,000 shares)	$2,000,000	($5 par, 400,000 shares)	$2,000,000
Paid-in capital	1,000,000	Paid-in capital	1,000,000
Retained earnings	4,000,000	Retained earnings	4,000,000
Net worth	$7,000,000	Net worth	$7,000,000

[14]With a stock dividend, *EPS* falls, and if the price/earnings (*P/E*) ratio is the same, the stock price will fall. We will take a closer look at this in the context of stock splits.

[15]A stock split is sometimes considered a large stock dividend. In fact, the NYSE defines a stock dividend greater than 25% as a stock split.

splits primarily to lower the price of the stock so that it is in an optimal trading range. Consider a stock that was selling at $160 before a split. Management might feel that the stock is too expensive for most investors and lowers it to $80 with a two-for-one split or to $40 with a four-for-one split. Presumably, because the stock will now be more affordable, the increased demand for the stock will put upward pressure on its price.

Companies may also split their stock simply to increase the number of shares outstanding. A company that is contemplating being listed on the NYSE may find this appealing. To be listed on the NYSE, a company must have a minimum number of shares outstanding, and a stock split is one way of increasing this number in a short period.

Reverse splits are another form of stock split, except that now the objective is to reduce the number of shares outstanding and increase the par value per share. For example, if the Beta Scan Corporation (Table 17·4) announced a one-for-two reverse split, stockholders would get one new share for every two they currently own. Beta Scan's par value per share would now double to $20, and the total number of shares outstanding would fall to 100,000. Again, net worth is unaffected.

Some companies announce stock reverse splits to avoid the "penny stock" label. Stocks selling on, say, the OTC market for below $10 are often labeled penny stocks and are generally considered to be very speculative. Many institutional investors are not allowed to invest in these stocks. With a reverse split, a company can appeal to these potential investors. However, most participants in the marketplace regard a reverse split as a desperate attempt by a company to prop up its sagging stock price. Whether or not this is true depends on the company's record of past earnings and the potential for future earnings growth.

Corporate Share Repurchase

Very often, corporate **share repurchase** is viewed as an alternative to paying dividends. If a firm has some surplus cash (or if it can borrow), it may choose to buy back some of its own stock. Such repurchases of stock can be accomplished in one of two ways: by means of a tender offer or by direct operations in the stock market. In any event, repurchased stock becomes **treasury stock** and plays no real part in the firm's day-to-day affairs. Treasury stock carries with it no voting rights and is not eligible for dividend payments.

◼ HIGHLIGHT
HENRY FORD'S DIVIDEND POLICY

Although dividend payments are not presently a legal requirement for corporations, this was not always true. The fascinating story of Henry Ford's dividend policies is an interesting aside to the dividend policy discussion in the text.

In 1916, stockholders John and Horace Dodge brought suit against the Ford

Motor Company for not paying a "reasonable" dividend. From an adverse decision in a lower court the case was appealed in the Supreme Court of Michigan, and early in 1919, Ford was ordered to pay a delayed dividend of $19 million with interest at 5% from the date of the first decision. The Supreme Court's decision stated that nonpayment of dividends to the stockholders was, considering the remarkable profits, "illegal and arbitrary."

Angered by this ruling, Henry Ford vowed to eliminate all other shareholders in his company by repurchasing shares, regardless of cost. On his original investment of less than $2,500, Couzens received $29 million from Ford. His sister, Mrs. Haus, who had put in $100 in 1903, received $200,000. Anderson and Racklam each made $12.5 million on their original $5,000 investment and the Dodges took in $25 million on their $10,000 investment. All of this was in addition to $30 million paid to them as shareholders over 16 years.

How did Ford pay for this expensive repurchase? Even the incredible Ford Motor Company could not come up with an immediate $75 million in cash. To finance this repurchase, Ford embarked on a brilliant idea involving his Model T car.

Ford first borrowed $75 million from Old Colony in Boston and Chase Securities in New York, agreeing to repay the loan in April 1931. However, the Great Depression began in 1929. To avoid defaulting on the bank loans, Henry Ford ordered his company to produce 90,000 Model T cars at incredible speed. These cars were to be shipped off to the dealers even though the dealers had not asked for them. The cars were to be transported at the receiver's expense and cash was expected upon delivery.

The dealers, anticipating a deluge of cars they had not ordered, threw up their hands in despair and challenged Ford's demands. Ford responded with a warning. If they did not take the cars and pay for them in cash, they would lose their franchises. In complete helplessness the dealers raised the cash through local banks. Thus Henry Ford received the cash to finance his repurchase from local banks all over the country.

Source: Compiled from information in *Henry Ford: A Great Life in Brief* by Roger Burlingame (New York: Alfred A. Knopf, 1955). From the Harry Ransom Collection, University of Texas at Austin. The research assistance of Van Harlow is gratefully acknowledged.

The "good-buy" argument is sometimes advanced as a reason for stock repurchase. Management, if it feels that current stock prices are depressed, may invest in this good buy through a repurchase. For example, the Tandy Corporation has, on several occasions, repurchased its own stock:

What is the rationale behind the decision to repurchase shares? Tandy management and directors believe the shares represent an attractive investment for the Company and its stockholders. At prices prevailing in recent years, which have been quite modest multiples of current earnings relative to historical norms, the purchase of shares with borrowed funds will enhance the future return on equity and earnings per share growth because the profit margins of the Company are in excess of the interest costs of the funds borrowed.

A Statement of Financial Policy, Tandy Corporation Annual Report

However, this rationale for repurchase has serious problems. For one thing, when shares are repurchased, there is upward pressure on the price. At the same time, if the firm is forgoing better investments to effect this repurchase, downward pressure is put on the stock price. Which effect will dominate?

There are also several ethical questions that arise. If management feels that its stock is undervalued, then clearly it has some information that the marketplace does not have. Since it is reasonable to assume that management has access to information about the company that outsiders cannot get, does this make repurchase insider trading? Insider trading is unfair to certain investors. In the case of a stock repurchase, if management buys undervalued stock, then shareholders who did not sell realize a capital gain. All that has happened is a transfer of wealth from selling to nonselling shareholders. No value has been created.

Sometimes stock repurchases are justified on the grounds that the company needs the stock to institute employee stock option plans. This reason is questionable: Why not issue new shares, instead, to employees who exercise their options?

Finally, stock repurchases, it is sometimes argued, are a way of altering the firm's debt–equity ratio. For a firm that wishes to increase its financial leverage, one alternative is to issue new debt and use the proceeds to buy back some common stock. However, it must be pointed out that this is seldom done.

Learning Check for Section 17·2

Review Questions

17·7. Explain the three broad dividend payment procedures used by corporations.

17·8. Why do managers like to follow a stable dividend policy?

17·9. What does it mean to say that dividends have informational content?

17·10. What is the significance of the ex-dividend date, the declaration date, and the date of record?

17·11. Stock dividends and stock splits increase the stockholders' wealth. True or false? Why or why not?

17·12. What are some of the commonly advanced reasons for repurchasing shares? Do these arguments deserve merit? To what extent?

New Terms

Date of record	Ex-dividend date	Payment date
Declaration date	Information content	Stock dividends
Dividend reinvestment	of dividends	Stock splits
plans (DRPs)	Legal listing	Treasury stock

SUMMARY

Do Dividends Affect Firm Value?

The relationship between dividend payments and stock prices is not entirely clear. In perfect and efficient capital markets, dividends are irrelevant and it is unnecessary for management to worry about an optimal dividend policy. When market imperfections are recognized, however, the situation does not become any clearer. Some imperfections, such as transactions costs and the legal requirements of some institutional investors, encourage larger dividend payouts, whereas other imperfections, such as contractual constraints, encourage greater retention. In addition, the impact of several managerial considerations makes the relationship between stock prices and dividend policies even more unclear.

Dividend Payment Policies and Procedures

In general, most managers, justifiably or unjustifiably, prefer stable dividend policies. Perhaps this is because dividend changes convey information that affects stock prices. Dividends need not be paid in cash. Stock dividends and stock splits, considered alternatives to cash dividends, are really accounting rearrangements that have no appreciable effect on the wealth of the stockholders. Corporate share repurchases, achieved either through tender offers or by direct operations in the market, are another alternative to dividend payments. Although several reasons have been advanced for share repurchases, most of them are not satisfactory. Many believe that share repurchases are driven by complex tax considerations. These tax-based arguments, too, are not fully understood.

PROBLEMS

17•1.   Prepare a list of the factors that managers must take into account in making the dividend payment decision.

17•2.   All else remaining constant, how should an increase in the corporate tax rate affect a firm's optimal dividend policy?

17•3.   Company *A* declares a dividend on May 10, 1986, to all stockholders on record on May 14. If Howard Smith buys the stock from Ralph Biggy on May 16, who is entitled to the dividend?

17•4.   What is the impact of stock dividends and stock splits on stockholders' equity?

17•5.   The Zetamax Corporation has expected earnings of $4.5 million. It plans a total investment outlay of $3 million this year. Historically, Zetamax has had a dividend payout ratio of 25%. Calculate the amount of dividends that the company will distribute.

17•6.   ABC Company's 1986 annual report showed that the company had originally issued 300,000 shares ($4 par) at $16 per share. Over time, the company's accumulated earnings had amounted to $3 million. If the board of directors now declares a four-for-one stock split, prepare the stockholders' equity section of the balance sheet for ABC before and after the split.

17•7.   XYZ Company has issued 100,000 shares ($2 par value) at $15 per share. The company's retained earnings amount to $5 million and its current stock price is $50 per share. If the company declares a 15% stock dividend, show how the stockholders' equity section of the company's balance sheet will appear before and after the stock dividend.

17•8.   Conrad Doenges owns 200 shares of GMC stock. If GMC declares a dividend of $5 per share (the current price of GMC is $65), estimate the price of the stock on the ex-dividend date. (Assume that the stock price is constant until then.) Has Conrad lost money because his stock is worth less?

READINGS

BAKER, W. KENT, AND PATRICIA L. GALLAGHER, "Management's View of Stock Splits," *Financial Management*, Summer 1980, 73–77.

BLACK, FISHER, AND MYRON SCHOLES, "The Effects of Dividend Yield and Dividend Policy on Common Stock Prices and Returns," *Journal of Financial Economics*, May 1974, 1–22.

BRITTAIN, J. A., *Corporate Dividend Policy* (Washington, D.C.: The Brookings Institution, 1966).

COPELAND, THOMAS E., "Liquidity Changes Following Stock Splits," *Journal of Finance*, March 1979, 115–141.

LEWELLEN, WILBUR G., KENNETH L. STANLEY, RONALD C. LEASE, AND GARY G. SCHLARBAUM, "Some Direct Evidence on the Dividend Clientele Phenomenon," *Journal of Finance*, December 1978, 1385–1399.

LINTNER, JOHN, "Distribution of Incomes of Corporations among Dividends, Retained Earnings, and Taxes," *American Economic Review*, May 1956, 97–113.

LITZENBERGER, R. H., AND K. RAMASWAMY, "The Effects of Dividends on Common Stock Prices: Tax Effects or Information Effects," *Journal of Finance*, May 1982, 429–443.

LOOMIS, C. J., "A Case for Dropping Dividends," *Fortune*, June 15, 1968, pp. 181ff.

MILLER, M. H., AND M. S. SCHOLES, "Dividends and Taxes," *Journal of Financial Economics*, May 1974, 1–2.

PART VII

Working Capital Management

18

Working Capital Management

In Chapter 6 we examined the firm's balance sheet and saw that the firm's assets and liabilities were divided into short-term and long-term categories. This division is used in many areas of finance, including asset investment decisions. Long-term asset investment—the capital budgeting process—was discussed in Chapters 10 and 11. This chapter begins the discussion of short-term asset investment decisions, commonly called **working capital management.**

In practice, the term **working capital** refers only to current assets. However, we will use this term more broadly to refer to both current assets and current liabilities. The term **net working capital** will be used to refer to the difference between a firm's current assets and current liabilities.

We will examine why working capital is important for the firm and the factors affecting the firm's working capital decisions. As we will see, the working capital decision concerns not only the amount of current assets a firm should have, but also the degree to which these current assets should be supported by short-term or long-term debt.

This chapter has four sections, whose scope and objectives are as follows:

SECTION 18·1: *The Importance of Working Capital.* This section shows why working capital decisions are important. Not only do firms have a large portion of their total assets in current assets, their managers must spend a great deal of their time making working capital decisions.

SECTION 18·2: *Short-Term Financial Decisions and Value Maximization.* This section contains an overview of working capital management and policy and its relationship to value maximization. We explain why short-term and long-term decisions are separated. The difficulties in connecting short-term decisions with value maximization are then discussed.

SECTION 18•3: *Why Current Assets and Current Liabilities Are Required.* In this section, we consider why firms invest in current assets. The idea of the operating cash conversion cycle, which measures the time it takes for the initial cash outflows for goods and services to be realized as cash inflows from sales, is examined, and the notions of permanent and temporary current assets are introduced.

SECTION 18•4: *Deciding on an Appropriate Working Capital Policy.* In the final section, we examine a firm's asset mix decision and the financing mix decision in a risk–return framework. The asset mix decision concerns the firm's mixture of short- and long-term assets. The financing mix decision concerns the mix of short- and long-term liabilities to finance the firm's short-term assets. We also discuss the interrelationship between these two decisions.

SECTION 18•1 *The Importance of Working Capital*

MANAGERIAL EFFORT

Many surveys have indicated that managers spend considerable time on day-to-day problems that involve working capital decisions. One reason for this is that current assets are short-lived investments that are continually being converted into other asset types. For example, cash is used to purchase inventory items; these inventory items eventually become accounts receivable when they are sold on credit; and finally, the receivables are transformed into cash when they are collected. With regard to current liabilities, the firm is responsible for paying these obligations on a timely basis. Taken together, decisions on the level of different working capital components become frequent, repetitive, and time consuming.

LIQUIDITY

A firm's net working capital is also often used as a measure of its liquidity position. That is, it represents the risk or probability that a firm will be unable to meet its financial obligations as they come due. Therefore, the more net working capital a firm has, the greater its ability to satisfy creditors' demands. Moreover, because net working capital serves as an illiquidity risk measure, the firm's net working capital position will affect its ability to acquire debt financing. For example, commercial banks often impose minimum working capital constraints in their loan agreements with firms. Similarly, bond indentures may contain such restrictions.

PROPORTION OF TOTAL FINANCING

One measure of working capital's importance is the extent to which corporations use it. Table 18•1 contains composite common-size balance sheets for the manufacturing, mining, and trade industries. As shown, current assets and liabilities represent sizable commitments for these firms. For example, over 40% of their total assets are devoted to current assets, while current liabilities comprise about 25% of their total financing.

However, these aggregate figures disguise the relative importance of working capital to firms with different product lines and different asset bases. Table 18•2a demonstrates the marked variation in the mix and level of working capital components even in the same industry. About the only generalization that can be made is that as the percentage of current assets becomes higher, the percentage of current liabilities also increases. Table 18•2b points out that working capital requirements are especially important to smaller firms even within the same industry. That is, small firms tend to use a higher percentage of both current assets and current liabilities. This means that efficient working

TABLE 18•1 Working Capital Components as a Percentage of Total Assets and Liabilities

	Fourth Quarter 1983	Fourth Quarter 1984
Assets		
Current assets		
Cash	3.0	2.7
Marketable securities	3.3	3.1
Accounts receivable	15.4	15.0
Inventories	17.1	17.6
Other current assets	2.8	3.0
Total	41.6	41.4
Fixed assets	58.4	58.6
Total assets	100.0	100.0
Claims on assets		
Current liabilities		
Accounts payable	9.1	8.7
Notes payable	3.2	3.6
Accrued taxes	1.6	1.6
Other current liabilities[a]	11.7	10.9
Total	25.6	24.8
Long-term liabilities	25.3	26.1
Stockholders' equity	49.1	49.1
Total claims on assets	100.0	100.0

[a]Includes current installments on long-term debt, excise and sales taxes, accrued expenses, etc.

Source: *Quarterly Financial Report for Manufacturing, Mining and Trade Corporations* (Washington, D.C.: U.S. Department of Commerce, April 1985).

TABLE 18·2 Working Capital Components as a Percentage of Total Assets by Industry and by Firm Size

a. By Industry

	Manufacturers			Retail			Service		
	Soft Drinks	Steel Foundries	Toys	Restaurants	Groceries	Furniture	Motel–Hotel	Air Transport	Computer Software
Current assets									
Cash and marketable securities	9.6	9.0	9.5	10.9	8.8	5.4	5.9	8.1	12.0
Accounts receivable	16.0	19.7	29.0	5.0	4.9	21.8	4.3	20.5	35.5
Inventory	13.6	16.8	34.1	6.8	33.4	51.0	2.3	7.1	8.8
All other current	1.9	3.5	2.3	2.0	1.9	1.4	1.9	2.9	5.0
Total	41.1	49.0	74.9	24.7	49.0	79.6	14.4	38.6	61.3
Current liabilities									
Accounts payable	13.2	11.4	13.0	11.5	20.4	16.9	4.0	13.8	14.2
Notes payable	3.3	7.3	14.3	5.8	4.5	12.0	4.4	6.6	9.1
Accruals	4.6	5.2	6.6	8.3	5.7	4.8	3.6	4.9	9.9
All other current	6.6	6.5	6.4	11.2	8.0	11.1	9.3	12.5	11.8
Total	27.7	30.4	40.3	36.8	38.6	44.8	21.3	37.8	45.0

b. By Asset Size

	Manufacturers: Soft Drinks		Retail: Restaurants		Service: Motel–Hotel	
	<$1,000,000	All	<$1,000,000	All	<$1,000,000	All
Current assets						
Cash and marketable securities	11.8	9.6	11.4	10.9	7.2	5.9
Accounts receivable	21.7	16.0	4.9	5.0	5.3	4.3
Inventory	15.9	13.6	7.3	6.8	2.8	2.3
All other current	2.8	1.9	1.8	2.0	1.6	1.9
Total	52.2	41.1	25.3	24.7	16.9	14.4
Current liabilities						
Accounts payable	15.5	13.2	11.8	11.5	5.0	4.0
Notes payable	2.4	3.3	7.0	5.8	5.8	4.4
Accruals	6.5	4.6	8.8	8.3	4.0	3.6
All other current	5.0	6.6	12.5	11.2	13.9	9.3
Total	29.4	27.7	40.1	36.8	28.8	21.3

Source: Robert Morris Associates, *Annual Statement Studies,* copyright 1983. RMA cautions that the studies be regarded only as a general guideline and not as an absolute industry norm. This is due to limited samples within categories, the categorization of companies by their primary Standard Industrial Classification (SIC) number only, and different methods of operations by companies within the same industry. For these reasons, RMA recommends that the figures be used only as general guidelines in addition to other methods of financial analysis.

capital management is even more critical for them than for larger firms. (See the highlight "Computers and Working Capital Management: An Indispensable Combination of the Future.")

■■ *HIGHLIGHT*

*COMPUTERS AND WORKING CAPITAL
MANAGEMENT: AN INDISPENSABLE COMBINATION
OF THE FUTURE*

Computers are increasingly becoming the most important instrument in the daily life of the financial manager. A new generation of treasury workstations is rapidly moving its way into the office of the treasury manager—*expert systems* which will enable managers to perform a substantial number of routine tasks without necessarily being physically present, thereby providing them with more time to spend on such central issues as improved cash flow and productivity. The system, which is based on a number of preprogrammed heuristics for working capital management, is capable of making decisions automatically. It will provide management with vital synthesized information in corporate summaries. But more important, it will identify surpluses and deficits of funds, decide on amounts of transfers, and channel these into their most productive uses. Furthermore, the system will monitor zero-balance accounts and the amount of float. The objective is to reduce valuable personnel and computer time and thereby make financial operations more efficient.

An additional area of increasing popularity of the computer is in the commercial paper market. Instead of issuing commercial paper by the slow and inefficient process of drawing up documents, some of the major corporations and banks have recently set up an innovative scheme for the buying and selling of commercial paper in the marketplace—the commercial paper computerized network. Commercial paper transactions are handled electronically, thus eliminating the physical transfer of documents. The network is already being used by such companies as American Express and the Ford Motor Credit Company. There are many advantages to this market network, both short term and long term. Since transactions are instantaneous, there is no float. Through extensive use of passwords and codes, it appears that the system is relatively safe, even in today's world of hackers and other "computer pirates." Errors are rectified immediately without having to go through the trouble of changing documents. The long-term implications of this computerized market are perhaps more important. Through this system the future role of commercial paper dealers will become increasingly redundant. This will be manifested in a trend toward direct placement and, consequently, avoidance of implicit costs such as placement fees and flotation costs. We will ultimately face a commercial paper market with swaps (short-circuiting the dealer) and lower spreads, where the only significant cost will be that of information.

Source: Compiled from *Cash Flow*, October and November 1985. The research assistance of Christian Eidenert is gratefully acknowledged.

Learning Check for Section 18•1

Review Questions

18•1. Why do managers often separate short-term and long-term decisions? Is this separation desirable?

New Terms

Net working capital	Working capital	Working capital
Working capital	management	policy

SECTION 18·2 *Short-Term Financial Decisions and Value Maximization*

Conceptually, short-term decisions on current assets and current liabilities should be made in a manner similar to long-term investment and financing decisions. A current asset is simply another type of investment that ties up cash. It is an investment that should provide a return commensurate with its risk. Therefore, the capital budgeting rules developed in Chapters 10 and 11 should also apply here; an asset's initial investment is balanced against its discounted benefits and costs. Similarly, current liabilities are just another source of financing, which have costs and risks much like those of long-term sources of financing.

WHY SHORT-TERM AND LONG-TERM DECISIONS ARE OFTEN SEPARATED

Historically, financial theory has separated decisions concerning current assets and current liabilities from long-term decisions. A basic justification for this separation is that current assets are fundamentally different types of investments. For example, current assets constitute a continuously fluctuating level of liquid assets that is rapidly transformed from one form to another. Long-term investments, on the other hand, occur irregularly over time, involve readily identifiable or specific assets (e.g., a fully automatic lathe) and are highly illiquid. In simple terms, current assets represent reversible investments, whereas fixed assets are irreversible investments.

Although this argument has some truth, separate treatment has the unfortunate consequence of not necessarily being consistent with a firm's objective of value maximization. More important, the link between working capital decisions and value maximization becomes obscured when such decisions are viewed in isolation. What is required is a conceptual framework or understanding of how working capital decisions affect firm value. Such decisions, unfortunately, are more difficult to link clearly to shareholder wealth maximization.

WORKING CAPITAL MANAGEMENT AND SHAREHOLDER WEALTH MAXIMIZATION

While there are some theoretical problems inherent in valuing working capital items, the fact that the basic principles of long-term asset investment decisions should apply equally well to short-term asset decisions should not be ignored. This means that an asset investment should be made whenever its benefits exceed its costs. Although quantifying this trade-off is more difficult for short-term assets, the decision criterion is still: Invest in an asset if its *NPV* is positive.

The first problem in applying this rule arises in establishing the *useful life* of a current asset. If the investment is being considered as part of a capital budgeting project, its useful life is the same as the useful life of the project.[1] But what if a current-asset decision is being made separately, without being related to a fixed-asset investment in terms of time? A practical solution is to treat the current asset as an ongoing permanent investment whose benefits will continue for the foreseeable future. As Chapter 1 emphasized, one of the most important advantages of the corporate form of organization is that it has an ongoing life, independent of the lives of its shareholders. Thus, the current assets of the firm may be considered to have an indefinite life. This assumption implies that n, the useful life of the current asset, will approach infinity and $\Delta CFAT_t$, the incremental cash flows to the firm from these current assets, will become an annuity in perpetuity.

The remaining, and stickier, problem involves determination of the risk and thus the appropriate discount rate to apply to the incremental cash flows, $\Delta CFAT$. This is not easy because such flows do not "trade" and are not valued separately, as is a security in the market. This issue is addressed in Chapter 19.

The emphasis in this chapter is on the practical considerations in determining the risks and returns associated with working capital decisions. Further, the discussion focuses on the appropriate levels of each current asset rather than on specific assets. Fortunately, decisions on the mix of current and long-term financing are far less troublesome because the distinction between the two is largely one of maturity and of management's attitude toward the risks associated with each source.

Learning Check for Section 18·2

Review Questions

18·2. Integrating working capital management into a value-maximizing framework is not easy. Why?

18·3. What is (are) the simplification(s) required to evaluate working capital decisions in a value-maximizing framework?

---

[1] Recall that in evaluating a capital budgeting project in Chapters 10 and 11, a net working capital requirement was treated as part of the initial investment and then as a terminal cash flow.

SECTION 18•3 # *Why Current Assets and Current Liabilities are Required*

From Table 18•2 it is clear that business firms invest in varying degrees in current assets. The level and nature of these investments depend on the firm's product types, its operating cycle, the levels of sales and operating expenses, and management policy. As sales increase over time, more cash, receivables, and inventories will usually be needed. Even within a firm's normal operating cycle, seasonal sales patterns cause the level of current assets to be relatively high or low at any particular point. Moreover, the firm's credit and inventory policies, and how efficiently it manages its current assets, can drastically affect a firm's working capital needs. For example, a conservative toy manufacturer may maintain a high level of inventory to satisfy unexpected demands or to hedge against delays in acquiring new inventory. A more aggressive or more efficient toymaker, on the other hand, may function with a much lower invest-ment in inventories.

But why are current-asset investments required? The answer is that they provide the liquidity necessary to support the realization of the expected returns from a firm's long-term investments. The cash flows associated with long-term investments are uncertain and irregular, and it is the nonsynchronous nature of the cash flows that makes working capital necessary. Otherwise, a mismatch between cash inflows and outflows could cause a liquidity crisis. This, in turn, could disrupt or reduce the longer-term returns expected from a firm's fixed-asset investments. Current assets therefore act as a buffer to reduce the mis-match between cash outflows for goods and services and the cash receipts gener-ated by sales revenues.

Cash outflows are fairly predictable. For example, goods purchased on credit require payment by a known date. The same holds for accruals (e.g., wages and taxes) and short-term loans. The problem stems from the difficulty in forecasting cash inflows because sales demand is more uncertain. The result is that more current assets, representing future cash receipts, must be held to meet the more predictable (scheduled) payments for maturing liabilities.

THE OPERATING CASH CONVERSION CYCLE

A useful way to illustrate a firm's operating cash flow problem is to describe it in terms of the concept of the operating cash conversion cycle.

KEY CONCEPT: The **operating cash conversion cycle** measures the time it takes for the initial cash outflows for goods and services to be realized as cash inflows from sales.

The conversion cycle captures the fact that different working capital components have different life expectancies and are transformed to liquidity flows at different rates. Referring to Figure 18•1, assume that an investment in new equipment is used to expand production and sales. Before any benefits (cash inflows) from this capital expenditure are received, cash outflows for labor and materials must be incurred to produce a finished product. This product may then sit in inventory for weeks or months before it is sold. Moreover, if it is sold on credit, the original cash expenditures will still be tied up (invested) in accounts receivable. Only when the credit customer pays his bill does the firm finally receive a cash inflow from its fixed investment. This is the imbalance in cash outflows and inflows that necessitates current-asset investments.

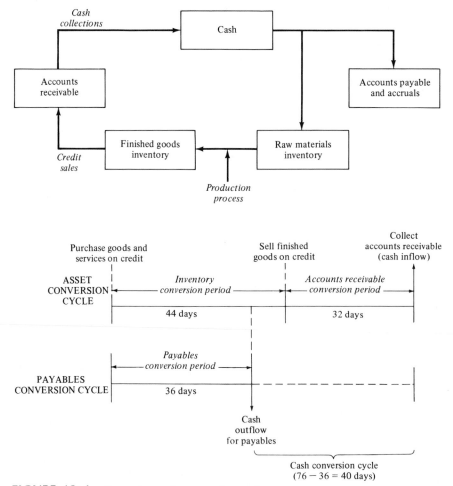

FIGURE 18•1 Operating cash conversion cycle.

Example 18•1 Calculating the Net Cash Conversion Rate

Assume that a firm has annual credit sales of $1,825,000. If sales are nonseasonal, a sales rate of $5,000 per day is implied (with a 365-day year). Further, assume that its working capital position, less cash balances, is as follows:[2]

Accounts receivable	$160,000	Accounts payable	
Inventory	220,000	and accruals	$180,000
	$380,000		$180,000

To see how quickly the operating cash flows through this firm, we need to determine how fast each account turns over. The accounts receivable conversion rate is 32 sales days ($160,000/$5,000), while the inventory conversion rate is 44 sales days ($220,000/$5,000).[3] These conversion rates are expressed in sales days to give an idea of how long it will take a current asset to be transformed from one form to another. In this example, it takes 32 + 44 = 76 days in sales for cash to flow through the current-asset conversion cycle; that is, it takes 76 days from the commitment of cash for materials to the receipt of cash collected from sales.

With regard to current liabilities, goods and services are usually purchased on credit, and it must be determined how long the firm defers these payments. The payables conversion periods for its accounts payable and accruals average 36 sales days ($180,000/$5,000). The combined result is a net cash conversion cycle of 40 days:

CONVERSION PERIOD

Accounts receivable	32 days
Inventory	44 days
Asset conversion rate	76 days
Payables conversion rate	−36 days
Net cash conversion rate	40 days

---

[2] Inventory and accounts payable numbers have been adjusted upward to recognize that we are working with "sales dollars" rather than "cost dollars." This "grossing up" is done easily:

Inventory in sales dollars = inventory in cost dollars/contribution margin

[3] These calculations are related to the turnover ratios studied in Chapter 7. The accounts receivable conversion rate is the average collection period, while the inventory rate is the inventory turnover ratio (assuming that only information on sales, and not on the cost of goods sold, is available) divided into 365 days.

IMPLICATIONS OF THE NET CASH CONVERSION RATE

This residual time indicates that a shortfall in cash flow equal to 40 sales days must be financed in some way or a liquidity crisis will occur after 36 days. One solution is to utilize spontaneous sources of financing further by deferring payments on trade credit payables. However, most firms are limited in the extent to which they can do this without impairing their credit rating. The more typical solution is to arrange a negotiated source of short-term credit, such as a bank loan, to finance the remaining working capital investments. This financing need could be reduced, of course, if management were able to use its current assets more efficiently (e.g., by increasing its inventory turnover), because the asset conversion period would decrease.

If, on the other hand, the asset conversion period becomes greater than 76 days without a simultaneous lengthening of the payables conversion period (or if management decides that a minimum cash balance of $40,000 is needed), additional financing over an even longer period will be required. Therefore, a longer cash conversion cycle will reflect a greater commitment to cash and noncash current-asset investments, and a concomitant increase in the need to finance these investments with current liabilities.

TEMPORARY CURRENT ASSETS AND PERMANENT CURRENT ASSETS

From the description of the cash conversion cycle, it appears as if the investment in current assets would drop to zero as the cycle ends. This would happen only if sales stopped and the firm went out of business. However, each current asset is like a "reservoir" that never empties completely because its level of investment fluctuates with the rate of cash inflow and outflow. If the inflows are greater than the outflows, the investment level increases. For example, if there is an unexpected jump in sales, inflows into accounts receivable will temporarily be greater than outflows; hence the investment level will increase. On the other hand, if inflows are less than outflows, the investment level will decrease. For instance, if an unanticipated surge in cash expenditures occurs, the firm's cash balances would temporarily be drawn down.

KEY CONCEPT: **Temporary current assets** fluctuate with the operational needs of the firm.

This discussion illustrates that at any point in time, a minimum level of investment in current assets will always be needed if the firm is to continue its operations. This continuous level of current assets is referred to as *permanent current assets*, and they are as permanent as the firm's fixed assets.

KEY CONCEPT: **Permanent current assets** refers to the minimum level of current assets required to maintain a firm's daily operations.

As in Example 18•1, a portion of the current assets will be temporary and will fluctuate over the firm's operating cycle. The degree of fluctuation will depend on the rate of change in sales and expenses due to such factors as seasonal influences. Figure 18•2 describes this relationship for a retail merchandise firm. Notice that around the Easter, school-year, and Christmas selling seasons, current assets temporarily inflate to accommodate the seasonal increase in inventories and accounts receivable. After the selling season, inventory levels are low and accounts receivables decline as sales decline during the interim periods. This split between temporary and permanent current assets has important implications when deciding what a firm's working capital policy is for managing its current assets and liabilities. This issue is explored next.

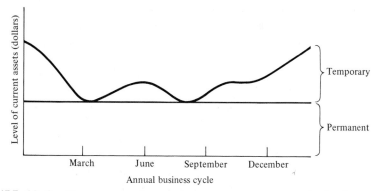

FIGURE 18•2 Temporary and permanent current assets over the firm's annual business cycle.

Learning Check for Section 18•3

Review Questions

18•4. What factors make it necessary to maintain current assets?

18•5. What is the operating cash conversion cycle? What does it measure? How can it be used?

18•6. Distinguish between temporary current assets and permanent current assets.

New Terms

Net cash conversion cycle

Operating cash conversion cycle

Permanent current assets

Temporary current assets

SECTION 18·4 *Deciding on an Appropriate Working Capital Policy*

The greater the uncertainty associated with a firm's cash inflows, the greater the margin of safety that will be required. This margin of safety can be provided by increasing the proportion of liquid assets and/or lengthening the maturity pattern of its financing sources. Both strategies affect the firm's risk and returns. More current assets lead to greater liquidity but represent lower-yielding investments. Long-term debt usually has a higher explicit cost but lower risk than does short-term debt.

Therefore, the primary consideration in developing an overall working capital policy is the risk-return trade-off associated with:

1. The appropriate mix between current and fixed assets.

2. The appropriate mix between short- and long-term financing required to fund the current-asset investments.

It is also important to note that *risk* here refers to the risk of illiquidity or default rather than to the systematic risk discussed in earlier chapters.

RISK-RETURN TRADE-OFF IN THE ASSET MIX DECISION

Fixed-asset investments are undertaken to generate future returns that will enhance firm value. As stated before, such undertakings often require investments in current assets to control for adverse short-term developments that arise from an imbalance in cash flows. Otherwise, the favorable long-run benefits from fixed assets may never be realized. But what is the appropriate mix between short- and long-term investments? Generally, the greater the firm's commitment to current assets, the greater its liquidity. But the return on current assets is usually less than the return on fixed (earning) assets. This implies that although the firm can reduce its risk of illiquidity with a relatively higher current asset investment, it does so only by reducing its return on invested capital.

Example 18·2   Risk and Return at Different Current-Asset Levels

Assume that a firm is considering two different working capital plans, as depicted in Table 18·3. Notice that the two policies differ only with regard to

TABLE 18·3 Risk-Return Trade-Off for Different Mixes of Current and Fixed Assets

	Conservative Asset Policy (Lower Risk, Lower Return)	Aggressive Asset Policy (Higher Risk, Higher Return)
	Balance Sheet Effects	
Current assets	$ 40,000	$ 20,000
Fixed assets	80,000	80,000
Total assets	$120,000	$100,000
Current liabilities	$ 10,000	$ 10,000
Long-term debt	30,000	30,000
Equity	80,000[a]	60,000[b]
Total claims	$120,000	$100,000
	Income Statement Effects	
Net income	$30,000	$30,000
Measures of liquidity	*Decreasing Liquidity*	
1. Percent current assets[c]	33.3	20.0
2. Net working capital[d]	$30,000	$10,000
3. Current ratio[e]	4:1	2:1
Measures of profitability	*Increasing Profitability*	
1. Earnings per share[f]	$7.50	$10.00
2. Rate of return on equity[g] (book value)	37.5%	50.0%

[a] 4,000 shares at $20.
[b] 3,000 shares at $20.
[c] Current assets ÷ total assets.
[d] Current assets − current liabilities.
[e] Current assets ÷ current liabilities.
[f] Net income after taxes ÷ shares outstanding.
[g] Net income after taxes ÷ book value of equity.

the level of current assets.[4] Furthermore, to focus only on the asset-mix decision, assume that a higher investment in current assets is financed by equity. (This allows reported income to be unaffected by how the investment is financed.) Referring to the bottom half of Table 18·3, it can be seen that as the percentage of total assets invested in current assets decreases from 33.3% to 20%, the various measures of liquidity indicate that the firm becomes less liquid. The net working capital position falls from $30,000 to $10,000, and the current ratio drops from 4:1 to 2:1. In other words, a conservative policy will

---

[4] To simplify matters, assume that any additional investment in current assets is placed in cash. This will neutralize any increased returns that might be forthcoming from higher sales stimulated by higher inventory or accounts receivable.

provide a lower risk of illiquidity because net working capital and the current ratio are relatively higher.

In contrast, the profitability measure indicates that a lower risk of illiquidity occurs only by penalizing return performance. That is, a conservative policy provides a 37.5% return on equity, while a more aggressive stance gives a 50% return on equity. Therefore, a relatively higher level of current assets produces a favorable effect on liquidity, but at the expense of reducing the rate of return on equity.[5] This exemplifies once again the familiar trade-off between risk and return; risk-reduction techniques invariably result in lower potential returns.

RISK-RETURN TRADE-OFF IN THE FINANCING-MIX DECISION

A second determinant of a firm's overall working capital policy is the mix of short- and long-term financing used to fund current assets. Generally, the cost of short-term credit is less than the cost of long-term debt. One reason is that trade credit normally has no explicit cost. Another reason is that the interest rate on short-term debt such as bank loans is typically less than the interest rate on long-term debt.

Nevertheless, greater reliance on short-term versus long-term debt has a greater risk of illiquidity. First, there is the possibility that a firm may not be able to refinance its short-term debt when it matures. When the debt needs to be repaid, the firm could be having financial problems, such as an extended labor strike or an economic recession that has caused sales, and hence cash inflows, to decrease. Such difficulties may prevent the firm from having the required funds. In fact, reduced cash inflows may have forced the firm to borrow more from banks to maintain its liquidity. Thus the more frequently a firm refinances its debt, the greater the risk of illiquidity. Second, short-term rates vary more than long-term rates. This means that cash outflows for interest expenses will be more uncertain, since they will vary from period to period. In contrast, payments on long-term debt are known for certain over the entire period during which the debt is outstanding and can be more carefully planned for in advance. That is, the firm has greater flexibility in repaying and refunding long-term liabilities than with short-term debt.

Example 18•3   Risk and Return for Different Financing Mixes

To show the effect of the firm's financing mix on its risk and return, consider the conservative asset policy in Table 18•3, but now hold constant the

---

[5] Because a theoretical consensus is lacking on the potential benefits of liquidity in enhancing firm value, we have focused on the effect of liquidity on accounting rather than on market-based returns.

investment decision (i.e., the percentage of current assets to total assets is fixed). As Table 18•4 shows, the conservative financing policy uses 16% long-term debt to support the current-asset investment, while the aggressive policy calls for a 10% bank loan. The bottom half of this tables indicates that the more conservative policy has a lower degree of illiquidity, as evidenced by a higher net working capital position ($30,000) and current ratio (4:1). However, because this policy uses more costly long-term debt, net income is less and hence the return on equity is lower than under the aggressive policy. Thus the risk of

TABLE 18•4   Risk-Return Trade-Off for Different Mixes of Short- and Long-Term Financing

	Conservative Financing Policy (Lower Risk, Lower Return)	Aggressive Financing Policy (Higher Risk, Higher Return)
	Balance Sheet Effects	
Current assets	$ 40,000	$ 40,000
Fixed assets	80,000	80,000
Total assets	$120,000	$120,000
Accounts payable	$ 10,000	$ 10,000
Notes payable—bank (10%)	0	30,000
Current liabilities	$ 10,000	$ 40,000
Long-term debt (16%)	30,000	0
Equity (10,000 shares)	80,000	80,000
Total claims	$120,000	$120,000
	Income Statement Effects	
Net operating income (*NOI*)	$ 64,800	$ 64,800
Less: Interest expenses[a]	4,800	3,000
Taxable income	$ 60,000	$ 61,800
Less: Taxes (50%)	30,000	30,900
Net income	$ 30,000	$ 30,900
Measures of liquidity	*Decreasing Liquidity*	
1. Percent current assets[b]	33.3	33.3
2. Net working capital[c]	$30,000	0
3. Current ratio[d]	4:1	1:1
Measures of profitability	*Increasing Profitability*	
1. Earnings per share[e]	$3.00	$3.09
2. Rate of return on equity[f]	37.5%	38.6%

[a] Interest expense on long-term debt is 0.16 × $30,000 = $4,800, while interest expense on the short-term bank loan is 0.10 × $30,000 = $3,000.
[b] Current assets ÷ total assets.
[c] Current assets − current liabilities.
[d] Current assets ÷ current liabilities.
[e] Net income after taxes ÷ shares outstanding.
[f] Net income after taxes ÷ book value of equity.

illiquidity can be reduced by resorting to the use of long-term debt, but only by also reducing the firm's profitability.

RISK-RETURN TRADE-OFFS WHEN COMBINING THE CURRENT ASSET–LIABILITY MIX DECISION

The preceding discussion treated current-asset and financing decisions separately in a static framework. These decisions, however, are interrelated and often simultaneous in nature. As Figure 18·2 showed, the firm's level of current assets fluctuates over its operating cycle because of seasonal demand for its products. This implies that its short-term financing needs will also vary. Given these additional considerations, how does one determine the best overall working capital policy? Alternatively stated, what is the appropriate level of net working capital? The answer to this question requires simultaneous consideration of the current-asset and current-liability decisions.

Basically, four different policies may be adopted: a matching policy, a conservative policy, an aggressive policy, and a balanced policy. Each policy, and the factors to be analyzed, will now be examined. Furthermore, a modified version of Figure 18·2, as well as the information in Tables 18·3 and 18·4, will be used to illustrate each policy.

TYPES OF NET WORKING CAPITAL POLICIES

Once the firm's management has decided on its mix of current assets and long-term assets, it must decide on how to finance its current assets. There are several financing plans that management could adopt. We will cover four of the most common types.

A Matching Policy[6]

A matching policy matches the maturity of a financing source with an asset's useful life. Short-term assets should be financed with short-term liabilities, while long-term assets should be funded by long-term financing sources.

Notice that if this policy were adopted, net working capital would be zero and the current ratio would be 1. Most financial managers would find this to be imprudent because a larger amount of current assets versus current liabilities is needed to serve as a buffer against the relatively less predictable cash inflows from sales. Another reason, discussed earlier, is that a portion of current assets is permanent and therefore should be financed long term.

Figure 18·3 depicts the logic of the matching policy: Temporary current

---

[6] This is often called a *self-liquidating policy*.

566

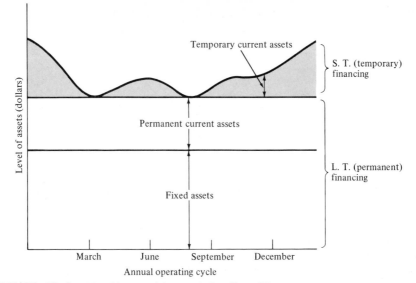

FIGURE 18·3 Matching working capital policy. All temporary current assets financed by short-term financing sources; all long-term assets and permanent current assets financed by long-term financing sources.

assets should be funded by spontaneous sources of financing (such as payables and accruals), as well as short-term borrowings, if need be; permanent current assets and fixed assets should be financed by long-term debt and equity.

The matching policy assumes, somewhat unrealistically, that the implied cash flow pattern is known with certainty. It also assumes that management can readily determine at any time which portion of current assets is a temporary investment and which is permanent. In practice, however, the temporary expansion and contraction of these assets may differ, so that a smaller or larger permanent current asset requirement will result. Added to this are the uncertain borrowing costs and the possibility that adequate credit may not be available when needed.

A Conservative Policy

A conservative policy ignores the distinction between temporary and permanent current assets by financing almost all asset investments with long-term capital (Figure 18·4). Under this policy, temporary swellings in current assets that cannot be covered by spontaneous financing sources are supported by long-term financing. When the level of current assets contracts, any surplus funds are invested in short-term marketable securities.

Referring to the conservative policy described in Table 18·4, it can be seen that this policy greatly reduces the risk of illiquidity and eliminates the firm's exposure to fluctuating loan rates and the potential unavailability of short-term

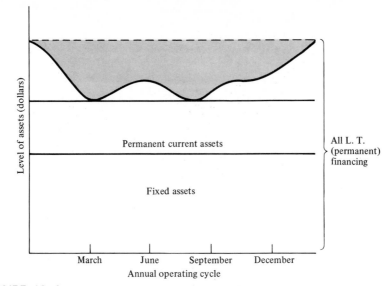

FIGURE 18•4   Conservative working capital policy.

credit. On the other hand, a conservative policy is less profitable because it has a higher financing cost. First, long-term funds have a higher explicit (or implicit) cost, whether they consist of long-term debt or equity. Second, this cost differential is not normally offset by the returns earned on marketable securities. The reason is that short-term financial assets earn less than it costs to finance them with long-term securities.

An Aggressive Policy

An aggressive policy takes the other extreme position of resorting to short-term liabilities to finance not only temporary but also part or all of the permanent current-asset requirement (Figure 18•5). Table 18•4 shows that this aggressive policy is an attempt to increase the return on equity by taking advantage of the cost differential between short- and long-term debt. Of course, such a strategy increases the risk of illiquidity because the firm must continuously refinance its short-term loans at an unpredictable interest rate. An imbalance in cash flows generated from operations, whether due to an internal reason (overinvestment in accounts receivable) or an external factor (economic slowdown), could produce a liquidity crisis. Moreover, a temporary period during which short-term interest rates are higher than long-term rates, as in the early 1980s, would eliminate the attractiveness of this policy's higher profitability and further enhance its risk of illiquidity.

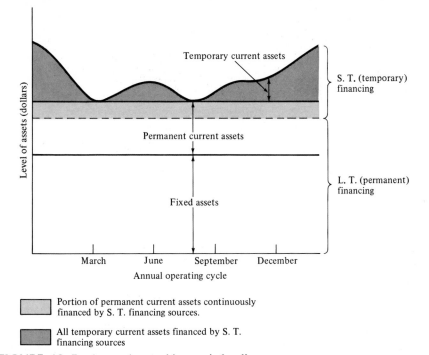

FIGURE 18•5   Aggressive working capital policy.

A Balanced Policy

Because of the impracticalities in implementing the matching policy and the extreme nature of the other two policies, most financial managers opt for a compromise position. Such a position is the balanced policy. As its name implies, management adopting this policy balances the trade-off between risk and profitability in a manner consistent with its attitude toward bearing risk.

As illustrated in Figure 18•6, long-term financing is used to support permanent current assets and part of the temporary current assets. Thus short-term credit is used to cover the remaining working capital needs during seasonal peaks. This implies that as any seasonal borrowings are repaid, surplus funds are invested in marketable securities. The portion above the dashed line represents short-term financing, while the troughs below it represent short-term holdings of securities.

This policy has the desirable attribute of providing a margin of safety not found in the other policies. If temporary needs for current assets exceed management's expectations, the firm will still be able to use unused short-term lines of credit to fund them. Similarly, if the contraction of current assets is less than expected, short-term loan payments can still be met, but less surplus cash will be available for investment in marketable securities. In contract to the other

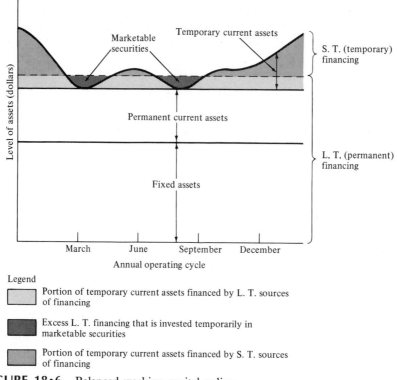

Legend

□ Portion of temporary current assets financed by L. T. sources of financing

■ Excess L. T. financing that is invested temporarily in marketable securities

▨ Portion of temporary current assets financed by S. T. sources of financing

FIGURE 18·6 Balanced working capital policy.

working capital policies, a balanced policy will demand more management time and effort. Under the policy, the financial manager will not only have to arrange and maintain short-term sources of financing but must be prepared to manage the investment of excess funds.

THE APPROPRIATE WORKING CAPITAL POLICY

The analysis so far has offered insights into the risk profitability trade-off inherent in a variety of different policies. Just as there is no optimal capital structure that all firms should adopt, there is no one optimal working capital policy that all firms should employ. Which particular policy is chosen by a firm will depend on the uncertainty regarding the magnitude and timing of cash flows associated with sales; the greater this uncertainty, the higher the level of working capital necessary. In addition, the cash conversion cycle will influence a firm's working policy; the longer the time required to convert current assets into cash, the greater the risk of illiquidity. Finally, in practice, the more risk averse management is, the greater will be the net working capital position.

The management of working capital is an ongoing responsibility that involves many interrelated and simultaneous decisions about the level and financing of current assets. The considerations and general guidelines offered in this chapter should be useful in establishing an overall net working capital policy.

Learning Check for Section 18•4

Review Questions

18•7. Evaluate the following statement: "A firm can reduce its risk of illiquidity with higher current-asset investments, but the return on capital goes down."

18•8. What are the risk-return trade-offs involved in choosing a mix of short- and long-term financing?

18•9. There are four different policies that managers must consider in designing their working capital policy. Explain the features of each policy. What are the advantages and disadvantages of each policy?

New Terms

Aggressive policy	Balanced policy	Financing-mix decision
Asset-mix decision	Conservative policy	Matching policy

SUMMARY

The Importance of Working Capital

Working capital refers to current assets and current liabilities. Net working capital is the difference between current assets and current liabilities and is a measure of a firm's liquidity. Working capital plays a major part in the firm's operations. Current assets comprise a substantial proportion of the firm's total assets. Because of the high turnover of current assets, managers spend a substantial amount of time on working capital decisions.

Short-Term Financial Decisions and Value Maximization

Investments in current assets must, theoretically, be made in a manner similar to the *NPV* approach used for deciding on long-term assets. Practically, short-term and long-term asset decisions are separated. To simplify the analysis, it is often convenient to treat an investment in current assets as an ongoing or permanent investment.

Why Current Assets and Current Liabilities Are Required

The operating cash conversion cycle is a useful tool for measuring the time it takes for the initial cash outflows for goods and services to be realized as cash inflows from sales. The net cash conversion rate identified using this approach indicates the shortfall in cash flow, which must be financed in some way.

Deciding on an Appropriate Working Capital Policy

The amount of net working capital a firm should have depends on the amount of risk the company is willing to take. Four different policies—a matching policy, a conservative policy, an aggressive policy, and a balanced policy—can be followed. The greater the risk taken, the greater the potential for larger returns. Working capital decisions must be made after careful evaluation of the advantages and disadvantages of each policy individually in light of other qualitative considerations.

PROBLEMS

18•1. The Kaler Appliance Store is considering the acquisition of a personal computer and associated software to improve the efficiency of its inventory and accounts receivable management. Andrea Kaler estimates that the initial cash outflow for the computer and software will be $15,000, and the associated net cash savings will be $3,000 annually.
   (a) If Kaler's discount rate for the cash flows associated with this project is 12% and the $3,000 savings will occur for only 10 years (at which time the computer and software are valueless), should she buy the computer?
   (b) What if the project lasts 10 years but the discount rate is 16%?
   (c) What if the project lasts forever and the discount rate is 12%?
   (d) What if the project lasts forever and the discount rate is 16%?

18•2. Phineas Phogg of the Fat Freddie Gourmet Shoppe is considering an expansion of inventory to boost sales. This expansion would require an initial outlay of $20,000 and would generate a permanent net increase in annual cash flow of $2,500.

(a) Should Phineas undertake the expansion of inventory if his discount rate for this project is 10%?

(b) Should Phineas undertake the expansion of inventory if his discount rate for this project is 15%?

(c) At what discount rate would Phineas be indifferent to the expansion project?

18·3. Jimmy Hilliard, manager of the Hilliard Racquetball Club, is considering lowering the usage fee for the courts. He estimates that this will result in an immediate (one-time) cash flow of $18,000 from new membership fees. On the other hand, the annual net cash flow from usage fees is expected to fall by $3,000 indefinitely (because of the lower fees).

(a) Should Jimmy lower the usage fee if his discount rate for this project is 15%?

(b) Should he lower the usage fee if his discount rate for this project is 20%?

(c) At what discount rate would he be indifferent to lowering the usage fee?

18·4. David Cordell, manager of the Berylium Records Store, currently has the following balance sheet:

Cash	$ 10,000	Accounts payable	$ 10,000
Marketable securities	5,000	Notes payable	20,000
Accounts receivable	20,000	Current liabilities	30,000
Inventory	40,000	Long-term debt	60,000
Current assets	75,000	Common stock	60,000
		Retained earnings	50,000
Fixed assets	125,000		
Total assets	$200,000	Total liabilities and stockholders' equity	$200,000

David plans an expansion that will increase cash by $3,000, accounts receivable by $7,000, and inventory by $15,000. Furthermore, the financing for this expansion will come from some combination of notes payable and long-term debt.

(a) What is Berylium's level of net working capital now (i.e., before the expansion)? What is the current ratio now? What is the quick ratio now?

(b) Suppose David finances the entire expansion with notes payable. What is the new level of working capital? The new current ratio? The new quick ratio?

(c) Suppose David finances the entire expansion with long-term debt. What is the new level of working capital? The new current ratio? The new quick ratio?

(d) What will the new amount of notes payable be if David chooses to keep the current ratio the same as it is now?

(e) What will the new amount of current liabilities be if David chooses to keep the quick ratio the same as it is now?

18·5. The Crary Seafood Company has annual sales of $1,440,000. Its average levels of accounts receivable, inventory, and accounts payable are as follows (these levels are expressed in terms of sales dollars):

Accounts receivable	$52,000
Inventory	14,000
Accounts payable	28,000

(a) Assuming a 360-day year, what are average daily sales?

(b) How many days of sales are represented by accounts receivable?

(c) How many days of sales are represented by inventory?

(d) How many days of sales are represented by accounts payable?

(e) What is Crary's net cash conversion rate?

(f) Suppose that sales and the current accounts shown are all to increase by 25%. What would the new net cash conversion cycle be?

18·6. Ratliff McNubb, general manager of television station IBEM, is about to undertake an aggressive advertising campaign that will require increasing the level of accounts receivable by $30,000. Ratliff has to decide whether to finance this increase by borrowing the $30,000 with a one-year 12.5% bank note or by issuing long-term bonds with a 14% coupon rate. Following is a summary of IBEM's projected financial statements under each of the two plans.

	12.5% Bank Note Plan	14% Long-Term Bond Plan
Cash	$ 5,000	$ 5,000
Accounts receivable	50,000	50,000
Net fixed assets	45,000	45,000
Total assets	$100,000	$100,000
Accounts payable	$ 10,000	$ 10,000
Notes payable (12.5%)	40,000	10,000
Current liabilities	$ 50,000	$ 20,000
Long-term debt (14%)	20,000	50,000
Equity (10,000 shares)	$ 30,000	$ 30,000
Total liabilities and stockholders' equity	$100,000	$100,000
Net operating income (*NOI*)	$ 9,000	$ 9,000
Interest	7,800	8,250
Taxes (40%)	480	300
Net income	$ 720	$ 450

(a) Calculate the level of net working capital and the current ratio of the two plans. Which plan would you say is more risky?

(b) Calculate *EPS* and return on (book value of) equity for both plans. Which plan would you say is more profitable?

(c) Suppose that IBEM pays out all its earnings as dividends and its balance sheet and *NOI* at the end of the year are the same as they are today. Find the level of net working capital, current ratio, *EPS*, and return on (book value of) equity under the bank note plan if one year from today the interest rate on one-year bank notes is 16%.

18•7. The Corporeal Foods Company is considering certain changes that will result in increased automation of food processing and canning. This change will require an additional investment of $40,000 in fixed assets, but it will allow the level of current assets to decrease by $40,000 because of an increase in operating efficiency. Corporeal currently has current assets of $160,000, fixed assets of $240,000, and current liabilities of $100,000. Further, Corporeal's board of directors has estimated that investment in fixed assets yields 18% on average. Hence Corporeal's return on total assets is now

$$\frac{\$160,000}{\$160,000 + \$240,000}(0.08) + \frac{\$240,000}{\$160,000 + \$240,000}(0.18) = 14\%$$

(a) Calculate Corporeal's present current ratio and level of working capital.

(b) Calculate Corporeal's current ratio, level of working capital, and return on total assets if the change to increased automation is made. Will the change increase or reduce the liquidity risk? Will it increase or reduce profitability?

18•8. The MacMinn Crane Company has a wide variation in current asset components during the four seasons, as shown here:

	Spring	Summer	Fall	Winter
Cash	$10,000	$10,000	$ 10,000	$ 30,000
Accounts receivable	50,000	20,000	60,000	100,000
Inventory	20,000	40,000	60,000	10,000
	$80,000	$70,000	$130,000	$140,000

MacMinn has fixed assets of $120,000.

(a) What is MacMinn's level of permanent current assets?

(b) Suppose that MacMinn has chosen to adopt a conservative working capital policy, financing all net working capital requirements with long-term debt. What is MacMinn's level of long-term financing during each of the four seasons? What is MacMinn's current ratio during each of the four seasons?

(c) Suppose that MacMinn has decided on an aggressive working capital policy, financing all fixed assets and one-half of permanent current assets with long-term financing and the rest of its assets with short-term financing. What is MacMinn's level of long-term financing during each of the four seasons? What is MacMinn's level of short-term financing during each of the four seasons? What is MacMinn's current ratio during each of the four seasons?

(d) Suppose that MacMinn has chosen to adopt a matching working capital policy, financing all fixed assets and permanent current assets with long-term financing and the rest of its assets with short-term financing. What is MacMinn's level of long-term financing during each of the four seasons? What is MacMinn's level of short-term financing during each of the four seasons? What is MacMinn's current ratio during each of the four seasons?

(e) Suppose that MacMinn has chosen to adopt a balanced working capital policy, using long-term financing in the amount of 1.75 times fixed assets, and financing any assets in excess of this amount with short-term financing. If 1.75 times fixed assets exceeds the level of total assets, the excess is invested in marketable securities. What is MacMinn's level of long-term financing during each of the four seasons? What are MacMinn's level of short-term financing, level of marketable securities, and current ratio during each of the four seasons?

18•9. Allen Motors last year had sales of $7,200,000 and current assets and liabilities as follows:

Cash	$ 20,000	Accounts payable	$ 80,000
Marketable securities	10,000	Notes payable	120,000
Accounts receivable	60,000		$200,000
Inventory	450,000		
	$540,000		

Assume that the levels of cash, accounts receivable, inventory, and accounts payable change in the same proportion that sales do (e.g., if sales are 10% higher next year, you would also expect each of these four accounts to be 10% higher).

(a) What is the current ratio now?
(b) If sales increase by 10%, what will the new current ratio be?
(c) To what value must sales fall for the current ratio to fall to 2.0?
(d) To what value must sales fall for the current ratio to fall to 1.0?

READINGS

KALLBERG, J. G., AND K. PARKINSON, *Current Asset Management* (New York: Wiley-Interscience, 1984).

RICHARDS, V. D., AND E. J. LAUGHLIN, "A Cash Conversion Cycle Approach to Liquidity Analysis," *Financial Management*, Spring 1980, p. 32–38.

VANDER WEIDE, J., AND S. F. MAIER, *Managing Corporate Liquidity* (New York: John Wiley & Sons, Inc., 1985).

19

Current Asset Management: Cash and Near-Cash Items

Higher interest rates and a changing economic climate in the 1980s have drawn closer attention to the performance and escalating costs of firms' current-asset investments. Having presented an overview of working capital management in Chapter 18, we now begin our discussion of current assets: cash, marketable securities, accounts receivable, and inventory. In this chapter we analyze cash and near-cash assets. Chapter 20 discusses the remaining two components of current assets: accounts receivable and inventory. As in earlier chapters, decision-making rules affecting these investments are developed with the underlying goal of shareholder wealth maximization.

This chapter examines the three major topics pertaining to cash management:

1. The efficient collection and disbursement of operating cash.

2. The optimal level of operating cash balances.

3. The investment of temporary, excess cash in near-cash assets such as marketable securities.

The three sections of this chapter will cover each of these topics in detail.

SECTION 19•1: *The Efficient Collection and Disbursement of Operating Cash.* In this section, an overview of the cash management process is presented. The reasons for holding cash are examined, followed by a detailed discussion of the cash management decision. The section concludes with an analysis of the efficient collection and disbursement of cash, with particular emphasis on the concept of float.

SECTION 19•2: *The Optimal Level of Operating Cash Balances.* Cash is a nonproductive asset in that it earns no return; however, as shown in Section 19•1, the firm needs cash balances to function. This section demonstrates how to determine the appropriate level of cash balances for the firm to hold by balancing the costs and benefits of holding cash.

SECTION 19•3: *Investing Excess Cash in Marketable Securities.* This section examines the investment of excess cash, cash that is not immediately needed for current operations, in marketable securities. The criteria used to select marketable securities and the types of these securities are examined.

SECTION 19•1 The Efficient Collection and Disbursement of Operating Cash

REASONS FOR HOLDING CASH BALANCES

Business firms usually hold cash balances for five reasons: (1) transaction purposes, (2) compensating balance requirements, (3) precautionary reserves, (4) potential investment opportunities, and (5) speculation.

Transaction Purposes

Firms need daily cash balances (checking accounts) to conduct their ordinary business transactions. These balances are used to meet cash outflow requirements for operational or financial obligations and to serve as temporary depositories for cash inflows from sales customers.

Compensating Balance Requirements

Commercial banks hold a firm's cash balances and provide the conduit for collecting and disbursing cash. In addition, these banks are a source of short-term financing. They not only charge for these services, they may also receive an indirect fee through compensating balances. A compensating balance is a set amount of cash that the firm must leave in its checking account at all times as part of a loan agreement. These balances provide banks with additional compensation because they can be reloaned or used to satisfy their reserve requirements.

579

Precautionary Reserves

Most firms hold extra cash in order to handle unexpected problems or contingencies due to the uncertain pattern of cash inflows and outflows. The extent of such buffer reserves depends on the predictability of cash flows; the less predictable the cash flows, the more cash will be held. Precautionary balances also depend on how quickly a firm can borrow additional cash. (Financially strong firms normally rely on prearranged lines of bank credit to satisfy most of this requirement.) If any cash balances are maintained for precautionary reasons, they are usually invested in near-cash assets such as marketable securities because precautionary reserves are not part of normal operations.

Potential Investment Opportunities

A firm may allow excess cash reserves to build up in anticipation of a future investment opportunity such as the acquisition of another firm or a major capital expenditure program. In addition, the proceeds from a new debt or equity offering may temporarily swell cash reserves while being allocated to planned investment projects.

Speculation

A firm's management may feel that some prices may soon change. These prices could be raw material prices, equipment prices, or even currency exchange rates. Managers desiring to profit from these expected price changes will delay purchases now and store up cash for use later when they expect prices to be lower.

CASH MANAGEMENT DECISIONS

Cash management decisions are based on forecasts of future cash inflows and outflows. As seen in Chapter 9, the principal way to anticipate cash needs is through the cash budget. Recall that a cash budget is used to forecast cash balances over the next three to six months on a daily, weekly, or monthly basis. It tells how much cash is expected, when, and for how long.

By analyzing the expected operating and financial cash receipts and disbursements in this budget, the financial manager is able to prearrange short-term financing to cover projected cash deficits or to fund short-term investments if excess cash is expected. Financial cash outflows such as fixed-rate interest payments and tax payments are very predictable. However, sales and expense forecasts are much more uncertain. It is this uncertainty that necessitates the development of a cash management program. Such a program must not only be responsible for the cash budget and its cash flow implications but must include a control system to continually gather and monitor the information on the firm's daily cash balances, cash receipts, and disbursals. In addition, the firm's portfolio of marketable securities must be evaluated continually. Figure 19•1 presents an expanded version of the cash cycle presented earlier in Chapter 18 to illustrate the various cash flows that must be managed.

The cash management decisions areas deal with:

1. The efficient collection and disbursement of operating cash.

2. The appropriate level of operating cash balances.

3. The investment of temporary excess cash in near-cash assets such as marketable securities.

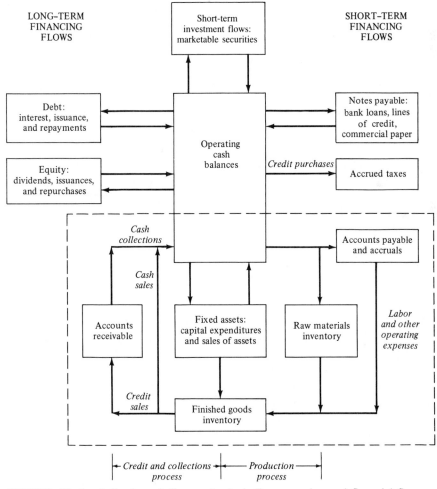

FIGURE 19•1 A firm's cash flow cycle, including operating and financial flows. The material within the dashed line contains the operating cash flow cycle.

These decisions must consider the trade-off between potential insolvency and the opportunity cost of forgone income from overinvesting in cash and near-cash assets. That is, large cash balances will minimize the risk of illiquidity but will reduce profitability and possibly firm value. Each of these decisions will now be discussed in greater detail.

MANAGEMENT OF CASH RECEIPTS AND DISBURSEMENTS

Ideally, a firm prefers to collect cash as soon as possible on its credit sales. In contrast, a firm prefers to delay payment on its purchases as long as possible without hurting its credit rating. This phase of cash management, then, focuses on accelerating cash receipts and slowing cash disbursements where possible. Because time is money, sophisticated money management strategies have been devised to implement this objective.

THE CONCEPT OF FLOAT IN CASH MANAGEMENT

As a firm deposits customers' checks in its bank account and issues its own checks, its book balance keeps changing. The bank also records these transactions, but its balance may differ systematically from the company's book balance. This difference between the bank and book balances is called *float*.[1]

There are four types of float that must be managed. A closer examination of them is useful because it explains why float exists in the first place.

Negative Float

Negative float increases the amount of cash tied up in the collection cycle and earns a zero rate of return. Negative float, which is undesirable and should be minimized as much as possible, consists of mail float, processing float, and clearing float.

Mail float represents the time during which a customer's check is in the postal system. As long as the check is in the mail, funds are not available for use.

Processing float represents the time it takes for the firm to deposit the customer's check in its bank. An efficient firm will not let customers' checks sit in storage, but will attempt to present them for payment as soon as possible.

Clearing float represents the time it takes for the deposited check to clear the banking system and become usable funds.[2] A firm has no direct control over

---

[1] Sometimes float is defined as the interval between the time when a check is written and when the check-writing firm's cash balance in the bank is actually reduced. We prefer to define float in dollar terms.

[2] Banks use either the Federal Reserve System or another clearinghouse to clear interbank checks. The clearing float created by this process has been considerably reduced because of requirements contained in the 1980 Depository Institutions Deregulation and Monetary Control Act. For example, the Federal Reserve must take no longer than two days to make funds available regardless of where the check was initially deposited.

clearing float; however, a firm experiencing excessive clearing float may change to a more efficient bank.

Positive Float

Positive float allows the firm to maintain control of cash for a longer period of time, thus earning a larger return. The major positive float we will examine is disbursement float, which represents the time between a firm's payment of a creditor's bill and when the payment clears the firm's checking account. Disbursement float reduces the firm's idle cash; thus, management should try to increase this type of float.

Example 19•1   Calculating Steady-State Float

Consider the case of Teeple, Inc. Table 19•1 shows Teeple's float situation. Teeple starts its operations on day 0 with a zero cash balance. It takes Teeple's bank two days to clear a deposited check; that is, the deposit clearing time, $CT^{dep} = 2$ days. To clear Teeple's disbursements, the bank takes four days, or the disbursement clearing time, $CT^{dis} = 4$ days.

On day 0, Teeple deposits a check for $100 and simultaneously issues a check for $100. Its book balance is thus zero. However, the bank will not record the deposit or the payment because of the processing float ($CT^{dep} = 2$ days) and disbursement float ($CT^{dis} = 4$ days). Total float is thus still zero.

On day 1, the same situation is repeated. No new entries are made in the bank's books, and the total float is still zero.

On day 2, the check deposited on day 0 is credited to the firm's account and the bank balance rises to $100. Total float is thus $100.

On day 3, the check deposited on day 1 is credited to the firm, and the bank balance rises to $200. The disbursement check has not yet cleared. Total float is thus $200.

TABLE 19•1   Illustration of Steady-State Float for Teeple, Inc.:
Company's Books

Day	Disbursements	Deposits	Cash Balance	Bank Balance	Float
0	$-100	$+100	0	0	0
1	-100	100	0	0	0
2	-100	100	0	$100	$100
3	-100	100	0	200	200
4	-100	100	0	200	200
If Teeple withdraws $200 on day 5,					
5	-100	100	-200	0	200

Deposit clearing time, $CT^{dep} = 2$ days
Disbursement clearing time, $CT^{dis} = 4$ days

On day 4, two things happen. The check deposited on day 2 is credited to the firm, and the check issued on day 0 is paid by the bank. The net change in cash in the bank's books is zero, so total float is still $200. In fact, the total float will not change after day 4 and will remain at $200. Thus Teeple has a **steady-state float** of $200.

The existence of a steady-state float of $200 will allow Teeple to withdraw $200 from the bank and invest it in, say, marketable securities that earn interest. Thus, if Teeple did this on day 5, the book cash balance would show -200 and the bank's balance would be $0. This illustrates the advantage of *playing float*, or profiting from managing the steady-state float. The firm has, in effect, "created" $200, which can be put to productive use.

The steady-state float can be estimated easily by using the following equation:

$$\text{Steady-state float} = (\text{average daily disbursements}) \times (CT^{\text{dis}} - CT^{\text{dep}}) \tag{19-1}$$

For Teeple,

$$\text{Steady-state float} = (\$100)(4 - 2) = \$200$$

verifying the calculation in Table 19•1.

STRATEGIES FOR ACCELERATING CASH COLLECTIONS

Accelerating cash collections is an attempt to reduce the negative float associated with the time it takes from the mailing of a customer's check until it becomes usable funds to the firm. A number of strategies are designed to do just this. Each has to be evaluated carefully in terms of its incremental costs relative to its incremental benefits.

Decentralizing Collections of Accounts Receivable

Most firms serve geographically dispersed customers. To reduce mail and processing float, many firms decentralize their collections operation by using a lockbox system, a local collection office, and/or preauthorized check payments.

Lockbox System With a lockbox system, the firm has its customers mail their payments to a post office box in a specific city (often located in a Federal Reserve Bank city to cut the clearing time). A local bank collects the checks from this box and deposits them in the firm's checking account. The advantage of a lockbox is that checks are deposited sooner (less mail float) and become usable funds more quickly than if a centralized collection operation is used (less clearing float, especially if checks are drawn on local banks). The main disadvantage is cost. Because bank fees for this service are related to the volume of checks deposited, lockboxes are too expensive if many small checks are involved.

Local Collection Office In this alternative, a firm sets up its own collection center to handle customers' remittances. This center can be an existing branch office or an entirely separate operation. Employees receive, record, and place all payments in a local depository bank. Moreover, the billing process may be speeded up if the local office also bills its regional customers. As with a lockbox, this system reduces mail and clearing float by strategically locating these systems where customers tend to cluster. The main distinctions between the two systems are cost and who processes the checks. With a lockbox system, a bank conducts all the processing for a monthly activity fee or a minimum required compensatory balance. With a local collection office, the firm must invest in personnel, equipment, and office space. Which system or mixture of systems is desirable depends on an incremental analysis of the costs and benefits from accelerating collections.

Preauthorized Check Payments A low-cost alternative for speeding collections when a firm receives a large volume of fixed payments from the same customers is to use preauthorized checks. Under a prearranged agreement, a firm is permitted to draw a specific amount from a customer's checking account at specified intervals. Remittances for periodic insurance premiums, lease payments, and mortgage payments are often made this way. This method allows a collecting firm to reduce greatly all three types of negative float; it has the added feature of increasing the certainty of a firm's cash inflows. (See the highlight "Preauthorized Payment Systems in the American Brewing Industry".)

■■ *HIGHLIGHT*

PREAUTHORIZED PAYMENT SYSTEMS IN THE AMERICAN BREWING INDUSTRY

A preauthorized payment system (PAPS) can be used effectively in any industry that has a stable customer base and in which the amounts collected are the same each month. It is not surprising, therefore, that insurance companies and mortgage companies have used PAPS for years. However, a recent pioneer using very flexible and dynamic preauthorized payments arrangements has been the brewing industry.

The G. Heilman Brewing Company, Inc. of LaCrosse, Wisconsin, was, in November 1980, the first of the brewers to use PAPS. Following Heilman's acquisition of Carling-National Breweries in 1979, it became increasingly difficult for the company to collect its accounts receivables. Later that year, Heilman's credit department actively investigated the feasibility of a PAPS with several major banks. When it was determined that such an arrangement was feasible, Heilman's treasurer tried to convince the chief financial officer and the executive vice-president that this arrangement was good for the company. After initial skepticism from top management, Heilman introduced its PAPS in November 1980.

Before the PAPS could begin, the company had to get customers to sign an authorization agreement. Heilman began its system by getting six beer wholesalers to sign the agreement. However, the system encountered considerable resistance; some customers objected to losing control over their bank accounts, some voiced concerns about security, and others "simply did not like the system." Heilman responded in different ways. Some customers were allowed a trial period to see whether they liked the system, while others were offered a one-time extension in credit terms for trying the system. Eventually, by late 1983, more than 85% of Heilman's wholesale customer base had signed up for the PAPS.

Heilman's success with its PAPS encouraged the rest of the industry to follow suit. The Miller Brewing Company (Milwaukee) began its PAPS in January 1982, and the Stroh Brewery Company (Detroit), Adolph Coors Company (Golden, Colorado), and Anheuser-Busch, Inc. (St. Louis) followed the trend in 1983. The Pabst Brewing Company was the last firm to initiate a PAPS system (late 1984). In promoting the use of their PAPS, some of these breweries offered their customers bigger discounts, sent "credits" as part of pricing promotions, and actively sought new subscribers to their systems.

Today, PAPS are considered fairly standard in the brewing business. In 1985, the American brewing industry had combined sales of around $1 billion. It has been estimated that the use of PAPS has resulted in a total savings of around $1 million per year for the industry as a whole.

Source: Compiled from the information contained in various issues of *Cash Flow*.

MECHANISMS FOR RAPIDLY TRANSFERRING FUNDS

Modern telecommunications has revolutionized the transfer of funds through the use of electronic funds transfer systems (EFTS). Once deposits are made, EFTS offer a number of options to move funds rapidly between accounts.

Sweep Accounts

Within a particular bank, sweep accounts allow a firm to drop its checking account balance to a minimum level at the end of each day. Any funds released by "sweeping" the account can then be invested overnight to earn interest income or be transferred to a centralized disbursement bank.

Wire Transfers

Interbank transfers of usable funds can be made in less than an hour through wire (telegram) transfers via a bank's or the Federal Reserve's wire system. Although mail float is reduced, wire transfers are expensive and are usually restricted to large dollar transfers on an infrequent basis.

Electronic Depository Transfer Checks (DTC)

To reduce clearing float, a DTC can be made through any number of EFTS networks. With a DTC, a local collection center can place customers' checks in a local depository bank and notify the firm's central bank (located near its headquarters) of the amount. The central bank then prepares a DTC for this amount, credits the amount to the firm's account, and transmits the DTC to the local depository bank for payment. The DTC's main advantage is that a one-day clearing time is possible rather than the normal two days through the Federal Reserve System.

STRATEGIES FOR CONTROLLING DISBURSEMENTS

Just as speeding collections helps convert accounts receivable into cash and reduces cash balances, slowing disbursements attempts to do the same thing. Within limits, a number of strategies can be utilized to control and slow down cash outflows. However, abusing the use of these strategies may irritate a firm's creditors to the point where its credit rating is jeopardized or its trade credit may be withdrawn.

Stretching Payables[3]

The place to begin is to establish a policy of paying accounts payable or accruals only when they are due. There is no benefit to paying sooner; in addition, the availability of cash for other investment purposes is reduced. Occasionally, paying bills late may be overlooked by creditors, but a regular habit of delinquency can only lead to problems.

Zero-Balance Accounts

Large corporations that have multiple branches or divisions often have many checking accounts in different banks. This may seem justifiable to conduct local operations, but excess cash balances and a loss of disbursement con-

---

[3]*Stretching* should not be interpreted to mean paying after the credit period. The term as used here refers to paying as late as possible within the credit period.

trol tend to occur. One way to eliminate these problems is to allow each operating entity to write checks on a special checking account that contains no funds. These accounts are all located at a central bank, so that at the end of each day, the negative balances created by the divisions' checks can be restored to zero by debiting a master account. Moreover, if the master account has a surplus of cash, it can be swept into an overnight investment. Better control over disbursements and excess balances results without usurping the payment authority of local operations. Figure 19•2 shows how a typical zero-balance arrangement might work.

Remote or Controlled Disbursing[4]

Originally, this type of disbursement was available only at banks with remote branches or correspondent banks or those that were located in a remote section of the country—hence the name. Rather than giving local operating units payment authority, all payments are centralized through one disbursement bank. Not only is mail and clearing float lengthened, but this float can be better controlled. As can be seen from Figure 19•3, the basic idea is simple. Disbursements are not funded until the day checks are presented for clearance and are covered by a same-day transfer of funds by the firm. In fact, most controlled disbursement points can provide the required information by late morning, so that the firm can still tap short-term credit sources if necessary. Furthermore, this disbursements method can be applied to many accounts, all of which can be funded with a single funds transfer.

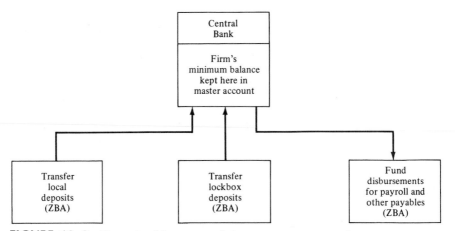

FIGURE 19•2   Example of how a zero-balance arrangement works.

[4]For further details, see S. F. Maier, "Insulated Controlled Disbursing," and S. F. Maier and D. M. Ferguson, "Disbursement System Design for the 1980s," in the November 1982 issue of the *Journal of Cash Management.*

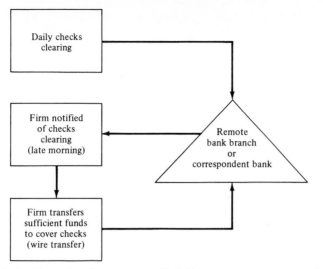

FIGURE 19·3 Example of how a controlled disbursement account works.

CONCENTRATION BANKING: AN INTEGRATED CASH MANAGEMENT SYSTEM

To attract large corporate customers, banks have begun to offer an integrated systems approach that utilizes the cash management strategies previously discussed. This systems approach is referred to as **concentration banking.** Figure 19·4 illustrates how the various strategies can be tied together to facilitate efficient cash management. For example, a firm may use a mixture of local office and lockbox systems for cash collections locally or regionally. Each day, the local depository or lockbox bank would transfer cash above a minimum or target balance to the firm's central concentration bank. These daily funds transfers could be made either by a wire transfer or DTC. The transferred funds would then be placed in a master account for disbursement to cover deficits in its zero-balance accounts or to cover checks drawn against its remote branch bank account. By accelerating cash collections for rapid transfer to a central concentration bank and by pooling these funds for controlled disbursement, a firm can achieve optimal float advantages and thus reduce operating cash balances to a minimum. Moreover, extensive reports are generated to provide data for better control purposes. Such a system is costly, however, so that all aspects of a concentration bank system are normally used only by the largest corporations. Nevertheless, every firm needs to evaluate these strategies to find the one(s) that are cost justifiable.

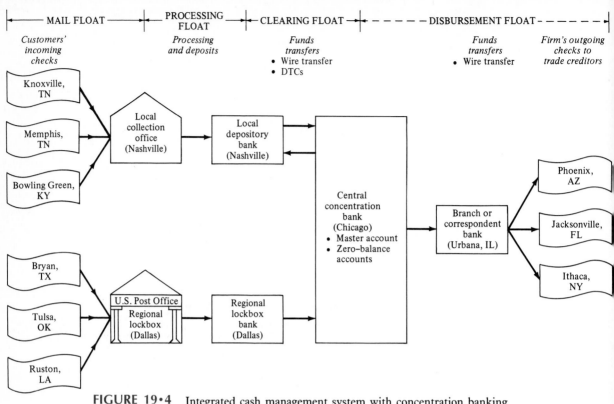

FIGURE 19·4 Integrated cash management system with concentration banking collection float.

Learning Check for Section 19·1

Review Questions

19·1.   Why do firms hold cash? What are the three cash management decisions confronting the financial manager?

19·2.   What is float? Distinguish between negative and positive float. How is the steady-state float calculated?

19·3.   Explain the various options open to a firm to speed up the collection of cash.

19·4.   What is concentration banking?

New Terms

Cash flow cycle	Electronic funds	Positive float
Clearing float	transfer system (EFTS)	Precautionary
Compensating	Float	reserve
balance	Local collection	Processing float
Concentration	office	Steady-state float
banking	Lockbox system	Sweep accounts
Depository transfer	Negative float	Zero-balance
check (DTC)	Mail float	accounts

SECTION 19·2   *The Optimal Level of Operating Cash Balances*

It should be clear by now that a firm should retain as little cash as possible, since cash is a nonproductive asset. Yet a firm cannot do without cash balances. A company needs cash to satisfy one or more of the requirements for holding cash discussed earlier. How does a manager decide on the optimum level of cash that the firm must maintain?

The **optimum cash balance** is determined by the larger of:

1. The sum of transactions balances and precautionary reserves.

2. Compensating balance requirements.

Thus, if a firm estimates its transactions balance and precautionary reserve requirements to be $40,000 and $60,000, respectively, and if the bank's compensating balance requirement is $80,000, the firm should hold an optimum cash balance of $100,000. Of course, the interesting questions pertain to determination of the transactions and precautionary balance requirements for the firm. These figures must be estimated by management based on a variety of subjective factors. It is not easy to suggest meaningful rules to arrive at dollar amounts for these cash balances. A company's transaction–precautionary balance depends on sales volume, the predictability of its cash flow forecasts, and the ease with which cash shortages can be covered by short-term borrowings. The higher the sales volume and the larger the number of transactions conducted, the larger the required cash balances. The greater the uncertainty associated with cash inflows and outflows, the larger the transactions and precautionary balances required. Predictable differences between daily inflows and outflows can be gauged by analyzing the past pattern of daily deposits and written checks. Variations in checking deposits may also provide guidance in deciding the average balances required. The ability to generate short-term credit by means of, say, overdraft privileges, wherein banks automatically extend loans to cover checks written in excess of available balances, will also affect the optimum cash balances.

MATHEMATICAL MODELS

One way to quantify these subjective considerations in determining the optimum cash balance is to formulate the question as an inventory decision problem so familiar to students of operations research.[5] It is not necessary to explore the inventory problem in detail. Instead, its application to the optimum cash balance question is discussed briefly.

Assume that the Zeta Corporation has a pool of funds (cash) that it uses to pay its bills. When the cash is exhausted, it replenishes its liquidity by selling marketable securities, which are short-term investments that earn interest and are easily sold. In deciding how much to hold in its pool of cash, Zeta must balance costs and benefits. Every dollar held by Zeta as cash forgoes the opportunity to earn interest by being invested in marketable securities. While an initial decision would therefore be to hold very little cash, there are disadvantages from this course of action. If Zeta runs out of cash, it has to sell some marketable securities to maintain liquidity. Selling these securities is not a costless exercise. Transactions costs may be significant, and the more often Zeta runs out of cash, the more often it incurs this cost.

Therefore, Zeta must attempt to have enough cash on hand to avoid excessive transactions costs from selling marketable securities, while at the same time not losing an excessive amount of interest by not investing in marketable securities. The optimal cash balance is therefore determined by equating the marginal cost of holding a dollar in cash with the marginal benefit of this extra liquidity. These costs and benefits may be quantified, and the optimal amount of cash computed.

If Zeta starts with a pool of $1 and ends up with zero (before it sells new T-bills to raise cash), the marginal cost of carrying cash is given as

$$\text{Marginal cost of carrying cash} = \text{average cash balance} \times \text{interest rate}$$

or

$$\text{Marginal cost of carrying cash} =$$

$$\left(\frac{\text{beginning cash balance} + \text{ending cash balance}}{2}\right) \times (\text{interest rate}) \quad (19\text{-}2)$$

$$= \left(\frac{1 + 0}{2}\right) \times \text{interest rate} = \frac{\text{interest rate}}{2}$$

[5]Chapter 20 examines inventory policies in more detail.

Thus, larger initial cash balances reduce Zeta's potential transactions costs. The marginal reduction in transaction costs for every dollar of initial cash balance is given as

$$\text{Marginal reduction in transactions costs} = \frac{\text{annual cash disbursements} \times \text{transactions costs per sale}}{(\text{Starting cash balance}^2)} \quad (19\text{-}3)$$

To find the optimum starting cash balance, equate equation (19-2) with equation (19-3) and solve:

$$\text{Optimum cash balance} = \sqrt{\frac{2 \times \text{annual cash disbursement} \times \text{transactions cost per sale}}{\text{Interest rate}}} \quad (19\text{-}4)$$

This is the optimum cash balance for Zeta.

Example 19·2   Calculating Optimum Cash Balances

Assume that Zeta disburses $2 million in cash every year and that every sale of T-bills costs $50. If the current risk-free interest rate is 10%, Zeta's optimum cash balance is given as

$$\text{optimum cash balance} = \sqrt{\frac{2 \times \$2,000,000 \times \$50}{0.10}}$$
$$= \$44,721$$

The reader can verify that Zeta's optimum cash balances will be larger if the transactions costs are larger or if the interest rate is lower. The reasoning in this situation should be clear.

Learning Check for Section 19·2

Review Question

19·5.   How does a manager determine the optimum level of cash balances?

New Term

Optimum cash balance

SECTION 19•3 *Investing Excess Cash in Marketable Securities*

Typically, cash in excess of requirements for transactions, precautionary balances, and/or compensating-balance purposes is temporarily invested in marketable securities.[6] Excess funds may build up during seasonal lows but will eventually be needed for expanding inventory and accounts receivable during seasonally high sales periods (excess transactions balances). On the other hand, excess cash may be held to cover uncertain financing requirements or to take advantage of a potential investment opportunity.

Of course, an alternative to holding excess cash for these purposes is to borrow short-term to finance uncertain cash requirements. Which approach is taken depends on management's overall working capital policy, as seen in Chapter 18. In this section, we take as given the working capital policy and the funds available for temporary investments.

DECISION CRITERIA

Many types of temporary, near-cash investments are available; thus the financial manager needs criteria for determining which ones best fit his or her needs. Since these investments are temporary stores of transactions and precautionary balances, the primary consideration is how quickly they can be converted to cash without loss of value (principal). This eliminates most long-term securities from consideration because their prices tend to vary widely. This leaves short-term debt securities such as money market instruments as the best choice. The three most important characteristics to consider are risk, marketability, and term to maturity.

Risk

When buying a debt instrument issued by a business entity, two types of risk affect the instrument's value over time: default risk and interest-rate risk. *Default risk* refers to the chances that the issuer may be unable to pay interest or principal on time or at all. (U.S. government issues have no default risk.) Given the reasons for investing excess cash, a firm will usually invest in marketable securities with little or no default risk. *Interest-rate risk* refers to fluctuations in a security's price caused by changes in market interest rates. As rates change, the value of a debt security will change in the opposite direction. If a firm is forced to sell a security after interest rates have risen, it will probably suffer a loss of principal. Only if a security is held to maturity and redeemed at par can interest-rate risk be avoided.

---

[6]Note that this implies that the amount of funds invested becomes a "residual" decision.

Marketability

Marketability refers to how quickly a security can be sold prior to maturity without a significant price concession. Some securities are very marketable, meaning that they may be sold quickly at or near their full value. Other securities are not very marketable, meaning that they may be difficult to sell quickly or that they may be sold only by giving a deep price cut. The major determinants of a security's marketability is the existence of an active secondary market for that security.[7] A firm investing in marketable securities wants to be able to obtain cash from the sale of these securities quickly and without losing value in the process. Firms therefore prefer to purchase highly marketable securities as temporary investments for cash.

Term to Maturity

Firms normally limit their marketable securities purchases to issues that have relatively short maturities (less than one year). The variability in fixed-income securities' prices tends to increase with an increase in the term to maturity because of interest-rate risk, as just discussed. Maturity dates of marketable securities held should coincide, where possible, with the length of time the excess funds are not needed. Maturities of 1 day, 10 days, or any number of days can easily be found.

Notice that yield or return was not mentioned as an important decision criterion. Highly marketable, low-risk securities have relatively low yields, but safety of principal is the main criterion for excess cash investments. Only after risk, maturity, and marketability have been considered should return be allowed to influence the final choice.

TYPES OF MARKETABLE SECURITIES

Money market instruments are usually the securities that most closely satisfy the foregoing criteria. Money market instruments are short-term securities. They are usually securities with maturities of up to one year, although some money market instruments have maturities up to five years (e.g., U.S. Treasury notes). Eight types of marketable securities will be described briefly. Table 19•2 contains a summary of their characteristics and historical yields. As seen in the last three columns, the yields on these instruments vary considerably over time. The reason is that yields depend on the state of the economy, business credit demands, inflation expectations, and monetary and fiscal policies.

[7]Chapter 1 contains a discussion of secondary markets.

TABLE 19·2 Summary of the Characteristics and Historical Yields of Various Money Market Instruments

Money Market Instrument	Issued Maturities	Minimum Denomination	Special Features	Historical Yields[a] (%)		
				1983	1984	1985
Treasury bills	91 and 182 days and 52 weeks	$10,000	No default risk; excellent marketability; discount instrument	8.61	9.52	7.48
Federal agency issues	Varies	$5,000	Low default risk; good marketability; coupon-bearing instrument	—	—	—
Banker's acceptances[b]	30 to 180 days	$25,000	Default risk is relatively small but varies with the issuing bank; good marketability for acceptances issued by larger banks	8.90	10.14	7.92
Large negotiable certificates of deposit[c]	30 to 180 days	$100,000	Default risk varies with issuing bank; up to $100,000 insured by Federal Deposit Insurance Corporation (FDIC); fair marketability; deposit plus accrued interest	9.07	10.37	8.05
Commercial paper[d]	30 to 270 days	$100,000	Default risk is the highest of the money market instruments but normally is low; poor marketability; discount instrument	8.88	10.10	7.95
Repurchase agreements	1 to 30 days	$500,000	Low default risk since lender holds the underlying securities and collateral; poor marketability because it is a two-party agreement, but is self-liquidating within a few days	[f]	[f]	[f]
Eurodollar loan deposits[e]	Overnight to 360 days	$1,000,000	Low default risk, but depends on issuing foreign bank (deposits uninsured); poor marketability; deposit plus accrued interest	9.57	10.75	8.27
Money market mutual funds	None	$1,000	Low default risk, but depends on the instruments held by the mutual fund's portfolio; good marketability; interest earned daily on shares issued	8.10	6.71	6.46

[a]Annual averages of monthly data, except as indicated
[b]Averages of the most representative daily offering rates of dealers. Rates of top-rated banks only.
[c]Three-month, secondary market.
[d]Three-month.
[e]Three-month.
[f]Yields are negotiable but usually less than the T-bill yield.
Source: Continental Bank's *Interest Rate Comparison*, various issues.

Treasury Bills

T-bills are debt obligations of the U.S. government used to finance fiscal deficits. They are issued with maturities of less than one year and are considered to be default free because they receive the full financial backing of the U.S. government. T-bills are sold as a discount instrument; that is, they trade at less than their redemption value, with the difference between the redemption and market values representing the interest received. The market for these securities is the largest, most liquid sector of the money markets. Because they are the safest and most marketable security, they have the lowest yield but are most widely held.

Federal Agency Obligations

Certain U.S. government agencies raise funds by issuing short-term instruments. These securities are relatively safe and have good marketability, although not as much as Treasury securities because they are guaranteed by the agencies themselves (although the U.S. government has a moral obligation to back them). Their slightly lower marketability and safety in comparison to Treasury securities causes them to have slightly higher yields. Examples of such agencies are the Government National Mortgage Association (Ginnie Mae) (GNMA), Federal Farm Credit Banks (FFCBs), and Federal Home Loan Banks (FHLBs).[8]

Banker's Acceptances

These discount securities are time drafts drawn on and accepted by a bank. They were designed to facilitate import-export trade business. Since acceptances are guaranteed by the issuing bank, their safety depends on that bank's financial strength. The secondary market is well organized, very active, and hence very liquid. Yields are usually higher than on Treasury securities of comparable maturity.

Negotiable Certificates of Deposit

Commercial banks issue large-denomination time deposits called *certificates of deposit (CDs)*, which entitle the holder to receive the amount deposited plus accrued interest upon maturity. They are negotiable because once they are issued, they can be traded in the secondary market. Maturities are set to fit the investor's needs. CDs of the largest banks are handled by government securities

---

[8]Of these agencies, only the FFCB issues coupon securities; all others are discount securities. In addition, it must be pointed out that unlike the other agencies, the GNMA is an arm of the Department of Housing and Urban Development (HUD), and its obligations are directly guaranteed by the Treasury.

dealers and are therefore highly marketable. Yields on CDs are generally above the rates on T-bills and federal agency issues.

Commercial Paper

Commercial paper consists of short-term unsecured promissory notes issued by large corporations and finance companies with high credit ratings such as the General Motors Acceptance Corporation (GMAC). Commercial paper is sold directly to investors by the issuer and through commercial paper dealers. The secondary market for commercial paper is weak. This low marketability plus a higher default risk results in higher yields than on most other money market instruments.

Repurchase Agreements

A repurchase agreement, or *repo,* is a negotiable arrangement (not a security) between a bank or securities dealer and an investor in which the investor acquires certain short-term securities (usually T-bills) with the understanding that the bank or dealer will repurchase these securities at a slightly higher price in a specified number of days. Their maturities are very short and are tailored to meet the investor's needs. A repo yield is slightly less than the rate (less a "haircut") that can be obtained from outright purchase of the underlying security. Repurchase agreements are relatively safe investments because a banker or dealer as well as the issuer of the security have to default before a loss is incurred.

Eurodollar Loan Deposits

Eurodollar deposits are interest-bearing (time) deposits in European banks or foreign branches of U.S. commercial banks. These deposits are denominated in dollars rather than in the local currency—hence the name *Eurodollar.* They generally carry higher interest rates than those found on U.S. time deposits. As with negotiable CDs, maturities and interest rates are negotiable. Marketability is limited, although an organized secondary market is developing. The default risk varies with the issuing bank.

Money Market Mutual Funds

As Table 19•2 indicates, most of the higher-yielding marketable securities are available only in relatively large denominations. Smaller firms with only limited funds to invest are unable to purchase these securities directly. An alternative is to purchase the securities indirectly through a money market mutual fund. These mutual funds pool the investments of many small investors and invest them in large-denominated money market instruments. Shares, much like common stock, are issued against this portfolio of securities. By purchasing these shares, a smaller firm can attain the higher yields offered on large-denominated securities for even very short periods of time. In addition, interest is earned daily and many mutual funds offer draft-writing privileges that allow the firm to earn interest on invested funds until the check clears. The default risk is slight but depends on the types of securities purchased by the mutual fund.

Learning Check for Section 19·3

Review Question

19·6. What are the popular marketable securities available in the marketplace? What are their distinguishing features? Compare them on the basis of three criteria: risk, marketability, and term to maturity.

New Terms

Banker's acceptance
Commercial paper
Eurodollar loan
  deposit

Federal agency
  obligation
Marketability
Marketable security
Money market
  mutual fund

Negotiable certificate
  of deposit (CD)
Repurchase
  agreement
T-bill

SUMMARY

The Efficient Collection and Disbursement of Operating Cash

Companies need to hold cash for a variety of reasons. This cash must be managed efficiently by the financial manager. Cash receipts must be speeded up and cash disbursements slowed down. In addition to playing the float, a manager can use lockboxes, local collection offices, preauthorized checks, and other modern electronic funds transfer procedures. Several techniques for slowing disbursements also exist. An integrated systems approach to cash management is concentration banking.

The Optimal Level of Operating Cash Balances

The optimum level of cash balances is determined as the larger of (1) the sum of transactions and precautionary balances and (2) compensating balance requirements. Mathematical models can also be used to determine the optimal cash balance.

Investing Excess Cash in Marketable Securities

Cash in excess of the firm's requirements should be temporarily invested in marketable securities. In making this short-term investment, the firm should consider the risk of the security, its marketability, and its term to maturity. There are numerous types of marketable securities; their characteristics vary widely.

PROBLEMS

19·1. The Jameson Building Supplies Company has annual sales of $9 million (all credit). On average, it takes five days for a customer's mailed check to be deposited. Mel Jameson believes that he can reduce this float time by two days through the use of a lockbox. The bank will charge a flat fee of $4,000 per year to perform this service.
   (a) What are average daily sales for January? (Assume a 360-day year.)
   (b) All of January's receipts from sales go into a money market mutual fund. By how much will the average balance in this fund increase if Mel adopts the use of the lockbox?
   (c) Suppose that the money market fund earns 10% per year. Should Mel enter into the lockbox agreement?
   (d) Should Mel enter into the lockbox agreement if the money market fund earns 10% but the lockbox reduces float by only one day?

19·2. Newman-Markups Department Store has annual credit sales of $27 million. John Harris, the collections manager, has estimated that it takes six days for a mailed payment to be credited to Newman's account and that this time can be cut to three days if Newman opens up a lockbox account with a local bank. The account in which the checks are placed earns 8% annually. The lockbox agreement calls for a monthly payment of $500 and, in addition, a monthly charge of $0.03 per check. Newman's currently processes 45,000 checks monthly. (Treat these expenses as if they occur at the beginning of the year.)
   (a) What are Newman's daily sales? (Assume a 360-day year.)
   (b) By how much will Newman's average bank balance increase if it adopts the lockbox?
   (c) Should Mr. Harris adopt the lockbox?
   (d) Suppose that Newman's has found that a regular 20% of its customers account for 80% of credit sales. Should Mr. Harris open up the lockbox and use it only for this 20% of the customers?

19•3. The Texron Oil Company is headquartered in Houston but has customers in Dallas, Fort Worth, El Paso, San Antonio, and Austin as well. Mark Hannah, the collections manager, is planning to open collection offices in these cities to speed up the collection process. The dollar volume of collections, the annual cost of running the collections center, and the reduction in float time for each city are as follows:

City	Annual Collections	Annual Cost of Center	Reduction in Float Time (Days)
Dallas	$300,000,000	$80,000	1
Fort Worth	160,000,000	76,000	2
El Paso	120,000,000	75,000	3
San Antonio	220,000,000	78,000	2
Austin	150,000,000	80,000	2

(a) Using a 360-day year, find the daily collections from each of the five cities.
(b) What marginal increase in deposits (because of reduced float) will each city's collection center contribute to Texron's deposits?
(c) Suppose that the rate earned on these accounts is 8%. In which cities (if any) should Mr. Hannah open up collection centers?

19•4. George Morgan is currently comptroller of Ducor, Inc. Ducor has two accounts with its bank: a demand deposit account, the balance of which earns no interest, and a money market fund, the balance of which pays 8% interest. There is a $10 fee for transferring any funds from the money market fund to the demand deposit account. Ducor's cash disbursements total $1 million annually.
(a) When George makes a transfer from the money market fund to the demand deposit account, what should the amount of the transfer be? How often will he make a transfer?
(b) What should the amount of the transfer be if the transfer fee is raised to $15? How often will George make a transfer?
(c) What should the amount of the transfer be if the transfer fee stays at $10 while the interest rate is raised to 10%? How often will George make a transfer?
(d) What should the amount of the transfer be if the transfer fee is raised to $15 and the interest rate is raised to 10%? How often will George make a transfer?

19•5. Andrew Senchack, financial manager of the Phoenix Renovation Service, has been keeping the firm's funds in the Sparrow Fund, a money market fund that pays 8% on deposits and has no charge for withdrawals. Andrew has found another fund, the Hawkeye Fund, which pays

10.5% on deposits but has a $20 fee for a withdrawal of any size. Phoenix has annual cash disbursements of $4 million. Andrew is considering establishing an account with Hawkeye, transferring funds to Sparrow only occasionally, and using the Sparrow account to handle daily transactions.

(a) Using a 360-day year, find the daily disbursement of funds.

(b) When Andrew makes a transfer, what will the size of the transfer be?

(c) How often will Andrew make transfers?

(d) If Andrew does not change to the Hawkeye Fund, what is his average balance in the Sparrow Fund (assuming the $4 million for disbursements is available at the beginning of the year)? What annual interest does this account earn?

(e) If Andrew establishes the Hawkeye account, what will be his average balance in Sparrow? His annual interest from Sparrow?

(f) What will be the average balance in Hawkeye? The annual interest from Hawkeye?

(g) What is the marginal dollar value of establishing the Hawkeye account?

19•6. Bob Dince, controller of the Carter Farming Group, currently keeps Carter's funds in a demand deposit account yielding 6% compounded annually. Carter's annual disbursements total $360,000, and this sum is deposited in the account at the beginning of the year and is used to pay bills as they come due. Bob is considering investing the money in T bills with an annual yield of 8.5%, selling T bills as necessary to replenish the demand deposit account. Suppose that it costs $45 to sell any dollar amount of T bills.

(a) What is the current average balance in the demand deposit account? What is the annual interest that this account earns?

(b) If Bob decides to buy the T bills, what is the dollar amount of T bills he will sell whenever he replenishes the demand deposit account? What are the average balance and annual interest in the demand deposit account?

(c) What is the average balance in the T-bill account? What is the annual interest earned from the T bills?

(d) Should Bob make this switch? What is the marginal dollar value of this decision?

19•7. The National Record Club (based in New York) has many mail-order customers in California and is losing substantial revenue as a result of the average of seven days between the time a customer deposits his payment and the time the deposit is credited to National's account in a New York bank. Accordingly, Socorro Quintero, collections manager for National, is trying to find a way to reduce this float time and has narrowed the solutions to (1) operating a collection center in Los Angeles or (2) opening lockbox accounts in the major California cities. Socorro estimates that a collection center in Los Angeles will require an annual expenditure of $70,000. Lockbox expenditures and new float time for each city are shown in the following table.

City	Float Time for Los Angeles Collection Center (Days)	Lockbox Expense	Float Time for Lockbox (Days)	Annual Receipts
Los Angeles	1	$25,500	1	$18,000,000
San Francisco–Oakland	2	15,000	1	10,000,000
San Diego	2	18,000	1	12,000,000
Santa Barbara	2	14,000	1	8,000,000
Pasadena	3	9,000	1	6,000,000

Any receipts are placed in a money market fund yielding 10%.
(a) Find the net marginal benefit of opening the Los Angeles collection center.
(b) Find the net marginal benefit of opening each lockbox.
(c) What should Socorro do?

Evaluating Cash Management Strategies

Determining whether to adopt a specific cash management technique is analogous to evaluating a replacement decision in capital budgeting. That is, a new technique or system is compared with an existing one in an incremental benefit-cost analysis. Typical costs are usually bank fees, employee salaries, and perhaps an investment in specialized equipment.[9] The primary benefit is the potential cash freed up by improving the float time. This released cash can be used to increase income or reduce costs. For example, released funds can be invested in short-term earning assets or used to repay short-term debt.

To assess a technique's feasibility, the *NPV* for the current-asset investment decision must be determined using the capital budgeting methods discussed in earlier chapters. However, to focus on the issues involved in evaluating a cash management technique, note first that many cash savings methods involve no fixed-asset investment (i.e., no depreciation); therefore, this equation can be simplified as follows:

$$NPV = \frac{\Delta CFAT_t}{RRR} - CFAT_0$$

$$NPV = \frac{(\Delta \text{revenues} - \Delta \text{expenses})(1 - T)}{RRR} \qquad (19A\text{-}1)$$

where ΔRevenues = change in annual before-tax cash inflows (income)

ΔExpenses = change in annual before-tax cash outflows (costs)

T = marginal tax rate

RRR = (after-tax) opportunity cost of capital[10]

The reader may ask why it is necessary to compute *NPV* if, as argued, $CFAT_0 = 0$ in most cases. Why not simply go with the new project as long as revenues exceed expenses? It is certainly true that the new system is to the firm's advantage as long as revenues are greater than expenses. However, calculating

---

[9]Some high-volume retailers have established their own check processing facilities that operate the same check-sorting and encoding equipment as bank lockboxes. When checks are high-volume, low-dollar payments, an in-house collection center can be a feasible alternative to a bank-operated facility.

[10]Since no investment is involved, taxes can be safely ignored (because $\Delta CFAT_0 = 0$) without affecting the decision. However, to be consistent with the earlier analysis of long-term investments in Chapters 10 and 11, we are staying with an after-tax framework. Moreover, if depreciable assets are involved, equation (19A-1) cannot be used because such investments are irreversible. The standard capital budgeting methods developed in Chapters 10 and 11 must be used in this case.

the *NPV* tells us how much of an advantage (in dollars) this really is. This is important if the firm is considering alternative cash management strategies.

UNCOLLECTED FLOAT ANALYSIS

The fundamental tool in determining the net benefits of any cash management technique is an **uncollected float analysis.** A collection float analysis measures the expected reduction in float in days and then translates these days into the potential cash released from uncollected cash balances. Similarly, a disbursement float analysis measures the expected increase in float in days and converts this into the potential cash released from available cash balances. More specifically,

$$\Delta F = C \times \Delta t \tag{19A-2}$$

where ΔF = change in average uncollected or available cash balances (released cash)

C = average daily check receipts or disbursements

Δt = change in average float time in days

For example, if a firm collects $146 million annually in sales, its average daily check receipts would be C = $146 million/365 days = $400,000 per day. If mail, processing, and clearing float average five days, the daily total uncollected balance associated with this float would be $2 million ($400,000 × 5). Now, if float could be reduced by two days, the reduction in float (or average uncollected balances freed up) would be

$$\Delta F = \$400,000 \times 2 \text{ days} = \$800,000$$

The before-tax change in annual cash income is the incremental income received by improving float time. This is given by

$$\Delta \text{Revenues} = \Delta F \times RRR \tag{19A-3}$$

or, from equation (19A-2),

$$\Delta \text{Revenues} = (\Delta C \times \Delta t) \times RRR \tag{19A-4}$$

In this case, the opportunity cost of capital can be viewed as the forgone interest income that could be earned by investing F, or the interest expenses that could be saved by using F to reduce short-term debt.

Example 19A•1 Estimating the Advantages of a Lockbox Arrangement

Recall that adopting a lockbox system is an attempt to benefit from an improved collection system to reduce mail, processing, and clearing float associated with converting receipts (checks) into available or usable funds.

Assume that Herculean Corporation's annual credit sales are $136,875,000, which are billed and collected through a centralized location. A collections study indicates that 700 checks per day are processed and deposited, on average, and that a regional lockbox network could reduce Herculean's float by two days. However, the lockbox banks will charge $0.20 per check to operate the lockbox system. If the released cash could be used to reduce short-term debt costs by 10%, should the system be adopted (the marginal tax rate is 50%)?

In this example, from equation (19A-1),

$$\Delta\text{Revenues} = \left(\frac{136,875,000}{365}\right)(2 \text{ days}) \times 0.10$$
$$= \$750,000 \times 0.10 = \$75,000$$

Note that "revenues" in this case come from a $75,000 decrease in interest expenses. To determine the change in cash expenses due to the banks' fees:[11]

$$\Delta\text{Expenses} = 700 \text{ checks} \times 365 \text{ days} \times \$0.20/\text{check} = \$51,100$$

Therefore, the *NPV* from equation (19A-1) is

$$NPV = \frac{(\$75,000 - \$51,100)(1 - 0.50)}{0.10} = \$119,500$$

The lockbox system should be adopted. But what if the lockbox banks also required $300,000 in compensating balances? Since these funds would be placed all year in a nonearning checking account, the compensating balances would act to reduce *F*, the $75,000 in released cash. Therefore, the net benefit would become

$$NPV = \frac{[\$75,000 - \$300,000(0.10) - \$51,100](1 - 0.50)}{0.10} = \$-30,500$$

The lockbox system should not be implemented.

---

[11]If adopting the lockbox system resulted in reducing any of the operating expenses associated with the centralized billing collection center, these expenses should be included here.

Example 19A•2   Stretching Payables

Stretching payables is an attempt to benefit from an increase in disbursement float. Assume that a cash manager discovers that her firm is paying off its accounts payable an average of two days early. If the firm changed this practice and paid them on their due date, what would be the effect on the disbursement float if credit purchases are $91,250,000 annually? If the available cash released could be invested in short-term securities at 12%, what would be the net benefit to the firm?

The average increase in disbursement float would be

$$\Delta F = C \times \Delta t$$
$$= (\$91,250,000/365 \text{ days}) \times 2 \text{ days} = \$500,000$$

and the *NPV* would be

$$NPV = \frac{\Delta \text{revenues}}{RRR} = \frac{\Delta F \times RRR}{RRR}$$
$$= \$500,000 \times \frac{0.12}{0.12}$$
$$= \$500,000$$

Learning Check for Appendix 19•A

Review Questions

19A•1. What is the procedure for evaluating cash management strategies? How is this procedure similar to capital budgeting?

19A•2. What is uncollected float analysis? What does it measure? How is this information useful to the firm?

New Term

Uncollected float analysis

PROBLEMS

19A•1. Ommi Corporation is considering a lockbox system. Its annual credit sales are $61,590,000. A study done by the corporation estimates that

31,500 checks are processed, on average, per day, and that a regional lockbox system could reduce Ommi's float by 3 days. Lockbox banks would charge $0.25 per check to operate the lockbox system. If the cash freed by the lockbox system could be used to reduce short-term debt on which Ommi pays 10% interest, should the lockbox system be implemented?

19A•2. Your boss, the owner of a sports equipment manufacturing firm, has asked you to see if you can improve his cash management. You easily determine that the firm makes $32,500,000 in credit purchases. You then find out that the owner has always believed in paying a bill as soon as it is presented. This practice results in the firm paying its payables 18 days before they are due. If the firm were to pay its payables only when due and the available cash released could be invested in marketable securities earning 9%, what would be the net benefit to the firm?

READINGS

BATLIN, C. A., AND SUSAN HINKO, "Lockbox Management and Value Maximization," *Financial Management*, Winter 1981, 39–44.

BAUMOL, W. J., "The Transactions Demand for Cash: An Inventory Theoretic Approach," *Quarterly Journal of Economics*, November 1952, 545–556.

KALLBERG, J. G., AND K. PARKINSON, *Current Asset Management* (New York: Wiley-Interscience, 1984).

MILLER, M. H., AND D. ORR, "A Model of the Demand for Money by Firms," *Quarterly Journal of Economics*, August 1966, 413–435.

MULLINS, DAVID WILEY, JR., AND RICHARD B. HOMONOFF, "Applications of Inventory Cash Management Models," in *Modern Developments in Financial Management*, ed. S. C. Myers (New York: Praeger Publishers, 1976).

NAUSS, ROBERT M., AND ROBERT E. MARKLAND, "Solving Lockbox Location Problems," *Financial Management*, Spring 1979, 21–31.

POGUE, G. A., R. B. FAUCETT, AND R. N. BUSSARD, "Cash Management: A Systems Approach," *Industrial Management Review*, Winter 1970, 55–76.

STONE, BERNELL K., "The Use of Forecasts for Smoothing in Control-Limit Models for Cash Management," *Financial Management*, Spring 1972, 72–84.

STONE, BERNELL K., AND NED C. HILL, "The Design of a Cash Concentration System," *Journal of Financial and Quantitative Analysis*, September 1981, 301–322.

VANDER WEIDE, J., AND S. F. MAIER, *Managing Corporate Liquidity* (New York: John Wiley & Sons, Inc., 1985).

20

Current Asset Management: Accounts Receivable and Inventory

Chapter 18 explains why working capital is important to support the operations of the firm. In Chapter 19, we examine two types of current assets: cash and near-cash items. In this chapter we conclude our discussion of current assets with an analysis of two important current asset items: accounts receivable and inventory. The management of these items is different from cash management in its details but similar in its general approach.

The two sections of the chapter are devoted to these current asset accounts.

SECTION 20•1: *Managing Accounts Receivable.* The various aspects of a firm's credit policy are covered in this section. First, the required analysis for a credit extension policy is discussed in detail. Then the factors involved in establishing a collections policy are outlined. Specific techniques for monitoring a firm's investments in accounts receivable are presented in Appendix 20•A.

SECTION 20•2: *Managing Inventory.* This section presents a brief overview of the management of inventory. A firm must ensure that it has sufficient inventory to support its operations. Inventory in excess of this amount is wasteful.

SECTION 20•1 *Managing Accounts Receivable*

The investment in accounts receivable results from a firm's credit sales, and its level indicates the extent to which its credit and collections policies are used to stimulate sales. For example, if a firm charges the same price for cash and credit sales, offering credit is in effect a price reduction.[1] Although less liquid than either cash or marketable securities, receivables are a major investment for many firms (refer to Table 20•1) that also involves a trade-off between risk and profitability. The issue is how much to invest in receivables in order to maximize shareholder wealth. Too little investment may deprive the firm of the marginal benefits from a higher sales level (reduced profitability). Too much investment may expose the firm to excessive costs by tying up valuable cash (increased liquidity risk).

Managing accounts receivable involves the following:

1. Establishing a credit extension policy.

2. Establishing a collection policy.

3. Monitoring the receivables investment.

Credit extension policies provide guidelines for granting credit, the terms of payment, and the amount of credit to extend to a customer. Collection policies provide guidelines for ensuring that customers pay their bills according to the credit terms. Monitoring the receivables investment involves evaluating and controlling the quality of the total receivables investment in order to detect any problems and to suggest corrective actions. These three areas of receivables management will now be investigated.

TABLE 20•1 Three Types of Credit Accounts Found in Credit Agreements

---

1. *Open book credit.* The most common type of credit is open book or open account credit. Goods and services are sold without a contract evidencing the transaction. An invoice provides an informal statement of the transaction.
2. *Installment credit.* Repayment is made by a series of regular (monthly) payments. Most of these arrangements are for a one-time purchase of an expensive item (e.g., a computer).
3. *Revolving credit.* Revolving credit is a hybrid of the first two wherein the indebtedness is classified as current as long as a minimum payment (a fraction of the outstanding balance) is made each month.

ANALYZING A CREDIT EXTENSION POLICY

Credit may be extended to an individual or to another firm. Credit granted to an individual is referred to as **consumer credit**. Credit extended to another firm is known as **trade credit**. The following discussion will focus on trade

---

[1] This reduction can occur in two ways. A direct reduction occurs if the firm offers a discount when the account receivable is paid off before a certain date. An indirect reduction occurs if no finance charge is assessed. In effect, a firm granting credit, say for one month, presents its customer with an interest-free loan because the customer continues for a month to have the use of this money, which can then be invested to earn interest income.

credit because the treatment of trade credit differs somewhat from that of consumer credit. A firm has limited liability and a life span greater than the lives of its management and owners. Moreover, trade credit is fairly sensitive to interest-rate changes, whereas consumer credit is largely affected by changes in income and unemployment. These and other distinctions affect the credit-granting (and collections) decision in different ways, making a complete discussion of both rather cumbersome. Table 20•1 summarizes the more common types of credit accounts.

Credit Standards

Credit standards are criteria that determine which customers will be granted credit and to what extent. A customer must meet or exceed the minimum credit standards. Ideally, a firm's credit standards will reject only those customers who ultimately would not pay their bills promptly or not at all (become *bad debtors*). First, no qualitative or quantitative method can predict the future bill-paying ability of a customer.[2] Second, attempting to implement "ideal" credit standards may result in a too stringent or too tight policy that may eliminate the risk of nonpayment (lower collection expenses and bad-debt losses) but may also eliminate potential sales to those rejected customers who would have paid their bills. At the other extreme, an excessively liberal policy may lead to higher sales, but greater bad-debt losses and collection costs would follow. Therefore, the trade-off between marginal benefits and costs dictates a balance between these two extremes.

A discussion of how a firm should establish its credit standards is beyond the intended scope of this book, because such standards depend on subjective and objective information. Nevertheless, credit standards often revolve around the "four C's of credit": (1) character—a customer's willingness to pay; (2) capacity—a customer's ability to generate cash flow; (3) capital—a customer's financial resources, such as collateral; and (4) conditions—current economic or business conditions. These four general characteristics are normally assessed by investigating different sources of credit information, subject to time and cost considerations. Table 20•2 describes the more common sources of credit information.

Some credit sources provide an overall credit rating. A key to the Dun & Bradstreet credit rating system is given in Figure 20•1. An example of a Dun & Bradstreet credit report on a firm is given in Figure 20•2. If such a credit report is not available on a customer, the firm's credit standards are applied to the credit information available on that customer and the probability of delinquent payment or a bad-debt loss is assessed. Based on this subjective analysis, a customer may, for example, be classified into a credit risk category, which in turn determines the credit amount or line of credit to be extended. Table 20•3 provides an example of one credit classification scheme. Many firms quantify

---

[2] Some credit-scoring models have shown some promise in predicting default; however, their predictions are not very accurate.

TABLE 20•2 Common Sources of Credit Information

1. *Financial statements.* A credit applicant is often asked to supply various types of financial information, such as audited balance sheets, income statements, and pro forma statements. Applying the financial analysis techniques studied in Chapter 5, the firm assesses the applicant's financial strength and ability to pay its obligations.
2. *Credit agencies.* An important source of credit information is credit agencies such as Dun & Bradstreet (D&B) that specialize in providing credit ratings and credit reports on individual firms. For example, Figure 20•1 contains an example of D&B's credit *rating* system, which provides a measure of an applicant's "financial strength" (net worth) and a composite credit appraisal (from "high" to "limited"). For an extra fee, an individual credit *report* can be obtained, such as that shown in Figure 20•2.
3. *Banks.* Banks will often provide a credit check for their customers. Larger banks maintain sizable credit departments that share information with each other. Limited credit information, such as loan repayment experience, can be obtained in this way.
4. *Trade associations.* Various trade associations keep records of member firms' credit experience with different suppliers. Information such as credit amount extended, payment experience (slow or prompt), and so on, can easily be obtained through such sources.

this process through the use of a credit-scoring system. Such a system assigns point values to different attributes that have historically been indicative of customers' payment behavior. Based on the total value of these points, a customer's credit application is accepted or rejected and, in some cases, placed in a classification scheme such as the one in Table 20•3.

Credit Terms

The second part of a credit extension policy establishes the terms on which credit is granted. Competitive conditions or industry standards often dictate such terms. In other instances, they may be related to the perishability or turnover of the products. Credit terms define the credit period and any discount offered for early payment. They are usually stated as "net t" or "d/t_1, n/t." The first example states that payment is due within t days from a specified date, usually the date of the good's receipt. The second allows a discount of $d\%$ if payment is made within t_1 days; otherwise, the full amount is due within t days. For example, "3/10, $n/30$" means that a 3% discount from the invoice amount can be taken if payment is made within 10 days; otherwise, full payment is due within 30 days.[3] Cash discounts are offered to reward early payments, and thereby to reduce the collection period and the amount invested in accounts receivable.

---

[3] Occasionally, the credit terms may specify an interest cost if payment is not received within the credit period. For example, "3/10, $n/30$, 15% over 30" indicates that an annual interest cost of 15% will be assessed on any amount outstanding after 30 days.

Key to Ratings

ESTIMATED FINANCIAL STRENGTH			COMPOSITE CREDIT APPRAISAL			
			HIGH	GOOD	FAIR	LIMITED
5A	$50,000,000	and over	1	2	3	4
4A	$10,000,000 to	49,999,999	1	2	3	4
3A	1,000,000 to	9,999,999	1	2	3	4
2A	750,000 to	999,999	1	2	3	4
1A	500,000 to	749,999	1	2	3	4
BA	300,000 to	499,999	1	2	3	4
BB	200,000 to	299,999	1	2	3	4
CB	125,000 to	199,999	1	2	3	4
CC	75,000 to	124,999	1	2	3	4
DC	50,000 to	74,999	1	2	3	4
DD	35,000 to	49,999	1	2	3	4
EE	20,000 to	34,999	1	2	3	4
FF	10,000 to	19,999	1	2	3	4
GG	5,000 to	9,999	1	2	3	4
HH	Up to	4,999	1	2	3	4

GENERAL CLASSIFICATION FOR ESTIMATED FINANCIAL STRENGTH AND COMPOSITE CREDIT APPRAISAL

ESTIMATED FINANCIAL STRENGTH			COMPOSITE CREDIT APPRAISAL		
			GOOD	FAIR	LIMITED
1R	$125,000	and over	2	3	4
2R	$50,000 to	$124,999	2	3	4

EXPLANATION

When the designation "1R" or "2R" appears, followed by a 2, 3 or 4, it is an indication that the Estimated Financial Strength, while not definitely classified, is presumed to be in the range of the ($) figures in the corresponding bracket, and while the Composite Credit Appraisal cannot be judged precisely, it is believed to fall in the general category indicated.

"INV." shown in place of a rating indicates that Dun & Bradstreet is currently conducting an investigation to gather information for a new report. It has no other significance.

"FB" (Foreign Branch). Indicates that the headquarters of this company is located in a foreign country (including Canada). The written report contains the location of the headquarters.

ABSENCE OF A RATING--THE BLANK SYMBOL

A blank symbol (--) should not be interpreted as indicating that credit should be denied. It simply means that the information available to Dun & Bradstreet does not permit us to classify the company within our rating key and that further inquiry should be made before reaching a credit decision.

EMPLOYEE RANGE DESIGNATIONS IN REPORTS ON NAMES NOT LISTED IN THE REFERENCE BOOK

Certain businesses do not lend themselves to a Dun & Bradstreet rating and are not listed in the Reference Book. Information on these names, however, continues to be stored and updated in the D&B Business Information File. Reports are available on such businesses and instead of a rating they carry an Employee Range Designation (ER) which is indicative of size in terms of number of employees. No other significance should be attached.

KEY TO EMPLOYEE RANGE DESIGNATIONS

ER 1	1000 or more	Employees
ER 2	500- 999	Employees
ER 3	100 - 499	Employees
ER 4	50 - 99	Employees
ER 5	20 - 49	Employees
ER 6	10 - 19	Employees
ER 7	5 - 9	Employees
ER 8	1 - 4	Employees
ER N		Not Available

Dun & Bradstreet Credit Services

DB a company of
The Dun & Bradstreet Corporation

FIGURE 20·1 Dun & Bradstreet's credit rating system.

Dun & Bradstreet, Inc.

BE SURE NAME, BUSINESS AND ADDRESS MATCH YOUR FILE

ANSWERING INQUIRY

This report has been prepared for:

SUBSCRIBER: 008-001042

THIS REPORT MAY NOT BE REPRODUCED IN WHOLE OR IN PART IN ANY MANNER WHATEVER.

DUNS: 06-647-3261
RETTINGER PAINT CORP

727 WHITMAN WAY
BENSON, MI 48232
TEL:313 961-0720

CARL RETTINGER, PRES

DATE PRINTED
AUG 13, 198-

WHOL PAINTS & VARNISHES

SIC NO.
51 98

SUMMARY

RATING	CC2
STARTED	1950
PAYMENTS	SEE BELOW
SALES	$424,612
WORTH	F $101,867
EMPLOYS	5
HISTORY	CLEAR
CONDITION	GOOD
TREND	STEADY

SPECIAL EVENTS
07/10/8- Business burglarized Jul 3 but $18,000 loss is fully insured.

PAYMENTS (Amounts may be rounded to nearest figure in prescribed ranges)

REPORTED	PAYING RECORD	HIGH CREDIT	NOW OWES	PAST DUE	SELLING TERMS	LAST SALE WITHIN
07/8-	Disc	30000	15000	-0-	2 10 N30	1 Mo
	Disc	30000	15000	-0-	1 10 N30	2-3 Mos
	Disc-Ppt	10000	5000	250	2 10 N30	1 Mo
	Ppt	10000	7500	-0-	30	1 Mo
06/8-	Disc	15000	7500	-0-	2 10 N30	2-3 Mos
05/8-	Disc	10000	5000	-0-	2 10 N30	1 Mo
	Ppt	1000	-0-	-0-	30	1 Mo

FINANCE
06/25/8- Fiscal statement dated May 31 198-:

Cash	$ 20,623	Accts Pay	$ 47,246
Accts Rec	55,777	Bank Loans	34,000
Inventory	92,103	Notes Pay (Trucks)	7,020
Current	168,503	Current	88,266
Fixt & Equip	13,630	COMMON STOCK	35,000
Trucks	8,000	EARNED SURPLUS	66,867
Total Assets	190,133	Total	190,133

Annual sales $424,612; Net profit $17,105. Monthly rent $3,500. Fire insurance on mdse & fixt $95,000; Equipment $20,000.

Prepared from statement(s) by Accountant: Steige Co., CPA's, Detroit, MI. Extent of audit, if any, not indicated.

--0--

On Jun 22 198-, John J Lawson defined monthly payments: $3,000 to bank, $400 on notes. Admitted collections slow but losses insignificant. Said inventory will drop to $60,000 by December. Expects 5% sales increase this year.

PUBLIC FILINGS
03/25/8- On Mar 17 198-, a suit in the amount of $200 was entered against subject by Henry Associates, Atlanta, GA (Docket #H27519). Involves merchandise which Lawson says was defective.
05/28/8- On May 21 198-, a financing statement (#H741170) was filed listing subject as debtor and NCR Corp., Dayton, OH as secured party. Collateral consists of equipment.

BANKING
06/25/8- Account long maintained, carries average balance low to moderate five figures. Unsecured loans to moderate five extended and now open.

HISTORY
06/22/8- CARL RETTINGER, PRES JOHN J LAWSON, V PRES
DIRECTOR(S): THE OFFICER(S)

Incorporated Michigan Feb 2 1950. Authorized capital consists of 3,500 shares common stock, no par value. Paid in capital $35,000. Officers own capital stock equally.

CARL RETTINGER born 1920 married. Employed by E-Z Paints, Detroit, MI, 12 years; five as manager until starting subject early 1950.

JOHN J LAWSON born 1925 married. Obtained accounting degree 1946 and then employed by Union Carbide, Chicago, Ill, until joining Rettinger at inception.

OPERATION

Wholesales paints and varnishes (85%), wallpaper and supplies. 500 local accounts include retailers (75%) and contractors. Terms are 2 10 net 30 days. Peak season spring through summer.

EMPLOYEES: 5, including the officers.

FACILITIES: Rents 7,500 sq. ft. one-story block structure, good repair.

THIS REPORT, FURNISHED PURSUANT TO CONTRACT FOR THE EXCLUSIVE USE OF THE SUBSCRIBER AS ONE FACTOR TO CONSIDER IN CONNECTION WITH CREDIT INSURANCE, MARKETING OR OTHER BUSINESS DECISIONS, CONTAINS INFORMATION COMPILED FROM SOURCES WHICH DUN & BRADSTREET, INC DOES NOT CONTROL AND WHOSE INFORMATION, UNLESS OTHERWISE INDICATED IN THE REPORT, HAS NOT BEEN VERIFIED. IN FURNISHING THIS REPORT, DUN & BRADSTREET, INC IN NO WAY ASSUMES ANY PART OF THE USER'S BUSINESS RISK, DOES NOT GUARANTEE THE ACCURACY, COMPLETENESS, OR TIMELINESS OF THE INFORMATION PROVIDED AND SHALL NOT BE LIABLE FOR ANY LOSS OR INJURY WHATEVER RESULTING FROM CONTINGENCIES BEYOND ITS CONTROL OR FROM NEGLIGENCE

FIGURE 20•2 Example of a Dun & Bradstreet credit report.

Costs and Benefits of a Credit Extension Policy

Costs The major costs of a credit extension policy can be grouped into four categories:

1. Cash discounts. A percentage of sales deducted as an incentive to encourage early payment.

TABLE 20·3 Example of a Classification Scheme by Credit Risk Category, Line of Credit, and Historical Payment Behavior

Credit Risk Category		Line of Credit to Grant	Historical Payment Behavior	
			Average Collection Period (Days)[a]	Bad-Debt Loss Ratio (%)[b]
Lowest	1	>$500,000	20	0.5
	2	<$500,000	30	1.5
	3	<$250,000	45	3.0
	4	<$100,000	60	6.5
	5	<$ 50,000	90	10.0
Highest	6	Reject		

[a] *Average collection period* measures the average number of days a current account is outstanding before it is paid off.
[b] *Bad-debt loss ratio* measures the percentage of outstanding credit sales that prove to be uncollectible and are written off as a charge against sales.

2. Credit and collection expenses. Administrative costs for conducting an in-house credit operation.

3. Bad-debt losses. Accounts that are uncollectible and written off as a charge against sales.

4. Financing costs. The *RRR* or opportunity cost of capital of funds tied up in a receivables investment.

Benefits Extending credit can be a potential sales tool for stimulating revenues and thereby increasing the cash flows (returns) to fixed-asset investments. Moreover, a credit policy may be needed to prevent an erosion in market share. If competitors offer credit on better terms, for example, a firm will be forced to follow suit simply to maintain its sales level. In contrast, restricting credit through more stringent standards or terms may produce net benefits if any reduced sales are more than offset by lower credit costs.

EVALUATING A CHANGE IN THE CREDIT EXTENSION POLICY

Deciding whether to adopt a credit policy normally involves comparing a new policy with an existing policy. Once again, it is the incremental benefits and costs that are relevant to this decision. Assume that the Herculean Corporation currently extends credit to those customers that fall in the four lowest credit-risk categories in Table 20·3 (categories 1 to 4). Management wants to know if it is more profitable to eliminate the marginal accounts by tightening its credit standards and restricting credit to the three lowest-risk categories. Table 20·4A summarizes Herculean's current and proposed credit policy details.

TABLE 20•4A Herculean Corporation's Proposed Change in Credit Policy

	Existing Policy	Proposed Policy
Credit standards	Categories 1–4	Categories 1–3
Average collection period	40 days	35 days
Bad-debt losses	4% of sales	2% of sales
Percent of sales taking discounts[a]	30	32

[a] That is, the percentage of sales being paid back in 10 days or less.

Such a move would affect sales negatively because the sales to customers in the highest-risk category (4) would be lost, but the amount of investment in receivables would decline. Moreover, the operating and credit costs should decrease. Collection and bad-debt expenses, in particular, are normally due disproportionately to servicing the lower-quality or marginal accounts. Therefore, the question is: Will the lost sales be more than offset by the decrease in expenses and receivables investment?

To answer the question, the total cash flows resulting from each policy are estimated first. Next, the cash flows from the current credit policy are subtracted from those of the proposed policy to determine the incremental cash flows associated with the proposed policy. Finally, the *NPV* of these incremental cash flows is estimated and an accept-reject decision made.

Referring to Table 20•4B, Herculean's current revenues of $136,875,000

TABLE 20•4B Worksheet for Evaluating Herculean's Proposed Changes (Thousands of Dollars)

	(1) Proposed Policy	(2) Current Policy	(3) Incremental Cash Flows (1) − (2)
Change in operating cash flows ($\Delta CFAT_t$)			
Δ Revenues	116,800	136,875	(20,075)
Δ Operating costs (70% of sales)	(81,760)	(95,812)	14,052
Δ Credit expenses			
Discounts taken[a]	(1,121)	(1,232)	111
Credit and collection	(2,100)	(3,400)	1,300
Bad debts[b]	(2,336)	(5,475)	3,139
Δ CFBT	29,483	30,956	(1,473)
Δ Taxes (40%)	(11,793)	(12,382)	(589)
Δ CFAT	17,690	18,574	(884)
Change in "initial investment" ($\Delta CFAT_0$)[c]:			
level of accounts receivables	11,200	15,000	(3,800)

[a] Proposed policy: $116,800 \times 0.32 \times 0.03 = \$1,121$
Current policy: $\$136,875 \times 0.30 \times 0.03 = \$1,232$
[b] Proposed policy: $\$116,800 \times 0.02 = \$2,336$
Current policy: $\$136,875 \times 0.04 = \$5,475$
[c] Proposed policy: $(\$116,800/365 \text{ days}) \times 35 \text{ days} = \$11,200$
Current policy: $(\$136,875/365 \text{ days}) \times 40 \text{ days} = \$15,000$

will drop to \$116,800,000 under the new credit policy, an incremental decrease in before-tax cash flows of \$20,075,000. On the other hand, operating and credit expenses will also decline. The net change in cash flow will be a decrease in cash flow after taxes of \$884,000. However, a smaller level of receivables will be required for two reasons: (1) lower sales and (2) a shorter credit period (average collection period). As the table indicates, these two factors cause the investment in receivables to fall by \$3.8 million.

As discussed in Section 18•2, the incremental cash flows can be treated as a perpetuity. If the firm's opportunity cost of capital is 10%, its *NPV* can be calculated as:

$$NPV = \frac{\Delta CFAT_t}{RRR} - \Delta CFAT_0$$

$$= \frac{\$-884,000}{0.10} - (\$-3,800,000) = \$-5,040,000$$

Therefore, by restricting credit to higher-quality credit risks, Herculean will end up reducing its firm value by over \$5 million. In other words, retaining the higher-risk customers is preferred, and the proposed credit policy should be rejected.

Finally, if relaxing a credit policy were being considered instead, the same evaluation scheme would apply, but the cash flow effects would be the opposite. For example, if Herculean's credit terms were changed from 2/10, *n*/30 to 1/10, 1/10, *n*/40, sales would be stimulated, but operating costs, credit expenses, and the cost of financing the higher level of sales (higher receivables investment) would also be greater.

FURTHER REFINEMENTS IN ANALYZING CREDIT POLICY CHANGES

A number of other considerations not formally recognized in the Herculean example need to be mentioned.

Changes in Net Working Capital

Whenever a credit policy change affects sales, working capital components other than accounts receivable may be affected. For example, if a policy change increases sales, the investments in operating cash balances and inventory may need to be increased to support the higher sales. Moreover, spontaneous financing such as current liabilities may also increase and may serve to offset the higher-current-asset investment. Therefore, a proper evaluation of a policy change should account for any change in net working capital requirements and should include it in the analysis as part of the initial investment.

Risk and the *RRR*

The primary risk associated with a credit decision is the chance that customers will not pay their bills. Because bad-debt losses are fairly predictable, the risk inherent in accounts receivable is relatively low. Presumably, restricting credit to higher-quality customers should reduce the variability in bad-debt losses and collection expenses. Nevertheless, we have ignored any differences in the variability of the cash flows under the two policies. Is this a correct procedure? No, but estimating the change in the *RRR* due to a credit policy change alone is very difficult.[4] In practice, risk differences are normally recognized by adjusting the *RRR* up or down according to a set of risk class designations (refer to the ad hoc method of estimating the *RRR* in Chapter 11).

Fixed versus Variable Costs

Estimating the incremental cash flows will usually involve only variable costs (those that increase directly with increased sales). In the earlier example, it was assumed implicitly that fixed costs remained unchanged because a sales decrease occurred. If a sales increase were involved, say with a relaxed credit policy, fixed costs might increase if the firm is operating near its capacity. If additional fixed costs result, they should also be included in the incremental cash flow analysis.

The Optimal Policy

The best or optimal policy in terms of maximizing shareholder wealth cannot be determined directly. Rather, the financial manager must evaluate alternative policies and move in steps toward the optimal credit extension policy. For example, Herculean might next see if relaxing its credit standards by extending credit to the highest-risk category (5) might improve its position. Finally, altering the present credit terms might be more profitable, but should they be relaxed or tightened? Only an incremental benefit-cost analysis can tell—as well as actual experience. Over time, the dynamics of a changing group of customers and a changing business environment may make a formerly optimal policy undesirable. This is why continual evaluation and monitoring of the investment in receivables are required—a topic that will be examined shortly.

ESTABLISHING A COLLECTIONS POLICY

Collecting accounts receivable is usually a routine task because most firms pay their bills on time. However, overdue accounts do occur, so collection procedures for these delinquent payments must be established, especially since this

---

[4]It is necessary to estimate the beta of the credit decision "project"—a difficult task.

affects the investment in receivables and hence the return. Collection procedures usually start with a second mailing indicating that the account is overdue, followed by a personal phone call or visit. If these efforts go unrewarded, the account may be turned over to a collection agency or direct legal action may be taken.

Key decisions for management include how long it will wait before labeling an account overdue and initiating the collection procedures and how aggressively it will pursue these accounts. Beginning too soon may antagonize customers. Aggressive collection efforts may reduce future sales and profits if customers are chased off to competitors. Changing business conditions will alter payment patterns (e.g., payments tend to slow down during an economic downturn), and often an otherwise creditworthy customer will allow a bill to become overdue for a good reason, perhaps through oversight or a misplacement of the bill.

The collection policy or methods adopted should be determined by the same incremental benefit-cost analysis used to evaluate the credit extension policy. The time and effort spent on collecting an individual account must be traded off against the expected benefits. Collection efforts can be expensive. While second or third letters or telephone calls are relatively inexpensive, collection agency or legal fees are substantial. Remember that the objective of a collection is not to minimize bad-debt losses; it is to maximize the value of the firm.

MONITORING THE RECEIVABLES INVESTMENT

As mentioned earlier, customers' payment patterns determine the level of investment in receivables and its return. For instance, a slow payment pattern will lead to an excessive investment and a lower rate of return. To manage its receivables efficiently, a firm must monitor and evaluate its receivable collections to detect any changes in its status and composition and to institute corrective actions where appropriate. One or more of several techniques involving the average collection period ratio, the aging schedule, or a collections schedule are typically used. These techniques for monitoring investments in accounts receivable are discussed in detail in Appendix 20•A.

Learning Check for Section 20•1

Review Questions

20•1. What are the three decision areas confronting an accounts receivable manager?

20•2. How would you evaluate a proposed credit extension policy in an *NPV* framework? What are some other important issues not considered in your *NPV* analysis?

New Terms

Consumer credit   Credit standards   Trade credit
Credit extension policy

SECTION 20•2   *Managing Inventory*

Just as with accounts receivable, the investment in inventory represents a sizable portion of many firms' total asset investment (refer to Table 20•1).

WHY DO FIRMS HOLD INVENTORIES?

Ideally, as with cash, firms should maintain zero inventory (why?). However, in practice, this goal is not feasible, as inventories must be held for several reasons.

Inventories in the Production Process

Irrespective of the item being produced by a company, a significant amount of inventory can be tied up in the production process in the form of unfinished goods.

Inventories in Shipment

Even finished goods that are in the process of shipment are inventory, and these inventories can be significant.

Inventories to Reduce Inventory Costs

Firms often hold inventory with the expectation of lowering the substantial fixed costs that accrue when ordering and/or producing additional inventories in the event of an unanticipated shortfall. These additional inventory costs can arise for a variety of reasons.

Acquisition Costs Acquisition costs are the costs incurred in the process of acquiring the item(s) to be held in inventory. Examples of acquisition costs include the purchase price of the inventory, transportation costs, production costs, and the costs of placing purchase orders (management time, telephone calls, paperwork).

Holding Costs Holding costs include all costs associated with holding the item in inventory until sold. The costs of storage, security costs, and insurance are examples.

Shortage Costs Shortage costs are costs that are incurred when the firm cannot honor a customer's order because the item is out of stock. Shortage costs can be direct (lost revenues, higher production and transportation costs) or indirect (lost revenues because of customer dissatisfaction). These costs can be substantial and must be incorporated explicitly into any analysis of inventory policy.

Management costs can be substantial for companies that have hundreds of inventory items on hand. To facilitate inventory handling and control, many firms use sophisticated computerized inventory management systems. Of course, implementing such a system can itself be costly.

THE ROLE OF THE FINANCIAL MANAGER IN INVENTORY DECISIONS

First, it must be noted that day-to-day operations of inventory management rarely include the financial manager. Rather, the financial manager's responsibility is to evaluate the overall investment in inventory. Intuitively, it would seem that excessive inventories reduce the risk of production delays or stockouts and hence should increase firm value. However, the additional carrying costs may wipe out any gains. Similarly, inadequate inventories increase risk and may negatively affect firm value. But the offsetting benefit of lower carrying costs needs to be considered. Managers must constantly strive to balance these benefits and costs and to allow inventory to increase as long as reduced costs and risks are more important than the cost of carrying that level of investment.

Although managing inventory appears to fall within the realm of financial management, especially since it requires an investment of costly funds, this is not how it is normally treated in practice. In contrast to other current assets, inventory is considered the direct responsibility of other functional areas, such as purchasing, production, or marketing. In fact, inventory decisions in large firms are often made jointly among the different functional managers, with the financial manager playing a somewhat passive role (if any).

VALUE-MAXIMIZATION CONSIDERATIONS

Conceptually, an argument can be made that the financial manager should be more involved because an opportunity cost of funds is tied up in inventory. Therefore, should not the inventory decision be treated like other asset decisions? Should not its risk and return be considered in a capital budgeting framework? If so, what is the link between inventory decisions and shareholder wealth maximization?

The link between decisions on the optimal level of inventory or inventory policy and value maximization is unclear. Most textbooks focus on models that minimize total costs by determining the optimal inventory level or the optimal time or amount to order. But *optimal* here has no reference to the effect on firm value. Instead of going through these (sometimes elaborate) models, we will merely indicate in general terms what the role of the financial manager should be in managing inventories.

Because of the problems of integrating inventory decisions into our standard value-maximization framework, we adopt a modified goal of inventory management in the remainder of this chapter.

THE GOAL OF INVENTORY MANAGEMENT

KEY CONCEPT: The goal of **inventory management** is to minimize the total cost of an investment in inventory.

Because inventory is a reversible investment that continually fluctuates in size, inventory decisions usually focus on determining its optimal level. Therefore, the incremental benefits of carrying inventory, such as more flexible production scheduling or marketing efforts, must be balanced against the incremental costs (and risks) of holding inventory, such as storage, handling, and reordering costs, as well as obsolescence and spoilage.

Recognize that with very large inventories, a firm forgoes the opportunity to use the funds in other productive investments. A fundamental question in inventory management is how many units to order at a time. If large amounts of inventory are ordered each time, the dollar amount in inventories rises and the firm's total holding costs increase. On the other hand, if too few units are ordered, the firm will incur excessive acquisition costs. An optimal order quantity (also called the **economic order quantity,** *EOQ*) is one that balances the excessive acquisition costs associated with small order quantities and the excessive holding costs that arise with large order quantities. Figure 20•3 shows how these costs react to the size of the inventory order placed. The total costs of inventory, which is the sum of ordering costs and holding costs, will at first decline. Above a certain order size, however, total costs will increase. The optimal order quantity (*EOQ*) is the point where total costs are minimized, as shown in Figure 20•3.

To find the *EOQ* several models have been developed. A brief overview of the most popular model—the *EOQ* model—is provided next.

THE EOQ MODEL

The *EOQ* **model** is a simple model commonly used to find the optimal ordering quantity. The idea underlying this model is fairly simple. First, the total cost is expressed in terms of the quantity ordered, and then the quantity that yields the lowest total cost is identified as the *EOQ*. The *EOQ* can be determined either by finding the total costs associated with each order quantity or by using an *EOQ* equation:[5]

---

[5] Since the derivation of this formula is along the lines of the derivation of equation (19-4), it will be left as an exercise to the interested reader.

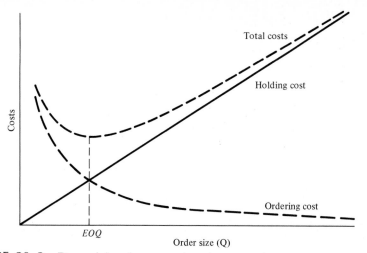

FIGURE 20·3 Determining the economic order quarterly.

$$EOQ = \sqrt{\frac{2DC_A}{C_H}} \qquad (20\text{-}1)$$

where D = total per period demand

C_A = acquisition costs per order

C_H = holding cost per unit

Both of these methods will now be examined in an illustration.

Example 20·1   Calculating the EOQ Two Ways

Johnston Soft Drinks distributes about 150,000 cases of its cola drink to its 10,000 retail outlets in the Midwest and the Pacific northwest. Johnston purchases its cola drink from a major bottling company at a cost of $5.25 per case (including transportation). Management has estimated that the cost of warehousing, insurance, theft, taxes, and damage (holding costs) amounts to 20% of the firm's average investment in inventories over the year. It is also estimated that the company incurs an acquisition cost of $30 per order. How many cases should Johnston order each time?

METHOD 1

STEP 1. Find the Firm's Average Investment in Inventories

As can be seen in Figure 20·4, if Johnston starts with Q cases and depletes the inventory gradually to zero before reordering, the average inventory over

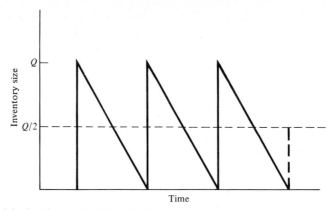

FIGURE 20·4   Graph depicting the assumption of steady demand on inventory.

any period will be (beginning inventory + ending inventory)/2, or $(Q + 0)/2 = Q/2$.

STEP 2. Find the Average Holding Costs

Since the average inventory is $Q/2$, the average holding costs would be $(Q/2) \times C_H$, where C_H represents the holding cost per unit. For Johnston, the average holding cost per unit would be 20% of $5.25 = $1.05, and the average cost therefore amounts to $(Q/2) \times \$1.05 = \$0.53Q$.

STEP 3. Find the Annual Acquisition Cost

If D denotes Johnston's annual demand (150,000 cases) and Q is the quantity ordered each time, the number of orders Johnston will have to place is D/Q. The annual acquisition costs will therefore be $(D/Q) \times C_A$, where C_A is the acquisition cost per order. For Johnston, the annual acquisition costs thus amount to $(150,000/Q)(\$30) = \$4,500,000/Q$.

STEP 4. Calculate the Total Costs

$$\text{Total costs} = \text{total holding costs} + \text{total acquisition costs}$$
$$TC = \$1.05Q + \$4,500,000/Q$$

Table 20·5 shows the total costs for different values of Q. As can readily be seen, the *EOQ* for Johnston is 2,900 cases of cola. That is, the total costs to Johnston are minimized when Johnston orders 2,900 cases per order.

METHOD 2

A more precise *EOQ* number can be obtained directly, using equation (20-1):

TABLE 20·5 Total Costs for Different Order Quantities

Order Quantity, Q	Holding Cost, 0.53Q	Acquisition Cost, $4,500,000/Q	Total Costs
500	$ 265	$9,000	$9,265
1,000	530	4,500	5,030
1,500	795	3,000	3,795
2,000	1,060	2,250	3,310
2,500	1,325	1,800	3,125
2,900	1,537	1,552	3,089
3,000	1,590	1,500	3,090
3,200	1,696	1,406	3,102

$$EOQ = \sqrt{\frac{2 \times 150,000 \times 30}{1.05}} = 2,928$$

Although the formula method appears to provide a more accurate *EOQ* number, the practical significance of the difference in an *EOQ* of 2,900 units (from Table 20·5) and 2,928 units obtained via the formula is negligible. This difference may conveniently be ignored in many instances, especially since the *EOQ* was calculated under two simplifying assumptions: that demand is distributed uniformly over the year and that there is no uncertainty regarding cost/demand numbers.

SOME REFINEMENT OF THE EOQ MODEL

There are several subtleties in the preceding illustration that were ignored. For example, a more comprehensive analysis would have taken into account the lead time—the delay between order and receipt of the cases of cola. If it takes on average three days for an order to be processed and delivered, it is obvious that Johnston should place an order before its inventory levels reach zero. Johnston should place an order three days before the date of receipt of the new shipment. Another consideration that may have to be factored into an *EOQ* analysis is the impact of quantity discounts that suppliers sometimes offer on large orders. With such discounts, Johnston's *EOQ* may be larger than 2,928 cases, as the discounts effectively lower the acquisition costs. In addition, safety stocks requirements can complicate the analysis further. Recall that the *EOQ* model discussed earlier did not explicitly consider the fact that demand uncertainty exists. Uncertainty can be recognized in an *EOQ* model by allowing the company reserve to accommodate unexpected increases in demand. Of course, the use of safety stocks will increase the firm's average investment in inventories. The procedures used to recognize these additional complexities in *EOQ* analysis will not be examined here.

Learning Check for Section 20•2

Review Questions

20•3. Why do firms hold inventories? What are the costs of holding inventory?

20•4. What is the goal of inventory management? Why do we depart from the goal of shareholder wealth maximization?

20•5. What is the *EOQ* model? What are the assumptions underlying this method for calculating optimal inventory?

New Terms

Acquisition costs

Economic order quantity

EOQ model

Holding costs

Shortage costs

SUMMARY

Managing Accounts Receivable

A credit extension policy requires an analysis of credit standards, credit terms, and the costs and benefits of extending credit. Management must establish an appropriate collections policy and, in addition, monitor its investments in accounts receivable by using one or more available techniques: the average collection period ratio, an aging schedule, or a collections schedule.

Managing Inventory

Conceptually, inventory decisions, too, should be made in a capital budgeting framework by estimating the opportunity cost of funds tied up in inventory and the benefits of increasing inventory. Because the link between inventory management and value maximization is not clear, the goal of the financial manager is usually to minimize overall costs. In this regard, the *EOQ* model may be useful. However, as a practical matter, financial managers seldom have much input into inventory decisions. The production engineers in the operations departments typically decide on inventory levels.

PROBLEMS

20•1. Steve Smith is credit manager for the southeast branch of the Earnest, Pearce, and Brown Clothing Stores. The stores currently under Steve's responsibility have annual credit sales of $60 million. Operating costs total 90% of sales. The average collection period is 40 days and bad-debt losses total 2% of sales. The Mueller Credit Corporation has guaranteed that it can reduce the average collection period to 30 days and bad-debt loss to 0.5% of sales. However, Steve estimates that the changes necessary to implement the Mueller proposal will reduce annual credit sales to $50 million. Any reduction in current assets will allow Steve to reduce current liabilities by the same amount. The estimated cost of short-term credit is 10%. Mueller Credit will charge an annual fee of $75,000 for their service. Steve is determining the marginal benefits and costs of hiring Mueller before making a final decision. If Mueller is hired:
   (a) What is the marginal savings from the reduced bad-debt loss?
   (b) What is the marginal savings from the reduced investment in accounts receivable?
   (c) What is the marginal expense of lost sales?
   (d) What should Steve do?

20•2. The Sipra Audio & Video Equipment Store is considering a change in credit policy to stimulate sales. Annual sales are currently $5 million, and 85% of this amount are operating costs. The average collection period is currently 20 days, and bad-debt losses currently total 1%. Naim Sipra, owner and manager of the store, is considering relaxing the credit standards with one of three plans:

Plan	Sales	Average Collection Period (Days)	Bad-Debt Loss (%)
A	$6,000,000	25	1.5
B	6,750,000	30	2.2
C	7,250,000	36	3.0

Any money saved from a reduction in accounts receivable will be invested in marketable securities yielding 8%. Find the net marginal cash flow for each of the three plans (compared with the current operations). Which plan should Naim choose?

20•3. Bobby Wolff, manager of Ace Groceries, has some extra space in one store and is trying to decide between opening a pharmacy and a record and tape department. The relevant data are as follows:

627

	Pharmacy	Record and Tape Department
Average age of inventory	30 days	90 days
Average collection period	30 days	60 days
Bad-debt loss	1%	2%
Annual sales	$540,000	$450,000
Operating cost as percentage of sales	0.60	0.50

Bobby estimates that any investment in current assets has an opportunity cost of 12%.
- (a) What is average level of inventory for each plan measured in sales dollars? Measured in terms of the cost of goods sold dollars?
- (b) What is the average level of accounts receivable for each plan?
- (c) What is the cost of the required increase in current assets for each plan?
- (d) What is the bad-debt expense for each plan?
- (e) What is the gross profit (sales − cost of goods sold) for each plan?
- (f) What plan should Bobby choose?
- (g) What plan should Bobby choose if the opportunity cost of investing in current assets is only 6%?

20•4.   Westmark Jewellers plans to liberalize its credit policy by extending its current 30 day credit period to 60 days. The company expects that this will increase its current sales (all credit) of $348,000 by 30%. Unfortunately, however, bad debts are also expected to rise to 5%, up from the current level of 2% of total sales. The company's operating cost of 35% of sales and its credit collection costs of $4,500 are expected to remain the same. The company is in the 30% tax bracket and it requires all investments to return 10%. Would you advise the company to go ahead by the liberalization plan? Why? Exactly how much richer or poorer will the company be if it relaxes its credit policy?

20•5.   Tom Buffington, the new inventory manager for NordicDesigns, a paint company, has decided that the *EOQ* for the company is 200 ten gallon cans per order. He arrived at this number taking into account the company's ordering cost of $200 per order and its annual holding cost of $4 per can. How many cans does NordicDesigns sell? How many orders will the company have to place to meet its requirements?

20•6.   Audio Mart, a discount electronics chain based in Tacoma, Washington, sells only one brand of stereo amplifier which it buys in large quantities from its manufacturer at a total (including transportation) cost of $125 each. Audio Mart sells around 4000 amplifiers annually. Warehousing, security and the cost of maintaining a warranty service department approximate 20% of the firm's average investment in inventories over the year. In addition, the company incurs a "handling fee" of $800 for every order placed with the manufacturer.

(a) How many amplifiers should Audio Mart buy with each order?
(b) How many such orders should it place during the year?
(c) What is Audio Mart's total "handling fee" expense for the year?
(d) What would Audio Mart's total expense be if it placed orders for 100 amplifiers each time?

APPENDIX 20•A *Monitoring of Accounts Receivable: Aging and Collection Schedules*

Two measures studied in Chapter 7 are widely used to monitor a firm's overall level of accounts receivable: the average collection period and the aging schedule of accounts receivable. A third and more refined method, referred to as a **collections schedule,** breaks down receivables in terms of the actual month in which the sale was made rather than aggregating them, as the first two measures do.

AVERAGE COLLECTION PERIOD

The average collection period (in days) is defined as

$$\text{Average collection period} = \frac{\text{accounts receivable}}{\text{annual credit sales}/365}$$

and indicates the average number of days required to collect a due account. This measure is useful in monitoring receivables by comparing it to the firm's credit terms or an industry average and by observing its behavior over time. As with any financial ratio, deviations from the norm require further investigation of the reason(s) for this behavior. For example, if credit terms are 1/10, *n*/30 but the average collection period is 46 days, an inquiry into why collections are being delayed is clearly warranted. Perhaps the credit or collection policy has become too lax and lower-quality credit customers are beginning to have a disproportionate effect on the payment experience.

A further refinement that increases the collection period's sensitivity to the recent payment experience is to calculate daily sales by using an averaging period over the last 30 to 90 days rather than annually. Increased sensitivity has a cost, though, because the collection period will be affected by seasonal and random fluctuations in the daily sales rate. This means that the collection period may appear to be lengthening even though the credit and collections policies or the payment experience have not changed. Allowances for seasonal behavior must be developed if this measure is to retain its usefulness.

AGING SCHEDULE

A more detailed picture of the accounts receivable status and composition can be derived by creating a distribution of the receivables by age (days outstanding) in dollar and percentage amounts. Table 20A•1 is an example of an **aging schedule.** One way to use this schedule is to compare it with the firm's

TABLE 20A·1   Aging Schedule of Accounts Receivable

Number of Days Outstanding	Dollar Amount of Accounts Receivable Outstanding	Percent of Total Accounts Receivable
0–30	$32,500	62.8
30–45	11,000	21.3
45–60	5,500	10.6
60–90	1,650	3.2
90 or more	1,100	2.1
	$51,750	100.0

current credit terms. If they call for net 30, this implies that 37.2% of its receivables are past due, an excessive amount. Not only does it cost the firm to carry them, but the probability of default increases the longer the account goes unpaid. In fact, the 2.1% in receivables falling in the "90 days or more" age category should be examined closely to determine whether they are collectible or are potential losses.

The aging schedule has the same drawback as the average collection period—it is influenced by the seasonality of sales. For example, when the sales rate increases, the "less than 30 days" accounts will inflate and will decrease when the sales rate falls. Therefore, the proportions in each age category will be different at different times of the year. Unfortunately, an aging schedule does not tell us what caused a change in the proportions. Is it because the sales rate has changed, is it because one customer's payment pattern has changed, or is it some combination of these two? Since the main objective of monitoring receivables is to identify the actual payment pattern and its effect on the level of receivables, a more refined technique is needed.

A COLLECTIONS SCHEDULE APPROACH[6]

A **collections schedule** eliminates seasonal sales effects by combining information on monthly credit sales and the actual payment pattern in order to identify what proportion of the receivables balance is due to each (earlier) month's sales. The first step is to establish the payment pattern by creating a time distribution of cash flows that result from each month's credit sales. As shown in Table 20A·2, this payment pattern describes the proportion of credit sales in a given month that becomes cash flows in that month and in subsequent months. For example, reading across the rows in part (a), January's credit sales of $1,200 were collected over three months as cash flows of $240 in the current month (cash sales) and $840 and $120 (in February and March), respectively.

[6] For further details on this method, see B. K. Stone, "The Payments-Pattern Approach to the Forecasting and Control of Accounts Receivable," *Financial Management*, Autumn 1976, 65–82.

TABLE 20A·2 Monthly Payment Pattern from Credit Sales by Dollar and Percentage Amounts

a. Monthly Payment Pattern by Dollar Amount

Month of Sale	Total Credit Sales	January	February	March	April
From prior months		$1,000	$ 200		
January	$1,200	240	840	$ 120	
February	3,000		660	2,040	$ 300
March	2,100			420	1,450
April	2,400				480
Monthly cash inflows		$1,240	$1,700	$2,580	$2,230

b. Monthly Payment Pattern by Percentage of Monthly Credit Sales

Month of Sale	Total Credit Sales	January	February	March	April
January[a]	$1,200	20	70	10	
February	3,000		22	68	10
March	2,100			20	69
April	2,400				20

[a] The percentage of January sales collected in January through March is given by $240/$1,200 = 20%, $840/$1,200 = 70%, and $120/$1,200 = 10%.

Moreover, note that $960 ($840 + $120) of total sales represents credit sales that become accounts receivable.

To establish the payment pattern more clearly, however, the individual cash flows need to be recast as a percentage of sales, as in Table 20A·2b. To interpret this information, we need to follow the diagonals as indicated by the arrows. The diagonals show that cash sales in January through April tended to be 20 to 22% of total sales, while 68 to 70% were collected one month later and the remaining 10% two months later. What this table suggests is that the payment pattern has been very stable over time even though monthly sales have fluctuated substantially.

To carry the analysis further and see the effect that the payment pattern has on the end-of-month receivables balance, we now refer to Table 20A·3. In part (a) and reading down the columns, February's receivables balance is $2,460, which is simply the sum of the uncollected sales (still outstanding) from January and February. (The proportion of receivables arising from January's sales, for example, is found by finding the difference between total sales and the sales already collected; that is, $1,200 − $240 − $840 = $120, from Table 20A·2.)

Once again, it is useful to convert the dollar figures to percentages, based on the sales in the month in which they originated. This reveals the underlying receivables collection patterns. For example, 78% and 10% of February's sales were in the form of receivables at the end of February and March, respectively.

TABLE 20A·3 Monthly Receivables Balances by Month of Origin in Dollar and Percentage Amounts

a. Receivables Balances in Dollar Amounts

Month of Sale	Total Sales	January	February	March	April
From prior months		$ 200			
January	$1,200	960	$ 120		
February	3,000		2,340	$ 300	
March	2,100			1,680	$ 230
April	2,400				$1,920
Monthly receivables balance		$1,160	$2,460	$1,980	$2,150

b. Receivables Balances as a Percentage of Monthly Credit Sales

Month of Sale	Total Sales	January	February	March	April
January	$1,200	80	10		
February	3,000		78	10	
March	2,100			80	11
April	2,400				80

To evaluate how well the firm's collection policy is performing, we again follow the diagonals illustrated by the arrows. As might be expected from the stable payment pattern found earlier, the receivables collection behavior is relatively stable despite the fact that the level of receivables has fluctuated from month to month. By contrast, if the percentages along the diagonals had been decreasing, this would have indicated an improving collections pattern (i.e., sales were being collected quicker), and an opposite conclusion would have resulted if the percentages had been increasing.

ADVANTAGES OF THE COLLECTIONS SCHEDULE

Perhaps the best way to appreciate the advantages of the collections schedule approach is to compare this method with what the two traditional methods tell us. In Table 20A·4, the average collection period and the aging schedule for February–April are presented, using the same information as in Table 20A·3. Note that both the collection period and the aging schedule give a distorted view of the collections pattern. For example, the February–March results appear to signal a worsening condition, but this is misleading because we saw that the underlying payment or collections pattern is relatively constant. The reason these measures are distorted is that they are affected by the seasonal or random fluctuation in sales. Only the collections schedule approach gives the true picture by separating the sales rate effect from the receivables collection experience.

TABLE 20A·4 Comparing the Collections Schedule to the Average Collection Period and Aging Schedule

a. Average Collection Period

	February	March	April
Level of receivables	$2,460	$1,980	$2,150
Credit sales/30 days[a]	$100	$70	$80
Average collection period	25 days	28 days	27 days

b. Aging Schedule[b]

Number of Days Outstanding	Percentage of Total Accounts Receivable		
	February	March	April
0–30	95	85	89
30–60	5	15	11
	100	100	100

[a] For example, from Table 20A·3, the monthly sales rate for February is $3,000/30 days = $100 per day.

[b] For example, from Table 20A·3, the percentage of receivables in the "0–30 days" age category for February is $2,340/$2,460 = 95%, and for the "30–60 days" age category $120/$2,460 = 5%.

Learning Check for Appendix 20·A

Review Questions

20A·1. Should the average collection period be computed on an annual basis? Why?

20A·2. Is the aging schedule a better method of analyzing a firm's accounts receivables than the average collection period? Why or why not?

20A·3. What are some of the drawbacks of the aging schedule?

20A·4. What are some of the advantages of the collections schedule approach over both the average collection period and the aging schedule?

New Terms

Aging schedule   Average collection period   Collections schedule

PROBLEMS

20A·1. Deborah Davies, financial manager of Peoplico, noticed last June that many customers were negligent in paying their bills and hired David

Sokolow as accounts receivable manager. Six months have passed, and Deborah is now evaluating David's performance. Accordingly, she has constructed the following table of payments made since David's arrival at the firm.

Month of Sale	Total Credit Sales	July	August	September	October	November	December
				Collections Made			
July	$2,000	$1,000	$667	$200	$ 133		
August	1,800		936	612	198	$ 54	
September	1,500			825	540	120	$ 15
October	1,800				1,008	666	108
November	2,100					1,218	840
December	2,200						1,320

(a) Find the monthly payment pattern as a percentage of monthly credit sales.
(b) Construct a table of receivables balances in dollar amounts.
(c) Construct a table of receivables balances as a percentage of monthly sales.
(d) How would you characterize David's performance as credit manager?

20A·2. A table of receivables balances in dollar amounts for the first four months of operation of the Gillum Rug Cleaning Corporation is presented.

Month of Sale	Total Credit Sales	March	April	May	June
March	$1,600	$1,400	$ 600	$ 200	
April	1,800		1,500	650	$ 250
May	2,400			1,800	700
June	3,200				2,000

(a) What was the total receivables balance at the end of March, April, May, and June?
(b) Construct a table of receivables balances as a percentage of monthly credit sales. Is Gillum collecting its accounts receivable more or less quickly than when they began in March?
(c) Construct a table of the monthly payment pattern in dollars.
(d) Construct a table of the monthly payment pattern as a percentage of monthly sales.

READINGS

BATLIN, C. A., AND SUSAN HINKO, "Lockbox Management and Value Maximization," *Financial Management*, Winter 1981, 39–44.

BAUMOL, W. J., "The Transactions Demand for Cash: An Inventory Theoretic Approach," *Quarterly Journal of Economics*, November 1952, 545–556.

HILL, NED C., AND KENNETH D. RIENER, "Determining the Cash Discount in the Firm's Credit Policy," *Financial Management*, Spring 1979, 68–73.

KALLBERG, J. G., AND K. PARKINSON, *Current Asset Management* (New York: Wiley-Interscience, 1984).

KIM, YONG H., AND JOSEPH C. ATKINS, "Evaluating Investments in Accounts Receivable: A Wealth Maximizing Framework," *Journal of Finance*, May 1978, 403–412.

MILLER, M. H., AND D. ORR, "A Model of the Demand for Money by Firms," *Quarterly Journal of Economics*, August 1966, 413–435.

MULLINS, DAVID WILEY, JR., AND RICHARD B. HOMONOFF, "Applications of Inventory Cash Management Models," in *Modern Developments in Financial Management* ed. S. C. Myers (New York: Praeger Publishers, 1976).

NAUSS, ROBERT M., AND ROBERT E. MARKLAND, "Solving Lockbox Location Problems," *Financial Management*, Spring 1979, 21–31.

POGUE, G. A., R. B. FAUCETT, AND R. N. BUSSARD, "Cash Management: A Systems Approach," *Industrial Management Review*, Winter 1970, 55–76.

SACHDEVA, KANWAL S., AND LAWRENCE J. GITMAN, "Accounts Receivable Decisions in a Capital Budgeting Framework," *Financial Management*, Winter 1981, 45–49.

STONE, BERNELL K., "The Use of Forecasts for Smoothing in Control-Limit Models for Cash Management," *Financial Management*, Spring 1972, 72–84.

STONE, BERNELL K., AND NED C. HILL, "The Design of a Cash Concentration System," *Journal of Financial and Quantitative Analysis*, September 1981, 301–322.

VANDER WEIDE, J., AND S. F. MAIER, *Managing Corporate Liquidity* (New York: John Wiley & Sons, Inc., 1985).

21

Current-Liabilities Management

In Chapter 18 it was shown that working capital management involves decisions relating to the amount and composition of current assets (investment decision) and how these assets are to be funded (financing decision). In Chapters 19 and 20 we examined those factors that enable the financial manager to decide on the amount and composition of the current-asset investments. In this chapter we address the second aspect of working capital management, the financing decision.

Because current assets can be financed by any number of sources, the financial manager has to make two financing decisions regarding:

1. The desired proportion of short- and long-term financing sources.

2. The composition of short-term sources.

We address the "desired proportion" decision first. Once this decision is made, two other issues relating to the composition of short-term sources of credit can be examined:

1. What types of short-term credit to employ.

2. What mix of these alternative financing sources is appropriate.

The chapter consists of two sections:

Section 21•1: *General Considerations in Current-Liability Management.* There are both advantages and disadvantages to using short-term versus long-term financing. In this section, we discuss these advantages and disadvantages, and examine the costs and risks of using short-term credit. We then consider the various sources of short-term credit and the characteristics that distinguish them from each other.

Section 21•2: *Sources of Short-Term Credit.* In this section, we examine the different sources of short-term credit, with an emphasis on their availability and cost. We close with a discussion of the factors involved in deciding on the appropriate mix of short-term credit instruments.

SECTION 21•1 *General Considerations in Current-Liability Management*

FACTORS CONSIDERED IN DETERMINING THE PROPORTIONS OF SHORT- AND LONG-TERM DEBT

The first financing decision in working capital management involves the determination of the desired proportions of short- and long-term debt to fund current assets. Associated with this decision is the evaluation of the relative flexibility, costs, and risks of these two sources. In this section, some qualitative considerations involved in arriving at this decision are presented. Since several subjective considerations are involved, it is not easy to arrive at a simple formula that will enable the manager to make this decision.

Flexibility

Short-term credit is usually more flexible than long-term credit. For example, a short-term bank loan can be arranged much more quickly than a long-term loan such as a bond issue. More time is needed by lenders to make a thorough examination of the firm's financial position before granting any long-term credit. Lawyers need to write out, carefully and in detail, the loan agreement and any restrictions that may apply. This is because long-term lenders are making a commitment of funds for, say, 10 to 20 years, and funds raised through long-term financing are usually much larger than short-term borrowings. This process is very time-consuming. Therefore, if funds are needed quickly, the financial manager should consider short-term sources of funds.

Another consideration is the purpose of the funding. Long-term funds are usually not appropriate if the manager only needs to satisfy seasonal or cyclical requirements. Otherwise, idle (costly) cash will build up when the need for the funds diminishes. The firm could, of course, pay off the long-term liability early but, as Section 21•2 will indicate, this can be costly. Finally, long-term financing arrangements always contain provisions that may reduce management's future flexibility. Short-term credit, in contrast, rarely constrains management to the same degree.

Cost

Appendix 5•B discusses the term structure of interest rates: the relationship between short-term and long-term rates. As this appendix shows, short-term rates have historically been less than long-term rates. This relationship means that short-term debt usually costs less than long-term debt. Firms often choose short-term financing because they pay less interest for it than for similar long-term debt.

Second, long-term debt involves flotation or placement costs not normally associated with short-term debt. Third, if the firm finds itself in a position where long-term funds are no longer needed, the firm still incurs the interest expense. If it decides to repay the debt early (if possible), it may incur additional costs in the form of expensive prepayment penalties. With short-term credit, needless interest costs on idle funds can be avoided by paying off the debt immediately and without penalty.

Risk

Even though short-term credit is more flexible and often less expensive, firms typically view short-term debt as riskier. This perception stems from two sources.

Fluctuating Interest Rates While the level of short-term interest rates is typically lower than the level of long-term interest rates, short-term rates tend to fluctuate more over time. This causes the firm's interest expenses, and hence earnings, to be subject to more variation (risk) over time with short-term debt. When a firm borrows long term, its interest costs will be relatively stable because it "locks in" a certain interest rate.[1] This also avoids the chances of higher borrowing costs in the future.

Refunding the Debt Short-term debt exposes the firm to the risk of not being able to refund (refinance) it. When debt matures, the firm has the option of either paying it off, rolling it over, or arranging new financing. Heavy use of short-term debt can lead to a number of problems. More frequent debt servicing is required. Repaying maturing debt places greater demands on the firm's cash

---

[1]Of course, it may be a high rate that is locked in.

flows. If a firm finds itself facing a labor strike, a recession, or another financial problem, sales, and hence cash inflows, may be insufficient to fulfill its debt obligations. On the other hand, tight credit conditions in the banking system can restrict the supply of loanable funds. This means that it may be very difficult or impossible to refinance the debt with either the same or a different source. The result: operating and financial difficulties that may lead to insolvency or even bankruptcy. The more frequently debt must be refinanced, therefore, the greater the risk that the necessary funding will be unavailable.

SHORT-TERM CREDIT: TYPES, SOURCES, AND GENERAL CHARACTERISTICS

The importance of short-term financing was indicated in Chapter 18 when it was seen (refer to Table 18•2) that the typical firm (especially smaller firms and those in the wholesale-retail business) relies extensively on this form of financing to fund its operations. Short-term credit consists of obligations expected to be paid off within one year. These obligations appear as current liabilities on a firm's balance sheet, usually as accounts payable, accruals, and notes payable.

As shown in Table 21•1, there are several types and sources of short-term funds. A useful way to distinguish among them is to think in terms of (1) their availability, (2) their cost, (3) the degree of management discretion in utilizing

TABLE 21•1 Types and Sources of Short-term Credit

Type of Credit	Source of Credit (Creditor)	Cost	Degree of Management Discretion	Security Required
1. Accounts payable	Suppliers	Implicit	Spontaneous	Unsecured[a]
2. Accrued wages	Employees	Zero	Spontaneous	Unsecured
3. Accrued taxes	Governments: federal, state, local	Zero	Spontaneous	Unsecured
4. Deferred income	Customers	Zero	Negotiated	Unsecured

5. Notes payable:
  a. Bank loans
  b. Accounts receivable loans
  c. Inventory loans
	Commercial banks and other financial institutions	Explicit	Negotiated	Unsecured or secured

6. Commercial paper	Investors	Explicit	Negotiated	Unsecured

[a]Suppliers normally provide unsecured trade credit without a formal arrangement to indicate this indebtedness. Occasionally, they will require a promissory note to be signed to acknowledge the liability. In this case, this obligation will appear as "Notes payable—trade" on the balance sheet.

them, and (4) whether or not some form of security is required by the creditor, i.e., (**secured** or **unsecured** credit). These are the four aspects that the financial manager needs to evaluate in determining which sources to use.

Availability

Certain sources, such as accounts payable, are more readily accessible to firms with good credit records than other sources and hence are more likely to be available when needed. One source, accruals, is automatically available to all firms, whereas another, deferred income, is available only to firms whose normal industry practices require customers to make advances or deposits against the future delivery of goods or services. Some sources, such as bank loans, are guaranteed to be available once an agreement has been signed, and the dollar amount can usually be increased or decreased easily, as needed. Receivable and inventory loans normally are viewed as a "source of last resort" because they tend to be used by firms with poor credit ratings. Finally, one source, commercial paper, is available only to the largest firms with excellent credit ratings.

Cost

Financial managers attempt to minimize the cost of financing, which is usually expressed as an annual interest rate. It is rare for the cost of short-term credit to be zero; usually, such credit involves costs, either implicit or explicit. This means that the financing source with the lowest interest rate should be chosen. Accruals have no cost associated with them as long as timely payments are made. Accounts payable (trade credit) have an implicit cost if a cash discount is offered but not taken. Even a financing source such as a bank loan, which has an explicit cost in the form of an interest rate, may have additional terms such as discount interest or compensating balances, which cause the effective interest rate to be greater than the stated interest rate.

This means that the application of decision criteria to minimize the financing cost or annual interest rate is a bit more complex than it appears. Because different methods of stating interest charges and fees are used with short-term financing, it becomes difficult to compare the cost of alternative sources of credit. This raises two important questions:

1. What is meant by the **cost of financing?**

2. How is the **annual interest rate** determined?

Drawing on the concepts developed in Chapter 2 regarding the determination of interest rates, especially the simple (rather than compound) interest rate, a general procedure will now be outlined that can be used to convert the different terms on various types of short-term credit to comparable annual effective interest rates.

The annual interest (effective) rate (AIR) can be calculated as follows:

$$AIR = \left(1 + \frac{i}{m}\right)^m - 1 \qquad (21\text{-}1)$$

where AIR = annual compounded (effective) rate of interest

i = stated annual simple rate of interest

m = number of compounding periods in one year

i/m = simple interest rate per compounding period

Because most short-term credit is outstanding for only a short period of time (usually less than two to three months), the simple interest rate, i/m, can be used as an approximation of the effective (compound) interest rate given in equation (21-1). This means that approximating the AIR on any short-term source of credit implies computing

$$AIR = i\left(\frac{1}{m}\right) \qquad (21\text{-}2)$$

$$AIR = \frac{\text{interest costs per period (\$)}}{\text{usable loan amount}} \times \frac{360 \text{ days}}{\text{number of days funds borrowed}}$$

$$\left(\begin{array}{c}\text{effective interest rate}\\\text{per period}\end{array}\right) \times (\text{number of periods per year})$$

Although this formula appears to be straightforward, the key to its application is in the careful definition of the interest costs per period and the usable loan amount. For instance, the interest costs on a bank loan may include costs other than explicit interest expenses such as processing fees or other prepaid costs. Moreover, if this loan was for \$1 million, for example, and the bank required a \$200,000 compensating balance, the usable loan amount is only \$1,000,000 − \$200,000 = \$800,000. Therefore, this "adapted" way of calculating simple interest will be used in the remaining sections of this chapter.

Degree of Management Discretion

The third factor distinguishing the sources of short-term credit is the degree of management discretion than can be exercised in utilizing them. Short-term credit sources available to the firm can be described as either spontaneous or negotiated. **Spontaneous sources,** such as trade credit or accruals, arise in the normal course of business, without any action by management being required. These funds become available automatically simply by conducting business operations. For example, as a firm expands its sales, it normally obtains more materials from its suppliers. These increased inventory purchases will increase accounts payable. The firm's managers do not make a specific decision to borrow short-term funds; rather, they do so informally, as a natural effect of their decision to increase sales. Therefore, the amount of these funds tends to increase as the volume of business increases and to decline when the volume of business falls off. By contrast, obtaining **negotiated sources**—for example, bank credit, commercial paper, and receivables or inventory loans—requires management effort.

SECURITY REQUIRED

Unsecured Credit

Short-term credit may be either unsecured or secured. Unsecured credit includes all debt that has as security only the cash-generating ability of the firm: for example, trade credit, accruals, unsecured bank loans, and commercial paper. The lender simply places faith in the ability of the firm to repay the funds in a timely fashion. If the firm becomes insolvent and is forced to declare bankruptcy, the unsecured lender usually has only a small chance of recovering the amount owed.[2]

Secured Credit

Secured credit involves the pledging of specific assets, such as accounts receivable, inventory, or fixed assets, as collateral. If the borrower defaults on the obligation, the secured lender can seize and sell the collateral to fulfill the borrower's obligation. In a sense, then, lenders in a secured debt arrangement have two layers of security: the firm's cash-generating ability and the pledged assets' collateral value.

The following discussion of the sources of short-term credit is organized and presented in terms of the degree of management discretion that can be exercised in using them and in terms of the security that each requires. This allows us to focus on the remaining distinguishing elements of short-term credit: their availability and cost.

Learning Check for Section 21•1

Review Questions

21•1. What are some of the factors that complicate a manager's decision regarding the desired mix of short- and long-term debt?

---

[2]Exceptions include certain accruals, such as accrued wages and taxes. In these cases, if any debts of a bankrupt firm are repaid, employees and the government must be paid what is owed them before any other creditor's claim can be satisfied.

21•2. What are some of the factors that make short-term debt riskier than long-term debt?

21•3. List the various types of credit. For each type of credit, identify (a) the source, (b) the cost, (c) the security required, and (d) the degree to which each is spontaneous.

21•4. Would you expect to observe a relationship between the returns on secured and unsecured credit? Explain your reasoning.

New Terms

Annual interest rate	Refunding	Spontaneous
Cost of financing	Secured	sources of credit
Negotiated sources	credit	Unsecured trade
of credit		credit

SECTION 21•2 *Sources of Short-Term Credit*

SPONTANEOUS SOURCES OF SHORT-TERM CREDIT

Accounts Payable (Trade Credit)

Availability Trade credit occurs when a firm purchases goods or services on credit from another firm (supplier).[3] It is analogous to a charge account for a consumer. By accepting cash payment at some future date (i.e., with a time lag) rather than immediately, the supplier assumes the role of a lender. This indebtedness appears as an account payable on the balance sheet of the purchaser and as an account receivable on the balance sheet of the supplier.

Almost all firms use trade credit as a method of financing. Although the extent of its use varies by industry, trade credit accounts for approximately 40% of the total current liabilities of business corporations. It is used extensively for

---

[3]Trade credit is extended in connection with goods purchased for resale. This distinguishes it from related forms of credit. For example, a firm may purchase on credit equipment to be used in its production process rather than to be resold to others. This type of credit normally involves an installment loan contract with periodic payments of interest and principal. This is not trade credit. Similarly, consumer credit is excluded from the definition of trade credit.

several reasons. First, it is a continuous source of financing. That is, although the amount varies with fluctuations in purchases, the firm always has some accounts payable; as some accounts are paid, new purchases create new payables. On the other hand, bank credit used to meet peak seasonal needs is paid off once these needs have diminished.

Another reason is that trade credit is more available than negotiated sources of short-term credit. As purchases of goods and services increase in anticipation of increased production and sales, accounts payable will increase automatically.

Example 21•1   Calculating the Financing Provided by Trade Credit

Suppose that a firm purchases an average of $3,000 a day on terms of "net 30"; that is the items must be paid for in 30 days after the invoice date. This means that its suppliers provide $3,000 × 30 days = $90,000 in short-term financing. Now assume that the firm's sales, and hence purchases, double. In this case, its accounts payable or trade credit will also double to $180,000, providing additional financing of $90,000.[4]

Cost   Most trade credit occurs as an open account whereby goods are shipped to the purchaser with only an invoice indicating the amount of indebtedness (i.e., the obligation is not acknowledged in writing).[5] Even though it bears no interest, trade credit on an open account is not formally costless; rather, it is implicit in the terms of credit agreed to by the borrower and suppliers. Let us now consider the effect of two credit terms—the discount policy and the credit period—on the implicit cost of trade credit.

1. *No trade discount offered.* If the credit terms are "net 30," for example, the cost is implicit in the price paid for the goods or services. That is, as shown in Chapter 20, a firm that extends credit to its customers incurs the expense of operating a credit department and financing its accounts receivable. Just as with any other cost of doing business, the buyers of the supplier's products ultimately bear this cost in the form of higher prices. Nothing is free. However, if the firm has the alternative of buying the same goods at a lower price for cash, it can calculate the implicit credit cost and then decide to buy the goods on either

---

[4]Another way this source of financing can increase is if the credit period is extended from 30 to 45 days. Note that by lengthening the credit period, additional financing of $3,000 × (45 − 30) days = $45,000 is generated.

[5]Another form of trade credit is the promissory note, wherein the purchaser formally signs a note indicating the amount due. These notes usually involve an explicit interest cost and a specific maturity date. This type of credit is not used very frequently because of the added cost it entails. Usually only firms with a poor credit rating are forced to use this form of trade credit. It appears on the balance sheet as "Notes payable—trade."

cash or credit terms, depending on which alternative is more reasonable. More-over, it should be noted that if there is no difference between the cash and credit prices, the purchaser bears the credit cost whether or not credit is extended by the supplier.

2. *Trade discount offered.* More commonly, the credit terms provide for a net period with a trade discount. If the supplier allows a discount for prompt payment, an implicit cost is incurred if the discount is not taken.

Example 21•2 Calculating the Cost of Trade Credit

Consider a firm that buys its supplies on credit terms of "2/10, *n*30." For every $100 owed, the firm can "save" $2 if it pays off its account within 10 days. On the other hand, if the discount is not taken, the firm has another 30 − 10 = 20 days to pay off the account in full. This means that the firm receives 20 days in financing, but the cost of this financing is the discount lost. This forgone discount is, in effect, a penalty or interest cost.

To illustrate what this implies in terms of an annual interest rate, equation (21-2) can easily be modified in terms of percentages.

$$AIR = \frac{\text{interest costs per period}}{\text{usable loan amount}} \times \frac{360 \text{ days}}{\text{number of days funds borrowed}} \quad (21\text{-}3)$$

$$= \frac{\text{discount } (\%)}{100\% - \text{discount } (\%)} \times \frac{360 \text{ days}}{\text{net period} - \text{discount period}}$$

$$= \frac{2}{100 - 2} \times \frac{360 \text{ days}}{30 - 10} = 36.73\% \text{ per year}$$

Thus the interest rate being charged on the 20 days' worth of credit is 37.2 on an annualized basis. What if the trade discount were 3% instead of 2%? Using equation (21-3), we find that

$$AIR = \frac{3}{100 - 3} \times \frac{360 \text{ days}}{30 - 10} = 55.67\%$$

Clearly, both trade discount policies involve an expensive source of financing. Whenever sufficient cash flow is available or a bank loan can be arranged at a lower interest rate, there is a strong incentive to take advantage of a trade discount.

---

3. *Changing the credit period.* It is instructive to stay with the last example and examine what will happen if the credit terms are changed by making the credit period "net 60" (i.e., 3/10, *n*60).

From equation (21-3),

$$AIR = \frac{3}{100 - 3} \times \frac{360 \text{ days}}{60 - 10} = 22.27\%$$

Notice that by doubling the net credit period from 30 to 60 days, the annual interest rate is cut by more than half. The reason is that the same interest cost is incurred, but now the firm has 50 days rather than 20 days over which to spread the cost.

To summarize the ideas presented so far:

KEY CONCEPT: The cost of trade credit varies (1) directly with the size of the discount and (2) inversely with the length of time between the net credit period and the discount period.

ACCRUALS AND DEFERRED INCOME

Accruals

Availability A second source of spontaneous financing is accruals (accrued expenses), which represent liabilities for services that have been provided to the firm but have not yet been paid for by the firm. The most common expenses accrued are wages and taxes.[6]

Accrued wages represent money a firm owes its employees. In effect, employees provide part of a firm's short-term financing by waiting two weeks or a month to be paid rather than being paid every day. Although the amount of financing available from this source can be increased by lengthening the pay period, legal and practical considerations limit the extent to which this can be done.

Similarly, the level of financing available from accrued taxes is determined by the amount of the firm's tax liability and the frequency with which these expenses are paid. For example, federal income taxes must be paid quarterly (on January 15, April 15, etc.), but the firm can use accrued taxes as a source of funds between these payment dates. Payment of property and sales taxes varies from state to state. For example, corporations operating in Texas pay property taxes annually and sales taxes monthly.

Cost Accruals have no associated explicit or implicit cost. In effect, they are valuable to the firm because they are costless substitutes for otherwise costly short-term credit. This is especially true during periods of tight credit or high interest rates. For example, if bank credit costs 14%, $5 million in accruals would save the firm $5,000,000 \times 0.14 = $700,000 per year in interest expenses. Therefore, there is an incentive to accrue as many expenses as possible.

---

[6]Other expenses also accrue during the normal course of business, such as periodic interest payments on long-term debt, utility bills, and rental or lease payments paid at the end of the period rather than on a prepaid basis. For the average firm, these accrued expenses are relatively small compared with accrued wages and taxes.

Deferred Income

Availability In some industries, it is accepted practice to require customers to make advance payments or deposits for goods and services that a firm will deliver at a future date. Such payments are common with big-ticket items, such as jet aircraft, or with services. Because these funds increase the firm's liquidity (i.e., cash), they are a source of short-term financing. Such liabilities appear on the balance sheet as "Deferred income" (i.e., income to be earned when delivery to the customer is made) or "Customers' advances (or deposits)."

Cost Like accruals, deferred income usually has no explicit or implicit cost. Occasionally, interest may be paid at an agreed-upon rate. In this case, the liability is considered a negotiated source of financing.

NEGOTIATED SOURCES OF UNSECURED SHORT-TERM CREDIT

Unsecured Bank Credit

Availability After trade credit, the next largest source of short-term financing for corporations is commercial bank loans. Yet, whereas nearly all firms use trade credit, not all firms necessarily use bank credit. Short-term unsecured bank loans are typically used to fund seasonal buildups in the firm's investments in accounts receivable and inventories. Once these assets generate sufficient cash flow, the bank loans are paid off.

Commercial banks provide short-term business credit in essentially two forms: lines of credit and transaction (single-payment) loans. Both forms require a borrower to sign a promissory note that formally acknowledges the debt's amount and maturity, as well as the interest to be paid.

1. **Line of credit.** A line of credit is usually an informal agreement to lend up to a maximum amount of credit to a firm and is usually established for a one-year period. Although not legally binding on the bank, a line of credit is almost always honored. For example, on January 2, a financial manager may negotiate with the bank to provide up to $5 million in the coming year. On February 1, the manager signs a promissory note for $500,000 for 120 days. This amount is then deposited in the firm's checking account and is referred to as a **takedown** against the total credit line. Before the $500,000 is repaid, the firm may borrow additional amounts at any time as long as the total borrowed does not exceed the $5 million limit.

A special type of line of credit is a **revolving-credit agreement.** Its main distinction is that the bank makes a formal, contractual commitment to provide a maximum amount of funds to the firm. To secure this type of financing, the firm usually pays a commitment fee of 1/4 to 1/2% per year on the average unused portion of the commitment. The size of the fee is dictated by credit conditions (availability of funds) and the relative bargaining power of the two parties.

The line of credit and the revolving-credit agreement usually require a firm to "clean up" or pay off any loan amount at least once a year, usually for 30 to 45 days. This is done to assure the bank that the loan is only for seasonal needs. These forms of bank credit are renegotiated annually. At that time, the bank reviews the firm's future financing needs, usually by analyzing its cash budget projections, before granting a new credit line.

2. **Transaction (single-payment) loan.** The line of credit and the revolving-credit agreement are best suited for firms that have multiple financing requirements that need frequent funding in varying amounts. When a firm needs short-term funds for a specific purpose (e.g., interim financing to develop raw land), a transaction loan is usually more appropriate. Unsecured transaction loans are very similar to the other two forms of bank credit in terms of cost and maturity.

Cost Most bank loans carry an explicit interest rate, which historically has been based on a benchmark rate called the *prime rate*. The prime rate fluctuates over the life of the loan as interest rates change.[7] Bank loans may also include implicit interest charges such as discount interest, compensating balances, and commitment fees. The effective cost of interest will be higher in these cases than the stated interest rate.[8]

1. **Discount interest.** Banks sometimes charge interest on the basis of discount interest. In this case, the amount of interest charged is determined in the same way as simple interest, but interest is deducted from the initial loan amount rather than being paid at the end of the loan. This method increases the effective rate of interest.

Example 21•3 Discount Interest

Assume that a bank has lent a firm $100,000 for 90 days at an annual interest rate of 12%. The interest cost per period is $100,000 \times 0.12 \times 90/360 =$ $3,000, or 3% per 90 days.[9] If the loan were discounted, the annual interest rate would be determined from equation (21-2) as follows:

---

[7]Today this definition may not be entirely accurate, as several large firms (e.g., General Motors) have been able to borrow at rates below the prime rate.

[8]The cost of bank credit tends to vary by the size of the firm, the industry, and the geographical location. For example, the cost to a small firm is typically higher than the cost to a large firm, the reason being that the costs of loaning to a small firm are larger because of the fixed costs of processing a loan. That is, the fixed cost per loan dollar is higher for smaller dollar amounts. The other reason is that the business risk of smaller firms is greater than that of larger firms.

[9]It is common practice in the banking industry to charge interest on the basis of a 360-day calendar year.

$$AIR = \frac{\text{interest costs per period}}{\text{usable loan amount}} \times \frac{360 \text{ days}}{\text{number of days funds borrowed}}$$

$$= \frac{\text{discount interest paid}}{\text{initial loan amount} - \text{discount interest paid}} \times \frac{360 \text{ days}}{\text{number of days funds borrowed}}$$

$$= \frac{\$3,000}{\$100,000 - \$3,000} \times \frac{360}{90} = 12.37\%$$

Notice that the borrower receives $97,000 at the time of the loan but is expected to repay the full $100,000. The borrowing firm is thus charged a rate of interest based on the full-face amount of the loan but receives only a portion of that amount for actual use. As shown, this means that the effective interest will be higher—12.37% versus the stated 12% rate.

2. **Compensating balances.** In providing loans (as well as other services), banks often require firms to maintain a minimum average account balance called a **compensating balance** (refer to Chapter 19 for further discussion). The required amount is usually computed as a percentage of the customer's loan outstanding or as a percentage of the bank's commitment to future loans, as in a line-of-credit arrangement. A common rate is 20% against outstanding loans or 10% against a future commitment.

Example 21·4 Compensating Balances

Return to Example 21·3 to see what effect a 20% compensating balance requirement will have on the annual interest rate. Because a compensating balance reduces the loanable amount, just as the discount interest method does, the usable loan amount is

Usable loan amount = loan amount − discount interest − compensating balance
$$= \$100,000 - \$3,000 - 0.20(\$100,000)$$
$$= \$77,000$$

The *AIR* then becomes

$$AIR = \frac{\text{interest costs per period (\$)}}{\text{usable loan amount}} \times \frac{360 \text{ days}}{\text{number of days funds borrowed}}$$

$$= \frac{\$3,000}{\$77,000} \times \frac{360}{90} = 15.58\%$$

This clearly demonstrates that the stated interest rate 12% can be misleading if the financial manager is not careful in assessing all of a loan's interest charges.

▬▬ *HIGHLIGHT*

IMPLICIT PREPAYMENT PENALTIES:
THE "RULE OF 78"

Loan agreements very often contain an explicit prepayment penalty cost. Many financial institutions (savings and loan associations, credit unions, banks, etc.) that extend consumer loans, however, often claim that their loans do not have prepayment penalties. When the loan is paid off early, they often use the so-called rule of 78 to calculate the payoff amount. What most borrowers do not realize is that the rule of 78 implicitly carries a prepayment penalty.

The rule of 78 is a procedure that makes the required payoff on a loan higher than the actual balance. In Figure 1, curve A shows the unpaid balance at any time over the life of the loan. Curve B shows the payoff amount calculated using the rule of 78. The implicit penalty for paying off a loan at t is therefore the segment CD. Notice that this prepayment penalty is at a maximum somewhere in the middle of the loan's life. It is ironic that the rule of 78 was approved for use as a result of the Truth-in-Lending Act.

How can the prepayment penalty be calculated? The steps are as follows:

Step 1.

Calculate the total interest on the loan (I) as follows: $I = AL - P$, where A is the monthly payment, L is the life of the loan (months), and P is the amount borrowed.

Step 2.

Depreciate the interest using the sum-of-the-years'-digits method to calculate the interest remaining (I_R). I_R can be calculated using the formula

$$I_R = I\left[1 - \frac{t(2L + 1 - t)}{L^2 + L}\right]$$

where t is the time the loan has been outstanding.

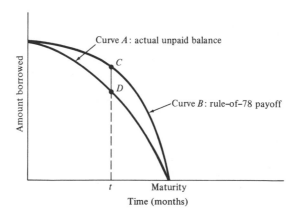

FIGURE 1

Step 3.

Calculate the payoff balance (B) as $B = (L - t)A - I_R$.

Step 4.

Calculate the prepayment penalty as penalty $= B - P_t$ where P_t is the unpaid (correct) balance at t.

Commercial Paper

Availability Commercial paper consists of short-term, unsecured promissory notes (IOUs) issued by firms that have a high credit rating. Generally, only the largest firms with greater financial strength qualify to issue commercial paper. Maturities can range from a few days up to nine months. Although commercial paper has no set denomination, it is usually issued in minimum amounts of $100,000.

In recent years, commercial paper has become an increasingly important source of short-term credit for many types of firms, such as finance, utility, and bank holding companies. By the end of 1984, nearly $250 billion in commercial paper was outstanding. Most commercial paper (over 75%) is issued by financial institutions and in bearer form; that is, the holder is the owner, and the issuer keeps no record of ownership. It can be issued so that it is payable to a specific investor. Commercial paper can be issued to lenders either directly by the borrower (direct placement) or indirectly through commercial paper dealers (dealer market).

The chief attraction of commercial paper to borrowers is its lower cost relative to bank financing. The interest rate on commercial paper is normally less than the prime rate. Its primary disadvantage is limited access to this source of credit. Even under ideal money market conditions, only the largest firms can sell commercial paper. This is because of its unsecured nature.

Cost Commercial paper is occasionally issued as a discount note, but typically it is issued as an interest-bearing security that has a stated coupon rate. At maturity, the amount owed by the borrower is the principal amount of the note plus accrued interest. The stated interest rate is closely tied to that of other money market instruments, such as T bills and negotiable CDs. A rule of thumb is that commercial paper is usually 1 to 3% below the prime rate. Moreover, it is even less expensive than a bank loan because the costs of preparing financial statements and negotiating with a bank are avoided. On the other hand, the issuer of commercial paper must prepay certain placement fees and flotation costs. These additional expenses serve to increase the implicit cost of commercial paper.

Example 21•5   Cost of Commercial Paper

Assume that the Espey Corporation plans to issue $100 million in commercial paper for 182 days at a stated (discounted) interest rate of 14%. If dealers will charge $100,000 in placement fees and flotation costs, the annual interest rate is calculated as follows:

STEP 1

$$\text{Interest cost per period} = \frac{\$100 \text{ million} \times 0.14 \times 182}{360}$$

$$= \$7,077,777$$

STEP 2

$$\text{Usable loan amount} = \text{loan amount} - \text{discount interest} - \text{prepaid expenses}$$
$$= \$100 \text{ million} - \$7,077,777 - \$100,000$$
$$= \$92,822,223$$

STEP 3

$$AIR = \frac{\text{interest costs per period (\$)}}{\text{usable loan amount}} \times \frac{360 \text{ days}}{\text{number of days funds borrowed}}$$

$$= \frac{\$7,077,777}{\$92,919,000} \times \frac{360}{182} = 15.1\%$$

Thus the effective cost of this credit source to Espey is 15.1%.

NEGOTIATED SOURCES OF SECURED SHORT-TERM CREDIT

Ideally, both the lender and the borrower prefer that a short-term loan remain unsecured if the creditworthiness of the borrower justifies it. For the lender, things are kept simple. For the borrower, an unsecured loan does not encumber its assets or restrict its future borrowing flexibility. Nevertheless, cases arise that require specific assets to be pledged as collateral before a short-term loan will be extended. For example, a firm may have reached the limit of its unsecured borrowing capacity. If additional unsecured credit cannot be justified, a bank may seek the pledge of specific assets before a larger loan is granted. The two most common assets pledged as collateral are accounts receivable and inventory.

Accounts Receivable Loans

Availability A firm's receivables are among its most liquid assets because they can be converted easily to cash. For this reason, lenders consider receivables as prime collateral for a secured loan. Two procedures are used in arranging for short-term financing that is backed by accounts receivable: pledging and factoring.

1. **Pledging receivables.** This is the simplest and least costly procedure to administer. The borrower merely provides a given dollar amount of receivables as collateral. If the lender provides a general line on a firm's receivables, all accounts are pledged as security for the loan. Because the lender has no control over the quality of the pledged receivables, the loan amount is a relatively small percentage of the receivables' face value (e.g., less than 50%).

A general line is the least complicated method of pledging receivables. A more complicated method is to require the borrower to submit invoices for lender approval prior to granting a loan. Only those invoices receiving lender approval can be pledged as collateral. Because the lender has some control over the collateral's quality, the loan amount will be a high proportion of the receivables' value (e.g., 80 to 90%).

2. **Factoring receivables.** Factoring accounts receivable involves selling them to a financial institution called a **factor.** Commercial finance companies and sometimes subsidiaries of commercial banks are the primary sources of this type of short-term credit. Although not strictly a secured loan because the receivables are sold rather than pledged as collateral, factoring has a comparable effect on the selling firm's cash flows. Consequently, firms tend to view factoring as an alternative to pledging accounts receivable.

Example 21•5 Cost of an Accounts Receivable Loan

The general manager of Harris Graphics (HG) needs to raise $60,000 in short-term borrowing from his accounts receivable. He currently has $120,000 in accounts receivable due in 90 days, and expects 2% of these accounts receivable to be uncollectable. If he factors $60,000 of these receivables, he will receive $54,000. What interest rate is he paying for this arrangement?

STEP 1

The net amount of the accounts receivable factored is:

$$(1 - \text{percentage amount uncollectable})(\text{amount of desired loan})$$
$$= (1 - 0.02)(\$60,000)$$
$$= \$58,800$$

STEP 2

The dollar amount of interest that HG pays to the factor is:

$$\$58,\!800 - \$54,\!000 = \$4,\!800$$

STEP 3

The *AIR* is:

$$AIR = \frac{\text{interest costs per period (\$)}}{\text{usable loan amount}} \times \frac{360 \text{ days}}{\text{number of days funds borrowed}}$$

$$= \frac{\$4,\!800}{\$54,\!000} \times \frac{360}{90} = 35.56\%$$

The *AIR* for factoring the accounts receivable is 35.56%.

Cost Accounts receivable loans generally carry an explicit interest rate 2 to 5% higher than the bank prime rate. Commercial finance companies may charge an even higher rate. Furthermore, the lender will usually charge a handling fee, stated as a percentage of the face value of the receivables processed. This fee is typically about 1 to 2% of the face value.

Because factoring involves the outright sale of a firm's receivables to a factor, the factor bears the risk of collection and, for a fee, services the accounts. This fee is stated as a percentage of the receivables' face value and is usually 1 to 3%. Offsetting this cost, though, is the fact that the lender provides credit services that eliminate or at least reduce the need for similar services by the borrower.

Inventory Loans

Availability Inventory loans are another source of short-term secured credit from financial institutions. In this case, a firm pledges part or all of its inventories as collateral. The extent to which this loan source is available depends on two factors. In accepting inventory as collateral, a lender is concerned with its resale value and the ability to control its use by the borrower, because these two factors determine the risk of loss to the lender if the borrower defaults on the loan.

The greater the resale value and the greater the lender's control, the larger the percentage of the cost of the inventory that the loan can safely represent. Resale value is affected by the inventory's perishability, risk of obsolescence, and marketability. For example, the absence of a ready resale market for a certain type of inventory subjects the lender to a high risk of loss from a forced sale. Therefore, such inventory will not have much (if any) loan value.

Control is affected by the type of financing arrangement. The three methods of achieving lender control are **floating liens, trust receipts,** and **warehouse receipts.** Table 21•2 provides a short description of these methods. They tend to differ primarily in the way the lien or title to the inventory is established.

TABLE 21•2 Characteristics of Different Types of Inventory Loans

1. *Floating lien.* The lender has a general claim on all the borrower's inventory. No administrative expense is involved because the lender need not monitor specific units of inventory. It offers little security because the lender does not hold title to the inventory and cannot control its size or disposition by the borrower.
2. *Trust receipt.* Lender control is increased because (1) the lender retains legal title to the pledged inventory, and (2) specific units of inventory are identified in writing on documents called trust receipts.
3. *Warehouse receipt.* Even stronger lender control exists because inventory is placed under the lender's physical as well as legal possession. The inventory being financed is shipped to a terminal or public warehouse that is controlled by the employees of the warehousing company. Inventory is released to the borrower only with the lender's authorization.

Cost The cost of securing borrowing by pledging inventories is quite high and varies greatly, depending on the legal and physical means by which the lien is placed, as well as the nature or quality of the inventory collateral. Borrowing against trust or warehouse receipts usually provides the least costly inventory loans. Interest rates tend to be 2 to 3% over the bank prime rate. Moreover, if warehousing fees are assessed, they tend to run 1 to 3% of the value of the inventory stored. Because a floating lien provides relative security, the cost of such loans is rather difficult to specify. A 3 to 6% interest rate above prime is a reasonable estimate. However, exceptions to this estimate may occur if the financial integrity of the borrower is judged to be high.

Learning Check for Section 21•2

Review Questions

21•4. What is the cost of forgoing a trade discount?

21•5. How is the cost of not taking a discount calculated?

21•6. "Accruals and deferrals should be used to the maximum." Do you agree? Why?

21•7. How do you calculate the annual interest rate for (a) discounted loans, (b) loans with compensating balances, and (c) commercial paper?

21•8. Accounts receivable can be a credit source in two different ways. Explain.

New Terms

Account receivable
  loans
Accruals
Deferred income
Discount interest
Factor
Factoring receivables

Floating lien
Inventory loans
Line of credit
Pledging receivables
Revolving-credit
Takedown

Trade credit
Transaction loan
Trust receipts
Unsecured bank
  credit
Warehouse receipts

SUMMARY

General Considerations in Current-Liability Management

All firms require the use of current assets. These current assets must be financed in one way or another. The manager of a company has to decide on the proportion of long-term to short-term liabilities that will be used to finance these current assets. In making this decision, flexibility, cost, and risk considerations must be taken into account. It is convenient to characterize short-term credit sources in terms of their availability, cost, the degree of management discretion they allow, and the security required.

Sources of Short-Term Credit

Trade credit is the largest source of spontaneous credit to a firm. By analyzing the terms of this short-term credit, the financial manager must find the opportunity cost of not taking any potential discounts. Accrued wages and accrued taxes are spontaneous sources that have no cost. Deferred income is another spontaneous costless source of short-term funds.

Bank credit is negotiated unsecured credit, and lines of credit allow firms access to this source of short-term funds. It is important to calculate the annual interest rate (AIR) of each type of bank loan before deciding on the type of bank credit to be used. If the bank uses discounted interest or requires compensating balances, the cost of the loan is increased.

Commercial paper is a promissory note that can be issued by large companies. The implicit cost of commercial paper can be determined by following a four-step procedure.

A company can also raise short-term funds from several secured credit sources. Accounts receivable loans and inventory loans are the most common forms of secured credit.

Regardless of the source of short-term funds, the manager must base his or her decision on the cost of the funds and weigh this against several qualitative factors (e.g., flexibility) before deciding on the composition of the firm's short-term liabilities.

PROBLEMS

21•1.   Your credit card has an interest rate of 1.5% per month.
   (a)   What is the approximate annual rate (or simple annual rate)?
   (b)   What is the effective annual rate (compounded annual rate)?

21•2.   The Dylan Tambourine Company has taken out a 60-day $2,000 note from the bank. The note calls for payment of $2,050 when due.
   (a)   What is the approximate annual rate (or simple annual rate)?
   (b)   What is the effective annual rate (compounded annual rate)?

21•3.   On August 1, you purchase some materials on terms of 1/10, n40.
   (a)   What is the last day on which you can pay and still take a discount?
   (b)   What is the amount of the discount?
   (c)   When is payment due if you do not take the discount?
   (d)   What is the approximate annual rate of interest that you are paying by failing to take the discount?

21•4.   Your firm, the Washington Appliance Store, has virtually unlimited access to short-term loans from the First National Bank of Commerce at a cost of 16%. Your two major suppliers offer the same prices, but at different terms of payment: The Heed Distributing Company offers terms of 2/10, n30, while Sitzes Wholesaling offers terms of 11/2/10, n60.
   (a)   What is the cost of forgoing the discount if you get your appliances through Heed?
   (b)   What is the cost of forgoing the discount if you get your appliances through Sitzes?
   (c)   What should you do?

21•5.   The Traynm Distributing Company offers a 2% discount on cash purchases and a 1% discount for payment within 20 days. If you take neither discount, payment must be made in 60 days.
   (a)   What is the cost of forgoing the cash discount and paying in 60 days instead?

(b) What is the cost of forgoing the 20-day discount and paying in 60 days instead?

(c) What is the cost of forgoing the cash discount and paying in 20 days instead?

(d) If the interest rate on short-term notes is 18%, what should you do?

21•6. The Waller Corporation purchases its raw materials with terms of 1/10, n40. What is the cost of forgoing the discount if they pay on the
(a) 15th day?
(b) 20th day?

21•7. What is the cost of forgoing a cash discount if the terms are
(a) 1/10, n20?
(b) 2/10, n30?

21•8. The Eng Manufacturing Company will need funds this fall to finance an increase in inventory. Kuo Eng anticipates a need of $160,000 for 90 days but wants to have available $250,000 in case more funds are needed. The Mercantile Bank is willing to extend this line of credit provided that Kuo leaves a compensating balance of 20% of the amount actually borrowed. The account that holds the compensating balance earns no interest. The simple interest rate on the loan is 14%. Assume a 360-day year.
(a) If Kuo borrows $160,000, how much of this amount is usable?
(b) How much would Kuo have to borrow to get $160,000 of usable funds?
(c) What line of credit must Kuo establish to have available $250,000 in usable funds?
(d) What annual interest rate is Kuo paying if he borrows an amount sufficient to generate $160,000 in usable funds?

21•9. Hoffman's Bait Shop needs to finance an increase in working capital in preparation for the fishing season. Owner Rodney Hoffman is seeking a revolving credit agreement with the Groos National Bank. He can establish a $200,000 line of credit with a commitment fee of $1\frac{1}{2}$% per year on the unused balance, or he can establish a $400,000 line of credit with a commitment fee of only 1%. In either case, the cost of borrowed funds is 15% per year. Rodney will need to borrow funds for only 90 days. The commitment fee is paid when the loan is taken out. Assume a 360-day year. What is Rodney's effective annual interest rate if he secures the $200,000 line of credit and actually borrows $100,000?

21•10. Alfred Cancer of the Brady Produce Company wishes to secure a $500,000 loan for a 60-day period. Gilbert Bernal of the Pumice National Bank has offered to make the loan as either a regular 15.5%,

60-day note or as a prepaid-interest, 15%, 60-day note. Which should he accept? What if the rate on the prepaid-interest loan is 15.25%?

21•11. The Milner-Barry Vending Company needs to raise $60 million for a period of 120 days. Irv Davidson, financial manager of Milner-Barry, is choosing between two plans for issuing commercial paper. The first calls for 16% annual interest with a dealer's commission of $150,000. The second calls for 15.2% discounted interest with a dealer's commission of $300,000. Which plan should Irv choose? What if the commission on the 15.2% commercial paper were only $200,000?

21•12. Don Grefe, financial manager of the Minihan Publishing Company, needs to raise $800,000. Fortunately, Minihan has $1.5 million of receivables due in the next 120 days. Don is considering pledging these receivables and getting a 15% loan or factoring $800,000 of the receivables. If he does the latter, he will receive only $750,000. Based on past experience, Don judges that 1.5% of the receivables will eventually be written off as bad-debt losses. What is the implicit interest rate of factoring the accounts receivable? Should Don factor or pledge the accounts?

21•13. The Campbell Sporting Goods Store currently pays its employees on the 1st and the 15th of every month and is considering paying wages monthly instead. (Assume that there are 30 days in every month.) Campbell has 340 employees, who are paid an average of $2,000 monthly. If Campbell's other sources of short-term credit have a cost of 12%, how much will Campbell save annually by making the switch to monthly wages?

21•14. Steve Stern of the Baird Boat Company is about to take out a 15% prepaid-interest loan for $600,000. What is the annual interest rate if the period of the loan is
(a) 30 days?
(b) 40 days?

21•15. Anita Ewing's electricity bill is for $120 and is due May 5. There is a 5% discount if the bill is paid by April 5. What is the implicit simple annual interest rate being paid by not taking the discount? The implicit compound annual interest rate?

READINGS

HAYES, D. A., *Bank Lending Policies, Domestic and International* (Ann Arbor, Mich.: University of Michigan, Bureau of Business Research, 1971).

MAIER, STEVEN F., AND JAMES H. VANDER WEIDE, "A Practical Approach to Short-Run Financial Planning," *Financial Management*, Winter 1978, 10–16.

MEHTA, DILEEP R., *Working Capital Management* (Englewood Cliffs, N.J.: Prentice-Hall, Inc., 1974).

MERVILLE, LARRY J., AND LEE A. TAVIS, "Optimal Working Capital Policies: A Chance-Constrained Programming Approach," *Journal of Financial and Quantitative Analysis*, January 1973, 47–60.

MOSKOWITZ, L. A., *Modern Factoring and Commercial Finance* (New York: Thomas Y. Crowell, 1977).

SMITH, KEITH Y., *Guide to Working Capital Management* (New York: McGraw-Hill Book Company, 1979).

YARDINI, EDWARD E., "A Portfolio-Balance Model of Corporate Working Capital," *Journal of Finance*, May 1979, 535–552.

PART *VIII*

Special Topics in Financial Management

22

Warrants, Convertibles, and Options

A complete study of finance must include a review of solutions to specialized financial problems. These solutions consist of special financial instruments and procedures that allow firms and individuals to obtain capital, to reduce risk, or to profit from speculative activities. The objective of this chapter is to provide students with an understanding of the concepts underlying these instruments and procedures.

We have previously dealt with aspects of long-term financing based on the more conventional forms of securities, such as common stock, preferred stock, and bonds. Although these types of securities represent the predominant means by which firms raise new capital, the early 1980s saw the growing use and popularity of alternative approaches in specialized financing situations. In this decade of creative financing, warrants and convertibles have become two popular securities issued by firms in an effort to raise funds in accord with their specific requirements. For the purposes of this chapter, these two forms of financing are discussed with respect to the issuing firm. Particular emphasis is placed on understanding the circumstances that tend to make warrants and convertibles an attractive financing medium. In addition, the basic features of these securities and the factors that affect their value are discussed briefly.

Options, which are traded between individuals[1] and not issued by corpora-

---

[1] *Individuals* in this context mean both single investors and corporations. Corporations may purchase options, just like single investors, and for the same reasons.

tions, have proved extremely popular vehicles for reducing risk and for speculation. These two objectives, which at first seem quite contradictory, make sense when we see how options allow risk-averse individuals and firms to transfer risk to speculators who accept risk in the expectation of making substantial profits.

This chapter consists of three sections:

SECTION 22·1: *Warrants.* In this section, the essential features of warrants are introduced and the uses of warrants are outlined. In addition, the value of warrants and the factors affecting their value are presented briefly.

SECTION 22·2: *Convertibles.* The terminology and special features of convertibles are introduced, and the uses of convertibles are discussed.

SECTION 22·3: *Options.* This section is a brief introduction to options. The basic concepts underlying options are introduced, along with relevant terminology. It is also shown that warrants and convertibles are special forms of options.

SECTION 22·1 *Warrants*

A **warrant** is a security issued by a corporation granting the holder of the warrant the right to purchase a specified number of shares of common stock at a specified price any time prior to an expiration date.

Warrants are typically issued with new common stock or debt offerings as part of a **unit.** For example, in 1982 the Trans World Corporation issued warrants in connection with its common stock offering. The company sold 1.8 million units, each consisting of one share of common stock and one warrant.

The specific rights conveyed by the corporation to the warrant holder are set out in a warrant agreement, which is analogous to the bond indenture discussed in Chapter 6.[2] The major features of these rights include the expiration date, the number of shares of common stock to which the warrant entitles its holder, and the stated price, known as the **exercise price,** at which these shares may be purchased.

The option to convert the warrant into shares of stock is limited to the life of the warrant. Generally, the expiration date is set 5 to 10 years from the date of original issue. It should be noted, however, that perpetual warrants are occasionally issued. Commonwealth Edison, for example, has issued perpetual warrants on its class *A* and *B* stocks that can be exercised any time into one-third of a share of its common stock for $30.00.

The exercise price is typically set 10 to 30% above the prevailing market value of the stock. For example, if Modular Packaging Corporation's common stock is selling at $40 per share, the exercise price of a new warrant issue might be set at $50 (25% above the existing market price). If the price per share of Modular's stock subsequently rises above the $50 exercise price, it would bene-

---

[2]The warrant agreement normally specifies certain restrictions on corporate behavior and stipulates how the outstanding warrants will be handled in case of mergers and acquisitions.

fit the warrant holder to exercise the option and purchase the stock. Alternatively, he could sell the warrant in the marketplace.

Although a warrant is an option to purchase common stock, warrant holders do not have any voting rights or rights to dividend payments. These rights can be acquired only through the purchase of the stock upon exercise of the warrant. The fact that warrant holders do not receive dividends implies that the value of warrants is not dividend protected. In other words, once the common stock goes ex-dividend, the value of the stock will drop by an amount approximately equal to that of the dividend payment, and hence the value of the warrant will decline.[3] This will be an important factor for a warrant holder in deciding when to exercise a warrant.

Although not dividend protected, warrants are normally protected against stock splits and stock dividends. If in the preceding example the Modular Packaging Corporation has a 2-for-1 stock split and the resulting price per share of common stock is $20, the exercise price of the warrant will be adjusted accordingly to $25.

Warrants can also be issued as part of or as an attachment to a bond or preferred stock offering. The warrant can be kept by the original purchaser of the bond or preferred stock, or in many cases can be detached from the debt instrument and sold separately in the open market. Warrants are traded over the counter and are listed on the American, New York, Chicago Board Option Exchange, and regional exchanges.

USE OF WARRANTS

Some of the factors influencing corporations in their use of warrants as a vehicle for financing can be anticipated in light of the preceding discussion regarding the basic features of warrants. Warrants offer the holder the possibility of participating in the future price appreciation of the stock. This characterizes them as **sweeteners** or **equity kickers** when attached to otherwise straight debt financing. The value of the warrant, and hence the value of this upside potential for the holder, often produces a benefit for the issuing corporation through a reduction in the coupon rate on a bond issue. In addition, warrants allow the company to issue its securities with less restrictive debt covenants. It is important to note that the investment characteristics of warrants (i.e., the bond and equity participation) appeal to a large number of investors. This increased marketability is another factor that tends to lower the coupon rate on the bond or the dividend rate on the preferred stock issue.

To illustrate, assume that a newly formed corporation (a *startup* company) with very little track record is faced with having to raise capital at a relatively high interest rate of 16%. If warrants are attached to a bond issue, the bondholders (i.e., the lenders) might be willing to accept a lower interest rate of, say, 12% in exchange for the right to equity participation. Obviously, this assumes that

---

[3]The relationship between the warrant price and the price of the underlying stock will be explored subsequently.

the lender has some expectation of future rewards. If there is no desire on the part of the lender to participate in the equity, the warrants might then be detached and sold in the marketplace to offset the reduced interest rate.

From the corporation's perspective, the reduction in the interest rate has lowered the cash flow drain due to debt capital and has perhaps made feasible an otherwise unattractive prospect for financing. This reduction in interest costs may be particularly important for a new or growing firm that has a constant need for capital.

As warrants are exercised, the corporation receives additional funds from the sale of stock to the warrant holder. The funds that the corporation receives are at a price lower than the current market value, yet above that prevailing at the time of the original warrant issue. These proceeds are received without incurring additional underwriting expenses, thereby lowering overall flotation costs. Thus the use of warrants can result in subsequent influxes of capital, causing the shifts in the firm's capital structure; the firm's financial leverage becomes smaller and smaller.

Although many firms with specific financing needs believe that the use of warrants makes financing cheaper, there is a possible adverse effect on the price of common stock with the use of warrants. Because the exercise of warrants results in the purchase of common stock below market value at some future point in time, there can be significant dilution of *EPS* and control to existing shareholders if the warrant issue is large relative to the number of outstanding shares. This potential result of the exercise of warrants can result in a decrease in the price of the common stock at the time of the warrant issue. For similar reasons, a large number of outstanding warrants may make it difficult or more expensive to undertake new equity financing.

As an illustration of the future effects on a firm resulting from a hypothetical warrant issue, Table 22•1 presents some financial statistics before and after the exercise of the warrants. Using the example of warrants for the Modular Packaging Corporation with an exercise price of $50, notice that, after exercise, the number of outstanding shares increases and there is an influx of additional capital. This results in lower *EPS* and a decrease in the leverage of the firm.

TABLE 22•1 Warrant Exercise Effects on Modular Packaging Corporation[a]

	Before Exercise	After Exercise
Liabilities	$ 50,000,000	$ 50,000,000
Common equity	50,000,000	62,000,000
Total assets	$100,000,000	$112,000,000
Warrants outstanding	240,000	—
Shares outstanding	1,000,000	1,240,000
Earnings	$20,000,000	$20,000,000
Earnings per share	$20.00	$16.13
Debt/total assets	0.5000	0.4464

[a]Assumes that each warrant entitles the holder to purchase one share of common stock for $50.

As a consequence of the more attractive financial aspects of warrants, they are often utilized in connection with mergers and acquisitions. By issuing warrants to the stockholders of the acquired firm, certain tax liabilities can be reduced while allowing the stockholders to participate in future gains. For similar reasons, warrants are often issued to venture capitalists.

VALUE OF WARRANTS

The value of a warrant and the factors that affect this value can be examined by returning to the example of Modular Packaging Corporation's warrants. Table 22·2 depicts a typical relationship between the price of the underlying common stock and the price of the warrant, assuming that other factors remain constant.[4] Also tabulated is the minimum value of the warrant and the warrant premium.[5]

The minimum value of a warrant represents the exchange value between the current stock price and the shares purchased at the exercise price. This minimum value may be expressed as

$$W_m = \begin{cases} (P_s - E)N & \text{for } E < P_s \\ 0 & \text{for } E > P_s \end{cases} \qquad (22\text{-}1)$$

TABLE 22·2 Value of Warrants[a]

Price of Stock, P_s	Price of Warrant, P_w	Minimum Value,[b] W_m	Warrant Premium, $P_w - W_m$
$10.00	$ 0.00	$ 0.00	$ 0.00
20.00	0.18	0.00	0.18
30.00	1.60	0.00	1.60
40.00	5.24	0.00	5.24
50.00	11.06	0.00	11.06
60.00	18.49	10.00	8.49
70.00	26.96	20.00	6.96
80.00	36.06	30.00	6.06
90.00	45.53	40.00	5.53

[a]Exercise price = $50.00.

[b]Minimum value = $\begin{cases} (P_s - E)N & \text{if } E < P_s \\ 0 & \text{if } E > P_s \end{cases}$

$N = 1$

[4]The relationship between the price of the common stock and the price of the warrant represented in Table 22·2 assumes that several factors, such as the variance of stock returns and the level of interest rates, remain fixed. Unless otherwise specified, these assumptions are made in all the other tables and figures in this chapter. The importance of these factors and their impact on warrant values are discussed later in this chapter.

[5]The minimum value of the warrant is also known as the *formula value, exercise value,* or *theoretical value.* The term *theoretical value* is a misnomer, however, since theory suggests that the warrant will trade typically at above the minimum value.

where W_m = minimum value of the warrant

P_s = current price of the common stock

E = exercise price

N = number of shares of stock that can be purchased by exercising the warrant

Examining Table 22•2 and assuming that $N = 1$, the minimum value of a warrant for a stock price of $80 and an exercise price of $50, for example, can be found from equation (22-1); that is,

$$W_m = (\$80 - \$50)(1) = \$30$$

The minimum value of the warrant from Table 22•2 is illustrated by the solid line in Figure 22•1. Note that the actual market price of the warrant is greater than its minimum value. The difference between these two is known as the **warrant premium.**

FACTORS AFFECTING WARRANT PRICES

Various factors affect the market value of warrants and the magnitude of the warrant premium. Three important ones are:

1. The variability of the common stock price.

2. The time remaining prior to expiration.

3. The dividend payment.

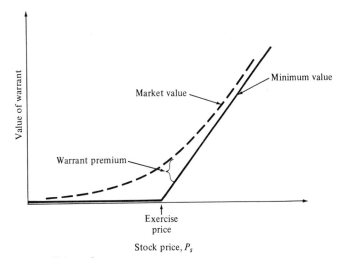

FIGURE 22•1   Value of warrants.

The importance of the variability of the stock price with respect to the value of warrants can be demonstrated by considering the investment leverage offered by warrants.[6]

The investment leverage aspect of warrants is illustrated in Table 22•3, which compares the potential gains from owning the stock with the gains from owning warrants for various magnitudes of price changes in the underlying stock, assuming that the warrants were priced at the minimum value. The table is constructed under the additional assumption that the stock sells initially for $51 per share. This stock price corresponds to a $1 minimum value ($W_m$) for the warrant given a $50 exercise price. These initial values are presented at the top of Table 22•3. If the stock price subsequently changes to the level represented in column 1, the warrant price will change in accordance with equation (22-1). The warrant price corresponding to each potential stock price in column 1 is presented in column 2. Column 3 shows the dollar gain/loss from the stock investment, while column 4 expresses these gains/losses in percentage terms. Columns 5 and 6 present, respectively, the dollar gain/loss and the percentage gain/loss from an investment in the warrant.

Comparing columns 4 and 6 in Table 22•3, it is apparent that warrants offer the holder a much greater degree of investment leverage than the common stock, while providing limited downside risk. For example, if the stock price goes up to $80, an investment in the stock would have provided a gain of 56.86%, while an investment in the warrant would have yielded a dramatic

TABLE 22•3   Leverage Provided by Warrants[a]

(1) Subsequent Stock Price	(2) Subsequent Warrant Price[b]	(3) Dollar Gain from Stock	(4) Percentage Gain from Stock	(5) Dollar Gain from Warrant	(6) Percentage Gain from Warrant
$ 0	$ 0	$−51	−100.00	$−1	−100
10	0	−41	−80.39	−1	−100
20	0	−31	−60.78	−1	−100
30	0	−21	−41.18	−1	−100
40	0	−11	−21.57	−1	−100
50	0	−1	−1.96	−1	−100
60	10	9	17.65	9	900
70	20	19	37.25	19	1,900
80	30	29	56.86	29	2,900
90	40	39	76.47	39	3,900
100	50	49	96.08	49	4,900
110	60	59	115.69	59	5,900
120	70	69	135.29	69	6,900

[a]Initial stock price when warrant is purchased = $51; exercise price of warrant = $50; initial warrant price = $1.
[b]Assuming that warrants are priced at the minimum value.

[6]The term *investment leverage* is used here to describe and compare the potential for gains and losses per dollar invested. This term should be distinguished from the operating and financial leverage concepts developed earlier.

2,900%. However, if the stock price falls to $10, the investment in the warrant would have yielded a higher percentage loss than the investment in the stock. Note, however, that neither investment can yield a loss in excess of -100% because of limited liability. This feature of warrants is summarized in the following key concept.

KEY CONCEPT: Warrants offer unlimited upside potential with limited downside risk.

Because of this attractive feature of warrants, investors are willing to pay a premium, and the warrant price gets bid up above the minimum value expressed in equation (22-1). The degree to which investors are willing to pay a premium is linked to the variability of the underlying stock price. As can be seen in Table 22•3, increases in the price of the common stock provide substantially greater percentage increases in the minimum value for any given warrant. On the other hand, downward movements in the price of the stock, and hence the warrant's minimum value, are bounded or limited to a maximum downside loss of 100%. Therefore, the higher the variability of the stock price, the greater the likelihood that the stock price will exceed the exercise price and provide gains to the warrant holder.

As the stock price increases above the exercise price, the investment leverage effect decreases and the price of the warrant approaches the minimum value. To illustrate this point, assume that the initial price of the stock is $100 (rather than $51, as in Table 22•3). This stock price implies a minimum warrant value of $50, since the exercise price is $50. A subsequent $9 increase in the price of the stock produces a minimum increase in the value of the warrant of $9, which corresponds to a gain of 18% ($9/$50). This contrasts dramatically with the 900% gain from a similar $9 warrant price increase indicated in Table 22•3.[7] This simple comparison serves to demonstrate the diminishing investment leverage effect with increasing stock price. It also illustrates why the investment leverage effect is at a maximum when the stock price is equal to the exercise price. It is at this point that the speculative nature of the warrant is at its greatest, and consequently, the warrant premium is at a maximum, as shown in Figure 22•1.

A closely related factor that affects the value of the warrant is the time remaining before expiration. Obviously, the longer the time interval, the greater the chance that the stock price will exceed the exercise price. As the expiration date nears, the warrant premium diminishes. Just prior to expiration, the warrant will, in fact, be priced at the minimum value described by equation (22-1). A third factor is the dividend yield of the common stock. Because warrant holders do not receive dividend payments, warrants are less attractive than stock. As the level of dividend payments increases, the warrant premium decreases and the value of the warrant moves closer to the minimum value.

---

[7]In Table 22•3 a $9 gain from the warrant corresponds to a percentage gain of 900%. This happens when the stock price is at $60.

Learning Check for Section 22·1

Review Questions

22·1. What are some of the basic features of warrants?

22·2. Why are warrants issued by corporations?

22·3. What are the factors affecting warrant prices? What is the minimum value of a warrant?

22·4. Explain the leverage feature inherent in warrants.

New Terms

Equity kickers	Sweetener	Warrant premium
Exercise price	Unit	
Expiration date	Warrant	

SECTION 22·2 *Convertibles*

A convertible security is a bond or preferred stock that, at the option of the holder, can be exchanged or "converted" into common stock. The number of shares of stock into which the bond or preferred stock may be converted is determined by the conversion ratio.[8]

Corresponding to the conversion ratio is the conversion price, representing the effective price at which the bondholders are obtaining the common stock upon exercising their option to convert. The relationship between these two terms can be expressed as

$$C = \frac{\text{face value of bond}}{R} \tag{22-2}$$

where R is the conversion ratio and C is the conversion price. Similar to the provisions of warrants, the conversion terms of most convertible bonds are set such that the conversion price is 10 to 30% above the market price of the common stock at the time of issue.

To illustrate the relationship of the conversion price with the conversion ratio expressed in equation (22-2), assume that the Modular Packaging Corporation issues 20-year convertible debentures with a $1,000 par value and a 10% coupon rate. The terms of the issue allow the holder the right of conversion at

---

[8]The discussion that follows is phrased in the context of bonds, but the same principles can be applied to the case of preferred stock.

$50 per share of Modular's common stock. The conversion ratio is, therefore,

$$R = \frac{\$1,000}{\$50} = 20 \text{ shares}$$

In other words, Modular's 10% bond may be converted into 20 shares of common stock at the option of the holder.

The conversion terms are usually adjusted for stock splits and stock dividends, as is the exercise price in the case of warrants. A 2-for-1 stock split occurring after the convertible issue of the Modular Packaging Corporation in the earlier example would result in a change of the conversion price from $50 to $25. Dividend payments are not received by convertible bondholders until after conversion. However, in contrast to warrant holders, they do receive interest payments on the bond.

Often the conversion terms include an acceleration clause that provides for increases or **step-ups** in the conversion price on designated dates. The $50 conversion price on Modular's convertibles might be fixed for five years, for example, then set at $55 for the next five years, and so on. Thus an acceleration clause results in conversion into fewer shares because as the conversion price increases, the conversion ratio decreases. The value of the conversion option consequently decreases as the conversion price increases. The convertible holder has an incentive to exercise his or her conversion option prior to the step-up (assuming that other factors make it financially attractive to do so). Through such a provision, therefore, the issuing corporation has more control over when the bonds are converted.

Another means by which a company can force conversion is by adding a call provision to the bond. A call provision entitles the firm to *call* the convertible, that is, buy it back at a certain prespecified price known as the *call price*. If the call price is lower than the current value of the stock obtained through conversion, the bondholder may decide to convert rather than risk a call by the company. This advantage for the firm is balanced by the higher interest rate it must pay to compensate bondholders for the possibility of having their bonds called. For a discussion of a situation in which a company may want to exercise a call provision, see the highlight "A New Trend in Callable Convertibles?"

▉▉ HIGHLIGHT

A NEW TREND IN CALLABLE CONVERTIBLES?

As seen in the text, companies often include a call provision on convertibles because it gives the firm the advantage of forcing conversion. Of course, the call price must be lower than the market value of the stock to make conversion attractive for the investor.

This logic has led investors to believe that their holdings will not be called if the underlying stock is trading at a price lower than the conversion price. Since conversion cannot be forced, investors often assume incorrectly that their convertibles will not be redeemed.

However, early in 1986, several convertible issuers called in their convertibles—not for the purpose of forcing conversion but to redeem them for cash. When such issues are called, investors lose the difference between the market value of the convertible and the call price, as well as the attractive preferred dividends or coupon interest. National Medical Enterprises, for example, called for redemption of its $12\frac{5}{8}$% convertible subordinated debentures due in 2001. Subsequent to this announcement the price of the debenture dropped dramatically, from about $113 to the call price of $100, a 12% loss. Similar but somewhat less dramatic losses were experienced when Recognition Equipment's 11% convertible subordinated debentures and PSA's $9\frac{1}{2}$% preferred stock were called in.

Why would a company redeem convertibles for cash? Companies may be seeking to refinance their debt at lower interest rates. Both Recognition Equipment and PSA issued new debt and common stock to finance this repurchase of the more expensive old debt.

If this recent trend of refinancing debt by calling in the convertible continues, investors holding on to high-coupon convertible debt or high-yielding preferreds should be aware that they face the risk of a call from the issuing company.

USE OF CONVERTIBLES

Convertibles are issued by firms for reasons similar to those for warrants. The conversion feature acts as a "sweetener" to the debt issue and often allows the issue to be made at a lower coupon rate and under less restrictive covenants than those of straight debt financing.

In essence, convertibles represent deferred equity financing. The management of a firm issuing convertibles is probably really interested in equity financing but, for whatever reasons, feels that the current stock price is too low to allow such financing. By issuing convertibles, management hopes that as the stock price increases and aligns with their expectations, convertible holders will exercise their option to convert and redeem their bonds for common stock. The net result, of course, is that the firm raises equity capital at a price equivalent to the conversion price, which, as mentioned, is typically 10 to 30% higher than the stock price at the time of issue. Naturally, if the price of the stock subsequent to the convertible issue increases much more than the conversion price, it would have benefited the firm simply to wait and issue stock.

On the other hand, if the price of the stock remains depressed and convertible holders do not exercise their option to convert, the firm is saddled with debt. This results in what is known as an *overhanging issue*. Such a situation makes it extremely difficult for a firm to undertake additional external financing. The firm, having issued convertibles with the hope of achieving an eventual increase in debt capacity upon conversion, finds itself in a more financially leveraged position than was originally intended. The debt service on the outstanding convertibles, coupled with a continuing depressed common stock price, make both equity and debt financing unattractive due to the increased costs associated with higher firm risk.

The successful use of convertibles, as in the case of warrants, can result in a shift in the capital structure of the firm. This will happen only if convertible holders exercise their option and debt is converted into equity. An important distinction between convertibles and warrants, however, is the fact that warrants bring in additional funds to the firm as they are exercised, whereas convertibles do not. Convertibles simply allow for a transformation of debt into equity through the conversion option.

To illustrate these conversion effects (and to contrast them with the effects on the firm using warrants presented in Table 22•1), various financial statistics are depicted in Table 22•4, using the convertible example for the Modular Packaging Corporation. Notice from this table that Modular's shares outstanding increase from 1 million to 1.2 million. Earnings, however, are unaffected. In this case, *EPS* and leverage decrease, but the overall capitalization of the firm remains the same.

TABLE 22•4 Conversion Effects on Modular Packaging Corporation[a]

	Before Exercise	After Exercise
Liabilities	$ 50,000,000	$ 40,000,000
Common equity	50,000,000	60,000,000
Total assets	$100,000,000	$100,000,000
Shares outstanding	1,000,000	1,200,000
Earnings	$20,000,000	$20,000,000
Earnings per share	$20.00	$16.67
Debt/total assets	0.5000	0.4000

[a]Assumes an outstanding convertible bond issue totaling $10,000,000 with a conversion price of $50 per share.

Learning Check for Section 22•2

Review Questions

22•5. What are some of the basic features of convertibles?

22•6. Why are convertibles issued by corporations?

New Terms

Callable convertible   Conversion price   Step-ups
Convertible security   Conversion ratio

SECTION 22•3 *Options*

Options provide a contractual right to purchase or sell any asset at a stated price subject to certain restrictions, such as the length of time for which this right is exercisable. Perhaps the most familiar form of options are those on common stock, which have a very active market on exchanges such as the Chicago Board Options Exchange (CBOE).

WHAT ARE OPTIONS?

To understand options on common stock, it is useful to consider another type of option, one that is much simpler—an option on a house.

Assume that you have identified a house that you would like to buy. Suppose that the house costs $125,000. You expect that it will take you 10 weeks to arrange for financing. To avoid the possibility that the builder will sell the house before that time, you ask the builder for a 10-week option on the house at $125,000. If the builder grants you the option, you can, at any time during the life of the option (10 weeks), buy the house for $125,000. If, for some reason, housing prices decline and the house is now worth only $110,000, you do not have to buy the house; you let the option expire, and no further action is necessary on your part. Recognize that obtaining such an option increases the possibilities for you, the buyer, and the builder will not give this option away for free. The builder may require $5,000 for this option, and this *option price* or *option premium* must be negotiated between you and the builder.

Notice that you, the option buyer, are, in effect, buying a type of insurance from the builder. The option allows you and the builder to share the risks. As the buyer of the option, you have the first call on the house at a fixed price, and you can simply walk away from the deal if you choose to do so, losing at most the initial investment (the option price). The builder is thus taking on some risk but is willing to do so for the $5,000 option premium. From this example of an option on a house, several characteristics of options can be observed:

1. Options are not free. The option premium is the value of the option.

2. Options have a fixed maturity; they expire on a certain date (the *expiration date*).

3. Options can be exercised before expiration at a prespecified price called the *exercise price* or *striking price*.

4. Options may or may not be exercised, depending on the difference between the market value of the underlying asset (house) and the exercise or striking price.

5. Options themselves do not affect the market value of the underlying asset.

OPTIONS ON COMMON STOCK

In contrast to the preceding example, the most common options are options on common stock. Options on common stock are becoming increasingly popular, and the trading volume on the CBOE has exceeded the turnover on the NYSE. There are two types of common stock options: call options and put options.

Call Options

KEY CONCEPT: A **call option** on a common stock allows the holder of the option to buy (*call*) a certain number of shares of the underlying stock at a prespecified price within a prespecified period.

Assume that an investor purchases a three-month call option on 100 shares of Hewlett-Packard stock at an exercise price of $35 per share when the stock price is $40. The option holder then has the right to purchase 100 shares of Hewlett-Packard for $35 at any time over the option's life, regardless of the actual price of Hewlett-Packard stock. This suggests that:

KEY CONCEPT: A call buyer expects the price of the underlying stock to rise above the exercise price.

The minimum value of the call option in this example must be $5. Why? Assume that the option price is $3. Then an investor could buy the option for $3, exercise it for $35, and sell the stock for its market price of $40, thereby making a profit of $2 immediately. To avoid these guaranteed profit opportunities, the option must sell for at least $5.

As it turns out, call options will sell for more than their minimum value (i.e., they are worth more than the difference between the stock price and the exercise price) if there is any time remaining before the option expires and if the stock price is greater than the exercise price.

Consider Table 22•5, which shows the prices and other relevant details of Hewlett-Packard call options as of June 8, 1988. On that day, Hewlett-Packard stock closed at a price of $58\frac{5}{8}$. Table 22•5 shows nine different call options (three different expiration dates for each of three different exercise prices) on the stock. Notice from the table that the options sell for more than their mini-

TABLE 22•5 Hewlett-Packard Call Options

Hewlett-Packard Stock Price[a]	Exercise Price (Striking Price)	Price of Call for Different Expiration Dates[b]		
		June	July	August
$58\frac{5}{8}$	$50	$7\frac{1}{2}$	$8\frac{5}{8}$	$9\frac{1}{4}$
58\frac{5}{8}	55	$3\frac{7}{8}$	$4\frac{3}{8}$	$5\frac{3}{8}$
58\frac{5}{8}	60	$\frac{9}{16}$	$1\frac{3}{4}$	$2\frac{5}{8}$

[a]Price per share.
[b]Price for option on 100 shares of stock.
Source: *Wall Street Journal,* June 9, 1988.

mum values. This is because there is always a possibility that the stock price will rise before the option expires. From Table 22•5 we also observe that:

1. The longer the remaining life of the call option, the larger the option premium. For example, consider the option with a $50 exercise price. The June option sells for $7\frac{1}{2}$, while the July option sells for $8\frac{5}{8}$. The August option is the most expensive at $9\frac{1}{4}$.

2. The larger the exercise price, the smaller the price of the option. Consider the June options on Hewlett-Packard. The $50 exercise price option costs $7\frac{1}{2}$, the $55 exercise price costs $3\frac{7}{8}$, and the cheapest option ($\frac{9}{16}$) is the option with the $60 exercise price.

Although not evident from Table 22•5, we will note two other properties of call options without giving any detailed explanations:

3. The call option price increases as the market value of the stock increases.

4. The call option price increases as the volatility of the stock increases.

Put Options

KEY CONCEPT: A **put option** on a common stock allows the holder of the option to sell (*put*) a certain number of shares of the underlying stock at a prespecified price within a prespecified period.

In contrast to a call option buyer:

KEY CONCEPT: A put buyer expects the price of the underlying stock to fall below the exercise price.

Table 22•6 shows the put option prices on Hewlett-Packard stock as of June 8, 1988. The symbol "r" in the table indicates that no options were traded on that day.

In contrast to a call option, the minimum price for a put option is the difference between the exercise price and the price of the underlying stock.

TABLE 22•6   Hewlett-Packard Put Options

Hewlett-Packard Stock Price[a]	Exercise Price (Striking Price)	Price of Call for Different Expiration Dates[b]		
		June	July	August
$58\frac{5}{8}$	$50	r	$\frac{3}{16}$	r
$58\frac{5}{8}$	55	$\frac{1}{4}$	$\frac{3}{4}$	$1\frac{7}{16}$
$58\frac{5}{8}$	60	2	$2\frac{3}{4}$	$3\frac{1}{2}$

[a]Price per share.
[b]Price for option on 100 shares of stock.
Source: *Wall Street Journal,* June 9, 1988.

THE ROLE OF EXCHANGES

The CBOE provides an active secondary market in options. Consider the case of an investor buying a Hewlett-Packard August option for 9\frac{1}{4}$. We already know that the investor has two alternatives: either exercise the option or permit it to expire. With secondary markets, the investor has a third alternative. He can sell the option in the marketplace at the prevailing option price. Thus an investor can get in and out of options before they mature. This would not be possible with an option on a house, as such options do not have established secondary markets. Another advantage of exchange-traded options is their low transactions costs. Buying and selling options through the CBOE's computerized network is relatively inexpensive (compared to the pre-CBOE commissions). Finally, since the CBOE guarantees the option, buyers and sellers can trade options without fear of default. All these advantages offered by exchange-traded options have resulted in a dramatic increase in options trading.

OPTIONS AND CORPORATE FINANCE

It is important to note that options do not play a direct role in the day-to-day operations of a company. The existence of Hewlett-Packard call and put options does not have any direct effect on Hewlett-Packard's *RRR* or cash flows. Options are not a source of financing to the firm (unlike warrants and convertibles). The presence of options on a company's stock may stabilize the price of the stock in the marketplace, but the financial manager has no direct control over this situation. Nevertheless, options can be used by financial managers in many ways. For example, pension fund managers can use options and options on indexes (not dealt with here) to lock in yields on their investments or to reduce the risk of their portfolios. However, the use of options in such situations takes us into an area well beyond the intended scope of this book.

WARRANTS AND CALLS AS OPTIONS

Warrants and convertibles, which were covered earlier in this chapter, represent special forms of call options. The factors affecting their value are the same as those that establish the value of any option. A very important distinction between warrants and convertibles and the stock options previously mentioned, however, is the **writer** of the option contract (i.e., the entity originating the option). In the case of warrants and convertibles, it is the firm that is writing the options and receiving the proceeds from this activity. By contrast, stock options are written by the individual shareholders, who negotiate these contracts in the secondary market.

Of the factors listed previously, only the last was not included in the discussion of the value of warrants and convertibles. Establishing a complete theoretical framework for the value of options is beyond the scope of this chapter; suffice at this point to note that as the risk-free interest rate rises, the market value of an option also increases.

Learning Check for Section 22·3

Review Questions

22·7. Warrants and convertibles are special forms of options. Do you see why?

22·8. What factors affect the value of an option?

22·9. Why should the variance in the price of the underlying asset affect the option's value?

New Terms

Call option   Option writer   Put option

SUMMARY

Warrants

Warrants and convertibles are forms of securities whose use provide firms with alternative means of raising capital in specialized financing situations. Often these situations are characterized by the need of firms to undertake additional financing in the face of inordinately high capital costs due to firm-specific risk or general market conditions. Through the use of warrants and convertibles, additional capital can be raised facilitated by offering bondholders the option of equity participation. In exchange for this option, bondholders often reduce the interest rate on the associated debt issue, thereby making the financing package more attractive from the firm's perspective.

The holder of a warrant has the right to purchase a specified number of shares of common stock at a specified price at any time prior to the warrant's expiration date. Warrants offer the holder the opportunity to participate in future price appreciation of the stock. The value of the warrant is affected by the variability of the common stock price, the time remaining to expiration of the warrant, and the dividend payment.

Convertibles

A convertible security is a bond or preferred stock that, at the option of the holder, can be exchanged for common stock. The number of shares of stock into which the bond or preferred stock may be converted is determined by the conversion ratio. Convertibles are issued by firms for reasons similar to those for issuing warrants. As with warrants, the value of the convertible is affected by the terms and provisions of the specific security, the variability of the common stock price, the time remaining until expiration of the convertible provision, and the dividend payment on the common stock.

Options

An option is the contractual right to purchase or sell an asset at a stated price subject to certain restrictions, such as the length of time for which this right is exercisable. Among the more popular options are those on common stock. A call option gives the holder the right to purchase a certain number of shares of a stock at a prespecified price for a prespecified period. A put option gives the holder the right to sell a stock at a prescribed price for a prescribed period. The existence of a strong secondary market in options has increased their popularity. Warrants and convertibles may be viewed as special forms of call options. Unlike call options that are written between two investors, warrants and convertibles are written by the company receiving the proceeds from the sale of the option.

PROBLEMS

22•1.   Warrants of the Escher Cheese Importing Company are trading for $4. The warrants entitle the bearer to buy one share of stock for $50. Can you draw an inference concerning share price?

22•2.   The Rusk Automobile Company currently has warrants outstanding that allow the bearer to purchase shares for $30. What can you say about the value of the warrant if the share price is currently
(a) $25?
(b) $30?
(c) $35?
(d) $40?

22•3.   Warrants of the Bournias Manufacturing Corporation have a subscription price of $60. The share price is currently $67 and the warrant currently trades for $9.50.
(a)   What is the formula value (or minimum value) of the warrant?
(b)   What is the warrant's premium?

22•4.   Following is a table of anticipated warrant values, given different values of a share of National Banknote.

Share Price	Warrant Value
$30	1
35	2
40	$3\frac{1}{2}$
45	$7\frac{1}{2}$
50	$11\frac{3}{4}$
55	$16\frac{1}{4}$
60	21

The warrant entitles the bearer to purchase one share for $40.

(a) Find the minimum or formula value for each of the share prices given.

(b) Find the warrant's premium for each of the share prices given.

(c) If the share price is currently $30, find the percentage change in share price and the percentage change in warrant value if the share price increases by $5.

(d) If the share price is currently $40, find the percentage change in price and the percentage change in warrant value if the share price increases by $5.

(e) If the share price is currently $50, find the percentage change in price and the percentage change in warrant value if the share price increases by $10.

22•5. Shares of the Simpson Auto Import Corporation currently trade for $27. Simpson also has outstanding warrants with an exercise price of $25 and a maturity of one year. These warrants currently sell for $4.

(a) How much will the warrant be worth just before it matures if the year-end share price is $0? $20? $25? $27? $30? $35?

(b) If you buy 100 warrants, what will your dollar profit or loss be if the year-end share price is $0? $20? $25? $27? $30? $35?

(c) If you buy 100 warrants, what will your return be if the year-end share price is $0? $20? $25? $27? $30? $35?

22•6. You have just received an inheritance of $10,000 and are thinking of investing it all in Mayto shares, which are currently trading for $50 each. However, you have also noticed that you can buy for $4 Mayto warrants with an exercise price of $50. Furthermore, you can invest any surplus funds in a money market fund yielding 10%.

(a) If you invest the entire amount in shares, how many shares can you buy?

(b) If you invest the entire amount in warrants, how many warrants can you buy?

(c) If you buy enough warrants to purchase the number of shares you could buy in part (a) and invest the rest of the inheritance in the money market fund, how much will you have in the fund?

(d) Find the value of each of the portfolios from parts (a), (b), and (c) if the year-end share price has the following values:

Year-End Share Price	Portfolio A (All Stock)	Portfolio B (All Warrants)	Portfolio C (Warrants and Money Market Fund)
$ 0			
40			
45			
50			
55			
60			
65			
100			

(e) Find the percentage returns of the portfolios and year-end stock prices specified in part (d).

Year-End Share Price	Portfolio A's Return	Portfolio B's Return	Portfolio C's Return
$ 0			
40			
45			
50			
55			
60			
65			
100			

(f) Can you draw any conclusions concerning the current warrant price of $4 from a comparison of portfolios A and C?

22·7. The Miller Insurance Company currently has a capital structure of $60 million in equity and $40 million in debt, both expressed in book-value terms. Miller is about to issue $20 million of $1,000 face-value bonds, each with a warrant attached that entitles the bearer to buy 10 shares at $50 each.
   (a) What will the capital structure be immediately after Miller issues the bonds?
   (b) If all the warrants are exercised in five years and no new shares or bonds are sold between now and then, what will the capital structure be in five years?
   (c) If Miller wishes to keep the subscription price at $50, how many shares must they allow the bearer of one warrant to buy if they

wish to have their current capital structure if all the warrants are exercised?

22•8. An 8% coupon bond convertible to 25 shares of common stock is trading for $877. The bond matures in 10 years. Assume that the face value of the bond is $1,000.
   (a) What can you say about the yield to maturity of nonconvertible but otherwise similar bonds?
   (b) What can you say about the current share price?

22•9. A 10% coupon bond that is convertible to 40 shares of common stock was issued six years ago. The bond has 14 years left to maturity. Today the share price is $29 and the yield to maturity of nonconvertible but otherwise similar bonds is 9%.
   (a) What is the conversion ratio of the bond?
   (b) What is the conversion price of the bond?
   (c) What can you say about the price of the bond today?
   (d) What can you say about the price of the bond if the yield to maturity on nonconvertible bonds with the same risk falls to 7% while stock price remains at 29?
   (e) What can you say about the price of the bond if the yield to maturity of nonconvertible bonds with the same risk stays at 9% but the price falls to $26?

22•10. Eight years ago the Centurion Services Corporation issued two classes of preferred stock, each with a $5 dividend. Class *A* was nonconvertible and was sold for $40 per share. Class *B* was convertible to two shares of common stock and was sold for $50 per share. At the time, common shares were trading for $20.
   (a) Today the yield on class *A* stock is 8% and common shares are trading for $31.25. What are the class *A* shares trading for? What can you say about the price of the class *B* shares?
   (b) Suppose that the yield on the class *A* stock drops to 5%, while the share price remains at $31.25. What are the class *A* shares trading for? What can you say about the price of the class *B* shares?
   (c) Suppose that the yield on class *A* stock rises to 15%, while the share price remains at $31.25. What are the class *A* shares trading for? What can you say about the price of the class *B* shares?
   (d) Suppose that the yield on class *A* shares remains at 8%, but the share price rises to $40. What are the class *A* shares trading for? What can you say about the price of the class *B* stock?
   (e) Suppose that the yield on class *A* shares remains at 8%, but the share price falls to $20. What are the class *A* shares trading for? What can you say about the price of class *B* stock?
   (f) What two events must occur for class *B*'s share price to fall to $40?

22•11. The Kinetico Corporation is issuing 20-year, 8% coupon convertible bonds at par. The bonds have a conversion ratio of 25. The common shares just paid a dividend of $0.50. Dividends are expected to grow at a 10% annual rate, and investors' required return on the stock is 15%.
(a) Using the Gordon growth formula, find the value of a share today.
(b) What do you expect the value of a share to be 10 years from now? (Hint: Find D11 and use the Gordon growth formula to find P10.)
(c) Will you convert the bond? Using the yield-to-maturity formula,

$$YTM = \frac{I + (B_n - B_0)/n}{(B_n + B_0)/2}$$

where I is the coupon payment, n the number of years to maturity, and B_j the value of the bond at time j, find the anticipated yield to maturity of this bond.

22•12. The Potentia Services Corporation's sources of capital are currently $7 million in equity and $3 million in long-term debt (both book-value figures). Potentia is about to issue $3.5 million of new 10-year convertible bonds.
(a) What proportion of Potentia's capital is provided by equity sources and what proportion by debt sources?
(b) What will Potentia's capital structure (proportions of equity and debt) be after issuing the new bonds?
(c) Suppose that in 10 years all the bonds are converted. What will Potentia's capital structure be? If they wish to retain today's capital structure, how much debt must they sell immediately after the bonds are converted?

22•13. John Polonchek is considering purchase of ETT's new issue of 20-year, 7% coupon bonds with a warrant. The warrant entitles the bearer to purchase 10 shares of ETT stock for $25 per share. John expects ETT shares to pay a $1 dividend at the end of the year and expects the dividends to grow by 8% annually. Furthermore, John feels that investors will require a 16% return on the shares.
(a) Using the Gordon growth formula, find the value of a share today.
(b) Find the value of a share in year 20. (Hint: Calculate D21 and use the Gordon growth formula.)
(c) Assume that John does not wish to sell or exercise warrants until the maturity date. Will he exercise them at the end of the 20th year? Using the yield-to-maturity formula [see Problem 22•11(c)], find John's yield to maturity on the bond.

22•14. Huret Instruments, Inc., has just issued at par a 20-year convertible bond with a sliding conversion ratio. The conversion ratio is 40 for the first 10 years, 30 for the next 5 years, and 25 for the last 5 years. The share price is currently $15 and is expected to grow by 8% per year.

(a) What is the conversion value (value of the shares for which the bond may be redeemed) of the bond just before the end of the 10th year? Just after the end of the 10th year?

(b) What is the conversion value of the bond just before the end of the 15th year? Just after the end of the 15th year?

(c) What is the conversion value of the bond just before it matures?

(d) Suppose that the bond has an 8% coupon and that if you buy the bond and eventually convert it, you will convert just before the end of the 10th, 15th, or 20th year. If your discount rate of valuing cash flows from the bond is 10%, in which year, if any, should you convert? Should you buy the bond at all? What if your discount rate is 9%?

22•15. Marion Lawson is considering issuing new Maxda, Inc. 20-year maturity convertible bonds. The bonds have a 10% coupon and will be sold at par. The conversion ratio is 35, and the share price is currently $20.

(a) Suppose that Mrs. Lawson decides to buy the bonds only if she can earn a 12% return. What must the conversion value of the bond be in 20 years to earn this return? What must the annual stock price appreciation rate be to reach this conversion value?

(b) Suppose that Mrs. Lawson decides to purchase the bonds only if she can earn a 14% return. What must the conversion value be in 20 years to earn this return? What must the annual stock price appreciation rate be to reach this conversion value?

READINGS

ALEXANDER, GORDON J., AND ROGER D. STOVER, "Pricing in the New Issue Convertible Debt Market," *Financial Management*, Fall 1977, 35–39.

BLACK, F., "Fact and Fantasy in the Use of Options," *Financial Analysts' Journal*, July–August 1975, 36–41, 61–72.

BLACK, F., AND M. SCHOLES, "The Pricing of Options and Corporate Liabilities," *Journal of Political Economy*, May–June 1973, 637–654.

BRENNAN, M. J., AND E. S. SCHWARTZ, "The Case for Convertibles," *Chase Financial Quarterly*, Spring 1982, 27–46.

GALAI, DAN, AND MIER I. SCHNELLER, "The Pricing of Warrants and the Value of the Firm," *Journal of Finance*, December 1978, 1333–1342.

INGERSOLL, JONATHAN E., "An Examination of Corporate Call Policies on Convertible Securities," *Journal of Finance*, May 1977, 463–478.

PUTNAM, B., "Managing Interest Rate Risk: An Introduction to Financial Futures and Options," *Midland Corporate Finance Journal* (Special Issue), 1982.

23

Mergers and Other Business Combinations

Mergers and acquisitions, or more typically just *mergers,* are generic terms referring to different types of business combinations wherein two or more firms combine to form one legal entity (corporation). The three types of business combinations that are discussed in this chapter are consolidations, mergers, and holding companies. Nevertheless, the term *mergers* will be used to account for all three types because the financial principles and implications to be discussed below apply equally well to all of them.

A merger can be viewed as an investment in a future growth opportunity. In Chapters 10 to 14 we examined decisions designed to achieve future growth by internal expansion—by enlarging or improving production and distribution of existing products or by developing new products. This chapter is concerned with decisions about future growth through external expansion—by acquiring another firm or only part of its assets. Internal expansion offers certain advantages, such as greater control over the asset expansion process and greater assurance of technological compatibility with existing operations. However, internal expansion usually requires a longer implementation period and incurs the uncertainties occasioned by building a new plant or developing a new product and its market acceptance. Acquiring a firm that already has the facilities or products desired can eliminate these concerns and often can be done more cheaply this way. By contrast, Table 23•1 presents a 10-year history of the expenditures by U.S. firms on internally generated investment relative to the amounts spent on acquiring other firms.

TABLE 23•1 U.S. Capital Expenditures for New Plant and Equipment (Internal Growth) versus the Value of All Mergers (External Growth), 1975–1982 (Billions of Dollars)

	Capital Expenditures	**Value of Mergers**
1982	$316.4	$53.8
1981	321.5	82.6
1980	295.6	44.3
1979	270.5	43.5
1978	231.2	34.2
1977	198.1	21.9
1976	171.4	20.0
1975	157.7	11.8

Source: *Statistical Abstract of the United States 1984*, 104th ed. (Washington, D.C.: U.S. Department of Commerce), and *Mergerstat Review, 1982* (Chicago: W. T. Grimm & Co.).

A growing firm may therefore be constantly interested in identifying potential acquisitions, and it is the financial manager who is called upon to evaluate a prospective merger. This chapter is divided into three sections.

SECTION 23•1: *Types of Business Combinations.* In this section the various types of mergers are defined and the reasons that mergers are undertaken are analyzed.

SECTION 23•2: *How a Merger Is Effected.* The mechanics of effecting a merger, in particular, friendly takeovers and hostile takeovers, are explained briefly.

SECTION 23•3: *Other Forms of Corporate Restructuring.* In the final section, we discuss several other popular forms of corporate reorganization. These forms of reorganization allow the firm to dispose of all or part of its assets or to become a private rather than a publicly traded firm.

SECTION 23•1 *Types of Business Combinations*

The term *merger* commonly refers to any business combination in which one or more of the firms involved do not survive in name. But technically:

KEY CONCEPT: A **merger** refers to the combination of two (or more) corporations in such a way that legally just one corporation survives, while the other is dissolved according to the laws of the state in which it is incorporated.[1]

---

[1]The term *acquisition* is sometimes used in reference to mergers. In the vernacular of the financial press, the word *mergers* is used quite broadly, while *acquisitions* normally refers only to the situation wherein one firm acquires another firm and the latter ceases to exist in name or as a legal entity, or only part of another firm's assets are purchased.

The legally surviving (*acquiring*) firm ends up owning the assets of the dissolved (*target*) firm, and only its name and common stock continue to exist. For example, a merger occurs when firm *A* purchases firm *B* and the surviving firm is firm *A*. The target firm is said to have been merged into the surviving firm, and its shareholders receive either shares of stock in the acquiring firm or some other form of compensation, such as cash.

In contrast:

KEY CONCEPT: A **consolidation** occurs when two (or more) corporations combine to create an entirely new corporate entity.

Following a consolidation, neither of the original firms continues to exist as a separate entity. Rather, they are dissolved and a new corporate entity is created according to the laws of the state in which it is incorporated. For example, a consolidation occurs when firm *A* combines with firm *B* in order to form firm *C*. Both *A*'s and *B*'s shareholders give up their respective shares and receive new shares in firm *C* or some other form of consideration.

KEY CONCEPT: A **holding company** is a firm that owns sufficient voting stock in one or more other companies so as to have effective control over them.

A holding company is frequently called the *parent* company, which controls the *subsidiary* companies. Depending on how widely dispersed the stock of the subsidiary is, effective control may be gained with as little as 10% ownership. In fact, control of some major corporations can be had for less than 10% ownership interest in them. Seldom does it require a full 51% ownership interest to maintain control in a publicly held corporation.

SPECIFIC TYPES OF MERGERS

During different periods in American corporate history, several types of mergers and acquisitions have enjoyed prominence. **Congeneric mergers** occur between firms that have *related business interests* and can be classified as being either horizontal or vertical. **Horizontal mergers** were prevalent around the turn of this century and consist of the combination of two firms engaged in the *same* business. The surviving firm continues in the same business but is simply larger. These horizontal mergers are most notably associated with the robber baron era in the late nineteenth century. During this period, large corporations such as U.S. Steel and Standard Oil joined their smaller competitors by way of mergers. This created monolithic concerns that ultimately gave rise to early antitrust legislation.

Vertical mergers, in vogue during the 1920s, occur when a firm acquires firms "upstream" from it, such as its suppliers, and/or firms "downstream" from it, such as its product distributors. This process may go all the way upstream to the suppliers of raw materials and downstream to those firms that sell to the ultimate consumer. Therefore, these mergers involve a vertical integration (combination) of two or more stages of production or distribution that are usually separate. The advantages are lower transactions costs, assured supplies, improved coordination, and higher barriers to entry (for potential competitors). The disadvantages are larger capital requirements, reduced flexibility, and loss of specialization.

Conglomerate mergers occur when *unrelated* businesses combine. The business world saw an explosion of conglomerate mergers in the 1960s. A prime example of a successful series of conglomerate mergers is the Teledyne Corporation, which became one of America's largest firms by having acquired many unrelated businesses. Today, this type of merger continues to be an important part of the total merger picture.

Compared to the ebb and flow of early merger activity, the dollar magnitude of today's mergers is enormous. In the early 1980s, industrial giants such as U.S. Steel–Marathon Oil, DuPont–Conoco, and Socal–Gulf have participated in this game. For example, Texaco's acquisition of Getty cost $10.1 billion, and the Socal–Gulf deal involved $13.2 billion.

ECONOMIC REASONS FOR COMBINING BUSINESSES

The underlying objective for a potential merger should be to maximize shareholders' wealth. The reasons given in contemplating a merger should be evaluated in terms of whether or not they contribute to this objective. As with any investment decision, the cost of merging with another firm should be in terms of the *NPV* of its expected future cash flows. Next we discuss a number of reasons used to explain why businesses combine their activities.

Operating Advantages

A merger may arise because of the economies of scale that may be achieved. This is the most often cited and easiest justification to explain a merger. **Economies of scale** refer to the reduction in the average cost of producing and selling a product as production volume increases. For example, overhead costs can typically be reduced because what were formerly two departments, such as accounting activities, can be collapsed into one. While the surviving department may be larger than the department of either of the premerger firms, it will typically be smaller than both of them together. Horizontal mergers often take advantage of reduced production costs by increasing the volume of production. By controlling suppliers or distributors, a vertical merger may take advantage of enhanced scheduling and inventorying opportunities.

Financing Advantages

A postmerger firm may be able to take advantage of new opportunities in the financial markets because of its increased size or efficiencies. For instance, two firms may be far from their optimal debt capacity: one overextended, the other underextended. By merging, they may achieve greater debt capacity. This, in turn, may lead to a lower cost of capital for the postmerger firm.

The postmerger firm may also be able to raise funds at a lower cost than that at which either of the premerger firms could have acquired funds. The reason is that increased size tends to reduce the risk of default. Moreover, a (larger) postmerger firm is able to issue new securities in larger dollar amounts and thereby at a *reduced flotation cost.* That is, the cost associated with issuing stocks and bonds normally decreases as the size of the issue increases.[2] However, it is doubtful whether these savings alone would be sufficient to justify a prospective merger.[3]

Enhanced Growth Opportunities

Companies may merge in order to grow at a rate faster or in a manner other than they could have achieved by internal expansion alone. Moreover, a merger may be a quicker and cheaper way to expand into new or related products or to acquire production facilities to increase production of already existing products. Building a new plant to produce a new product can take years and be very costly. There are also uncertainties associated with cost overruns, the quality of the plant to be built, and the acceptability of the product. When a firm acquires another firm, it can do so relatively quickly at a more certain price, providing a product in a more timely fashion.

Diversification

Some firms merge to diversify their operations and thereby smooth earnings that would otherwise fluctuate due to seasonal or economic cycles. For instance, an auto manufacturer might acquire a replacement-parts company with the idea that in favorable economic periods people buy new cars, whereas in recessionary times, people resort to maintaining their existing cars and hence sales of auto parts will increase. The postmerger firm's earnings would thus come from new-car sales in good times and from auto-parts sales in poor times. By diversifying its business activities, a firm's business risk is spread over more operations (reduced), which results in a favorable impact on share price.

Another motive for diversifying through mergers is to create investment opportunities for a firm with lagging sales. For example, the tire and rubber industry began a vigorous diversification program in the early 1980s as the

---

[2]The SEC estimated that the costs associated with issuing less than $500,000 in common stock on average exceeded 20% of the gross proceeds. For issues over $20 million, the costs were less than 5% of gross proceeds.

[3]Quite often a catchall term, *synergy,* is used to explain a prospective merger. *Synergy* refers to the notion that the whole is greater than the sum of its parts and simply means that the surviving firm's future earnings will be greater than the sum of the individual firms' earnings. Synergy results from the benefits that the operating and financing advantages of a merger offers, as well as nonquantitative benefits such as improved management.

longer-term outlook for the replacement tire market (three-fourths of total tire sales) began to wane. Uniroyal, one of the world's largest producers of natural rubber, invested heavily in chemicals, to the point where the profits derived from this source equaled those from its tire business.

As seen in earlier chapters, diversification can be used to reduce risk. While a firm's acquisition can reduce business risk, its shareholders can diversify their portfolio at less cost than the firm can. For this reason, financial theory suggests that diversification is not a sound justification to support a merger. However, diversification may contribute to the long-term health of a firm if it reduces the risk of illiquidity or bankruptcy.

Interestingly enough, in recent years, a major movement to "de-conglomerate" through asset deployments has taken place. Essentially, firms began *selling off* entire operating units that no longer fit into their long-term corporate strategy. Some simply wanted to respecialize, while others found that acquired businesses were not sufficiently profitable due to higher inflation and opportunity costs of capital. For example, while a business might have yielded a 14% return, a 17% opportunity cost of capital made this an undesirable investment.

Moreover, there was generally no lack of buyers.[4] A business rejected by one corporation could fit well into the operations of another. One of the larger asset deployments occurred when BSN-Gervais—a French firm—bought the Dannon Yogurt operations from Beatrice Foods. Beatrice was able to shrug off the mounting competition in the yogurt business and BSN-Gervais was able to gain a quick market access for its diverse dairy products.

Tax Advantages

An earlier form of the federal tax code offered considerable tax advantages to mergers between certain firms. There once was a brisk activity in corporations acquiring other corporations just to use the operating losses of the acquired company as an offset against the acquiring company's income. The purpose was to reduce the acquiring firm's tax liability. The target firm, with little prospect of earning enough to take advantage of its tax-loss carryforwards, and the acquiring firm could both benefit from a merger. In recent years, new federal tax laws have severely restricted the use of this operating loss deduction. Nevertheless, in limited circumstances, a corporation may still be able to use an acquired firm's tax losses to reduce tax liabilities. In these cases, a financial manager needs to be careful in analyzing the merger's tax consequences to be certain that the advantages accrue to the acquiring firm.

---

[4]In some cases, rather than selling the assets of the undesirable business, the firm *spun off* the assets in the form of a new company and issued the new company's shares to its shareholders as a dividend.

HOLDING COMPANIES

In contrast to mergers, controlling interest is the principal advantage of holding companies. Through its control, a holding company may be able to integrate certain functions of the held company with operations of other held companies. This results in achieving the benefits of economies of scale. In addition, the price paid per share of the held companies, and thus the capital requirements, are usually less than if all the shares were purchased outright.[5]

Through its controlling interest, a holding company can benefit from the leveraged ownership it offers by **pyramiding** its investment.[6] That is, control of a larger aggregation of operating assets may be obtained with a smaller investment in common stock than by using other forms of business combinations. For example, suppose that a holding company can control three (layered) operating companies, each with a market value of $100 million, with an average holding of 10% in each stock. If each held company was financed with 50% debt and 50% equity, these three companies, together worth $300 million, could be controlled by the holding company with only a $15 million investment in common stock [(0.10)(3)(0.50)($100 million)].

This seemingly extravagant arrangement is workable as long as the corporations are profitable at each level. However, just as control and its profitability are magnified, so are any losses. A loss at the lower level of the holdings can cause a collapse of the entire system. The reason is that extremely high leverage may be obtained through the use of debt financing by both operating companies and the holding company. Each partially debt-financed company multiplies the leverage at each level as the earnings stream rises through the holding company structure. Therefore, a small change in earnings per share (*EPS*) of the subsidiary companies produces a large change in *EPS* of the top holding company. In fact, this attenuated form of ownership was a popular method of ownership of public utilities in the 1920s and 1930s. As a result of many failures and related abuses, the Public Utility Holding Company Act of 1935 was enacted to prevent highly leveraged ownership of utilities.

One problem with holding companies is that if they own less than 80% of their held corporations, 15% of the dividends received from these held companies are subject to taxation. If the holding company has a 46% marginal tax rate, 6.9% [i.e., (0.15)(0.46)] of dividends received from its holding must be paid as taxes. This introduces another layer of taxation because when the holding pays dividends to its shareholders, they will be taxed at their marginal tax rate. With other business combinations, a transfer of cash funds (dividends) between operating companies is not taxed.

---

[5]Undue publicity, which tends to push up the price per share, may be avoided by purchasing the shares quietly over time. A notice of purchase and intent must still be filed with the SEC under certain conditions.

[6]A firm that is strictly a holding company is analogous to a mutual fund in that it has no business operations per se. Its only assets are the securities of other corporations. Texas Utilities is an example of a pure holding company.

Learning Check for Section 23•1

Review Questions

23•1. What is a merger? What are the different types of mergers?

23•2. What are the potential economic advantages from mergers?

23•3. What is a holding company? Holding companies are said to have an extra layer of taxation. What does this mean?

New Terms

Acquisition
Congeneric merger
Conglomerate merger
Holding Company

Horizontal merger
Merger
Parent company

Pyramiding
Subsidiary
Vertical merger

SECTION 23•2 *How a Merger Is Effected*

There are two ways to acquire another company: *purchase the assets* or *purchase the stock* of the target company. There are advantages and disadvantages to both methods, and in some cases only one of the methods may be available, such as in a tender offer versus a **friendly takeover.** Each method needs to be examined thoroughly by the financial manager to assess the most favorable method to employ.

A FRIENDLY TAKEOVER

Purchase of Assets

The purchase of assets method is fairly easy and flexible. Typically, the purchaser will enter into discussions with the management or board of directors of the target firm concerning the details of the purchase (sale). From the buyer's perspective, there are several advantages to this purchase arrangement. Foremost is that the acquiring firm can buy certain assets and not others. That is, only a portion of the target company is bought. The buyer can also avoid hidden or contingent liabilities of the target that would become its liabilities if the target were acquired outright. Moreover, it is easier to negotiate such a purchase since only the board of directors needs to agree to the deal. There are no minority shareholders involved (i.e., shareholders of the target firm who refuse to sell their ownership interest). In 1984, Carter–Hawley–Hale Stores, Inc. sold its lucrative Waldenbooks' assets to K Mart as a defensive ploy against its potential takeover by The Limited, Inc.

From the perspective of the target firm, there is a new element of flexibility. The consideration paid to the target in exchange for its assets, whether cash or securities, may be used for reinvestment purposes or distributed to the target's shareholders as a dividend.

Purchase the Stock

An acquiring firm may make an outright purchase of a target's stock. It can then maintain the target as a subsidiary company or division, or it can dissolve the target as a separate entity. It is the latter event that is technically defined as a merger.

Several drawbacks occur with this type of merger. The acquiring firm falls heir to the target firm's liabilities, including hidden and contingent liabilities. Whether or not the target's board of directors are approached, the shareholders must approve the merger. This requires the assent of a stipulated percentage of the shareholders (usually two-thirds) for the merger to be acceptable. Finally, the shareholders who refuse to give up their shares can become quite troublesome to the acquiring firm. These **dissenting shareholders** can, in fact, kill a prospective merger. They can seek redress in the courts to protect their interests if they feel that there has been fraud or an unfair price offered. Court battles are costly and time-consuming. Moreover, dissenting shareholders can simply refuse to sell, becoming *minority* shareholders and creating an ongoing headache for the acquiring firm.

A HOSTILE TAKEOVER

Tender Offer

If a target's board of directors is not receptive to a takeover, the acquiring firm can resort to a **tender offer.** A tender offer is the purchase of a target's stock through the secondary financial markets or directly from individual stockholders. A tender offer tends to be very costly. For one, the price(s) paid for the target's shares are usually relatively high because tender offers are made publicly through the financial press, brokers, and direct mailings. The greater publicity inspires greater demand for the shares by speculators, driving prices up. On the other hand, the ability to raid or secretly acquire the target's stock is limited. Federal regulations set out strict rules governing the acquisition of publicly traded stock.

Proxy Fight

Tender offers can also be expensive if the acquiring firm obtains only a portion of the target's stock and then proceeds to *force* a merger through a proxy fight. In a proxy fight, the acquiring firm's management approaches the target firm's shareholders and requests the right to vote their shares at the next shareholders' meeting. If the purchaser garners this right, it can oust the target's hostile directors and elect directors more receptive to a negotiated merger. The target's shareholders might even be induced to cooperate in such a plan if they favor the merger—further guaranteeing a successful merger.

Recent merger and acquisition activity, especially hostile takeovers, has spawned a new and unique language. The highlight "The Language of Mergers and Acquisitions" contains a description of some of the more colorful terms. For an example of how an antitakeover strategy is implemented, see the Highlight "Poison Puts as an Antitakeover Strategy."

■ *HIGHLIGHT*

THE LANGUAGE OF MERGERS AND ACQUISITIONS

The frenzied merger activity of the late 1970s and early 1980s produced a language unique to the field. For example:

1. *Blank check.* Authorizing issuance of new shares, usually preferred, at the discretion of the board of directors or even top management. Its most common purpose is to give friendly shareholders the necessary voting rights to help vote down a hostile takeover attempt.

2. *Shark repellants.* Amending the corporate charter or bylaws to make a takeover much more complex and costly, thereby discouraging it. For example, the amendment might require that more than a majority—a "super majority"—is required to approve a merger.

3. *Poison pill.* Creating a new class of security and subsequently implementing it if a takeover succeeds: for example, creating a new convertible that converts only if the takeover succeeds; hence it converts into the acquiring firm's shares, thereby effectively enhancing the exchange ratio dramatically in favor of the target shareholders. This strategy, because of its various permutations and possible consequences, has also been called the *doomsday machine.*

4. *"Scorched earth" strategy.* Implementing a defensive strategy that may threaten the very survivability of the target. Implementing this strategy causes massive problems for the target as well as the suitor.

5. *"Pac-Man" strategy.* Involving two companies trying to take over each other by buying the other firm's shares; each company tries to gobble up the other first. This strategy was immortalized in the Bendix–Martin Marietta takeover battle of 1982. This battle has been labeled the "Jonestown" strategy because of the suicidal debt burden that would have been the legacy of a successful Bendix–Martin Marietta corporation.

6. *Greenmail.* Accumulating a large block of a target's shares and threatening a fight to take over control of the firm, but with the hidden objective

of raising the market price of the shares and selling them for a premium. Texas oilman T. Boone Pickens was accused of this strategy in his apparent quest to take over Gulf in 1983 and 1984. The strategy was successful in that while the Pickens group did not wrest control from Gulf's management, he was instrumental in garnering hundreds of millions of dollars in profits for his investment group.

7. *White knight.* Coming to the rescue of a target firm threatened by a hostile takeover bid. The white knight usually acts at the request of the target and most commonly succeeds by acquiring the target itself.

8. *Crown jewel.* Refers to a very profitable or highly desirable division owned by the target firm that is especially sought after by the acquiring firm. In a defensive strategy employed by Carter–Hawley–Hale, Inc., a crown jewel in the form of Waldenbooks shops was sold to K Mart for $248 million in an attempt to thwart a takeover by The Limited, Inc.

■ *HIGHLIGHT*

POISON PUTS AS AN ANTITAKEOVER STRATEGY

The recent boon in takeover activity has been applauded by several stockholders who have benefited handsomely. However, many bondholders have suffered considerably. This is because acquiring firms typically use large amounts of debt to finance their takeover. The old bondholders' debt is perceived to have more risk, rating agencies downgrade the old debt, and the market value of the bonds tumbles.

To placate nervous bondholders, companies have attempted various new strategies, but one that is becoming very popular is the *poison put*. Bondholders who buy poison-put bonds can, in the event of takeover, put or redeem their debt under certain prespecified terms.

A recent example of a poison-put debt issue is W. R. Grace and Company's $250 million Eurobond issue with a poison-put provision. In fact, the company was forced to add the put feature at the insistence of potential debt holders. Sperry Corporation, another company that has been the subject of takeover speculation, is another example of a convertible debt issue with a poison-put provision.

Grace & Company's issue is convertible into common stock after five years. The debt holders can convert their debt into cash or Grace common stock if there is a "change in control." A change in control occurs, among other things, when "the company determines that any person is the . . . owner . . . of 30% or more of the outstanding stock."

Although Grace's poison put may not halt a potential takeover attempt, it undoubtedly introduces another layer of complexity in any takeover analysis. If bondholders choose to put their debt and convert to stock, an acquirer may have to issue new stock, thereby increasing the cost of the takeover.

★This information can be found on p. 13 of the W. R. Grace & Company prospectus, dated January 29, 1986.

697

Learning Check for Section 23•2

Review Questions

23•4.   Outline the different ways in which a friendly takeover can be effected.

23•5.   What are tender offers and proxy fights? Why do they take place?

New Terms

Dissenting shareholders	Friendly takeover	Proxy fight
	Hostile takeover	Tender offer

SECTION 23•3 *Other Forms of Corporate Restructuring*

In addition to mergers and acquisitions, there are several other popular forms of corporate reorganization currently in vogue. These include corporate sell-offs, liquidations, spin-offs, going private, and leveraged buyouts (LBOs). In this section, we provide a brief overview of these different forms of corporate reorganization.[7]

A SELL-OFF

KEY CONCEPT: A corporate **sell-off** is an exchange of assets for either cash or securities.

A sell-off of assets is simply a reverse merger from the point of view of the divesting firm. Although sell-offs are usually voluntary, sometimes a firm may be forced into an involuntary sell-off because of some regulatory action.

An example of a voluntary sell-off is the sale by Warner-Lambert of Entenmann's, a bakery business, to General Foods. A second example of a sell-off is the sale by INA Corporation of Hospital Affiliates International to Hospital Corporation of America. The sale of International Harvester's Solar Turbines International Division to Caterpillar Tractor, General Electric's sale of its metallurgical coal business, and Dun and Bradstreet's sale of its television stations are other examples.

Why do companies engage in a sell-off? Of the several reasons popularly advanced for sell-offs, two make economic sense. First, a company may be able to remove some diseconomies by selling off certain assets; second, a firm may

---

[7]This section draws heavily from the various excellent articles in the Summer 1984 issue of the *Midland Corporate Finance Journal.*

have found a buyer that is willing to pay more for the assets than its value to the seller. After reviewing the empirical evidence on sell-offs academic researchers have concluded that voluntary sell-offs increase the value of the selling companies.

The implications of this finding are that management should constantly review its assets and should consider selling assets if these assets will be worth more to some other company.

LIQUIDATIONS

KEY CONCEPT: A corporate **liquidation** represents the (usually) total sale of a company's assets.

A liquidation is thus an extreme form of a sell-off. Note that a liquidation is not the same as a shutting down of operations. In a liquidation the assets are sold to another firm and the proceeds are distributed to the company's stockholders. No reinvestment of the cash proceeds is involved. The organization ceases to exist in its current form. National Silver and Reeves Telecom are two firms that went through liquidations.

After analyzing the data on 25 liquidations between 1963 and 1982, Hite and Owers found that the market reacted strongly to liquidations. The evidence indicated that perhaps the firm's current organizational structure was not in the best interests of the shareholders. It was perhaps a recognition of this fact that motivated the companies to sell off their assets and return the proceeds to the investors.

SPIN-OFFS

KEY CONCEPT: A **spin-off** involves a separation of operations of a subsidiary from its parent.

Each separated unit acts as an independent corporation; however, there is no change in the ownership of the equity claims. That is, while the parent company gives up control of the subsidiary's operations, the shareholders maintain their proportionate ownership in both corporations.

Between 1963 and 1981 there were 93 voluntary spin-offs for companies listed on the American and New York stock exchanges. Such arrangements were initiated, for example, by Houston Oil and Mineral (which spun off Houston Oil Trust), Itek Corporation (which spun off its eyeglass manufacturing business—Camelot Industries Corporation—from its defense electronics business), and Valmac Industries (which spun off Distribuco, its food distribution subsidiary).

Several potential advantages of spin-offs have been cited. Some authors have suggested that there may be tax advantages, loosening of certain regulatory constraints, and increased managerial efficiencies from spin-offs. Empirical studies have revealed that a good number of spin-offs were motivated by tax-savings considerations.

GOING PRIVATE

When a public corporation becomes a private company it is said to have gone private. Although there are several transactions that qualify for this description we will discuss only pure going-private transactions here.

KEY CONCEPT: When the management (or major owner) of a corporation purchases the shares of outside stockholders and reorganizes the firm as a private company, it is said to have **gone private.**

A special form of going private is the leveraged buyout:

KEY CONCEPT: A **leveraged buyout (LBO)** is a going-private transaction in which the managers borrow funds from outside investors to buy out the shareholders.

There are several explanations that have been advanced for the going-private strategy. For small companies, the costs of having publicly traded stock can be expensive; registration costs, listing costs, and other costs arising out of the need to service stockholders can be large. Going private eliminates these costs. For example, the Congoleum Corporation went private in 1980 and the company estimated that the avoidance of annual reports, SEC filings, and so on, generated savings of between $6 and $8 million. Another explanation relates to incentive arrangements; by being both the owners and managers of the company, there is greater flexibility in designing incentive schemes. For example, a proxy statement for the buyout of Big Bear Stores contained a very innovative compensation scheme for management. With greater incentives, management has a greater interest in the firm's performance and well-being. In fact, managers may be willing to pay a premium to existing stockholders to afford them this joint owner-manager status. It is perhaps because of these potential benefits that recent academic research has found that, on average, public stockholders benefited from going-private transactions.

Learning Check for Section 23•3

Review Questions

23•6.   What is the difference between a merger and a sell-off?

23•7.   What are some advantages of a corporate spin-off?

23•8.   Is there a difference between going private and a leveraged buyout?

New Terms

Going private   Liquidation   Spin-off
Leveraged buyout   Sell-off

SUMMARY

Types of Business Combinations

The term *mergers* is often used loosely to refer to the various business combinations into which a firm can enter. Mergers are the result of corporate attempts to increase future growth through external expansion. Depending on the nature of the business combination, the terms *merger, consolidation,* or *holding company* may apply.

A merger between two companies with related business interests is a congeneric merger, while a horizontal merger takes place when two companies in the same line of business are combined. Vertical mergers occur when a firm acquires, say, its suppliers or distributors. When unrelated businesses combine, a conglomerate merger results.

Several reasons have been advanced for the increasing merger activity. Operating and financing advantages, the potential for enhanced growth opportunity, tax advantages, and diversification are advantages of mergers commonly cited. The diversification argument, however, raises several questions. For example, since investors can diversify on their own, why should companies do it for them?

How a Merger Is Effected

A merger can be effected through the purchase of a firm's assets or stock. A friendly takeover, one accepted by the target firm's management, may be accomplished by the purchase of the target firm's assets or stock. If the merger attempt is resisted by the target company, an unfriendly takeover can be effected via a tender offer, whereby the target's stock is purchased in the secondary market or directly from individual stockholders. A hostile takeover can also be accomplished via a proxy fight, in which acquirers seek to gain the votes of the target's shareholders and use them to vote out the target's hostile directors and elect directors more receptive to a negotiated merger.

Other Forms of Corporate Restructuring

There are several other popular forms of corporate reorganization. A corporate sell-off is an exchange of assets for either cash or securities. A corporate liquidation usually involves the total sale of a company's assets. A spin-off involves a separation of the operations of a subsidiary from its parent. A firm may

701

also go private, whereby a management group or major owner of a corporation purchases the shares of outside stockholders and reorganizes the firm as a private company. Another popular procedure is a leveraged buyout (LBO), whereby a group of managers borrow funds from outside investors to buy out the shareholders.

READINGS

DODD, PETER, AND RICHARD RUBACK. "Tender Offers and Stockholders Returns," *Journal of Financial Economics*, November 1977, 351–373.

HAUGEN, ROBERT A., AND TERENCE C. LANGETIEG, "An Empirical Test for Synergism in Merger," *Journal of Finance*, September 1975, 1003–1014.

HITE, GAILEN, AND J. OWERS, "Security Price Reactions Around Corporate Spin-off Announcements," *Journal of Financial Economics*, May, 1983, 409–436.

HOFFMEISTER, J. RONALD, AND EDWARD A. DYL, "Predicting Outcomes of Cash Tender Offers," *Financial Management*, Winter 1981, 50–58.

JENSEN, M. C., AND R. S. RUBACK, "The Market for Corporate Control: The Scientific Evidence," *Journal of Financial Economics*, April 1983, 5–50.

LINN, SCOTT C., AND MICHALE S. ROZEFF, "The Corporate Sell-off," *Midland Corporate Finance Journal*, Summer 1984.

MANDELKER, GERSHON, "Risk and Return: The Case of Merging Firms," *Journal of Financial Economics*, December 1974, 303–335.

MUELLER, DENNIS C., "The Effects of Conglomerate Mergers," *Journal of Banking and Finance*, December 1977, 315–347.

MYERS, S. C., "A Framework for Evaluating Mergers," in *Modern Developments in Financial Management*, ed. S. C. Myers (New York: Praeger Publishers, 1976).

SCHIPPER, K., AND R. THOMPSON, "Evidence on the Capitalized Value of Merger Activity for Acquiring Firms," *Journal of Financial Economics*, April 1983.

SHAD, S. R., "The Financial Realities of Mergers," *Harvard Business Review*, November–December 1969, 133–146.

24

Leasing

A primary concern for a growing company is the acquisition of physical and capital assets. These assets are presumably employed in an efficient manner in some type of productive activity such that shareholder wealth or total firm value is maximized. The decision to acquire assets is generally accompanied and intertwined with the problem of optimally financing this acquisition. Chapters 15 and 16 dealt with this problem in terms of the conventional forms of debt and equity. Alternative and hybrid forms of debt and equity instruments were also discussed in earlier chapters. Approximately 20% of new equipment acquired by companies is lease financed. Leasing represents yet another financing alternative, and one by which firms raise a substantial amount of capital. As will be seen, leasing can be viewed as a type of debt through which the firm is able to obtain the use of a physical asset, though not legal ownership. It is this use, however, not the actual ownership, that is of interest to the firm in pursuing its wealth-maximizing objectives.

This chapter presents briefly the different types of leasing arrangements in use today, the advantages of leasing, and the approaches to deciding whether an asset should be leased or purchased. When the proper framework has been established for evaluating leases, the firm can better achieve its prescribed objectives.

There are three sections in this chapter:

SECTION 24•1: *The Fundamentals of Leasing.* In this section, we introduce the terminology of leasing and consider the advantages of leasing, the different types of leasing arrangements in vogue today, and finally, some basic aspects of the tax code as it pertains to leasing.

SECTION 24•2: *Lease Analysis from the Lessee's Perspective.* In this section, we outline the procedures available to a firm in deciding between leasing and buying. Two equivalent approaches are presented.

SECTION 24•3: *Lease Analysis from the Lessor's Perspective.* The analysis of Section 24•2 is examined from the leasing company's perspective. As this section shows, the gains to the lessor are losses to the lessee, and the losses to the lessor are gains to the lessee.

SECTION 24•1 *The Fundamentals of Leasing*

WHAT IS A LEASE?

KEY CONCEPT: A **lease** is a type of rental agreement that typically involves a series of fixed payments that extend over several periods.

A lease represents a contract under which one party is entitled to use an asset for a specified period. In consideration of this use, the user is required to make periodic payments to the owner of the asset. Stated differently, a lease is a contract between a lessor and a lessee wherein the owner of an asset allows another party to use it for a leasing fee.

KEY CONCEPT: The **lessor** in a lease arrangement is the party that has the title to (i.e., owns) the property being leased.

KEY CONCEPT: The **lessee** in a lease arrangement is the party that has the use of the asset being leased.

Figure 24•1 compares leasing with purchasing, and illustrates the general relationship between the lessor and lessee and the use of an asset. Notice the similarities in the leasing and buying alternatives to the acquisition of an asset. If a company chooses to buy an asset, it has to raise the required capital by transacting in the capital markets. With the funds raised in this manner, it purchases (i.e., obtains the use, value, and title to) the asset from, say, an equipment dealer. This relationship contrasts with that of a lease purchase; if the firm decides to be the lessee in a lease contract, it simply enters into a lease contract with a leasing firm (lessor) and obtains use of the asset. The lessor, in this case,

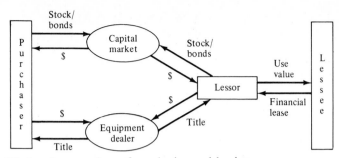

FIGURE 24·1 A comparison of purchasing and leasing.

has to raise the required capital for the purchase of the asset from the equipment dealer.

Consider the example of the Rhomberg Company, which requires the use of some expensive excavating equipment for, say, the next two years. One obvious alternative involves direct purchase of the equipment. However, if the company does not have the cash or if its credit sources are limited, it can perhaps raise new money in the capital markets by issuing stock or bonds. With the new funds, Rhomberg can buy the excavating machines. As an alternative, Rhomberg can approach Associated Leasing, Inc., and lease the equipment from this company by agreeing to specific terms spelled out in the lease contract or leasing agreement. Associated, in turn, will acquire the asset from the manufacturer in one of several possible ways. In this example, Rhomberg is the lessee and Associated Leasing is the lessor.

WHY LEASE?

If leasing is similar to borrowing, why do companies lease assets? How does one explain the phenomenal growth of the leasing industry in recent years? In addition to the potential economic advantages of leasing seen later in this chapter, there are several qualitative considerations that can make leasing attractive to a company. Some of these factors will now be discussed.

Increased Flexibility

A short-term lease is a cancellable lease that offers a firm flexibility. If Rhomberg expects to use the excavating machines for only a short time, it is perhaps not worthwhile to buy the machines and later sell them. With a cancellable lease, Rhomberg can return the machines to the lessor when it no longer needs them. This flexibility is especially attractive in the case of computer systems and other products undergoing rapid technological advances. If a technologically superior product comes to market, the firm can cancel the lease and enter into a new one for the new machine. Many managers cite flexibility as an important reason for leasing.

Certain Maintenance at a Known Cost

Leased equipment may include maintenance arrangements by the lessor, or alternatively, a maintenance contract can be purchased at a known cost.[1] This upper limit on the maintenance expenditure makes future cash flows less uncertain.

Lower Administrative Costs

A company can lower its organizational complexity and administrative costs through leasing. In very large operations, a company may find it more attractive to let some other party take care of the assets instead of having to create a new department within the firm to take care of the acquisition, maintenance, and eventual sale of the assets. Specialized leasing companies can usually do this job at a lower cost.

Lower Costs to the Lessor

There are several advantages available to the lessor that may not be available to the lessee. For example, if the lessor is an automobile leasing company, because of the typically large volume of cars purchased, automobile manufacturers usually offer their cars to these companies at "fleet rates." These rates may be much lower than the price that a company may have to pay for the car if it purchased it. In addition, because of the large volume, insurance rates, maintenance expenditures, the ease of eventual sale of the equipment, and so on, are more favorable to the lessor. These advantages can be passed on to the lessee in the form of lower lease payments.

An incredible number of incorrect justifications for leasing are often advanced. For example, "leasing defers capital expenditures," "leasing reduces property taxes," and "operating leases increase short-term incomes" are reasons commonly advanced for leasing. Leasing does not defer capital expenditures, although it does defer the expenditure of cash. However, the same effect can be achieved by borrowing. Although property taxes may be avoided by the lessee, the lessor pays the property taxes and this cost should be reflected in the lease payments. Thus this apparent cost-avoidance argument does not hold water. The fact that leasing can affect book income should have no impact on firm value. In efficient markets, investors can see through this fallacy. The *NOI* of the firm will determine the value of the company.

Until recently, leasing was viewed as a form of debt financing that does not show up on the balance sheet. In other words, it is considered a form of hidden debt. In this sense, leasing was considered to offer the advantage of off-balance-

---

[1] Of course, maintenance contracts are also available for assets purchased by the firm. However, for leased assets, maintenance contracts are often offered by the lessor and are typically cheaper than the contracts available through a third party.

sheet financing. However, with the advent of FASB 13 rule, capital leases (to be defined subsequently) are recognized as liabilities incurred by the firm and show up on the balance sheet.[2] When properly accounted for, analysts should treat leases as another factor contributing to increased financial leverage. Yet many managers believe that leases are not properly accounted for as debt in financial analyses. Whether this argument is valid is open to question. It is unlikely that a company can fool analysts by using this strategy.

TYPES OF LEASES

Several types of leases are utilized in financial markets. In general, they may be classified as:

1. Operating (or service) leases.

2. Financial (or capital) leases.

Special types of financial leases are the sale-leaseback, the direct lease, and the leveraged lease, to name but a few. These forms of leasing will now be discussed.

Operating Leases

Operating leases are characterized by the fact that the maintenance and service of the leased equipment are provided by the lessor; the cost of the maintenance and service are incorporated into the lease agreement or stated in a separate service contract. Typically, operating leases are for terms shorter than the usable life of the equipment. Since the lease payments do not ordinarily amortize the lessor's cost for the equipment, the returns to the lessor in addition to the lease payments are in the form of subsequent lease renewals or proceeds from the disposal of the equipment upon expiration of the lease.

Another common feature of operating leases is a cancellation clause that gives the lessee the right to cancel the lease agreement before expiration of the primary term. This has the effect of shifting the risks associated with technological obsolescence from the lessee to the lessor. Such a feature has important implications for both parties to the lease when the usefulness of the equipment is particularly exposed to technological advances such as those commonly seen in the computer industry.

Financial Leases

A **financial or capital lease** differs from an operating lease in that it is a noncancellable, longer-term lease that fully amortizes the lessor's cost for equip-

---

[2] FASB stands for Federal Accounting Standards Board, an organization that prescribes the correct accounting conventions in use today.

ment. Under this form of lease, service and maintenance are usually provided by the lessee. Further, the lessee may have to provide insurance and pay property taxes. In contrast to operating leases, financial leases typically have a term that corresponds more closely to the productive life of the asset. Automobile leases are an example of such financial leases.

Some financial leases provide for certain renewal or purchase options at the end of the lease term, although these options are subject to certain IRS restrictions. These and other tax considerations are discussed later in this chapter.

Sale-Leaseback Arrangement

A special type of financial lease often utilized by firms is the **sale-leaseback** arrangement. Under this arrangement, assets that are already owned by a firm are purchased by a lessor and leased back to the firm. The firm, as lessee, executes a lease agreement with the lessor, which ordinarily is a financial institution such as a commercial bank, insurance company, or leasing company.

The structure of this arrangement is analogous to a mortgage on the asset taken out by the lessee. Rather than making a series of payments to amortize a loan, however, the lessee makes a series of payments that amortize the lessor's acquisition costs and provide the lessor with a required return. By entering into this type of arrangement, the lessee firm (Rhomberg) can free the capital originally invested in the equipment.

Direct Leases

A **direct lease** is identical to the sale-leaseback arrangement, except that the lessee does not necessarily own the leased asset. The lessor already owns or acquires the asset, which is then provided to the lessee. Often the lessor is a manufacturer or a leasing company that is providing the asset and its financing to the lessee.

As an example, if Rhomberg had learnt that its competitor, Currie, Inc., had advertised the excavating equipment for sale, Rhomberg could ask Associated Leasing to purchase the asset from Currie and then lease it to Rhomberg.

Leveraged Leases

A **leveraged lease** is a special lease arrangement under which the lessor borrows a substantial portion of the acquisition cost of the leased asset from a third party. The *leverage* refers to the financial leverage used by the lessor in structuring the lease, and the risk associated with default by the lessee is partially borne by the third-party lender. Typically, leveraged leases involve only large assets due to the complexity and expense of structuring the lease arrangement. The third party financing the asset is usually an institution such as an insurance company or pension fund. Often this lender takes assignment of the lessor's interest in the lease and requires direct receipt of lease payments.

Returning to our preceding example, if Associated Leasing is unable to enter into the direct lease arrangement proposed by Rhomberg because it (Associated) is unable to come up with the capital to buy the equipment from Currie, Associated can finance its purchase of the excavating equipment with a loan from the Prudent Insurance Company. It can then enter into a direct lease with Rhomberg. This set of transactions constitutes a leveraged lease.

TAX CONSIDERATIONS IN LEASING

Taxes play a very important role in the structure of leases and in the value of leases to both the lessor and lessee. It is essential, therefore, to discuss certain IRS requirements imposed on lease agreements if one is to understand how and when various tax benefits associated with leasing can be captured and to whom these benefits apply.[3]

In general, a lease can be categorized as either a true lease or a conditional sale lease, depending on the nature of the lease agreement. The difference between these two types of leases is one of substance in the eyes of the IRS.

True Lease

Under a **true lease,** the lessee is able to deduct the lease payments fully for tax purposes. Further, the lessor may retain the tax depreciation deductions. In providing tax shields to the lessor, therefore, the true lease can, in certain cases, reduce the effective lease costs to the lessee. These costs and the benefits of leasing are discussed in the next section. A lease can qualify as a true lease provided that various IRS guidelines are met.

Five IRS requirements for a true lease are as follows:

1. The estimated fair market value of the leased asset at the expiration of the lease will equal or exceed 20% of the asset's original cost (excluding the effects of inflation or deflation).

2. The estimated remaining useful life of the leased asset beyond the term of the lease will equal or exceed 20% of the original estimated useful life of the asset and will be at least one year.

3. The lessee must not have the right to purchase the asset from the lessor at a price less than the fair market value.

4. The lessor must have a minimum "at risk" investment equal to at least 20% of the cost of the leased asset.[4]

5. The lease must provide a reasonable return to the lessor relative to the return on loans.

---

[3] This discussion of the tax aspects of leasing is kept to a minimum. The IRS guidelines have changed in recent years and are, of course, subject to future change. Since the actual details may vary in different lease situations, we outline only the general framework for recognizing these tax aspects. The tax adjustments used are very general, but they capture the substance of the current tax code.

[4] The "at risk" investment represents the lessor's equity interest in the leased asset.

Conditional Sale Lease

If any of the conditions just outlined are violated in a lease arrangement, the lease becomes a **conditional sale.** A conditional sale lease is one that is not particularly interesting in terms of the analysis of this chapter. It is viewed simply as an installment loan by the IRS if the previous guidelines are not met. In other words, the lessee is viewed as having, in fact, purchased the asset rather than having leased it, and the lessor is viewed as having financed this purchase via a loan. In other words, the IRS assumes that this is a regular purchase being labeled a lease simply for certain tax benefits.

For tax purposes, the lessee treats the property as owned and claims the depreciation. The lease payments are treated as loan payments, and the lessee may deduct only the portion that is equivalent to "interest" on the "loan." Therefore, for all intents and purposes, a conditional sale lease is a sale, and the analysis of such a transaction could be approached using the concepts discussed earlier in this book.

Learning Check for Section 24•1

Review Questions

24•1.   What are the advantages of leasing?

24•2.   What is the difference between operating and financial leases? What are some of the special forms of these leases?

24•3.   What are true and conditional sale leases?

New Terms

Capital lease	Lease	Operating lease
Conditional sale	Lessee	Sale-leaseback
Direct lease	Lessor	arrangement
Financial lease	Leveraged lease	True lease

SECTION 24•2 *Lease Analysis from the Lessee's Perspective*

There are two fundamental questions that a manager must answer in regard to the acquisition of physical assets: First, should an asset under consideration be acquired? Second, if the firm decides to acquire the asset, should it be purchased or leased? Putting this another way, since leasing is an alternative to borrowing, should the asset be lease financed or debt financed?[5]

A manager must pursue the alternative that is in the best interests of the stockholders. Thus the alternative that has the most favorable impact on firm value is the preferred alternative. To assess the impact of either alternative on firm value, an *NPV* analysis for leasing is required. This framework will now be developed.

To develop a framework for determining when leasing is financially attractive, the discussion will begin by considering financial leases.[6] As alluded to earlier, financial leases are substitutes for debt, since they provide for the use of an asset and commit the firm to a predetermined payment obligation. This fixed obligation forms the basis for our analysis of leases. Based on the concepts developed in Chapters 1, 2, and 3, any procedure for determining the value of leasing must include an examination of the cash flows resulting from the leasing decision.

Example 24•1   Calculating the Lessee's Cash Flows

Assume that Rhomberg requires the use of some excavating equipment for six years. The equipment costs $10,000. Rhomberg has previously determined the machine to be acceptable regardless of the way in which it is financed. That is, management has already determined the answer to the first of the two questions posed earlier. The question now facing Rhomberg is whether to finance the equipment with conventional debt (i.e., a term loan) or to lease it. The firm does not wish to use any equity to purchase the machinery. Rhomberg can borrow money at 12%. In addition, if Rhomberg buys the equipment, it can depreciate the equipment straight-line over the five years toward a zero salvage value.[7] Rhomberg is in the 25% tax bracket. Associated Leasing is amenable to a lease arrangement with Rhomberg under the following terms: life of lease, six years; annual lease payment, $2,200, with the first payment due upon signing the lease agreement.[8] The required analysis for this lease-versus-buy decision will now be examined.

Since leasing is a substitute for debt, the leasing decision can be approached by considering the opportunity costs of financing via a lease. If Rhomberg chooses to lease the equipment, it will lose the tax shield provided by depreciation—a benefit that would have accrued to Rhomberg if it had bought the

---

[5] This is not to imply that the firm should not pay for the asset in cash. Our intent here is to compare leasing with borrowing.

[6] Operating leases are more complex to value, since they are often cancellable; therefore, they are not discussed in this chapter.

[7] In this chapter and in the end of chapter problems it will be assumed that the entire asset value is depreciable.

[8] The lessor's decision to provide such a lease under these terms will be considered subsequently as a separate issue.

equipment. Also, there is a loss of the interest tax shield available through debt financing. However, the lease payments can be treated as an expense for tax purposes.

At this point, one could proceed by defining the total cash flows to the firm provided by leasing and by determining the appropriate *RRR* for use in discounting. Alternatively, lease and debt financing can be compared by examining the incremental (or decremental) cash flows incurred through leasing as compared to borrowing. This is sufficient, since the cash flows from the project itself are the same, regardless of the type of financing. Following this approach, therefore, the lease cash outflows (obligations of the firm) in period t, LCF_{Bt}, can be calculated as

$$LCF_{Bt} = \begin{cases} C - P(1 - T_B) & \text{for } t = 0 \\ -P(1 - T_B) - T_B D_t & \text{for } t > 0 \end{cases} \qquad (24\text{-}1)$$

where C = cost of the equipment leased

P = lease payment

D_t = forgone (lost) depreciation in period t

T_B = firm's (lessee's) marginal tax rate

LCF_{B0}, the initial (period 0) cash outflows from the lease arrangement, will be positive, as the firm gets the asset (effectively a cash inflow) without a net cash outlay. Since LCF_{Bt} represents cash outflows to the lessee, P and D_t will be negative.

For Rhomberg,

$$LCF_{B0} = \$10,000 - \$2,200(1 - 0.25) = \$8,350$$
$$LCF_{Bt} = \$-2,200(1 - 0.25) - (0.25)(\$2,000) = \$-2,150$$

Table 24•1 shows the details of the calculations implicit in the use of these equations for determining the lease cash flows.

It should be noted that the cash flow components of LCF_{Bt} may not possess the same risk. For example, the lease payment tax shield may be riskier than the lease payment if the firm will not have enough taxable income in future years to utilize the deduction. If that is the case, there will be separate discount rates for each of the respective cash flow items. For our purposes, we assume that all cash flows have the same risk. The question now is how to use the aforementioned lease cash flows in a decision framework such that the lease and debt financing alternatives can be properly evaluated.

TABLE 24•1   Lease Cash Flows to the Lessee

	Year					
	0	**1**	**2**	**3**	**4**	**5**
Equipment cost	$10,000					
Lease payment	−2,200	−2,200	−2,200	−2,200	−2,200	−2,200
Tax shield or lease payments[a]	550	550	550	550	550	550
Last tax shield on depreciation[b]	0	−500	−500	−500	−500	−500
Net cash flow	$ 8,350	$−2,150	$−2,150	$−2,150	$−2,150	$−2,150

[a]25% × $2,200
[b]25% × $2,000 annual depreciation

EVALUATION OF A LEASE VERSUS PURCHASE DECISION

Approach 1: The Equivalent Loan Approach

Since financing an asset via leasing is a substitute for debt financing, a comparison of the leasing and borrowing alternatives can be made by constructing an equivalent loan.

KEY CONCEPT: An **equivalent loan** is a loan whose net after-tax cash commitments imposed on the firm are identical to those imposed by leasing.

The idea underlying this approach to deciding between leasing and buying is simple. In the Rhomberg example, an annual cash outflow of $2,150 for five years generates a time 0 cash inflow of $8,350 for the company (see Table 24•1). The relevant question now is: What loan (i.e., what cash inflow) can Rhomberg get from its bank that will result in five annual cash payments of $2,150? The answer to this question will yield the equivalent annual loan. If the equivalent annual loan is greater than $8,350, Rhomberg should borrow from the bank and buy the equipment, if the equivalent annual loan is less than $8,350, Rhomberg should sign the lease agreement with Associated Leasing.

Calculating an equivalent loan is fairly straightforward. It is similar to the calculation of a uniform annual series, which we studied in Appendix 11•C. Since Rhomberg can borrow at 12% and since its tax bracket is 25%, the after-tax cost of the loan is 12% $(1 − 0.25) = 9.0\%$. Let the equivalent annual loan be X. Then

$$\$X = \$2,150(PVFA_{.09,5})$$

That is,

$$\$X = \$2,150(3.8897)$$
$$= \$8,362.86$$

The equivalent annual loan is therefore $8,362.86. That is, a loan of $8,362.86 from Rhomberg's bank will impose on Rhomberg a series of identical annual cash outflows as the lease.

Since the lease and the equivalent loan represent identical cash flow liabilities to the firm, one merely has to compare the net financing provided by the two alternatives, as shown in Table 24•2. Clearly, the leasing option available to the firm generates $12.86 less financing in this particular example. Thus the leasing alternative should be rejected and Rhomberg should fund the project with debt.

Approach 2: The Discounting Approach[9]

Another approach to evaluating financial leases is by discounting the lease cash flows with the appropriate discount rate. Let us begin by considering the lessee's before-tax cost of debt. Given that lease cash flows are debt-equivalent cash flows, it is appropriate to discount the after-tax lease cash flows with an after-tax discount rate. In this case, the after-tax cost of debt to the firm is $(1 - T_B)k_d$, since the payments on debt are tax deductible. As seen earlier, this works out to 9.0%.

Using $(1 - T_B)k_d$ as the appropriate discount rate, the *NPV* of the net after-tax lease cash flows from Table 24•1 is determined as follows:

TABLE 24•2 Comparison of Lease and Equivalent Loan Cash Flows

	Year					
	0	**1**	**2**	**3**	**4**	**5**
Lease cash flows[a]	$8,350	2,150	2,150	2,150	2,150	2,150
Equivalent loan cash flows	8,362.86	2,150	2,150	2,150	2,150	2,150
Difference	$−12.86	$0	$0	$0	$0	$0

[a] From Table 24•1.

[9] This approach is essentially the same as the previous approach; it makes the decision using *NPV* rather than the equivalent loan. The reader will notice the equivalence between the two approaches.

$$NPV = \$8,362.86 - \$2,150(PVFA_{.09,5})$$
$$= \$8,362.86 - \$2,150(3.8897)$$
$$= 0$$

a result that should come as no surprise.

Now determine the *NPV* of the lease. This is simply the net amount of financing provided by leasing less the present value of the lease cash flows. Since the lease alternative generates $8,350 in financing (Table 24•1) and requires net annual payments of $2,150, the *NPV* of this transaction is

$$NPV_B = \$8,350 - \$2,150(PVFA_{.09,5})$$
$$= \$8,350 - \$2,150(3.8897)$$
$$= \$-12.86$$

Since the *NPV* is negative, Rhomberg should not accept the lease financing but, instead, should borrow.

Learning Check for Section 24•2

Review Questions

24•4. How would you calculate the lease cash flows to a firm leasing an asset? Why?

24•5. Explain the equivalent loan approach to making a lease/buy decision.

24•6. What is the standard *NPV* approach to making a lease/buy decision?

New Term

Equivalent loan

SECTION 24•3 *Lease Analysis from the Lessor's Perspective*

What about the lessor's perspective on leasing? It is clear that the lessor will be willing to enter into a lease agreement provided that the project earns, at a minimum, his company's weighted-average cost of capital, $WACC_L$ (remember that the subscript L denotes the lessor as a lender).[10] Thus the lease will be

---

[10] Again, it is important to recognize that *WACC* is being used instead of *RRR* only to simplify the exposition. The implicit assumption here is that the lease project has the same risk level as the leasing company itself.

structured such that the implicit interest rate paid by the lessee will be at least the lessor's $WACC_L$.

The lessor's cash flows are analogous to those of the lessee, but with a reversal of sign. In addition, the lessor will be exposed to its own marginal tax rate, T_L. The cash flows to the lessor can therefore be denoted as

$$LCF_{Lt} = P(1 - T_L) + T_L D_t \tag{24-2}$$

Table 24•3 depicts these cash flows to the lessor under the assumption that the lessor has the same tax rate as the lessee (i.e., $T_L = T_B = 0.25$).

The value of the lease to the lessor in this example can be determined by discounting the lessor's cash flows, LCF_{Lt}, by the lessor's opportunity cost, $WACC_L$. Let us assume that $k_d = 0.12$, so that $WACC_L = (1 - T_B)k_d = 0.09$. Since the net cash outflow to the lessor at time 0 is $8,350 and the cash inflows amount to $2,160 per year for five years, the NPV of this project to the lessor is

$$NPV_L = \$-8,350 + \$2,150(PVFA_{.09,5}) = \$12.86$$

Notice that NPV_L is exactly the same as NPV_B except for the opposite sign. Thus, with $T_L = T_B$ and $WACC_L = (1 - T_B)k_d$, the gains to the lessor from leasing are exactly offset by the losses to the lessee (and vice versa). (See the highlight "The Growing Trend in Leasing Aircraft.")

TABLE 24•3 Cash Flows to the Lessor

			Year			
	0	**1**	**2**	**3**	**4**	**5**
Equipment cost	$-10,000					
Lease revenue[a]	2,200	2,200	2,200	2,200	2,200	2,200
Tax on lease revenue[b]	-550	-550	-550	-550	-550	-550
Tax shield on depreciation[c]		500	500	500	500	500
Net cash flow to lessor	$- 8,350	$2,150	$2,150	$2,150	$2,150	$2,150

[a] Lease payment required by lessor.
[b] $0.25 \times \$2,200 = \$550$
[c] $0.25 \times$ depreciation $= .25(2,000) = 500$

■ *HIGHLIGHT*

THE GROWING TREND IN LEASING AIRCRAFT

Since the 1986 tax bill eliminated several incentives for capital expenditures such as Investment Tax Credits and accelerated depreciation, many large companies have altered the manner in which they acquire the use of expensive equipment to run their businesses. Perhaps the most dramatic changes are taking place in the airline business which has seen a steep increase in the practice of leasing aircraft from operating lease companies. Major airline companies such British Airways, Lufthansa, Singapore Airlines, Malaysian Airlines and even small companies such as the Seattle-based Alaska Air Group have leased much of their aircraft needs. In 1981 about seven percent of all commercial aircraft deliveries went to lease companies; in the first half of 1988 this figure has already exceeded 50%.

Many of these companies have found leasing to be a more attractive alternative than an outright purchase through debt. Managers have argued that leasing increases their "flexibility" and many small undercapitalized companies have found it easier to lease than to buy aircraft. Of course, these smaller companies pay a higher lease rate, but apparently, they still find leasing attractive. America West Airlines, for example, says that its launch in 1983 would not have been possible if it had to purchase outright its $70 million of aircraft.

With the growing demand for leased aircraft the lessor market has seen some major new players. International Lease Finance Corporation of Beverly Hills, California, which pioneered the operating lease industry in 1972 received orders for $6.6 billion of aircraft in May 1988 alone. The GPA Group Ltd., based in Shannon, Ireland is another major leasing company currently managing $1.7 billion in aircraft that has been leased. Aircraft manufacturers themselves are becoming lessors—American Airlines' March 1987 $2.5 billion acquisition of 25 Airbus A300s and 15 Boeing 767s were leased from the manufacturers. A more interesting concept is the joint venture McDonnell Douglas Corp. has formed with GPA, known as Irish Aerospace, to facilitate leasing of its new MD-11 jumbo jets.

How long this leasing boom will survive is not clear. With increased demand for leased aircraft, lease rates have already started rising. Alaska Air Group found that its leasing rates shot up by 14% in one year. Alaska Air now has begun to rely less on leasing its aircraft. United Airlines, is another case in point: Its chief financial officer argues that "the cost is too much vis-a-vis the flexibility. It's easy to get leases, but you pay a lot of money for them."

Source: Compiled from information in "For Airplane Lessors, Business Is Greater", *The Wall Street Journal*, May 20, 1988.

Learning Check for Section 24•3

Review Question

24•7.   How would you calculate the cash flows to a lessor? Why?

SUMMARY

The Fundamentals of Leasing

Leasing represents an alternative form of debt financing for the firm. As a substitute for debt, therefore, its value to the firm relative to straight debt financing can be determined by comparing the lease to an equivalent loan. Alternatively, this value can be ascertained by discounting the lease cash flows at the appropriate discount rate (i.e., the firm's after-tax borrowing cost).

Leasing is advantageous for some firms. Leases may allow increased flexibility, cheap and certain maintenance, lower administrative costs, and to lower costs to the lessor.

Leases are generally placed in one of five categories. Operating leases stipulate that the maintainance and service of the equipment will be provided by the lessor. Financial leases are noncancellable agreements that fully amortize the lessor's cost of the equipment. In a sale-leaseback arrangement, a firm may sell its assets to a lessor and then lease them back. A direct lease is similar to the sale-leaseback arrangement, except that the lessee does not own the equipment. Finally, a levered lease is one in which the lessee borrows a substantial part of the acquisition cost of the leased asset from a third party.

Lease Analysis from the Lessee's Perspective

A manager seeking to acquire an asset must compare the advantages of leasing the asset and borrowing to obtain the asset, and pick the alternative that is in the best interest of the stockholders. The lessee's cash flows must be calculated and evaluated, using either the equivalent loan approach or the discounting approach.

Lease Analysis from the Lessor's Perspective

The cash flows accruing to the lessor must be examined in a manner similar to that of the lessee. The lessor will be willing to enter into a lease agreement only if the project earns, at a minimum, his companies weighted-average cost of capital. The lessor's cash flows are analogous to those of the lessee but with a reversal of sign.

PROBLEMS[11]

24•1.   Sally Wheeler needs to acquire the use of a crane for her construction business and cannot decide whether to buy or lease. The crane costs

---

[11] Some of the problems in this chapter require the use of a financial calculator.

$50,000 and can be depreciated straight-line to a zero salvage value in five years. Sally has a marginal tax rate of 34%. Lease payments are $11,000 annually.

(a) Find the net initial outlay and the tax shield on depreciation for each of the next five years if the crane is purchased.

(b) Suppose that the lease expense is payable at the beginning of each of the next five years and that the tax savings resulting from the lease deduction are recognized as the payment is made. Find the after-tax cash flow from the leasing alternative for each of the next five years.

(c) What is the amount of financing the lease provides? What is the decremental cash flow for each of the next five years?

(d) What should Sally do if her firm's before-tax cost of debt is 10%? What if it is 15%?

24•2. Linda Gillum has been assigned the task of acquiring the use of some laser equipment used for printing and binding by her employer, the Gambit Publishing Company. Linda can purchase the equipment for $120,000 and will depreciate it straight-line to a salvage value of zero in five years. Alternatively, it can be leased for $30,000 annually, payable and deductible at the beginning of each of the next five years. Gambit's marginal tax rate is 25%.

(a) What are the net initial outlay and the tax shield generated by depreciation each year if the equipment is purchased?

(b) Find the after-tax cash flow associated with the leasing alternative for each of the next five years.

(c) What is the amount of financing that the lease provides?

(d) What should Linda do if the before-tax cost of debt is 16%?

(e) What should Linda do if the before-tax cost of debt is 20%?

24•3. William Juraschek, co-owner of Topologico's Bar and Grille, intends to acquire the use of a margarita machine for each of his three current restaurants. The machines cost $30,000 each. If purchased, they would be depreciated straight-line to a salvage value of zero in five years. They are actually expected to last for eight years and to have a salvage value of zero at that time. The machines can be leased for $5,000 each per year, payable and deductible at the beginning of each year. Topologico's marginal tax rate is 34%, and the before-tax cost of debt is 16%.

(a) What is the net initial outlay associated with purchase of the machines? What is the tax shield generated by depreciation for each of the next eight years?

(b) What is the annual after-tax lease expense?

(c) What is the immediate savings incurred (financing provided) by the lease? What is the decremental cash flow for each of the next eight years?

(d) What should William do?

(e) What should William do if the machines are actually expected to last 10 years rather than 8 years?

24•4. Larry Moss, financial manager of Goring Industries, is trying to determine whether Goring should lease or buy five new trucks that are necessary for a six-year project that is being undertaken. The trucks cost $18,000 each. The trucks, if purchased, will be depreciated straight-line to a salvage value of $5,000 each at the end of six years. The lease payments would be $14,000 annually, payable at the beginning of each year. The tax savings from the lease deduction are recognized as the payment is made. Goring's marginal tax rate is 25%, and the before-tax cost of debt is 15%.

(a) Find the initial outlay and the subsequent after-tax cash flows at the end of each of the next five years if the trucks are purchased.

(b) Find the annual after-tax cash flow for the leasing alternative.

(c) Find the financing provided by the lease and the decremental cash flow for each of the next six years.

(d) What should Larry do?

24•5. Richard Wood, owner of the Victoria Child Care Center, Inc., is considering acquisition of 20 personal computers for a class he is developing. The computers can be purchased for $2,000 each and would be depreciated straight-line over a five-year period. Their anticipated value at the end of five years is zero. Alternatively, the computers can be leased for $10,150 annually, payable at the end of each year. The deduction is recognized as the payments are made. Richard's before-tax cost of debt is 15%.

(a) What is the initial outlay associated with purchase? What are the annual tax savings from depreciation if the Center's tax rate is 34%?

(b) What is the annual after-tax cash flow associated with leasing if the tax rate is 34%?

(c) What is the net financing provided by the lease? What is the decremental cash flow from the lease?

(d) Should Richard lease or buy the computers?

(e) What are the annual tax savings from depreciation if the Center's tax rate is 25%?

(f) What is the annual after-tax cash flow associated with leasing if the tax rate is 25%?

(g) What is the net financing provided by the lease? What is the decremental cash flow from the lease? What should Richard do?

24•6. The Ajax Leasing Company has just received an order from a client who wishes to lease four cement mixers for five years. Ajax can buy the cement mixers for $25,000. Ajax will depreciate them straight-line to a salvage value of zero in five years. Ajax will finance this project with debt; they can secure a five-year note at the prime rate of 16%. Lease payments will be received at the beginning of each year and are subject to taxation immediately upon receipt.

(a) What must Ajax's annual rental be if they are in the 34% tax bracket and the cement mixers have a salvage value of zero in five years?

(b) What must Ajax's annual rental be if they are in the 15% tax bracket and the cement mixers have a salvage value of zero in five years?

(c) What must Ajax's annual rental be if they are in the 34% tax bracket and the cement mixers have a salvage value of $4,000 each in five years?

(d) What must Ajax's annual rental be if they are in the 15% tax bracket and the cement mixers have a salvage value of $4,000 each in five years?

24•7. John Feo, financial manager of the National Delivery Service, needs to acquire the use of 200 Jeeps for the next six years. The Jeeps can be purchased for $12,000 and have an estimated salvage value of $3,000 each in six years. If purchased, the Jeeps will be depreciated straight-line to a salvage value of zero in three years. Alternatively, the Jeeps can be leased for $2,320 each annually, due at the beginning of each year. National's before-tax cost of debt is 16%, and their tax rate is 34%.

(a) Suppose that the tax deduction for the lease payments is recognized as the payment is made. What is the after-tax lease expense each year? What are the amount of financing provided by the lease and the decremental cash flow for each year? What should John do?

(b) Suppose that the tax deduction for the lease payments is not recognized until the next tax bill is due, one year after the payment is made (e.g., the payment made now is deducted one year from today, the payment made one year from today is deducted two years from today, etc.). What is the after-tax payment made today? What is the after-tax cash flow for each of years 1 to 5? What is the after-tax cash flow for year 6? What should John do?

24•8. Fill in the blanks for the following calculations of an equivalent loan. The tax rates remain the same for all five years. (Hint: Start with the last column and work backward.)

			Year			
	0	**1**	**2**	**3**	**4**	**5**
Principal balance (end of year)			$16,346.38	$9,327.16	$1,886.79	0
Interest (10%)	0				$932.72	$188.68
Tax shield on interest	0					
Effective after-tax interest expense	0					$113.21
Payment of principal	0			$7,019.22	$7,440.37	$1,886.79
Net cash flow		$-8,000	$-8,000	$-8,000	$-8,000	$-2,000

24•9.   Don Morrison of the Morrison Construction Company needs to acquire the use of a tractor for the next three years. Don has found a used tractor that he can purchase for $18,000. The tractor will be depreciated straight-line to a salvage value of zero in three years. Alternatively, Don can lease the tractor for $5,000 annually, due at the beginning of each year. The deduction for the lease payments is realized as soon as the payments are made. Don can take out a bank loan at a 15% interest rate. The company's marginal tax rate is 25%.
   (a)   What is the net financing provided by the lease?
   (b)   What is the after-tax lease payment at the end of each of years 1, 2, and 3? What is the tax shield generated from depreciation?
   (c)   Find the equivalent loan of the lease. Should Don lease or buy the tractor?

24•10.   Virginia Pierson is trying to decide whether to lease or buy a smelting oven for the construction of an electric plant. The oven costs $60,000 and would be depreciated straight-line to a salvage value of zero in five years. Virginia's firm's tax rate is 34%, and the before-tax cost of debt is 15%.
   (a)   What is the initial outlay required to purchase the oven?
   (b)   What cash flow will be generated from depreciation at the end of each of the next five years?
   (c)   Using the after-tax cost of debt, find the *PV* of all cash flows associated with purchase of the oven.
   (d)   Suppose that Virginia can lease the oven for $15,000 annually, payable at the beginning of each year, and the resulting tax deduction is recognized immediately. What is the after-tax lease payment? The *PV* of the after-tax lease payment? Should Virginia lease or buy?
   (e)   Suppose that Virginia can lease the oven for $13,000 annually, payable at the beginning of each year, and the resulting tax deduc-

tion is recognized immediately. What is the after-tax lease payment? Should Virginia lease or buy?

(f) What would the annual lease payment have to be in order for Virginia to be indifferent between leasing and buying?

READINGS

BOWER, R. S., "Issues in Lease Financing," *Financial Management*, Winter 1973, 25–34.

BREALEY, R. A., AND C. M. YOUNG, "Debt, Taxes, and Leasing—A Note," *Journal of Finance*, December 1980, 1245–1250.

FABOZZI, F. J., *Equipment Leasing: A Comprehensive Guide for Executives* (New York: Dow Jones-Irwin, Inc., 1982).

LEVY, HAIM, AND MARSHALL SARNAT, "Leasing, Borrowing, and Financial Risk," *Financial Management*, Winter 1979, 47–54.

LEWELLEN, WILBUR G., MICHAEL S. LONG, AND JOHN J. McCONNELL, "Asset Leasing in Competitive Capital Markets," *Journal of Finance*, June 1976, 787–798.

MILLER, MERTON H., AND CHARLES W. UPTON, "Leasing, Buying, and the Cost of Capital Services," *Journal of Finance*, June 1976, 761–786.

O'BRIEN, THOMAS J., AND BENNIE H. NUNNALLY, JR., "A 1982 Survey of Corporate Leasing Analysis," *Financial Management*, Summer 1983, 30–36.

SCHALL, L. D., "The Lease-or-Buy and Asset Acquisition Decisions," *Journal of Finance*, September 1974, 1203–1214.

25

International Financial Management

Over 85% of the world is not the United States. This observation suggests that in the absence of restrictive government regulations, American companies should be able to expand their sales markets significantly by going overseas, thereby improving their profit position. For example, the opening up of China's doors to U.S. firms has had the effect of dramatically increasing the market for Coca-Cola, as the new market has expanded by over 1 billion people. It is this potential for added profit that motivates American firms (or any nation's firms) to pursue lucrative overseas markets.

Because of the enormous resources invested by American companies overseas (especially in Europe), it is often said that the fate of some European economies is tied inextricably to the fate of the multinationals.[1] The power and influence of American multinational companies are immense. Every one of America's top 50 manufacturing companies (in sales) is multinational. IBM, Monsanto, Union Carbide, General Motors, Texas Instruments—the list goes on and on—are all American multinational companies.

But why do companies invest directly abroad? For example, why doesn't General Motors simply ship its locally produced cars to the United Kingdom instead of establishing manufacturing plants there? Why do American multina-

---

[1] Because of the enormous dependence of the European economy on U.S. firms, it is often said that "when the United States has a cold, Europe sneezes."

tional companies invest billions of dollars overseas, providing employment opportunities and economic advancement to those countries?

There are several reasons for investing abroad. The most obvious consideration is the principle of comparative advantage, which is usually provided as the classic reason for international trade. Comparative advantage suggests that each nation's workers should be used where they have the largest advantage or the smallest disadvantage relative to those of other countries. That way, all nations involved will benefit. It is generally felt that American businesses have certain managerial and technical skills that enable them to perform well in other countries. Thus, by directly investing abroad and using these resources in conjunction with their special managerial and technical skills, U.S. companies can use the principle of comparative advantage to their greatest benefit.

Another reason for overseas investing is the relative costs of capital and labor at home and abroad. With very high labor costs in the United States, companies tend to be more capital intensive (i.e., have more operating leverage, in the language of Chapter 8). For a labor-intensive product, American companies may find it more profitable to operate in a country such as Taiwan, where labor costs are relatively low. Operational constraints such as excessive transportation and insurance costs and government regulations can also induce a company to invest in plants overseas rather than at home.

Companies often manufacture abroad to avoid tariffs. To sell American-made computers in France may involve a tariff payment to the French government, while the same computer made in France may be exempt from this fee. Since tariffs put increasing upward pressure on the price of the final product, cost-conscious firms may be inclined to manufacture their products directly in the host countries. Tax laws can also make a big difference; with favorable taxation, companies have higher cash flows. Great Britain, for example, has often allowed multinationals to take any amount of annual depreciation that they needed to offset profits until the asset was fully depreciated. Finally, by investing abroad, the company gets some benefits from diversification. By spreading risks across several nations, firms are, in effect, creating a risk-reducing portfolio of investments for their stockholders.

In this chapter, we provide a very broad overview of the international finance environment and suggest some guidelines for financial decision making for American firms investing abroad.

SECTION 25•1: *The International Financial Environment.* In this section, we define exchange rates and examine the function of spot rates and forward rates. The major determinants of exchange rates and the political risks faced in international trade conclude the section.

SECTION 25•2: *The Multinational Firm.* This section presents the potential internal and external funding sources for multinational companies, the special features of international cash management techniques, and the various documents frequently used in international trade transactions.

SECTION 25•3: *Capital Budgeting for Multinational Companies.* The special considerations involved in making capital budgeting decisions for multinational companies are introduced in this section. Factors affecting the cash flows from projects and the problems with determining an appropriate discount rate for overseas projects are also reviewed. It must be stressed, however, that given the complexity of international financial management, this is simply a brief introduction to this topic.

SECTION 25•1 The International Financial Environment

EXCHANGE RATES

Different countries have different currencies, and all economic activity within a country is done in terms of the local currency. Frenchmen buy their wines in French francs, Englishmen buy stout in pounds, and the Japanese farmer would probably not accept any currency other than the yen. Hence a problem arises when one country does business with another. Americans may not want yen, so an American company that supplies soft drinks to Japan will have to convert its yen into dollars.[2] Obviously, there needs to be a rule for such currency conversions. This rate of conversion is the exchange rate. (See the highlight "The Evolution of the Current Exchange-Rate System.")

■ *HIGHLIGHT*

THE EVOLUTION OF THE CURRENT EXCHANGE-RATE SYSTEM

The world economy has undergone many changes over the years with regard to exchange-rate agreements. A brief review of the evolution of the current *floating rate* system is now presented. Since several countries have their own independent exchange rate rules even today, this historical review will provide some perspective on the exchange-rate systems of other countries today.

The Gold Standard (1880–1914)

The need for a formalized system for the settlement of international payments became clear in the free-trade era of the late nineteenth century. Britain was the first country to adopt the gold standard, but other countries joined in, so that by the 1880s all major trading countries were on a gold standard. The countries declared a par value for their currencies in terms of gold, thereby linking them

---

[2]For a discussion of the role of different currency types in the world economy, see S. P. Magee and R. K. S. Rao, "Vehicle and Non-Vehicle Currencies in International Trade," *American Economic Review;* May 1980, 368–373.

together in a worldwide fixed-exchange-rate system. The four main characteristics of the gold standard at that time were: (1) all monetary units were defined as a fixed quantity of gold; (2) there was free and unlimited coinage of gold; (3) all currencies were freely convertible into gold (*convertibility*); and (4) gold was freely imported and exported for private payment.

Interwar Period (1918–1939)

During World War I this gold standard system was disrupted; for both economic and political reasons the flow of private gold stopped. After the war and during a period of freely fluctuating exchange rates, the restoration of the gold standard became the prime economic objective of many countries. The restored gold standard, however, did not circulate gold coins; rather, countries were linked to gold by the central banks' promise to purchase and sell gold bullion at a fixed price. Some countries, Great Britain and France, for example, repegged their currencies at unrealistic prices with respect to the severe postwar inflation experienced in Europe. During the 1930s, country after country abrogated its banks' obligations to meet its note and deposit liabilities in gold. In 1934, the United States suspended convertibility of its currency and made it illegal for private citizens to hold gold except in its natural state or in coins with recognized value to collectors. World depression brought about competitive devaluations in an attempt to stimulate exports to increase the GNP. Exchange controls and tariffs were also utilized to protest domestic markets. With these economic pressures and the outbreak of World War II, the gold standard again disintegrated.

Bretton Woods (1944–1970)

In 1944, representatives from the United States, Great Britain, and other Allied nations held a conference in Bretton Woods, New Hampshire, to reach agreement on a new international monetary system. Their goals were to establish an arrangement that would be (1) multilateral with the agreement and participation of all major countries, (2) nondiscriminatory, (3) achieve stable currency rates, and (4) promote free trade. Under the Bretton Woods system, each country defined its currency in terms of the U.S. dollar, and the dollar, in turn, was pegged to gold at $35 per ounce. A central rate or par value was set, and the countries were committed to maintaining a market rate for their currencies within ±1% of the central rate. The International Monetary Fund (IMF) was established to monitor the member countries' exchange rates and to provide short-term loans to countries that were experiencing difficulty in maintaining par value because of balance of payments disequilibrium. Countries could adjust their par values, but only to correct "fundamental" disequilibrium in its balance of payments and only after prior approval from the IMF.

Bretton Woods, although essentially a gold standard system, established the U.S. dollar as a *key currency*. A key currency is defined as a currency that functions as a quotation currency or a unit of account, a transaction currency that may be used as legal tender to effect commercial transactions, and an asset currency that is held either as a private asset or an official reserve asset. Since the U.S. dollar was convertible into gold, countries were willing to accept the dollar as a reserve asset because it was "as good as gold." With the increased volume of international trade and investment in the 1950s, the growth of the gold stock obviously could not expand as rapidly as the need for monetary gold. However, countries could acquire dollar reserves by running balance-of-payments surpluses and accepting the dollar as payment. To provide liquidity to the world system in the form of increased gross reserves, the United States ran large balance-of-payments deficits that were financed through the exporting of gold and through foreign monetary authorities accepting dollar balances as reserve assets.

As long as other countries had confidence in the U.S. dollar and its convertibility, the system ran smoothly. By 1971, however, the U.S. gold stock had dwindled to approximately $12 billion, while foreign dollar holdings were up to about $60 billion. In August 1971, Nixon suspended gold convertibility and allowed the dollar to devalue. Thus the Bretton Woods system collapsed.

Smithsonian Agreement (1971–1973)

In an attempt to reestablish a fixed-rate system, the Smithsonian Agreement realigned exchange rates with significant changes from their value under Bretton Woods. Japan increased the yen value relative to the dollar by 17%, and Germany increased the deutsche mark (DM) value by 14% relative to the dollar. The U.S. dollar was devalued with respect to gold by slightly less than 8% from $35 to $38.02 per ounce of gold. Again, countries established a central rate with respect to the dollar, but with a 2¼% margin on either side of the par value. Nevertheless, the system was not adequate to withstand the pressures of the worldwide balance of payments disequilibrium, and it soon became apparent that a fixed-rate system was not sustainable. By March 1973, all the major currencies were allowed to float.

Managed Float (1973–present)

Under our current system, exchange rates float with market supply and demand. However, national monetary authorities may intervene in the foreign exchange market at their discretion to prevent disruptive exchange-rate movements.

There are several different exchange-rate policies today. Some currencies have continued to be pegged to a major currency or to a basket of currencies. A group of European countries have joined together in the European Monetary System, in which they maintain a fixed rate among themselves and float as a group with respect to the rest of the world currencies. This is referred to as a *joint float*. Still other currencies have adopted a *crawling peg*, which may best be described as a pegged currency with many mini-devaluations, adjusting frequently to reflect market conditions. The most frequent criticism of today's system is the volitility of the exchange rates. Nonetheless, the rapid growth in the volume of international trade since the advent of floating rates may be evidence that floating rates allow for sufficient absorption of serious shocks to the world economy, such as recession and inflation, without serious repercussions in international trade.

The exchange rate, which is set by demand and supply in the international capital markets, can be viewed conveniently as the price per unit of foreign currency. The price an American would have to pay in dollars for 1 Japanese yen is the dollar-yen exchange rate and is expressed as $/yen (dollars per unit of foreign currency). Sometimes exchange rates are quoted in terms of the number of units of foreign currency per dollar. For example, if the exchange rate is

$0.001/yen, the same exchange rate quoted in yen/$ is 1,000. Care must be taken to understand the manner in which the exchange rate is quoted.

Perhaps the most distinctive aspect of international management is that firms doing business overseas have the constant problem of exchange-rate fluctuations. We already know that the uncertainty in predicting cash flows even for a domestic company can influence virtually all financial decisions. Even if a foreign cash flow can be predicted accurately in terms of the foreign currency, the value of the cash flow in dollars is uncertain because managers do not know the future exchange rate. Since exchange rates permeate virtually every aspect of international finance, a large portion of the discussion in this section focuses on exchange rates.

In general, the principles for financial decision making that are applicable to a domestic company are just as applicable to a firm doing business overseas. However, the number of additional variables that must be taken into account makes the process considerably harder.

Spot Rates and Forward Rates

The exchange rates of major trading partners of the United States are quoted daily in the *Wall Street Journal*. Since the foreign exchange market's prices are constantly changing, the rate quoted is that of the previous day at 3:00 P.M. Eastern Standard Time. An example is shown in Figure 25•1. The *Wall Street Journal* quotes currencies both directly, or as U.S. dollars per unit of foreign exchange, and indirectly, or as foreign currency per U.S. dollar. On June 8, 1988, for example, the Danish krone was quoted at $0.1533. Figure 25•1 also shows that 1 U.S. dollar was equivalent to 6.5250 krone. Note that these two exchange rates are simply reciprocals of one another (6.5250 = 1/0.1533).

In discussing exchange rates, it is important to distinguish between spot exchange rates and forward exchange rates. Some of the exchange rates in Figure 25•1 are spot rates and others are forward exchange rates.

Foreign exchange may be purchased or sold for immediate delivery (at the spot exchange rate) or for delivery at a future date (at the forward exchange rate). For example, a business manager who needs to convert French francs (FF) into American dollars can do so immediately at the **spot exchange rate** (5.8185 FF to the dollar on June 8, 1988). On the other hand, if he expects to get the French francs 90 days from now, he may wish to avoid the uncertainty of the exchange rate at that time. In this case, the manager can still lock in a future exchange rate by agreeing today to sell francs in the 90-day forward market at an exchange rate called the **forward rate**. From Figure 25•1 again, this exchange rate was 5.8120 francs per dollar on June 8, 1988. The business manager is entering into a contract today in which he promises to sell francs for $1/5.8120 each on June 8, 1988. Thus he has eliminated exchange risk; rather than being dependent on the June 8 spot rate, he has locked in a price of 17.21 cents per franc.

Wednesday, June 8, 1988

The New York foreign exchange selling rates below apply to trading among banks in amounts of $1 million and more, as quoted at 3 p.m. Eastern time by Bankers Trust Co. Retail transactions provide fewer units of foreign currency per dollar.

Country	U.S. Dollar Equiv.		Currency per U.S. Dollar	
	Wed.	Tues.	Wed.	Tues.
Argentina	.1350	.1350	7.405	7.405
Australia (dollar)	.8060	.7990	1.2407	1.2516
Austria (schilling)	.08299	.08292	12.05	12.06
Bahrain (dinar)	2.6525	2.6525	.377	.377
Belgium (franc)				
Commercial rate	.02788	.02789	35.87	35.86
Financial rate	.02779	.02778	35.98	36.00
Brazil (cruzado)	.005869	.005914	170.40	169.09
Britain (pound)	1.8095	1.8130	.5526	.5516
30–day forward	1.8087	1.8122	.5529	.5518
90–day forward	1.8063	1.8091	.5536	.5528
180–day forward	1.8015	1.8035	.5551	.5545
Canada (dollar)	.8182	.8135	1.2222	1.2293
30–day forward	.8171	.8123	1.2239	1.2310
90–day forward	.8147	.8098	1.2274	1.2348
180–day forward	.8114	.8066	1.2324	1.2398
Chile (official rate)	.004057	.004057	246.47	246.47
China (yuan)	.2687	.2687	3.7220	3.7220
Colombia (peso)	.003404	.003404	293.79	293.79
Denmark (krone)	.1533	.1531	6.5250	6.5300
Ecuador (sucre)				
Official rate	.004008	.004008	249.50	249.50
Floating rate	.002099	.002099	476.50	476.50
Finland (markka)	.2459	.2457	4.0675	4.0700
France (franc)	.1717	.1730	5.8185	5.7795
30–day forward	.1720	.1731	5.8150	5.7760
90–day forward	.1721	.1732	5.8120	5.7735
180–day forward	.1722	.1734	5.8065	5.7665
Greece (drachma)	.007275	.007270	137.45	137.55
Hong Kong (dollar)	.1280	.1280	7.8095	7.8152
India (rupee)	.07360	.07348	13.59	13.61
Indonesia (rupiah)	.0005970	.0005970	1675.00	1675.00
Ireland (punt)	1.5600	1.5600	.6410	.6410
Israel (shekel)	.6309	.6309	1.5850	1.5850
Italy (lira)	.0007813	.0007868	1280.00	1271.00
Japan (yen)	.007962	.007968	125.60	125.50
30–day forward	.007987	.007994	125.21	125.09
90–day forward	.008035	.008040	124.46	124.38
180–day forward	.008104	.008108	123.40	123.34

FIGURE 25•1   Foreign exchange rates on June 8, 1988.

The forward markets can be used to reduce or eliminate exchange risk, although the process is not costless. This process is illustrated later in the chapter.

Major Determinants of Exchange Rates

Exchange rates are influenced by many factors; among the most important ones are the inflation rates, interest rates, balance-of-payments surpluses or deficits, and the level of international reserves. We now explore briefly the nature of the dependence of exchange rates on these variables.

Jordan (dinar)	2.7739	2.7739	.3605	.3605
Kuwait (dinar)	3.6284	3.6284	.2756	.2756
Lebanon (pound)	.002755	.002755	363.00	363.00
Malaysia (ringgit)	.3882	.3876	2.5760	2.5802
Malta (lira)	3.0994	3.0994	.3226	.3226
Mexico (peso)				
Floating rate	.0004405	.0004405	2270.00	2270.00
Netherland (guilder)	.5167	.5207	1.9355	1.9205
New Zealand (dollar)	.6960	.6960	1.4368	1.4368
Norway (krone)	.1601	.1599	6.2450	6.2540
Pakistan (rupee)	.05621	.05621	17.79	17.79
Peru (inti)	.03030	.03030	33.00	33.00
Philippines (peso)	.04757	.04757	21.02	21.02
Portugal (escudo)	.007133	.007133	140.20	140.20
Saudi Arabia (riyal)	.2663	.2663	3.7555	3.7555
Singapore (dollar)	.4959	.4955	2.0165	2.0182
South Africa (rand)				
Commercial rate	.4481	.4478	2.2316	2.2331
Financial rate	.3389	.3412	2.9500	2.9300
South Korea (won)	.001364	.001364	733.20	733.20
Spain (peseta)	.008834	.008834	113.20	113.20
Sweden (krona)	.1673	.1670	5.9770	5.9880
Switzerland (franc)	.6952	.7015	1.4385	1.4255
30–day forward	.6981	.7046	1.4325	1.4192
90–day forward	.7038	.7102	1.4208	1.4080
180–day forward	.7123	.7189	1.4039	1.3910
Taiwan (dollar)	.03500	.03500	28.57	28.57
Thailand (baht)	.03968	.03968	25.20	25.20
Turkey (lira)	.0007520	.000720	1329.81	1329.81
United Arab (dirham)	.2723	.2723	3.671	3.671
Uruguay (new peso)				
Financial	.002941	.002941	340.00	340.00
Venezuela (bolivar)				
Official rate	.1333	.1333	7.50	7.50
Floating rate	.03183	.03183	31.42	31.42
W. Germany (mark)	.5790	.5845	1.7270	1.7110
30–day forward	.5811	.5866	1.7209	1.7046
90–day forward	.5851	.5905	1.7091	1.6934
180–day forward	.5909	.5963	1.6924	1.6769
SDR	1.36501	1.36373	0.732594	0.733286
ECU	1.21057	1.21105	. . .	. . .

Special Drawing Rights are based on exchange rates for the U.S., West German, British, French and Japanese currencies. Source: International Monetary Fund.

ECU is based on a basket of community currencies. Source: European Community Commission. z–Not quoted.

Inflation Rates If the domestic price of goods rises faster than the price of foreign imports (i.e., domestic inflation is greater than foreign inflation), the demand for foreign exchange will be great, as will its price. This is because more and more of the cheaper foreign goods will be demanded by Americans. As the demand for the foreign currency, say the yen, rises, so does the price of the yen. If, however, domestic goods are relatively cheaper, demand for exports will increase, supplying the country with foreign currency. An increase in the supply of foreign exchange will lower its price, thereby pressuring the domestic currency to appreciate.

The **purchasing power parity (*PPP*) theory** explains this movement in exchange rates. Basically, this theory implies that goods of equal value in differing countries may be equated through an exchange rate. If a loaf of bread costs

$1 in the United States and 100 yen in Japan, the exchange rate must be 100 yen/$. A more useful form of the PPP theory is the relative form of the theory, which in equation form is

$$PPP_R = \text{spot rate} \times \frac{P_h}{P_f} \qquad (25\text{-}1)$$

where P_h and P_f represent the price indexes in country h and country f, respectively.

For example, in 1980 the dollar/peseta exchange rate was $0.0126/peseta. The Spanish price index (PI) for October 1984 was 169.3, while the U.S. price index was 117.6 using 1980 as a base year [PI(1980) = 100]. If Spain is treated as country h and the United States is country f, the PPP rate would be

$$PPP_R = \$0.0126/\text{pesata} \times \frac{117.6/100}{169.3/100} = 0.0088$$

The actual rate at the end of October 1984 was $0.0059/pesata. The discrepancy may be due either to the exchange rate, which does not reflect purchasing power parity, or more likely, the spot rate did not reflect purchasing power parity and this discrepancy was magnified by the equation. However, the PPP theory is very useful in explaining exchange-rate changes and pressure for change over time.

The purchasing power parity theory is a useful predictor of future exchange rates. If the current exchange rate in Mexico, for example, is $0.005/peso and Mexico's expected inflation rate is 30% annually while the United States expects an inflation rate of 7%, the purchasing power parity theory would indicate an exchange rate of approximately $0.004/peso in one year:

$$\$0.005/\text{peso} \times \frac{1.07}{1.3} = \$0.0041/\text{peso}$$

Interest Rates The second major factor in determining exchange rates is the relative interest rates. For example, if yields (interest rates) are relatively higher in the United States than in Great Britain, English short-term funds will be attracted to the United States as English businesses attempt to earn higher returns on their cash holdings. As a result, there will be an increased demand for the dollar by pound holders, and the price of the dollar in pounds (one divided by the direct U.S. exchange rate) will go up.

Looking at this from another angle, since fewer dollars are required to purchase a pound, the dollar appreciates while the pound depreciates. Because of market supply and demand conditions, interest rates will reflect the expected changes in the exchange rate. More specifically, forward and spot rates will adjust to reflect parity between similar risk investments in different countries.

The **interest-rate parity theory** may be stated as (when exchange rates are expressed as dollars/foreign currency)

$$\frac{\text{spot rate} \times (1 + \text{foreign yield})}{\text{forward rate}} = 1 + \text{home yield}$$

or

$$\frac{S \times (1 + i_f)}{F} = 1 + i_h$$

This equation may also be expressed as

$$\text{forward rate} = \text{spot} \times \frac{1 + \text{foreign yield}}{1 + \text{home yield}} \qquad (25\text{-}2)$$

$$F = S \times \frac{i_f}{i_h}$$

To illustrate, suppose that on December 31, 1984, you were considering investing $100,000 for one year in either U.S. Treasury bills at 9.58% or the German money market at 5.6%. The current spot rate is 0.3177 dm/$. The forward rate at which you would be indifferent to the transaction would be 0.3061. Using the equation above yields.

$$F = \frac{1}{0.3177} \times \frac{1.0560}{1.0958} = \$3.033/\text{dm or } 0.3297 \text{ dm/\$}$$

If the forward rate deviated significantly from this value, traders in the market can make profits. Foreign exchange dealers, however, are always looking for these types of discrepancies, and by acting on them quickly, tend to force the market to equilibrium.

Balance-of-Payments Surpluses and Deficits   The balance-of-payments positions also have a major impact on exchange rates. If a country is running a large or persistent deficit in either the current account[3] or on the overall settlements balance,[4] there is pressure to devalue the currency. There will be both internal and external pressure to devalue the currency, thereby reducing imports and increasing exports to bring the current account into balance. Conversely, if a country has been running a surplus, it is, in effect, supplying the rest of the world with real goods and services while accepting paper claims from foreign currency. Reducing the amount of goods and services available while increasing

---

[3]The *current account* is a record (prepared by the U.S. Department of Commerce) of all international sales of goods and services between the United States and its trading partners.

[4]The *settlements balance* is the net result of activities involving the current account, short-term capital flows, and errors and omissions involved in transactions made, but for which specific measurements are unavailable.

the money supply will lead to inflation, pressuring policymakers to appreciate the currency to remedy the situation.

Level of Reserves The final factor is the level of reserves that the monetary authority possesses. If a country observes its currency depreciating in the foreign exchange market and has economic reasons to support or stabilize its currency, it may step in and buy its foreign exchange with its accumulated reserve assets. However, the country can "prop up" its currency only as long as it has reserves available. Therefore, it cannot support an artificially high exchange rate indefinitely through market intervention.

POLITICAL RISKS

Firms conducting international business must consider not only economic factors but also political factors. In the context of the domestic corporation, we have already seen how operating risk and financial risk can affect a firm's cash flows. A company doing business overseas runs both of these risks and, in addition, faces two other types of risk. As already seen, exchange-rate risk enters into virtually every intercountry transaction of the firm. Another type of risk that is unique to an international company is political risk. It is important to recognize that in one form or another, political risk affects the potential outcome of overseas investments. This risk should therefore be recognized in all foreign investment decisions.

Blocked Funds

Blocked funds can represent one form of political risk. Companies doing business overseas are at the mercy of the local government, which may completely prohibit the withdrawal of funds from that country. An example of this is the U.S. government's freezing of all Iranian bank accounts in the United States during the 1980 hostage crisis. The possibility of blocked funds can have a strong adverse effect on the profitability of a company's operations in that country, even if eventually it is allowed to repatriate the funds to the parent company.

Expropriation

Expropriation in its most blatant form is an extreme form of funds blockage. The local government simply takes over the company, and the multinational is helpless. Chile, a few years ago, expropriated American copper operations in that country, and Libya nationalized American oil interests. Unanticipated actions by local authorities can affect the cash flows from the subsidiary and, consequently, the value of the parent company.

At least to some extent, firms can cope with political risk in a variety of direct and indirect ways. By involving more of the local population in both ownership and management, the risks can be somewhat minimized. Alternatively, the multinational firm can obtain political risk insurance from a variety of agencies. The Overseas Private Investment Corporation (OPIC), for example, will insure multinational companies against the risk of funds freezing, expropriations, and changes in foreign laws. Other potential insurance sources include the Foreign Credit Insurance Association (FCIA) and Eximbank. In addition, the Agency for International Development (AID) may provide companies with some protection of their direct foreign investments in certain countries.

Learning Check for Section 25·1

Review Questions

25·1. What are spot and forward exchange rates?

25·2. What are the factors affecting exchange rates?

25·3. What is political risk, and how can companies cope with this risk?

New Terms

Blocked funds	Forward rate	Purchasing power
Exchange rate	Interest rate	parity
Expropriation	parity	Spot rate

SECTION 25·2 *The Multinational Firm*

With a general understanding of the international environment of the firm, we are now in a position to look at specific corporate financial management issues as they pertain to multinationals.

MULTINATIONAL FINANCING

The potential sources of financing for a company with international operations are best treated in two categories: internal financing (from the parent) and external financing (from nonparent sources).

Internal Financing

American corporations doing business overseas can, in general, use funds supplied entirely by American individuals and institutions. That is, the firm can use its internally (i.e., domestically) generated funds for overseas investment unless there are explicit restrictions imposed on the firm by stockholders or bondholders.

In recent years, however, there has been an increasing tendency for U.S. companies to finance their foreign subsidiaries with a minimum of equity capital. The bulk of financing has been via debt capital. Several reasons have been advanced to explain this phenomenon. For one thing, debt capital generally has the advantage that interest payments are tax deductible in the foreign country. Managers have also felt that there is a smaller risk of expropriation by a foreign government when most of the capital is debt capital. Governments might be discouraged from expropriating the capital resources of the company if they faced the threat of upsetting other agencies and perhaps even their own citizens. Another advantage of debt financing is that it provides the parent company some measure of protection against devaluation. If a currency gets devalued, the parent will have to come up with fewer dollars to pay off the debt. Also, cost considerations apparently favor the use of debt for overseas operations. Until recently, the cost of debt (interest rates) has been lower in the United States than in most other countries. Finally, American companies with extensive plant facilities overseas have been encouraged by host governments to borrow from local merchant banks under some very favorable terms.

With the exception of Japan and London, the majority of foreign equity markets are small in relation to the U.S. equity markets. Yet U.S. companies do sell stock in overseas markets for a variety of reasons. There is a common feeling among managers that companies gain tremendously from local ownership. When the residents of the host country feel that they own a significant portion of the firm, the company tends to get more favorable treatment from the local government. In addition, the sales for these companies are supposedly improved as the citizens of the local country buy more products from "their" company. Employee loyalty is also said to improve. Finally, several governments insist that a certain proportion of the firm must be owned by local citizens.

Interestingly, most international financial managers concede that their choice of debt versus equity financing decisions is determined primarily by the parent company's view of the tax ramifications of the capital structure and the local subsidiary's assessment of the local sociopolitical and environmental realities (See the highlight "Investing in Foreign Companies.")

◼ HIGHLIGHT

INVESTING IN FOREIGN COMPANIES

Many investors prefer to diversify their stock investments not only across various American companies but also across various international securities. This international diversification can be done in three ways:

1. Americans can invest abroad directly by working with an *international broker*. Stocks trading on the stock exchanges in Germany, Japan, Hong Kong, or the United Kingdom can be bought or sold fairly easily.

2. A second alternative is to invest in *mutual funds* that devote some of their portfolio to foreign securities. This method of investing abroad amounts to buying professional management. There are many specialized mutual funds that investors can choose from; the Templeton World Fund, Scudder International, Keystone International, and T. Rowe Price International Fund are some large institutions that offer international diversification.

3. A third alternative is to purchase *American depository receipts* (**ADRs**). These are securities issued by American banks acting as depositories for shares of a foreign corporation held overseas. In selling an ADR to an American national, the bank is guaranteeing that the stated number of shares of the particular foreign company have been deposited in the bank's foreign office. The bank agrees to act as custodian of these shares as long as the ADR is outstanding. ADRs allow Americans to invest abroad and allow foreigners to raise capital in the United States. Many ADRs are traded on the NYSE, the AMEX, and the OTC markets. The most popular ADRs in the United States are South African gold mining stocks. Some foreign companies with ADRs traded in the United States are the following:

Bowater Corporation	British Petroleum	Canon
Bank Leumi	Beecham Group	Biogen
De Beers	Dunlop Holdings	Kubota
Dresdner Bank	Fuji Photo	Honda
Kirin Brewery	Matsushita	Unilever
Nippon Electric	Pioneer Electronics	Nissan Motors
KLM Royal Dutch	Sony Corporation	TDK
Vaal Reef Mining	Royal Dutch Petroleum	Kloof Gold
Telefonos de Mexico	Glaxo Holdings	Santos

External Financing

There are three primary sources of external financing for multinationals: commercial banks in the host country, the Eurocurrency and Eurobond markets, and the various international lending agencies.

As with U.S. markets, the source of external funds depends on whether short-term or long-term financing is needed. The two sources of short-term funds are commercial banks and the Eurocurrency market.

Commercial Banks In the Host Country Commercial banks abroad perform essentially the same functions as domestic banks. This classification includes local banks, foreign branches of U.S. banks, and Edge Act subsidiaries.[5] Euro-

---

[5]Edge Act corporations are financial institutions incorporated in the United States under the Edge Act. These companies are owned by commercial banks. Most of their income is from overseas. American banks like to establish Edge Act corporations because this allows them to conduct certain overseas business that is otherwise prohibited by American banking laws.

pean banks usually allow longer-term loans than U.S. banks and offer both commercial banking and investment banking services.

Eurocurrency and Eurobond Markets The **Eurocurrency markets** provide for the borrowing of **Eurodollars,** usually through lines of credit or revolving credit arrangements in which the bank charges a commitment fee as well as interest on the principal borrowed. The Eurodollar is defined as a dollar-denominated deposit held in a bank outside the United States[6] There is an active market for these deposits, especially in Europe. The rate paid on Eurodollars is quoted in terms of the London Interbank Offer Rate (LIBOR), the rate that large London banks charge each other for Eurocurrency loans. Loans to large multinational companies are usually quoted in terms of LIBOR plus a percentage for the risk premium based on the borrower's creditworthiness.

The primary advantage of Eurodollar deposits is that they are not under the scrutiny of U.S. regulatory agencies and therefore have no reserve requirements or FDIC insurance premiums required against them. With the associated lower costs, banks may offer a higher rate for these deposits, making them very attractive for holders of excess dollar liquidity. Processing and overhead costs for loans are also lower because only large corporations with high credit standings may participate; thus, borrowing may be at an attractive rate as well.

International bond markets and development banks provide intermediate-to long-term sources of funds for the multinationals. An international bond is any bond sold outside the country of the borrower. There are two types of international bonds: the foreign bond and the **Eurobond.** The foreign bond is a bond issued in the currency of the country in which the bond is sold or traded. These bonds are traded in the secondary market in the country of issue. The primary difference between these and domestic bonds is that the issuer is a foreign government or corporation, and the bonds are subject to the security regulations of the country in which they are issued.

The Eurobond is denominated in a currency different from that of the country or countries in which it is issued. Typically, it is internationally syndicated and the secondary market exists among the banks that deal in Eurobonds. Like Eurocurrency, Eurobonds have fewer regulatory requirements and therefore have lower transaction costs.

Development Banks With the problems experienced by commercial banks in lending to the less developed countries (LDCs), it is likely that additional capital to facilitate growth will come increasingly from international agencies and from the governments of the developed countries. There are several groups of lending agencies, including the World Bank group, regional lending agencies, and national development banks. Although many of these groups lend to the governments, the funds are used to fund development programs in which many multinationals are involved. Some international lending agencies lend directly to private enterprises as well.

---

[6]Interestingly, some people include even the deutsche mark deposits in Europe under the term *Eurodollar.*

1. The World Bank Group. The International Bank for Reconstruction and Development (IBRD), also referred to as the *World Bank*, was formed in 1944 along with the International Monetary Fund (IMF). It usually finances the foreign exchange portion of projects for less developed countries.

2. The International Finance Corporation (IFC). The IFC was formed in 1956 as a supplement to the World Bank for higher-risk loans. It makes nonguaranteed loans to private enterprises in developing countries.

3. Regional lending agencies. The Inter-American Development Bank (IDB) and the Asian Development Bank (ADB) promote economic growth in Latin America and Asian countries, respectively. The United States is a member of both groups. The loans are available to private and public entities in the member nations.

4. National development banks. Eximbank (the Export-Import Bank) provides financial assistance for buyers of U.S. exports to support economic growth in the United States. The bank provides direct long-term financing for foreign borrowers to purchase U.S. exports at a rate that is usually less than that available to foreign borrowers in their own country.

5. The Agency for International Development (AID). AID provides loans to foreign governments and other qualified borrowers for economic development projects at rates that are usually lower than international money market rates.

6. The Private Export Funding Corporation (PEFCO). PEFCO provides intermediate-term financing of U.S. exports.

7. Foreign national development banks. Banks such as the United Kingdom's Industrial Reorganization Corporation, France's Credit Nationale, Germany's Kreditanstalt fur Wiederaufbau, and Italy's Instituto Mobiliare Italiano provide programs to encourage their countries' exports, similar to the U.S. Eximbank and AID.

CASH MANAGEMENT FOR A MULTINATIONAL COMPANY

To many financial managers of multinational companies, international cash management is both a rewarding challenge and a major source of frustration. This is because the efficient handling of large sums of cash can result in significant cost savings to the firm; however the methods of handling cash, in particular cash transfers, vary from country to country, and managers are faced with a perplexing array of complications regarding cash transfers.[7] Nevertheless, much

---

[7]For example, American managers in Latin America often complain that there are no standardized check-clearing times, phone balance verification is undependable, mail systems are poor, many banks share a common computer terminal, and so on.

progress is being made in increasing the quality of cash-handling procedures, with American banks such as Citibank, Chase, Bank of America, and Manufacturers Hanover Trust taking the lead.

The principles of cash management studied in Chapter 19 also apply to the firm with overseas operations. However, as in other areas, the multinational dimension adds new complications. A major problem faced by a company with subsidiaries in different countries is the coordination of an efficient flow of funds between the various offices. Idle cash at any location should be minimized, and all surplus funds should be channeled to a cash center. (Lockbox arrangements are not widely available in many countries.) In Europe, Switzerland is a popular cash center, while for Asian operations Hong Kong is popular. The choice of an overseas cash center must be made very carefully. Ideally, the cash center should be in a country with a stable government that does not impede the flow of funds into and out of the country. The local currency in the cash center should also be strong and readily convertible into other currencies. This will help the firm minimize exchange risk. In addition, this country should have an active money market so that excess funds can readily be invested to earn interest. Another important feature is that the local government taxes income only at the source, not every time funds are brought into the country.

Multinational managers also play the float, but transfer times for international funds are much longer. This is often a very serious concern to managers because the longer transfer times not only tie up the funds that could otherwise be put to use but also increase the exchange risk. For many years, international funds transfer messages were sent by cable. In 1977 the Society for Worldwide Interbank Financial Telecommunication (SWIFT) was formed. SWIFT is a computerized arrangement for speedy (within minutes) funds transfers between 800 European, North American, and Latin American banks. In addition, SWIFT is used extensively to transfer debit-credit information between bank accounts. The Clearing House Interbank Payments System (CHIPS) is another arrangement widely used for international funds transfers. Any credit manager can instruct her bank to initiate a CHIPS payment on her behalf—and the transaction will be completed the same day. There are also an increasing number of international banks that can actively work with the company in designing its working capital policies. In particular, transfer times can, for a fee, be dramatically reduced. The company must decide whether this fee is justified by the benefits of speeded cash transfers.

Intercompany netting is another practice gaining popularity among U.S. managers because it cuts down the costs associated with expensive exchange conversions. In simple terms, *netting* refers to the process of offsetting one subsidiary's receivables with another subsidiary's payables. With this type of book entry, the multinational has smaller actual cash transfers among its various offices.

The **reinvoicing center** is a relatively new phenomenon that is gaining widespread acceptance. Suppose that an American firm is supplying aircraft parts to Italy and the price was set in lira. The American company would sell the contract to its invoicing center (located perhaps in Switzerland), which would pay the company in dollars and then collect Italian lira from the purchaser. The actual shipment of goods would take place from the United States to Italy, without the involvement of the reinvoicing center. An intracompany exchange rate (usually stable) set by the reinvoicing center would determine the dollars that the American company would get. The advantage of this arrangement is that the company's foreign exchange risk can be handled at one centralized level. In addition, this center can carefully plan funds transfers such that the company's tax liability is minimized. Although countries such as Switzerland encourage the formation of reinvoicing centers, many countries have banned both reinvoicing centers and the practice of intercompany netting.

Thus the financial manager must first identify the cash management options available and the alternatives that are ruled out. Then a cost-benefit analysis of the various alternatives will help identify the appropriate methods to be pursued.

FINANCING INTERNATIONAL TRADE

International trade transactions involve different types of risks than domestic trade and therefore require alternative settlement techniques. In domestic transactions, sales are usually made on a cash basis or through open-account trade credit. These terms are unacceptable to importers and exporters because of the time lag between contract and delivery of goods and lack of adequate information to make responsible credit decisions. Additionally, in the event of default, settlement through international courts may be cumbersome and costly. For these reasons, importers and exporters have adopted the use of several documents to facilitate international trade; the three most important documents are trade drafts, bills of lading, and letters of credit.

Documents Commonly Used in International Trade

Trade drafts are written orders initiated by the exporter notifying the importer of the exact amount and time at which the importer or its agent must pay. If the exporter (drawer) orders payment "on sight," or immediately, by the importer (drawee), it is referred to as a **sight draft.** If the draft is payable at a specific future date after presentation, it is referred to as a **time draft.** A time draft may be accepted by either the importer or a bank. If it is signed by the importer, the importer acknowledges his obligation to pay and the draft is called a **trade acceptance.** If the importer's bank accepts the draft, the bank agrees to pay the exporter, thereby substituting its creditworthiness for that of the importer, and the draft is referred to as a **banker's acceptance.** Figure 25•2 shows a specimen sight draft.

A banker's acceptance represents an unconditional promise of the bank to make payment on the draft at maturity. It is created in connection with payment from a buyer to a foreign seller. An acceptance implies that an internationally known U.S. bank agrees to make the payment at a certain date to the seller

```
Bank in Lima Credit ABZ-6033

$ 1,000.00 (U.S.)                    New York, September 1,    19 _ _

    At sight _____    Pay to the order of

            Ourselves  (A)

    One thousand and 00/100 - - - - - - - - - - - - -  Dollars

To: Morgan Guaranty              G. T. Tyler Company
(C)   Trust Company                                      (B)
    New York, N.Y.    SPECIMEN
```

FIGURE 25·2 Sample of a sight draft. (The American Bankers Association, *Letters of Credit*, Book 3. Washington, D.C., 1968, p. 77. 1968 American Bankers Association. Reprinted with permission. All rights reserved.)

overseas. Figure 25·3 shows a sample banker's acceptance. Suppose that a company in New Jersey plans to import shoes from Italy. Since the importer in Hoboken does not know the Italian shoemaker, he approaches a bank and asks for **acceptance credit.** If the bank agrees, it sends a *letter of credit* (to be defined) to the Italian company, guaranteeing the payment. The Italian firm is author-

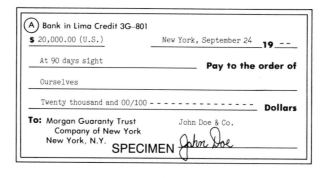

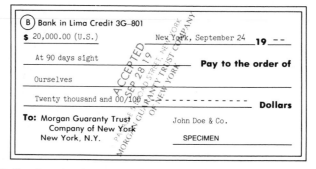

FIGURE 25·3 Sample of a banker's acceptance. (The American Bankers Association, *Letters of Credit*, Book 3. Washington, D.C., 1968, p. 35. 1968 American Bankers Association. Reprinted with permission. All rights reserved.)

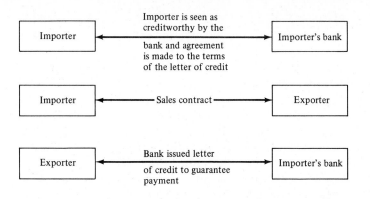

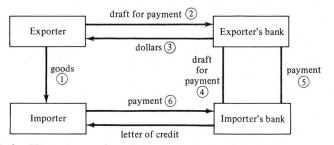

This arrangement may be further reinforced by a letter of confirmation by the exporter's bank. In this case, the exporter's bank guarantees the payment of the importer's bank. The relationships may be illustrated as follows:

FIGURE 25•4 How a letter of credit arrangement works.

ized to draw a time draft on the bank. Upon the presentation of proper documents showing that the shoes have been shipped, the U.S. bank agrees, for a fee, to accept the draft for payment. The draft can also be sold by the importer to his local bank at a discount and the funds obtained immediately. In this way, he can obtain payment for the shoes even before the U.S. importer has paid for them. Banker's acceptances also have an active secondary market in New York.

A **bill of lading,** the next major international trade document, serves three purposes: (1) it provides a receipt of goods from the exporter to the shipper; (2) it acts as a contract between the carrier and the exporter, indicating that the carrier will transport the goods for a fee; and (3) it may convey legal title to the goods. Bills of lading may be either straight or to order. A **straight bill of lading** does not convey legal title to the goods and tends to be used in shipping to affiliates when merchandise has been paid for in advance. An **order bill of lading,** on the other hand, conveys title to the merchandise only to the party to whom the document is addressed. Typically, when dealing with an unknown importer, it is addressed to the exporting firm. Therefore, the exporter retains title to the merchandise until payment is made, at which time the bill of lading is signed over to the party making payment. This arrangement allows the exporter to sell goods to the importer without releasing title until the payment is made.

Letters of credit are the third way to reduce the risk of noncompletion of contract. Basically, letters of credit are issued by a bank on behalf of an importer. Once the bill of lading and other proper documents have been received by the bank, the bank substitutes its promise to pay for that of the importer. The exporter then has a financial arrangement only with the importer's bank, not with the importer. The relationships are shown in Figure 25•4. The letter of credit does not guarantee the underlying commercial transaction; it is simply a promise to pay upon presentation of certain documents. The banks involved have a responsibility to examine the documents with reasonable care, but they are not responsible in any way for the goods being shipped.

These three documents—the trade draft, the bill of lading, and the letter of credit—have all greatly facilitated international trade because they reduce the risks involved in dealing with unknown parties.

Learning Check for Section 25•2

Review Questions

25•4. What are the sources of external financing for a multinational corporation?

25•5. What are some of the unique aspects of multinational cash management?

25•6. What are the unique arrangements common in international trade financing?

New Terms

ADR	Letter of credit	Straight bill
Banker's acceptance	LIBOR	of lading
Bill of lading	Order bill	SWIFT
CHIPS	of lading	Time draft
Eurobond	Reinvoicing centers	Trade acceptance
Eurocurrency market	Sight draft	Trade drafts
Intercompany netting		

SECTION 25•3 *Capital Budgeting for Multinational Companies*

The process of capital budgeting for a foreign operation is, in theory, identical to a situation involving a domestic investment analysis—identify the cash flows that are generated by an investment and find the *NPV* of the investment after adjusting for risk. The risk adjustment can be done either in the cash flows or by increasing the discount rate upward. If the *NPV* is positive, the project is a worthwhile endeavor.

Unfortunately, this analysis, although correct, is more difficult to implement in the case of multinational firms. There are several new variables involved, and developing a simple framework for making these decisions is not an easy task. Because of the complexity of the environment, estimates of cash flows have a wider margin of error, and estimation of the risks is likely to be difficult. Rather than try to develop quantitative frameworks for making capital budgeting decisions in this environment, we will identify several special considerations that must be borne in mind in making the *NPV* analysis. Careful attention to these factors can help the financial manager make a better decision using the *NPV* criterion.

CASH FLOW CONSIDERATIONS

The important issue to remember in making foreign investments is that the ultimate objective of the manager should be to enrich the shareholders of the parent company. Thus the value of foreign investments to stockholders depends crucially on the cash flows that can be repatriated either immediately or at a later date to the home country. Thus the possibility of funds blockages or expropriation must be clearly recognized in estimating potential cash flows. Of course, as we have seen, firms can minimize this risk through insurance. However, insurance is not free, and this expense must be treated as a cash outflow in capital budgeting decisions.

The opening up of a new overseas operation can sometimes result in an indirect cost to the firm. For example, if an American car manufacturer sets up a new plant in Brazil, it is with the expectation that the new sales of cars to the Brazilians will increase the company's revenues. For example, this investment may increase the car maker's revenues by 12%. Yet this estimate of the new revenue is not the relevant incremental revenue to the car maker. Because the cars are being made in Brazil, the parent company will lose some of its original exports to Brazil, thereby resulting in an indirect cost. The incremental revenues for this proposed investment should therefore recognize this potential reduction in the revenues of the domestic company. Putting it another way, if the firm has the ability to generate some of its revenues from the proposed project independent of that project, the indirect costs from taking on that project should be recognized properly in calculating the incremental cash flows.

Two unique features of international financial cash flows are **supervisory fees** and **royalties.** These are contractually arranged periodic remissions of funds by the subsidiary to the parent company and represent a "fee" for, say, the supervision on patent use. These fees are simply devices that multinational companies have used to protect themselves in repatriating funds back home. Since they are fees (rather than profits), local governments are less likely to prevent this cash drain from the subsidiary in the host country into the coffers of the multinational. These periodic cash inflows to the parent firm should therefore be part of the capital budgeting decision. In many cases, however, this fee is set at an artificially high level. In such cases, where this cash flow is not really tied to the merits of the project but instead represents an accounting adjustment by management, the fee and royalty amounts should be adjusted downward in the *NPV* analysis of the project.

Along the same lines, a **tie-in sale** is a fairly common arrangement that parent firms have with their subsidiaries. A tie-in sale may require the subsidiary to buy certain materials from the parent. Tie-in sales can be useful to the parent because they may enable it to supply the product at the lowest possible cost; in other instances, tie-in sales arrangements ensure that quality components are supplied to the subsidiary. For example, a capital investment in Mexico to manufacture hand-held calculators may require the Mexican subsidiary to buy the electronic chips from the parent in the United States. Presumably, the parent feels that the quality of its product is superior. In situations such as this, again, care must be taken in calculating the incremental cash flows from the proposed project. The benefits to the parent are the net flows from the overseas project.

Sometimes the parent company may choose to transfer its used equipment to the new foreign subsidiary. Equipment transfers can be advantageous to the parent because the parent may be able to realize higher salvage values in the foreign country. How does one recognize the cost of this transferred machinery in the capital budgeting analysis? The relevant cost that must be charged to the project is not the depreciated book value of the machinery; instead, the opportunity cost of acquiring a similar piece of equipment in the foreign country is the appropriate cost.

The tax laws of the local country are obviously a major determinant of the profits and cash flows generated by a project. The complexity in making tax adjustments to profits is heightened by the fact that tax adjustments must be made at two levels: at the level of the host country and again when the profits are repatriated back to the United States. Tax laws relating to international investments are extremely complicated and are not presented in this book.[8] It is important to remember, again, that the tax adjustments must ultimately be viewed in light of their effect on the cash flows to the parent.

DISCOUNT-RATE CONSIDERATIONS

As we know so well, capital budgeting analyses are not meaningful without the use of a properly specified discount rate (opportunity cost) to find the *PV*s of the cash flows generated by an investment. The proper discount rate includes a riskless interest rate plus a premium for bearing risk. In the case of domestic capital budgeting, the discount rate can be estimated by, say, the CAPM. How

---

[8]U.S. tax laws regarding profits and losses on translation gains and forward contracts require the definition of *functional currency*. FASB-52 is the accounting standard adopted in these matters. For a summary of the tax aspects of international transactions, see Martin A. Miller, *GAAP Guide* (San Diego, Calif.: Harcourt Brace Jovanovich, Inc., annual).

does one find the proper discount rate to be applied to a multinational company's investment overseas? The relevant risk of the investment should first be estimated and then an appropriate risk premium identified. In a strict sense, one needs to develop an international capital asset pricing model (ICAPM) to do this correctly. Such models do exist, in fact, but their use is severely limited. For a variety of reasons, this approach of risk adjustment—adjusting the discount rate upward for risk—is not recommended. The risks in international finance are much more difficult to estimate, and world markets are not as highly integrated as various domestic financial asset markets. Therefore, it may be better to adjust the cash flows downward for risk in making the *NPV* calculations. These cash flow adjustments must reflect the political risks, the tax implications for cash flows, and the other factors specific to multinationals.

In summary, cash flow adjustments are preferred purely on the grounds of pragmatism. There is more information available than can meaningfully be used to make cash flow adjustments; however, risk adjustments to the discount rate are severely hampered by the problems of using this information properly to quantify the relevant risks of the investment.

Learning Check for Section 25•3

Review Questions

25•7.   What are some of the special features of multinational investment cash flow estimation?

25•8.   What are the problems involved in determining the opportunity cost (discount rate) of investing abroad?

New Terms

ICAPM   Supervisory fees   Tie-in sale
Royalties

SUMMARY

The International Financial Environment

Since American businesses are in search of greater profits and cash flows, overseas markets are very attractive. In addition, because of several potential advantages to investing abroad, multinational companies establish subsidiaries in many foreign countries. The financial manager of the multinational company, like his or her domestic counterpart, should remember that the objective of the subsidiary is to increase the wealth of the parent company and, consequently, that of its shareholders.

The financial principles used in running an overseas operation are similar to those applicable to a domestic company, except that foreign business analyses are greatly complicated by a variety of tangible and intangible considerations unique to foreign operations.

Perhaps the biggest concern facing multinational finance managers is the constant uncertainty associated with exchange risks and political risks. Several strategies can be employed to cope with these uncertainties, at least to some extent. Hedging techniques reduce the exchange risk. Political risks can be reduced either directly, via insurance, or indirectly by structuring company operations in such a way that these risks are minimized.

The Multinational Firm

Cash management for multinational companies is a challenging task for managers. Several measures, such as the establishment of cash centers, reinvoicing centers, and intercompany netting, are worthwhile strategies to increase efficiency. International trade is often facilitated by the extensive use of four documents: trade drafts, banker's acceptances, bills of lading, and letters of credit. These documents greatly reduce the risks involved in dealing with unknown parties.

Capital Budgeting for Multinational Companies

Capital budgeting analyses for multinationals can be quite complicated. Unique aspects of international cash flows relate to supervisory fees and royalties, tie-in sales, equipment transfers, and tax laws. These cash flows are adjusted downward for risks in the analyses. The risks of international finance are difficult to estimate. It is thus better to adjust for these risks by reducing the estimates of the cash flows rather than by attempting to adjust the discount rate.

PROBLEMS

25•1. Today the exchange rate between British pounds and American dollars is $1.40 per pound. One year ago the exchange rate was 0.625 per dollar.
(a) What is the indirect (i.e., implied) exchange rate for pounds today?
(b) What was the direct exchange rate for pounds one year ago?
(c) Has the dollar strengthened or weakened relative to the pound during the last year?

25•2. Three years ago, the exchange rate between Austrian schillings and Czechoslovakian koruna was 3 schillings per koruna. Today the exchange rate is 0.4 koruna per schilling.

(a) What was the indirect exchange rate between schillings and koruna three years ago from the perspective of someone in Austria?

(b) What is the direct exchange rate between schillings and koruna today from the perspective of someone in Austria?

(c) Has the schilling strengthened or weakened relative to the koruna during the last three years? If that trend continues at the same rate, what will the direct and indirect exchange rates be in three years from the perspective of someone in Austria?

25•3. Today the direct exchange rate for Swiss francs is $0.50 per franc, and the direct exchange rate for Japanese yen is $0.004 per yen.

(a) What is the indirect exchange rate for Swiss francs?

(b) What is the indirect exchange rate for Japanese yen?

(c) What is the exchange rate between Swiss francs and Japanese yen, expressed as a direct rate to someone in Tokyo? To someone in Geneva?

25•4. In 1968 the direct exchange rate for French francs was $0.40 per franc. At that time the U.S. consumer price index was 100 and the French consumer price index was also 100. In 1983 the U.S. consumer price index was 225 and the French consumer price index was 280.

(a) Using the purchasing power parity theory, estimate the direct exchange rate for French francs in 1983.

(b) Suppose that the inflation rate for each country stays the same for the period 1983–1998 as it was during the period 1968–1983. Estimate the direct exchange rate in the year 1998.

(c) Suppose that the inflation rate for each country stays the same for the period 1983–2013 as it was during the period 1968–1983. Estimate the direct exchange rate in the year 2013.

25•5. The current exchange rate between Brazilian cruzieros and American dollars is 1,032 cruzieros per dollar. Four years ago the American consumer price index was 260; today it is 332. Four years ago the Brazilian consumer price index was 361; today it is 2,737. Using the purchasing power parity theory, estimate the exchange rate between cruzieros and dollars four years ago.

25•6. In 1984 the indirect exchange rate for Swedish kroner was 8.5 kroner per dollar. The U.S. consumer price index was 230 and the Swedish consumer price index was 160. In 1979 the U.S. consumer price index was 180 and the Swedish consumer price index was 120. Using the purchasing power parity theory, estimate the direct exchange rate for Swedish kroner in 1979.

25•7. Today the direct exchange rate between U.S. dollars and Saudi Arabian rial is $0.25 per rial. The 180-day forward rate for rials is $0.24 per rial.
(a) Use the interest-rate parity theory to estimate the rate on Saudi Arabian 180-day government securities if the U.S. 180-day T-bill rate is 9%.
(b) Use the interest-rate parity theory to estimate the rate on U.S. 180-day T bills if the rate on Saudi Arabian 180-day government securities is 16%.

APPENDIX 25·A *Exposure Management*

The floating-exchange-rate system currently prevalent has brought about a new twist in financial risk management; now managers of international operations must take into account foreign exchange risks in addition to business and financial risks. There are two basic ways that exchange-rate fluctuations can affect the value of accounts: actual transactions that involve currency conversions, and translations of foreign-currency-denominated financial statements of a subsidiary into the parent company's currency. These two types of **exposure risks** are illustrated in the following examples.

TYPES OF EXPOSURE RISKS

Transaction exposure risks occur when a company has accounts receivable or payable in foreign currencies. If a Texas firm exports goods to a London firm and the invoice is denominated in dollars, the Texans are protected against exchange-rate changes. However, if the invoice is in British pounds (£), the Texas firm has an exposed position. Assuming that the invoice was for goods priced at £80,125, and assuming that the exchange rate dropped from $1.2481/£ to $1.1565/£, instead of receiving $100,004 for the merchandise, the Texas exporter would receive $92,665 (£80,125 × $1.1565/£), a loss of $7,339.

Translation exposure risks occur when the balance sheet is translated into the parent company's currency for the purposes of consolidation, performance evaluation, taxation, and so on. A subsidiary whose currency has been weakened by inflation from a ratio of 1:2 to a ratio of 1:1.5 would appear to be worth only three-fourths of its initial value. Although this does not represent an actual cash loss because the currency value has only been translated, not converted, there is no difference for financial reporting purposes.

Firms obviously could not survive in the international arena if they left their positions completely unprotected. Therefore, multinationals use a number of methods to shield themselves from exchange-rate fluctuation risks.

HEDGING

Hedging is one of the most often used methods of protecting the firm's claims on foreign currency against the unfavorable impact of unexpected exchange-rate fluctuations. Two frequently used techniques are the forward market hedge and the currency option market hedge.

Forward Market Hedge

The primary purpose of the **forward market hedge** is to limit financial loss due to unexpected changes in the exchange rate. The forward market allows the party making or receiving payment to eliminate the uncertainty of that payment.

Example 25A•1   Forward Market Hedge

Suppose that a U.S. exporter contracts to sell machinery for 3,500,000 DM to a German business on November 13, 1984. As part of the terms of the contract, the exporter agrees to accept payment in six months in deutsche marks. The U.S. firm may either sell marks 180 days forward to lock in their dollar value, or it may assume the exchange-rate risk and convert the 3,500,000 DM at the spot rate on May 13, 1985. Observing the 180-day forward rate given on November 13, 1984 ($1/2.8785 DM), the firm would lock in a price today of $1,215,911 for delivery on May 13, 1985.

$$3,500,000 \text{ DM} \times \left(\frac{\$1}{2.8785 \text{ DM}} \right) = \$1,215,911$$

If the firm had assumed the exchange-rate risk, it would receive $1,137,472 on May 13, 1985.

$$3,500,000 \text{ DM} \times \left(\frac{\$1}{3.0775 \text{ DM}} \right) = \$1,137,287$$

Therefore, by assuming the risk, the American firm lost $78,624 (ignoring the transaction cost of entering the forward market).

The Currency Options Market Hedge

The currency options market operates in a manner similar to the forward market, except that it allows the firm the choice of either exercising the option or letting it expire. Currency options may be viewed as insurance against downside risk, which may be obtained for a fee or premium. For example, if a Japanese exporter expects to receive payment in dollars in three months, he may wish to buy a put option (put options give the holder the right to sell currency at a given rate, while call options give the holder the right to buy currency at a given rate). If, in three months, the spot exchange rate is less than the option exchange rate, the Japanese importer will exercise his option. Conversely, if the spot rate three months hence is greater than the option rate, the importer will allow his option to expire and perhaps realize an additional profit if the spread is adequate to cover the option premium.

PROBLEMS WITH HEDGING

Hedging, however, has both inherent problems and usage problems that make it a method to be used with caution. To hedge the exposed position, the exposure must be accurately measured. Translation exposure is fairly easily measured. The liabilities are subtracted from the assets on the balance sheet, and the remainder is the exposed position. Transaction exposure is more difficult because one must determine the actual cash flows and project future cash flows based on future sales, future purchases, credit assumptions, dividend payments, debt principal involving foreign currency, and so on. After the exposed position is measured, the exchange rate applicable to the exposed position must be predicted. Predicting the movement of exchange rates is very complex. Studies comparing forward rates to the actual spot rate in the future to test the predictive power of forward rates have not been very promising.

Aside from these inherent problems, there are errors common in hedging practices. First, there is a tendency to hedge only the downside risk, separating it from the upside risk, which results in unnecessary hedging. Second, decisions are usually made on the basis of single currencies, if not single transactions. To avoid suboptimization, there is a need to centralize hedging policies. Centralization in a global operation, however, is difficult and often unwise, sacrificing both flexibility and speed. Third, companies tend to overhedge because the exposed position is defined too broadly by accounting rules. There is little debate over covering current assets and current liabilities; however, covering inventories and long-term debt may be questionable. Cases where inventory is wrongly considered to be exposed would be either inventory exported for dollars or inventory sold solely within a country. In the latter case, devaluation is usually followed by price increases that offset the effects of the devaluation. Covering long-term debt seems justifiable only when the borrowed funds are exported or go into short-term assets.

For all of these reasons, hedging, either through the forward market or the currency options market, should not be relied upon by the international financial manager as the sole method of protecting against exchange-rate fluctuations.

ALTERNATIVE EXPOSURE MANAGEMENT TECHNIQUES

Balance Sheet Trade-Offs

When threatened with the prospect of currency devaluation, a subsidiary may reduce its cash and short-term assets without much damage to its liquidity requirements. Other actions may also be taken, but their costs may outweigh their benefits; for example, if inventory is cut to lower the exposed position, the reduced production and lower sales effectiveness may be more costly than the gain from the smaller exposed position in inventories.

Lags and Leads

One of the most fundamental concepts in international financial management is to position assets in a strong currency and liabilities in a weak currency.

This may be achieved in the current accounts with the methods of lagging and leading. Basically, leading consists of collecting of foreign currency collectibles before they are due when the foreign currency is expected to devalue, and paying foreign currency payables before they are due when the currency is expected to strengthen. Lagging, on the other hand, involves delaying receivables in the expectation of strengthening currencies and delaying payables in the expectation of weakening currencies. Because all firms want their currencies to be in a strong position, lagging and leading are often accomplished more easily through related entities. Accounts payable and accounts receivable may relate to intercompany purchasing and sales, dividends, debt principal, interest, fees, royalties, and so on. This technique again illustrates the concept of interest-rate parity in that it is not always wise to borrow where the interest rates are the lowest; low interest rates usually denote a strong currency, and if the currency appreciates via-à-vis the parent company's currency, it will be more expensive to pay off the principal. Therefore, low interest rates may be more than offset by currency appreciation.

Budgeting and Billing

The two methods just discussed are largely a function of the strength of the firm and the demand for its product. In a market with a high price elasticity, firms may attempt to price their goods high enough to allow for a certain amount of exchange loss. If the company is large enough to demand it, home currency billing is preferable. Toyota of Japan, for example, demands yen for their exported cars in some areas of the world, thereby avoiding transaction exposure completely. Relatively few firms, however, are in a position to afford these luxuries in protection.

Clearinghouse System

The **clearinghouse** is a centralized affiliate that conducts transactions between foreign subsidiaries or firms. It maintains a stock of currency enabling one participant to purchase the goods of a foreign participant, each dealing in its own currency, thereby eliminating the transaction risks by shifting all risk to the clearinghouse. Since it has a stock of many currencies, the clearinghouse's foreign exchange exposure is lessened because the fluctuations in various exchange rates tend to be offsetting. The main disadvantage of this system is that it is basically a centralized bartering arena and, as such, may not meet the needs of a highly diversified corporation. Clearinghouses usually deal with subsidiaries that have similar products or are in vertical distribution systems.

Currency Portfolios

The avenues open to foreign exchange managers are not mutually exclusive; currency portfolio management is offered in conjunction with hedging as a way to reduce the cost of hedging. The portfolio effect causes the variation in returns on this combination of currencies to be less than the sum of the variations in the currencies when taken separately, thereby reducing exchange risks. Figure 25A•1 illustrates this point. The reader will immediately recognize that the diversification argument described here is identical in principle to the discussion in Chapter 13.

The **currency portfolio** approach to hedging may render the need for forward market hedging unnecessary. A very elementary example illustrates this point. Two managers, one using the traditional hedging approach and the other the currency portfolio approach, are presented with the following situation. The managers have a short position (net debtors) in the German mark, which is expected to appreciate vis-à-vis the dollar, and a long position (net creditors) in the Swiss franc, which will probably also appreciate. The manager using the traditional approach will probably hedge the German mark to avoid losses. The currency portfolio manager will do nothing with the long position, reasoning that the correlation coefficient of the currencies is positive, almost 1. Thus the currencies should move together, the short and long positions offsetting, and eliminate the need (and cost) for hedging.

Unfortunately, the portfolio theory is not as simple as canceling out the effects of the movement of two exchange rates. In fact, two of its weaknesses are its complexity and its complicated application. However, with computers becoming a basic element in the modern manager's array of business tools, these barriers to acceptance have essentially been eliminated.

Finally, it is necessary to reemphasize that these methods—hedging, balance sheet trade-offs, leads and lags, home country billing, budgeting for exchange-rate changes, the currency clearinghouse system, and the currency portfolio theory—are not mutually exclusive. They may all be used concurrently in protecting the international firm from both translation and transaction exposure risks.

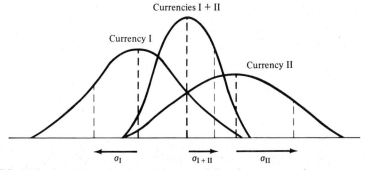

FIGURE 25A•1   Risk reduction with a portfolio of two currencies.

Learning Check for Appendix 25A•1

Review Questions

25A•1 Distinguish between transaction exposure and translation exposure.

25A•2. Explain how hedging can be used to protect a company from exchange risk. Is hedging easy?

25A•3. What are some other common exposure management techniques? What are the advantages and disadvantages of each?

New Terms

Clearinghouse	Exposure risks	Hedging
Currency options market hedge	Forward market hedge	Transaction exposure
Currency portfolios		Translation exposure

PROBLEMS

25A•1. Three years ago the exchange rate between Egyptian pounds and U.S. dollars was 1.5 pounds per dollar. At that time the interest rate on high-grade three-year U.S. CDs was 10% annually, and the rate on Egyptian CDs of equivalent risk was 12% annually.
  (a) Using the interest-rate parity theory, estimate what the forward rate for Egyptian pounds must have been three years ago.
  (b) Estimate today's exchange rate.

25A•2. Today the 180-day U.S. T-bill rate is 9% per year and the rate on 180-day Pakistan government securities is 16% per year.
  (a) Estimate the 180-day forward rate for rupees if the direct spot rate is $0.07 per rupee.
  (b) Estimate the spot rate for rupees if the 180-day forward rate is $0.09 per rupee.

25A•3. The exchange rate between Greek drachmas and U.S. dollars was 40 drachmas per dollar six years ago. At that time the U.S. consumer price index was 232 and the Greek consumer price index was 164. Today the U.S. consumer price index is 331 and the Greek consumer price index is 437. Today's interest rate for six-year U.S. CDs is 9% and the rate for six-year Greek CDs of equivalent risk is 15%.

(a) Estimate today's spot rate for drachmas.

(b) Estimate the six-year forward rate for drachmas.

25A•4. The Bank of Hong Kong has made an offer to the Jefferson Food Corporation to accept payments from the firms that import food from Jefferson. Currently, it takes an average of 10 days to receive these payments and convert them to dollars. Under the terms of the offer, the Bank of Hong Kong would collect the payments, convert them to dollars, and deposit them in a special account denominated in dollars, thus reducing the float time to one day. The fee for this service would be $10,000 annually. In addition, the account would pay only 8.75% annually (most other savings accounts in Hong Kong pay 9% annually). Jefferson collects the dollar equivalent of $800,000 per month and has a cost of capital of 9%. Should they take advantage of the bank's offer? What side benefits would acceptance of the offer bring?

25A•5. The Tessio Exporting Company of Italy has a banker's acceptance from the Physical Bank of New York that can be redeemed for 600,000 lira in 90 days. Tessio's local bank has offered to buy the banker's acceptance for 575,000 lira. What financing rate is Tessio paying by taking advantage of this offer?

25A•6. The Columbia Lumber Company has contracted to sell lumber to the Saskatchewan Construction Corporation for 500,000 Canadian dollars in six months. The current direct exchange rate is $0.75 per Canadian dollar, and the six-month forward rate is $0.74 per Canadian dollar.

(a) If Columbia does not contract in the forward market and the spot rate in six months is $0.79 per Canadian dollar, how many U.S. dollars will they receive in six months?

(b) If Columbia does not contract in the forward market and the spot rate in six months is $0.69 per Canadian dollar, how many U.S. dollars will they receive in six months?

(c) If Columbia does contract in the forward market and the spot rate in six months is $0.79 per Canadian dollar, how many U.S. dollars will they receive in six months?

(d) If Columbia does contract in the forward market and the spot rate in six months is $0.69 per Canadian dollar, how many U.S. dollars will they receive in six months?

25A•7. You have $100,000 that you can invest in a two-year CD for 11%. A friend has pointed out that you could invest the $100,000 for two-year English CDs for 15%. The current spot rate is $1.25 per pound, and the two-year futures rate is $1.18 per pound.

(a) Do the English CDs really offer a better rate of return than the U.S. CDs?

(b) Is there a way to guarantee a higher return than the 11% offered by U.S. CDs?

READINGS

ALIBER, ROBERT C., *Exchange Risk and Corporate International Finance* (New York: John Wiley & Sons, Inc., 1978).

EITEMAN, DAVID K. AND ARTHUR I. STONEHILL, *Multinational Business Finance* (Reading, Mass.: Addison-Wesley Publishing Company, Inc., 1982).

FOLKS, WILLIAM R., JR., AND RAMESH ADVANI, "Raising Funds with Foreign Currency," *Financial Executive*, February 1980, 44–49.

MENDELSOHN, M. S., *Money on the Move, The Modern International Capital Market* (New York: McGraw-Hill Book Company, 1980).

OBLAK, DAVID J., AND ROY J. HELM, JR., "Survey and Analysis of Capital Budgeting Methods Used by Multinationals," *Financial Management*, Winter 1980, 37–41.

RODRIGUEZ, RITA M., AND E. EUGENE CARTER, *International Financial Management* (Englewood Cliffs, N.J.: Prentice-Hall, Inc., 1979).

SHAPIRO, ALAN C., "Financial Structure and Cost of Capital in the Multinational Corporation," *Journal of Financial and Quantitative Analysis*, June 1978, 211–226.

SHAPIRO, ALAN C., *Multinational Financial Management* (Boston: Allyn and Bacon, Inc., 1982).

Appendix A: Mathematical Equations

In this appendix, we reproduce the derivation of certain formulas that are used in the text. We then present several formulas to determine time value factors for interest rates and/or time periods not covered in the time value tables in Chapter 2.

Derivations

PRESENT VALUE (PV) OF A PERPETUITY (EQ. 2-9)

Consider a perpetual cash flow per period of CF and a discount rate of $k\%$. The PV of this perpetuity is given as

$$
\begin{aligned}
PV_{\text{perpetuity}} &= CF(PVF_{k,\,1}) + CF(PVF_{k,\,2}) + CF(PVF_{k,\,3}) + \cdots + \\
&\quad CD(PVF_{k,\,\infty}) \\
&= CF[(PVF_{k,\,1}) + (PVF_{k,\,2}) + (PVF_{k,\,3}) + \cdots + \\
&\quad (PVF_{k,\,\infty})]
\end{aligned}
\tag{A-1}
$$

Substituting in the formula for the PV factors gives us

$$
PV_{\text{perpetuity}} = CF\left[\frac{d1}{(1+k)^1} + \frac{1}{(1+k)^2} + \frac{1}{(1+k)^3} + \cdots + \frac{1}{(1+k)^n}\right]
\tag{A-2}
$$

Multiplying both sides of Eq. (A-2) by $(1 + k)$ gives us

$$(1 + k)\, PV_{\text{perpetuity}}$$
$$= CF\left[1 + \frac{1}{(1 + k)^1} + \frac{1}{(1 + k)^2} + \frac{1}{(1 + k)^3} + \cdots + \frac{1}{(1 + k)^{n-1}}\right] \quad \text{(A-3)}$$

Subtract Eq. (A-2) from Eq. (A-3) to get

$$(1 + k - 1)\, PV_{\text{perpetuity}} = CF\left[1 - \frac{1}{(1 + k)^n}\right] \quad \text{(A-4)}$$

As n goes to infinity, the term $1/(1 + k)^n$ goes to zero, making the right-hand side of Eq. (A-4) CF, so that

$$PV_{\text{perpetuity}} = \frac{CF}{k}$$

GORDON VALUATION MODEL (EQ. 4-7)

The proof of the Gordon valuation model begins with Eq. (4-6):

$$S_0 = \frac{Div_1}{1 + k_s} + \frac{Div_1(1 + g)}{(1 + k_s)^2} + \cdots + \frac{Div_1(1 + g)^\infty}{(1 + k_s)^\infty}$$

This equation may be written as

$$S_0 = \frac{Div_0(1 + g)}{1 + k_s} + \frac{Div_0(1 + g)^2}{(1 + k_s)^2} + \cdots + \frac{Div_0(1 + g)^n}{(1 + k_s)^n}$$
$$= Div_0\left[\frac{(1 + g)}{1 + k_s} + \frac{(1 + g)^2}{(1 + k_s)^2} + \cdots + \frac{(1 + g)^n}{(1 + k_s)^n}\right] \quad \text{(A-5)}$$

Multiplying both sides of Eq. (A-5) by $(1 + k_s)/(1 + g)$ gives

$$\left(\frac{1 + k_s}{1 + g}\right)S_0 = Div_0\left[1 + \frac{1 + g}{1 + k_s} + \frac{(1 + g)^2}{(1 + k_s)^2} + \cdots + \frac{(1 + g)^{n-1}}{(1 + k_s)^{n-1}}\right] \quad \text{(A-6)}$$

Subtracting Eq. (A-5) from Eq. (A-6) gives

$$\left(\frac{1 + k_s}{1 + g} - 1\right)S_0 = Div_0\left[1 - \frac{(1 + g)^n}{(1 + k_s)^n}\right]$$

or

$$\left(\frac{1 + k_s - 1 - g}{1 + g}\right)S_0 = Div_0\left[1 - \frac{(1 + g)^n}{(1 + k_s)^n}\right] \qquad \text{(A-7)}$$

Assuming that $k_s > g$, notice that as n goes to ∞ the term [$\star$] on the right-hand side of Eq. (A-7) becomes 1.0. Thus

$$\left(\frac{k_s - g}{1 + g}\right)S_0 = Div_0$$

which, when rearranged, yields

$$S_0 = \left(\frac{Div_0(1 + g)}{k_s - g}\right) = \frac{Div_1}{k_s - g}$$

THE BREAK-EVEN POINT (EQ. 8-5)

We begin with the equation for the firm's net operating income (*NOI*), Eq. (8-4):

$$NOI = S - TC$$
$$= PQ - (F + VQ)$$

At the break-even point $NOI = 0$ and the break-even quantity becomes $Q^\star$. Thus

$$0 = PQ^\star - (F + VQ^\star)$$

or

$$PQ^\star = F + VQ^\star$$

Solving for $Q^\star$ gives

$$PQ^\star - VQ^\star = F$$
$$Q^\star(P - V) = F$$
$$Q^\star = \frac{F}{P - V}$$

THE DEGREE OF OPERATING LEVERAGE (DOL) (EQ. 8-6)

Equation (A-8) gives the formula for the *DOL*:

$$DOL = \frac{\%\Delta NOI}{\%\Delta S} \qquad \text{(A-8)}$$

Since $NOI = [Q(P - V) - F](1 - T)$, $\Delta NOI = \Delta Q(P - V)(1 - T)$. Thus

$$\%\Delta NOI = \frac{\Delta NOI}{NOI} = \frac{\Delta Q(P - V)}{Q(P - V) - F} \qquad \text{(A-9)}$$

Since $S = PQ$, $\Delta S = \Delta QP$. Thus

$$\%\Delta = \frac{\Delta S}{S} = \frac{\Delta Q}{Q} \qquad \text{(A-10)}$$

Combining Eqs. (A-9) and (A-10), we obtain

$$DOL = \frac{\%\Delta NOI}{\%\Delta S} = \left(\frac{\Delta Q(P - V)}{Q(P - V) - F} \right)\left(\frac{Q}{\Delta Q} \right) = \frac{Q(P - V)}{Q(P - V) - F}$$

THE DEGREE OF FINANCIAL LEVERAGE (DFL) (EQ. 8-7)

Equation (A-11) gives the formula for the *DFL:*

$$DFL = \frac{\%\Delta NI}{\%\Delta NOI} \qquad \text{(A-11)}$$

Since $NI = [Q(P - V) - F - I](1 - T)$, $\Delta NI = \Delta Q(P - V)(1 - T)$. Thus

$$\%\Delta NI = \frac{\Delta NI}{NI} = \frac{\Delta Q(P - V)}{Q(P - V) - F - I} \qquad \text{(A-12)}$$

The $\%\Delta NOI$ is given in Eq. (A-9). Combining Eqs. (A-9) and (A-12), we obtain

$$DFL = \frac{\%\Delta NI}{\%\Delta NOI} = \left(\frac{\Delta Q(P - V)}{Q(P - V) - F - I} \right)\left(\frac{Q(P - V) - F}{\Delta Q(P - V)} \right)$$
$$= \frac{Q(P - V) - F}{Q(P - V) - F - I}$$

THE DEGREE OF COMBINED LEVERAGE (DCL) (EQ. 8-8)

Equation (A-13) gives the formula for the *DCL:*

$$DCL = \frac{\%\Delta NI}{\%\Delta S} \qquad (A-13)$$

Combining Eqs. (A-10) and (A-12) gives

$$DCL = \left(\frac{\Delta Q(P - V)}{Q(P - V) - F - I}\right)\left(\frac{Q}{\Delta Q}\right) = \frac{Q(P - V)}{Q(P - V) - F - I}$$

RELATIONSHIP BETWEEN THE RISK OF THE FIRM AND THE RISK OF EQUITY (EQ. 14-3)

Since the firm's assets can be viewed as a "portfolio" of debt and equity, the asset beta of the firm can be determined using Eq. (13-1):

$$\beta_A = (\text{proportion of debt})(\beta_D) + (\text{proportion of equity})(\beta_E) \quad (A-14)$$

Because of the assumption of riskless debt $(\beta_D = 0)$, Eq. (A-14) reduces to

$$\beta_A = \frac{D}{D + E - TD}(0) + \frac{E}{D + E - TD}(\beta_E)$$

$$= \frac{E}{D + E - TD}(\beta_E)$$

which, by a simple rearrangement of terms, becomes

$$\beta_E = \beta_A\left(1 + \frac{D}{E}(1 - T)\right)$$

THE ECONOMIC ORDER QUANTITY (EOQ) MODEL (EQ. 20-1)

The ordering costs are $C_A(D/Q)$. The holding costs are $C_H(Q/2)$. The economic order quantity (EOQ) is determined by setting ordering costs equal to holding costs and solving for Q.

$$\text{Ordering costs} = \text{holding costs}$$

$$C_A \frac{D}{Q} = C_H \frac{Q}{2}$$

Solving this equation for Q gives

$$Q = \sqrt{\frac{2DC_A}{C_H}}$$

In Chapter 2 we introduced four tables for computing present and future values for both single amounts and annuities. When faced with a problem that uses an interest rate or time period not covered in these tables, the student must rely on a financial calculator or on a formula to compute the necessary values. Table A-1 contains the formulas for calculating any of the interest factors introduced in Chapter 2. These formulas can be used for fractional interest rates (e.g., 7.31%) or fractional time periods (e.g., 18.351 years).

TABLE A·1   Calculation of Future Value and Present Value Interest Factors

Interest Factor	Formula
Future value of lump sum, $FVF_{i,n}$	$(1 + i)^n$
Future value of annuity, $FVFA_{i,n}$	$\dfrac{(1 + i)^n - 1}{i}$
Present value of lump sum, $PVF_{i,n}$	$\dfrac{1}{(1 + i)^n}$
Present value of annuity, $PVFA_{i,n}$	$\dfrac{1 - [1/(1 + i)^n]}{i}$

Appendix B:
Answers to Odd
Numbered Problems

2•1. $4,690.10
2•3. $2.53
2•5. $4,290.96
2•7.   14.2 years ≈ 14 years
2•9.   (a) $2,000 from five years ago (b) $1,000 from 10 years ago
       (c) $3,000 now
2•11. (a) $477.93 (b) $477.93 (c) $477.93
2•13. $6,274.55
2•15. $5,142.69
2•17. $10,660.69
2•19. $17,530.70
2•21. $11,103.75
2•23. $416.67
2•25. (a) $111.62 (b) $91.73 (c) Buy in 30 months
2•27. 11.98%

3•1. $7,722.00
3•3. $19,500
3•5.   (a) $1,000 (b) Leave the money in the money market mutual fund.
3•7.   The project should still be accepted.
3•9.   Choose The Cloisters.
3•11. Purchase from Tunney

4•1.   Common Stock = $300,00, Paid in Capital = $121,000, Retained
       Earnings = $68,000, Treasury Stock Purchased = −$145,200
4•3.   8.75%
4•5. $17.50

4•7.   15%
4•9. $15.00
4•11. $38.00

5•1.   (a) 9.0% (b) 9.0% (c) 9.1%
5•3. $1,196.36
5•5. $876.66
5•7.   7.99% ≈ 8.00%

6•1.   (a) $1,200 (b) $7,200
6•3.

	Dec. 31, 1987	Dec. 31, 1988
Long-Term Debt	$60	$65
Preferred Stock	20	20
Common Stock	60	70
Retained Earnings	40	42
Total	$180	$197

6•5.   Retained Earnings = $25
6•7.   (a) $100 (b) $32 (c) $19.2 (d) $179.2
6•9.

	1984 Jet Electro %	1984 Industry %
Net Sales	100.0%	100.0%
Cost of Goods Sold	72.8	73.1
Gross Profit	27.2%	26.9%
Operating Expenses:		
Selling	3.7%	4.1%
General & Administrative	8.6	6.6
Depreciation	3.1	5.7
Total Operating Expenses	15.4%	16.4%
Net Operating Income	11.8%	10.5%
Interest	5.6	4.6
Taxable Income	6.2%	5.9%
Taxes	2.5	2.4
Net Income	3.7%	3.5%

6•11. (a) $23,000 (b) $78,000
6•13. Ending Balance = $205,000
6•1A. (a) $33,170 (b) 0.2591 (c) 0.39
6•3A. (a) $13,500 (b) $11,250, 0.075 (c) Issue Debt
6•1B. (a) $11,500 (b) $46,000
6•3B. (a) $2,000 (b) $4,000 (c) 25%

7•1.   (a) Current = 3.13; B: Quick = 1.67; W: Debt/Equity = 0.76; W:
       Times Interest Earned = 8.25; W: Average Collection Period =
       1.02; B: Inventory Turnover = 57.56; W: Fixed Asset
       Turnover = 15.54; W: Operating Profit Margin = 0.031; W: Net
       Profit Margin = 0.016; W: ROA = 0.167; W: ROE = 0.258; W
     (b) The ratios that are most out of line with the industry average are

the current, quick, debt-equity, times interest earned, and inventory turnover.

7•3. Inventory = $100; Accounts Receivable = $150; Net Plant and Equipment = $600; Total Assets = Liabilities + Stockholders' Equity = $1,000; Long-Term Debt = Common Stock = $300; Net Income = $10; Fixed Costs = $300

7•5. Do not lend the money.

7•7. (a) *Ancel* (OPM = 0.025, NPM = 0.01, ROA = 0.075, ROE = 0.0828)
  Starks (OPM = 0.340, NPM = 0.12, ROA = 0.1417, ROE = 0.1600)
  (b) Purchase Starks.

8•1. (a) 230,000 Copies per Month (b) 170,000 Copies per Month
  (c) $1,200 = NOI
  (d) 200,000 Copies per Month, $1,750 = NOI

8•3. (a) 20 Units per Month, $1,500 = NOI, 5.0 = DOL (b) 19 Units per Month, $1,500 = NOI, 4.1667 = DOL

8•5. (a) 2,000,000 Units per Month (b) 3.6667 = DOL

8•7. (a) NI for all equity = $270,000, NI for the 50%-50% plan = $126,000
  EPS for all equity = $0.450, EPS for the 50%-50% plan = $0.252
  DFL for all equity = 1.00, DFL for the 50%-50% plan = 2.14
  (b) 98,286

9•1. Expected Cash Inflows: May = $5,210; June = $4,790; July = $4,675

9•3. Cash Surplus (Deficit): Jan = $0; Feb = $50,000; Mar = $80,000; Apr = $25,000

9•5. Sept. cash balance = $300
  Net cash flows over the quarter = $−11 ($−1 in Oct., $26 in Nov., $36 in Dec., all from the cash flow budget in problem 9-4)
  Therefore, ending cash balance = $300 + ($−11) = $289
  0.65($840 + 920 + 900) − ($266 + 294 + 322 + 216 + 228 + 252) = $151
  ($197 + 225 + (0.3 * $900) − ($532) = $160
  ($18 + 9 + 13) − ($164) = −$124
  ($197 + 225 + 270) − ($172 + 197 + 225) = $98 (payment of accounts payable)
  $52 − 52 = 0 (taxes payable)

9•7. Cash = 0.04125: Accounts Receivable = 0.05167: Inventory = 0.04267: Accounts Payable = 0.04367: Wages Payable = 0.00475
  Level of cash = $569,250: Level accounts receivable = $713,046:
  Level inventory = $588,846: Level accounts payable = $602,646:
  Level wages payable = $65,550
  Other accounts that will change are gross fixed assets (by 200,000), accumulated depreciation (by 162,000), and retained earnings [by

.02(.6)(13,800,000) = 165,600]. Hence the pro forma balance sheet for Dec. 31, 1989 is:

Cash	$569,250	Accounts Payable	$602,600
Marketable Securities	257,000	Wages Payable	65,550
Accounts Receivable	713,000	Notes Payable	316,000
Inventory	588,800	Current Liabilities	$984,150
Current Assets	$2,128,050	Long Term Debt	1,500,000
Gross Fixed Assets	6,368,000	Common Stock	2,300,000
Less: Accumulated Depreciation	2,014,000		
Net Fixed Assets	$4,355,000	Retained Earnings	1,668,680
Total Assets	$6,482,050	Total Liabilities & Stockholder's Equity	$6,452,750

The excess of (Total Assets) over (Total Liabilities and Stockholder's Equity) of $6,482,050 − 6,452,750 = $29,300 represents additional financing that must be secured during the year of 1989.

10•1. (a) $130,000 (b) $107,500 (c) $145,000
10•3. $11,250 = CFAT, −$16,500 = Net Cash Flow from Replacement
10•5. (a) $11,125 = ΔCFAT
(b) $\Delta CFAT_1 = \$11,125$, $\Delta CFAT_2 = \$12,625$, $\Delta CFAT_3 = \$11,025$, $\Delta CFAT_4 = \$10,065$, $\Delta CFAT_5 = \$10,065$, $\Delta CFAT_6 = -\$1,155$
10•7. (a) $340,000 (b) $75,312.50 (c) $90,000
(d) $\Delta CFAT_1 = \$80,000$, $\Delta CFAT_2 = \$87,500$, $\Delta CFAT_3 = \$79,500$, $\Delta CFAT_4 = \$74,700$, $\Delta CFAT_5 = \$74,700$, $\Delta CFAT_6 = \$71,100$, $\Delta CFAT_{7-8} = \$67,500$
10•9. (a) $90,000 (b) $217,500 (c) $21,000 (d) $100,000

11•1. (a) $200,000 = Initial CF, ΔCFAT = $24,500, $120,000 = Terminal CF (b) 8.16 (c) 10.31% (d) −$22,930 (e) 0.7921 (f) 7.81%
11•3. (a) $340,000 (b) $75,312.50 (c) $90,000 (d) 4.51 (e) 22.59% (f)−$49,470.62 (g) 15.24%
11•5. (a) $217,500 (b) $21,000 (c) $100,000 (d) 10.36 (e) −$66,645.80 = NPV, 0.6936 = PI (f) −$93,332.80 (g) 5.45%
11•7. (a) $1,750,000 = Initial CF, $343,750 = Annual CF, $750,000 = Terminal CF
(b) The curve crosses NPV = 0 at an interest rate of approximately 17% = IRR.
11•9. The IRR is approximately 10%. (A calculator determined that the actual IRR equals 9.7%)

12•1. 12% = E(R)
12•3. 4.57% = E(Dividend Yield)
12•5. (a) The decision is unclear. (b) Choose to buy the old restaurant.
12•7. Vulcan would probably be preferred. Vulcan's returns are negatively correlated with the returns of the market and would serve to reduce portfolio risk relatively more than inclusion of Goodwealth.

12•9. (a) $11\% = E(R_A)$, $10 = E(R_B)$: (b) $\sigma_A^2 = 0.6\%^2$, $\sigma_B^2 = 2.4\%^2$ (c) $\sigma_P^2 = 0.864\%^2$

12A•1. (a) $17.1\% = E(R_A)$, $15.4\% = E(R_B)$, $16.2\% = E(R_M)$
  (b) $\sigma_A^2 = 5.99\%$, $\sigma_B^2 = 3.10\%$, $\sigma_M^2 = 1.40\%$
  (c) $\sigma_{AM} = 8.38\%^2$, $\sigma_{BM} = 4.12\%^2$
  (d) $\rho_{AM} = 1.00$, $\rho_{BM} = 0.95$

13•1. (a) $E(R_M) = 16\%$ (b) $E(R_M) = 19\%$ (c) $E(R_M) = 22\%$
13•3. $R_f = 9\%$
13•5. (a) $E(R_X) = 14.0\%$ (b) $E(R_Y) = 18.0\%$ (c) $E(R_Z) = 20.0\%$
  (d) $E(R_P) = 17.2\%$ (e) $\beta_P = 0.90$ (f) $E(R_P) = 17.2\%$
13•7. (a) $E(R_M) = 18\%$ (b) $E(RF_{Gord}) = 22\%$ (c) $E(RF_M) = 22\%$
  (d) $E(RF_{Gord}) = 26\%$
13•9. $P_0 = \$40.82$
13•11. $\beta_P = 1.4$, $E(R_P) = 18.4\%$
13•13. $P_0 = \$18.69$

14•1. (a) WACC $= 16.2\%$ (b) WACC $= 14.0\%$
14•3. (a) NPV(W) $= \$25,940$, NPV(X) $= \$10,650$, NPV(Y) $= \$27,530$, NPV(Z) $= \$12,050$. If each of these projects is independent, then we should adopt W, X, Y, and Z. If they are mutually exclusive, then we should adopt only Y.
  (b) NPV(W) $= -\$470$, NPV(X) $= -\$13,325$, NPV(Y) $= -\$2,995$, NPV(Z) $= \$22,700$. We should not accept any of these projects because they all possess negative NPVs.
  (c) The "NPVs" calculated are not really NPVs. This result obtains because the discount rate utilized is not market determined.
14•5. (a) WACC $= 12\%$ (b) WACC $= 13\%$
14•7. (a) $E(R_X) = 14\%$, $E(R_Y) = 12\%$ (b) NPV(X) $= \$4,032$, NPV(Y) $= \$3,257$
14•9. $E(R_{Proj}) = 17.6\%$, NPV $= \$39,454,545$
14A•1. $k_d = 7.63\%$
14A•3. $k_s = 14.48\%$
14A•5. WACC $= 10.25\%$
14A•7. WACC $= 12.95\%$

15•1. (a) PV of Tax Shield $= \$216,288$, $V^L = \$10,216,288$
  (b) PV of Perpetual Debt $= \$500,000$, $V^L = \$10,500,000$
15•3. Pollard is $3.75 m more valuable than Geraci.
15•5. (a) Annual Tax Savings $= \$0.15$ m (b) Total Tax Savings $= \$1.5$ m

16•1. (a) 2,000,000 (b) EPS $= \$0.75$, EPS $= \$1.13$ (c) Interest $= \$2,400,000$ (d) $\$0.70$ (e) It will always be true that debt is more attractive, as measured by EPS, than equity at relatively low levels of NOI. (f) NOI $= \$9,600,000$
16•3. (a) EPS $= \$0.86$, EPS $= \$1.20$ (b) EPS $= \$0.88$, EPS $= \$1.19$
  (C) $\$224.5$ m
16•5. (a) Preferred Dividend $= \$3,125,000$, NOI $= \$4,166,667$

(b) EPS for Plan 1 = $6.75, EPS for Plan 2 = $6.81
EPS for Plan 1 = $8.25, EPS for Plan 2 = $8.47
(c) NOI = $41.67 m

16·7. If we have access to funds that will enable us to cover our short-term deficits, then the financing plan is feasible

17·1. Transactions costs, flotation costs, institutional restrictions, the firm's financial resources, flexibility, access to equity capital, control of the firm, ability to borrow, past dividend policy and inflation. This list is not exhaustive.

17·3. The dividend will be paid to Mr. Biggy.

17·5. $375,000

17·7. After the stock dividend, Com stock = $230,000; Paid-in-capital = $2,020,000; Ret Earn = $4,250,000; Total stockholders' equity = $6,500,000

18·1. (a) $1,951 (b) −$500 (c) $10,00 (d) $3,750

18·3. (a) −$2,000 (b) $3,000 (c) 16.7%

18·5. (a) $4,000 (b) 13.0 (c) 3.5 (d) 7.0 (e) 9.5 (f) 9.5

18·7. (a) 1.60, $60 k (b) 1.20, $20 k, 15%

18·9. (a) 2.7 (b) 2.851 (c) $4,475,520 (d) $1,759,680

19·1. (a) $25 m (b) $50 k (c) Accept (d) Reject

19·3. (a) Dallas = $833,333; Fort Worth = $444,444; El Paso = $333,333; San Antonio = $611,111; Austin = $416,667
(b) Dallas = $833,333; Fort Worth = $888,889; El Paso = $1,000,000; San Antonio = $1,222,222; Austin = $833,333
(c) Dallas = −$13,333; No: Forth Worth = −$4,889; No: El Paso = $5,000; Yes: San Antonio = $19,778; Yes: Austin = −$13,333; No

19·5. (a) $11,111.11 (b) $80,000 (c) 7.2 days (d) $320,000 (e) $40,000, $3,200 (f) $1,960,000, $205,800 (g) −$112,000

19·7. (a) $8,333 = Net Benefit
(b) Los Angeles = $4,500, San Francisco-Oakland = $1,667, San Diego = $0, Santa Barbara = −$667, Pasadena = $1,000
(c) Choose the L.A. collection center.

20·1. (a) −$950,000 (b) $250,000 (c) −$1,000,000 (d) $125,000

20·3. (a) Pharmacy: Sales = $45,000, CGS = $27,000
Record and Tape: Sales = $112,500, CGS = $56,250
(b) Pharmacy: Average A/R = $45,000
Record and Tape: Average A/R = $75,000
(c) Pharmacy: Change in Fixed Assets = $8,640
Record and Tape: Change in Fixed Assets = $15,750
(d) Pharmacy: Bad Debt Expense = $5,400
Record and Tape: Bad Debt Expense = $9,000
(e) Pharmacy: Gross Profit = $216,000
Record and Tape: Gross Profit = $225,000

(f) Accept the Pharmacy
(g) Accept the Record and Tape Department
20•5. Demand = 400, Order = 2

21•1. (a) 18% (b) 19.56%
21•3. (a) August 11 (b) 1% (c) September 10 (d) 12.12%
21•5. (a) 12.24% (b) 9.09% (c) 18.18% (d) 9.09%
21•7. (a) 36.36% (b) 36.37%
21•9. 15.06%
21•11. Choose plan A under either commision schedule.
21•13. Savings = $20,400
21•15. Simple Interest = 63.16%, Compound Interest = 85.06%, Accept the Discount

22•1. Less than $54
22•3. $W_P = \$2.50$
22•5.

S_P	$P_W \approx \max\{S_P - \$0), \$25\}$	$Pf_W = P_W - \$4$	$(Pf_W * 100)/\$400$
$ 0	$ 0	−$4	−100%
20	0	−4	−100
25	0	−4	−100
27	2	−2	−50
30	5	1	25
35	10	6	150

22•7. (a) Prop of Equity = 50% and the Prop of Debt = 50% (b) Prop of Equity = 53.8% and the Prop of Debt = 46.2% (c) 30
22•9. (a) 40 (b) $25 (c) The price must be greater than $1,160 (d) Price = $1,262.36 (e) The price will be greater than $1,077.86 but less than $1,160.
22•11. (a) $11.00 (b) $28.60 (c) The return will be 10% > 8.6%
22•13. (a) $12.50 (b) $58.26 (c) Exercise
22•15. (a) CV = $2,440.27, g = 6.4% (b) CV = $4,638.60 g = 9.9%

24•1. (a) Price = $50,000, Depr = $10,000, Shield = $3,400 (b) After-Tax Lease Payments = $7,260 (c) Financing Provided by Lease = $42,740
Find the decremental cash flow.

Year	1	2	3	4	5	6
Decremental cash flow	$42,740	$10,660	$10,660	$10,660	$10,660	$ 3,400

(d) Lease the crane in either case.
24•3. (a) Initial Outlay = $90,000, Depr = $18,000, Tax Shield = $8,160 (b) After-Tax Outflows = $9,900

(c)

Year	1	2	3	4	5	6	7	8
Decremental cash flow	$81,000	–$18,060	–$18,060	–$18,060	–$18,060	–$18,060	–$9,900	–$9,900

(d) Lease the Machines (e) Lease the Machines

24•5. (a) Initial outlay $40,000, Annual depr = $8,000 Tax Savings per
Annum = $2,720

(b) After-tax cost of leasing = $6,699 (c) Financing provided by
leasing = $33,301

Year	1	2	3	4	5	6
Decremental cash flow	$33,301	$9,419	$9,419	$9,419	$9,419	$2,720

(d) Lease the computer (e) Depreciation = $2,000 (f) After-Tax Cost
of Leasing = $7,613 (g) Buy the Computer

24•7. Lease the Jeeps (b) Buy the Jeeps

24•9. (a) Initial Outlay = $18,000, After-Tax Outlay = $3,750, Net
Financing = $14,250

(b) Annual Depreciation = $6,00, Tax Shield = $1,500, (c) Lease the
tractor

25•1. (a) 0.7143 pounds (b) $1.6 (c) The dollar has strengthened.

25•3. (a) 2 francs per dollar (b) 250 yen per dollar (c) 0.008 francs per yen

25•5. 173.8 cruzeiros per dollar four years ago

25•7. (a) Home Yield = 13.54% (b) Foreign Yield = 11.36%

25A•1. (a) 1.5833 pounds per dollar (b) 1.5833 pounds per dollar

25A•3. (a) 74.71 drachmas per dollar (b) 103.04 drachmas per dollar

25A•5. 17.39% simple interest, 18.57% compound interest

25•7A. (a) The English CD is a very good deal.

(b) See the Solutions Manual.

Appendix C: Glossary

Accelerated cost recovery system (ACRS). Detailed guidelines that the firm must follow when depreciating assets for tax purposes.

Accounting rate-of-return (AROR). Used to related the after-tax profits provided by a project to its average investment.

Acquisition. The takeover of one company by another.

Acquisition costs. Costs incurred in the process of acquiring item(s) to be held in inventory.

Additional paid-in capital. Amount paid for stock above its stated par value.

Ad hoc approach. Method providing an approximation to the conceptually correct method of estimating the risk-adjusted discount rate.

Agency costs. Inefficiencies caused by conflicts between participants in a business.

Agency problems. Difficulties that arise when there is a separation of ownership and control of a firm.

Agency theory. Theory that identifies potential conflicts between participants in a business and examines how the undesirable consequences of potential conflicts can be reduced.

Agents. Managers who act on behalf of stockholders in running a firm.

Annual percentage rate (APR). *See* Effective interest rate.

Annuity. Series of equal cash flows at regular intervals.

Annuity due. Annuity in which payments are made at the beginning of each period.

Articles of incorporation. Document that creates a private corporation according to the general corporation laws of the state.

Articles of partnership. Written contract for a partnership that specifies agreement to salaries, contributions to capital, distribution of profit and losses, and dissolution of the partnership.

Asset utilization ratios.   Used to indicate how efficiently management utilizes its assets in generating revenues by relating or comparing sales to different types of assets.

Average collection period.   Used to measure the efficiency of a firm's credit policy.

Average return.   Calculation of the expected return from an investment.

Balance sheet.   Listing at a specific point in time of the book value of the assets of a firm and the claims on these assets.

Bankruptcy.   The condition under which an individual or firm is unable to pay debts.

Beta coefficient.   Measure of the sensitivity of an asset to market conditions; it is the relevant risk measure for calculating an asset's required rate of return.

Bill of lading.   Trade document used in international transactions.

Blocked funds.   Capital invested in foreign countries that is restricted from being withdrawn from those countries.

Bond.   Long-term debt instrument representing money borrowed by a firm from investors.

Bondholder.   Person or group that lends debt capital to a firm.

Break-even analysis.   Procedure used to tell the manager how profits will vary when production costs, sales volume, and selling price vary.

Break-even point.   Point at which net operating income equals zero; at this level of production and sales, total operating costs equal revenues from operations.

Break-even quantity.   *See* Break-even point.

Business organization.   Collective endeavor consisting of contractual relationships among the various parties involved in some productive activity.

Call option.   Instrument that allows the holder to purchase a particular stock at a prespecified price within a certain period.

Call provision.   A feature of corporate bonds that allows the company to pay off the debt before maturity.

Capital.   Productive resources that a firm uses to produce goods or services.

Capital asset pricing model (CAPM).   Model of the relationship between systematic risk and expected return. A basis for valuing financial assets.

Capital budgeting.   Process of selecting projects that can increase a firm's value.

Capital expenditure.   Cash outflows associated with a long-term investment or capital budgeting projects.

Capitalism.   Economic system characterized by individual and corporate ownership of most of the economy's capital as opposed to government ownership.

Capitalizing.   Finding the present value of a stream of cash flows.

Capital lease.   *See* Financial lease.

Capital outlay.   Initial startup funds for a new project.

Capital rationing.   Process whereby a firm allocates a limited amount of capital to wealth-maximizing projects.

Carryback. Process by which the deductions or credits of one taxable year are applied against the tax liability in an earlier year.

Carryforward. A tax rule that allows an expense to be recognized at a later time period when revenue is received.

Cash dividend. Payment of a firm's earnings in the form of cash to stockholders.

Cash flow. Total dollar amount of funds available for the firm to put to productive uses.

Cash flow budget. Forecast of cash receipts and cash expenditures over specific intervals.

Characteristic line. Regression line showing the average relationship between the returns on a stock and the returns on the market.

Chief financial officer (CFO). A member of the board of directors who is responsible for all financial operations.

Clearing float. The time it takes for a deposited check to clear the banking system and become usable funds.

Clearinghouse. Centralized affiliate that conducts transactions between foreign subsidiaries or firms.

Clientele effect. The phenomenon that stocks with stable dividend policies will attract those investors that favor that policy.

Coefficient of variation (CV). Ratio of the standard deviation of returns to expected returns.

Collections schedule. Used for breaking down receivables in terms of the actual month in which the sale was made rather than aggregating them.

Combined leverage. The joint effect of operating and financial leverage.

Common-size statement. Balance sheet or income statement in which items are expressed in percentages rather than dollars.

Common stock. Security representing an ownership interest in a corporation.

Common stock certificate. Document or financial security that a stockholder keeps as proof of ownership in a corporation.

Compensating balance. Average balance desired by a bank to be kept on deposit in exchange for holding credit available.

Competitive bid. Sealed bid that contains price and terms of a prospective contractor.

Complementary proposals. Projects in which the cash flows together exceed the sum of the cash flows that would be generated from either project individually.

Compounding. Adding interest to principal at time intervals for the purpose of establishing a new basis for subsequent interest computations.

Computer simulation. Computer methods that allow one to examine the impact of changes in all possible combinations of variables.

Conditional sale. Sale in which the vendee receives possession and right of use of the goods sold, but transfer of title to the vendee is dependent on performance of some condition, usually full payment of purchase price.

Congeneric mergers. Mergers occurring between firms that have related business interests and can be classified as being either horizontal or vertical.

Conglomerate mergers. Mergers occurring when unrelated businesses combine.

Consolidation. Event that occurs when two or more corporations combine to create an entirely new corporate entity.

Consumer credit. Credit granted to an individual.

Contribution margin. Used to denote the dollar amount that each unit sold will contribute to meeting fixed costs.

Controller. Chief accountant of a company.

Conventional project. Project with an initial net cash outflow followed by a series of net cash inflows.

Conversion ratio. Equals the number of shares of stock into which a convertible security (bonds or preferred stock) may be converted.

Convertible bonds. Bonds that permit bondholders to change their debt to equity at prespecified prices.

Corporation. Legal entity, chartered by a state or the federal government, and separate and distinct from the persons who own it.

Correlation. Statistical association between two series of numbers.

Correlation coefficient. Statistic that measures the strength of the association between two series of numbers.

Cost-reduction proposal. An investment that will lower a firm's operating costs.

Coupon interest rate. Stated annual rate of interest paid on the par value of a bond.

Coupon stripping. Separation of coupon payments from the face value of the bond.

Covariance. Measure of the relationship between assets; it is calculated as the product of the correlation between the assets and the respective standard deviations.

Coverage ratios. Used to measure the degree to which fixed payments are "covered" by operating profits.

Credit extension policies. Guidelines for granting credit, the terms of payment, and the amount of credit to extend to a customer.

Creditor. One who has extended credit to a company.

Credit scoring. Procedure that combines ratios by assigning a predetermined weight to each ratio value and summing these weights to arrive at an overall credit rating.

Credit standards. Criteria that determine which customers will be granted credit and to what extent.

Cumulative preferred stock. Stock whose dividends, if omitted because of insufficient earnings or for any other reason, accumulate until paid out.

Date of record. Date on which stockholders are eligible to receive the cash dividend.

Debentures. Bonds that are not secured by the assets of a firm.

Debt. Obligation to pay.

Debt capital. Funds borrowed to finance the operations of a business.

Debt insurance.   A surety bond purchased from an insurance company for its entire debt issue.

Debt-to-assets ratio.   Debt ratio that uses the book value of assets (debt plus equity) in the denominator.

Debt utilization ratios.   Used to measure a firm's degree of indebtedness.

Declaration date.   Date on which the board declares the dividend for the next quarter.

Default.   When a firm is unable to make required payments, either interest or principal.

Default risk.   Risk that an investor accepts that a company will not be able to fulfill its financial agreements.

Deficiency memorandum.   Written notice from the Securities and Exchange Commission to a prospective issuer of securities that the preliminary prospectus needs revision or expansion.

Degree of combined leverage (DCL).   Percentage change in net income for a given percentage change in sales.

Degree of financial leverage (DFL).   Percentage change in net income for a given percentage change in net operating income.

Degree of operating leverage (DOL).   Percentage change in net operating income for a given percentage change in sales.

Depreciation.   Allocation of the historic cost of an asset over its economic life, the period over which it is expected to provide benefits to its owner.

Direct lease.   Situation when the lessor already owns or acquires an asset, which is then provided to the lessee.

Discount bond.   Bond offered below face value.

Discounting.   (1) Finding the present value of a cash flow. (2) An institution lending money to a business with a customer's debt obligation to the firm as security on the loan.

Discount rate.   Rate used to convert future cash flows to present values.

Diversification.   Process of reducing risk by forming portfolios of imperfectly correlated assets.

Dividend payout ratio.   Ratio of dividends paid out to total earnings (net income).

Dividends.   Earnings and profits of a corporation appropriated for distribution among shareholders, usually paid quarterly.

Dividend reinvestment plan (DRP).   Automatic reinvestment of shareholder dividends in more shares of the company's stock.

Divisible projects.   Projects that can be partially accepted.

Double taxation.   Effect of federal tax law whereby earnings are taxed at the corporate level, and then taxed again when stockholders receive dividends.

Due diligence.   Practice by investment bankers of fully investigating all aspects of a firm before raising capital for the company.

Economic order quantity (EOQ).   Inventory decision model to calculate the optimum amount to order based on fixed costs of placing and receiving an order, carrying cost of inventory and the sales.

Economic profit. Equal to the profit in excess of the profit that could have been made from the best alternative foregone.

Economies of scale. Reduction in the average cost of producing and selling a product as production volume increases.

Effective interest rate. Interest rate that recognizes the nominal or annual interest rate plus the extra interest gained because of compounding.

Efficient market. Market in which the value of an asset reflects all available information. In such a market it is impossible to generate excess returns consistently.

Equilibrium. Status of a market in which there are no forces operating that would automatically set in motion changes in the quantity demanded or the price that currently prevails.

Equity. Ownership.

Equity capital. Stockholders' or owners' investments made in an organization.

Equity kicker. *See* Sweetener.

Equivalent loan. Loan whose net after-tax cash commitments imposed on the firm are identical to those imposed by leasing.

Eurobond. Bond that pays interest and principal in Eurodollars.

Eurocurrency. Money deposited by corporations and national governments in banks away from their home countries.

Eurodollar. U.S. dollar held as a deposit in a European commercial bank.

Ex ante return. Return that one expects to receive from a certain investment.

Excess returns. Economic profits expressed as a percentage of initial investment.

Ex-dividend date. Fourth business day preceding the date of record; date established by the securities industry.

Expectations theory. Theory stating that current interest rates reflect expectations about future interest rates.

Expected holding period. Length of time an investment is expected to be owned.

Expected return. Average return from the investment calculated as the probability-weighted sum of all potential returns.

Ex post return. Actual return received from an investment.

Expropriation. Strongest form of blocked funds—a country nationalizes the assets of the investing firm.

Face value. Actual stated value of the bond; typically $1,000.

Factoring. Type of financial service whereby a firm sells its accounts receivable to a factoring company, which then acts as principal, not as agent.

Fair rate of return. Level of profit that a utility is allowed to earn as determined by federal and/or state regulators.

Financial assets. Resources such as cash or loans that are needed to acquire real assets.

Financial lease. Lease in which the service provided by the lessor to the lessee is limited to financing equipment.

Financial leverage. The ability of the firm to magnify the sensitivity of net income to changes in net operating income.

Financial management. Art and science of making financial decisions for a company.

Financial ratio analysis. Systematic use of ratios to interpret financial statements so that the existing and historical strengths and weaknesses of a firm can be determined.

Financing decision. Answers about what securities to issue to a company and what mix of short-term credit, long-term debt, and equity best facilitates the effort to meet the firm's objectives.

Fixed-asset turnover ratio. Used to indicate how well the investment in long-term (fixed) assets is being managed.

Fixed-charge coverage ratio. Considers the extent to which all fixed financial charges are covered.

Fixed operating costs. Costs that do not depend on the number of units produced within a given range of production.

Float. Difference between the bank's balance for a firm's account and the balance the firm shows on its books.

Forward market hedge. Method used to limit financial loss due to unexpected changes in the exchange rate.

Free-enterprise system. Economic system wherein people are allowed to organize and operate (invest) at a profit without excessive government intervention.

Funds flow analysis. Examines the changes in net working capital through the use of a statement of changes in financial position.

Gordon valuation model. Formula for calculating stock price under the assumption of a constant perpetual growth rate.

Gross profit. Sales minus the cost of producing the goods sold.

Hedging. Method of protecting the firm's claims on foreign currency against the unfavorable impact of exchange-rate fluctuations.

Holding company. Firm that owns sufficient voting stock in one or more other companies so as to have effective control over them.

Holding costs. Costs associated with holding the item in inventory until sold.

Homemade dividends. Situation when a stockholder obtains cash by selling some of his/her stock.

Homemade leverage. Situation when an investor who borrows money and buys the stock of an unlevered firm can, in effect, replicate the leverage of the firm.

Horizontal mergers. Combination of two firms engaged in the same business.

Horizontal revenue expansion proposal. Proposal that increases a firm's revenues from an area unrelated to the firm's existing business activities.

Human capital. Intangible assets of the firm, such as dedicated workers and management skills.

Imperfectly correlated. Projects that have a correlation coefficient of less than 1 are imperfectly correlated.

Implementation phase. Occurs when the company makes the required arrangements to take on a new project.

Income bonds. Obligation on which the payment of interest is contingent on sufficient earnings from year to year.

Income statement. Report of a firm's performance by measuring the profits (losses) generated over a period of time.

Incremental cash flows after taxes. Net cash flows that occur if and only if a project is accepted.

Independent proposals. Projects in which the acceptance of one has no effect whatsoever on the cash flow of the other.

Indivisible projects. Projects that must be accepted or rejected in their entirety.

Industrial-development bond. Bond issued by a state or local government to finance plants and facilities that are then leased to private businesses.

Initial public offering (IPO). Corporation's first offering of stock to the public.

Interest payments. *See* Interest rate.

Interest rate. Ratio of the payment for the use of financial capital to the amount borrowed.

Interfirm analysis. Used to interpret ratio values by comparing a firm's financial ratios to related firms' comparable ratios at a point in time.

Internal rate of return (IRR). Discount rate that makes *NPV* equal to zero.

Intrafirm analysis. Used to interpret ratio values by examining the behavior of a firm's ratios over time.

Intrinsic value. True value of tangible materials.

Inventory management. Operating to minimize the total cost of an investment in inventory.

Inventory of resources. Statement of a firm's future purchasing power.

Inventory turnover ratio. Used to determine whether too much or too little is invested in inventories.

Investment banker. Firm, acting as underwriter or agent, that serves as intermediary between an issuer of securities and the investing public.

IRR. *See* Internal rate of return (IRR).

IRR rule. Accept a project if the *IRR* is greater than the required rate of return; otherwise, reject the project.

Legal listings. Process of being included in a list of potential investment candidates.

Lessee. In a leasing arrangement the party that has the use of the asset being leased.

Lessor. In a leasing arrangement the party that has the title to the property being leased.

Letter stock. Category of stock that derives its name from an inscription on the face of the stock certificate, indicating that the shares have not been registered with the Securities and Exchange Commission and, therefore, cannot be sold to the general public.

Leveraged buyout (LBO).   Going-private transaction in which the managers borrow funds from outside investors to buy out the shareholders.

Leveraged lease.   Special lease arrangement under which the lessor borrows a substantial portion of the acquisition cost of the leased asset from a third party.

Limited liability.   Legal exemption of stockholders from financial liability for the debts of the firm beyond the amount they have individually invested.

Limited partnership.   Limited partners generally assume no monetary responsibility beyond the capital originally contributed to the partnership.

Line of credit.   Agreement whereby a financial institution promises to lend up to a certain amount without the need to file another application.

Liquidity.   Ability to be converted rapidly to cash.

Long-term solvency.   Measure of a firm's ability to meet its long-term obligation.

Mail float.   Time during which a customer's check is in the postal system.

Marginal tax rate.   Tax rate on an additional dollar of income.

Market portfolio.   Contains all assets in the economy properly weighted to represent their proportionate market values.

Market segmentation theory.   Theory suggesting that the marketplace for debt offerings is divided into three segments: short, intermediate, and long term.

Market values.   Current market price of any asset: the maximum cash proceeds obtainable from selling the assets.

Maturity date.   Date that bonds become due. The amount of principal borrowed is repaid on this date.

Merger.   Combination of two or more corporations in such a way that legally just one corporation survives.

Mortgage bond.   Tax-exempt security sold by municipal and state authorities for the purpose of providing low interest rate mortgage loans to qualified individuals.

Mutual exclusivity.   Exists when the acceptance of one project automatically rules out the acceptance of another project.

Negative float.   Increases the amount of cash tied up in the collection cycle and earns a zero rate of return.

Negotiated deal.   Process of bargaining that precedes an agreement.

Net income (NI).   Net profit before taxes minus taxes.

Net present value (NPV).   Present value of cash inflows minus the present value of cash outflows. Represents the economic profit adjusted for risk and timing.

Net operating income (NOI).   Income from property or business after operating expenses have been deducted, but before deducting income taxes and financing expenses.

Net profit before taxes (NPBT). Also known as "taxable income," it is all revenues (operating and nonoperating) minus all expenses (operating and financial).

Net profit margin. Income after all costs have been deducted.

Net working capital. Difference between current assets and current liabilities.

NOI-EPS analysis. Method that helps the financial manager evaluate the impact of various plans over a range of net operating income levels.

Nominal interest rate. Equals that stated interest rate, not taking into account compounding or inflation.

Nonconventional project. Project that is not a conventional project. *See also* Conventional project.

Nonoperating income. Income not directly related to the firm's day-to-day operations e.g., rent from leased land.

NPV profile. Graph that displays the *NPV*s for a project at different discount rates.

NPV rule. Rule that accepts projects with *NPV*s greater than zero and rejects all others.

Operating cash conversion cycle. Time it takes for the initial cash outflows for goods and services to be realized as cash inflows from sales.

Operating cash flows. Net benefits (incremental cash flows after taxes) received over a project's economic life.

Operating expenditures. Cash outlays that produce no benefits beyond the current period.

Operating lease. Type of lease in which the lessor handles all maintenance and servicing.

Operating leverage. Magnification in net operating income resulting from small changes in sales; exists because of fixed costs.

Operating profit margin. Used to determine the percentage of each sales dollar that is represented by operating profits.

Opportunity cost of capital. Relevant discount rate to be used for financial decision making; it is the rate of return forgone from the next best alternative; equal to the required rate of return (RRR).

Optimal capital structure. That debt-to-equity or debt-to-value ratio at which the value of a firm is maximized.

Ordinary annuity. Sequence of uninterrupted, equal cash flows with payments (receipts) occurring at the end of each period.

Outstanding issue. *See* Seasoned issue.

Overvalued. Description of a stock whose current price does not seem justified.

Partnership. Organization of two or more persons who pool resources to form a business.

Par value. Face value or stated value of a bond or common stock. It is usually equal to $1,000 for bonds.

Payment date. Date on which the firm actually mails the dividend checks.

Penny stocks. Stock that typically sells for less than $1 per share.

Percent of sales forecasting method. Constructing pro forma financial statements by assuming that the relevant items maintain a constant percentage relationship to sales.

Permanent current assets. Portion of a firm's current assets that is needed to maintain the firm's daily operations.

Perpetuity. Series of equal periodic cash flows that continues forever.

Physical capital. Financial assets and real assets.

PI rule. Accept a project if the index is greater than 1; otherwise, reject the project.

Portfolio. Collection of two or more assets.

Positive float. Allows the firm to maintain control of cash for a longer period of time, thus earning a larger return.

Preemptive rights. Rights specified in the charter of a corporation, granting to existing shareholders the first opportunity to buy a new issue of stock.

Preferred stock. Part of the capital stock of a corporation that has priority over the remaining stock, or common stock, in the distribution of dividends.

Premium bond. Bond with a selling price above face or redemption value.

Price risk. Situation where bondholders may have to sell their bonds above or below their purchase price, depending on the level of interest rates in the economy at a particular time.

Primary market. Financial market where initial issues of financial securities are sold.

Prime lending rate. Interest rate that banks charge to their most creditworthy customers.

Private information. Specialized information. Private information should not be confused with insider information, the use of which is illegal.

Private placement. Process by which a company finds a small group of large, usually institutional investors to provide the entire amount of new capital it seeks.

Privileged subscription. Right of existing shareholders of a corporation, or their transferees, to buy shares of a new issue of common stock before it is offered to the public.

Probability distribution. Statement of the different potential outcomes for an uncertain variable, together with the probability of each potential outcome.

Processing float. Time it takes for the firm to deposit the customer's check in his/her bank.

Profit. Positive difference that results from selling products and services for more than the cost of producing these goods.

Profitability index. Equal to the present value of cash inflows divided by the present value of the cash outflows.

Profitability ratio. Used to measure the overall record of management in producing profits.

Profit maximization. Objective of a firm to maximize accounting profits. This is not necessarily the same as maximizing shareholder wealth.

Pro forma balance sheet. Projected balance sheet for a future date.

Pro forma statement. Projected income statement for a future period.

Project. Single proposal or a collection of economically dependent proposals.

Project financing. Form of lending usually for a complicated operation. Since the lending is project specific, so is the timing of repayment.

Property rights. Rights to the ownership and stewardship of, and profits from, land, capital, and other goods.

Proposal. Alternative that is under consideration.

Proprietorship. Business owned by a single person.

Prospectus. Formal written offer to sell securities that sets forth the plan for a proposed business enterprise and other relevant facts.

Purchasing power parity (PPP) theory. Theory implying that goods of equal value in differing countries may be equated through an exchange rate.

Put option. Investment that allows that holder to sell a particular stock at a prespecified price within a certain period.

Pyramiding. Use of financial leverage to finance purchases of additional investments.

Quick ratio. Considers only assets that can be readily converted to cash and is therefore a stricter test for liquidity.

Rate of return. *See* Internal rate of return (IRR).

Real assets. Physical assets (plant, equipment); in contrast to financial assets.

Realized return. *See* Ex post return.

Red herring. First document released by an underwriter of a new issue to prospective investors.

Refunding operation. Process of a company replacing an entire old issue with a new one.

Registration statement. Document explaining the purpose of a proposed public offering of securities.

Regulated companies. Companies that cannot change their rates charged to customers without the approval of the appropriate regulatory agency.

Relevant risk. Portion of the asset's total risk that is relevant for the determination of opportunity costs.

Replacement proposal. Cost-savings proposal.

Required rate of return (RRR). Minimum rate of return that the project must yield to justify its acceptance.

Residual theory of dividends. Theory in which dividend policy is a residual from investment policy.

Restrictive covenants. Conditions that bondholders impose on the firm when they buy bond issues.

Retained earnings. Net profits kept to accumulate in a business after dividends are paid.

Retention ratio. Ratio of retained earnings to total earnings for the period; 1 minus the payout ratio.

Return on assets (ROA). Measures the after-tax returns on an investment without regard to the manner in which the assets were financed.

Return on equity (ROE). Return earned on a company's common stock investment for a given period.

Revolving credit. Loan account requiring monthly payments of less than the full amount due.

Rights offering. *See* Privileged subscription.

Risk. Measurable uncertainty: in finance, it refers to the variability of returns from an investment.

Sale-leaseback arrangement. Arrangement where assets already owned by a firm are purchased by a lessor and leased back to the firm.

Scattergram. Diagram showing relation between two quantities.

S corporation. Corporation with a limited number of stockholders that elects not to be taxed as a regular corporation and meets certain other requirements.

Seasoned issue. Securities that have been outstanding for sometime, i.e., not new issues.

Secondary market. Financial market in which existing securities can be bought and sold.

Security. (1) Property pledged as collateral. (2) A document endorsing ownership.

Seed capital. Startup funds for a new business.

Semifixed operating costs. Costs that include both fixed and variable elements within a relevant range of activity.

Semivariable costs. *See* Semifixed operating costs.

Sensitivity costs. Examination of the sensitivity of some variable to changes in another variable.

Shelf registration. A rule that allows a company to register an entire issue with the Securities and Exchange Commission and to then sell them in smaller amounts at its discretion.

Shortage costs. Costs incurred when the firm cannot honor a customer's order because the item is out of stock.

Short-term solvency. Measure of a firm's ability to meet its short-term obligations.

Sinking fund. Fund used to accumulate the cash needed to pay off a bond or other security.

Spin-off. Form of corporate divestiture that results in a subsidiary or division becoming an independent company.

Spread. Difference between the proceeds an issuer of a new security receives and the price paid by the public for the issue.

Standard deviation. Square root of the variance of a probability distribution.

Standby commitment fee. Sum required by a lender to provide a commitment.

Stated interest rate. Equals the annual interest rate, not taking into account compounding.

Statement of retained earnings. Financial statement that reconciles the balance in retained earnings account at the beginning of the income statement period to the balance at the end of the period.

Stock. Document or financial security that a stockholder keeps as proof of ownership in a corporation.

Stock dividend. Payment of stock to a firm's existing shareholders.

Stock market. Financial market where investors buy and sell shares of stock.

Stock split. An increase in the total number of outstanding shares of a company; increases in the number of shares investors hold, but doesn't necessarily increase the value of their investment.

Stockholder. Individual or organization with an ownership position in a corporation.

Stockholders' equity. Also known as "net worth," it is the difference between assets and liabilities; what would be left over if all liabilities were paid off. Can be measured in book or market values.

Straight-line depreciation. A depreciation method that spreads the historic cost of the asset evenly over its economic life.

Substitute proposals. Projects in which the cash flows from taking on two projects are less than the sum of the cash flows generated by the two projects individually.

Supervisory fees. Contractually arranged periodic remissions of funds by the subsidiary to the parent company.

Sweetener. Feature added to a securities offering to make it more attractive to purchasers.

Systematic risk. The relevant risk for pricing an asset: depends on the extent to which an asset's returns are affected by general economic conditions.

Take-up fee. Sum required by a lender that depends on the number of underwritten rights handled.

Tangible benefits. Assets having physical existence, such as cash, real estate, or machinery.

Taxable income. *See* Net profit before taxes (NPBT).

Tax shields. Amount of depreciation charged against income, thus protecting that amount from tax.

Technical analysis. Process of using historical stock price data to predict stock price behavior.

Temporary current assets. Assets that fluctuate with the operational needs of the firm.

Tender offer. Offer made by another firm or investor to purchase shares of a firm's stock for a specified price, usually above the current market price.

Terminal cash flows. Cash flows that are expected to occur at the point when a project's useful life ends.

Term loans. Borrowings on which fixed amounts of principal and interest are paid regularly over the life of the loan.

Tie-in sale. Common arrangement between parent firms and their subsidiaries, possibly requiring the purchase of certain materials from the parent company.

Times interest earned ratio. Used to measure how many times interest expenses are earned or covered by profits.

Total risk. Undiversifiable risk plus diversifiable risk.

Trade credit. Credit extended to another firm.

Trade draft. Written orders initiated by the exporter notifying the importer of the exact amount and time at which the importer or its agent must pay.

Transaction exposure. Risks that occur when a company has accounts receivable or payable in foreign currencies.

Translation exposure. Risks that occur when the balance sheet is translated into the parent company's currency for the purposes of consolidation, evaluation, taxation, and so on.

Treasurer. Person responsible for managing the firm's current assets, evaluating investment proposals, and negotiating with banks for short-term loans and with underwriters for long-term loans and stock issues.

Treasury stock. Common or preferred stock that had been issued by a company and later reacquired.

True lease. Situation where the lessee is able to deduct the lease payments fully for tax purposes.

Undervalued. Security selling below its liquidation value or the market value that analysts believe it deserves.

Underwriter. To assume risk of buying a new issue of securities from the issuing corporation or government entity and reselling it to the public.

Uniform Partnership Act. Law adopted by most states that lays out the legal rules pertaining to partnerships.

Unique risk. Risks that are specific to the company in question.

Unlimited liability. Proprietors and partners have financial liability for the debts of the firm beyond the amount they have individually invested.

Unsystematic risk. Risk that is company-specific: can be eliminated through diversification.

Valuation. Process of capitalizing the cash flows provided by an asset.

Value of the firm. Market value of a firm's debt and equity.

Valuing an asset. Finding the present value of the cash flows provided from that asset.

Variable operating costs. Expenses that vary directly with the level of production and sales.

Variance. Sum of the probability-weighted squared deviations from the mean in return from an investment.

Venture capitalists. Source of financing for start-up companies or other ventures that entail some risk but offer the potential for above average profits.

Vertical mergers. Situation where a firm acquires firms "upstream" from it, such as suppliers, and/or firms "downstream" from it, such as product distributors.

Vertical revenue expansion proposal. Proposal to increase a firm's revenue by increasing the production of an existing product.

Warrant. Security issued by a corporation granting the holder of the warrant the right to purchase a specified number of shares of common stock at a specified price any time prior to an expiration date.

Weighted-average cost of capital (WACC). The cost of each component of capital used by the firm multiplied by the proportion of that component in the firm's capital structure.

Welfare of the stockholders. Concern with maximizing the stockholders' profits.

Yield curve. Graph showing the term structure of interest rates by plotting the yields of all bonds of the same quality with maturities ranging from the shortest to the longest available.

Zero-coupon bonds. Security that makes no periodic interest payments but instead is sold at a deep discount from its face value.

Index